Law's Ethical, Global and Theoretical Contexts

Law's Ethical, Global and Theoretical Contexts examines William Twining's principal contributions to law and jurisprudence in the context of three issues which will receive significant scholarly attention over the coming decades. Part I explores human rights (including torture), the role of evidence in human rights cases, the emerging discourse on 'traditional values', the relevance of 'Southern voices' to human rights debates, and the relationship between human rights and peace agreements. Part II assesses the impact of globalization through the lenses of sociology and comparative constitutionalism, and features an analysis of the development of pluralistic ideas of law in the context of privatization. Finally, Part III addresses issues of legal theory, including whether global legal pluralism needs a concept of law, the importance of context in legal interpretation, the effect of increasing digitalization on legal theory, and the utility of feminist and postmodern approaches to globalization and legal theory.

Upendra Baxi is Professor of Law Emeritus at the Universities of Warwick and Delhi.

Christopher McCrudden FBA is Professor of Human Rights and Equality Law at Queen's University, Belfast and William W. Cook Global Law Professor at the University of Michigan Law School.

Abdul Paliwala is Emeritus Professor at the School of Law, University of Warwick and a visiting professor at Birkbeck University of London.

William Twining, photographed by Karen Twining Fooks

Law's Ethical, Global and Theoretical Contexts

Essays in Honour of William Twining

Edited by

UPENDRA BAXI, CHRISTOPHER MCCRUDDEN AND ABDUL PALIWALA

CAMBRIDGE
UNIVERSITY PRESS

CAMBRIDGE
UNIVERSITY PRESS

University Printing House, Cambridge CB2 8BS, United Kingdom

Cambridge University Press is part of the University of Cambridge.

It furthers the University's mission by disseminating knowledge in the pursuit of education, learning and research at the highest international levels of excellence.

www.cambridge.org
Information on this title: www.cambridge.org/9781107116405

First published 2015

A catalogue record for this publication is available from the British Library

Library of Congress Cataloguing in Publication data
Law's ethical, global, and theoretical contexts : essays in honour of William Twining / edited by Upendra Baxi, Christopher McCrudden, and Abdul Paliwala.
pages cm
Includes bibliographical references and index.
ISBN 978-1-107-11640-5
1. Twining, William, 1934– 2. Law – Philosophy. 3. Law and ethics. 4. Law – Moral and ethical aspects. 5. Law – Interpretation and construction. 6. Human rights. 7. Constitutional law. I. Twining, William, 1934– honouree. II. Baxi, Upendra. III. McCrudden, Christopher. IV. Paliwala, Abdul.
K231.L395 2015
340′.1–dc23

2015012816

ISBN 978-1-107-11640-5 Hardback

Contents

Preface *page* vii
Notes on Contributors xiv

1 **An intellectual journey with William Twining: an interview** 1
Manuel Atienza and Raymundo Gama

Part I Human rights 19

2 **Resituating Twining's discovery of Bentham's Fragment on 'torture' amidst the twenty-first-century CE 'Terror Wars'** 21
Upendra Baxi

3 **Human rights and traditional values** 38
Christopher McCrudden

4 **Southern voices in transitional justice: a critical reflection on human rights and transition** 73
Fionnuala Ní Aoláin

5 **Human rights and Latin American Southern voices** 90
Oscar Guardiola-Rivera

Part II Globalizations 113

6 **Towards a socio-legal theory of indignation** 115
Boaventura de Sousa Santos

7 **Towards a cosmopolitan pluralist theory of constitutionalism** 143
Gavin W. Anderson

8 **The state and constitutionalism in postcolonial societies in Africa** 165
Yash Ghai and Jill Cottrell

9 **Comparative law, rights and the environment** 196
John McEldowney

10 **Homage and heresy from a licensed subversive: theorizing paradigm change in transnational economic regulation** 213
Jane Kelsey

Part III Legal theory 239

11 **Digital thoughtways: technology, jurisprudence and global justice** 241
Abdul Paliwala

12 **Twining on Llewellyn and Legal Realism** 265
Frederick Schauer

13 **Theorizing as activity: transnational legal theory in context** 280
Peer Zumbansen

14 **Does global legal pluralism need a concept of law?** 303
Roger Cotterrell

15 **How to do things with legislation, or, 'Everything depends on the context'** 320
David Miers

16 **How to do things with standards** 335
Jeremy Waldron

17 **Glimmers of an awakening within analytical jurisprudence** 354
Brian Z. Tamanaha

Appendix: A bibliography of William Twining 367
Penelope Twining
Index 379

Preface

> My personal political views have been reasonably 'progressive' throughout my adult life, but, unlike many colleagues, I have normally tried to distance these views when writing about academic matters, partly because my academic ideology gives primacy to values of tolerance and open-mindedness in this context, partly because the kind of approach I favour can itself accommodate a wide spectrum of political views, and partly because most of my working life has been spent as an expatriate in situations in which one has been expected to exhibit diplomatic restraint. [1]

At the celebration of William Twining's eightieth birthday at the Institute of Advanced Legal Studies in London, we offered William an IOU: a Festschrift as his birthday present. The original plan was to present the book itself, but due to circumstances beyond our control it was a promise of pleasures yet to come! In the event, we are delighted that this volume is seeing the light of day. We very much hope that William will see it as a promise suitably fulfilled. This collection of essays for William Twining is a happy confluence of two tributaries: a critical jurisprudential project of Christopher McCrudden and a more global South-focused project of Upen Baxi and Abdul Paliwala.

We are delighted that this tribute to William Twining is being published in his eighty-first year. It is traditional in such a celebration for the editors to attempt to provide a biography of the person whose work is being celebrated – a task that in William's case would be a complex one indeed. Fortunately, William has provided us with an intellectual autobiography in his perceptive interview with Manuel Atienza and Raymundo Gama, published here in English for the first time. The picture that emerges from reading the interview, together with the scholarly contributions to this book, is of an intellectual who is a pre-eminent Renaissance man among legal scholars: a bricoleur whose breadth of engagement and vision can be best described as principled eclecticism.

His legal theory combines Hartian positivism, Llewellynite realism and Benthamite utilitarianism with contemporary ideas about globalisation and

[1] William Twining, 'Introduction: Wandering Jurist' in *Law in Context: Enlarging a Discipline* (Cambridge University Press, 1997) 2.

social justice that are derived from scholars such as Boaventura de Sousa Santos, Amartya Sen and his *Southern Voices* (Abdullahi An-Na'im, Upendra Baxi, Francis Deng and Yash Ghai).[2] Underlying his transformation of the way we look at evidence and legal rules is American Realism, but a Realism linked to ideas derived from Bentham and Wigmore, neither of whom can be considered part of the Realist tradition as we know it, at least today. His engagement with legal pluralism is inspired by Llewellyn's anthropological *Cheyenne Way*, but enhanced by direct engagement with social anthropology and his experiences in Tanzania and the Sudan. It is this experienced engagement which inspired him to debunk the approach to customary law in which an expert sat with a group of male elders, asked ethnocentric questions based on Anglo-Saxon concepts and wrote down the answers, which then became Restatements of Customary Law.[3] Twining's ethnographic pluralism is combined with an understanding of globalisation and social justice in order to generate ideas about global legal pluralism. All these aspects of William's work are reflected in the chapters included in this volume.

It is a particular pleasure that the book is appearing in the *Law in Context* Series, which William founded with Robert Stevens in the late 1960s.[4] The invention of Law in Context was rooted in disenchantment with Salmond's *Law of Torts*, an engagement with American Legal Realism in Chicago and direct experience of the Sudan and Tanzania – ideas subsequently honed at Queen's University, Belfast and Warwick Law School. Twining tells the story of how the *Law in Context* Series was invented.[5] The idea for the book series was initiated in conversations with Stevens in Dar es Salaam in 1965. However, It was Patrick Atiyah, his friend and colleague in his previous academic engagement in the Sudan, who asked the most pertinent contextual question: 'How can I find out whether English businessmen take consideration seriously when I am isolated in this place? . . . How can one make sense of *Felthouse v Brindley* in Khartoum?' Years later, in 1970, Atiyah, who became a Warwick professor, was to publish the remarkable volume on *Accidents Compensation and the Law*, the first of this transformative book series.[6]

We believe that this volume captures the range of Twining's ideas on law, justice, human rights and globalisation, and we shall leave further consideration of these themes to our contributors. But we do wish in this Preface to engage a little more than the other contributions do with William's outstanding contribution to legal education as a pedagogist, an innovative educational practitioner and an activist reformer. Twining has discussed his engagement with legal education especially in two volumes: *Blackstone's Tower* published in

[2] William Twining, *Human Rights: Southern Voices* (Cambridge University Press, 2009).
[3] William Twining, 'The Restatement of African Customary Law: A Comment' (1963), 1 *Jo. Modern African Studies* 221.
[4] William Twining, 'Reflection on Law in Context' in Twining, *Law in Context* (n 1) ch. 3.
[5] Ibid. [6] Patrick Atiyah, *Accidents, Compensation and the Law* (Weidenfeld, 1970).

1994 and *Law in Context: Enlarging a Discipline* published in 1997.[7] His intellectual eclecticism is closely linked to his pedagogical eclecticism. Twining's critique of the University of Oxford, where he received his legal education, was that 'there was little sustained discussion of legal education by law teachers, let alone by law students.'[8] Nevertheless, he recognized the value of the Oxford system in promoting intellectual engagement and freedom. Thus H. L. A. Hart's linking of analytical philosophy to jurisprudence introduced 'vigorous intellectualism in the study of law'.[9] Moreover, the Oxford system of tutorials and self-education gave him a sense of intellectual freedom and enabled him to read widely in and beyond the law. This notion of intellectual freedom continues to be central to Twining's pedagogy.

The University of Chicago Law School was another formative influence. His experience there, he says, both exposed and provided for some key missing ingredients in my legal education up to then: the linking of law to the social sciences; a dialectical approach to every issue; a highly intellectualized but nevertheless realistic approach to legal practice and the law in action; a demonstration of the interdependence of theory and practice; and a concern for justice. This combined experience formed the intellectual basis for his approach to legal education in Khartoum and Dar es Salaam.[10] In Khartoum his attempt to make the course more interesting by using apparently 'relevant' English cases with stories of camels in the zoo such as M'Quaker v Goddard[11] led to his realization that the issue of context required more than superficial engagement. He describes how he 'threw down a challenge: is that how Sudanese feel about camels? A hand went up. "Aha," I thought, "at last I have got a response." But instead it was a question: "Please, sir, why was the camel in a zoo?" At that moment some scales fell away from my eyes. What had a camel in a zoo to do with the Sudan? Or circus elephants or performing fleas or slanderous parrots or carbolic smoke balls or the rule against perpetuities? What was I doing teaching all this artificial and irrelevant frippery to Sudanese students?'

It was in Dar es Salaam, however, that the idea of an intellectually and politically relevant law in context was given an impetus by the then President, Julius Nyerere. Twining writes that Nyerere's expectation of the University of Dar es Salaam, and of the Law School, 'was clear'. He continues: 'we should teach East African Law in context – and context here meant the historic break with colonialism, local circumstances and problems, and the ideology of the first Independence Government. The University should aspire to international standards of excellence, to traditional (western) academic values, but it must

[7] William Twining, *Law in Context* (n 1); William Twining, *Blackstone's Tower: The English Law School* (Sweet & Maxwell, 1994).

[8] Twining, 'Introduction: Wandering Jurist' (n 1) 3. [9] Ibid. 4. [10] Ibid. 7.

[11] [1940] 1 KB 687; 'The Camel in the Zoo' in Twining, *Law in Context* (n 1) 27.

contribute to nation building, focus on African problems and conditions, and study law in its local context.'[12]

Even while in Dar es Salaam he continued his engagement with Karl Llewellyn, with whom he studied in Chicago and whose papers he was organizing after Llewellyn's death. This engagement with American Realists continued during his brief stint at Yale Law School, followed by professorships at Belfast and Warwick, and culminated in the publication in 1973 of *Karl Lewellyn and the Realist Movement* in the *Law in Context* Series.[13] This period provided both an intellectual and practical engagement with legal education in the United States and the United Kingdom. The Llewellyn book provides a considered analysis of United States legal education from Langdell through the Realist and Dewey-inspired Columbia Curriculum Reform movement to Lasswell and MacDougall's policy approach at Yale.

Twining's *Law in Context* Series provides key insights into William's own approach to teaching and legal education. His overall perspective reflects, firstly, his general commitment to a pedagogy that promotes intellectual freedom. Secondly, he suggests the need for a sociology of legal education which also explores it in terms of what its graduates are going to be doing, whether acting as pericleans or plumbers in the law, or even working outside the legal professions.[14] Thirdly, there is the promotion of the study of law in context. This involves rethinking the traditional classification of law subjects to introduce new ideas such as international commercial transactions, broadening the focus of attention so that legal doctrines are rarely studied without reference to the social situations, the problems, the policies, and the processes that constitute the context of their operation. It involved, too, reconsideration of the techniques of teaching and examination to enable students to have room for independent exploration, and a switch from emphasis on knowledge of rules of law to emphasis on the acquisition of skills including both intellectual and clinical skills.[15]

At the Queen's University, Belfast, then at Warwick Law School, and subsequently at University College London, together with his many international engagements, he put these ideas into his own educational practice and supported educational developments in each of these law schools, in the United Kingdom and globally. At Queen's, his teaching of jurisprudence and courses on 'Juristic Technique' emphasised new approaches to rule handling, subsequently to become the innovative book, co-written with David Miers, then at

[12] William Twining, 'McAuslan in Context: Early Days in Dar and Warwick [Later Days in 43 countries]' in Valerie Kelley and Thanos Zartaloudis (eds), *Essays in Honour of Patrick McAuslan* (forthcoming, 2015).

[13] William Twining, *Karl-Llewellyn and the Realist Movement* (Weidenfeld, 1973).

[14] See William Twining, 'Pericles and the Plumber' in *Law in Context* (n 1) ch. 4.

[15] William Twining, Katherine O'Donovan and Abdul Paliwala, 'Ernie and the Centipede' in J. A. Jolowicz, ed., *Division and Classification of Law* (Butterworths, 1970), 10; William Twining, 'Pericles and the Plumber' and 'Legal Skills and Legal Education' in *Law in Context* (n 1) ch. 4 and ch. 9.

Queen's, *How to Do Things with Rules*.[16] A further innovation at Queen's was his encouragement of Abdul Paliwala to teach 'Computers and Law' as a segment of the jurisprudence course. Twining also supported the establishment of the Ballymurphy and Springfield Social Action Centres as early examples of law clinics in the United Kingdom. His membership of the Armitage Committee, which established the Northern Ireland Institute for Professional Legal Studies, enabled him to implement his belief that legal professionals required training in skills that could not just be absorbed by osmosis during an apprenticeship.[17]

At Warwick, under the leadership of Geoffrey Wilson, *Law in Context* came into its own. Every member of the Law School was required to develop their own interpretation of a contextual approach to law.[18] William had already been involved in discussions with Wilson about the establishment of a different type of Law School before arriving there in 1972.[19] For William, it meant refashioning the jurisprudence and legal methods courses, but his most significant contribution was a reinvention of an evidence course, using Bentham and Wigmore, to develop what he terms a 'modified Wigmorian analysis'.[20] The initial intellectual results of these pedagogical endeavours were the innovative books *Rethinking Evidence* and *Analysis of Evidence*[21] but the real innovation was in the nature of experiential teaching, involving sociological and psychological experiments to take students beyond traditional rule-based approaches.

Such innovative approaches were combined with the twin Realist notions of 'context' and 'skills' in legal education. They permeated the School's clinical programmes, as part of the 'skills' revolution in legal education. In *Legal Skills and Legal Education,* William set out his skills thesis.[22] 'The time is ripe,' he wrote, 'for academic lawyers to take the lead in making direct learning of "skills" a central component of every stage of legal education and training.' He continued: 'Such a change will involve not only shifts of emphasis in curriculum but, more importantly, changes in attitudes and competencies of law teachers, as well as new institutional and collective arrangements.'[23]

The law in context and skills approaches to legal education, of which he was an important advocate, have had a significant influence throughout legal education in the United Kingdom and beyond, without replacing the dominant

[16] William Twining and David Miers, *How to Do Things with Rules* (Weidenfeld, 1976).
[17] Twining, 'Introduction: Wandering Jurist' (n 1) 13. [18] Ibid. 14. [19] Ibid. 13.
[20] William Twining, 'Taking Facts Seriously' in *Law in Context* (n 1) ch. 5.
[21] William Twining, *Rethinking Evidence: Exploratory Essays* (Northwestern University Press, 1994); Terence Andersen, David Schum and William Twining, *Analysis of Evidence* (Little Brown, 1991).
[22] Twining in *Law in Context* (n 1) ch. 9; see also Rajeev Dhavan, Neil Kibble and William Twining, *Access to Legal Education and the Legal Profession* (Butterworths, 1989).
[23] Ibid. 181.

doctrinal approaches to law teaching.[24] The *Law in Context* Series, in particular, provides a vehicle for contextual legal education everywhere, and helps to promote more contextual cases and materials books in the United Kingdom. Also of considerable significance was the diasporic effect of law teachers and students moving from Warwick and influencing other law schools in the United Kingdom and abroad, with William himself subsequently moving to University College, London.[25] He became even more convinced of the need for law teachers to develop more innovative approaches to teaching and learning, and while at University College, London he developed an innovative Law Teachers' Programme. Subsequently, Warwick took the lead in promoting innovation in legal education with the establishment of national centres, including the Law Technology Centre and the UK Centre for Legal Education. The underlying ethos of the centres was informed by William's ideas on the combination of context and skills, and Twining remained an active member of the Advisory Board of the UK Centre for Legal Education.

Twining's approach to legal education has always encompassed the importance of reform and reorganization at both the academic and professional stages. In particular, he perceived very early that it was not just the academic stage that needed a skills revolution, but also the professional stage. The latter had no tradition of research and development, so that, as he wrote, 'almost nothing is known about how effective, efficient or worthwhile such teaching is.'[26] Twining's Hamlyn Lectures, entitled *Blackstone's Tower,* were a strong plea for the integrated reform of both the academic and professional stages of legal education.[27] His active consultative engagement with the Lord Chancellor's Advisory Committee on Legal Education resulted in the Committee's first report reflecting much of Twining's educational principles as the basis for a comprehensive approach to legal education and training at both stages.[28] These included the need for intellectual integrity and independence of mind, core legal knowledge (including general principles, nature and development of law, analytical and conceptual skills), contextual knowledge (including law's social, economic political, philosophical, moral and cultural contexts), legal values (encompassing ethical and social justice values) and professional skills (including acting like a lawyer and appropriate engagement with practice situations).

[24] His many international contributions to legal education include India. See e.g. Marc Galanter, Savitri Goonesekera and William Twining, *Report of the Expert Panel on the Running of the National Law School University of India* (Bangalore: National Law School University, 1996).

[25] Among the movers were Patrick Atiyah to Oxford, Patrick McAuslan to LSE and Birkbeck, Martin Partington to Bristol, Francis Snyder to University College, London, Avrom Sherr to Liverpool and to the Institute of Advanced Legal Studies, Sol Picciotto to Lancaster, David Farrier and Mike Chesterman to New South Wales and Yash Ghai and Jill Cottrell to Hong Kong.

[26] Twining, 'Legal Skills and Legal Education' in Twining (n 1) ch. 9 180.

[27] Twining, Blackstone's Tower (n 7).

[28] Lord Chancellor's Advisory Committee on Legal Education and Conduct, *First Report on Legal Education and Training* (HMSO, 1996) 78.158.56.101/archive/law/files/downloads/407/165.c7e69e8a.aclec.pdf accessed 15 February 2015.

Unfortunately, the report had a mixed impact, especially in relation to the professional stage, and William himself remained sceptical of its achievements, as he has been of the most recent Legal Education and Training Review.[29] His clarion call has been consistent throughout his career, and it retains its clarity and importance: the need for a thorough intellectual engagement with the multiple needs of, and the factors affecting, all stages of legal education. Paul Maharg suggests, and we agree, that 'Twining has set us a challenge, no less difficult now than it was in 1967. Taken seriously, the challenge may well lead to a remarkable transformation, a sea-change: the lawyer as Periclean plumber.'[30]

In putting this celebration together we have incurred many debts. We would like to thank, in particular, Penelope Twining for her encouragement and for allowing us to publish her Bibliography of William's published work. We are also most grateful to Karen Twining Fooks for providing the photograph of William which faces the title page. The editors would like to thank the authors for their contributions and our respective institutions for enabling us to work on this project: for Upendra Baxi, the University of Warwick and the University of Delhi; for Christopher McCrudden, the Queen's University of Belfast, the Leverhulme Trust for a three-year Major Research Fellowship for 2011–14, the Straus Institute, New York University for a Fellowship for the year 2013–14, and the *Wissenschaftskolleg zu Berlin* (Institute for Advanced Studies) for a Fellowship for the year 2014–15; for Abdul Paliwala, the University of Warwick and Birkbeck University of London, where he has been a visiting Professor. We express our gratitude to Cambridge University Press, in particular Finola O'Sullivan, who supported the project, and Jonathan Ratcliffe and Richard Woodham as well as Sri Hari Kumar Sugumaran of Integra Software Services, who saw it through to the end. Finally, we would like to thank William himself: without his inspiration and friendship over the years, this work would not have been possible; and equally, for his assistance to the editors and authors once the secret of the Festschrift was out!

Upendra Baxi
Christopher McCrudden
Abdul Paliwala
March 2015

[29] Twining, 'Thinking about law schools: Rutland Reviewed' (1998), 25 *Jo. Law and Society* 1; Legal Education and Training Review Independent Research Team, *Final Report: The Future of Legal Services Education and Training Regulation in England and Wales* (LETR, June 2013) www.letr.org.uk/the-report/ accessed 15 February 2015; Pete Smith, 'LETR: the role of academics in legal education and training: 10 theses' (2014), 48: 1 *The Law Teacher* 94–113; and 'IALS Event: The Role of Academics in Legal Education and Training' *Lawsync* 2013 www.lawsync.com/2013/11/11/ials-event-the-role-of-academics-in-legal-education-and-training/ accessed 15 February 2015.

[30] Paul Maharg, 'Sea-Change' (2011), 18 (1–2) *International Journal of the Legal Profession* 139 at 156.

Notes on Contributors

Gavin W. Anderson is Senior Lecturer at the School of Law, University of Glasgow

Manuel Atienza is Professor of Legal Philosophy at the University of Alicante

Upendra Baxi is Emeritus Professor at the University of Warwick and Emeritus Professor at the University of Delhi

Roger Cotterrell FBA is Anniversary Professor of Legal Theory at Queen Mary University of London

Jill Cottrell has retired from law teaching and is now a Director of the Katiba (Constitution) Institute, Kenya

Raymundo Gama is Professor of Law at the Instituto Tecnológico Autónomo de México

Yash Ghai FBA is Emeritus Professor of Public Law at the University of Hong Kong, Director and Chair of the Advisory Board of the Katiba Institute and Chair of the Advisory Board of the Commonwealth Human Rights Initiative

Oscar Guardiola-Rivera is Senior Lecturer in Law at the School of Law, Birkbeck University of London

Jane Kelsey is Professor of Law at the University of Auckland

Christopher McCrudden FBA is Professor of Human Rights and Equality Law at Queen's University, Belfast and William W. Cook Global Professor of Law at the University of Michigan Law School

John McEldowney is Professor of Law at the School of Law, University of Warwick

David Miers is Emeritus Professor of Law at Cardiff University

Fionnuala Ní Aoláin is Dorsey & Whitney Professor of Law at the University of Minnesota Law School and Professor of Law at the University of Ulster's Transitional Justice Institute

Abdul Paliwala is Emeritus Professor of Law at the School of Law, University of Warwick and Visiting Professor at Birkbeck University of London

Frederick Schauer is David and Mary Harrison Distinguished Professor of Law at the University of Virginia

Boaventura de Sousa Santos is Professor of Sociology at the University of Coimbra, Portugal and Distinguished Scholar of the Institute for Legal Studies at the University of Wisconsin Law School

Brian Z. Tamanaha is William Gardiner Hammond Professor of Law at Washington University Law School

Penelope Twining has been married to William Twining for fifty-eight years

Jeremy Waldron FBA is University Professor at New York University School of Law

Peer Zumbansen is Professor of Transnational Law at the Dickson Poon School of Law, King's College London

1

An intellectual journey with William Twining: an interview

Manuel Atienza and Raymundo Gama

Introduction

In December 2009 we asked William Twining to give an interview for the journal *Doxa, Cuadernos de Filosofía del Derecho*. We followed the format used with many other legal philosophers interviewed in the last decades (Bobbio, Hart, von Wright, Carrió, Bulygin, Raz, Alexy, MacCormick, Finnis...) and covered several aspects of his intellectual biography, as well as central problems within legal theory. We believed then, as we believe now, that an interview with William Twining would be significant for Continental and Latin American legal theorists and jurists, given his contributions to legal theory, intellectual history, legal method, legal education, evidence and globalisation. Twining accepted enthusiastically and answered all the questions in depth (with the exception of the last query, which he answered in a concise but fascinating way), providing valuable insights into several aspects of his life, work and thinking. The result was a revealing interview whose interest goes beyond our initially intended readership, extending to other audiences and contexts as well.

In May 2010, Twining went to Alicante to give a lecture on Wigmore's chart method and the logic of proof in the Legal Argumentation course of the University of Alicante. He discussed the niceties of the chart method with an audience of professors and lawyers from Spain and several Latin American countries. We all had the impression that we were attending a memorable lecture, from which one could take an important lesson: the fundamental assumptions of the method are basically the same, irrespective of whether it is a common law or a civil law system. We are very glad that the interview appears now in English as a separate chapter in this volume. As for the title of this piece, we believe that it may serve as an invitation to an intellectual journey with an outstanding legal scholar.

Interview with William Twining

1. Professor Twining, we would like to begin this interview with some biographical notes. Can you give us some information about your background?

I was born in Uganda in 1934. I sometimes say that I had a colonial childhood, an anti-colonial adolescence, a neo-colonial start to my career, and a post-colonial middle age. This is open to more than one interpretation, but the facts are that the first ten years of my life were spent in Uganda and Mauritius; that I went to school and university in England, but spent several holidays and vacations in East Africa; that from 1958 to 1965 I taught law first in Khartoum, then in Dar-es-Salaam; and that since then I have maintained contacts and interest in several countries in Eastern Africa – Sudan, Tanzania, Kenya, Uganda and, to a lesser extent, Rwanda and Ethiopia. I have not written much about this, but it remains an important part of my background.

2. How did you decide to study Law?

I drifted into Law. I wanted to escape from a rigorous but joyless classical education. I wished to study History, but my father – a self-taught historian – dismissed it as a non-subject. Law appeased his desire for practicality and my elder brother offered me his notes.

3. We would like to ask you about your experience at Oxford. Who were the professors who most inspired you as an undergraduate and, in particular, what was your relationship with H. L. A. Hart?

I went up to Brasenose College, Oxford in 1952, the year that H. L. A. Hart was elected to the Corpus Chair of Jurisprudence. Law in Oxford was at an early stage of its post-War development. Teaching was mainly centred in individual colleges and was very uneven in intensity and rigour. I was lucky because Brasenose had a strong tradition in Law. My closest contacts as an undergraduate were with two Roman lawyers, both of whom became Professors of Comparative Law. J. B. K. M. (Barry) Nicholas was my main tutor; he was an excellent Socratic teacher. Professor F. H. Lawson was an important mentor. Ronald Maudsley taught me what little English law I learned and G. D. G. Hall stimulated my interest in Legal History. I was well taught, but within a narrow tradition that was far removed from legal practice and social reality.

Towards the end of my second year I attended Professor Hart's lectures, which became the precursors of *The Concept of Law*.[1] I was fascinated and learned for the first time that Law could be intellectually interesting. I spent much of the summer of 1954 puzzling over Hart's inaugural lecture on 'Definition and Theory in Jurisprudence',[2] helped by a fellow undergraduate, Michael Woods, who later became a respected philosopher. I was captivated, indeed obsessed, by what was then crudely called 'linguistic analysis'.

[1] H. L. A. Hart, *The Concept of Law* (2nd edn including Postscript). (Oxford University Press, 1961/1994).

[2] H. L. A. Hart, 'Definition and Theory in Jurisprudence' (Inaugural Lecture). (Oxford University Press, 1953). Reprinted in Hart, *Essays in Jurisprudence and Philosophy* (Oxford University Press, 1983), ch. 1.

It was entirely due to Hart that I became a jurist. To begin with, I was a devoted disciple. Later, our relations were ambivalent. I have always recognized the value of conceptual analysis and have greatly respected Hart's intellect – indeed I was awed by him – but from an early stage I felt that something was missing. In the 1970s and 1980s Hart and I worked closely and cordially together on the definitive edition of Bentham's *Collected Works*,[3] but he was both puzzled and disappointed by my enthusiasm for Karl Llewellyn. His attitude towards me visibly cooled after 1979, when I published an article in the *Law Quarterly Review*,[4] which diplomatically and indirectly expressed my reservations. It is difficult for a former pupil to say that his teacher is not fulfilling his potential. This was the subtext of my essay, especially in regard to Hart's failure to bridge the divide between analytical jurisprudence and socio-legal studies. My final judgement on Hart was: 'Pellucid intellect, narrow agenda'.

4. In this context, what is your opinion of Nicola Lacey's biography of Hart?

Part of the key to my disappointment is to be found in Nicola Lacey's superb biography: *H. L. A. Hart: The Nightmare and the Noble Dream.*[5] For me, this is a very sad book. It brilliantly evokes Hart's background and the contexts in which Hart's career developed, especially Oxford in the period 1945 until his death in 1992. It reveals a great deal about his troubled inner life. There has been some rather muted controversy about the question of how far an intimate biography of a respected jurist is appropriate or relevant to understanding his work. My own view is that the details of his personal life throw little light on his juristic ideas, but they go a long way to explaining the trajectory of his career: why, for example, *The Concept of Law,* which was conceived as a mere prolegomenon, came to be treated as his *magnum opus*; his obsession with only one of his many critics, Ronald Dworkin; and his relatively early abandonment of intellectual work at the frontiers of his subject in favour of public service, academic administration and editing Bentham (a task for which he was ill-suited). For me, Lacey's biography tells a tragic story of a potential unfulfilled.

[3] Jeremy Bentham (1748–1832),*The Collected Works of Jeremy Bentham.* (Charlottesville, VA: InteLex Corporation; University College, London: Bentham Committee).

[4] William Twining, 'Academic Law and Legal Philosophy: The Significance of Herbert Hart' 95 *Law Quarterly Rev.* (1979) 557 reprinted in Twining, *The Great Juristic Bazaar: Jurists' Texts and Lawyers' Stories* (Aldershot: Ashgate, 2002), ch. 4.

[5] Nicola Lacey, *A Life of H.L.A. Hart: The Nightmare and the Noble Dream* (Oxford University Press, 2004).

5. What aroused your interest in Legal Realism and what was the significance of your relationship with Karl Llewellyn? Could you describe the academic atmosphere at the University of Chicago? Did you find a lot of differences with education at Oxford?

I graduated from Oxford in 1955, shortly before I was twenty-one. I did not know what I wanted to do or be. The main options at the time seemed to be to practice at the Bar, to pursue an academic career in Law, to seek work in Africa (probably in education), or to try to become a writer. I disliked the atmosphere of the Inns of Court, I was not really interested in law, there were few jobs in 'acceptable Africa' (i.e. not South Africa or the Rhodesias) in the era of decolonization, and writing offered no means of support. Eventually I combined Africa, law teaching and writing, but for two years after graduation I in effect 'dropped out'. I did some part-time teaching in Oxford, travelled widely in Europe and Africa and pursued an intensive, eclectic course of reading and self-education in which literature, philosophy, African history, politics and anthropology featured at least as much as law and legal theory. Towards the end of this period I opted to do postgraduate work in the United States.

It was largely by chance that I went to Chicago and worked with Karl Llewellyn. Professor Lawson was responsible for placing promising Oxford graduates in leading American law schools. Knowing of my interest in Jurisprudence, he asked me: which living American jurists did I most admire? I needed notice of that question, as I was largely ignorant of American legal theory, except for caricatures of American Realism, which was treated as a form of jazz jurisprudence – easy to criticise, but not worth taking seriously. After some investigation I came back to Lawson with two names: 1. Lon Fuller at Harvard; 2. Karl Llewellyn at the University of Chicago. The latter institution offered me a Fellowship, so in September 1958, newly married, I went there.

Was I predisposed to be attracted to Llewellyn and American Legal Realism? Not consciously. There were, however, some prior influences. First, while I was an undergraduate my brother had encouraged me to read Wolfgang Friedmann's *Law and Social Change in Contemporary Britain*[6] and similar works, including Maine's *Ancient Law*.[7] These were attractive, but unsettling, because they seemed to have almost no connection with what I was studying for my BA in Jurisprudence at Oxford. Later I came across *The Right of Property*[8] by a Danish jurist, Vinding Kruse, which included some rather poor photographs of houses and other buildings. A law book with *pictures* was a new and disturbing idea. Closely related to this, after graduation I

[6] Wolfgang Friedmann, *Law and Social Change in Contemporary Britain* (London: Stevens and Sons, 1951).

[7] Henry Sumner Maine, *Ancient Law: Its Connection with the Early History of Society and its Relation to Modern Ideas* (10th edn 1884) (London: J. Murray, 1861).

[8] Vinding Kruse, *The Right of Property* (London, New York: Oxford University Press, 1939).

experienced a series of culture shocks about the divide between what I had learned at Oxford and the practice of law. To give just one example: the eleventh edition of *Salmond on Torts*[9] was the main textbook on that subject. It was an admirable expository work – clear, succinct, even interesting. Nowhere did it mention that in negligence litigation a very high percentage of cases (today over ninety percent) are settled by negotiation out of court; that in most litigated cases at least one insurance company is in the background; that availability of legal aid influences patterns of torts litigation; and that most disputed torts claims turn on questions of fact rather than questions of law. This book was *unrealistic* in ways that are not fully captured by abstract distinctions between theory and practice or the law in books and the law in action. Throughout my academic career, getting more of the action into the books has been a central concern. Patrick Atiyah's *Accidents, Compensation and the Law* (now in its seventh edition)[10] is one of the most successful attempts to integrate legal doctrine with issues of policy and the 'realities' of litigation. It provides a sharp contrast with *Salmond on Torts*.

There is a third, less obvious, reason why I may have been predisposed to favour Legal Realism: my African background. I was born in Uganda, spent part of my late adolescence in East Africa, and even had some exposure to what later became known as African law. One did not need to be very alert or sensitive to realize that, despite British influence, law in East Africa (Kenya, Tanzania and Uganda were classified as 'common law countries') was radically different from law in England and Wales and that many of the differences can only be explained by reference to what is vaguely labelled 'context' – history, culture, economic conditions and politics. It is no coincidence that many of the leading members of the Law in Context movement in the United Kingdom spent part of their early careers in Africa or other colonial and post-colonial countries.

The University of Chicago, the Law School and the Windy City all provided new experiences. The University, financed largely by Rockefeller money, ruthlessly pursued Excellence; it did this in an abrasive dialectical fashion, so that one found that whenever one opened one's mouth one's assumptions were liable to be challenged, even at breakfast. The Law School fitted that culture. It was also more grown-up and professional than undergraduate Oxford. The students were older, worked harder, and were more competitive and ambitious than those I was used to. Orally, they were more articulate and forthcoming than English students, but fortunately for a bemused Oxonian they had not learned how to write. At the time I did not realize that the faculty included some of the most famous names in American academic law: Dean Edward Levi, Harry Kalven, Max Rheinstein, Kenneth Culp Davies, Walter Blum and

[9] John William Salmond, *Salmond on the Law of Torts* (11th edn). (London: Sweet and Maxwell, 1953).

[10] Patrick Atiyah, *Accidents, Compensation and the Law* (7th edn, P. Cane, 2006). (Cambridge University Press, 1970).

Malcolm Sharp, as well as Karl Llewellyn and his formidable wife, Soia Mentschikoff. I found nearly all of them friendly, approachable and not unduly concerned about their reputation. When I arrived I had simply assumed the superiority of Oxford and it took me a long time to learn otherwise.

It also took some time to grasp some profound ideological differences. In England I considered myself quite progressive, but I had often had to be on the defensive because I was not a wholehearted socialist or Marxist. In Chicago I encountered free market economics for the first time. In 1957–8 the first shoots of what became Law and Economics were sprouting. Dean Edward Levi was the impresario; Aaron Director was the vehicle, or –as I saw it – the hatchet man. Some of my encounters with Director may be of interest.

When I arrived in Chicago, I found that my faculty supervisor had put me down to do Director's course on 'The General Theory of Price'. I consulted some fellow students, who told me that this was the easiest course to pass in the Law School, provided you agreed with the instructor. Outraged, I confronted my supervisor: 'I thought that I had come to the University of Chicago, not the University of Moscow,' – this was the year of Sputnik – 'I am told that you pass Mr Director's course only if you agree with him. I disagree with him.' I won that encounter, was excused the course, and never learned any economics – a serious mistake.

The second episode occurred when a group of foreign students was taken to see a well-known programme for urban renewal. This involved replacing acres of slums with 'low cost housing'. It was clear to me that the former inhabitants could not have afforded the rents. We were not told what happened to them. At a party after this outing, I raised this question with my neighbour, who turned out to be Aaron Director. He said: 'They were not economically fit to survive.' At first, I thought this crass caricature of Darwin was intended as a joke. It was not. I never recovered from this first encounter with economic fundamentalism.

The third episode took place a few years later when I returned to Chicago to give some lectures and inspect Karl Llewellyn's papers. On my arrival from Dar-es-Salaam, jet-lagged and unshowered, I was met by Denis Cowen, the Director of the New Nations Program, who said: 'You must come to the Law School immediately; Aaron Director is giving a lecture on "Economic Development in Africa".' 'But he has never been to Africa,' I objected. I went. Director started by stating the familiar postulates of Friedmanite economics: economic development can only take place under certain rigorous conditions for a free market economy. He then proceeded to spell out the logical implications of his premises. When he finished, I got up wearily and said: 'I have not been to *all* of the African countries that Mr Director was talking about; but I have lived in some and have visited others, and I can say categorically that not a single government has in the past, does now, or is ever likely to accept his starting premises.' I sat down. 'I was talking economics, not politics,' was the succinct reply.

There is not space to give an adequate account of my experiences in Chicago, so let me move on to Karl Llewellyn. I have written about him and our relationship at great length elsewhere, so let me be brief. In 1957–8 more than half my timetable was taken up by other courses, but I took Llewellyn's course on 'Law in our Society' and spent a fair amount of time reading and researching under his direction. After his death I got to know him much better by putting his papers in order (1963–4), writing his intellectual biography and dealing guardedly, but intimately, with his widow, Soia Mentschikoff. Llewellyn and I got on very well together: he was intrigued by my interest in Africa and found my loyalty to Hartian jurisprudence a challenge. In retrospect, I recognize that his vision of law offered to fill in most of the shortcomings in my early legal education that I had sensed but not articulated. Obviously, there are specific ideas that I have assimilated, used or even refined in my own work: the law jobs theory; juristic method; styles of judging and argumentation; type fact situation; horse sense (uncommon sense based on experience); his interpretation of 'realism'. Apart from such specifics and our personal relationship, it was also a matter of attitude: he was *proud* of being a lawyer (a new idea to me); he was familiar with German law, but *loved* the common law all the more; he was *fascinated* by details of how things worked (crafts, techniques, technology); jurisprudence is about understanding law, rather than contributing to philosophy (not all questions that are jurisprudentially interesting are philosophically interesting); 'realism' was not a philosophy nor a doctrine nor a theory of law nor an epistemology, but rather a way of looking: see it fresh, see it whole, see it as it works. His philosophical underpinnings were close to classical pragmatism, especially John Dewey. He had moral and political commitments, but they were not doctrinaire. One of his favourite aphorisms was: 'Technique without ideals is a menace; ideals without technique are a mess.'

In writing about the topic, I emphasise a distinction between 'realism' as a concept and American Legal Realism as a label for the ideas of a few individuals at a particular period in American history – mainly between 1915 and about 1940. Some of the myths about American Legal Realism just do not fit the facts: that it was only or even mainly concerned with adjudication of questions of law; that it was a philosophy or a School or a theory of law; that it was a form of skepticism; and, I would add, that strange, parochial idea, that concern with being 'realistic' is an American exclusive. Llewellyn was responsible for the label and, in part, for inviting generalisations about the ideas of some quite disparate thinkers, whose most distinctive ideas were not shared by others – Jerome Frank's fact-skepticism, Leon Green's theory of causation, Underhill Moore's 'scientific fact research', and Llewellyn's law-jobs theory.

6. Apart from Hart and Llewellyn, would you include any other philosopher or jurist that has played an important role in your intellectual development?

It is difficult to distinguish between affinity and influence, and influence is often unconscious. When I think of all the teachers, writers, collaborators, colleagues, friends and critics to whom I owe intellectual debts, I sometimes feel like a sponge assimilating any liquid that comes its way and exuding a pale, diluted, contaminated mixture when squeezed. Apart from Hart and Llewellyn, I have conversed with, taught and written about so many jurists that it is difficult to single out two or three. Bentham has been a regular sounding board, but I am not a Benthamite. R. G. Collingwood's *Autobiography*[11] made a striking impact when I read it shortly after I graduated – my emphasis on standpoint, the idea of reading and writing about texts as a form of self-definition, a particular approach to reading juristic texts (the historical, the analytical and the applied) and some ideas about historical reconstruction are all in part attributable to him. Jerome Frank, John Henry Wigmore, Bentham again and David Schum all feature prominently in my work on Evidence, as does thirty years of friendship and collaboration with Terry Anderson. Over a similar period, Susan Haack has been my main philosophical sounding board, especially in relation to epistemology and pragmatism. My close friend, the late Neil MacCormick is discussed below. David Miers is a long-term close collaborator. In recent years I have been entranced by the writings of Italo Calvino, who has helped me greatly in sorting out my ambivalences about 'post-modernism': I value multiple perspectives, I recognize almost infinite complexity, I believe that imagination is required for understanding, but underneath I am an old-style cognitivist who distinguishes between epistemology and ontology.

7. Before we proceed to talk about your conception of Jurisprudence, could you provide a general overview of your work? What would you say are your most important works and under what circumstances did they arise? Would you say there have been different periods in your academic work?

At first sight, my writings appear to fall into three main categories: legal theory, including intellectual history (e.g. *Karl Llewellyn and the Realist Movement*,[12] *The Great Juristic Bazaar*,[13] *General Jurisprudence*);[14] writings about law as a discipline – i.e. legal scholarship, legal theory and legal education (e.g.

[11] R. G. Collingwood, *An Autobiography* (Oxford University Press, 1938/2002).

[12] William Twining, *Karl Llewellyn and the Realist Movement* (2nd edn) (Cambridge University Press, 2014).

[13] William Twining, *The Great Juristic Bazaar: Jurists' Texts and Lawyers' Stories* (Aldershot: Ashgate, 2002).

[14] William Twining, *General Jurisprudence. Understanding Law from a Global Perspective* (Cambridge, New York: Cambridge University Press, 2009).

Blackstone's Tower,[15] *Law in Context: Enlarging a Discipline*);[16] and evidence and proof (e.g. *Analysis of Evidence*[17] (with Anderson and Schum); and *Rethinking Evidence*).[18] Those listed here are the most substantial; which of them are significant is for others to judge.

However, there are other patterns that cut across these categories. In particular, while some of my writings are relatively detached works of scholarship or theorising (e.g. most of the writings about Llewellyn, Bentham, and the Anglo-American tradition of evidence scholarship), others are by-products of more activist enterprises, such as campaigning for reform in legal education, advancing legal education in Africa and the Commonwealth, trying to broaden academic law publishing, or to influence policies on legal records or access to legal education. Editing the *Law in Context* series, helping in the development of law schools in Dar-es-Salaam, Warwick and elsewhere, were practical ways of advancing causes, which I also wrote about. For over fifty years I have been involved in what Americans call 'Law and Development', in a variety of capacities, but I have made only modest contributions to the scholarly literature. *Analysis of Evidence* and *How To Do Things With Rules*[19] (with David Miers) are concrete manifestations of an interest in teaching intellectual skills to law students and more generally in the idea of 'legal method' broadly conceived.

Similarly, my career falls into recognizable periods, which do not coincide neatly with my intellectual interests. Very roughly, between 1958 and 1965, I taught law in Sudan and East Africa, but I have maintained my interest in that region for much longer. Between 1963 and 1973 my main scholarly project was on Karl Llewellyn and this was mostly carried out in Chicago, New Haven and Belfast. While in Belfast (1966–72) my interests in Jeremy Bentham, legal education and 'law in context' developed significantly in addition to working on Llewellyn. My work on Evidence began at Warwick (1972–82) and continued at University College London, where I have been based since 1983, but I was also involved in a range of other activities. About 1995 I began to explore the implications of so-called 'globalisation' for legal theory and law as a discipline and I deliberately revived some of my Eastern African interests in connection with this.

Some of the main themes in my writings cut across these periods and subject matters. I am not conscious of having 'developed' in the sense of radically changing my views since the mid-1960s, but clearly my later work on evidence,

[15] William Twining, *Blackstone's Tower: The English Law School* (London: Sweet and Maxwell, 1994).

[16] William Twining, *Law in Context: Enlarging a Discipline* (Oxford University Press, 1997).

[17] T. Anderson, D. Schum and W. Twining, *Analysis of evidence* (2nd edn) (New York: Cambridge University Press, 2008).

[18] William Twining, *Rethinking Evidence: Exploratory Essays* (2nd edn) (Cambridge University Press, 2006).

[19] William Twining and David Miers, *How to Do Things With Rules* (4th edn) (London, New York: Cambridge University Press, 2010).

globalisation and jurisprudence could not have been anticipated even twenty years ago. In 1972 Soia Mentschikoff, Karl Llewellyn's widow, became Dean of the University of Miami Law School. She recruited a number of Chicago graduates, including myself as a regular visitor, to assist in transforming the institution along Llewellynesque lines. For over thirty years I have continued to visit – mainly in the Spring, for I am also a Montesquieuite, who believes in the importance of climate. This arrangement has kept me in touch with Llewellyn's legacy, including collaboration and co-teaching Analysis of Evidence with Terry Anderson (also a pupil of Llewellyn's), and has given me the opportunity to develop my ideas through a seminar on 'Globalisation and Law'.

8. What is your conception of Jurisprudence and what would you say are the main tasks for a legal theorist?

The goal of an academic discipline is to advance and disseminate understanding of the subject matters of that discipline. This applies to the discipline of law. I favour a broad and open-ended interpretation of 'understanding law' in this context, involving multiple perspectives and diverse subject matters. Jurisprudence, in this view, is the theoretical part of law as a discipline. A theoretical question is a general question, one posed at a relatively high level of abstraction. Abstraction is a relative matter. 'Legal philosophy' roughly designates that aspect of Jurisprudence that deals with very abstract questions. It is an important part of Jurisprudence, but it is only one part. Some questions, such as 'What is justice?', 'What is a valid argument?', are philosophical questions. 'What constitutes a valid and cogent argument on a question of law?' is part philosophical, in part depends on the meaning of 'a question of law', which in turn depends on how that is conceived in a given legal tradition or a particular legal system. 'What constitutes a valid, cogent and appropriate argument about a question of law in the Supreme Court of the United States or the Cour de Cassation in France?' requires some local legal knowledge and sensibility. In my experience, very few jurists have made significant contributions to philosophy and only a handful of philosophers have sufficiently immersed themselves in legal materials to contribute much to understanding law. So I deplore the practice of treating legal philosophy as co-extensive with Jurisprudence – or the only interesting part. Jurists should be concerned with jurisprudentially interesting questions, not just philosophically interesting ones.

In my view, Jurisprudence can usefully be viewed as a heritage, as an ideology, and as an activity. In any given intellectual tradition there is a vast heritage of texts, debates, arguments and ideas. Much juristic activity is devoted to engaging with selected texts – interpreting, explaining, comparing, assessing, conversing with, criticizing and using them. One purpose of engaging with juristic texts is to clarify one's own ideas. An important justification for getting students to read such texts is as an exercise in self-definition, to relate their beliefs about law to their more general beliefs –about the cosmos, morality, politics and so on – to ideology in a non-pejorative sense. Sometimes, of course, one finds that some texts are ideological in a Marxian sense, enterprises of self-interested legitimation.

For disciplined, charitable reading of juristic texts I favour a Collingwoodian approach involving three stages: the historical, the analytical and the applied. The first stage involves setting a particular text in the context of the author's time, situation and concerns (what was biting him/her?). The analytical stage involves putting the text to the question: the reader converts the author's concerns into questions: What questions does this text address? What answers does it suggest? What are the reasons for the answers? Then: Do I agree with the questions? Do I agree with the answers? Do I agree with the reasons? At the third stage, the reader explores the implications and detailed applications of answers and ideas supplied by the text. This helps to clarify the contemporary significance of the text, but also serves as a test of the validity, cogency and relevance of the text to the reader's concerns.

Theorising as an activity, doing jurisprudence, involves posing, re-posing, arguing about and answering general questions relating to law at various levels of abstraction. Engaging with selected texts in our heritage – or from other legal or intellectual traditions – is one important way of carrying out the activity. Texts are an important, but not always indispensable, resource in this respect. There are other routes, such as reflecting on questions in the abstract, analyzing concrete examples, conversing, arguing or debating with colleagues and so on. Theorising has several functions or jobs: constructing total pictures (synthesizing); clarification and construction of individual concepts and conceptual frameworks; developing normative theories, such as theories of justice or human rights; constructing, refining and testing empirical hypotheses; developing working theories for participants (e.g. prescriptive theories of law-making or adjudication); and so on – wherever thinking at a relatively general level contributes to understanding. Perhaps the most important function is articulating, exposing to view and critically assessing important assumptions and presuppositions underlying legal discourse generally and particular aspects of it – not only issues about law in general, but also the assumptions and presuppositions of sub-disciplines, as has been happening recently in fields obviously affected by globalisation, such as comparative law and public international law. This critical function can usefully be applied to one's own work as well as to others – there is a need for a self-critical legal studies movement.

9. Do you consider yourself a positivist, and if so, in which sense?

Labelling thinkers is nearly always an inexact enterprise and, as you suggest, 'positivism' has many meanings and associations. If it means a perspective that is amoral, indifferent to morality or scientistic, then clearly I am not a positivist. I have worked in the shadow of Bentham, Hart and Llewellyn, three quite different individuals who are usually allocated to a broad positivist tradition. In some contexts, I accept versions of the separation thesis and the social sources thesis that have been attributed to Hart's *The Concept of Law*, but with reservations. I share with Hart the belief that we need a vocabulary for giving accounts of the realities of the law in action. One needs to be able to describe regimes of governance and how they operate in practice as well as having a vocabulary for evaluating them. Indeed, it is difficult to understand how one can assess a foreign or exotic legal order without first obtaining accurate information about its rules and how it operates in practice. I also broadly share Hart's view that one should not romanticizse legal phenomena: '[T]he identification of the central meaning of law with what is morally legitimate, because orientated towards the common good, seems to me in view of the hideous record of the evil use of law for oppression to be an unbalanced perspective, and as great a distortion as the opposite Marxist identification of the central case of law with the pursuit of the interests of a dominant economic class'.[20] However, sharp distinctions between is and ought, between law and morality, are conceptually problematic and, in my view, break down in some contexts. For example, they do not hold in reasoning about questions of law in hard cases; even in fact-determination not all 'questions of fact' are value free. Similarly, while distinctions between observer and participant perspectives are helpful, they too can be problematic.

Of course, a good deal of legal theory, legal scholarship and legal education is participant-oriented. For example, in Anglo-American legal education we regularly ask our students to adopt the standpoints of, *to pretend to be*, legislators, judges, advocates, legal advisers and various kinds of users of law. For some of these participants, the idea that they should aspire to make the system 'the best it can be' is attractive. Many such roles can be conceived as having normative elements. However, even in such contexts some distinction between is and ought is needed; for example, an internal critic arguing for reform of a particular law or a legal adviser concerned to give a client realistic advice. Ronald Dworkin's conception hardly fits tax advisers, partisan advocates, dissidents, and some other users of a legal system. Most non-positivist theories, like Dworkin's, are participant oriented in this sense. In *General Jurisprudence* I explicitly adopted a positivist position in considering how to construct reasonably inclusive overviews (or mental maps) of legal phenomena from a global perspective. This was a descriptive enterprise. Understanding law involves embracing both aspiration and reality, not just one of them. So I am a positivist some of the time in some contexts, but the label is not very informative.

[20] H. L. A. Hart 1983, supra note 2 at 12.

10. Let's talk about one of your more recent books, *General Jurisprudence: Understanding Law from a Global Perspective*. To what extent do you think the challenges of globalisation have changed the way of understanding the Law?

General Jurisprudence (2009)[21] can be read as the continuation, but not quite the culmination of a project that ostensibly began in the mid-1990s, but the roots of which can be traced back through my involvement in various supra-national activities concerning the global South or the Third World in the 1970s and 1980s, to working in Eastern Africa before that, to my colonial childhood and adolescence. The book was preceded by essays collected in two books (*Globalisation and Legal Theory* (2000)[22] and *The Great Juristic Bazaar* (2002))[23] and has been succeeded by a reader on four Southern jurists (*Human Right: Southern Voices* (2009)),[24] and several further essays. The central question addressed in the book is: what are the implications of 'globalisation' for law as a discipline and jurisprudence as its theoretical part? The book is written from the standpoint of a Western, common law oriented jurist, concerned about the health of his discipline in his own country and more generally in the West. It is *not* an attempt to construct a global theory of law.

The 'plot' can be briefly summarized as follows: if one interprets 'globalisation' to refer to the complex processes that are making the world more interdependent, then one needs to recognize that most of these processes are taking place at sub-global levels and that we lack adequate concepts and data for making many truly 'global' generalisations about legal phenomena. For law, some of the most significant sub-global patterns relate to such phenomena as former empires, diasporas, religions, trading blocs, regions, language spread, and legal traditions –almost none of which are global in a literal geographical sense. If one adopts a global perspective in order to construct a broad contextual overview, a jurist needs to conceptualise 'law' in a reasonably open and inclusive manner that includes some idea about non-state law, to differentiate between different levels of relations and ordering that to some extent reflect these sub-global patterns, and to recognize their complexities and our relative ignorance about most of the phenomena. This leads one not only to be suspicious of loose talk about 'global Law', 'global law firms' and 'global institutions', and confident universalist claims, but also to question some widespread, often ethnocentric, assumptions underlying Western traditions of academic law –for example, that law consists only of two forms: the municipal law of nation states and classical international law; that we live in a secular age rather than one of religious revival; that Western legal concepts fit non-Western legal orders.

[21] William Twining 2009, supra note 14.

[22] William Twining, *Globalisation and Legal Theory* (London: Butterworth and Evanston: Northwestern University Press, 2000).

[23] William Twining 2002, supra note 13.

[24] William Twining, ed., *Human Rights, Southern Voices* (Francis Deng, Abdullahi An-Na'im, Yash Ghai and Upendra Baxi) (New York: Cambridge University Press, 2009).

Part of my argument is that a new generation of jurists is reinterpreting some canonical Western jurists critically from a global perspective. Tamanaha starts with Hart's premises but pares away nearly all of his criteria of identification of law. Pogge, by challenging Rawls' conception of societies as self-contained units, has developed a variation of Rawls' principles of justice applied to supra-national institutions that is much more radical than Rawls' own *The Law of Peoples*.[25] Peter Singer has explored the implications of Benthamite utilitarianism from a global perspective. I have done something similar for Hart and Llewellyn. And Santos has developed a 'common sense' theory based on a strange mixture of Max Weber and post-modernism. This emphasises the continuities as much as the disjunctures in appraising our heritage from a global perspective. In addition, thinking about law in the world as a whole makes comparative law central to understanding law and makes some topics more salient, such as diffusion, pluralism and surface law – whether strong claims to convergence, unification or harmonization of laws apply mainly to surface phenomena. However, law as a practice-oriented discipline concerned with detailed practical problems will continue rightly to be largely focused on specific issues arising in 'local' (both geographical and intellectual) contexts at a variety of levels. The implications of globalisation vary significantly for different kinds of legal specialism and will make some supranational and transnational fields more important.

11. What would you say have been your main contributions to the study of Evidence?

I joined the University of Warwick Law School in 1972. The institution was committed to 'broadening the study of law from within' in all subjects. Before I arrived, I was asked: 'Which field of law are you going to Warwickize', meaning rethink in a broader way than its orthodox or traditional treatment. The choice soon narrowed to Land Law or Evidence. I had no specialized knowledge of either. My colleague, Patrick McAuslan, wished to approach Land Law from a Public Law perspective – and in time did so with distinction. So I took Evidence. This became my main focus of attention for fifteen years. From the start I conceived of this as a case study of the general enterprise of broadening the study of law. The first step was to construct an ideal type of orthodox Anglo-American approaches to the study of Evidence, to articulate their underlying assumptions, and to assess them critically. For example, the subject of Evidence in law was treated as co-extensive with the Law of Evidence – mainly the rules governing admissibility. The contested jury trial (a wholly exceptional event) was treated as the paradigm case for the application of the exclusionary rules. Rules constituted the whole subject matter of Evidence. The concept of 'legal reasoning' was limited to argumentation about questions of

[25] John Rawls, *The Law of Peoples* (Cambridge, MA: Harvard University Press, 1999).

law (typically in 'hard cases') and reasoning about questions of fact was ignored or dismissed as mere common sense. This ideal type was narrowly conceived and easy to criticize. The real challenge was to construct a coherent conception of Evidence in legal contexts to replace that orthodoxy.

As I was historically inclined, my next question was: has anyone tried to do this before? The answer was that for two hundred years after the publication of the first treatise, Chief Baron Gilbert's *The Law of Evidence* (1754),[26] there had been numerous attempts to develop a 'theory of evidence', some of which had been quite broadly conceived. So, rather than try to 'reinvent the wheel,' I devoted some attention to intellectual history. I examined the assumptions underlying leading Anglo-American treatises on Evidence from 1754 to the 1970s and constructed a further ideal type of the assumptions underlying 'The Rationalist Tradition of Evidence Scholarship' to which the ideas of almost all common law specialists had approximated. The tradition was heavily influenced by Bentham, especially the premise that the direct end of adjudication is rectitude of decision, i.e. the correct application of rules to facts that were probably true. In short, the enterprise involved the pursuit of truth by rational means on the basis of inferential reasoning from evidence. Bentham argued that there should be no rules of evidence. This was considered too extreme, but the scope of the Law of Evidence narrowed considerably over time. Nevertheless, in the English academic tradition the assumption persisted that rules (or, more broadly, doctrine) constituted the subject matter of the discipline of law. In 1972, during a highly charged debate on reform of criminal evidence in England, the leading evidence scholar, Sir Rupert Cross, stated: 'I am working for the day when my subject is abolished.' This provided a splendid foil for my work, for how could scholars *abolish* the subject of Evidence in law? What would one study about Evidence if there were no rules?

The two outstanding figures in the Anglo-American tradition were Jeremy Bentham and John Henry Wigmore. So I wrote a book about them (*Theories of Evidence: Bentham and Wigmore* (1985))[27] and used each of them as a reference point for developing my own ideas. Bentham inspired the model for the Rationalist Tradition. His proposals for reform were considered to be too radical, but almost every change over the next two centuries has moved in the direction that he indicated, but at a slower pace. Bentham also provided a foil for considering non-utilitarian and various skeptical perspectives. Wigmore divided the subject of Evidence in law into two parts: the Principles of Proof and the Trial Rules. Although he was revered for over fifty years as a scholar in respect of the latter, hardly anyone had paid much attention to his Principles of Proof, including his 'chart method' of structuring and constructing arguments about disputed questions of fact in complex cases.

[26] Jeffrey Gilbert, *The Law of Evidence* (Dublin, 3rd edn, 1769) (London, 1754).

[27] William Twining, *Theories of Evidence: Bentham and Wigmore* (London and Stanford, CA: Stanford University Press, 1985).

I developed my theoretical ideas about Evidence over 30 years mainly through a series of essays, many of which are collected in *Rethinking Evidence*.[28]

My interest in Evidence started at roughly the same time as the development of 'the New Evidence Scholarship' in the United States. In the early years this was mainly concerned with issues about probabilities and proof, with quite sharp divisions between Baconians (inductivists) and Pascalians (who believe that all probabilistic reasoning is in principle mathematical – with further divisions between Bayesians, frequentists and other schools of statistics). I joined in these debates, as I did in relation to later concerns about the relationship between narrative and argument in legal fact-finding, but my main concerns were broader.

Ironically, having set out on a seemingly radical programme, I found myself reviving and defending some key aspects of the Anglo-American tradition that had been forgotten: Bentham's view of the ends of adjudication, Thayer's vision of the Law of Evidence as a series of disparate exceptions to a principle of free proof, and Wigmore's chart method. All of these go beyond conceiving of the subject of Evidence in law solely or mainly in terms of rules. In retrospect, I mildly regret not having devoted more attention to the details of the surviving rules of Evidence, which still remain the main focus of professional examinations in the United States and of most specialists in the field. My argument that the exclusionary rules are an important, but only a small, part of the subject might have been more persuasive. Instead, in recent years I have devoted more attention to the idea of Evidence as an evolving multi-disciplinary field. This has been the subject of an ambitious programme at University College London since 2003 (*Evidence, Inference and Inquiry*).[29]

12. You had a close relationship with Neil MacCormick. If you were asked to write a paper in his honour, what aspects of his personality and work would you emphasise?

Neil MacCormick was an outstanding jurist, a close friend, and in many respects a kindred spirit. We mourn his death at a relatively young age. It is some consolation that he was able to complete the quartet of books which encapsulated his ideas and will be perceived as his monument. He was admired, praised and loved by a wide range of diverse people for a number of different things: as a teacher; as a public intellectual; as a democrat; as a committed Scottish nationalist and European; and, to use one of his favourite expressions, one who contributed to the gaiety of nations. I greatly valued his friendship and learned much from his jurisprudence. I regret that, despite planning to do so, we only collaborated on one published essay.

[28] William Twining 2006, supra note 17.

[29] P. Dawid, M. Vasilaki and W. Twining (eds), *Evidence, Inference and Inquiry* (Oxford University Press, 2011).

Intellectually, we were quite different, but complemented each other. His main interests beyond law were in philosophy, politics and Scotland; mine were more in history, literature, anthropology and Africa. If I admitted to having a general theory of law it would be quite close to his conception of an institutional normative order. He was an excellent philosopher, but unlike some contemporary analytical jurists his conception of philosophy was in the spirit of the Scottish Enlightenment rather than a more narrowly conceived form of conceptual analysis. This meant that he was genuinely concerned to bridge the gap between analytical and social scientific perspectives on law, not only at the abstract level of philosophy.

In his later writings, MacCormick seemed to have deserted his earlier legal positivism. In my view, this should be interpreted as a shift of emphasis rather than as a radical departure. MacCormick's shift reflected his passionate, activist commitment to certain liberal democratic values; it did not involve a rejection of the need for relative detachment on the part of scholars. But he was concerned to emphasise that expositors, teachers and jurists are often second-order participants in their own legal systems and that in these roles it is incumbent on them to make a system's aspirations guide their activities. As indicated above, I have no objection to this view, but it is not appropriate for more detached or 'external' perspectives. Comparative lawyers, historians and empirical researchers into law should be committed to the values of scholarship, but need a more detached stance towards the phenomena they study, for most law is a product of other people's power.

13. To finish this interview we would like to ask you to give a piece of advice to people who are starting their academic careers in legal theory. What would be your message for young legal theorists?

Think!

Part I
Human rights

2

Resituating Twining's discovery of Bentham's Fragment on 'torture' amidst the twenty-first-century CE 'Terror Wars'

Upendra Baxi[1]

1. Introduction

I have known William Twining for many decades. At my first meeting with him in Hong Kong, at a conference on legal education, he asked me what my priorities were as a new Vice Chancellor of the University of Delhi. He recalls fondly to this day that I said I wanted to achieve two things: one was to de-feudalize the university; the other was to see happy faces around me on the campus. He used to quote this many a time and asked, with a twinkle in his eyes, whether I had fulfilled these promises. He is himself a happy man and, not unlike me, likes others to be jolly, although there are times when he can become anxious or even indignant. Twining has a phenomenal memory, and I received an intimation of it when he was engaged in the project that subsequently became *Southern Voices* (he happily called Francis Deng, Yash Ghai, Abdullahi An-Na'im and me his 'subjects'). He likes not merely intellectual adventures; when Penelope and William Twining met on a recent visit, they had travelled *via* Somalia and had navigated the pirates successfully.

I met William Twining in print a long time ago, before meeting him in person, as many others have done, and I learnt a lot from him. Twining's contributions to the world of law and legal theory are truly legendary. I rediscovered Karl Llewellyn and American Realists through his truly great intellectual biography of Llewellyn. I rediscovered the virtues of conventional comparative jurisprudence through Twining's writings (I call it 'conventional' only because this genre usually ignores 'Uncle' Marx and Marxians). I find the links (which he draws only partly explicitly) between British analytical jurisprudential thinkers and globalization always interesting and, at points, very exciting. *Via* Twining, I realized why no law teaching is complete without teaching the law of evidence, which among other things teaches us 'how to do things with rules'. (He even went to the lengths of explaining to me, when I was sojourning at Washington College of Law in the United States, why it was

[1] I wish to place on record my appreciation of Professors Christopher McCrudden and Abdul Paliwala for their sage counsel, and to acknowledge Mr Vausjith Ram (fourth-year student of the National Law School of West Bengal), who helped me with some suggestions at the proof stage.

important to co-teach evidence with an ex-CIA agent. I was not persuaded.) Having attended some of his classes, I learnt a good deal from his approaches to law teaching and research in the Third World, my favourite being the article partly entitled 'Pericles and the Plumber', presented at the conference on legal education in 1972 in Pune, India. I can vouch (if any reassurance is needed) for the fact that he is appropriately postcolonial in his approach.

2. Bentham's Fragments

In this chapter, I focus on Twining's discovery of Bentham's fragments on 'torture' (hereafter called 'Fragments'). The timing of this discovery is significant, coinciding with his days at Queen's University Belfast and his experience of State and non-State terror in Northern Ireland in its long civil war. I explore this excavation for personal as well as intellectual reasons. The personal reason is that this is the only article in which Penelope Twining, his wife, is a co-author, testifying to her early scholarship and her contribution generally to William's work.[2] The broader intellectual reasons are many. Among these are Bentham's own views on the justification of torture, Twining's relation with this, and Bentham's legacy as received and revived in twenty-first-century wars *of* and *on* terror.[3]

Twining was the first to highlight two 'Fragments' of Jeremy Bentham written during 1785–80,[4] at that time unpublished.[5] Twining's interests were many sided, as the commentary on Bentham's 'Fragments' reveals. He was correct in suggesting that English jurisprudential writers (in Karl Llewellyn's terms, the 'jurisprudes') had not taken the problem of torture seriously and that they blithely assumed that the practice of torture was non-existent or *de minimis*.[6] There was a sharp distinction drawn at the time of his writing between the 'theory of punishment' (which was a dominant preoccupation) and 'torture' (which was ignored).[7] At least four preliminary questions arise. First, why did the Twinings publish these 'Fragments' from Bentham? Second, why did Twining not follow up his interest, particularly in the wake of the 9/11

[2] Although she has taken responsibility only for the Bentham MS, her contribution to the overall essay is far from being marginal.

[3] See, for this distinction, Upendra Baxi, *Human Rights in a Posthuman World: Critical Essays* 159–96 (Delhi: Oxford University Press, 2007).

[4] See William and Penelope Twining, 'Bentham on Torture' 25 *Northern Ireland Legal Quarterly* 305 (1973). This article is referred to hereafter simply as 'Twining'. Twenty-five years later, in the spring of 1804, Bentham again pursued the matter in a fragment 'Of Torture' and the more substantial draft, 'Means of extraction for extraordinary occasions' to March 1804 and 27 May 1804 respectively. These two texts have not been published, with the exception of three crucial sentences from the latter, which were printed in a footnote to the work of the Twinings and made much of, as we see later, by Alan Dershowitz.

[5] Burns' magisterial effort to do the complete works had then reached the fifth volume: see note 17 of Twining.

[6] Twining, at 305–6. [7] Id., at 307.

attacks on the USA? Third, why did Bentham even consider writing these as 'Fragments'? And, fourth, why should we read these 'Fragments' today?

The answer to the question of why we should read the 'Fragments' today is relatively clear. Torture is routine in the nation state (in jails and police precincts). It goes almost unrepressed; impunity is the hallmark of the practice of torture. It is also widely practised in declared and undeclared states of war and warlike situations across borders. All this is despite the fact that the normative prohibition contained in the near-universal UN Convention against Torture (CAT, hereafter) prohibits torture, as committed by public officials. And since 9/11, despite protestations that 'torture' (in the sense of infliction of severe pain, whether physical or psychological) is to be used only in a hypothetical ticking bomb situation, it continues to be more widely practised. It is also more widely discussed, and this discussion itself raises an ethical problem. There is little escape from intellectual respectability being lent to practices of torture. Slavoj Zizek was right when he said that 'essays . . . which do not advocate torture outright, [but] simply introduce it as a legitimate topic of debate, are even more dangerous than an explicit endorsement of torture'.[8] William Twining would surely have agreed to disagree; for him, not to discuss justifiable torture in rare cases would be to condone its usage in routine contexts, and such contexts have become disturbingly routine now with the terror wars.

Why did Bentham write the 'Fragments'? The answer to this question must be left to Bentham's corpus managers; they all agree that Bentham never completed these 'Fragments'. What the 'Fragments' say about the justification of torture is open to reconstruction – a compelling circumstance was that Bentham could not bring to bear a *full* utilitarian justification of torture; he did not consider inter-state relations and international law, and in 'Fragments' his attention was focused on exceptional cases. I discuss this in the next sections in some detail.

Twining's subsequent lack of interest in the subject of torture is relatively clear. Twining refers to the Irish experience in his 'Philosophy' and in *General Jurisprudence* he reiterates Bentham. Does this mean that his interest was

[8] Slavoj Zizek, *Welcome to the Desert of the Real*, 103 (London: Verso, 2002). But see Jeremy Waldron, *Torture, Terror, and Trade-Offs: Philosophy for the White House* (Oxford University Press, 2012). Twining would agree: for example, he writes: 'sometimes been regrettably persuasive when playing the role of Devil's Advocate. Thus talking about torture can have undesirable practical consequences or, when it has no significant consequences, it may be compared to fiddling while Rome burns': see William Twining and Barrie Paskins, 'Torture and Philosophy', *Proceedings of the Aristotelian Society, Supplementary Volumes*, 52: 143–94 at 143 (1978). He there offers utilitarian 'justification' in the critique of Paskins: see Barrie Paskins, 'What's Wrong with Torture?', *British Journal of International Studies*, 2: 138 (1976). I do not here take into account what Twining offers by way of 'the general theory of torture', with which Barry Baskins differs: much of what Twining says reiterates his analysis of Bentham. This article, referring in particular to Twining, will be referred to hereafter as 'Twining, Philosophy'. See also William Twining, 'The contemporary significance of Bentham's *Anarchical Fallacies*', *Archiv für Rechts- und Sozialphilosophie* 61: 325 (1975).

primarily in Bentham and not so much in torture? As a decent human being, Twining, of course, abhors torture; but as an intellectual, he finds torture to be an ambiguous concept. In his latest book,[9] Twining highlights the salience of torture as a theoretical problem in jurisprudence and social theory but does not go much beyond the 1973 torture article. Certainly, his later work, whether pre- or post-9/11, does not refer extensively to the problem of justification or the practice of torture. We do not know, for example, what Twining thinks of Alan Dershowitz, whose deployment of Benthamite torture warrants we consider later. Even so, we may infer that, not unlike Bentham, Twining would have privileged Bentham's 'justification' of recourse to torture in exceptional circumstances. But what was Bentham's position? It is to this that I turn first.

Even as I do so, I would like to state that this chapter does not narrate the causes and consequences (the history) of torture; the contemporary history of torture and the full contexts of the contemporary war *on* and *of* terror; its impact on the tormentor, the tormented and society at large; and the role of religion and the sacred in the justification of torture and terror. These are crucial areas, but here the focus is on the Bentham–Twining-type justification of torture in extremis or abnormal situations, when alternatives to its practice are not decisively adjudged morally superior.

3. Bentham's definition of torture

Jeremy Bentham had a horror of the seductive force of unanalyzed terms; his work always begins, and is littered, with stipulative definitions of terms he wishes to use. Torture was certainly not an exception; indeed, a precise definition of the term seemed necessary for him to avert the risks of confusion and sentimental waffle. He defines torture as follows: 'Torture, as I understand it, is where a person is made to suffer Torture, any violent pain of body in order to compel him to do something what or to desist from doing something which done or desisted from the penal application is immediately made to cease.'[10]

Torture is identified with the 'violent pain of body' of an individual. It is not clear why Bentham does not include mental torture in his definition. Perhaps he thought that all pain is physical and what is considered 'psychological' or mental is also physical pain. (I am not sure that my Delhi dentist fully agrees with Bentham. He displays a placard that reads: 'some pains are physical / some pains are mental / But there is one pain – dental / which is both physical and mental!') It is not clear whether Bentham is anti-Cartesian, denying the body/mind distinction; what is clear is that, for him, at least violent bodily pain is torture. This modern definition provided by the United Nations Covenant on Torture, Cruel and Unusual and Degrading Punishment or Treatment

[9] See William Twining, *General Jurisprudence: Understanding Law from a Global Perspective* 211–12 (Cambridge University Press, 2009).

[10] Twining, at 309.

(CAT),[11] on the other hand, extends to psychic pain, which Bentham's definition rigorously excludes.

At the same time, both Bentham and the Convention exclude what may be called group torture: the reasons for this exclusion are unclear and, as a rule, unjustifiable. The problem of group torture – official and social practises inflicting severe mental or physical pain on targeted communities – has little or no theoretical interest to Bentham or Twining, but is real enough as concerns minorities, whether ethnic, linguistic, religious, disabled or sexual. A part of this problem is addressed directly or indirectly through other international human rights instruments; directly in conventions such as the Genocide Convention, and indirectly in conventions such as those for the elimination of discrimination against women or racial discrimination conventions.

Bentham builds into his definition only compulsive torture (that is violent bodily pain) inflicted in order to 'compel him to do something what or to desist from doing something which done or desisted from the penal application is immediately made to cease'. This means that it should always be within the power of the victim to do something or desist from doing something in order to make the torture stop. Although Bentham agrees that the power may be fallibly exercised and may in fact be abused or misused, going beyond the use of torture for compulsive purposes, he does not consider that this justifies not conferring such powers in the first place.[12]

The definition is 'extensive', that is, it deals with violent bodily pain inflicted by persons in civil society as well as by agents of the state. This move normalizes such violent pain, which occurs routinely. It is important to stress that Bentham does not write merely about the use of torture by the state; he thinks that the practice of torture as defined by him is widespread in civil society.[13] There are cases in 'which it is customary to apply it, and in which nobody suspects the use of it to be improper', such as child beating by the mother or nurse.[14] It may be right for Bentham to speak of customariness in an era in which human rights law had not been invented; certainly, corporal chastisement of minors and violence against women now stand normatively

[11] But see Jeremy Davis, who observes 'ambivalence in Bentham's early torture writings over the question of whether or not interrogational torture is always effective. Bentham's indecisiveness about whether or not sufficiently intense physical pain is guaranteed to determine the behavior of its victims goes to the heart of his thought'. See Davis, 'The Fire-Raisers: Bentham and Torture', *Interdisciplinary Studies in the Long Nineteenth Century*, 19: 15 (2012) DOI:http://dx.doi.org/10.16995/ntn.643

[12] Twining, at 312–13; also see Twining, 'Philosophy' at 146–8 (where he discusses four fallacies) and pp. 151–62 (where he analyzes, Bentham-like, paradigmatic notions of torture and its elements). But see, for contemporary definitional predicaments, analyses as opposed as Jinee Lokaneeta, 'A Rose by Another Name: Legal Definitions, Sanitized Terms, and Imagery of Torture', *Law, Culture and the Humanities* 6:2 245–73 (2010) and Melanie Richter-Montpetit, 'Beyond the Erotics of Orientalism: Lawfare, Torture and the Racial–sexual Grammars of Legitimate Suffering', *Security Dialogue* 45:1, 43–62 (2014).

[13] Id., at 310. [14] Id., at 310–11.

outlawed at the bar of international human rights law. Without going into detailed analysis of these examples or generally addressing unjustifiable torture, it is important to acknowledge that Bentham always compares the legal with the moral and the popular sanctions.[15] If civil society generally accepts torture within its own domains, it is vain to expect state and law to completely check or arrest it. Bentham was probably the first British thinker to address both the extraordinary and banal (to deploy Hannah Arendt's difficult classification[16]) aspects of the use of torture.

Bentham does not accept torture, inflicted as punishment or in exceptional circumstances, where it is 'indeterminate'. The act of torture must be determinate: it must have a moment of beginning and a moment of cessation. And if at all resorted to, it must be effective as a tool for gathering information. In this way begins the consideration of justification, if any, for torture. As Twining says: 'For Bentham, the paradigm case of torture involves a situation in which the purpose (coercion) can be achieved immediately.'[17]

The 'imposition of violent bodily pain' is not easily decodable, as Bentham readily admits. Such pain is a matter of degrees. In more modern terms, 'disorientation, isolation, and brainwashing' (to use Twining's words) may or may not lead to a confession by a 'terrorist'. Such maltreatment is increasingly regarded as degrading, cruel and inhuman treatment, and not 'torture' in the Benthamite sense. Besides, as Twining points out, torture 'can be inflicted, for example, to incapacitate the victim, to terrorize others, . . . to compel public statements, as an outlet for feelings of vengeance, or of frustration or for sadistic impulses, or for more obscure unconscious motives, or perhaps as a matter of senseless routine ostensibly to serve some rational purpose or other in circumstances in which it could not in fact be fulfilled'.[18] There is thus normative agreement between Bentham, Twining and others that if torture is

[15] See Upendra Baxi, 'Introduction' to Jeremy Bentham, *Theory of Legislation* (Lexis/Nexis, 1975; reprinted 2013).

[16] See, Hannah Arendt, *The Origins of Totalitarianism* (New York: Harcourt Brace Jovanovich, 1951), 3rd edn with new prefaces; Id., *Eichmann in Jerusalem: A Report on the Banality of Evil* (New York: Viking Press, 1963; revised and enlarged edition, 1965); see also, Bernard J. Bergen, *The Banality of Evil: Hannah Arendt and 'The Final Solution'* (London: Rowman & Littlefield, 1998).

[17] Twining, at 340.

[18] Twining, at 341. I do not deal with the important aspect of whether or not torture belongs to the genre of theory of punishment to which Bentham's 'Fragments' give excessive attention and which William Twining reciprocates to some extent. My difficulties with a theory of punishment are several. First, each 'theory' sets out multiply stated general aims. Thus, in deterrence theory, retribution is present and much depends on whether we state deterrence as general or as individual. Second, these different theories of punishment come into conflict with one another, and this conflict is insoluble. Third, there are, or seem to be, no agreed advance principles of justice which privilege one theory over another. Fourth, the practice of administration of criminal justice is seldom consistent on why and how we punish – a psychoanalytic account suggests that we do not know why we punish: on these, see Albert Ehrenzweig, *Psychoanalytic Jurisprudence* (New York: Oceana, 1971); certainly, Albert demonstrated this to a telling effect in the case of the death penalty in an insanity cell. H. L. A. Hart guides us to a different point of view: see Hart, *Essays on Punishment and Responsibility* (Oxford University Press, 1968).

to be justified at all, it ought to be rendered determinate and ought not to continue beyond achievement of its stated purpose.

4. Utilitarian 'justification' of torture

Having invented the Principle of Utility, Bentham is the first thinker to apply the principle to torture, as his 'Fragments' reveal. The 'Fragments' conclude with the words: 'On this subject as much as on most others it behoves us to be on our guard not to be led astray by words. There is no approving it in the lump, without militating against reason and humanity: nor condemning it without falling into absurdities and contradictions.'[19] No 'approving it in the lump' characterizes Jeremy Bentham's cautious approach to the subject. The contrary stance militates 'against reason and humanity' because: (a) torture as corporal treatment (punishment as chastisement) was practised in civil society institutions; (b) the market or economic institutions or systems may themselves be viewed as claiming similar powers and impunities; and (c) only in rare situations interrogational and custodial torture by state officials may even be justifiable. He thus placed a heavy burden of reason on those who would rule out at the threshold any talk that condemns torture in the 'lump'. This essay would trespass beyond its purpose if it were to attend fully to considerations canvassed by propositions (a) and (b) above ~~and to those urged by proposition (a) above~~. We can note, however, that the expression 'cruel' or 'degrading punishment or treatment now covers what was earlier called 'chastisement', practised as a matter of right and status.[20]

In this chapter, I focus primarily on interrogational and custodial torture by state officials. In general, Bentham does not favour interrogational or custodial torture for many cogent reasons but he makes an exception when he tentatively justifies the use of interrogational torture for extracting information. Bentham wrote specifically in the context of the immediate aftermath of the Irish Rebellion of 1798. As Jeremy Davis puts it: 'The probable reason why "Means of extraction" anticipates so powerfully the contemporary scene is that Bentham outlined his fully fledged version of the ticking bomb case as a direct response to a cycle of insurgency and counter-insurgency that had shaken the British imperium and that was still bloodily ongoing in 1804.'[21] (As an aside, it is intriguing that Bentham wrote specifically in the context of the immediate aftermath of the Irish Rebellion of 1798, whilst Twining's discovery of the 'Fragment' occurs in the wake of the mid-twentieth-century Civil War in Northern Ireland.)

[19] Twining, at 337.

[20] See Christopher McCrudden, 'Human Dignity and Judicial Interpretation of Human Rights', 19(4) *European Journal of International Law 655* (2008); and see Id. (ed.), *Understanding Human Dignity* (Oxford University Press/British Academy | Proceedings of the British Academy Vol. 192, 2013).

[21] See note 11 at [5].

Bentham suggests that there are two cases in which interrogational torture 'may be properly applied'. The first case (for which he formulates at least ten rules[22]) 'is where the thing which a Man is required to do, a thing which the public has an interest in his doing, is a thing which for a certainty is in his power to do; and which therefore so long as he continues to suffer for not doing he is sure not to be innocent'. It is noteworthy that in this formulation the key elements are *power* and *interest.* Without both being present, torture, according to Bentham and Twining, is not justifiable. The care with which this case is enunciated is noteworthy: Bentham does not think torture in routine situations is justifiable.

Clearly, the ten rules which Bentham formulates, towards the implementation of this case, relate to the power (act of will) invested in the tormented to part or not to part with *secular* information. If what is required lies beyond the power of the would-be tormented, then torture is not justified. When an act of terror is attributed to the Divine Will (theological voluntarism that upholds the Divine Positive Law), and the human will – of the pious perpetrator – is merely an instrument of the Divine, then it would not be within the power of the individual to resist it and imparting information about other human agents, similarly devout, would be a breach of faith. This is the quintessence of religion-based terror today and it is inappropriate to deploy Bentham to justify torture in that context.

Leaving aside the question concerning *power*, the question of public *interest* is at one stage answered by Bentham in favour of recourse to torture by public officials in suggesting that the public interest decidedly demands this. Bentham assumes (and so does Twining[23]) that public or general interest in ticking bomb situations demands the exceptional regime of torture. Outside such manifestly clear cases, which are rare (as Bentham himself admits), the 'public' or 'general' interest is difficult to decipher; its import is not usually clear or compelling.

The term 'the public' in this context is confusing. There are many *publics* and they have different *interests*; the 'public interest' mystifies the processes by which interests of several publics are aggregated as one. In a democracy, it is the task of the state and bureaucracy to construct or to determine what the public interest at any given time is or demands; contestation by citizens over what the public interest may be and in what it lies (often by citizens, and going in the name of 'public opinion') is considered the stuff of liberal democracy. Bentham was aware of this, but whether he had a theory of state or bureaucracy is a matter of some debate.[24] Students of Bentham rarely discuss his

[22] For an analysis of quasi-punishments, see Twining at 343–4.

[23] In fact, one of his (joint) books deals with the dirty bomb scenario in the context of the law of evidence (Cambridge University Press, 1998).

[24] See L. J. Hume, *Bentham and Bureaucracy* (Cambridge University Press, 1981); H. L. A. Hart, *Essays on Bentham* (Oxford: Clarendon Press, 1982); Nancy L. Rosenblum, *Bentham's Theory of State* (Cambridge, MA: Harvard University Press, 1978).

'Fragments' on torture in relation to governments, governance and governmentality.[25] In any case, whether 'the' public interest requires torturing the innocent, who may be regarded as a terrorist, and when public processes are consistent with formal and substantive due process, are matters of considerable variance within and across nations.

The second case, according to Bentham, is where:

> a man is required what probably though not *danger of its* certainly it is in his power to do; and for the not doing of which... *is less* possible that he may suffer, although he be innocent; but which the *than the opposite danger* public has so great an interest in his doing that the danger of what may ensue from his not doing it is a greater danger than even that of an innocent person's suffering the greatest degree of pain that can be suffered by Torture, of the kind and in the quantity permitted to be employed. Are there in practice any cases that can be ranked under this head? If there be any, it is plain there can be but very few.[26]

This is an elaborate formulation, in which Bentham can be said to speak in the tongue of a comparativist. Bentham in effect says that an innocent individual (one about whom we are not certain conclusively or beyond reasonable doubt that she/he is in possession of true knowledge) can be tortured where not torturing him or her would engage in endangering the public. Admittedly, such cases would be 'rare' but only empirical studies will show this (for Bentham's times or ours). Yet, it would appear that a mere belief of the prosecutor or of the public at large (if such a being exists in the first place) would authorize torture of the innocent person. This would yield the conclusion that if the public interest in obtaining the required information is so great that a would-be tormented has it in his/her power, he/she may be tormented; but a person not in possession of such power (an innocent person) may also be tormented if pubic interest is sufficient. The suffering of the innocent posed very much the same problem for a good utilitarian as it does for a student of theodicy.[27] The question always is what constitutes the public interest and whatever that is when it is 'sufficient' to subject a human being to practices of torture.

5. Enter Dershowitz

While William Twining did not contribute significantly to the subject of torture after the discovery of Bentham's 'Fragments', Alan Dershowitz makes much of interrogational torture in the context of a ticking bomb theory. He relies on the Twinings' discovery but also underscores a few sentences in

[25] Most of the writings on Bentham on state, especially post-Foucault, importantly stress the Panopticon as a way of reading governments and governance.

[26] Twining, at 312–13 (emphasis added).

[27] St Thomas Aquinas introduced this problem in terms of the sufferings of the just: see, St Thomas Aquinas, *The Literal Exposition on Job: Scriptural Commentary on Providence*, Anthony Damico (trans.) (Atlanta, GA: Scholar's Press, 1989).

Bentham dealing with judicial torture. Dershowitz relies on the Israeli experience[28] but generalizes his case for the war on terror.[29] He has been renamed by some 'Torquemada Dershowitz'.[30] The indictment of being a 'Torquemada' (the infamous mediæval tormentor of the Inquisition) identifies Dershowitz as advocating 'permissible' and non-lethal torture, such as 'sterile needles being inserted beneath the nails to cause excruciating pain without endangering life'.[31] He has systematically rejected this appellation.[32] There are many difficulties in reading Dershowitz, but a combined reading of his two texts – one the famous *Why Terrorism Works*[33] and the second his response to Professor Strauss[34] – suggests some clarity concerning his position, however historically insufficient it might be.[35]

Conceptually, Dershowitz is right to reiterate that on so important a matter we all should avoid confusing 'empirical observations (what I think will happen as a matter of fact)' with 'normative proposals (what I think should happen as a matter of morality)'.[36] Normatively, he would 'like to see its use minimized'.[37] Dershowitz, however, introduces the distinction between lethal and non-lethal torture. The former is not justifiable. On non-lethal torture, he is more nuanced. His argument has two stages.

First, as an empirical matter, 'at least moderate forms of non-lethal torture are in fact being used by the United States and some of its allies today'. These would be justified at the bar of public opinion, 'if we ever confronted an actual case of imminent mass terrorism that could be prevented by the infliction of torture'. In those circumstances, he predicts, 'we would use torture (even lethal torture), and the public would favour its use.'[38] If this conclusion is empirically sound (either true or false), 'time will probably tell'.[39] Dershowitz then, secondly, presents his 'conditional normative position', which is that if the state in fact is using custodial torture, and if this 'would in fact be used in an

[28] See Alan Dershowitz, 'Is it necessary to apply "physical pressure" to terrorists – and to lie about it?', *Israel Law Review* 23, 192–200 (1989).

[29] See Alan Dershowitz, 'Is there a torturous road to justice?', 8 November 2001, available at www.groups-beta.google.com/group/alt.impeach.bush/msg/814527884aa6c904; *Shouting Fire: Civil Liberties in a Turbulent Age* (New York: Little Brown, 2002); *Why Terrorism Works* (New Haven: Yale University Press, 2002); 'Tortured Reasoning' in Levinson, S., ed., *Contemplating Torture: an introduction*, 257–80 (2004); *Preemption: A Knife That Cuts Both Ways* (New York: Norton, 2006).

[30] A reference made by Jed Babbin, 'The Silence of the Lambs: Torture is Not Appropriate Treatment for Terrorists', *Washington Times*, 21 March 2002, at A19. 'Torquemada Dershowitz then defines the liberal view of "permissible" torture, saying that it would be limited to "non-lethal means, such as sterile needles being inserted beneath the nails to cause excruciating pain without endangering life".'

[31] See Jed Babbin, supra note 30. [32] See note 30, supra.

[33] Alan M. Dershowitz, *Why Terrorism Works* (Yale University Press, 2002).

[34] Alan M. Dershowitz, 'The Torture Warrant: A Response to Professor Strauss', *New York Law School Review*, 48: 275 (2003); referred to hereafter simply by the author.

[35] Markus Wagner, 'The justification of torture. Some Remarks on Alan M. Dershowitz's *Why Terrorism Works*', *German Law Journal* 4: 5, 515 (2003).

[36] Supra note 32 at 277. [37] Ibid. [38] Dershowitz, 277. [39] Ibid.

actual ticking bomb mass terrorism case', it would be normatively better 'to have such torture regulated by some kind of warrant, with accountability, record-keeping, standards and limitations'. This, he avers, is different from the old, abstract Benthamite debate, concerning the justification of the interrogational – or, indeed, any – form of torture. It 'is not so much about the substantive issue of torture as it is over accountability, visibility and candour in a democracy that is confronting a choice of evils'.[40] Although Dershowitz is strongly opposed to brutality, testifying and prisoner rape warrants, he would say a 'heuristic yes' if requiring a warrant would subject these horribly brutal activities to judicial control and accountability'.[41] He recognizes a 'downside: legitimating a horrible practice that we all want to see ended or minimized'.[42] The downside consist of a dilemma, at least in 'democratic' society: either 'these horrible practices continue to operate below the radar screen of accountability, and avoid "legitimation"' or 'we try to control the practice by demanding some kind of accountability, [and thereby] we add a degree of legitimation to it while perhaps reducing its frequency and severity'[43]. He concludes: 'There is no easy answer'.[44]

There are several difficulties with the 'conditional normative' that would authorize non-lethal torture. Application of 'severe pain, psychological or physical', rightly continues to be prohibited under the CAT. Perhaps Dershowitz would approve a modification of CAT that would permit judicial warrants that authorize such infliction. But this is not as easy as it sounds. He does not fully appreciate the context of CAT, which goes back to the First and Second World Wars, the struggle over decolonization and development, and the postcolonial killing fields of the various phases of the Cold War. The gathering consensus concerning the outlawry of cruel, degrading treatment and punishment and acts of torture reflected in the CAT was based on an international consensus of a large number of ratifying states and subsequent developments in international law such as the Rome Treaty and the Statute of the International Court of Justice which created crimes against humanity. Treaty law can of course be changed, but the normative agreement of states against torture is rather robust, even amidst the American 9/11 aftermath.[45]

[40] Ibid. [41] Dershowitz, 278. [42] Dershowitz, 277–8. [43] Dershowitz, 278. [44] Ibid.

[45] But see Mark Osiel, *The End of Reciprocity: Terror, Torture, and the Law of War* (Cambridge University Press, 2009). See also Ruth Bleckley, 'Dirty Hands, Clean Conscience? The CIA Inspector General's Investigation of "Enhanced Interrogation Techniques" in the War on Terror and the Torture Debate', *Journal of Human Rights*, 10:544–61 (2011). See also Eric Stover and Laurel Fletcher, *Guantánamo and Its Aftermath: U.S. Detention and Interrogation Practices and Their Impact on Former Detainees Report* (University of California, Berkeley: Human Rights Center, 2008); Gisli H. Gudjonsson, *The Psychology of Interrogations and Confessions* (Hoboken: Wiley, 2003); Philip A. Quigley, 'Enhanced Interrogation: Torture Policies of the United States' *e-Research: A Journal of Undergraduate Work* 3: 2, Article 4 (2014); James P. Terry, 'Torture and the Interrogation of Detainees' *Campbell Law Review*, 32: 4, 595 (2010); Jinee Lokaneeta, *Transnational Torture: Law, Violence, and State Power in the United States and India* (New York University Press, 2011).

While it is true that the CAT does not affirm the categories of lethal and non-lethal torture, and it instead speaks of affliction of 'severe' pain and 'suffering', the United States' exceptionalism in equating 'severe' as 'prolonged pain' or suffering and proceeding to construe it as non-lethal pain or suffering[46] has come under severe criticism. Prescinding this momentarily, it is clear that similar problems would ensue for many constitutional bills of rights. The distinction between categories does mark a difference in kind; but nonlethal torture admits of several degrees, and to treat non-lethal as a 'lump' (in Bentham's withering term) is a grave error. The difficulties in arriving at a precise delineation of non-lethal torture are massive indeed. Because non-lethal torture can, and does, include several practices, a schedule of such practices – ranging from postural discomfort, sleep deprivation, frequent waterboarding, threat or use of sexual aggression, threats of murder of the tortured or their relation or acquaintance – would need to be specified and approved. An active judiciary may overturn in part or as a whole such legislatively drawn schedules if found offensive to constitutional guarantees. Alternatively, judicial schedules may be developed case by case. Severe difficulties haunt any proposals for judicial warrants as judicial activism in matters of security and terrorism is not a rare occurrence even in constitutional democracies.

Commenting on the CIA Inspector General's 2004 *Special Review of Counterterrorism, Detention and Interrogation Activities* (hereafter, 'IG report'),[47] Ruth Blakeley has recently concluded that as regards 'enhanced interrogation techniques', 'efforts to legalize torture under controlled conditions are futile, since there is little assurance that its use can be contained.' In any event, she says, 'its use is rarely aimed at thwarting imminent threats, and it is far from clear that it yields any evidence that could not be obtained through legitimate means.'[48] Blakeley finds that, based on the IG's own report,

[46] Under S 3(2) of the Torture Victim Protection Act 1999, the term 'torture' means 'any act, directed against an individual in the offender's custody or physical control, by which severe pain or suffering (other than pain or suffering arising only from or inherent in, or incidental to, lawful sanctions), whether physical or mental, is intentionally inflicted on that individual for such purposes as obtaining from that individual or a third person information or a confession, punishing that individual for an act that individual or a third person has committed or is suspected of having committed, intimidating or coercing that individual or a third person, or for any reason based on discrimination of any kind'.

This definition broadly follows Article 1 of the 1984 UN Convention Against Torture and Other Cruel, Inhuman and Degrading Treatment or Punishment. See *Price* v. *Socialist People's Libyan Arab Jamahiriya*, 294 F.3d 82, 92 (D. C. Cir. 2002); see also S. Rep. No. 249, 102nd Cong., 1st Sess., at 3 (1991); *United States* v. *Belfast*, 611 F.3d 783, 807–9 (11th Cir. 2010), cert. denied, 131 S. Ct. 1511 (2011).

[47] Office of the Inspector General. *Special Review: Counterterrorism Detention and Interrogation Activities* (Washington, DC: Central Intelligence Agency, 2004). See also the recent Senate report, *A Review of the FBI's Involvement in and Observations of Detainee Interrogations in Guantanamo Bay, Afghanistan, and Iraq: Committee Study of the Central Intelligence Agency's Detention and Interrogation Program* (2014).

[48] Blakeley, supra note 45 at 545.

non-lethal 'torture is extremely difficult to control once permission is granted for its use', and that this, therefore, 'raises deep questions about Dershowitz torture warrants proposal'.[49] She finds very questionable the three key assumptions used in justification of such techniques:

> firstly, that torture is effective as a means of securing intelligence to thwart imminent security threats, secondly, that the use of torture can be controlled, thereby limiting its use, and, thirdly, that by legitimizing some torture, officials involved in its use would be unlikely to face recriminations. The IG report offers the first empirical evidence from the War on Terror against which these theoretical assumptions can be tested.[50]

These empirically-based observations cannot be brushed aside in any advocacy or 'justification' of torture. In particular, the utilitarian justification of torture depends on its effectiveness; when that empirical claim is incapable of being sustained, the ground beneath the utilitarian justification simply vanishes.

6. Ontological positions

The philosophical (whether ethical or moral) question is whether torture, custodial or interrogational, is ever 'justified'. As against the ticking bomb scenarios, 'moral absolutists', writes Oren Gross, 'must maintain their support for the absolute ban on torture even when the outcome of abstaining from the use of torture is truly catastrophic'.[51] Whether what 'is' should affect the construction of that which ought to be remains a central question. A moral 'ought' that is not derived from the empirical 'is' is certainly possible.[52] There are many versions of this ontological position, but all conclude that torture authorized by state or the ruler (whether lethal or non-lethal) is morally wrong in any or all circumstances. Consequences – good or bad – do not matter in this moral reasoning. How things *are* does not affect the moral regard for how things *ought* to be.

However, this poses difficult questions about the basis of *the normativity of the normative*. Suspending these meta-questions, there are several different justifications for an absolute (under no circumstances) proscription of

[49] Ibid.

[50] Id., at 546. But see, for an important analysis, Fritz Allhoff, 'Empirical Objections to Torture: A Critical Reply', *Terrorism and Political Violence*, 26: 621–49 (2014).

[51] Oren Gross, 'The Prohibition of Torture and the Limits of Law' in S. Levinson, ed., *Torture: A Collection*, Chapter13 (Oxford University Press, 2004).

[52] See Eugen Ehrlich, 'Fundamental Principles of Sociology of Law' 86 (W. L. Moll, trans.) 5 *Harvard Studies in Jurisprudence* (1936) with an introduction by Roscoe Pound; Julius Stone, *Social Dimensions of Law and Justice* 551 (Sydney: Maitland, 1966), which names the motto, in slight variation, as the 'normative tendency of the factual'. See also Roger Cotterrell, *Living Law: Studies in Legal and Social Theory* (Farnham: Ashgate, 2008). See also N. Srivinasan, 'The Juristic and Political Ideas of Duguit', *The Indian Journal of Political Science* 1:1, 1–22 (1939). For a recent analysis of the normative and the factual see Adrian Vermeule, 'Connecting Positive and Normative Legal Theory', *Journal of Constitutional Law* 10:2, 387–98 (2008).

interrogational and custodial torture: those that place primary importance on the cruelty involved, or the breaches of physical integrity, or the violation of constitutional democracy that torture involved, or the violation of the idea of human rights. To review each would require a separate article; all I can offer here is a vignette of these justifications.

Some put cruelty first. Although the view of Judith Shklar that putting cruelty first is a modern virtue, and that many rightly regard cruelty 'as the most vicious of all vices' as it 'makes political action difficult beyond endurance, may cloud our judgment, and may reduce us to a debilitating misanthropy',[53] David Luban maintains that torture is 'the living manifestation of cruelty', and the 'peculiar horror of torture within liberalism arises from the fact that torture is tyranny in microcosm, at its highest level of intensity'. Further, the history of torture reinforces this horror because torture has always been bound up with military conquest, regal punishment, dictatorial terror, forced confessions, and the repression of dissident belief – a veritable catalogue of the evils of absolutist government that liberalism abhors. For all these reasons, it should hardly surprise us that liberals wish to ban torture absolutely – a wish that became legislative reality in the Torture Convention's insistence that 'nothing can justify torture'.[54]

It is similar, but not the same, to argue for an absolute prohibition of torture from the first premise of bodily integrity. Relying in part on the suffering and distress of victims during the Holocaust, Bob Brecher asks us to take the destruction of such integrity as comprising the wrong of torture:

> It is the whole of the process of torture in which treating him as not a person consisted; and to describe it as such is already to make a normative claim that no person ought to be treated like that. Why not? Because, and this claim is a factual one, it breaks them, it destroys the person they are... [T]orturers, that is to say, turned... [the tormented] his personhood against him, and in doing so made him into someone else. That is how... [the tormented] ... survived, as someone else; others do not.[55]

On this view, it is irrelevant whether torture is 'minimal' or 'maximal'.[56] And one can readily extend this justification to psychic integrity of the self.

The justification for an absolute prohibition from human rights is complicated, because while lawpersons talk about human rights law and

[53] JJudith N. Shklar, *Ordinary Vices*, 43 (Belknap Press, Harvard University, 1985).

[54] David Luban, 'Liberalism, Torture, and the Ticking Bomb', 91 *Va. L. Rev.* 1438 at 1439–40 at 1430. (2005).

[55] Bob Brecher, *Torture, Death and Philosophy*, p. 82 (London: Blackwell, 2007).

[56] Brecher cites, at p. 85, the following from Seamus Miller:

'The difference between minimalist and maximalist torture is that in the former case the victim's will is broken only temporarily and in a contained manner, and their consequent humiliation is limited, i.e., they survive the trauma and are able to get on with their lives. However, in the maximalist case the victim's autonomy and self-identity are damaged irretrievably. Accordingly, the victim – even if alive and physically well – has not survived intact qua autonomous self.'

jurisprudence, philosophers talk about the *idea* of human rights. This is an important discussion, generally analyzed elsewhere.[57] At the level of the idea of human rights, individual human dignity appears to be a prime candidate supporting the non-negotiable prohibition of the practice of torture. If dignity may only be protected via democratic constitutionalism, then the issue of what constitutes 'democracy' becomes very crucial, as any reader of Darius Rejali well knows.[58] Whatever the complexity and contradictions of democracy (for example, between plebiscitary and 'real' democracy, existing democracy and 'democracy to come', 'agonal' versus 'antagonistic' democracy, and democracy and 'mobocracy'), at the core of the notion lies the idea that torture shall be absolutely prohibited. If there is any cross-cultural or transcendent universal, it is the normative outlawry and prohibition of state torture.

7. Twining's position

There are some significant differences between Jeremy Bentham and Twining's Bentham. Unlike Bentham, Twining does not go into the matter of torture in civil society. In part, Twining implicitly associates torture as usually practised and even justified in civil society (to women, children, sexual minorities, disabled persons and others) with inhuman, degrading and cruel treatment or punishment. Nor has Twining much time or inclination for the studies of sadism or masochism that pervades so much of erotic pleasure, where seeking erotic joys that make the infliction of pain on others or oneself, as Michel Foucault once put it, part of 'the gloomy festival of punishment'.[59]

Putting these differences to one side, however, for Twining, the central contribution of Bentham was to pose the problem of justification of torture in exceptional situations, and in this Twining and Bentham adopt similar positions. For Twining, as for Bentham, the interference with autonomy and liberty is central: 'as a conceptual matter the point of torture is the infliction of pain for purposes of coercion'. While decrying the infliction of 'extreme pain and humiliation' for 'reasons other than coercion (e.g. sadism or revenge)' or

[57] Upendra Baxi, 'Reinventing Human Rights in an Era of Hyperglobalization' in Connor Greaty and Costas Douzinas (eds), *The Cambridge Companion to Human Rights Law*, 150–70 (Cambridge University Press, 2012). See also Sumner B. Twiss, 'Torture, Justification, and Human Rights: Toward an Absolute Proscription' *Human Rights Quarterly* 29:2, 346–67 (2007); Walter Kälin, 'Late modernity: Human Rights Under Pressure?' *Punishment & Society* 15(4) 397–411 (2013).

[58] See his classic study, *Torture and Democracy*. Princeton University Press (2009). See also Pierre Vidal-Naquet, *Torture: Cancer of Democracy* (Middlesex: Penguin Books, 1963); *La Torture Dans la Rėpublique* (Paris: Editions Francois Maspero, 1972); Noam Chomsky and Edward Herman, *The Washington Connection and Third World Fascism: The Political Economy of Human Rights*, vol. I (Boston, MA: South End Press, 1979); *After the Cataclysm. Postwar Indochina and the Reconstruction of Imperial Ideology. The Political Economy of Human Rights*, vol. II (Nottingham: Spokesman, 1979); see also note 64.

[59] See also Talal Asad, 'On Torture, or Cruel, Inhuman, and Degrading Treatment' *Social Research* 63: 4, 1081–1109 (1996).

the infliction when 'pointless (e.g. part of a routine in which the original purpose has been forgotten)' as 'strictly speaking extensions of the concept of torture', Twining stresses 'the ambiguity of the concept and the variety of purposes and motives for which this kind of extreme treatment is used in practice'. Twining continues in the Benthamite tradition of very limited justification for torture, subsequently pioneered by many especially in times of terror. Like Bentham, however, it is a nuanced and limited justification. He reiterates that 'institutionalized torture is endemically subject to abuse' (i.e. once established, it is almost inevitably used beyond any situation in which its infliction could be justified), and that this 'supports a consequentialist argument for an "absolute" prohibition, such as that under Article 3 of the EHCR'.

Conclusion

To conclude, I would wish to offer at least four caveats to Twining's analysis. First, Twining's insistence that Bentham offered a rigorous philosophy of torture is understandable, but questionable. Certainly, Bentham offered a theory of utility and considered torture as a special case of that theory. But it is doubtful if he offered any 'philosophy' of torture, unless one regards any exercise in justification (providing good reasons for belief or action) as all that there is to doing philosophy.[60]

Second, as we have seen, it is not clear how recourse to Bentham may help any deontological thinkers – broadly, persons who regard 'torture' of humans as normatively impossible of any justification being violative of a human being.

Third, like Bentham, Twining writes in a hard, muscular way about torture. He says: 'If the problem of reducing or abolishing torture is to be tackled effectively, what is needed is not "the effusion of a hard heart operating upon a cloudy mind," but tough minds working in the service of tender hearts. Perhaps Bentham's treatment of torture may help to stimulate efforts in this direction.'[61] 'Tough' minds are usually conceived as being *male* and *hard*: both Bentham and Twining seem to regard 'torture' (both perpetrators and victims) as a pre-eminently male affair; they regard the rights talk as an affair of the tender-hearted, whereas torture, and its 'justification', may only be addressed by tough-minded thinkers. I do not know the ways in which feminist readings approach Bentham (though utilitarianism is grist for the feminist ethical and philosophical mill), but I do know that leading feminist critiques urge that we take institutional violence as seriously as emotional intelligence and

[60] Twining, after all, harbours a deep suspicion of philosophy. He concludes 'Twining, Philosophy' (at 161) with the observation: 'The purpose of this paper has been to suggest that philosophers too have something to contribute to the development of such a theory. And such a contribution might, in its turn, help to clarify for us non-philosophers the question: What are good philosophers good for?'

[61] Twining, at 306. The matter in quotation marks is from Bentham, 'Supply without Burthen' in *Jeremy Bentham's Economic Writings* (ed. Stark), Vol. I, p. 335, cited by H. L. A. Hart, note 18, at 16 infra.

sentimental logics,[62] and invite us to take the ethics of care and the ethics of human rights equally seriously.[63]

Fourth, for Twining, whatever does not fall within 'torture' is covered extensively by CAT's prohibition of inhuman, cruel and unjust treatment or punishment. As regards 'coercive interrogation' (including waterboarding), '[w]hether or not some of these techniques amounted to "torture", several of them clearly amounted to inhuman or degrading treatment under public international law'. But this position is not without some difficulties. This approach has been seen by some as 'legally untenable', ignoring 'important jurisprudential developments emphasizing the prohibited purposes behind torture as the principal element distinguishing it from other forms of ill-treatment'. Furthermore, 'even more troubling, however, is the perverted effect this approach has had on debates over torture itself, making it too often the centrepiece of discussion at the cost of "lesser" but more common abuses'.[64]

That said, Bentham's 'Fragments,' and Twining's commentary on them, warrant more sustained attention and certainly beyond the terror wars, although ever since 9/11's 'crime of New York' (as Alain Badiou calls it) there has been a renewed effort at drawing a continuum between 'domestic' and 'international' terror. I disagree with many of their positions, but William and Penelope Twining continue, and will continue, to be recognized as the discoverers as well as the first commentators on Bentham's 'Fragments'. They have done a great service to an eminent cause serving both human rights and the *right to be human* – which, on my analysis, is the very foundation of all human rights known to law and jurisprudence.[65]

[62] See *The Body in Pain: The Making and Unmaking of the World* (New York: Oxford University Press); Christine E. Gudorf, 'Feminist Approaches to Religion and Torture' *Journal of Religious Ethics* 613 (2011); Clare McGlynn, 'Rape As Torture?: Catherine Mackinnon and Questions of Feminist Strategy' *Legal Studies* 16:71–85 (2008); Basuli Deb, 'Transnational Feminism and Women Who Torture: Reimag(in)ing Abu Ghraib Prison Photography' *Postcolonial Text*, 7:1 (2012).

[63] See e.g. Carol Gilligan, *In a Different Voice: Psychological Theory and Women's Development* (Cambridge, MA: Harvard University Press, 1982); Sara Ruddick, 'Remarks on the Sexual Politics of Reason' *in Women and Moral Theory* (Eva Feder Kittay and Diana T. Meyers, eds) (Totowa, NJ: Rowman & Littlefield, 1987): Jean Elshtain, 'Against Androgyny', *Telos* 47 (1981); Martha C. Nussbaum, *Women and Human Development* (Cambridge University Press, 2000); Id., *Frontiers of Justice: Disability, Nationality, Species Membership* (Belknap Press, Harvard University, 2006); Helga Kushe, Peter Singer and Maurice Rickard, 'Reconciling Impartial Morality and a Feminist Ethic of Care' *The Journal of Value Inquiry* 32: 451–63 (1998): Upendra Baxi, 'Justice and Care: The . . . Rosalind Wilson Memorial Lecture' *India International Quarterly* 37: pp. 118–32 (2010) and additional literature therein cited.

[64] Christian de Vos, 'Mind the Gap: Purpose, Pain, and the Difference between Torture and Inhuman Treatment' *Human Rights Brief* 14:2 (2007). Manfred Nowak, 'What Practices Constitute Torture?: US and UN Standards' *Human Rights Quarterly* 28.4 809–41 (2006).

[65] See Upendra Baxi, 'From Human Rights to the Right to be Human: Some Heresies' in Upendra Baxi and Geeti Sen (eds), *The Right to be Human* (Delhi: Lancers Press and India International Centre); reprinted in Upendra Baxi, *Inhuman Wrongs and Human Rights: Unconventional Essays* 1–17 (Delhi: Har-Anand, 1994). See also William Twining, *Human Rights, Southern Voices: Francis Deng, Abdullahi An-Na'im, Yash Ghai and Upendra Baxi* (Cambridge University Press, 2009).

3

Human rights and traditional values

Christopher McCrudden

1. Introduction

The relationship between 'traditional values' and 'human rights' is conceptually difficult, politically contested and legally important. For supporters of such values, the argument in favour of according them weight in the human rights context is clear. The fact of tradition brings with it a normative power, which gives rise to a good reason for those believing in the tradition to act in conformity with that tradition.[1] But is bringing an idea like 'traditional values' together with 'human rights' simply wrong-headed? Some people certainly think that we should not even be considering them together. They pepper advocates of traditional values with increasingly difficult questions. Human rights are clearly normative, specifying an 'ought', but why should we think of 'tradition' as having any normative weight? Are there any good reasons why the larger society should take into account the fact that a practice is based on tradition in deciding whether or not to override it in the name of human rights? Shouldn't we simply think of 'traditional values' as a descriptive, rather than a normative, category?

When advocates point to particular traditional values that we might respect, such as caring for the old, protecting children and encouraging solidarity, the response is robust. To the extent that traditions embody acceptable values, any reference to the values being 'traditional' is redundant. It is not because the values are *traditional* that gives them any normative significance, it is suggested, but the fact that the values are independently valuable. Where the traditional practices are *consistent* with human rights, they can be supported, but not because they are traditional. Where the traditional practices are *harmful* to human rights, they should not be given any weight.

The claims that need to be established by those supporting the normativity of 'traditional values', therefore, are difficult: that tradition carries with it not just a good reason for acting in a certain way, but a good reason for acting that does not depend simply on the content of a particular traditional value.[2] The

[1] This does not necessarily mean that it should trump other reasons for acting. Think of it as a *prima facie* obligation to act in conformity with that tradition.

[2] A similar claim is often made for law: that law provides a reason for acting that does not depend on the quality or content of the law.

critical questions become: what might the normativity of tradition be based on for those who follow it? Why and how should it be given any normative weight at all by others who do not believe in the tradition? Does 'tradition' provide good reasons for acting for adherents to that tradition, and good reasons for non-adherents to permit adherents to engage in practices that the tradition demands? Is there any added value that traditional values bring to the human rights project? These are some of the questions that this essay explores, in the context of the recent debates over the scope and meaning of human rights stimulated by the three 'traditional values' resolutions (hereafter referred to as 'the Resolutions') passed by the UN Human Rights Council in 2009, 2011 and 2012, which were the result of a highly controversial initiative spearheaded by Russia.[3]

There is, however, another dimension to this chapter. As we shall see, much of the support for the Resolutions comes from what can broadly be called the global South. In several books, particularly *Human Rights, Southern Voices*, and *General Jurisprudence: Understanding Law from a Global Perspective* William Twining has explored the question of how to reconcile human rights norms with belief systems embedded in the global South (including 'traditional values'), and in doing so has drawn attention to intellectuals from that part of the world, in particular Francis Deng, Yash Ghai, Abdullahi An-Na'im and Upendra Baxi. I suggest that those who take an interest in the legitimate concerns that significant sections of the global South have about the human rights project – concerns partly reflected in the 'traditional values' Resolutions – would do well to pay more attention to the 'Southern voices' on whom Twining rightly focuses attention.

This chapter is structured as follows: in part 2, I consider the recent Resolutions supporting 'traditional values'. These Resolutions are the peg on which I hang an initial discussion of the relationship between tradition and human rights, drawing on the work of Ghai. In part 3, I unpack the different sources that are seen to generate support for 'traditional values', distinguishing between national sovereignty, religious practice, traditional societies and conservative political thought. In part 4, I return to consider the approach to traditional values that appears to be emerging at the United Nations, identifying different approaches that frame the current debates. In this context, I consider recent human rights scholarship, in particular from the global South, that considers the relationship between traditional values and human rights, drawing on the work of An-Na'im, and Deng, contrasting their work with that of Tom Zwart. In part 5, drawing on sociological and philosophical critiques, I distinguish two conceptions of 'tradition' along several axes: tradition as a reflection of the past, versus tradition as a reflection of the present;

[3] The United Nations Human Rights Council passed the resolution A/HRS/16/L.6 entitled 'Promoting human rights and fundamental freedoms through a better understanding of traditional values of humankind', 24 March 2011. Previous resolution: 12/21 of 2 October 2009. Later resolution: 21/3 of 27 September 2012.

tradition as substantive content, versus tradition as the act of transmission; and tradition as a descriptive and empirical category, versus tradition as a normative orientation toward action. In part 6, I tentatively suggest an alternative approach to traditional values that is both truer to important aspects of human rights but sensitive to legitimate concerns arising in the global South. Part 7 concludes.

2. 'Traditional values' resolutions by the UN Human Rights Council

Several Resolutions of the Human Rights Council attempt to have the notion of 'traditional values' accepted into international human rights discourse. These Resolutions seek to have several concepts at the heart of human rights law, in particular 'dignity', 'freedom' and 'responsibility', interpreted through the lens of the idea of 'traditional values', which is left undefined. Traditional values are seen, in this approach, as the foundation for the pursuit of global human rights. The family, community, society and educational institutions are identified as having an important role in maintaining and passing on these traditional values. States are called on to strengthen the role of these institutions through adopting adequate positive measures. In particular, dignity is seen, in these Resolutions, as having the potential to rebalance international human rights back towards the local and the indigenous, weakening the pull of a homogenizing, universalist and liberal agenda.

Previous debates on cultural relativism and ethnocentrism

These Resolutions, at one level, might be seen merely as the most recent of a long line of attempts to restate cultural-relativist and rights-sceptical positions on human rights. From the time of the debates surrounding the adoption of the Universal Declaration on Human Rights in 1948, there have been recurring critiques of human rights universality. The 1947 statement by the Executive Board of the American Anthropological Association set the tone, stating that rights must be integrated in different societies, by 'the only right and proper way of life that can be known to them, the institutions, sanctions and goals that make up the culture of their particular society'.[4] Since then, there have been recurring set-piece conflicts between universalist and relativist positions: for example, on the meaning and practice of 'democratic' rights,[5] on the

[4] American Anthropological Association, Executive Board, *Statement on Human Rights Subcommittee to the Commission on Human Rights* (1947). See now the AAA Committee for Human Rights, *Declaration on Anthropology and Human Rights* (1999).

[5] Roger Lloret Blackburn, *Cultural Relativism in the Universal Periodic Review of the Human Rights Council*, ICIP Working Papers 2011/3, Institut Català Internacional per la Pau, Barcelona, September 2011.

appropriateness of a 'cultural defence' to certain criminal offences,[6] and on the existence and weight to be attached to supposedly collectivist 'Asian values'.[7]

These particular disputes set much of the framework within which subsequent debates have tended to be conducted: How far does Western human rights theory incline too much to individualism at the expense of communitarianism? Do different cultures and civilizations differ significantly in their foundational values? Is the language of human rights 'the best medium for cross-cultural discourse and dialogue'?[8] Often, these conflicts pit voices in the global South against what are characterized as liberal Western human rights discourse. But there is also a constant drumbeat of rights-scepticism from *within* the West, particularly from those who consider that rights-talk encourages what Mary Ann Glendon described as '[a] near aphasia concerning responsibilities'.[9]

None of these earlier debates, however important, involved human rights in geo-political disputes of quite such significance as those regarding the compatibility of Shari'ah law with international human rights standards. Even before the events of 9/11, conflicts between Islamic values and, for example, the European Convention on Human Rights, had resulted in considerable doubt being cast on the consistency of Shari'ah with (European) fundamental rights.[10] Post 9/11, however, these issues have been seen in a somewhat different light: one where militant Islam is seen by some as posing a threat to national security as well as Enlightenment values in many Western states. The intensity of the debate and the apparent irresolvability of the disputes have threatened to derail the human rights project.

Doctrinal developments in human rights law

To some degree, the Resolutions in the Human Rights Council are to be understood as reactions to these political debates. In other respects, however, the Resolutions have novel aspects. In particular, the Resolutions are reactions to recent developments in international human rights practice and human rights theory.

First, human rights practice. Prior to the 1980s, international organizations, states and NGOs had interpreted 'human rights' as broadly inapplicable to many 'traditional' practices. Broadly speaking, international human rights law had relatively little to say, either pro or con, about 'traditional values'. This

[6] Alison Dundes Rentein, *The Cultural Defense* (Oxford University Press, 2005).

[7] See e.g. *The Bangkok Declaration*, Final Declaration of the Regional Meeting for Asia of the World Conference on Human Rights, A/CONF.157/ASRM/8, A/CONF.157/PC/59 (7 April 1993).

[8] Twining, General Jurisprudence, 199.

[9] Mary Ann Glendon, *Rights Talk: The Impoverishment of Political Discourse* (Free Press, 1991), xi.

[10] *Refah Partisi (the Welfare Party) v. Turkey*, Application no. 41340/98, et al., 31 July 2001 (Chamber); upheld by the Grand Chamber, 13 February 2003.

distance resulted from several different strands of the then dominant interpretation of human rights: first, human rights primarily applied to actions by the state or state-sponsored bodies, not to non-state actors; second, human rights primarily imposed negative obligations on the state rather than positive obligations; third, human rights primarily related to the protection of civil and political rights, such as those found in the International Covenant on Civil and Political Rights, rather than those found in the International Covenant on Economic, Social and Cultural Rights (such as the right to health); and, fourth, there were 'private' areas such as sexual morality and intra-family relations that were regarded as inappropriate for international intervention and were considered firmly within the sphere of national sovereignty.

The result was to leave large swathes of activity regarding women and sexual minorities, for example, unaddressed in international human rights discourse. Perhaps the best known such issue was that relating to female genital cutting, which was long off-limits as an issue of international human rights concern.[11]

Since the 1980s, each of these elements in the dominant interpretation of human rights has been strongly challenged: actions by non-state actors were increasingly seen, at least by NGOs, as included within the sphere of international human rights activism; positive obligations on states to ensure the adequate implementation of rights within their jurisdictions by all, including 'private' actors, became commonplace in human rights discourse; partly as a result, socio-economic rights attracted significantly greater attention than before; and international human rights actors considered it legitimate for human rights norms to address issues in the 'private' sphere, and, indeed, to make them a central focus of their attention.

These changes have led to two important, but potentially conflicting, developments. On the one hand, there is now substantial human rights practice, particularly in the area of indigenous rights, upholding some cultural rights, including 'traditional values'.[12] One of the more important developments in this context was the Assembly of Heads of State and Government of the Organization of African Unity, meeting in Nairobi, Kenya, in June 1981, which adopted the Banjul Charter on Human and People's Rights. Article 17(3) provides specifically that 'The promotion and

[11] Madeline Baer and Alison Brysk, 'New Rights for Private Wrongs: Female Genital Mutilation and Global Framing Dialogues' in Clifford Bob, *The International Struggle for New Human Rights* (Penn Press, 2009) 93.

[12] In particular the decision by the African Commission on Human and Peoples' Rights concerning the Endorois indigenous community of Kenya, Communication No. 276/2003, *Centre for Minority Rights Development (Kenya) and Minority Rights Group International on behalf of Endorois Welfare Council v Kenya*, AHRLR (2009) 75, (2010) 49 I.L.M. 861, in which the Commission relied on Article 17 ACHPR which obliges the state to 'promote and protect traditional values recognized by a community', at para. 241. Cited, with approval, by the Inter-American Court of Human Rights, *Pueblo Indígena Kichwa de Sarayaku v. Ecuador,* Sentencia de 27 de junio de 2012, para. 216.

protection of morals and *traditional values* recognized by the community shall be the duty of the State.'[13]

On the other hand, as a result of these changes in human rights practice, women's rights and the rights of marginalized sexual minorities increasingly came to dominate human rights discourse (at least in Western states and in international organizations). There has been a parallel move, therefore, to ensure that cultural rights should not threaten these emerging international human rights standards. When these developments were combined with a noticeable reduction in the guilt that Western states felt over their former colonialism, 'traditional' practices came more into the firing line. Since then, there has been a persistent attempt by international and regional organizations with norm-creating human rights responsibilities to ensure that human rights standards trump conflicting 'traditional' practices in the global South, whether religious, cultural or customary. This has resulted in a plethora of texts[14] and interpretative statements,[15] as well as national judicial practice, reflecting this position. Indeed, at the same time as the Human Rights Committee was passing its Resolutions on traditional values, the Committee was passing other Resolutions in the context of efforts to prevent child marriages and forced marriages, in which 'traditional values' were seen as undermining human rights standards.[16] Again, one of the best-known examples of this trend is that relating to female genital cutting.[17]

[13] Emphasis added. In addition, article 18(2) provides (in part): 'The State shall have the duty to assist the family which is the custodian of morals and *traditional values* recognized by the community.' (emphasis added).

[14] See e.g. CEDAW, 1979, Art. 5; CRC, Art. 24(3); African Charter of the Rights and Welfare of the Child, 1990, Art. 1(3), Art 21; Protocol on the Rights of Women in Africa, 2003, Art. 2(2), Art 4(2)(d); African Youth Charter, 2006, Art. 13(3)(f), Art. 20(1)(a); Inter-American Convention on the Prevention, Punishment and Eradication of Violence Against Women, 1994, Art. 6, Art. 8; Council of Europe Convention on Preventing and Combating Violence Against Women and Domestic Violence, 2011, Art. 12, Art. 42. See generally, Federico Lenzerini, *The Culturalization of Human Rights Law* (Oxford University Press, 2014), 127–132.

[15] See e.g. the CESCR's interpretation of the ICESCR: 'no one may invoke cultural diversity to infringe upon human rights guaranteed by international law, nor to limit their scope', and 'limitations to the right of everyone to take part in cultural life may be necessary in certain circumstances, in particular in the case of negative practices, including those attributed to customs and traditions, that infringe upon other human rights,' General Comment No. 21, at 18, 19.

[16] HRC Resolution 24/23, Strengthening efforts to prevent and eliminate child, early and forced marriage: challenges, achievements, best practices and implementation gaps, A/HRC/24/2, 27 January 2014, referring to 'harmful traditional practices, perceptions and customs that are obstacles to the full enjoyment of human rights, in particular of women and girls.'

[17] Lest this be thought only to affect 'traditional' practices in Africa, however, the relatively recent decision in Germany, calling male circumcision solely for religious reasons into question on the grounds that it is contrary to the rights of the child, shows the potential for 'traditional' practices, widespread in Western culture and affecting males, also to be called into question. Cologne Regional Court (*Landgericht*), Decision 151 Ns 169/11 (2012), English translation available at: ukhumanrightsblog.com/2012/06/27/german-court-rules-childs-religious-circumcision-was-unlawful-analysis. The English courts have, so far, proven more cautious about

Growing uncertainty over normative foundations of human rights

Another significant part of the context that helps us understand the 'traditional values' Resolutions concerns human rights theory. In part because of the substantive expansion of human rights, in part because of their increased domestic and global political significance, there is growing uncertainty over the normative foundations of human rights. There are significantly different, and frequently conflicting, theoretical understandings of what we mean by this concept.[18]

At least three different approaches are currently identifiable. First, there are more limited institutional and source-based approaches: international human rights law is that which takes place in certain institutions interpreting specific sources, using shared interpretative techniques that apply in any other area of international law. This approach is reflected, too, in so-called 'political' theories of human rights, in which human rights are those norms the breach of which would justify international intervention into the otherwise sovereign sphere of national decision-making.

Second, there are broader approaches, sometimes called 'orthodox' or 'naturalistic' theories, in which human rights are based on an understanding that all persons have certain rights simply by virtue of being human. International human rights law is the instantiation in law of this understanding of the human person, the interpretation of which demands that extra-legal normative judgments will be centrally engaged.

Third, there are discourse-based approaches, in which relatively open-ended international human rights standards provide the opportunity for contested views to be debated and argued about; in this context, human rights norms are continually reinvented and resolutions are at best temporary and provisional. Related to this approach is an 'agreement'-based theory, in which human rights are those moral norms that a particular community has agreed to be sufficiently important to warrant being accorded the status of human rights.

As we shall see, this uncertainty over the normative foundations of human rights plays a significant role in providing an opening for those supporting the 'traditional values' Resolutions in three respects: first, the pluralism of theoretical approaches makes it difficult to argue convincingly that advancing traditional values falls foul of 'the' foundational principles of human rights, since there is no consensus as to what these are; second, the fact that the architecture of human rights theory is still evolving means that it is appropriate for these foundations to be re-examined in light of experience, and readjusted as necessary;[19] and, third, as we shall see, each of the competing theories

restricting circumcision for religious purposes; see *SS (Malaysia) v Secretary of State for the Home Department* [2013] EWCA Civ 888.

[18] I draw this brief description from Charles Beitz, *The Idea of Human Rights*.

[19] Obiajulu Nnamuchi, 'Towards a New Human Rights Paradigm: Integrating Hitherto Neglected Traditional Values into the Corpus of Human Rights and the Legitimacy Question', 14 *Chicago-Kent Journal of International and Comparative Law* 24, at 34.

identified can be interpreted as supporting one of the arguments in favour of traditional values being recognized by human rights.

New geo-politics: role of Russia and the Russian Orthodox Church

The final part of the jigsaw is the role of Russia. The Resolutions were not generated from within Africa, Asia or the Middle East, from which the previous relativistic arguments attracted most support, but from Russia, which had not seemed particularly attracted to a strong relativist position. Indeed, following the collapse of the Communism and the adoption of a constitutionalism that embraced constitutional rights, there was a strong push to join the major international human rights regimes, including the Council of Europe and the European Convention on Human Rights, as indications of these countries' acceptance of universal human rights after the dark days of Stalinist repression. Since that first flush of enthusiasm, however, Russia has seen much dirty linen being displayed before international and regional human rights bodies. This has resulted in a string of findings of human rights violations, particularly by the European Court of Human Rights. Coming at a time when Russia, in particular, is strongly reasserting its national interests internationally, and reinventing a narrative of national sovereignty, the external scrutiny of human rights bodies, and their 'interference', is perceived as threatening and unwelcome. Under President Vladimir Putin, Russia appears to be prepared to make a virtue out of this conflict with European human rights obligations, putting Russia forward as the leader of an informal ideological bloc (including many of its neighbours, China, and several states from the global South) that supports 'traditional values.'[20]

Although these concerns covered the gamut of human rights issues, decisions by the European Court of Human Rights on issues touching on religion were particularly sensitive because of the increased importance of the Orthodox Church, particularly in Russia, after the fall of Communism. Not only was the Russian *Government* increasingly antagonistic to the trend of human rights interpretation at the regional and international level, the Russian

[20] The relevant portion of President Putin's Annual Presidential Address to the Federal Assembly, 12 December 2013 eng.kremlin.ru/news/6402 (accessed 9 January 2015) is worth detailing in full: 'This destruction of traditional values from above not only leads to negative consequences for society, but is also essentially anti-democratic, since it is carried out on the basis of abstract, speculative ideas, contrary to the will of the majority, which does not accept the changes occurring or the proposed revision of values. We know that there are more and more people in the world who support our position on defending traditional values that have made up the spiritual and moral foundation of civilisation in every nation for thousands of years: the values of traditional families, real human life, including religious life, not just material existence but also spirituality, the values of humanism and global diversity. Of course, this is a conservative position. But speaking in the words of Nikolai Berdyaev, the point of conservatism is not that it prevents movement forward and upward, but that it prevents movement backward and downward, into chaotic darkness and a return to a primitive state.' See further Masha Gessen, 'Russia is remaking itself as the leader of the anti-Western world', *Slate*, 30 March 2014.

Orthodox Church was an enthusiastic ally in its scepticism, particularly over issues concerning sexual morality, women's rights and the family. The *Lautsi* case, in which Italy was required to defend the practice of displaying the crucifix in a public school before the European Court of Human Rights, was a key galvanizing moment. The Chamber decision holding the display to be contrary to the European Convention on Human Rights was overturned by the Grand Chamber after significant pressure from an ecumenical coalition of Christian Churches, including the Orthodox Church, apparently demonstrating that public engagement could, on occasion, turn the human rights tide.

It is no accident, therefore, that the Resolutions were introduced by the Russian government into the Human Rights Council at the urging, and with the active support, of the Russian Orthodox Church. Indeed, the speech by Russian Orthodox Metropolitan Kirill, Chairman of the Department for External Church Relations of the Moscow Patriarchate, to the Human Rights Council in March 2008 is often credited as a key moment in launching the campaign.[21]

An initial reaction

What should we make of these Resolutions? The scholarship of Yash Ghai, the first of Twining's 'Southern voices' to play a significant role in the critique that I offer in this paper, suggests a political analysis of these developments. His earlier criticism of those states supporting 'Asian values' as a counterweight to human rights seems equally applicable to at least some of the states supporting the recent Resolutions: that they are engaging in diversionary tactics, attempting to justify their authoritarian regimes in the face of internal and external criticism. As Twining put it, discussing Ghai's analysis, Ghai considered that '[h]uman rights rhetoric may be used – sometimes cynically manipulated – to further particular interests or, as in the Asian values debate, to give legitimacy to repressive regimes by emphasizing the right to self-determination of sovereign states . . . [M]uch state effort is devoted to artificially creating a common culture as a prop for national unity.'[22]

This seems as applicable to Vladimir Putin's Russia now as it was to Lee Kuan Yew's Singapore in the 1990s. But before concluding that this is all that can be said about the 'traditional values' Resolutions, it is, perhaps, worth reflecting a little more. I suggest in this chapter that, despite Ghai's scepticism, there may be a danger in dismissing arguments based on 'traditional values' too cavalierly. We may be in danger of throwing out the baby with the bathwater.

[21] Russian Orthodox Church, UN Human Rights Council 7th Session Geneva, 18 March 2008 Panel discussion on Human Rights and Intercultural Dialogue, 18 March 2008 (official translation provided by the Russian Orthodox Church).

[22] Twining, *General Jurisprudence*, 410.

3. Different ways of understanding the appeal of 'traditional values'

We need to begin any deeper analysis of 'traditional values' by considering the several different meanings reflected in the debates about the Resolutions. Although united in supporting 'traditional values', supporters diverged in what precisely they seek to support with 'traditional values', and why they are considered to be valuable in the human rights context. In this section, I suggest that we can identify at least four ways of conceptualizing the ideas of 'traditional values' as reflected in these debates: as a way of expressing the values of the *nation*, as a way of expressing *religious* values, as a way of expressing the values of '*traditional*' *societies*, and as a way of expressing *conservative* values.

National values

The first meaning understands 'traditional values' as those values that particular states regard as important, often sufficiently important to incorporate into their national law and practice. The claim that we should recognize 'traditional' values and weigh them highly becomes, in this context, a claim that international or regional human rights institutions should give more recognition and weight to the values that particular states hold dear, even when they depart from an emerging consensus based on the practice of other states.

Robert Marsh has suggested, for example, 'that people's adherence to ... traditional values can be seen both as a reaction to the Western values to which they have been exposed, and as symptomatic of a *nation-building* struggle that involves in part a positive evaluation of indigenous reactions to the cultural invasion of the modern West'.[23] Support for 'traditional values' in this sense becomes another way of expressing concerns about the erosion of national sovereignty in the sphere of norm creation and interpretation, bolstered by arguments from democracy (where that exists). One way of interpreting the decision by the Grand Chamber of the European Court of Human Rights in the *Lautsi* case, for example, is to view it as supporting traditional values of this type. European states were given considerable discretion to permit public schools to continue to display a crucifix in their classrooms as a symbol of national values, despite objection from parents, using the doctrine of the 'margin of appreciation'.

Whilst this understanding of 'traditional values' may satisfy those concerned with protecting national sovereignty,[24] it does little to address other

[23] Robert M. Marsh, 'Civilizational Diversity and Support for Traditional Values', 8 *Comparative Sociology* (2009) 267, 268 (emphasis added).

[24] Although, even here, the extent of the Court's discretion in choosing whether and how to allow this margin of appreciation renders it suspect. In the abortion context, for example, the ECtHR has become somewhat less generous in the extent of the margin of appreciation allowed to states, e.g. A, B, C v Ireland, Application no 25579/05, (2011) 53 EHRR 13.

understandings of why 'traditional values' should be protected since it places the *state* in the driving seat, allowing it to decide which, if any, 'traditional values' to uphold. So, for example, the ECtHR's use of the margin of appreciation to address issues concerned with abortion,[25] or the wearing of Islamic dress,[26] or conscientious objection to same-sex relationships,[27] recognizes the diversity of the values upheld in different *national* traditions. As the ECtHR stated in the *Leyla Sahin* case, concerning the wearing of Islamic dress: 'Rules in this sphere will consequently vary from one country to another according to *national* traditions and the requirements imposed by the need to protect the rights and freedoms of others and so maintain public order . . . Accordingly, the choice of the extent and form such regulation should take must inevitably be left up to a point to *the State* concerned, as it will depend on the specific domestic context.'[28] But this does little to ensure that human rights norms will protect 'traditional values' that a state does not value.

Religious practice

A second way of conceptualizing 'traditional values' is to view them as synonymous with long-standing religious beliefs and practices adopted by one or more of the major world religions; for supporters, these values correspond to an ultimate truth. The claim that we should recognize and weigh highly such 'traditional values' becomes, in this context, a claim that international or regional human rights institutions should give more recognition and weight to the values that particular religions hold dear, even when they depart from an emerging consensus based on the practice of states. 'Traditional values', in this sense, becomes another way of expressing concerns about the supposedly declining respect accorded by regional and international bodies to religious beliefs in the sphere of norm creation and interpretation. There is a significant degree of sympathy with the language of the Resolutions, understood in this way, in the Christian global South, particularly in Africa, and among Islamic states. One way of interpreting resistance to claims that there is a human right to same-sex marriage, for example, is on the basis that it requires a profound change in the understanding of marriage held by substantial sections of the major world religions, and the interpretation of human rights norms should give considerable weight to this.

Those seeking to further 'traditional values' in this sense are likely to see their claims as resting ultimately on arguments from 'religious freedom', but using the language of 'traditional values' rather than 'religious freedom' is seen as preferable. It appears to be becoming increasingly difficult to use 'freedom of

[25] *Vo v France*, Application no. 5392/00, (2005) 40 EHRR 12, at 82.

[26] *Leyla Sahin v Turkey*, Application no 44774/98, (2007) 44 EHRR 5.

[27] *Eweida v United Kingdom*, Application no 48420/10, (2013) 57 EHRR 8. The author was Junior Counsel for Ms Ladele in this case before the ECtHR.

[28] *Leyla Sahin v Turkey*, at 109 (emphasis added).

religion and belief' protections: 'freedom of religion' has become individualized, so that it becomes the freedom of belief of particular individuals to hold the beliefs they do, rather than providing protections for institutionalized religion as such; and several jurisdictions restrict severely the extent to which 'freedom of religion' extends to the protection of *practices* as opposed to the protection of beliefs. Using 'traditional values' language rather than 'religious freedom' is also more likely to lead to support from other states and constituencies that do not share religious presuppositions. Although originating in Russia, the strategy is one that seeks to appeal beyond Russia and beyond Orthodoxy.

'Traditional' societies

A third way of conceptualizing 'traditional values' is to view them as more akin to the cultural values held by localized communities of people in 'traditional' societies in Africa, Asia and Latin America. 'Traditional values' in this sense may or may not overlap with the religious values promoted by the major world religions, and they may, or may not, be considered by those holding them to be based on indigenous *religious* beliefs; they may simply be *cultural* beliefs devoid of any clear religious backing. So, too, 'traditional values' in this sense may, or may not, overlap with the values incorporated in state law in the countries in which these communities live. Examples of 'traditional values' in this sense include concepts such as *dheng* (or *dheeng*) among the Dinka people of South Sudan, or the idea of *ubuntu* in South Africa, concepts which we shall revisit subsequently.

Those seeking to further 'traditional values' in this sense are likely to support their claims by referring to those norms that seek to protect indigenous peoples and their right to 'self-determination', and to cultural rights as imbedded in such documents as the International Covenant on Economic, Social and Cultural Rights. Both these sets of protections were strongly influenced by the 'winds of change' leading to decolonialization. They are nearly always subject to a general human rights override, however, particularly where they come up against the rights of women, children and (increasingly) sexual minorities. In addition, resorting to the rights of 'indigenous peoples' does not capture the full range of 'traditional' practices to be protected. As a result, the Resolutions are attractive because they are seen as a potentially more effective way to influence the interpretation of human rights law in ways that will accord greater weight to such 'traditional values' without these limitations.

Conservative values

A fourth meaning of 'traditional values' is closer to conservative political arguments that have been commonplace in western democracies at least since the eighteenth century, and that we associate with thinkers such as

Edmund Burke. 'Traditional values' in this sense is a way of capturing a conservative orientation towards the defence of institutions and practices that have survived.[29] Because they have survived, conservatives consider that there should be a presumption that they are functionally useful in some way, and that we should be careful to understand what those functions are before we change them. Not to be careful in this way, changing institutions and value systems whose functions we do not fully understand, is likely to lead to unfortunate, unintended consequences that could, and should, have been avoided.[30]

Conservatives do not base their defence of traditional values on faith, or culture, or the nation, or democracy. Nor do they necessarily support any particular set of values or institutions. Rather, they seek to challenge liberal and progressive reforms on the basis of human reason, stripped of what they would see as the blinding effects of progressive liberal ideology or theory. Conservatives are not necessarily opposed to reform; they are not reactionaries in this sense. But change should be based on experience, particularly historical experience. These experiences are also likely to vary over time and place; it is not surprising, therefore, that different societies will reach different conclusions as to how best to order social life. Conservatism tends, therefore, towards particularism, context and complexity, eschewing universalistic assumptions. Conservatives' reaction to 'human rights' is likely to be similar to Burke's criticism of 'natural rights'. '[A]s [men's] liberties and the restrictions [on them] vary with times and circumstances and admit to infinite modifications, they cannot be settled upon any abstract rule; and nothing is so foolish as to discuss them upon that principle.'[31]

Consensus and divergence

We should notice something important about these different ways in which traditional values are considered to be important. With regard to certain issues, they may well significantly overlap. Take the issue of same-sex marriage. Each of the four approaches to 'traditional values' would take a different route, but they are likely to be united in opposing any such change originating at the international level. So, too, each of the four approaches would adopt different reasons why 'the family' is important, but they would be likely to coalesce around its centrality to social life as the transmission mechanism of practices

[29] I have benefitted especially from Jerry Z. Muller's Introduction to his edited collection, *Conservatism: An Anthology of Social and Political Thought From David Hume to the Present* (Princeton University Press, 1997). I am grateful to Steve Aschheim for bringing it to my attention.

[30] A recent example of this approach can be seen in the opinion of the United States Supreme Court delivered by Kennedy J. in *Town of Greece v Galloway*, 134 S. Ct. 1811 (2014).

[31] Edmund Burke, *Reflections on the Revolution in France* (1790), reprinted in Jerry Z. Muller, ed., *Conservatism* (Princeton, 1997), at 99.

and norms.[32] Because of this convergence, and the difficulty of knowing precisely where 'national values' end and 'religious values' or 'traditional values' begin, there is a tendency to think that they may all simply coalesce in theocratic constitutionalism.

In other contexts, on other issues, this overlap is much less apparent, and they conflict. 'Traditional values', in the sense of upholding *religious* values, may well be hostile to the state-centred approach (think of the opposition by the Holy See to proposals by Islamic states to criminalizing blasphemy[33]), to the indigenous culture approach (think of the opposition by Christian missionaries to female genital cutting in Kenya[34]), and to the 'conservative' approach (think of the conservative political opposition to the religious enthusiasm of Quaker attempts to abolish the slave trade[35]). What is, perhaps, particularly intriguing about the recent attempt to establish 'traditional values' in the Human Rights Council at the United Nations is the extent to which it involves the use of transnational and international mechanisms, using universalistic language, to bind together a coalition of temporary and particularistic interests under a common banner. For this reason, the potential for them all to coalesce is reduced.

4. Diverging approaches to traditional values at the United Nations

Having considered various dimensions of 'traditional values,' we turn now to consider the complex *relationship* between such values and human rights. We shall be primarily concerned with how this relationship has been conceived during the debates on the 'traditional values' Resolutions. But to help us understand the choices made, it will be useful first to consider the possible relationships more systematically. Conceptually, there are four principal ways in which 'human rights' and 'traditional values', understood in the four ways set out in the previous part, might be thought to function in relationship with each other. (In developing this taxonomy, my debt to William Twining's analytic distinctions between different types of 'cultural relativism' will be clear.[36])

[32] This potential for significant overlap can be seen in the operation of American constitutional law. As long ago as the late 1970s, Cole Durham was arguing that a 'rapprochement' could and should be effectuated between liberal individualism and the value of the family, pointing to several examples where tradition was used by the Supreme Court as an important element in determining the scope of constitutional rights. W. Cole Durham, 'Comment: The Relationship of Constitution and Tradition', 53 *Southern California Law Review* (1979–80) 645, 653.

[33] A/C.3/63/SR.46, para. 33.

[34] Baer and Brysk, note 11 above, at 95 (describing the unsuccessful attempts to restrict female genital cutting in Kenya in the 1920s).

[35] See Adrian Hastings, Alistair Mason and Hugh Pyper (eds), *The Oxford Companion to Christian Thought* (Oxford University Press, 2000) at 675.

[36] Twining, *General Jurisprudence*, 412 (he credits Yash Ghai with formulating these distinctions, but they are Twining's own formulation). The quotations that follow are taken from this source.

Analytical position 1: 'Human rights' are based on 'traditional values', which should be seen as at the root of universal human rights. This is often linked to the adoption of what Twining called 'strong cultural relativism', that is a position in which rights are seen to 'depend on culture rather than upon universal norms'.

Analytical position 2: 'Human rights' may conflict with 'traditional values', and in this conflict 'human rights' should triumph. This is often linked to a position that cultural differences do indeed exist, but only (the Western concept of) human rights 'is acceptable as a basis for universal norms'. The degree of importance that is attached to embeddedness of human rights in Western culture will determine whether this is considered to be a strong cultural relativist position or a universalist position.

Analytical position 3: Universal norms exist, and 'traditional values' provide important evidence both that different cultures possess such overlapping values, and what these norms are, from which a common core of human rights can be extracted. Twining refers to this as 'moderate cultural relativism'. Where 'traditional values' conflict with such overlapping universal norms they should be rejected, but the degree of such conflict should not be exaggerated. In many cases, traditional values can and should be harmonized with human rights standards by internal reinterpretation of the traditions from which the traditional values come.

Analytical position 4: There is conflict between 'traditional values' and 'human rights' but an enriched version of rights can and should be developed dialectically out of this tension, leading 'towards a new form of universalism' that draws on both sets of norms. Twining termed the methodology by which this fourth approach might be developed, 'intercultural discourse'.

Emerging approaches at the United Nations

Three distinct approaches emerge in the United Nations debates, echoing three of the analytical positions we've just identified: in the first, 'traditional values' serve to support particularist, conservative reinterpretations of human rights standards, reflecting the first analytical position; in the second, opponents of the Resolutions clearly prioritize Western conceptions of human rights, and regard them as trumping 'traditional values', reflecting the second analytical position; in the third approach, 'traditional values' are instrumentalized in the service of international universalism, reflecting the third analytical position. To help understand these positions more clearly, I shall begin with the second, before turning to the first and the third. We shall see that only the fourth analytical position is not well represented in the debates; we shall subsequently demonstrate that this gap opens up possibilities for future developments.

Opposition to the 'traditional values' Resolutions

The 'traditional values' proposals are seen by critics as seeking 'to impose an ideological monopoly', serving 'as a platform to bring together Orthodox Christian conservatives, Protestant fundamentalists and conservative [Roman] Catholics' and supported by a broad coalition of states, primarily from the global South.[37] Although there is convincing evidence that different religious traditions and different societies 'give rise to cultural zones with *distinctive* value systems',[38] each can nevertheless agree that 'their' particular traditions should be preserved. 'Traditional values' has thus become the slogan for an essentially conservative, even reactionary, movement opposed to what is seen as the liberal, internationalizing agenda of Western human rights activists.

The Resolutions of the Human Rights Council were perceived by some, in particular, as an attempt to turn the clock back, or at least to stop further development of human rights norms in areas regarding women and sexual minorities.[39] The European Union, for example, in reiterating its understanding of human rights as 'universal', and its view that 'States have a positive obligation to promote and protect these rights', consistently pointed to the 'potential harm posed by the concept of traditional values of such values in undermining the universality and inalienability of human rights',[40] and to the negative impact on the implementation of human rights, 'especially those concerning violence against women, sexual orientation, gender identity, age and disability'.[41] This danger was increased, given that there 'was no clear-cut, universally agreed definition,' the EU argued, of what was meant by 'traditional values'.[42] They are 'inherently subjective and specific to time and place'.[43]

In addition to EU resistance, the United States was also prominently against the Resolutions, and there was significant opposition from a loose coalition of human rights NGOs, mostly Western, which shared with the EU and the US an understanding that supporting 'traditional values' would lead to a weakening of women's rights and LGBT rights. Traditional values are seen by them as barriers to the achievement of human rights because the human rights project

[37] *Summary of information*, para. 71 (comments of Russian LGBT Network).

[38] Ronald Inglehart and Wayne E. Baker, 'Modernization, Cultural Change, and the Persistence of Traditional Values', 65(1) *American Sociological Review* 19, at 49 (emphasis added).

[39] See e.g. the statement by Zimbabwe at the Human Rights Council supporting the Resolutions, 27 February 2013, in which that support was set in the context of Zimbabwe's opposition to 'the issue of LGBT that is increasingly taking centre stage in discussions not only in the HRC, but across the entire UN system'.

[40] EU Statement to the Human Rights Council, 13 September 2013.

[41] UN High Commissioner for Human Rights, Summary of information from States Members of the United Nations and other relevant stakeholders on best practices in the application of traditional values while promoting and protecting human rights and upholding human dignity, A/HRC/24/22, para. 3.

[42] Para. 3. [43] Para. 3.

is seen as transformative, even transgressive, and therefore sceptical of values, beliefs and practices that are perceived as 'irrational survivals of old customs'.[44] The transformative potential of human rights thus casts *prima facie* doubt on traditional values, *because* they are traditional. From this perspective, the human rights project is seen as embracing the insistence of Enlightenment philosophers, 'that the rational, empirical pursuit of true knowledge required a throwing off of traditional authority, which demands the surrender of one's capacity for independent thought and renders one incapable of making new contributions to knowledge'.[45] This approach is particularly strong in some feminist approaches to human rights, in which references to the 'traditional' are nearly always pejorative.[46]

Opponents were faced with two rather different approaches, both broadly supportive, at least in principle, of an initiative based on traditional values. It is to these that we now turn.

'Traditional values' as particularist, conservative reinterpretation of international human rights

There are several key aspects of the speech by the Russian Orthodox Metropolitan Kirill to the Human Rights Council in March 2008[47] that set the scene for the subsequent discussions and that explain some of the original thinking behind his attempt to involve the Human Rights Council. We see, in this critical original move towards securing traditional values in the UN, the strong influence of both the national and religious understandings of traditional values examined previously, as well as the clear adoption of the first analytical position discussed earlier.

First, Metropolitan Kirill claims that a close identity exists between the appeal of human rights and the central tenets of Christianity. Christianity, indeed, is seen as the origin of the values that are now expressed in human rights documents. Second, a claim is made that the development and implementation of human rights principles, such as human dignity, are increasingly diverging from this original grounding in religious values, as attempts are made to separate them from their origins, and religion is becoming marginalized and privatized. Third, the influence of 'extreme feministic views and homosexual attitudes', together with the increasingly important role of a small group of experts and NGOs, means that the approach of those whose role it is

[44] Marsh, Contemporary Sociology, 269.

[45] R. Bauman, 'Tradition, Anthropology of', *International Encyclopedia of the Social & Behavioral Sciences* (2001), 15819.

[46] See e.g. Hilary Charlesworth and Christine Chinkin, *The Boundaries of International Law: A Feminist Analysis* (Melland Schill Studies in International Law) (Manchester University Press, 2000), passim.

[47] Russian Orthodox Church, UN Human Rights Council 7th Session Geneva, 18 March 2008 Panel discussion on Human Rights and Intercultural Dialogue, 18 March 2008 (official translation provided by the Russian Orthodox Church).

to develop and interpret human rights norms increasingly diverges from the opinion of believers, and the moral norms accepted by most people. Fourth, the way in which human rights are interpreted should not privilege any particular national approach to the implementation of human rights but should, instead, recognize that different nations have different experiences, and different histories, which also need to be taken into account in the development of national human rights systems.

In Resolution 12/21 of 2 October 2009, the Human Rights Council requested the UN High Commissioner for Human Rights to convene a workshop on traditional values and human rights, which was held in October 2010, and a summary of the discussions was reported to the Human Rights Council by the High Commissioner. Professor Tom Zwart of Utrecht School of Law presented a seemingly different approach to that proposed by Metropolitan Kirill during this workshop.[48] Zwart's approach, which he terms the 'receptor approach', 'starts from the premise that, by relying on local socio-cultural arrangements during the implementation stage, human rights production will be enhanced and reinforced rather than diminished'.[49] This can be done by 'identifying and making visible, domestic social arrangements supporting and protecting human rights that are already in place'. Zwart's 'receptor approach' assumes 'that international human rights will be most effective if they are able to lock on to socio-cultural receptors in diverse cultures, which will allow them to play a role in the societies concerned'.[50]

Initially, therefore, Zwart's approach *appears* to fit clearly within the third analytical position sketched out above. But, in a critical move, he argues, echoing Metropolitan Kirill, that if and when these arrangements 'fall short of the international human rights requirements, . . . *elements must be added to the existing institutions rather than attempting to replace them with Western-centered solutions*'.[51] This is significantly different from the third analytical position in privileging local understanding of values over international standards, and brings Zwart back into broad support for Metropolitan Kirill's approach.

Debates in the Human Rights Council were significantly influenced by both these approaches. In Resolution 16/3 of 24 March 2011, the HRC 'affirmed that

48 An article based on this is: Tom Zwart, 'Using Local Culture to Further the Implementation of International Human Rights: The Receptor Approach', 34(2) *Human Rights Quarterly* (2012) 546.

49 Ibid., 547. This theory raises significant issues that lie beyond the scope of this chapter, particularly those surrounding the difficult question of the 'vernacularization' of human rights, i.e. how human rights are internalized in the popular consciousness of different societies, Lucia Michelutti, 'The vernacularization of democracy: political participation and popular politics in North India', (2007) 13 Journal of the Royal Anthropological Institute (n.s.) 639, at 639. For a discussion of 'vernacularization' of human rights in the context of women's rights, see Sally Engle Merry, *Human Rights and Gender Violence: Translating International Law into Local Justice* (University of Chicago Press, 2005).

50 Ibid., 548. 51 Ibid., 547.

dignity, freedom and responsibility are traditional values, shared by all humanity and embodied in universal rights instruments'.[52] It also 'recognized that the better understanding and appreciation of these values contribute to promoting and protecting human rights and fundamental freedoms'.[53] The Council requested the Advisory Committee to prepare a study 'on how a better understanding and appreciation of traditional values' could contribute to the promotion and protection of human rights. The Advisory Committee established a drafting group on 12 August 2011. In December 2011, a draft was completed by the Rapporteur, Vladimir Kartashkin, and submitted to the Advisory Group.[54]

The draft report defined 'tradition' as 'all the elements of social and cultural heritage handed down from generation to generation and preserved within States, societies and population groups over long periods. Traditions include certain social conventions, behavioural norms, ideas, customs and ceremonies.'[55] From the human rights perspective, such traditions may be positive, negative or unrelated to human rights norms, depending 'each time on the specific circumstances'.[56] In a move that clearly reflected aspects of the approach advocated in Metropolitan Kirill's speech, dignity, freedom and responsibility are seen in Kartashkin's draft report as 'traditional values of humankind' which, by being recognized as such, 'makes them universal in nature and promotes the universal acceptance of human rights'.[57] In a critically important move, all international human rights agreements 'must be based on, and not contradict' these traditional values, and therefore any violation of these standards would render these agreements invalid.[58] Practically, too, unless human rights norms are to be seen as foreign and unacceptable, the links between traditional values and human rights norms must be strengthened. In a key paragraph, the Rapporteur concludes: 'no single approach to implementing human rights can be applied in all countries or to all peoples. Attempts to impose a single standard system for their implementation, under the pretext of the universal application of human rights, will lead to disagreements and conflict, and will undermine the inalienable nature of those rights.'[59]

Whilst it is not entirely clear what the Rapporteur's argument is, and it requires a degree of reconstruction to make it plain, the bare bones of the approach he sketches out in the draft report do emerge. It is important, initially, to understand what is *not* being argued in his draft report. First, the point of the 'traditional values' move is not primarily to reinforce the idea that the human rights regime should protect limited examples of specific

[52] Resolution 16/3, Human Rights Council. [53] Ibid.

[54] Preliminary study on promoting human rights and fundamental freedoms through a better understanding of traditional values of humankind: Prepared by Professor Vladimir Kartashkin, Rapporteur of the drafting group of the Advisory Committee, A/HRC/AC/8/4, 12 December 2011.

[55] Para. 7. [56] Para. 19. [57] Para. 74. [58] Para. 77. [59] Para. 79.

'traditional values', such as the rights of indigenous communities to the preservation of their own cultural norms. Conceptually, the Rapporteur does not see that move as particularly innovative, since several international instruments and judicial decisions do this already. Second, the point of the 'traditional values' move, as suggested by the Rapporteur, is not simply that 'human rights' have historically been influenced by 'traditional values' – again, that point has been made in the past and does not necessarily give rise to any conclusion that human rights should *currently* be interpreted in light of this. Third, the point of the 'traditional values' move is not to assert that, where 'human rights' and 'traditional values' conflict, 'traditional values' should necessarily trump in all circumstances; that would be a step well beyond what the existing legal texts, national or international, could support and would require a revolution in the drafting of human rights instruments. Fourth, the point of the 'traditional values' move is not a jurisdictional argument that 'human rights' and 'traditional values' simply operate in different spheres, and that the relationship between the two should be one where neither gets in the way of the other.

Rather, the radical move that the Rapporteur appears to want to make is to reorientate human rights *interpretation* by legitimizing 'tradition' as one of the normative foundations of human rights. Before proceeding further, we need to remind ourselves that it is not only the concept of 'tradition' that is contested, giving rise to different understandings, with different normative implications. As we have seen earlier, this is also the case with the concept of 'human rights' itself. The Rapporteur takes advantage of the current uncertainty over the normative foundations of human rights. He attempts to supplement, if not replace, the three main theories discussed earlier, with a fourth, based on the idea of 'traditional values'. In this approach, we understand what human rights are, at a fundamental level, by understanding 'traditional values'. 'Traditional values', in this understanding, become a significantly important source of interpretation of the grand meta-principles of human rights (dignity, freedom and equality). We interpret these meta-principles properly, therefore, when we interpret them in light of these 'traditional values'. 'Traditional values' are incorporated, in Federico Lenzerini's well-judged phrase, within the 'molecular structure' of rights.[60]

The Rapporteur's draft report thus involves an important move to have 'dignity' interpreted in a way that recognizes the variability of the understandings that different societies have of the implications of what it means to be human. Since human rights are seen as being based on 'human dignity,' the implication is that human rights will therefore differ significantly between societies. Transnational efforts (particularly by human rights NGOs) to produce a common approach on such deeply contested issues as abortion, capital

[60] *The Culturalization of Human Rights Law*, 189 (referring to the 'cultural factor' rather than 'traditional values').

punishment, same-sex marriage and affirmative action are seen as ignoring the deep differences between societies on the meaning and implications of human dignity, and should therefore be resisted. Prominent among supporters of this approach are those who have an understanding of human rights based in natural law, and particularly those with links to the Roman Catholic and Orthodox Churches. Thus, natural law is seen as supporting state-based support for families, state-based opposition to same-sex marriage, parental control of education, and opposition to abortion. In all these cases, it is seen as the role of the state to support what is 'traditional', interpreted as what is 'natural'.[61]

Instrumentalizing traditional values in the service of international universalism

The approach adopted by the Rapporteur was not, however, the approach taken by the Advisory Committee of the Human Rights Council. In August 2012, the Advisory Committee 'took note' of the Rapporteur's study and requested the drafting group to finalize the study in light of discussions held by the Committee, and to report back to the Advisory Committee. Meanwhile, it asked the Human Rights Council to defer its consideration until receipt of its final draft.[62] In December 2012, the Advisory Committee submitted its study.[63] This study revealed divided views and both the negative and positive impact that traditional values may have on human rights is discussed. The preferred way forward is set out in the Conclusions to the Advisory Committee's study.

For the Advisory Committee, the role that traditional values could usefully play is set out in the context of a general concern that 'people's awareness, acceptance and implementation' of the universal human rights proclaimed in the Universal Declaration of Human Rights and international covenants needs to be increased, and its view that 'a better understanding and the promotion of positive traditional values underpinning such universal norms and standards could have a useful role to play' in doing so.[64] Human rights education and training could usefully draw on 'familiar positive traditional values' derived from the local context, 'thus enhancing their acceptability and eliminating the negative perception that human rights are foreign or alien concepts'.[65] In addition, states 'should respect the cultural diversity and pluralism that exist

[61] See e.g. UN High Commissioner for Human Rights, Summary of information from States Members of the United Nations and other relevant stakeholders on best practices in the application of traditional values while promoting and protecting human rights and upholding human dignity, A/HRC/24/22 (hereafter *Summary of Information*), para. 38–39 (Acción Solidaria comments), para. 47 (Catholic Family and Human Rights Institute).

[62] Report of the Advisory Committee on its ninth session, 6–10 August 2012, A/HRC/AC/9/6, para. 9/4.

[63] Study of the Human Rights Advisory Committee on promoting human rights and fundamental freedoms through a better understanding of traditional values of humankind, A/HRC/22/71, 6 December 2012.

[64] Para. 74. [65] Para. 77.

within communities and societies as a source of enrichment and value added to the social and cultural fabric of these communities and societies, as well as of marginalized and vulnerable groups'.[66] We see clearly that the approach that the Advisory Committee adopts locates it firmly in the third analytical position discussed earlier.

This is confirmed by key aspects of the rest of its report. States, according to the Advisory Committee, have the responsibility to 'take sustained and systematic action to modify or eliminate stereotypes and negative, harmful and discriminatory practices justified by traditional values'.[67] Obstacles to the realization of human rights were especially notable 'in certain areas where the population continues to live according to centuries-old traditions and customs in conditions of poverty and deprivation'.[68] Whilst 'distinctive features of different cultures and religions should be accorded respect', this was only on condition that 'they are consistent with international human rights standards', and are without prejudice to the 'responsibilities of States to promote, protect and fulfil universal human rights in their respective countries and to cooperate at the international level'.[69] Balancing the positive and negative required 'a constant dialogue between different countries and peoples'.[70] In Resolution 21/3, the HRC requested the Office of the UNHCHR to collect information from states and others on best practices in the application of traditional values, which was prepared and submitted in June 2013.[71]

What we see emerging from the Advisory Committee's report, therefore, is a conservative argument of a different type from that reflected in the Rapporteur's draft report. The Advisory Committee's report suggests that, because traditional institutions and value systems have survived and have been valued, this may mean that they can be useful for new purposes. In this case, the new purpose is the transmission of (universal, international) human rights values into the local context, in order to render them more acceptable and thus more likely to be implemented and enforced in practice. Referring to traditional values may therefore serve as an effective mechanism for assisting in the promotion of the human right in question.

Voices from the global South

The approach that the Advisory Committee adopted fits much more clearly that proposed by Francis Deng and Abdullahi An-Na'im than the approach that Zwart, Metropolitan Kirill or the Rapporteur proposed.

Francis Deng, writing about the Dinka in South Sudan, is a prominent early exemplar of the approach that the Advisory Committee ended up adopting. Twining describes how Deng 'illustrated in a vivid and specific way the more

[66] Para. 78. [67] Para. 76. [68] Para. 79. [69] Para. 79. [70] Para. 80.
[71] *Summary of information.*

general theme of the complex relationship between long-established traditional values and modern conceptions of human rights'.[72] For Deng, Twining continues, 'human rights and principles of democracy are universal, but only at a very abstract level'.[73] 'In short, a cultural approach to human rights and democracy involves seeing tradition as supplementing abstract values and principles.' Deng, he suggests, identifies several ideas, *cieng* and *dheng*, that he regards as having the power to 'concretise, localise, and enrich abstract notions of human dignity'.[74] '[F]or institutions and particular norms to be accepted as legitimate and to be effective they must be debated, interpreted, and applied within the concepts and internal logic of local cultures. However, this does not preclude using universal standards as a basis for judging particular features of a culture or tradition.'[75] Although 'Deng acknowledges that, judged by the standards of human rights norms, some aspects of Dinka culture are open to criticism',[76] he 'argues that traditional Dinka values are basically compatible, in most respects, with the values underlying the Universal Declaration of Human Rights and related conventions and declarations'.[77]

So too, Abdullahi An-Na'im has adopted a somewhat similar approach. An-Na'im has also suggested that the human rights movement cannot be effective 'so long as there is a perception of exclusive Western authorship of the concept of human rights and its normative implications'.[78] These rights are unlikely to be accepted by Muslims, for example, unless they are seen as supported by Islamic texts. As Twining puts it, An-Na'im considers that 'the legitimacy of human rights standards will only be plausible . . . if members believe that they are sanctioned by their own cultural traditions. Since people understand things through their own cultural lenses, such legitimacy can mainly be attained by dialogue and struggle *internal* to the culture.'[79] There is a need, therefore, to 'strengthen the cultural legitimacy ... of international human rights standards'.[80]

This rapprochement is possible because, according to An-Na'im, 'despite their apparent peculiarities and diversity, human beings and societies share certain fundamental interests, concerns, qualities, traits and values that can be identified and articulated as the framework for a common "culture" of universal human rights.'[81] 'The criteria I would adopt for identifying universal human rights,' An-Na'im writes, 'is that they are rights to which human beings

[72] Twining, *General Jurisprudence*, 393. [73] Ibid., 389. [74] Ibid., 389. [75] Ibid., 389.

[76] Ibid., 390. A striking example is provided by Jeffrey L. Deal, 'Torture by Cieng: Ethical Theory Meets Social Practice among the Dinka Agaar of South Sudan', 112(4) *American Anthropologist* 563 (2010).

[77] Twining, *General Jurisprudence*, 377.

[78] Abdullahi A. An-Na'im, 'Human Rights and the Challenge of Relevance: The Case of Collective Rights', in *The Role of the Nation State in the 21st Century: Human Rights, International Organizations, and Foreign Policy* (Monique Castermans-Holleman et al. (eds), 1998), 7.

[79] Twining, General Jurisprudence, 399. [80] Ibid., 403.

[81] An-Na'im, *Human Rights in Africa*, 21.

are entitled by virtue of being human. In other words, universal standards of human rights are, by definition, appreciated by a wide variety of cultural traditions because they pertain to the inherent dignity and well-being of every human being, regardless of race, gender, language, or religion.'[82] In the case of Islamic law, for example, various different and conflicting messages are sent, depending on which texts are cited, with texts of the Qur'an and Sunna of the Medina period contrasting with the texts of the Qur'an of the Mecca period. This opens up the opportunity for internal dialogue within the Islamic tradition. Unless the basis of modern Islamic law 'is shifted away from the former, there is no way of avoiding drastic and serious violation of universal standards of human rights.'[83] Although the circumstances in which an out-and-out breach of human rights standards occurs can, therefore, be minimized, in certain circumstances this will be the case. Where that is the case, 'the internal struggle cannot and should not be settled by outsiders,'[84] although the external human rights standard remains the ideal that Muslims should aim to achieve in time.

As Lenzerini also suggests: 'when human rights are rationalized according to the terms of reference proper of a given culture – i.e. are attributed a meaning which is culturally intelligible in the light of the intellectual patterns of the community (of course, without altering their purpose) – their goal, content, and role are better understood by the members of the society. As a result of this process, human rights are empathized by the society and incorporated within its cultural substrate, in the sense that they are assimilated by the community and felt as natural components of their everyday life.'[85] This approach resonates well with evidence from the sociology and anthropology of human rights that appears to suggest that, in certain conditions, the ability of local actors to reframe international norms as local leads to more effective implementation of those norms.[86]

The approach adopted by Metropolitan Kirill, Zwart and the Rapporteur differs from these approaches in two respects. First, Zwart et al. reject the understanding of those who consider that the human rights regime articulates a particular set of moral or philosophical or political preferences which each state is required to adopt. Unlike Deng and An-Na'im, then, Zwart et al. leave open whether there is a philosophical set of commitments underpinning international human rights norms, and allows states, in Zwart's words, to 'remain loyal to their own philosophical conviction to the extent that the legal regime allows them', provided they implement 'the regime of human rights grounded in positive law'.[87] Second, they also differ from Deng and An-Na'im in not adopting a discourse-based approach, where a process of internal discourse and inter-cultural dialogue would be used to develop a universal

[82] An-Na'im, *Islamic Reformation*, 164. [83] Ibid., 179. [84] An-Na'im, *Promises*, 109.
[85] *Culturalization of Human Rights Law*, 217–8.
[86] Baer and Brysk, above, at 102 (describing campaigns against female genital cutting).
[87] Zwart, Using Local Culture to Further the Implementation of International Human Rights, 553.

consensus (An-Na'im is the example he uses here). In these approaches, argues Zwart, 'if there is a conflict between the two, traditional culture will have to give way to international human rights.'[88] As we have seen, this is precisely what he, Metropolitan Kirill and the Rapporteur want to avoid.

5. Two conceptions of tradition

Whilst these conceptualizations go some way towards explaining the complicated politics and philosophy of the traditional values debates in the United Nations, and enable us to separate various different strands of argument, we need to dig deeper still. In particular, we have not yet defined what is meant by 'tradition', being largely satisfied with providing examples of different ways in which 'traditional values' play a role. But what is meant by the idea of 'tradition' in each of these contexts? Is there a common understanding of 'tradition', and can attempts to define it at a higher level of generality help us to understand what is going on in the context of 'traditional values' at the United Nations?

For the purposes of this discussion, I shall not distinguish sharply between 'tradition' and 'custom',[89] largely because the material I am dealing with usually does not make a clear distinction between the two, using them almost interchangeably, and to impose such a distinction in retrospect would be misleading. I shall suggest that there are two competing conceptions of tradition, thus broadly conceived, and I shall suggest that, at the centre of the debate in the United Nations over the 'traditional values' Resolutions, we find therefore not just a debate over the nature of human rights, but also over the nature of tradition itself; a debate as to which of these two competing conceptions of tradition to adopt.

An orthodox understanding of tradition

Edward Shils proposed a sociological definition of the concept in 1981. For Shils, a tradition was that which is 'transmitted or handed down from the past to the present'.[90] One way of viewing a tradition, drawing on this definition, is that it is a reflection of the past, with a substantive, unchanging content. There

[88] Ibid., 547 (emphasis added). Somewhat earlier, Jason Morgan-Foster, 'A New Perspective on the Universality Debate: Reverse Moderate Relativism in the Islamic Context' (2003), 10 *ILSA J Int'l & Comp* L 35, proposed something similar in the context of a discussion of the relationship between human rights and Islamic law.

[89] Contrast Eric Hobsbawm, 'Introduction: Inventing Traditions' in Eric Hobsbawm and Terence Ranger (eds), *The Invention of Tradition* (Cambridge University Press, 1992), 1 at 2 (who insisted they be kept separate). Hobsbawm's distinction between 'tradition' and 'custom' may well correspond with my distinction between 'orthodox' and 'alternative' conceptions of tradition.

[90] Edward Shils, *Tradition* (Faber, 1981), 12. See further R. Bauman, 'Tradition, Anthropology of', *International Encyclopedia of the Social & Behavioral Sciences* (2001), 15819.

are additional aspects of this approach to tradition that often seem to be associated with this definition. Tradition is seen as irrational, because it is viewed as clinging to the past simply because it is the past. The past that is to be preserved by tradition is usually understood as primarily concerned with substantive content: traditional marriage, sexual constancy, etc. As a result, it is frequently seen as better understood as a descriptive rather than as a normative category. Combined together, we can call this the 'orthodox' understanding of the idea of tradition. Ironically, perhaps, it is this view of tradition that both the Rapporteur and the opponents of the Resolutions appear to share.

An alternative understanding of tradition

Drawing on recent sociological and philosophical scholarship, I want to suggest, however, that there is now a significant challenge to this orthodox view of tradition, and that a different way of thinking about tradition better explains some aspects of the current debates over the 'traditional values' Resolutions. There are four significant challenges to the orthodox concept that this alternative understanding presents. Out of these negative challenges an alternative conception emerges. As a result, tradition comes to be seen as a legitimate normative orientation toward action.

First, tradition is seen less as a reflection of the past than as a way of understanding the present. Richard Bauman, for example, has described how anthropological inquiry has moved to view tradition and related notions 'as symbolic, interpretive constructions in and of the present through the invocation of links to a meaningful past'.[91] So, too, Langlois considers that contemporary sociology is less concerned to view contemporary uses of tradition as embedded in an actual past and 'now integrates tradition into analyses of ongoing social change. In recent works, tradition is used to define a type of society (be it theoretical or empirical).'[92]

Second, tradition is seen not as static but often as in flux. Traditions change over time. For Langlois, '[t]radition is a transmitted heritage which survives and orients contemporary actions, but this heritage is often transformed.'[93] Traditions often have, as Patrick Glenn has pointed out in his study of 'legal traditions', a relatively stable core but no fixed boundaries.[94] Major traditions are often complex, incorporating traditions within traditions. They usually contain a mechanism by which aspects of the tradition are interpreted. They also often incorporate a conception of change and a method by which change

[91] Richard Bauman, 'Tradition, Anthropology of', *International Encyclopedia of the Social & Behavioral Sciences* (2001), 15819.

[92] S. Langlois, 'Traditions: Social', *International Encyclopedia of the Social & Behavioral Sciences* (2001), 15829.

[93] Ibid.

[94] Twining's discussion of Glenn in *General Jurisprudence* is particularly useful, pp. 80–83.

comes about, sometimes through selective incorporation of external ideas. There is often a degree of tension between what might be thought of as the doctrinal, or idealized, understanding of the tradition, and the social practice of those in the tradition; a tension that also requires to be managed, not infrequently resulting in change in the social practice or, perhaps more frequently, in the way in which the doctrine is articulated.[95]

Third, tradition is seen as an example of rationality rather than irrationality. We have seen that to act on the basis of 'tradition' has been seen as irrational, a criticism that was characteristic of Enlightenment thought. However, Raymond Boudon has advanced a contrary argument.[96] He suggests that there are five different kinds of rationality: utilitarian rationality, teleological rationality, axiological rationality, traditional rationality and cognitive rationality. As Langlois, explains: 'All of these types of rationality describe the good reasons why the actor is driven to act in a certain way. . . . Custom and habit can also incite individuals to act in a certain way. Therefore, when one speaks of traditional rationality – "it has always been that way" – he is speaking of one type of rationality among others.'[97]

Fourth, tradition is seen as less concerned with the substantive content of the tradition and more with the act of transmission of the tradition. Terrence Tilley distinguishes between two different elements in 'tradition': the act of transmission (in Latin, *traditio*), and the content handed down (in Latin, *tradita*).[98] Both liberal critics and conservative supporters miss critical aspects of the complex normativity of tradition that come more clearly into view when *tradita* and *traditio* are separated. Liberals who reject the normativity of tradition, on the one hand, consider it largely in the form of the *tradita*, missing the critical importance of the process of transmission as itself having

[95] There are several important examples of the importance of not considering traditions as static. For example, those who criticized 'Asian Values', such as Amartya Sen, considered that the proponents underestimated the extent to which 'Asian' cultures included several competing strands of political thought. Proponents were considered to be presenting a falsely monolithic, authoritarian reading of the cultures concerned. Amartya Sen, Human Rights and Asian Values: What Lee Kuan Yew and Li Peng Don't Understand About Asia, July 14 and 21, *New Republic*, 33 (1997). So too, as we have seen, Islam has been said to incorporate competing understandings of the tradition. In addition to An-Na'im, cited earlier, see also Mahmood Monshipouri, The Politics of Culture and Human Rights in Iran: Globalizing and Localizing Dynamics, in Mahmood Monshipouri, Neil Englehart, Andrew J Nathan, and Kavita Philip (eds), *Constructing Human Rights in the Age of Globalization* (ME Sharpe, 2003), 113.

[96] R. Boudon, Action, in R. Boudon, ed., *Traité de sociologie* (Presses Universitaires de France, 1992), 21–55; R. Boudon, *Raison, Bonnes raisons* (PUF, Paris, 2003); R. Boudon, *Essais sur la théorie générale de la rationalité* (Presses Universitaires de France, 2007); R. Boudon and F. Bourricaud, (1986), *Dictionnaire critique de la sociologie* (Deuxième édition, Presses Universitaires de France, 1986).

[97] S. Langlois, 'Traditions: Social', *International Encyclopedia of the Social & Behavioral Sciences* (2001), 15829.

[98] See e.g. Terrence W. Tilley, *Inventing Catholic Tradition* (Maryknoll: Orbis, 2000). The normativity of tradition has been extensively explored in Catholic theology because of the important function of tradition within Catholicism as a source for Catholic teaching.

normative value irrespective of the normativity of the *tradita*. On the other hand, the distinction between *tradita* and *traditio* also helps explain the approach of some of those who support tradition from a conservative perspective, for they too appear to emphasize the value of the *tradita* rather than that of the *traditio*.

Emphasizing *tradita* rather than *traditio* results in conservative support and liberal antagonism towards arguments based on traditional values because of an important dimension of the orthodox understanding of tradition discussed earlier, viz the extent to which tradition is static:

> to think primarily or exclusively of tradition as *tradita* is to suggest that what is important about tradition is what is handed down . . . and the knowledge of what is handed down, not the practices by which these things are handed down. In this sense, if tradition is to maintain its identity, then it must keep the things it hands down the same. Hence, *tradita* often leads to the notion that tradition is an ossified given or hypostatized content.[99]

Emphasizing *traditio*, on the other hand, does not necessarily bring with it this conservative baggage:

> What is missing from an understanding of tradition as a 'thing' to be 'handed down' in a supposedly 'uncorrupted' form is recognition of the malleable, inculturated and lived character of tradition as communicative and identity-shaping. Traditions shape beliefs, attitudes and actions of those persons who participate in them. In turn, individuals and communities reshape traditions in the very process of reception, transmission and enactment. The key insight for understanding tradition as a process that is necessarily open and responsive to context is the concept of practice.[100]

Normativity of tradition

There are, then, two radically different conceptions of tradition that emerge. The second conception, challenging the first, enables us to see more clearly why tradition is thought to provide a reason for action for those who share in that tradition, as well as why we should accord normative weight to it. Recently, philosophers have begun to explore the normativity of traditions 'that include norms of practice and behavior', and the recent work by Samuel Scheffler is particularly rich in this regard.[101] Scheffler attempts to answer the question: 'What is it about traditions that leads people to treat them as reason giving?' He finds many 'different factors that may contribute to the perceived

[99] Mark Medley, 'Catholics, Baptists, and the Normativity of Tradition: A Review Essay, Perspectives on Religious Studies', *Journal of the NABPR*, 119, 122.

[100] Ibid., 122.

[101] Samuel Scheffler, 'The Normativity of Tradition' in Samuel Scheffler, *Equality and Tradition: Questions of Value in Moral and Political Theory* (Oxford University Press, 2010), 287.

normative authority of a tradition'.[102] His understanding of tradition is firmly within the second conception of tradition.

Traditions, he suggests, 'serve to establish and entrench certain social conventions'[103] and in doing so 'facilitate social interaction and make it easier to achieve various individual and collective goals'.[104] Traditions may take the form of 'collective habits' that 'enable us to settle without excessive and repetitive deliberation on courses of action that have, on balance, proved successful in the past'.[105] We gain, he suggests, 'deliberative efficiency by relying relatively unreflectively on past practice as a defeasible guide to future conduct'.[106] Traditions 'may be regarded as a repository of experience and of the kind of wisdom that comes from experience'.[107] 'Subscribing to a tradition and acting in accordance with that tradition,' Scheffler suggests, 'may be ways of expressing one's loyalty to others who adhered to the tradition and to whom such adherence was important'.[108] We subscribe to the tradition in order to identify with, and keep close to, those in the past whom we respect; we respect them by following the traditions they followed.

Traditions not only embody values; they also provide for when those values come into effect and how those values are to be fulfilled. Establishing 'customs and conventions regarding the time and manner in which we fulfill' these values, reduces 'the indeterminacy of the norms and burdensomely discretionary character of the demands that they make of individuals'.[109] Traditions may be followed because the tradition 'has played a formative role in a person's development' and the person 'may come to feel that what the tradition stands for is also what he or she stands for'.[110] It comes 'to occupy a central place in the person's self-conception'.[111] Acting on tradition 'may be experienced as a requirement of personal integrity'.[112]

Scheffler's explanations, thus far, sound distinctly centred on the benefits that an individual gains from acting according to a tradition, irrespective of whether there is a current collective dimension to the tradition, but these do not exhaust Schaeffler's account. Several of his explanations depend on the fact that traditional practices are, 'by their nature collective enterprises'.[113] Thus, traditions provide important ways of enabling one to better deal with 'the vastness and impersonality of the universe and the precariousness and insignificance of our own place in it',[114] by connecting ourselves to the past and the future: 'In acting in accordance with the traditional practice, the individual acts not only as she has acted in the past and as she will act in the future, but also as others acted before she was born and will act after she is dead.'[115] The collective

[102] Ibid., 291. [103] Ibid., 291.
[104] Ibid. An example is the tradition in most communities, at least until recently, of having one day each week that did not involve work and business; a 'day of rest'.
[105] Ibid., 292.
[106] Ibid., 292. An example might be the tradition of wearing a school uniform at British schools, often justified in similar terms to these.
[107] Ibid., 292. [108] Ibid., 294. [109] Ibid., 293. [110] Ibid., 294. [111] Ibid. [112] Ibid.
[113] Ibid., 302. [114] Ibid., 297. [115] Ibid., 300.

dimension is also critical insofar as these traditional practices 'are sustained not only by the allegiance of many adherents over long periods of time, but also by the adherents' mutual recognition of one another as collaborators in a shared enterprise'.[116] This collective dimension reinforces this mutual connectedness. For Scheffler, a strong appeal of association with a tradition lies, significantly, in helping some to feel part of something that is bigger than themselves: 'One of its functions is to call attention to the limits of our egoism. We want to care about, and to value, things other than ourselves and our own flourishing.'[117]

In particular, Scheffler sees the normativity of tradition in the *traditio* rather than the *tradita*. Not surprisingly, therefore, because he identifies the normativity in the *traditio*, Scheffler emphasizes the extent to which 'all traditions change over time and new generations always find ways to modify a traditional legacy in light of changing circumstances and outlooks.'[118] It also explains why he considers that 'it would be a mistake to take an unduly dismissive attitude towards tradition as such or to view participation in a tradition as amounting to nothing more than a form of blind conservatism.'[119] Unfortunately, there is little evidence of this alternative conception of tradition in the United Nations debates, either from proponents or opponents of the 'traditional values' Resolutions.

6. The path not (yet) taken

We have noted in the earlier parts of this chapter that two significant elements are largely missing from the United Nations debates. The first is the possibility of a dialectical relationship between traditional values and human rights: one in which the conflict between them results in the emergence of a new understanding (the fourth analytical position discussed earlier). The second missing element is an understanding of tradition that reflects anything other than the orthodox conception. The alternative conception of tradition hovers in the wings, waiting to be articulated and operationalized, but it is the orthodox, conservative understanding of tradition that dominates the debates.

How might incorporating these two missing elements into the 'traditional values' debate help us to address their relationship with human rights in a more satisfactory way than the Human Rights Committee has so far succeeded in doing? Would incorporating these missing elements in any way change the debate? My tentative suggestion, in this part, is that the alternative conception of 'traditional values' can be useful in challenging key aspects of the current human rights project, but in ways that differ considerably from those that we have encountered so far. The alternative conception of tradition may enable us to develop an approach to 'traditional values' that more clearly addresses some of the motivations that underlie the move to adopt 'traditional values', without reverting to the approach advocated by Metropolitan Kirill.

[116] Ibid., 302. [117] Ibid., 304. [118] Ibid., 307. [119] Ibid., 309

So far, we have assumed, largely because this is the way the United Nations debate has been conducted by proponents and opponents of traditional values, that it is human rights that are progressive and transformative, and that it is traditional values that are conservative and regressive. But what if the position is in fact the reverse, and it is the case that human rights are conservative and traditional values are progressive? In that changed paradigm, the two missing dimensions mentioned in the previous paragraph take on an added importance. It is time to turn to the third set of Southern Voices to whom Twining has introduced us. At this point, Upendra Baxi and Boaventura de Sousa Santos enter the frame, and to this pair I will add Martii Koskenniemi. With their help, we can step back from the details of the Resolutions and their current political context, and place current dissatisfactions with human rights in a broader context.

In different ways, they have identified a similar discontent: the human rights project, they suggest, needs to be saved from instrumentalization. This occurs when, as Baxi suggests, 'human rights discourse becomes commodified, professionalized by technocrats, and sometimes hijacked by powerful groups'.[120] Koskenniemi has pointed to a similar set of concerns: '[W]hile the rhetoric of human rights has historically had a positive and liberating effect on societies, once rights become institutionalized as a central part of political and administrative culture, they lose their transformative effect and are petrified into a legalistic paradigm that marginalizes values or interests that resist translation into rights-language.'[121] Without addressing these problems, its authority and legitimacy may well evaporate, as it will not only fail to live up to its own emancipatory promise but also risks becoming a barrier to realizing the good through other strategies.

Both Baxi and Santos suggest that, in certain regions of the world, there is a noticeable trend: international human rights standards and globalization currently walk hand in hand. In particular, the instrumentalizing of human rights to serve the interests of global capital has contributed to the current backlash against the human rights project in these areas. And human rights discourse needs little modification to be seen as serving to legitimate free-market liberalism: not only are freedom of contact and freedom of property an obvious part of this discourse, but other core elements of civil and political rights are also drawn on, in particular the ideal of the autonomous individual making his or her way in the world, unencumbered by state regulation or oppressive communitarian responsibilities. In this context, human rights, defined primarily as rights to freedom and liberty, feature strongly, as do concepts like the 'rule of law' and a view of the government as the primary abuser of rights. 'One of the consequences of this is that it re-enforces the hegemony of civil and political

[120] Twining, *General Jurisprudence*, 377, citing Baxi.

[121] Martii Koskenniemi, 'The Effects of Rights on Political Culture' in Philip Alston, ed., *The EU and Human Rights* (Oxford University Press, 1999), 99.

rights over socio-economic and cultural rights. For instance . . . rights that are necessary for the operation of the market are promoted ahead of others.'[122] Foremost in putting forward this intimate connection between human rights and globalized economic liberalism are such international organizations as the World Bank and the International Monetary Fund, but other parts of the United Nations and some NGOs are not above sending a similar message. Their critique is a powerful one, seeing the current human rights project as neoliberal and supportive of some highly problematic aspects of globalization.

In order to meet these dangers, Baxi argues, the human rights project needs to re-engage 'with the experience of suffering and the needs of those who should be the main beneficiaries – the poor and the oppressed'.[123] Although different in many ways, Santos shares with Baxi a desire to develop a role for human rights law that is also essentially emancipatory, and has written extensively in support of this project. Santos' major work in English, *Toward a New Common Sense*,[124] argues even more broadly that modern society's reliance upon law, politics and science to both regulate and emancipate society has reached a crisis point and can no longer provide answers to current social problems. He engages in a series of sociological analyses of law in order to illustrate the need for a profound theoretical reconstruction of the notion of legality based on locality, nationality and globality, showing how global developments (including international human rights law) can be given their proper place in the sociology of law, and suggesting a new set of social structures that might sustain the emancipatory elements that he considers have disappeared from modern society. Santos' in particular, has developed an important theory of subaltern cosmopolitanism, in which local social movements opposed to the rise of economic globalization develop an alternative emancipatory cosmopolitan consciousness. Remember that his attempted reconstruction of the notion of legality is based on locality, nationality and globality.

Santos is vague, however, as to how this can be put into effect in practice. Is it possible, for example, for a *progressive* agenda to be built partly on using 'traditional values'? His theory is not developed explicitly in the context of a discussion of 'traditional values', but it takes on a certain resonance when combined with the recent sociological analyses discussed earlier which indicate that the group of those who support traditional values overlaps significantly with the group of those who would be regarded as subaltern by Santos. Marsh quotes Hardt and Negri, who observed in 2000 that 'the current global tendencies [meaning economic globalization] . . . are experienced by some as

122 Oche Onazi, 'Good Governance and Marketisation of Human Rights: A Critique of the Neoliberal Normative Approach' (2009)(2), *Law, Social Justice & Global Development Journal*, available at www.go.warwick.ac.uk/elj/lgd/2009_2/onazi.

123 Twining, *General Jurisprudence*, 377.

124 Boaventura de Sousa Santos, *Toward a New Legal Common Sense* (2nd edn, 2002, *Law in Context* Series, Cambridge University Press), a title whose first edition was originally published by Routledge (New York).

a kind of liberation but by others as an exacerbation of their suffering . . . [P] opular support for fundamentalist projects . . . [has] spread most widely among those who have been further subordinated and excluded by the recent transformation of the global economy.'[125] In support, Marsh convincingly demonstrates that traditional values (in the areas of religion, family and gender) are most often supported by older people, those of lower socio-economic status, and those living in less developed societies, in Islamic states, Sub-Saharan Africa, and Latin America.

One example must suffice. Mahmood Monshipouri has distinguished between 'localizers' and 'cosmopolitans' using Iran as an example. Localism arose, he argues, out of the 'paradoxes and uncertainties associated with globalization'.[126] Localizers are 'deeply suspicious of the global human rights discourse', seeing these rights as 'culturally specific',[127] 'a Western creation rooted in Western values imposed on the non-Western world'.[128] Women's rights are such a lightning rod in part because localizers view women as 'the specific vector of globalization's attack on the Islamic culture'.[129] '[P]olitical and socioeconomic equality of the sexes is unnatural' and an idea of complementarity is promoted, in which men and women have different roles, functions and duties. The cosmopolitans, on the other hand, 'generally argue the need to modify Islamic practices and principles so as to reconstruct cultural traditions, reconciling the traditional with the modern of the global environment'.[130] They seek for a more 'progressive reading of the Sharia',[131] and 'relentlessly maneuvered within the cultural, religious, and political limits of Islamic tradition, seeking a different interpretation'.[132]

Can traditional values help in developing Baxi's preferred role for human rights? Well, possibly, but there is no certainty that they will encourage this progressive path. For Marsh, adherence to 'traditional values are a form of protest, even when the holders of those values do not act out their protests in the form of social movements'.[133] In particular, the alternative conception of tradition discussed above permits approaches to traditional values to emerge that enable human rights to be used to *challenge* aspects of modernity as opposed to being its uncritical cheerleader.[134] Consider the approach adopted by the South African Constitutional Court.[135] There has been a persistent attempt to draw on the traditional indigenous African concept of *ubuntu* in the process of interpreting the South African Constitution's human rights protections. And *ubuntu* has been used to support interpretations that are notably progressive, for example in the area of economic and social rights, allowing human rights to be developed to challenge aspects of the South African Government's free-market liberalism.

[125] Marsh, 301, quoting Michael Hardt and Antonio Negri, *Empire* (Harvard University Press, 2000), 150.
[126] Monshipouri, 123. [127] Ibid., 124. [128] Ibid., 124. [129] Ibid., 129. [130] Ibid., 126.
[131] Ibid., 131. [132] Ibid., 134. [133] Marsh, 301. [134] See, for example, Onazi, above.
[135] Also noted in Onazi, above.

In their recently published study of the use of *ubuntu* in the Constitutional Court, Drucilla Cornell and Nyoko Muvangua argue that *ubuntu* has, in particular, acted as important source for the interpretation of human dignity in the South African Constitution, and that there is currently a resurgence in its use.[136] The importance of the concept, for our purposes, arises from its function in permitting understandings of how to take forward 'traditional values' in the legal interpretation of human rights. *Ubuntu* serves as an example of how an indigenous, traditional value can serve not only as a 'grounding ideal of the entire Constitution and, indeed, as a justiciable constitutional principle',[137] but one that is, 'at its core', 'transformative'[138] of society. 'Traditional values', we can see, do not necessarily entrench a hierarchical or patriarchal *status quo*. In particular, *ubuntu* has served as a basis for an expanding Constitutional jurisprudence concerning socio-economic rights, one that on occasion 'resists some of the worst aspects of the values, or lack thereof, of neoliberal capitalism'.[139]

Several fragmentary examples from the United Nations 'traditional values' consultation illustrate aspects of an emerging approach that chimes with an understanding of traditional values as potentially progressive challenges to aspects of human rights modernity. What appears to be a common element in these different approaches is the notion that ideas of solidarity and relationality are critical foundations of human rights that 'traditional values' challenge human rights to support. As articulated by Onazi, this 'entails institutionalizing processes where values of kinship, solidarity, cooperation, reciprocity, sympathy and trust can be strengthened and furthermore channeled to the processes through which human rights are provided'.[140] In its response to the Human Rights Committee's call for information on traditional values, for example, Syria referred to its vision of the good society, where there is 'respect towards and care of older persons and neighbours' with '[p]oor people and orphans . . . financially supported . . . [and] [c]hildren . . . given good care and kindness'.[141] Human Rights Watch, an NGO, 'appreciated the notion of

[136] Drucilla Cornell and Nyoko Muvangua, 'Introduction: The Re-Cognition of uBuntu' in Drucilla Cornell and Nyoko Muvangua (eds), *uBuntu and the Law: African Ideals and Postapartheid Jurisprudence* (Fordham University Press, 2012), 1.

[137] Ibid., 9. [138] Ibid., 10.

[139] Ibid. at 19, citing as an example the decision of the High Court in *City of Johannesburg v Rand Properties (Pty) Ltd* 2007 (SCA), Jajbhay J.: 'uBuntu speaks to our interconnectedness, our common humanity and the responsibility to each that flows from our connection. This in turn must be interpreted to mean that in the establishment of our constitutional values we must not allow urbanization and the accumulation of wealth and material possessions to rob us of our warmth, hospitality and genuine interests in each other as human beings.' See also how, in *Barkhuizen v Napier* 2007 (5) SA 323 (CC), Ngcobo J., human dignity was interpreted as supporting freedom of contract, but because *ubuntu* was seen as giving meaning to human dignity, contractual relationships were subject to the need to 'do simple justice between the contracting parties,' resulting in the Court overriding unreasonable or unfair time limitation clauses, even when agreed to by both parties.

[140] Onazi, above. [141] *Summary of Information*, para. 26.

"traditional values of mankind" as that [which] connected human rights to the broader context of humanitarianism reflecting the values of goodness, empathy, respect, care, mutual support, tolerance and trust. Those values were the entry point for a human rights discourse to evolve.[142] The Peoples' Welfare and Development Society, another NGO, 'underlined the positive contribution of traditional values such as faith, cooperation, simplicity and mutual respect on . . . the fight against human rights violations'.[143]

7. Conclusion

My argument, in brief, has been as follows: the 'traditional values' Resolutions have potentially disturbing implications for the future interpretation of human rights, and are therefore rightly regarded with suspicion. Having seen at close quarters the darker side of traditional values, and of religious faith, we should remain conflicted by the relationship between traditional values and human rights in political and legal affairs. The Human Rights Council's 'traditional values' Resolutions threaten to further divide rather than unite. Nevertheless, to dismiss these Resolutions simply as malign attempts to undermine human rights would be a mistake, as they indicate a deep unease with aspects of the human rights project that needs to be taken seriously. Traditional values can be an important source of a radical critique of human rights: a critique from which, in a dialectical way, an approach to human rights can emerge that may be truer to its transformative and subversive credentials. Understanding, and appreciating, the Southern Voices to whom William Twining introduced us can play a major role in making progress. Reorientation of the human rights project towards concern for the exploited, drawing on traditional values embedded in societies and cultures throughout the world, could be an important way in which the traditional values debate produces a more positive outcome; one that supports ideals that the human rights movement should see as central to its mission.

[142] Ibid., para. 60. [143] Ibid., para. 68.

4

Southern voices in transitional justice: a critical reflection on human rights and transition

*Fionnuala Ní Aoláin**

William Twining famously reminded us that '[t]he dominant Western scholarly and activist discourses about human rights have developed largely without reference to other standpoints and traditions.'[1] He cautioned that claims to the universality of human rights should pay heed to other traditions, listening closely to the local and the specific, and seek out the voices of those who could meaningfully interpret and create distinct 'Southern' perspectives. His clarion call seems fortuitously placed as contemporary emphasis on transitional justice and rule of law discourses have taken on much of the same kind of presumed universality, and are produced at a substantial distance from those places and people that are most likely to be the subjects of transition and role of law proselytizing. In parallel, as Mark Fathi Massoud has noted, just as 'human rights law [seems] to be promoted as a kind of carpet under which the dust and trauma of the war would be swept and left behind',[2] so too has transitional justice become the fixer for war and authoritarian ills in the post-Cold War era.

This essay sets out to explore the ways in which Southern voices, central to William Twining's vision of an integrated cosmopolitan legal order, are heard (or not) in the cacophony of sound that comprises transitional justice theory and practice. In one sense, what follows is a study of marginality and exclusion, and carries some sense of *déjà vu* as transitional justice repeats old and known patterns of legal hegemony in new, generally Southern, places and spaces. These places and spaces include sites emerging from violent conflict, fragile states, and states in the tenuous process of building new legal and political

* This essay pays homage to the collection of papers edited by William Twining to which my home institution, the Transitional Justice Institute (TJI), Belfast contributed in some small part. Professor Twining was Leverhulme Emeritus Professor at TJI for one year (2007–8) and during that time we had the pleasure to host him as part of our intellectual community and to bring Yash Ghai, Upendra Baxi, Abdullahi An-Na'im and Francis Deng to Belfast for an intensive multi-day seminar. Professor Twining was also a great supporter of the Institute from its inception and gave advice consistently and thoughtfully through the early years of establishment and consolidation.

1 William Twining, ed., *Human Rights, Southern Voices* (Cambridge University Press, 2009) 1.

2 Mark Fathi Massoud, *Law's Fragile State Colonial, Authoritarian, and Humanitarian Legacies in Sudan* (Cambridge, 2013) xi–xii.

orders following the adoption of comprehensive peace agreements.[3] Just as international law has been described as favouring 'a falsely rigid, ahistorical, selectively chosen set of self-justificatory texts and practices whose patent partiality raises the question of exactly whose interests are being served and who come out on top',[4] critical approaches to transitional justice emphasize its elite grounding, its fundamental consistency in supporting status quo rules of international law, and the centrality of the public/private divide to addressing systemic human rights violations. Drawing on Massoud's theory that legal systems in their intact liberal conception do not exist in failed states but rather that law plays a multiplicity of roles in maintaining and legitimizing repressive regimes,[5] I assess the ways in which transitional justice may both combine a new cosmopolitanism in times of the transition yet repeat old habits, albeit in highly revised garb. In this context, I probe the extent to which repressive and old conflict regimes move strategically to manipulate law and legal resources to maintain elite interests, even in the face of what appear to be substantive reviews of and revisions to the legal order in transitional settings. They are often aided and abetted by institutions and states from the global North, whose multiplicity of interests in these sites span the economic, the strategic, the political and the symbolic. In this telling, transitional justice theory and practice is an integral part of the legitimization that accompanies change, and its limited dialogue with local legal orders reflects Upendra Baxi's long-standing critique of human rights discourses as being commodified, professionalized by humanitarian technocrats, and – most worryingly – hijacked by powerful groups and states.[6]

1. A short transitional justice history

Transitional Justice is a field that has rapidly expanded, and that has both the fortune and disadvantage of being termed a contemporary 'industry'.[7] 'Transition' ('going across') implies a journey with beginning and end points. In early conceptualization, the journey of transitional justice was from authoritarianism to democracy,[8] with 'justice' challenges focused on authoritarianism's legacy of human rights abuses. This produced scholarly and policy

[3] V. Boege and others, 'On Hybrid Political Orders and Emerging States: State Formation in the Context of Fragility' in Martina Fischer and Beatrix Schmelzle (eds), *Building Peace in the Absence of States: Challenging the Discourse on State Failure* (Berghof Research Center, 2009).

[4] Arati Rao, 'The Politics of Gender and Culture in International Human Rights Discourse' in Julie Peters and Andrea Wolper (eds), *Women's Rights, Human Rights: International Feminist Perspectives* (Routledge, 1995) at 174.

[5] Austin Sarat and Thomas R. Keirns (ed), *Law's Violence* (University of Michigan Press, 1993).

[6] *Southern Voices* supra note 1, 157–209; Upendra Baxi, *The Future of Human Rights* (1st edn, Oxford University Press, 2002).

[7] See Paul Gready, The Era of Transitional Justice: The Aftermath of the Truth and Reconciliation Commission in South Africa and Beyond (Routledge, 2011).

[8] Cf. Samuel Huntington, *The Third Wave: Democratization in the Late Twentieth Century* (University of Oklahoma Press, 1991); Phillip Schmitter, Guillermo O'Donnell and Laurence

concentration on such questions as amnesty, criminal accountability, truth processes and lustration, the analytical leitmotif being 'how to promote accountability and truth without destabilizing transition.'[9] It was implicitly assumed that such transitions were endogenous – driven principally by forces within the state and internal to it. In the post-Cold War period, the discourse of transition was applied to movement from conflict to peace (and typically in parallel to more liberal forms of governance). With this came a focus on post-conflict reconstruction, 'demilitarization, demobilization and reintegration' (DDR), reparations, and accountability for conflict-related crime. Overlapping, and in parallel, came a developing focus on rule of law reform, and on the construction of memory in highly conflicted societies. From these various streams a rich literature emerged, incorporating both in-depth explorations of these areas outlined above and a sustained focus on the field's theoretical underpinnings. At its core lay a concept that could be termed 'paradigmatic transition':[10] a shift from an authoritarian state structure (whether conflicted or not) to peaceful democracy.

Despite this initially quite narrow focal point for transitional justice politics and practice, the expanding universe of transitional justice is now understood as relevant to a variety of sites. In post-Cold War settings, it is now associated with the move away from armed conflict to co-existence, even where the thresholds of violence do not meet the stringent criteria of the law of armed conflict.[11] There is also evidence of its extension into democratic settings, or at least the use of transitional justice mechanisms to address sustained human rights abuses within democratic polities, though, as I explore below, this may often be to circumvent stringent accountability rather than to advance it.[12] Its relevance now seems particularly acute in settings where violence or repression occurs within tightly bounded communities, when harms are not only perpetrated by strangers or those who are external to a community, but also when the most destruction is perpetrated by relatives, neighbours and those in the extended 'known' community.[13]

Whitehead, *Transitions from Authoritarian Rule: Comparative Perspectives* (Johns Hopkins University Press, 1986).

9 Lustration is one of a number of terms (such as 'vetting', 'screening' and 'administrative justice') used to describe processes that exclude or purge certain officials of prior regimes and other human rights violators from public office. See generally Alexander Mayer-Rieckh and Pablo de Greiff (eds), *Justice as Prevention: Vetting Public Employee in Transitional Societies* (Social Science Research Council, 2007).

10 A term coined by Ní Aoláin and Campbell as describing a rather staid understanding of the transitional justice arena. See Fionnuala Ní Aoláin and Colm Campbell, 'The Paradox of Transition in Conflicted Democracies' [2005] 27 HRQ 172.

11 Cf. Fionnuala Ní Aoláin, Naomi Cahn and Dina Haynes, *On the Frontlines: Gender, War and the Post-Conflict Process* (Oxford University Press, 2011).

12 See e.g. Kim Stanton, 'Canada's Truth and Reconciliation Commission: Settling the Past' (2011), 2(3) *IIPJ* ir.lib.uwo.ca/cgi/viewcontent.cgi?article=1034&context=iipj accessed 11 January 2015.

13 See Kimberly Theidon, *Intimate Enemies: Violence and Reconciliation in Peru* (University of Pennsylvania Press, 2013).

Transitional justice is also emerging as a repeat player in a number of sites, as the notion of post-Transitional Justice (also termed 'late Transitional Justice') has assumed greater potency in consolidated Latin American democracies.[14] In this telling, there is accountability engagement beyond the transitional justice models of the 1980s and a reopening of what were generally understood as 'closed deals' on amnesty, impunity and accountability. As a result, an emboldened range of actors, strategies and institutions have led calls for revisiting transitional accountability, creating new trajectories and timelines on the transitional clock.

Despite these expansions of the field, some scholars and practitioners have argued for much less ambitious goals for and understandings of Transitional Justice. Adrian Vermeule claims that Transitional Justice at very best can only operate as 'rough justice'. Vermeule's instincts are readily identifiable to those operating at the coal face of transition – namely that the perfect transition is rarely available and that 'preference satisfaction is not the yardstick by which ordinary people judge.'[15] More broadly, with Eric Posner he has distinctly challenged the notion of any exceptionality inherent in transitional justice as doing justice differently.[16] Despite this claim that transitional justice is merely a species of ordinary law, the argument to conventionality is tenuous, and the exceptional in transitional justice seems exceptionally hard to ignore.[17] Even the less ambitious versions of transition share multiple common traits with their more ambitious scholarly fellow travellers. In parallel, the pared-down vision remains substantially disconnected from the situated contexts of transitions and the local communities that have experienced direct harms. A narrowed vision still mandates a set of priorities and values for the field, and sets a clear hierarchy on what can be achieved, primarily by legal means, via transitional justice mechanisms.

One response to the elite-driven nature of the academic and policy analysis of the field has been the 'transitional justice from below' motif, which has addressed the important role of grassroots organizing and mobilization in the successes (and failures) of transitional justice claims.[18] On preliminary inspection, transitional justice from below might seem 'to take a modest first step towards de-parochializing . . . [the] juristic cannon' of transition justice.[19] For

[14] Cath Collins, *Post-Transitional Justice: Human Rights Trials in Chile and El Salvador* (Penn State University Press, 2010).

[15] Id. at 154.

[16] See also Eric Posner and Adrian Vermeule, 'Transitional Justice as Ordinary Justice' [2004], 117 *HLR* 761.

[17] Ruti Teitel, *Transitional Justice* (Oxford, 2000).

[18] Kieran McEvoy and Lorna McGregor (eds), *Transitional Justice from Below: Grassroots Activism and the Struggle for Change* (Hart Publishing, 2008). While the book provides an important critical analysis of standard scholarly transitional justice work, it is notable that the majority of the scholars represented in this collection come from North American or European universities, with a couple of notable exceptions, e.g. Catalina Diaz, 'Challenging Impunity from Below: The Contested Ownership of Transitional Justice in Colombia' at 189.

[19] *Southern Voices*, supra note 1 at 1.

example, a scholarly focus on community-led initiatives is an important one, and undercuts some of the elite actor concentration that has dominated transitional justice discourses in such key areas as peace agreements, DDR and Amnesty negotiations. But, regrettably, transitional justice from below still has much work to do if it is to fully address the embedded ethnocentric tendencies of the canon as it has emerged.

Elite focus remains a problematic aspect of both mainstream and 'from below' perspectives. As Kris Brown and I have argued elsewhere, transitional agreements – primarily though not exclusively peace agreements – increasingly function as necessary scaffolding and limiting straitjacket in one handy package, preventing disintegration in highly fractured societies but also stunting growth.[20] The pragmatism of certain forms of elite and non-state actor power-sharing has, we argue, had a singular effect on deepening nationalist identity and rewarding its expression through political power that enables clientalism, resilience and the intensification of traditional identities and militant expressionism.[21] The structured reproduction of ethnonational identities may be harmless in itself, but it may be accompanied by tight boundary-making and the fostering of politically-charged narratives of threat and historical hostility. Thus, we argue that the elite accommodation of power-sharing, and especially consociationalism, has a much shallower reach into transitional settings than the spectacle of former combatants uniting in government suggests.[22] In this context, it remains prescient to pay attention to the work being done at the micro civic and social level in transitional societies as a counterbalance to the concentrations of elite dominance, and broader effects that follow on the quality and experience of transition.

In the context of the work on 'transitional justice from below' it is worth noting that much of the scholarly work represented in this vein comes from the post-conflict/transitional setting of Northern Ireland. The production of knowledge here is, I suggest, cast slightly differently and in ways that cut across a neat North/South divide. As a protracted internal armed conflict (where the threshold of conflict as a matter of humanitarian law was disputed) taking place within an established Western democracy (the United Kingdom), whose history involves legacies of entrenched social and economic discrimination, disenfranchisement and a post-colonial legacy, as well as fractious cultural and religious divides, this site is atypical. It does not fit into neat binaries and the subjects of transition are not distanced from the scholarly and policy producers

[20] Kris Brown and Fionnuala Ní Aoláin, 'Through the Looking Glass: Transitional Justice Futures through the Lens of Nationalism, Feminism and Transformative Change' [2015], 1 *IJTJ* 127.

[21] One counterexample is the Colombian litigation by an assorted group of nongovernmental organizations and right-wing political actors that sought to prevent the governance reward for a non-state militant group. 'Colombia Court Bars Rebels Guilty of Atrocities from Public Office' *Reuters* (Bogota, 6 August 2014) www.reuters.com/article/2014/08/07/us-colombia-farc-court-idUSKBN0G703Q20140807 accessed 11 January 2015.

[22] For an analysis of courts and consociationalism see Christopher McCrudden and Brendan O'Leary, *Courts and Consociations: Human Rights versus Power Sharing* (Oxford, 2013).

of knowledge. The narrow gap between the producers of transitional discourses and the subjects of transition in Northern Ireland is unusual. This stellar scholarly engagement, a form of presence strongly and consistently modelled by William Twining,[23] tells us much about the importance of grassroots engagement, presence and validation as a means to bridge the gap in knowledge production and experienced realities of harm in societies where systematic atrocity crime is a lived reality. It also brings attention to the salient fact that the means to produce knowledge in many transitional societies are limited and the gap in empowered engagement is immeasurably wider in some transitional sites compared with others. Perhaps what the close connections between the producers of knowledge about transition, civil society and the experience of the conflict itself in Northern Ireland teaches us is the importance of those connections, and the value of intimacy between producers of 'knowledge' and the subjects of harm. This kind of 'active research' model, one that commits to knowledge building in partnership with the communities and individuals who experience harm, affirms the broader need for an ethics of research in divided, transitional and conflicted societies.[24] This implicit ethic of knowledge production, always a hallmark of William Twining's work, is one that can and should make a lasting imprint across legal fields, including transitional justice.

2. Missing in action

As we think about the 'missing pieces' of Transitional Justice, there is an evident under-conceptualized state of the field with respect to particular place and spaces. A number of general observations can be made on what has been lost, ignored or under-appreciated in defining the contours of transitional justice theory and practice. These disregarded elements have a particular salience for the roll-out of transitional justice in Southern settings.[25] The dearth of attention to these dimensions of transitional processes functions to obscure Southern voices in transitional justice theorizing, thereby rendering a partial and selected visibility to the vast number of geographical locales in which transitional justice processes are applied. I canvass these general

[23] It is worth noting that William Twining encouraged this type of engagement and it was reflected in his own life's work, e.g. William Twining, et al., *Emergency Powers: a Fresh Start Fabian Tract* (London: Fabian Society, 1972).

[24] This requires, I suggest, going beyond existing theoretical understanding of grounded research practice; see e.g. Barney G. Glaser and Anselm L. Strauss, *The Discovery of Grounded Theory: Strategies for Qualitative Research* (Aldine, 1967).

[25] A good cross-section of transitional justice work sites is found in the work of the New York-based International Center for Transitional Justice (ICTJ) www.ictj.org/our-work. Listed countries include Burundi, Cote d'Ivoire, The Democratic Republic of Congo, Kenya, Liberia, South Africa, Sudan and Uganda. In Latin America, countries include Argentina, Brazil, Colombia, Guatemala and Peru. In Asia, work is pursued in Afghanistan, Myanmar, Cambodia, Indonesia, Nepal and Timor-Leste. In the Middle East and North Africa, work sites include Algeria, Egypt, Iraq, Israel and the Occupied Palestinian Territory, Lebanon, Morocco and Tunisia.

limitations and then address the implications of such gaps for the visibility and influence of 'Southern voices' in transitional justice.

In her study of transitional justice interventions, Rosaline Shaw has observed that much of the applicable academic work is characterized by a 'high altitude' approach.[26] From this observation, I take it that much less attention has been paid to the routine ways of *doing* transitional justice in transitional societies than to the abstract study of broadly demarcated transitional justice (TJ) mechanisms. Attention to routine practices and the domestication of TJ has been sidestepped by the foregrounding of the 'input' and 'output' of international institutions.[27] This approach, combined with a lack of sustained attention to the specific cultural contexts absorbing TJ (including the institutional cultures doing the transposition of transitional justice theory to practice), means that there is sparse understanding of how local settings realize, adapt and reframe the concepts and practices of the field. The distance from local, ordinary and everyday instances demonstrate how the input of international institutions remains 'aloof and apart from the social and political relations in which they are immersed and embedded'.[28] As Tobias Kelly and Marie Dembour have succinctly articulated, international justice never exists 'above and beyond the local' and it is 'inherently given shape and meaning in specific local contexts'.[29] I acknowledge that the 'local' remains an important mantra in some transitional justice work, and case studies of various transitions and mechanism in particular country settings abound,[30] but this is not quite the same thing as fundamentally addressing the theoretical implications of local specificity in transitional justice theory and practice.

A defined feature of transitional justice theory and practice has been a persistent emphasis on naming, acknowledging and accounting for certain kinds of human rights violations over others. However, the encapsulation of human rights violations in repressive or conflicted states has generally mapped onto the civil and political rights that have been prioritized by the preponderance of states as having agreed enforcement traction in international law. This process typically marginalizes accounting for numerous other harms and

[26] Rosalind Shaw and Lars Waldorf, 'Introduction' in *Localizing Transitional Justice: Interventions and Priorities after Mass Violence*, ed. Rosalind Shaw and Lars Waldorf (Stanford, CA: Stanford University Press, 2010) 2.

[27] This is a particularly salient observation with respect to international criminal law. There are notable exceptions. See e.g. Louise Chappell, 'Nested Newness and Institutional Innovation: Expanding Gender Justice in the International Criminal Court' in M. Krook and F. Machay (eds), *Gender, Politics and Institutions: Towards a Feminist Institutionalism* (Palgrave, 2011) 163–180.

[28] Jonneke Koomen, 'Language Work at the International Criminal Court' (2014) 16 *IFJP* 581–60, 583.

[29] T. Kelly and Marie Dembour, 'Introduction: The Social Lives of International Justice', in M. B. Dembour and T. Kelly (eds), *Paths to International Justice: Social and Legal Perspectives* (Cambridge University Press, 2007) 1–25 at 6.

[30] Erin Baines, 'The Haunting of Alice: Local Approaches to Justice and Reconciliation in Northern Uganda' [2007], 1 *IJTJ* 91.

generally leaves social, economic and cultural rights violations at the margins of transitional justice accounting.[31] I have argued elsewhere, in the context of addressing the harms experienced by women in repressive and transitional settings, that there is a pressing need to articulate both a cogent theory of harm that is sufficient to address the depths of gendered harms, and to make such a theory generalizable to the myriad of conflict and repressive contexts in which harms are encountered.[32] More broadly, in the context of Southern transitions, it seems particularly apt to draw attention to the centrality of material inequality and the lack of redistribution in post-colonial contexts where abject poverty, sustained economic disenfranchisement and lack of access to social and political capital are enduring legacies. There is an obvious point relevant to post-colonial settings, foregrounded by victims' groups in a number of African transitional settings, which articulates the view that transitional justice programmes 'ought to deal with injustices that originated as far back as the colonial and precolonial encounters'.[33] This challenge, central to the resolution of long-standing social and economic injustices, begs the broader question of what the chosen starting point for harms will be for the purposes of transition, and who benefits and who loses on the line-drawing.

Another appreciably overlooked dimension of the transitional justice oeuvre has been attention to non-state actors in framing the terms, experience and success of transition in multiple settings. Theoretical and policy explorations from Ruti Teitel's foundational work onwards assume the centrality of the state to the framing of transitional justice discourse.[34] In this telling, one needs to reform and remake the state (and law), and in this transition/transformation one gets (potentially) the remaking of law and legal institutions. The state, in the classic discourse that emerged around the failings of the authoritarian states in Latin America in the 1970s, is in need of rescue.[35] In the examples that both fed and spawned the discourse of state rescue through transition, the classic sites of transitional justice transformation – namely amnesty, truth commissions and reconciliation – were the means to restore the state and the normality of the

[31] See e.g. Ismael Muvingi, 'Sitting on Powder Kegs: Socioeconomic Rights in Transitional Societies' [2009], 3 *IJTJ* 163; Tafadzwa Pasipanodya, 'A Deeper Justice: Economic and Social Justice as Transitional Justice in Nepal' [2008] *IJTJ* 378; Christine Chinkin, 'The Protection of Economic, Social, and Cultural Rights Post-Conflict' (Paper for the Office of the High Commissioner on Human Rights Women's Human Rights and Gender Unit, 2008); R. Duthie, 'Toward a development-sensitive approach to transitional justice' [2008] *IJTJ*, 292.

[32] Fionnuala Ní Aoláin, 'Advancing Feminist Positioning in the Field of Transitional Justice' (2012), 6 *IJTJ* 205.

[33] Khanyasela Moyo, 'Mimicry, Transitional Justice and the Land Question in Racially Divided Former Settler Colonies' [2014], *IJTJ* 1, 7.

[34] Ruti Teitel, *Transitional Justice* (Oxford University Press, 2000).

[35] Samuel Huntington, *The Third Wave: Democratization in the Late Twentieth Century* (University of Oklahoma Press, 1991); N. J. Kritz, ed., Transitional Justice: How Emerging Democracies Reckon with Former Regimes (3 vols., United States Institute of Peace Press, 1995). More recently, see Gretchen Helmke and Steven Levitsky (eds), *Informal Institutions and Democracy: Lessons from Latin America* (Johns Hopkins University Press, 2007).

liberal legal and political order. Part of what facilitated the discourse of transition was also the idealized 'clean break' phenomenon, whereby the transition was the break and the site of change ultimately bringing the state back to order and stability. Despite the centrality of the state to the development and maturing of transitional justice discourses, the state has not in practice had a complete monopoly on the framing of the transitional context or its solutions. The non-state actor has been distinctly less visible in framing and articulating the theory and practice of transitional justice. It states an obvious reality that the non-state actor has significant purchase in transitional societies.

As I have noted elsewhere,[36] there are broadly three main categories of non-state actor that have considerable shape and influence on the transitional landscape. The first is the non-state armed group. The purchase of the non-state armed group is largely negative but extraordinarily powerful. In a number of the Southern states in transition, the non-state actor rivals the formal power of the state in its capacity to act militarily and to exercise quasi-state-like functions. The non-state armed group may hold territory, perhaps even instituting a parallel justice system or quasi-state-like institutions (indeed, even where not directly linked to violent non-state groups, the operations of local legal systems and institutions are generally viewed with suspicion as a competitor by the fragile state). In this narrative, the non-state actor is the outsider (to the state), is violent, oppositional, seeks change often in radical ways, and may be fractured and highly unstable to the existing legal and political order. The second broad category of non-state actor with purchase over the transitional landscape is civil society. One paradoxical and highly relevant lens has been the broadly positive view of civil society groupings, and women's groups in particular, taken by elite actors in conflict management and ending processes. Civil society groups are often supposed to be agents of positive social change in relation to the ending of violence, or as conduits to facilitate conversations towards a cessation of hostilities with less palatable violent actors. The third broad category of non-state actor is the international community, in its political (intergovernmental organizations such as the United Nations) and economic (multinational corporations) manifestations. In practice, the political and material resources of the international community become very important in the inclusion and privileging of certain local non-state actors, and the marginalization or exploitation of other non-state actors. Thus, the finer details of the relationship between the international and local can be determinative of the transitional distribution of political power. In paying sustained attention to the importance and depth of presence by non-state actors, not only are core prejudices of transitional justice discourses more fully revealed, but the modalities of engagement themselves are more fully exposed.

[36] Fionnuala Ní Aoláin and Catherine O'Rourke, 'Gendered Justice and the Non-State Actors' in Michael Reed and Amanda Lyons (eds), *Contested Transitions: Dilemmas of Transitional Justice in Colombia and Comparative Experience* (International Center for Transitional Justice, 2013) 115–143.

Reflecting on these developments in recent years, the intellectual histories of transitional justice comprise various starting points and various threads of concentration on justice, accountability, the role of memory, reconciliation, and repair.[37] In many of these narratives, victimhood rhetorically stands at the moral centre of TJ's normative analysis. In important ways, the vocabulary of transitional justice (truth, acknowledgement, repair, reconciliation) appears to offer a universal language to mediate stories of violence and harm and translate the experiences across linguistic, geographical and social divides.[38] In Transitional Justice, the very term 'victim-centred' is a concept that is repeatedly used to validate or evaluate response to human rights violations.[39] It is a concept associating TJ with speaking truth to power, acknowledgement of harms, breaking silence, ensuring reparation, and rebalancing power relations. Yet, individual satisfaction and engagement with transitional justice by scholars and policy makers is both over- and under-estimated, and getting a firm handle on the engagement and satisfaction of victims with the modalities and outcomes of transitional justice mechanisms is an elusive enterprise. The focus on victims thus prompts the question of what victims want and need in any particular context in the immediate aftermath of systematic and sustained human rights violations. Who speaks for and about victims in such circulations?

While the 'textbook' transitional justice response might suggest an easy and common repertoire of claims among victims across transitional settings, growing empirical knowledge suggests otherwise.[40] For example, a study in the Central African Republic surveying attitudes to reparations found that women were more likely than men to demand apologies and punitive measures for those responsible for violations and to demand recognition of their suffering than men.[41] In the DRC, victims have acknowledged the importance of symbolic reparations and public apology, but at the same time underscored the need for 'tangible benefits to address the more concrete needs of victims, to

[37] Jon Elster, *Closing the Books: Transitional Justice in Historical Perspective* (Cambridge University Press, 2004); Paige Arthur, 'How "Transitions" Reshaped Human Rights: A Conceptual History of Transitional Justice' [2009], 31 *HRQ* 321; Ruti Teitel, 'Transitional Justice Genealogy' [2003], 16 *HHRJ* 69.

[38] For a pithy analysis of the role of language and translators in 'translating' harms for the purposes of international criminal justice, see Jonneke Koomen, 'Language Work at International Criminal Courts' [2014], 16 *IFJP* 581.

[39] Brandon Hamber, *Transforming Societies After Political Violence: Truth, Reconciliation and Mental Health* (Springer, 2009).

[40] See e.g. James Cavallaro and Stephanie Erin Brewer, 'Re-evaluating Regional Human Rights Litigation in the Twenty-First Century: The Case of the Inter-American Court' (2008), 102 *AJIL* 768; Jack Snyder and Leslie Vinjamuri, 'Trials and Errors: Principle and Pragmatism in Strategies of International Justice' [2003], 28 *IS* 5.

[41] Progress of the World's Women, at 7 (*citing* Patrick Vinck and Phuong Pham, Human Rights Center University of California, Berkeley 'Building Peace, Seeking Justice: A Population-Based Survey on Attitudes about Accountability and Social Reconstruction in the Central African Republic' (2010)).

which a symbolic component might be attached.'[42] In one study, by the Trust Fund for Victims in the Central African Republic, it was found that women prefer individual approaches to reparations over collective remedies.[43] The examples illustrate gendered, intersectional, country-specific and context-specific differences in victim priorities. Moreover, these examples point to some disjunction between the overwhelming emphasis on criminal accountability and impunity discourses in scholarly discourses in the global North, and the range of distinct priorities and demands in sites that have experienced conflict and cyclical peace processes in the global south.[44] It is not by accident that the analysis, normative development and enforcement of reparations for harms have fallen significantly behind in transitional justice discourse and practice: there is significant discomfort with providing reparations by international institutions, and reparations figure low in the priorities of states providing aid, humanitarian support and post-conflict reconstruction funds.[45] The unease can be connected to fears about the acceptance of responsibility that follows from assuming obligations for repair, as well as unwillingness to inherit the liabilities of prior regimes or provide salve for the harms caused by particularly nefarious individual human rights violators.[46] This is but one set of examples whereby externally set priorities for transitional justice (including sequencing or choices of mechanisms) trump local priorities for transitional justice. These priorities and values are exemplified by deploying one set of transitional mechanisms over others – a process which occurs at a sizeable distance from the sites of transition and with little meaningful exchange with those who have experienced 'torture and tyranny, deprivation and destitution, pauperization and powerlessness, desexualization and degradation'.[47]

Despite the debates within contemporary Transitional Justice scholarly and policy domains, there is a sustained absence of critical and non-mainstream voices from many of the key scholarly and policy sites where the field is named, fixed and applied. In spite of the notable absences from elite knowledge production there is much greater expression of critical left, situated, post-colonial, site-specific and feminist voices to be garnered across many of the local engagements with transitional justice than are generally revealed in visible TJ scholarly and

[42] UN Office of the High Commissioner for Human Rights, *Report of the Panel on Remedies and Reparations for Victims of Sexual Violence in the Democratic Republic of Congo* (2011) para. 150 www.peacewomen.org/assets/file/Resources/UN/vaw__reportofthepanelonremediesandreparationsforvictimsofsexualviolenceinthedrctotheohchr_march2011.pdf accessed 11 January 2015.

[43] The Trust Fund for Victims, *Reviewing Rehabilitation Assistance and Preparing for Delivering Reparation: Programme Progress Report* (International Criminal Court, 2011) www.trustfundforvictims.org/sites/default/files/imce/TFV%20Programme%20Report%20Summer%202011.pdf accessed 11 January 2015.

[44] See Karen Engle, 'Transforming Reparations for Conflict-Related Sexual Violence: Principles and Practice' (2015), *98 HHRJ 97*.

[45] See Fionnuala Ní Aoláin, Catherine O'Rourke and Aisling Swaine, 'Transforming Reparations for Conflict-Related Sexual Violence: Principles and Practice' (2015), 98 HHRJ 97.

[46] Id.

[47] Upendra Baxi, *The Future of Human Rights* (1st edn, Oxford University Press, 2002) at 6.

policy discourses. The majority of the voices that have entrée into transitional justice conversations are those of the Western/non-transitional 'here' speaking to the experiences and choices of the non-Western, 'othered' 'there'. The 'subaltern peoples' are distinctly missing and are spoken *for* and *to* but are rarely given meaningful space to speak to the experience of suffering on their own terms.[48] The challenge is not only theoretical, but is compounded by the fact that an uncritical and narrowly liberal conception of the transition directs our gaze away from the cultural, material and geo-political sites in which transitional justice practices have emerged. These sites have become the subject for protracted angst, in part because of a heightened sensitivity to human suffering, but it can at times be deceptively easy to give heightened attention to suffering without fundamental engagement with the causes of that suffering or with any view to structural amelioration. In simple terms, the sites that transitional justice most often engages with are the exotic 'other' of locales, subjects, conflicts and repressions elsewhere (never in the Western 'here').[49] The export of rule of law and transitional justice discourse can reflexively deploy an uncritical, liberal and hierarchical positioning with little capacity to recognize its own hegemony and privilege.[50]

Transitional justice discourse, in all its standard forms and straightjackets, thus demands critical interrogation. Specifically, seeing transitional justice as a form of discursive colonization, whereby its language and 'tool box' appropriate and codify knowledge in ways that exclude and produce hierarchies of value through the course of political transition, should be recognized.[51] A fully articulated postcolonial challenge to the hegemonic reach of legal liberalism as represented by mainstream transitional justice is emerging primarily from Southern feminist scholars,[52] and yet scholars and practitioners in the global North remain largely uninformed of this critique's relevance.

48 Here I borrow Baxi's terminology, and his reliance on Gramsci's use of the term.

49 As I have noted elsewhere in my work, this is particularly acute with respect to transitional justice discourses addressing violence against women. See e.g. Fionnuala Ní Aoláin, 'Advancing Feminist Positioning in the Field of Transitional Justice' (2012), 6 *IJTJ* 205.

50 On rule of law exports and the challenges for women in particular, see Michael Hamilton and Fionnuala Ní Aoláin, 'Gender and the Rule of Law in Transitional Societies' [2009], 18 *MJIL* 380.

51 *See* Christine Bell, Colm Campbell and Fionnuala Ni Aoláin, 'The Battle for Transitional Justice: Hegemony, Iraq and International Law' in John Morison, Kieran McEvoy and Gordon Anthony (eds), *Judges, Transition and Human Rights* (Oxford University Press, 2007) 147.

52 For an early articulation of what such an approach would encompass, see Khanyasela Moyo, 'Feminism, Postcolonial Legal Theory and Transitional Justice: A Critique of Current Trends' [2012], 1 *IHRLR* 237; Khanyasela Moyo, 'Mimicry, Transitional Justice and the Land Question in Racially Divided Former Settler Colonies' [2014], *IJTJ* 1; see also Pascha Bueno-Hansen, *Feminist and Human Right Struggles in Peru: Decolonizing Transitional Justice* (University of Illinois Press 2015, forthcoming).

3. Southern voices in transitional justice

It still remains to be seen what the fulsome articulation of voices from outside the global North would bring to the discussion of transitional justice in the global South. What we can surmise is that colonialism, sequential transition, intergenerational harms, land rights, subsistence rights, the relationship of transition to development, the complexity and compounded nature of gendered harms, and the responsibility of states and entities in the global North in terms of supporting, enabling and prolonging conflict and repression through the provision of funds, weapons, political cover and selective humanitarian intervention all figure prominently in the emerging analysis. In parallel, the relevance of transitional justice to the hegemonic practices of states in the global North (generally not the preoccupation of transitional justice theory and practice) is opened up.

There has been little differentiation between transitional justice processes driven primarily by a country's internal dynamics (e.g. 1980s Chile), and those driven largely by outside actors (e.g. Japan in 1945). In previous work Colm Campbell and I have termed the former 'endogenous' and the latter 'exogenous'.[53] Yet, to conflate the two risks simplification to the point of distortion: trial processes in exogenous situations (typically involving some form of international tribunal, utilizing international criminal law) are likely to have quite different dynamics from those in endogenous processes (typically, domestic tribunals employing national law). Transitional justice theory and practice frequently conflates the two with quite substantial consequences for ascribing agency and capacity to endogenous processes.

A largely under-appreciated form of transitional justice that is, by its nature, exogenous involves the forceful removal of an authoritarian regime by a democratic state, and the installation of democratization and transitional justice processes in the target state.[54] A benign example is the post-war creation of the Federal Republic of Germany (FRG) out of the zones occupied by the Western Allies. This followed shortly after the Nuremberg trials, and overlapped with those under Control Council Order No. 10 and with a 'de-Nazification' process. A much more contentious recent example is the US–UK intervention in Iraq, entailing not only invasion and elections but also trials of former regime members and the highly controversial and ultimately discarded 'de-Ba'athification' processes. The contemporary salience of this intervention lies partly in the degree to which it involves the exercise of hegemonic power by the world's most powerful democracy, strongly supported by another leading democracy (the United Kingdom). Crucially, however, the justification of manifest aggression by the target state was absent in this case (in contrast with the

[53] Ní Aoláin and Campbell, supra note 10.

[54] This analysis was first developed by Christine Bell, Colm Campbell and Fionnuala Ní Aoláin, 'The Battle for Transitional Justice: Hegemony, Iraq and International Law' in Morrison and McEvoy and Anthony (eds), *Human Rights, Democracy and Transition: Essays in Honour of Stephen Livingstone* (Oxford University Press, 2007).

wartime cases of Germany and Japan). Rather, as claims over 'weapons of mass destruction' waned, the imperative to 'democratize' and bring 'justice' were increasingly relied upon. Such assertions were open only to the democratic state, which could buttress its position by reliance on emerging international law norms about a 'right to democratic governance' and the value of 'transitional justice'. It could also point to broader tensions about the compatibility of non-democratic regimes with the robust protection of generally agreed human rights obligations. 'Transitional justice', therefore, became partly the justification for the exercise of hegemonic power, enhancing the salience of the state's deployment of the discourse.

Yet, in the aftermath of regime change, and its abject failure, the human rights excesses of the democratic state were largely placed beyond the reach of both regular and transitional justice mechanisms. There has been some accounting in the United Kingdom, specifically concentrated within the terms of defining the extraterritorial reach of the European Convention on Human Rights to the actions of military actors in Afghanistan and Iraq. However, this kind of partial and individualized adjudication loses sight of the broader state collapse followed by state rebuild mandate engaging the military in both countries. Transitional justice is externalized and not internalized in any meaningful way. In the United States, the originator of military expansions and use of force, impunity reigns. There is a broad political consensus on de facto amnesty for military and political actors, virtually no criminal prosecutions of substance, and ongoing obfuscation of the facts of the harms caused. There is little support for the kinds of necessary compensations that ought to follow for systematic torture, extra-judicial killing, extensive detention without trial and a myriad violations engaging both derogable and non-derogable rights under international human rights law.

These contemporary realities require acknowledgement of the dynamics accompanying contemporary political processes whereby deployment of the rhetoric of 'transition' is perceived as beneficial to achievement of the hegemon's goals. In theory, of course, the risks may point both ways and would give rise to a hazard whereby the democratic hegemon might be faced with transitional justice-like dilemmas in relation to its *own* violations, in addition to dilemmas affecting the target state. In practice, there has been patchy evidence of this, despite the evidence that the United States as hegemon has consistently used law-based arguments in its transitional justice justifications and deployed a rhetoric of law and justice while acting unlawfully. The evidence that transitional 'justice' has done little to stem the excesses of powerful Northern states operating in and around Southern states may simply reflect what critical scholars have consistently argued: namely that international law (and now read transitional justice) has little residual 'pull' on hegemons.[55]

[55] Cf. With regard to centrifugal and centripetal tensions in law, Christopher McCrudden, 'State Architecture: Subsidiarity, Devolution, Federalism and Independence' in Mark Elliott and David

Examination of transitional justice discourse in Iraq has an analytic currency in respect of this 'Southern-focused' analysis: firstly, it throws light on the nature of the hegemonic project and its relationship to law. Secondly, it provides a new perspective on the fluidity of contemporary transitional justice discourses and their openness to manipulation. It also starkly reveals the absence of Southern voices in transitional justice discourses. Most importantly, it shows the importance of transitional justice discourse to the hegemonic project, revealing a point of resistance for those asserting the normative force of international law in general and the importance of its human rights norms in particular.

In addressing the other challenging dimensions of transitional justice's *oeuvre*, it is useful to address the ways in which 'the pivots of liberalism' remain the end results of TJ, and more specifically what TJ, shot through with liberal democratic discourse, contributes to places and spaces that share little liberal or democratic heritage. In response to this framing, it is useful to unpack broad themes within this liberal discourse. Liberalism presupposes the individual citizen (as opposed to the state or communal group) as the primary unit in society. While there is room for the individual's sovereignty to be overridden, this emphasis on the individual as opposed to a 'collective' is what sets the liberal schema apart from other ideologies. As Brown and I have argued elsewhere, '[t]aking the individual as its normative base, liberalism then postulates that individual freedoms should be promoted, and indeed are universal. Acknowledging that individuals' interests can clash, it argues for tolerance, pluralism and equal opportunities.'[56] An attached tendency is that liberalism retains a certain 'whiggishness': a belief in reformability and progression.[57] While this is a simplified thumbnail sketch, it captures something of the amalgam of the liberal discourse. One can readily see that its point of origin is the global North, or more specifically the industrialized nations of Europe and North America. It is here that critics of the 'liberal peace' have entered. Chandra Lekha Sriram was the first to bring this critical lens to bear on Transitional Justice discourse and practice, pointing out that the liberal peace was conjoined to transitional justice in the peace-building schema constructed by international actors.[58] These international actors have complex motives and goals in the use of transitional justice frames, and the extent to which local actors retain any substantial control over the contours of the 'deals' made (and substantially enabled, supported and financially propped up by key states and institutions) is debatable.

Feldman (eds), *The Cambridge Companion to Public Law* (Cambridge University Press, 2015, forthcoming).

56 Brown & Ní Aoláin, supra note 20.

57 Norberto Bobbio, *Liberalism and Democracy* (Verso, 2005); Jose G. Merquior, *Liberalism, Old and New* (Twayne, 1991).

58 Chandra Lekha Sriram, 'Justice as Peace? Liberal Peacebuilding and Strategies of Transitional Justice' [2007], 21 *GS* 579.

Sriram and others warn that transitional justice, much like the liberal peacebuilding model with which it partners, has insidious effects, not least that it is often a poor fit for local legal and political cultures contributing to sustained instability in post-conflict societies.

Conclusion

The expansion of transitional justice is still a work in progress, and insofar as the new expansive approach remains inadequately developed and affirmed, several weaknesses associated with the traditional accountability matrix remain.[59] Some of these limitations have been outlined above, but it could also be explicitly underscored that transitional justice remains unduly selective. This weakness follows largely from the uneven attention paid by powerful states to different transitional societies. In certain (usually marginal) post-conflict or post-repression states, the absence or deficiencies of accountability mechanisms are created or compounded by powerful outside actors, whereas in other contexts, powerful states have endorsed the idea of calling rights violators to account. This selectivity is manifested by the creation of criminal justice mechanisms such as ad hoc war crimes tribunals for some states, but not for all. The point is not that international or hybrid legal tribunals are entitlements of transitional societies and therefore ought to be guaranteed by international actors, but rather that choices in fact define whether they are created in the first place. Second, traditional transitional justice is partial. Even where accountability is sought, at best only a fraction of those who have committed serious human rights violations may face trial or 'truth.' For many societies this compromise of 'some truth and some justice' is an agreed concession to allow for an end to atrocities and to provide a route to reconciliation with adversaries who do not come with clean hands. The partiality invariably creates tensions with the stated commitment to 'victims' and the victim-centred nature of transitional justice theory and practice. Moreover, as this essay has explored above, once one acknowledges partiality, there is a need to deeply unpack the layers of partial justice and to track the patterns of 'who gets' and who does not. Finally, transitional-justice-as-accountability may be characterized as myopic – in particular, the practice catches only a small fraction of the context that enables human rights violations to take place. Most evidently, expansive transformations may not be uniformly positive, particularly if driven by external (including international) political communities while also lacking an organic internal dimension. Nevertheless, there is good reason to hope that the success of transitions will be more deeply felt when a multitude of measures come into play in a way that responds to the real

[59] Fionnuala Ní Aoláin, 'Unseen Justice – The Depth of Change in Transitional Societies', 22 *Ethics & International Affairs* 213–222 (2008).

needs of fractured societies and to those communities and individuals who have experienced the greatest harms.

Given all these caveats, one might easily advocate the abandonment of transitional justice and a move to other frames and mechanisms of accountability and acknowledgement.[60] This essay ends on the positive note that while there is much revision to be done, and greater access to the language, creation and forms of transitional justice to be encouraged, there is also significant room for that revision, review and restatement in a field that is still being created, and that in many fundamental respects remains unsettled. Thus, as one Southern scholar has recently noted:

> . . .[whe]reas transitional justice's foundational concepts, namely human rights, justice, liberal democratization and rule of law, were invented by patriarchal societies and colonial masters and are sometimes appropriated for neocolonial ends, transitions create opportunities for members of former colonies to input into this discourse[61]

William Twining's lifelong commitment to surfacing Southern voices, reframing his own work in the context of those contributions and ideas, being prepared to question accepted scholarly canons at every point as he engaged 'geographies of injustice',[62] consistently addressing representation and the importance of critical voice, and the unfailing desire to counter parochialism, stands as a clarion call to scholars of transitional justice to hear, to read, to respond and to engage on the same terms.

[60] Some moves in this direction can be seen from the recent spurt of scholarly enthusiasm for *jus post bellum* as an organizing frame of justice and accountability in post-conflict societies.

[61] Moyo, *Mimicry*, supra note 33 at 2.

[62] The term belongs to Upendra Baxi but is deployed by Twining, *Southern Voices*, supra note 1, at 212.

5

Human rights and Latin American Southern voices

Oscar Guardiola-Rivera

1. Is law ethnocentric?

Recognized as a master in the emerging discipline of comparative jurisprudence, which he helped to create, William Twining set out to write about law and institutions from a truly global perspective. This meant resisting the urge to assume that it is possible to continue doing sound work in legal theory, or the philosophy and sociology of rights and institutions, solely from within Western traditions.

The standpoint of Western legal–political traditions vis-à-vis other practices of law and the political ontologies of the world remains unclear. All too often, Western law and politics presents itself not only as one among various ways of regulating human relations, but also as the unique representative of human regulation. That is, as being the one that measures and defines all the multitude of normative ways in the world, having the capacity to travel everywhere and be more or less universally applicable. Twining's lesson challenged such facile representations. He argued that to accept the profoundly influential character of the rich heritage of Western legality and socio-political theory did not mean having to deny that, from a global standpoint, academic law and practice appear to be 'generally parochial, narrowly focused and even unempirical'.[1] The canon and heritage of Western jurisprudence and social–political theory not only appear narrow and parochial when viewed from a global perspective, but they also, as Twining sharply observed, 'tend ... towards ethnocentrism'.[2]

What does it mean to say that Western law tends towards Eurocentrism and ethnocentrism? A tendency is an inclination towards a particular type of behaviour; a proclivity or predisposition. Building upon Twining's insight I am going to argue in this paper that what predisposes the canon and heritage of Western jurisprudence and socio-political theory towards the particular (i.e. ethnocentrism, Eurocentrism) is not its claim towards universality. Rather, it is the specific form of unity and uniqueness assumed by Western law that

[1] W. Twining, *General Jurisprudence: Understanding Law from a Global Perspective* (2009).

[2] W. Twining, *General Jurisprudence: Understanding Law from a Global Perspective* (2009) xi. See also *Human Rights, Southern Voices* (2009) 1–3.

predisposes it towards a particular ethnocentric behaviour. Western law is seen not as one element among others in the set of humanity's normative ways, but as the one that defines and measures what counts as part of the set, as the very standard of humanity: an understanding which it projects upon the other peoples it encounters around the world.

The intersection opened up by the convergence between law and anthropology is a good place to search for instances of such an inclination, to criticize them, and in the process to try to recover the standpoint of a more universal view of nature and the human. Twining's position, second to none within Western Anglo-Saxon jurisprudence and socio-political philosophy, is a powerful example of the ways in which the empirical and comparative study of ontologies and normative cosmologies – pioneered by anthropology – has challenged, even subverted, Western legal protocols and assumptions about what counts as human, as well as its own standpoint as the one and true representative of such a standard.

Such protocols and assumptions about the unity of mankind, and the moral importance of one's location on the planet vis-à-vis others, were derived from Christianized Greek metaphysics. They were then applied to the definition of the human in the sublunary, worldly or 'secular' realm by the sixteenth-century jurists and theologians who helped to determine the modern cosmopolitan framework in the wake of the 1550 debates in Valladolid, Spain. Such debates considered the consequences of the encounter between Europeans and Amerindians, and in particular the validity of European claims towards global hegemony. In the process, these jurists and theologians, and their successors in the Netherlands and elsewhere in Europe, invented human geography, geopolitics and modern international law.[3] Sixteenth-century jurists, navigators, cosmographers and theologians determined the cosmopolitical perspective, as well as its basic assumptions concerning the unity of the many beings, peoples and landscapes of the world. This proved influential, indeed quite decisive, in the specific setting of global colonization and empire by European powers. Often taken for granted in mainstream Western legal and social–political theory, such a perspective has been the subject of sustained criticism. This has emerged not only within contemporary anthropology but also in the inter-disciplinary forms of comparativism and legal anthropology practiced by realists in the Americas and elsewhere. In this respect, at least, Twining has proven to be a worthy successor of Bronislaw Malinowski's *Crime and Custom in Savage Society*, Karl Lewellyn and E. Adamson-Hoebel's *The Cheyenne Way*, the more contemporary *The Life of the Law* by Laura Nader, and, more

[3] For the sixteenth-century roots of modern law, specifically international and cosmopolitan law, see P. Fitzpatrick, 'Latin Roots: The Force of International Law as Event' and O. Guardiola-Rivera, 'Absolute Contingency and the Prescriptive Force of International Law, Chiapas-Valladolid, ca. 1550' in *Events: The Force of International Law*, F. Johns, R. Joyce and S. Pahuja (eds), with a foreword by M. Koskenniemi (Routledge-Cavendish, 2010), ch. 3 and 4.

generally, the intellectual attitude exemplified by Claude Lévi-Strauss's classic *Tristes Tropiques*.

In *Tristes Tropiques*, Lévi-Strauss told a story about the 'absolute, total and intransigent dilemmas by which the men of the sixteenth century felt themselves to be faced', which is thoroughly apposite to the question concerning the tendencies towards ethnocentrism present in Western law from its very inception in early modernity.[4] According to Lévi-Strauss, 'commission after commission was sent out to determine the nature' of the inhabitants of the New World. In the course of what was tantamount to a psycho-sociological inquiry, 'conceived according to the most modern standards', the colonists were required to answer a series of questions, says Lévi-Strauss, 'the purpose of which was to find out if, in their opinion, the Indians were or were not' capable of living like Castilian peasants – that is, crucially, like autonomous economic agents. 'All the replies were negative', the anthropologist tells us. The Amerindians refused to work in accordance with the economic imperatives of the time. They carried perversity 'to the point of giving away their possessions'. The alleged lack of a work ethic similar to that of Protestants and counter-reformist Catholics, and the apparent absence of notions of private property, were just the tip of the iceberg. According to the sociological inquiry carried out by these thoroughly modern commissions, the aborigines 'eat human flesh, and have no form of justice'.[5]

The point is clear: for these fact-finding commissions, composed of jurists and Christian theologians who followed the protocols of what we now call the social sciences, Amerindians had no 'law' and were either outside of humanity or occupied a lower place in its internal moral hierarchy, being a less perfect, unrealized form of the human. This was evidenced by their practices: their refusal to enjoy without sharing; their symbolic practices concerning the righting of communal wrongs and the treatment of prisoners captured in warfare; and most of all their refusal to hold any belief concerning the unity of God, King and Law. Muslims may hold the wrong beliefs, observed the Christian jurists and theologians doing their fieldwork in the Americas from the sixteenth century onwards, but in comparison to Amerindians at least they showed constancy in their beliefs.

Jurists and Christians theologians, as well as their more liberal successors, either ignored or disavowed the ways in which the Amerindians' refusal to believe, accumulate or to conquer evil by externalizing it in a figure of absolute enmity (captives, even those intended for execution, would be given wives and spend years as members of the community) were linked to Amerindian demands for reciprocity between human groups (extended in some cases to nonhumans). In this respect, what the proto-sociologists and jurists of the sixteenth century missed was the emergence of the rule as rule in the context of

[4] C. Lévi-Strauss, *Tristes Tropiques* (Penguin Modern Classics, 2011) [1955] 75 ff.

[5] C. Lévi-Strauss, *Tristes Tropiques*, 75–6.

gift-economies rather than exchange-economies, the recognition of which required the ability to assume the existence of an alternative viewpoint. Due to their intransigent focus on a specific form of unity (setting constant and faithful belief in God, the Sovereign and his Law, whether excessive or moderate, as the unique standard of humanity) our thoroughly modern jurists and sociologists were blind to alternative viewpoints.

Arguably, mainstream practices of Western law, although nominally secular, continue to be obsessed by a specific form of unity that is derived from its roots in Western Christian theology: whether one believes too much or too little still serves as a unique indicator of the place one occupies in the hierarchy of humanity. Belief is a standard. One is set apart from all others in the globe, in the very act of defining and measuring such others against the constancy of belief as a unique standard of humanity. Consider, for instance, the focus of security laws and 'responsibility' doctrines. These hijack the universalist impulse of human rights law at home and abroad in the service of particularist views concerning the alleged threat posed by foreign immigrants and cultures, all too often identified as 'fundamentalist' enemies, to the allegedly weak, moderate, liberal polities of the Judeo-Christian West. The framework of such laws and doctrines is the alleged struggle between those who believe too much and cannot make their specific religion a private affair and those who believe too little and manage to privatize belief. In principle, there is no space for questioning this basic framework that separates the peoples of the world between religious privatizers and fundamentalists, or to consider the challenge posed to it by the existence of religions without belief such as those observed among pre-Columbian Amerindians. If the spectrum of possibilities that frames current emphases on security laws and responsibility doctrines at home and abroad runs from too much belief, exemplified by the alleged fanaticism of Eastern law, to too little belief in the case of liberal Western law, then it turns out that the former has no monopoly over religious inspiration. Western law too has never been secular.

The story about the modern, constant, sovereign subject that Western commissioners expected but failed to find among Amerindians is also a story about how this subject is able to privatize religion and belief, rather than prevail over it. With religion neutralized and relegated to the inner sanctum of constant, isolated subjectivity, the question arises: what will replace the fading social bond? What can now gather us in a disenchanted, technocratic world without moral virtues? This was the problematic question that law inherited from the work of sociologists Emile Durkheim and Max Weber after the crises of the 1930s and World War II, taken up by such leading figures as H. L. A. Hart, whose lectures Twining attended at Oxford.[6]

[6] See N. Lacey, *A Life of HLA Hart: The Nightmare and the Noble Dream* (Oxford University Press, 2006).

The more globalized and disenchanted the world became, 'the more society sought solace and refuge in religion and religious movements', which sought an answer to the thin morality of 'secular' modern societies in the thick, strong and constant unity of belief in God, King, and Law.[7] Normative accounts informed by political theology have continued to haunt 'the epistemic certitude and assurances of sociology, and western society', and thus, also, of sociologically-minded Western understandings of law and normativity. This is so 'not because religion is a historical and developmental vestigial order that modern society cannot digest, but precisely because religions remain as modern as contemporary society'.[8]

This insight is important in order to provide an answer to our question concerning Western law's ethnocentric tendencies – part and parcel of the project of modernity as an imperial and colonial project – referred to by Twining. More specifically, there are two tendencies that converge within Western law as part of the project of modernity: an imperial propensity to externalize evil, on the one side, and the legal, institutional use of religion as a normative political technology that determines as much the horizon of the social as the horizon of the subjective. In particular, religion as a normative technology contributes decisively in the production and inscription of certain types of subjectivity, the incorporation of the other into ourselves.

It is at this point that the insights of anthropology deploy their most radical and critical force within Western academic law. For it turns out that modern concerns with the cannibalistic practices of Amerindian others were in part a mirror of the religious wars of seventeenth-century Europe, focused on rival understandings of the Eucharist.[9] Such externalization of internal conflicts upon evil others in the seventeenth century is arguably of the same kind as the externalization upon fundamentalist religious others of our internal concerns with immigration in the current era of globalization. But religion as a normative, political, modern and colonial technology also concerns the making visible of the constant, temperate soul – of enlightened human natures – against the darkness of bodies in the torrid zones of the world. As Mendieta argues, in such technical procedure of the inscription of subjects to law, 'the skin confesses the soul'.[10]

[7] E. Mendieta, 'Imperial Somatics and Genealogies of Religion: How We Never Became Secular' in *Postcolonial Philosophy of Religion*, P. Bilimoria and A. B. Irvine (eds), (Springer Science+ Business Media B. V. 2009), 231–246, at 233.

[8] Ibid.

[9] Hans Staden, *Hans Staden's True History: An Account of Cannibal Captivity in Brazil*, trans. N. L. Whitehead and M. Harbsmeier (Duke University Press, 2008), Introduction, xv.

[10] E. Mendieta, 'Imperial Somatics and Genealogies of Religion: How We Never Became Secular', 239. Mendieta is talking here about ethnography and genealogy, methodologies that developed their explanatory force in the fields of anthropology and history. He says: 'Genealogy allows us to understand how is it that the soul is the prison of the body, and how is it that the skin confesses the soul, in such a way that the skin and the body always betray the truths that constitute us as subjects.' See also his 'Geography Is to History as Woman Is to Man: Kant on

Modern Western law remains haunted by a singular experience of religion, as evidenced by its deployment of a particular technology of subjective inscription: one that tends to allow for the externalization of internal conflicts about the consequences of too little belief in society, by projecting them upon monstrous others who threaten us because they believe too much – from sixteenth-century cannibals to twenty-first-century immigrants as well as fundamentalist religious or political fanatics. Immigrants and religious or political fanatics are represented to modern audiences through mass media as monstrous others with which no relationship, other than force, is possible; their darker intentions reveal the vulnerability and weakness of liberal societies without strong moral values.

The implication is that to make the truth of our liberal values count over the superstitious beliefs of others in darker places left behind by the march of history, moderate values must be strengthened – become less moderate and tolerant – and even forcibly imposed. And if our moderate values can be imposed, that is because these 'others' are culturally backward, incapable of true meaning and are meaningless instead.

Let's understand by 'otherness' or 'alterity' something more essential and concrete: the universal condition for reciprocity. In such a condition, others aren't just the obscure object of our desires, sympathy or antipathy, but have desires of their own, produce meaning and have the ability to respond. Their words, their meanings, their ways and responses cannot be denied or disavowed. For words aren't just some neutral medium of communication, but bearers of value. As such, they're offered to others as something that comes from inside, as a gift. It is in the act of exchanging gifts, words, communicating and making alliances through marriages or in ritual confrontation, that reciprocity emerges. We engage in reciprocal relations not because we share the same values, actually or potentially, but because we need the act of sharing to transform ourselves just as we transform our environments. Alterity means that no relation with a natural environment is a one-way street. And if we must also be ready to be transformed then no place of origin, or shared account of origins, should hold moral priority. The West has no privileged moral position.

If others and their environments were incapable of meaning then our relations with them would have only one sense and direction: our way, our Western way. Their alterity itself would be meaningless, insofar as the only others that matter to us are those who, being able to hold on with constancy to some recognizable belief in the unity of God, Law and the Sovereign, can transact business with us and exchange goods and ideas on the basis of trustworthy contracts. Specifically modern legal technologies – prison, confession, mandates, interventions, contracts – are thus linked with normatively

sex, Race, and Geography' in *Reading Kant's Geography*, S. Elden and E. Mendieta (eds), (SUNY Press, 2011), 345–68.

structured regimes of truth-telling inscribed in terms of skin colour, supposedly revelatory of geopolitical location and capacity. Western law thus tends towards ethnocentricity, as Twining suggested, in this very precise way.

2. There are other ways: from the Cheyenne Way to the Chilean Way

Absent from the picture of legal and political globalization that focuses on strengthening moderate liberal values in a world of global contracts and exchanges, divided between those who believe too much and those who believe too little, is the insight of anthropologists. They observe the universality of a politics of law and reciprocal relations arising not only, or not at all, from a system of exchanges of beliefs and goods, but rather from solving the problem of how to manage relations among humans, and between humans and nonhumans, in situations of meaningful alterity.

The story of the emergence of such an insight is linked to the history of contemporary anthropology itself, in its relation with law. Here we can distinguish between three stages in that history, associated with the work of three different generations of anthropo-legal scholars. Malinowski was the single most important figure in setting the stage for the contemporary anthropological study of law, in much the same way that Lévi-Strauss is for anthropology in general. The work of the first generation – Malinowski, Lévi-Strauss, Llewellyn and Hoebel – demonstrated two things that anthropology and comparative ontology now view as self-evident: that all societies can be presumed to have a politics of law and reciprocal relations, regardless of the presence of Western trappings; and that anthropology's signature methods – field ethnography and decolonial genealogy – can be 'profitably applied to the study of law' and the management of co-productive relations between human groups and between these and nonhumans.[11]

The work of their worthy successors – people like William Twining, Simon Roberts, Boaventura de Sousa Santos and Eduardo Viveiros de Castro – constitutes the most important contribution to the destruction of the narrow province of jurisprudence and its reconstruction on the basis of localized comparativism, decolonial genealogy and field ethnography. This second generation – including Twining – has taken the emphasis on co-production and doing/making (the focus on problems and what is done about or made through them, known in academic law as the 'case method') to its most creative conclusion: that 'being' is both making and in the making, with human groups co-producing each other as well as their environments through the invention of technical devices to solve common problems in concrete situations of meaningful alterity and conflict.

[11] J. M. Conley and William O'Barr, 'A Classic in Spite of Itself: The Cheyenne Way and the Case Method in Legal Anthropology', *Law & Social Inquiry*, Vol. 29, No. 1 (Winter, 2004) pp. 179–217.

In this understanding, 'being' is not the result of a singular act of creation or enlightenment taking place somewhere, followed by its diffusion everywhere else through procedures of transplantation, downloading or hybridization that ultimately resemble the form of a pact or a contract.[12] Importantly, the idea of 'being' as the result of a unique act of creation followed by diffusion through consented borrowing, transplantation or downloading, invites us to think of innovation in terms of a disjunction, in space and time, between the creative moment taking place somewhere and its calculable repetition or absolutely incalculable difference elsewhere. In such a schema, consent represents the calculability or authorization (by the author) for repetition elsewhere in order to contain incalculability as a hazard.

On the contrary, the idea of 'being' as a process of generalized inscription and creolization suggests another answer to the question of how something other than the calculable, legal and ordered would come about, given that in principle there is nothing outside of the calculable, the legal and the ordered. The practical devices we invent in order to solve problems and conflicts (for instance, laws and rights) need to be understood not merely as formal procedures of authorization and the containment of hazardous incalculability or risk, but rather as technical actions, surfaces of inscription, or tools of technical differentiation. To explain: these are technologies that trigger different spacings, delays and rhythms. This is what legal philosopher Hans Lindahl has called borders, limits and fault lines, including, centrally, those that delimit and organize subjects and bodies into different classes, orders and races, cultures or skin colours within a collective natural or social sequence.[13]

Put more simply, this second generation of explorers of law, politics and reciprocity across cultures and natures has shown us that our social and natural bonds would be as airy as clouds if there were only contracts between individual subjects guaranteed by their mutual trustworthiness or their ability to hold on to their truth-beliefs. There are also things, technical things and objects, which stabilize our relations, and other ways to demarcate and slow

[12] See on this W. Twining, *Human Rights, Southern Voices: Francis Deng, Abdullahi An-Na'im, Yash Ghai and Upendra Baxi* (Cambridge University Press, 2009). Notice, in the introduction, Twining's emphasis on Ghai's experience of postcolonial constitution-making and political materialism versus notions of a 'culture of human rights', as well as on Baxi's injunction to take suffering seriously – in fact a call for a fundamental identification to the other – in contrast to sentimental, benevolent and liberal calls for cross-cultural dialogue. For the distinction between creolization – a fundamental identification to the other, division and multiplication – and hybridity – the mere combination and addition of same and other – see: E. Viveiros de Castro, *The Inconstancy of the Indian Soul. The Encounter of Catholics and Cannibals in 16th Century Brazil* (Chicago: Prickly Paradigm Press, 2011), and Jane A. Gordon, *Creolizing Political Theory. Reading Rousseau Through Fanon* (Fordham University Press, 2014). See also B. de Sousa Santos, *Epistemologies of the South: Justice Against Epistemicide* (Boulder: Paradigm Press, 2014). On decolonial genealogies, see E. Mendieta, 'Imperial Somatics and Genealogies of Religion: How We Never Became Secular' in *Postcolonial Philosophy of Religion*, P. Bilimoria and A. B. Irvine (eds), (Springer Science+ Business Media B. V. 2009), 231–46.

[13] See H. Lindahl, *Fault Lines of Globalization: Legal Order and the Politics of A-legality* (Oxford University Press, 2013).

down the time and place of our revolutions. Laws, legal ways and human rights exemplify such things. The next step is to better our understanding of law and its religious matrix as a political technology that produces embodied subjects and orders them, selecting some and deselecting others for the purposes of managing relations among humans and between humans and nonhumans in contexts of radical alterity.

Now, a third generation has taken such a step in the field of human rights, building on Twining's work on 'Southern Voices'.[14] For some time now, he and I have been talking about the need to extend and intensify the work started in *Human Rights, Southern Voices*, in the direction of *Latin American* Southern voices. Helped by many others,[15] I have been trying to do just that. The provisional results can be seen and reviewed in a trans-disciplinary trilogy that began in 2009 with the more philosophical *Being Against the World*, followed in 2010 by the ethnographic travelogue *What If Latin America Ruled the World?*, and concluding in 2013 with a narrative non-fiction work titled *Story of a Death Foretold: The Coup Against Salvador Allende, 11 September 1973*.

These works share a similar standpoint, focusing methodologically on the historical–comparative and genealogical–discursive study of institutions. This is an interpretive approach that challenges the predominance of so-called Rational Choice Theory and methodological individualism in the social sciences. It starts from the observation of a common set of problems. These stem from the persistent disavowal of objects ripe for historical comparative research across areas of the world, such as in the areas of law, policy and rights by those who insist that it is possible to do work in legal and political theory solely from the perspective of a parochial canon of Western theory and practice oblivious to its own predisposition. We can see this approach in the theories of, and practice derived from the work of, the Law and Economics school, Social Choice theorists, and cost–benefit analyses.[16]

The interpretive approach I espouse agrees with those exploring legal conceptions, social bonds and institutions in non-Western parts of the globe, from

[14] W. Twining, *Human Rights, Southern Voices* (Cambridge University Press, 2009).

[15] Chief among them the sociologist Boaventura de Sousa Santos, philosophers Eduardo Mendieta, Linda Martín-Alcoff, Drucilla Cornell and Lewis R. Gordon, historians Eric Hobsbawm, Marcus Rediker, Joanna Bourke and Peter Linebaugh, Brazilian anthropologist Eduardo Viveiros de Castro, Argentinian political theorist Ernesto Laclau and geneticist Yulia Kovas.

[16] See, for instance, Eric Posner's rational choice-based approach to international relations and international law. For historical comparativism, J. Mahoney and D. Rueschemeyer, *Comparative Historical Analysis in the Social Sciences* (2003). For the compatibility between historical comparative analysis, post-structural discourse theory, discursive institutionalism and other similar approaches see M. E. Hedayat, *The Exceptionalist Collective Imaginary: Hegemonic Battles and Costa Rica's Democratic Institutional Development*, PhD thesis submitted to the Department of Government of the London School of Economics (London: June 2014) pp. 25–40. For genealogy, see E. Mendieta, 'Imperial Somatics and Genealogies of Religion: How We Never Became Secular', 237–9.

a wide variety of disciplines, including hard sciences such as genetics as well as the life and earth sciences, but also anthropology, the philosophy of religion and literature. From these we learn that certain epistemic disconnects, *idées fixes* and automatic reflexes add to the basic constraints already faced by transnational commentators. As the American legal ethnographer Jorge Esquirol puts it, as regards the specific case of academic law, such epistemic disconnects operate within and without academia. They 'truncat[e] fuller debate about questions of law' in other parts of the world, and displace 'wider discussions over alternative policies, competing interests, and the distributional impacts of rules and institutions,' privileging instead a rather narrow set of perspectives, positions and prescriptions.[17]

The points made in the previous paragraphs also constitute the best introductory framework for the aims of the following sections of this chapter. Like the approaches mentioned earlier (general jurisprudence, law and globalization, historical comparativism, the philosophical and scientific study of networks) and inspired by them, I shall now explore a specific case of Latin American Southern voices in the human rights context: that of the second Russell Tribunal (Russell II), assembled in the wake of the events surrounding the 1973 *coup d'état* against Salvador Allende and the Chilean Way.[18]

Following Twining, I believe that this specific case, adopting a historical, comparative and genealogical perspective, yields a number of crucial lessons, to be learned and applied in the construction of an alternative vision and agenda for theorizing about law, political ideas and institutions. This allows for interpretive approaches, and argues for a more careful consideration of body, place, locality and inscription (*via* concrete forms of generalized writing, archiving, marking, sequencing and transcribing) than abstract (especially probabilistic and type-sociological) models in the social sciences allow. In this spirit, it concerns itself with Latin America as a specific locality for the appearance (in speech and writing) of Southern voices in human rights. However, it does not intend to develop a full-blown case study of historical comparison between the countries of this region or between this region as a whole and some other global grouping. The second half of this paper shares with the previously mentioned approaches, especially with Twining's *General Jurisprudence*, the thesis that most processes of 'globalization' take place at sub-global (e.g. Southern, specifically Latin American) levels and that a healthy cosmopolitan discipline of law and political theory (here including cosmopolitical philosophy) should encompass all levels of social relations and the normative orderings of such relations.

In honouring Twining's pioneering work by taking it in a hitherto ignored direction, this chapter hopes to contribute to the critical review and extension

[17] J. Esquirol, 'Writing the Law of Latin America' (2009), 40 *TGWILR* 3, 694.

[18] A more complete exploration of this specific case remains beyond the particular space limits of this paper.

of the Western canon of jurisprudence, social theory and political philosophy. Crucially, this can be done by taking into account, as Twining did, some of the more or less general problems of conceptualization, comparison and generalization, and the relationship between the local and the global. More pointedly, it also initiates a reflection on justice, law and globalization (global social justice) from within a specific tradition. Going beyond the aim of extending the canon, it is my objective to position Latin American Southern voices in human rights not simply as an alternative 'type' – one that could or should be added to others in order to form some sort of rainbow epistemic coalition – but rather as a 'bomb'. The aim here is to explode the boundaries, borders, limits and fault lines assumed by mainstream political philosophy and legal theory.[19]

3. The Chilean Way, the Inseparability Thesis and the Russell Tribunal

During a 1974 interview with the journalist Jorge Raventos, the famed Argentinian writer Julio Cortázar clarified his more general intellectual perspective. 'My standpoint,' he said, 'is that politics and ethics are inseparable.' He was responding to a question formulated by Raventos, concerning the politically critical function of writers, thinkers and academics, their militancy and activism, in the face of violence and oppression.[20] In the background were Cortázar's experiences as one among the group of Latin American writers and intellectuals that took part in the deliberations of the Russell II Tribunal, together with Gabriel García Márquez and Juan Bosch among others.

This citizen's tribunal considered evidence, explored the principles of the Nuremberg tribunals and used them critically in order to rule on the systematic violation of human rights, peoples' and indigenous rights in Latin America during the 1970s. Russell II had been convened in the wake of the furious violence unleashed during and after the *coup d'état* that unseated the socialist president of Chile, Salvador Allende, on 11 September 1973, and the increase in counterrevolutionary repression elsewhere in Latin America. It built, at least indirectly, on the critical heritage of the reports written by Frankfurt School lawyers and theorists for the US prosecution team during the Nuremberg Trials and, more directly, on the legacy left behind by Jean-Paul Sartre and Bertrand Russell during the first Russell Tribunal.[21]

[19] See on 'types' and 'bombs', B. Latour, 'Perspectivism, "Type" or "Bomb"?', *Anthropology Today*, vol. 25, issue, 2. Also, Eduardo Viveiros de Castro, 'The Untimely, Again', an introduction to Pierre Clastres, *Archeology of Violence*, Semiotext(e), 2010, 9–51.

[20] J. Cortázar and J. Raventos, 'Entrevista a Julio Cortázar', *Revista Redacción*, Junio de 1974.

[21] F. Neumann, H. Marcuse and O. Kircheimer, *Secret Reports on Nazi Germany: The Frankfurt School Contribution to the War Effort*, R. Laudani, ed., with a foreword by R. Geuss (Princeton University Press, 2013). For Sartre's 'ethics of the least favoured' in the context of his participation in Russell I, his wider philosophical project and the slippage from it towards the 'ethics of the other' and the 'human rights turn' of the 1980s, see P. Arthur, *Unfinished Projects: Decolonisation and the Philosophy of Jean-Paul Sartre* (Verso, 2009).

Russell I had condemned US intervention in Vietnam as an act of genocide on the basis of the Nuremberg principles, warning that its specific form of violence was closely connected to the demands of a global form of capitalism then under construction. Russell II extended the argument to the case of intervention in the Americas, condemning counterrevolutionary violence and the use of the 'state of siege' or 'state of exception' in countries such as Chile, Brazil, Bolivia, Uruguay, Guatemala, Haiti, Paraguay, the Dominican Republic, Puerto Rico, Nicaragua, Argentina and Colombia, which it ascribed to the defence of private, multinational commercial and financial interests. Crucially, it shifted Russell I's ethical and practical stance in favour of the least favoured towards a more militant law and politics, targeting racism, extractive neo-colonialism, the financialization of the global economy, and counterrevolutionary violence, as well as their theological–political, legal and economic justifications.[22]

Such a shift, hitherto ignored by students of the culture, legality, philosophy and institutions of decolonization and resistance in the 1960s and 70s, was and remains extremely significant. On the one hand, it set the stage for a confrontation between the anti-political ethics of abstract legality and individualistic subjectification, which would become dominant during the last two decades of the twentieth century and the first decade of the twenty-first. And on the other, it paved the way for the ethical politics and legality of militancy and desubjectification that, harkening back to the legacy of the 1960s and 70s, is carving out a space of its own on the stage of the global revolts of the second decade of the twenty-first century.

It is no accident that the flight towards an abstract ethics of disembodied humanity (often appearing as the dominant discourse of human rights) with no place and no concrete collective politics other than the constant movement of capital flows, occurred just as globalist ideology and counterrevolutionary disillusion was taking hold. Similarly, it is not by chance that the call to revisit the radical orientation of the militant politics of desubjectification, heard among student movements and emerging political sectors in the Americas, Asia and Europe, coincides with the end of 'capitalist realism' after 2008, the global revolts of 2011–13, the increase in geopolitical tensions and the backlash against neoliberalism in Latin America a little earlier.

The political ethics and legality referred to in Cortázar's clarification of standpoint, which declares that ethics, law and politics are inseparable (hereafter called the 'Inseparability Thesis') is one that takes seriously collective claims made by peoples living in suffering, under poverty, racial discrimination and socio-economic oppression. In this respect, Cortázar's Inseparability Thesis resonates with Upendra Baxi's claim in Twining's *Human Rights, Southern Voices* that human rights futures are dependent upon giving voice

[22] See P. Arthur, *Unfinished Projects: Decolonisation and the Philosophy of Jean-Paul Sartre* (Verso, 2009).

to suffering, as a concrete force and effect, the result of bad history, and must therefore engage in a discourse of suffering that is militant, i.e. one 'that moves the world'.[23] Another aspect in which Cortázar's thesis, emerging from the experience of Russell II, chimes with Southern voices such as Baxi's, is on its emphasis on the historical character of injustice and justice, over and above all theodicy narratives and eschatological claims.

Cortázar argues that the collective claims and demands of those wronged by past history are the concrete basis for rights and for doing justice in the present and the future. The Inseparability Thesis considers people in their multiple nature, their motley character. It views their demands as connected to their concrete situation in history: the ways in which they have been marked, individuated, selected or deselected by more or less legally sanctioned forms of subjectification and plunder. These were the 'least favoured' identified by Sartre's reworking of the Nuremberg principles during Russell I. Moreover, the emphasis on economic exploitation at the heart of global interventionism, justified in the name of the end-history of humanity by the institutional narratives of the West, provided Cortázar and the other jurors of Russell II with an important opportunity. The legacy of Nuremberg and Russell I was connected with the plea of indigenous and other oppressed peoples, the Chilean Way, and the future of human rights in a world in which the rights of multinationals carry more weight than those of their human victims, and in that sense the post-human world of what Cortázar called 'the multinational vampires'.

The Latin American writers who participated in Russell II picked up on Sartre's point and interpreted it through the experience of what had happened in Chile. They focused on the effects of Allende's decision to nationalize natural resources – copper – until then in the hands of multinationals and the banks. Allende's policy of nationalization, which combined elements of the legal critique of the Eurocentric bias of international law with insights from the Dependency school of economics, Marxist views on mining rents derived from quasi-monopolistic positions, and decolonial views concerning financial violence in international contexts,[24] subscribed to the legal doctrine of 'excess profits'.

Basically, the policy targeted above-average profits obtained by beneficiaries whose unjustly acquired gains continued to appreciate in value after the perpetrators of past evils have been driven away through wars of independence, anti-slavery or anti-colonial struggle. 'Excess profits' relates also to a

[23] W. Twining, *Human Rights, Southern Voices*, 158.

[24] See, for instance, F. Fanon, *The Wretched of the Earth* (London: Penguin Modern Classics [1961] 2009) 75–84. Making an explicit analogy with the case of reparations paid by the Germans to Israel for crimes committed by the Nazis, Fanon spoke of 'a double realisation: the realisation by the colonised peoples that it is their due, and the realisation by the capitalist powers that they must pay' (81). Also, P. Baran and E. Hobsbawm, 'Un manifeste non-communiste', *Les Temps Modernes* 193, June 1962, 1226–61.

crucial legal problem concerning feasible schemes of reparative justice. A crucial difference between the Chilean perspective and that of the multinationals on the issue of nationalization was that for the latter this was a simple matter of compensating for predictable future losses after the takeover, while for the former the takeover was a matter of reparative justice at the heart of post-colonial legal and political institutions, based on rights of conquest and property claims. The value of compensation after takeover should thus be weighted against the value of above-average profits obtained by current beneficiaries of past injustice.

At first, law tends towards the position that if there are good reasons to recognize historical injustice through reparations, these should be minimal and symbolic. The passage of time, issues of causality, financial viability and compounding of interest suggest these should never be taken as paving the way for restoring social justice in general. But, in Property Law, students are exposed to cases of 'adverse possession', in which the occupation of someone else's space (for instance, in the case of colonization) becomes a legal entitlement. There, the question is whether law cuts remedies off (for instance, through the prescription of a right to conquest) or allows for them (for instance, via takeovers and restitutions). Nationalization, as practiced in Chile in the 1970s in the cases of lands and mining, was but an example of backward-looking restitution, well grounded in the canon of property law by the early twentieth century. The specific case of copper nationalization was an application of legal theories of restitution according to which it would be unjust for beneficiaries of a perceived wrongdoing – e.g. under colonialism, neo-colonialism or apartheid – to keep the portion of their accumulated gains that exceeds the damages their surviving victims might claim. This would amount, as pointed out also by the Frankfurt critical reporters of the Nuremberg era, to profiting from a crime.

4. Making global social justice now

Allende's doctrine of excess profits was promulgated under Decree 92 of 28 September 1971. At the time, copper was quite profitable for US multinationals Anaconda and Kennecott, not least because of the war in Vietnam.[25] In 1969, Anaconda invested 16.6% of its global portfolio in Chile, but obtained 79.2% of its profits there; Kennecott invested 13.2% and made 21.3% of its total profits there. The Chilean Decree was based on UN General Assembly Resolution 1803/1962 on 'Permanent Sovereignty over Natural Resources'. This recognized the right of peoples to recover and use their basic resources, allowing for compensation to be established in accordance with the rules of the state

[25] S. Allende cited in V. Farías, *La izquierda chilena (1969–1973) Documentos para el estudio de su línea estratégica* (Santiago: Centro de Estudios Públicos, 2000) 983–977 and M. Amorós, *Compañero Presidente*, 214.

undertaking the nationalization and establishing the courts of that country as the appropriate venue for any resulting conflict.[26] Decree 92 provided for compensation and excess profit to be calculated on the basis of balance sheets available after 5 May 1955, when Law 11.828 created a Copper Department and it began recording data concerning profits. In the previous decades, copper mining companies had operated without significant regulation. Innovatively, the Decree addressed the circumstances in which benefits of past injustice have accumulated, in which the number of the original indigenous victims is ever decreasing, and in which individual victims would have difficulty proving losses on the scale of the cumulative gains that were thereby produced.

Challenging Western legal common sense on the issue of just compensation and the constructive value of unjustly accrued wealth, the Allende doctrine can be seen as giving those suffering from historical grievances that persist in the global market economy the right to demand compensation now rather than later against those who tend to treat the past as a series of catastrophes repeated over time, including ours, without end or solution. For those who hold such views, 'the time of rectifying the past is never now'.[27] This is important insofar as such permanent delay – interregnum, to use Thomas Hobbes' terms – has been conceptualized by constitutional lawyers like Carl Schmitt in the case of Nazi Germany or Jaime Guzmán in Pinochet's Chile, as a time of exception. In such exceptional times, they argue, appealing to Roman Law and sixteenth-century justifications of colonialism (viewed through the prism of twentieth-century fascism), it is legitimate to suspend liberties and opt for the lesser evil.

Such readings of past history and precedent make a mockery of the Nuremberg Principles and the holocausts (Jewish, Spanish, indigenous, and so on). They condemn human rights futures to a form of 'transitional justice' that ultimately defends as moral the position that nothing should come (politically and legally) after doing 'just enough to achieve political stability'.[28] The dubious model for such a kind of justice has been, precisely, the Chilean 'transition' after the coup. Later on, that model and its economic sidekick, the trickle-down theory of economic justice, would be imported everywhere else in the world. It has become the normal state of affairs since the late twentieth century.

Transitional and trickle-down models insist that arguments of justice must disregard all past history, and that political attempts to eradicate inequality should be avoided for moral reasons: to stave off the repetition of the genocidal past. The result is an untenable separation between ethics and

[26] UN General Assembly Resolution 1803 (XVII), 14 December 1962. According to A. Kilangi, the resolution resulted form the UNGA's focus on 'the promotion and financing of economic development in under-developed countries . . . and in connection with the right of peoples to self-determination in the draft international covenants on human rights'. At www.untreaty.un.org/cod/avl/ha/ga_1803/ga_1803.html.

[27] R. Meister, *After Evil*, 255–8.

[28] R. Teitel, 'Transitional Justice Genealogy', *Harvard Human Rights Journal* 19, 2003, 69–94; and *Transitional Justice* (Oxford University Press, 2000), also cited by R. Meister, *After Evil*, 259–76.

politics that in our time tends to be identified with standard human rights discourse and security humanitarianism. Crucially, the historicism of current human rights and security humanitarianism with respect to the sacrificial past evacuates history; it limits our awareness about particular moments of historical injustice that would inspire us to do something about it here and now, including forcing a resolution to overcome our habit of keeping what we already have at all costs.

This kind of historical awareness is the basis of remedial equality, as Baxi, Ghai and Twining, among others, explain. 'It simply assumes that most inequality is the result of past history', says human rights theorist Robert Meister, 'and that most of history was bad'.[29] But once we start to correct for particular moments of historical injustice, we can legitimately ask: why should we not do away with inequality altogether? 'Were we to treat material equality as both an approximation and a cap on remedial justice,' Meister argues, 'then the most a disadvantaged group can legitimately desire is that its ongoing disadvantage be wiped out.'[30] And once we recognize that the many unequal advantages enjoyed by the beneficiaries of past injustice, such as Kennecott and Anaconda in the case of Chile, could not be justified starting now, then the obvious question becomes the one Allende asked in terms of a doctrine of excess profits: why not put law to revolutionary use? Start with the recovery of common sources of wealth, such as copper or oil, use the revenue to force a public discussion on the role of markets in society, and then, perhaps, decide that not all goods are properly valued as mere instruments of use or profit; this, of course, was the original point of the Amerindians' refusal to work and their tendency to give away their possessions.

Nowadays, we could, perhaps should, force such a discussion in the cases of knowledge and education, health, family life, nature and art. We need such a discussion, too, in the case of civil liberties or human and post-human rights and duties that attempt to regulate relations not only among humans but also between humans and nonhumans and entire ecosystems in the context of climate change. Certainly, we would agree that these things are not properly or completely valued only as commodities. The point is not so much to destroy property *tout court*, but rather the more humble one that 'some things in life are corrupted or degraded if turned into commodities'.[31] A similar train of thought led Allende to issue his doctrine on excess profits. At its basis lies the kind of historical and existential awareness of contingency that characterized Allende's political character and attitude more generally. Such awareness accompanied also Sartre's conception of genocide in 1968, and García Márquez and Cortázar's conclusion at the end of Russell II that historical justice is optional, and that, as the former put it, the time and place comes

[29] R. Meister, *After Evil*, 258. [30] Ibid.

[31] M. Sandel, *What Money Can't Buy. The Moral Limits of Markets* (Allen Lane, 2012) 10. Also, J. Cortázar, *Papeles Inesperados* (Alfaguara, 2013) 268–9, and against the widespread rejection of remedial justice on the basis that all history is irremediably catastrophic, 276 and 282–3.

'where the races condemned to one hundred years of solitude will have, at last and forever, a second opportunity on earth'.[32]

5. Rethinking rights for the world of multinational vampires

According to the Latin Americans taking part in Russell II, even though the US had not perpetrated the acts in Chile directly, it was privy to a broader counterrevolutionary framework that regarded all attempts to right historical wrongs and achieve remedial equality, carried out under a variety of names (liberation, Third World-ism, people's rights, democratic socialism, indigenous rights, armed struggle) as attacks against the US and its economic interests. Thus, the US government could be found guilty of all violence carried out in the name of anti-communism, with the *caveat* that the use of force directed by the Americans wasn't simply a case of Cold War paranoia, but rather responded to the economic projections of multinational corporations.

The understanding of rights was extended from the 'rights of man' to include 'people's rights', a notion that introduced into rights discourse the rules concerning permanent sovereignty over natural resources and the 'excess profits' legal doctrine, recognized by most countries in the UN General Assembly as the kernel of the project of permanent decolonization. Russell II further declared that the American government and the multinationals had created a state of 'permanent intervention and strategic domination with the intention to assure the highest economic benefits'.[33] The general state of permanent intervention and domination referred to in Russell II had its particular instantiation in the state of exception and internal war alleged by the Chilean Junta as justification for Allende's overthrow. In fact, the widespread use of the state of exception and other forms of legal exceptionality were understood by Russell II as constituting the legal–political framework within which the 'permanent militarization' of international relations and internal politics was justified in countries like Chile or Colombia *vis-à-vis* their American neighbours.

[32] G. García Márquez, 'La soledad de América Latina. Estocolmo, Suecia, 8 de diciembre 1982' in *Yo no vengo a decir un discurso* (Barcelona: Mondadori, 2010) 29. In that closing paragraph of his Nobel lecture, as at the outset, he refers to Allende's death. See also J. Cortázar, *Fantomas contra los vampiros multinacionales* (México: Excelsior, 1975) 58, and *Apéndice. Sentencia del Tribunal Russell II, 1974–1975*, 69–77, at 76. There is now an English translation of the text by J. Cortázar: *Fantomas versus the Multinational Vampires. An Attainable Utopia*, trans. by D. Kurnick (Los Angeles: Semiotext(e), 2014).

[33] *Tribunal Russell II Sobre la situación de los países de América Latina*, appendix to J. Cortázar, *Fantomas contra los vampiros multinacionales*, México, Excelsior, 1975, 71–7. There is a recent English edition, published by Semiotext(e) in 2014. The sentence is available in digital format at www.literaberinto.com/cortazar, accessed 28 September 2012. Available also, together with other highly relevant documents, in the archives of the Leilo Basso Foundation in Rome. See also, P. W. Kelly, *When the People Awake. The Transnational Solidarity Movement, the Pinochet Junta, and the Human Rights Moment of the 1970s*, University of Chicago: Latin American History Seminar, March 2009, 35, available at www.humanrights.uchicago.edu/Baro/PatrickWilliamKelly, accessed 15 July 2014.

According to the Tribunal, 'the application of such legal measures is caused by the pressure exercised on behalf of private interests . . . seeking to exploit natural resources'.[34] The connection made by the Tribunal between the discourse of legal exceptionalism, the increasing militarization of international/internal conflicts, and economic globalization under the auspices of multinationals, is central. For it reveals the creative influence of the critical language used in the 1940s by the Frankfurt legal advisers to the US team during the Nuremberg trials, combined with autochthonous discourses of permanent decolonization harking back at least to the revolutions of the nineteenth century and the legacy of indigenous resistance against conquest and colonization.

It is worth recalling that Frankfurt advisers like Otto Kircheimer and Herbert Marcuse had seen the defence of the economic liberty of powerful agents as the root cause of the violations that had taken place during the Nazi regime. This was, precisely, the view taken by the Russell II Tribunal. For them, just as in the 1930s, the political representatives of extractive industries and capitalist interests had demanded tolerance for their intolerant positions and defended liberties that in fact sowed the seeds of exploitative oppression. From the 1970s onwards, the self-defined defenders of market liberties appealed to a quasi-theological discourse that combined religious and market libertarianism, and interpreted such liberties in the spirit of orthodox radicalism: as the natural law and order of the one true faith, and the only alternative.

In the case of Latin America, such a discourse had been inspired by the conservative and restorative ideologies of 1930s Europe, chief among them fascism and Iberian falangism. Conservative forces directed these against progressive attempts to create a social sector of the economy that could coexist with, but also limit, the expansionist tendencies of the (globalized) private sector of the economy, while avoiding the shortcomings of a *dirigiste* public sector. In Chile, the so-called 'Social Area' would comprise the copper mining industries, nitrates, iron and coal, recently nationalized under the 'permanent sovereignty' and 'excess profits' legal doctrines. It would also include part of the finance sector, commerce and trade, strategic monopolies, and the economic activities that conditioned social and economic development, such as energy and oil, construction, communications, paper, and transport. To operate this Social Area, alongside an area of private property and another one of mixed property, was a daunting task. It required, as Chilean jurist and Allende's chief advisor Eduardo Novoa Monreal put it, 'the invention of new blueprints for development oriented towards the construction of socialism'.[35]

The fact that a lawyer was one of the main architects of the Chilean Way in government is not without consequence. The 'blueprint' for the creation of the Social Area was to be a legal one, put into practice under the auspices of

[34] J. Cortázar, *Fantomas contra los vampiros multinacionales*, 73.
[35] E. Novoa Monreal et al., *La vía chilena al socialismo* (México: Siglo XXI, 1973) 44.

existing domestic legal powers and the relevant rules of international law at the time. Beginning with the epoch-making UN Declaration on the Granting of Independence to Colonial Countries and Peoples in 1960, the declared equivalence between independence (or self-determination) and human and peoples' rights, based on solidarity between peoples seeking independence for the sake of a new humanity beyond the confines of national borders, centred around issues of development and economic independence. This is why it is possible to speak today of at least two fundamentally opposed traditions of human rights and internationalism emerging out of the post-war context of the first half of the twentieth century.

On the one hand, there was the position maintained in the 1950s by colonial and neo-colonial powers that they could bind themselves to human rights in a legal covenant without fear that this would mean that the UN, especially its more pluralistic General Assembly, could interfere in their affairs. As a Belgian delegate put it at the time, in accordance with this position, human rights 'presuppose a high degree of civilisation ... often incompatible with the ideas of peoples who had not yet reached a high degree of development'. In accordance with statements such as this, rights should be understood as the exclusive province of developed (that is, colonial and neo-colonial, mostly Western) countries. To allow their use by underdeveloped peoples, for instance against their condition as subjects of empire or economic dependence, would be an attempt 'to lead them abruptly to the point which the civilised nations of today had only reached after a lengthy period of development'.[36] The link between development and rights in this view is but a repetition of the narrative that maintains that there are two sorts of people in the world and only one of them (the civilized, Judeo-Christian part) should inherit the earth and benefit from its riches. It keeps the applicability of human rights and economic independence or self-determination out of the picture, out of empire, and out of any meaningful discussion about the principles of government and global governance.

Though, at first, this was the position shared by some of the drafters of the Universal Declaration of 1948, e.g. Eleanor Roosevelt and the French jurist René Cassin, it did not prevail. A second position, beginning in the second half of the twentieth century, linked economic independence or self-determination with discourses of rights. This was a bid to take nineteenth-century ideas of the Rights of Man and the post-war construction of human rights in a more historically just direction: to bring about a new and more inclusive humanity, which would count within it the peoples who had for so long been considered backward, or not to have reached the right degree of development. This position built on nineteenth-century examples of wider legal universalism, such as those present in the 1804 Haitian Constitution written after the slave

[36] S. Moyn, *The Last Utopia. Human Rights in History* (The Belknap Press at Harvard University, 2012) 96.

revolution of 1801. Specifically, this position drew on the experience common to the majority of peoples in the world, that 'under the rule of powers which regarded themselves as qualified to teach others lessons, the world had known only oppression, aggression and bloodshed', as it was put by an Afghani delegate during the heated 1952 debates of the UN General Assembly on this issue.[37]

A corollary of this position, developed by rights theorists and anti-racism activists in the 1960s such as Frantz Fanon, was that former and current colonial and neo-colonial powers had a duty to pay reparations to plundered peoples, and the latter had a correlative right to apply forms of remedial justice and equality at the level of global transfers of capital that resulted, and still result, from the more or less overt use of violence by such powers. In October 1963, Argentinean economist and diplomat Raúl Prebisch, a powerful presence in the UN, coined the term 'new international economic order' in order to refer to the concrete actions and reforms that it would be necessary to undertake at the level of the rules of international relations in order to make north–south relations more equal.[38] These were the 'new blueprints for development' referred to by Novoa Monreal in Chile in the 1970s.[39]

6. Conclusion: voices for a human rights future in a post-human world

It is worth remembering the voices heard at the Russell II Tribunal. In the course of its deliberations, Salvador Allende's 1972 speech at the UN General Assembly on nationalization and the legal doctrine of excess profits were linked with the work of the *dependentista* economists, the Chilean and Latin American experience of the 1970s and the critical strands within the Nuremberg trials. These were brought to bear on the grim reality of a world in which a minority literally sucks the life out of the majority.

Writers like Cortázar had no illusions about the power of the Russell Tribunal or the human and peoples' rights discourse it helped to develop. In the absence of 'even a handful of [United Nations] Blue Helmets to stand between the bucket of shit and the prisoner's head', he said, it was difficult to avoid feeling that the human rights culture coming after the previous 'exceptional' emergency was simply not enough.[40] In coming to terms with what

[37] S. Moyn, *The Last Utopia. Human Rights in History*, 97.

[38] Edgar J. Dosman, *The Life and Times of Raúl Prebisch, 1901–1986* (Montreal, London and Ithaca: McGill-Queen's University Press, 2008) 485–6. See David Pollock, Daniel Kerner and Joseph L. Love, 'Raúl Prebisch on ECLAC's Achievements and Deficiencies: An Unpublished Interview' in *Revista CEPAL*, 75, December 2011, 9–22, at 19 and 21. See also S. Griffith-Jones, J. A. Ocampo and J. Stiglitz, 'Introduction' in *Time for a Visible Hand: Lessons from the 2008 World Financial Crisis* (Oxford University Press, 2010) p. I.

[39] Oscar Guardiola-Rivera, *Story of a Death Foretold. The Coup Against Salvador Allende, 11 September 1973* (London, New Delhi & New York: Bloomsbury) ch. 13.

[40] J. Cortázar, *Fantomas contra los vampiros multinacionales*, available at www.literaberinto.com /cortazar, accessed 13 August 2012.

happened in Chile, the members of Russell II confronted a fork in the road. They could either go down the road of a human rights culture, prosecuting others to show that theirs is not a culture of impunity – but this was a road based on feelings of impotence, guilt about always being too late and an anxiety to pre-empt the next holocaust – or else they could go down the road that started in Nuremberg, passing through the events of 11 September 1973 in Chile. This shows the way to the future: to encourage underlings and whistle-blowers to document and question illegal orders and bad laws; to bring to justice the politically and economically more powerful; to make justice more, rather than less, urgent; not to disavow the dreams and desires of the many on which their past struggles were based; and to provide the conditions for the development of what Baxi has called 'crimes against development'. These would be directed against the more favoured everywhere, and would establish a prosecuting counsel ready to act against old and new tyrants, including our less recognizable economic tyrants, north as well as south.

To their credit, the members of Russell II went for the second option. In the earlier part of the twentieth century it had become clear, thanks to the work of critical theorists informing the prosecution team during the Nuremberg trials, that we could not speak of Nazism (and thus also of racism) without referring to global capitalism as well.[41] Similarly, thanks to the work of Southern voices such as those that gathered at Russell II in the second half of the twentieth century, we cannot think of modernity, law and globalization without considering also colonialism and the decolonial turn of the majority of the peoples of the world.

Twining's Southern Voices project indicated that the majority of the peoples of the world have expressed themselves in a complex language. This language of pluralism, Third World-ism, popular coalition politics, decolonial and Southern turn, and transformative uses of law such as those made in Chile between 1970 and 1973, builds on the legacy of critical theory's involvement in the Nuremberg trials.[42] The Inseparability Thesis that emerged from Russell II is part of that legacy of human rights and Southern Voices. It asks that the claims of peoples and the many be given more weight than those of the wealthy and the powerful. In doing so, it recognizes that, for the most part, modern history has been written by the victors and is, therefore, not only biased, false, 'tending towards ethnocentrism' as Twining put it, but also uninspiring, incapable of producing human rights futures and making history.

From the standpoint taken in this paper, inspired by Twining's Southern Voices project, the mainstream story of law in modernity is biased and false also because it hides the fact of the impotence of the powerful and their

[41] See F. Neumann, H. Marcuse and O. Kircheimer, *Secret Reports on Nazi Germany: The Frankfurt School Contribution to the War Effort*, R. Laudani, ed., with a foreword by R. Geuss (Princeton University Press, 2013).

[42] See n. 11. See also U. Baxi, *Human Rights in a Post-human World: Critical Essays* (Oxford University Press, 2009).

ultimate inability to impose their laws. As Eduardo Mendieta says, echoing the best of contemporary critical theory and the Southern turn of people like Twining and de Sousa Santos, 'modernity is the Aesopian name for a violent historical process in which colonialism, genocide, and ecocide went hand in hand with two other fundamental processes: the spiritual conquest of the peoples to be subjugated, and what we can call epistemic gerrymandering'.[43] Conversely, the fable of law and modernity tells a tale that dismisses the actions of those who are attaining existence and liberty, and 'who prove every day, precisely, that the greatest power in the world is incapable of imposing its laws', as Sartre put it.[44]

If the writing of modern Western legal theory and history has at least contributed to maintaining the conditions of non-existence of the peoples of the non-Western world, then in different but related ways, Sartre, the writers of Russell II, Twining, de Sousa Santos, Mendieta and others are describing the fable of modernity as a process of inscription, individuating people, selecting some and deselecting others from a more integral unity of humanity. But these people in turn seek to negotiate, escape from and radically transform the laws imposed upon them, all the while transforming themselves.

[43] E. Mendieta, 'Imperial Somatics and Genealogies of Religion: How We Never Became Secular' in *Postcolonial Philosophy of Religion*, P. Bilimoria and A. B. Irvine (eds), 231. He refers to the cartographies, cosmographies and other technical graphs and processes of inscription (from grammar to money) described by W. Mignolo in his *The Darker Side of the Renaissance: Literacy, Territoriality, and Colonization* (The University of Michigan Press, 1995).

[44] J.-P. Sartre, *Il n'y a plus de dialogue posible*, 18–19.

Part II
Globalizations

6

Towards a socio-legal theory of indignation

Boaventura de Sousa Santos[1]

In this chapter, I present a rough draft of a socio-legal theory of law in the light of the newest wave of social protests that took place between 2011 and 2013 in different countries and regions of the world. They were so intense and dispersed in 2011 that Christopher Chase-Dunn (in 2013)[2] characterized this period as the 'World Revolution 2011', a date equivalent to other important eruptions of popular mobilization and protest, such as 1789, 1848, 1917, 1968 and 1989, leading on to structural changes in the world at large. I start by characterizing these social protests by identifying their different genealogies. I then present the challenges they pose to the critical theories of law in general and specifically to those proposed by William Twining and myself. In the third part I suggest what I call a sociology of emergences[3] in order to construct the socio-legal theory of law that might be implicit in the social protests. In the final part, I try to respond to the challenges concerning my own theorizing and speculate on what Twining's response might look like.

1. The indignation revolts

The protests I have in mind are the Arab Spring in North Africa and the Middle East,[4] the Occupy Wall Street movement, subsequently

[1] This paper was completed in the framework of the research project 'ALICE – Strange Mirrors, Unsuspected Lessons' (alice.ces.uc.pt), co-ordinated by me at the Center for Social Studies (CES) of the University of Coimbra, Portugal. The Project has received funding from the European Research Council under the European Union's Seventh Framework Programme (FP/2007-2013)/ ERC Grant Agreement n. 269807. A first version of this paper was presented to the *World Congress of Sociology of Law*, Toulouse, 3 September 2013. In preparing this version, I benefited from the precious comments of Christopher McCrudden, Upendra Baxi, Abdul Paliwala and Maria Irene Ramalho, and from the research assistance of Margarida Gomes.

[2] Christopher Chase-Dunn, 'The World Revolution of 2011: Assembling a United Front of the New Global Left', *IROWS Working Paper #82* (2013) irows.ucr.edu/papers/irows82/irows82.htm accessed 8 July 2013.

[3] Boaventura de Sousa Santos, *Epistemologies of the South. Justice against Epistemicide* (Boulder -London: Paradigm Publishers, 2014) [hereafter, Santos 2014].

[4] John R. Bradley, *After the Arab Spring: How Islamists Hijacked the Middle East Revolts* (New York: Palgrave Macmillan, 2012) [hereafter, Bradley 2012a]; and *The New Arab Revolt: What Happened, What It Means, and What Comes Next* (New York: The Council on Foreign Relations, 2012) [hereafter, Bradley 2012b]. See also Lynn Noueihed and Alex Warren, *The Battle for the Arab Spring: Revolution, Counter-Revolution and the Making of a New Era* (New Haven: Yale University Press,

expanding to many other cities in the USA,[5] the *indignados* movement in Southern Europe[6] and finally, in June 2013, the massive

2012); Kenneth M. Pollack, *The Arab Awakening: America and the Transformation of the Middle East* (New York: Brookings Institution Press 2011); K. Seigneurie, 'Discourses of the 2011 Arab Revolutions', *Journal of Arabic Literature* (2012) 43, pp. 484–509; Kurt Weyland, 'The Arab Spring: Why the Surprising Similarities with the Revolutionary Wave of 1848?', *Perspectives on Politics* (2012) 10/4, pp. 917–34; Nirvana Tanoukhi and Ali Mazrui, 'Arab Spring and the Future of Leadership in North Africa', *Transition* (2011) 106 Side A: Fifty Years, pp. 148–62; Randall Kuhn, 'On the Role of Human Development in the Arab Spring', *Population and Development Review* (2012) 38(4), pp. 649–83.

5 Jenny Pickerill and John Krinsky, 'Why Does Occupy Matter?', *Social Movement Studies: Journal of Social, Cultural and Political Protest* (2012) 11, pp. 279–87; Chris Hedges, 'The Revolutionaries in Our Midst', *Truthdig* (2013) www.truthdig.com/report/item/the_revolutionaries_in_our_midst_20131110 accessed 10 November 2013; Ronald Walter Greene and Kevin Douglas Kuswa, 'From the Arab Spring to Athens, From Occupy Wall Street to Moscow: Regional Accents and the Rhetorical Cartography of Power', *Rhetoric Society Quarterly* (2012) 42:3, pp. 271–88; Lee Edelman, 'Occupy Wall Street: "Bartleby" Against the Humanities', *History of the Present* (2013) 3/1, pp. 99–118; Craig Calhoun, 'Occupy Wall Street in perspective', *British Journal of Sociology* (2013) 64 (1), pp. 27–38; Todd Gitlin, *Occupy Nation, the Roots: The Spirit and the Promise of Occupy Wall Street* (New York: Harper Collins Publishers, 2012); Todd Gitlin, 'Occupy's Predicament: The Moment and the Prospect for the Movement', *British Journal of Sociology* (2013) 64 (1), pp. 3–25 [hereafter, Gitlin 2013a]; Todd Gitlin, 'Reply to Craig Calhoun', *The British Journal of Sociology* (2013) 64 (1), pp. 39–43 [hereafter, Gitlin 2013b]; Bernard Harcourt, 'Political Disobedience', *Critical Inquiry* (2012) 39 (1), pp. 33–55; Janet Byrne, ed., *The Occupy Handbook* (New York: Back Bay Books, 2012); Keith Gessen, Sarah Leonard, Carla Blumenkranz, Mark Greif, Astra Taylor, Sarah Resnick, Nikil Saval and Eli Schmitt (eds), *Occupy! Scenes from Occupied America* (New York: Verso, 2011); Sarah van Gelder, ed., *This Changes Everything: Occupy Wall Street and the 99% Movement* (San Francisco: Berrett-Koehler, 2011); Writers for the 99%, *Occupying Wall Street: The Inside Story of an Action That Changed America* (New York: O/R Books, 2012); Alasdair Roberts, 'Why the Occupy Movement Failed' *Public Administration Review* (2012), pp. 754–62; W. J. T. Mitchell, 'Image, Space, Revolution: The Arts of Occupation', *Critical Inquiry* (2012) 39, pp. 8–32; Michael Taussig, 'I'm so Angry I Made a Sign', *Critical Inquiry* (2012) 39, pp. 56–88; Mignon Nixon, 'Anatomic Explosion on Wall Street', *October* (2012) 142, pp. 3–25; Jenny Pickerill and John Krinsky, 'Why Does Occupy Matter?', *Social Movement Studies: Journal of Social, Cultural and Political Protest* (2012) 11 (3–4), pp. 279–87.

6 On the protest and mobilizations in Spain, Portugal and Greece, see SuNotissima, Quodlibetat, Axebra, Arnau Monty, TakeTheSquare, Alcazan, Toret and Simona Levi, *Tecnopolítica, Internet y R-Evoluciones. Sobre la Centralidad de Redes Digitales en el #15M* (Barcelona: Icaria, 2012); Ernesto Castañeda, 'The Indignados of Spain: A Precedent to Occupy Wall Street', *Social Movement Studies: Journal of Social, Cultural and Political Protest* (2012) 11 (3–4), pp. 1–11; Ángel Calle Collado, ed., *Democracia radical. Entre vínculos y utopías* (2011) Icaria, Barcelona and 'Las naturalezas (ya no tan subterráneas) del 15M', *Viento Sur* (2012) 123, pp. 61–9; G. Charnock, T. Purcell, and R. Ribera-Fumaz, *The Limits to Capital in Spain: Crisis and Revolt in the European South* (New York: Palgrave Macmillan 2014); Marta Cruells, and Pedro Ibarra (eds.), *La democracia del futuro. Del 15M a la emergencia de una sociedad civil viva* (Barcelona: Icaria. 2013); Mayo Fuster Morell, 'The Free Culture and 15M Movements in Spain: Composition, Social Networks and Synergies', *Social Movement Studies: Journal of Social, Cultural and Political Protest* (2012) 11 (3–4), pp. 386–92; María José Gámez Fuentes, 'Feminisms and the 15M Movement in Spain: Between Frames of Recognition and Contexts of Action', *Social Movement Studies: Journal of Social, Cultural and Political Protest* (2015) 1, pp. 1–7; Sandra González-Bailón, et al., 'Broadcasters and Hidden Influentials in Online Protest Diffusion', *American Behavioral Scientist* (2013) 57 (7), p. 943–65; Kostis Kornetis, 'Is there a future in this past? Analyzing 15M's intricate relation to the Transición', *Journal of Spanish Cultural Studies* (2014), pp. 1–16; Pablo La Parra Pérez, 'Revueltas lógicas: el ciclo de movilización del 15M y la práctica de la democracia radical', *Journal of Spanish Cultural Studies* (2014), pp. 1–19; I. Peña-López, M. Congosto and P. Aragón, 'Spanish Indignados and the evolution of 15M: towards

protests in Brazil around public transportation and public services in general.[7]

It is not my purpose to develop a full characterization of the different revolts and protests, their historical context, social composition, political orientation, forms of mobilization, discourses and narratives of resistance and alternative. I will limit myself to a few analytical observations that may help to ground the main argument of this chapter. In the last forty years, Western-centric theories of social movements have proposed a key distinction between old and new social movements.[8] Though differing on many issues, such theories tend to

networked para-institutions' in J. Balcells, A. Cerrillo y Martínez, M. Peguera, I. Peña-López, M. J. Pifarré de Moner and M. Vilasau (eds), *Big Data: Challenges and Opportunities*, Proceedings of the 9th International Conference on Internet, Law & Politics. Universitat Oberta de Catalunya (Barcelona: UOC-Huygens Editorial, 2013), pp. 359–86; Carlos Taibo, 'The Spanish *Indignados*: A Movement with Two Souls', *European Urban and Regional Studies* (2013) 20, pp. 155–8; Raimundo Viejo Viñas, 'Indignación. Política de movimiento, nueva ola de movilizaciones y crisis de representación' in Prats Rivas, E. Fermín, María de los Ángeles Mascott Sánchez and Efrén Arellano Trejo (eds), *La actuación del legislativo en los tiempos de crisis* (México: CESOP, 2012), pp. 123–56; José Manuel Mendes, 'Movimentos Sociais e Cidadania Crítica em Portugal: da Reelitização à Emancipação Social?', *Le Monde Diplomatique* (2013) Portuguese Edition, August 2013; Dimitrios Theodossopoulos, 'Infuriated with the Infuriated? Blaming Tactics and Discontent about the Greek Financial Crisis', *Current Anthropology* (2013) 54 (2), pp. 200–21; Carles Feixa, Inês Pereira and Jeffrey Juris, 'Global citizenship and the "New, New" social movements Iberian connections', *Young November* (2009) 2 17, pp. 421–42 [hereafter Feixa, Pereira and Juris, 2009]; Monedero, Juan Carlos, '¿A dónde va el 15M? Viento en las velas del movimiento', *Comiendo Tierra* (2013), www.comiendotierra.es/2013/05/15/a-donde-va-el-15m-viento-en-las-velas-del-movimiento accessed 15 May 2013; Julia Nuño de la Rosa, 'Movimientos sociales y democracia al otro lado del espejo: entrevista a Antoni Aguiló', *Oxímora* (2014) 4, pp. 111–25; Carlos Antonio Aguirre Rojas, 'Las revueltas populares de 2011 en perspectiva histórica', *Rebelión* (2012), www.rebelion.org/docs/146953.pdf accessed 26 March 2012. See also Cristina Fominaya Flesher, 'Debunking Spontaneity: Spain's 15-M/Indignados as Autonomous Movement', *Social Movement Studies: Journal of Social, Cultural and Political Protest* (2014) 14 (2), pp. 1–22 [hereafter, Fominaya Flesher 2014a]; *Social Movements and Globalization: How Protests, Occupations and Uprisings are Changing the World* (Basingstoke: Palgrave Macmillan, 2014) [hereafter, Fominaya Flesher 2014b] and 'España es diferente: Podemos y el 15-MPart', *Público* (2014) blogs.publico.es/el-cuarto-poder-en-red/2014/06/09/espana-es-diferente-podemos-y-el-15-m accessed 9 June 2014) [hereafter, Fominaya Flesher 2014c].

7 Pedro Fiori Arantes, 'Da (Anti) Reforma Urbana brasileira a um novo ciclo de lutas nas cidades', *Correio da Cidadania* (2013), www.correiocidadania.com.br/index.php?option=com_content&view=article&id=9047%3Asubmanchete091113&catid=72%3Aimagens-rolantes accessed 8 November 2013; Carlos Vainer, 'Mega-Eventos, Mega-Negócios, Mega-Protestos. Uma Contribuição ao Debate sobre as Grandes Manifestações e as Perspectivas Políticas', *ETTERN* (2013), www.ettern.ippur.ufrj.br/ultimas-noticias/196/mega-eventos-mega-negocios-mega-protestos accessed 24 June 2013; Marco Weissheimer, 'Não há um "movimento" em disputa, mas uma multidão sequestrada por fascistas', *Carta Maior* (2013), cartamaior.com.br/?/Coluna/Nao-ha-um-'movimento'-em-disputa-mas-uma-multidao-sequestrada-por-fascistas/28748 accessed 21 June 2013; Carlos Porto-Gonçalves and Fernando Luís Monteiro Soares, 'Sejamos realistas, exijamos... que se vayan todos... Pela Reinvenção da Política' *Contrapunto* (Montevideo: Centro de Formación Popular del Oeste de Montevideo Comisión Sectorial de Extensión y Actividades en el Médio Universidad de la República, 2013); Denílson Araújo Oliveira, 'Algumas palavras sobre as manifestações e conflitos sociais no Rio de Janeiro a partir de Junho de 2013', *Ensaios de Geografia* (2013) 2 (3).

8 Doug McAdam, John McCarthy and Mayer N. Zald (eds), *Comparative Perspectives on Social Movements Political Opportunities, Mobilizing Structures, and Cultural Framings* (New York: Cambridge University Press, 1996); Doug McAdam, Sidney Tarrow and Charles Tilly, *Dynamics*

agree on labelling the labour movement as old, and the movements that emerged in the late sixties of the past century, in the aftermath of the student movement, as new, such as the women's, ecological, peace, gay and lesbian movements. According to such theories, the old movements emerged from the contradictions of industrial society. They are working-class-or lower-class-based, and are focused on economic or materialistic issues (production and distribution issues). They seek to have an impact on public policy and, thus, on the state as well. The new social movements emerged from the contradictions of post-industrial society. They are old or new middle-class-based (peripheral to or outside of the labour market). They are less interested in politics in the narrow sense of party politics (civil society orientation) and they focus instead on cultural, life style, identity issues (social reproduction and life world issues). Although organized along very different logics, both old and new movements have some degree of institutionalization, even if the new social movements tend to resist bureaucratization. Even though they may organize protests and campaigns of different types, they are not reducible to them.

I have criticized, elsewhere, some of the analytical and conceptual ideas grounding these characterizations.[9] Here I would like to focus on the double Western-centric character of these theories. Even if the two types of movements may coexist in a given country at a given time, the categories used ('old' and 'new') point to an historical sequence. This sequence may indeed correspond to the sociological and political realities of the global North (Europe and North America) but it has very little to do with the social conditions elsewhere. In the global South – most of which was under European colonial rule until the mid-twentieth century or even the late twentieth century, in the case of countries subjected to Portuguese colonialism – and even in the Southern European countries that were subjected to fascistic dictatorships for many decades, old and new social movements emerged virtually at the same time. Moreover, the distinction between materialistic and non-materialistic issues is highly problematic outside the global North.[10] There are many movements

of Contention (New York: Cambridge University Press, 2001); J. Habermas, 'New Social Movements', *Telos* (1981) 49: 33–37; Alain Touraine, 'An Introduction to the Study of Social Movements' *Social Research* (1985) 52 (4), pp. 749–87; Ernesto Laclau, 'New Social Movements and the Plurality of the Social', in David Slater, ed., *New Social Movements and the State in Latin America* (Amsterdam: CEDLA, 1985); Chantal Mouffe, 'Towards a theoretical interpretation of New Social Movements' in S. Hanninen and L. Paldán (eds), *Rethinking Marx* (Berlin: Argument-Sonderband, 1984), pp. 139–43; Alberto Melucci, 'The New Social Movements: A Theoretical Approach', *Social Science Information* (1980) 19, pp. 199–226.

9 Boaventura de Sousa Santos, *The Rise of the Global Left* (London: Zed Books, 2006) [hereafter, Santos 2006].

10 Referring specifically the case of Brazil, Bernd Reiter affirms that the concept of 'new social movements' characterized by a focus on identity cannot readily be transferred to a Latin American context. Latin America never experienced the postmaterialist turn that led some to call certain European social movements 'new'. In addition, as the case of black organizing in Brazil demonstrates, identity-based Latin American social movements are much older than the literature suggests. What was indeed a Latin American novelty of the 1980s was the massive emergence of nongovernmental organizations (NGOs). In the case of Brazil, these

that, on the surface, by their thematic or type of organization, may be labelled as new movements; yet they are, indeed, involved in political economy issues, issues of production and distribution, which directly confront the capitalist state. For example, ecological movements throughout the global South are struggling against megaprojects, land grabbing, deforestation and the depletion of natural resources; they seek to defend their ancestral rights to water, land and territory. Theirs is an 'ecologism of the poor', as Joan Martinez Alier calls it,[11] involving materialistic or economic issues as well as cultural, identity or life style issues.

In the last decade, and following the same sequencing logic, a third category of social movements has emerged: the 'newest social movements',[12] or the '*new* new social movements'.[13] Richard Day[14] has forcefully argued that the radical activism that emerged in late 1990s and early 2000s represents a new type of collective actions characterized by its radical stance, although it has roots reaching back to the new social movements of the 1960s – feminisms, the US civil rights movement, Red Power, anticolonialism, gay and lesbian struggles – as well as further back to 'older' traditions of Marxist and anarchist socialism. He has in mind the protests in Seattle in 1999 against the World Trade Organization (WTO) during the meeting of the G8 countries. According to him, these mark the point at which a new militancy erupted onto the surface of an otherwise serene liberal democratic polity. These were followed in the next decade by many mobilizations of similar and different types but always guided by autonomist, anarchist repertoires of struggle.

organizations emerged in response to new financial opportunities provided by international donors and the coercive and paternalistic actions of states, a reality that the concept of new social movements is unable to capture. Both the long history of identity-based organizing and the emergence of NGOs can be explained by focusing on political opportunities and changing protest repertoires (Bernd Reiter, 'What's New in Brazil's "New Social Movements?"', *Latin American Perspectives* (2011) 38 (1), pp. 153–68).

[11] Joan Martinez Alier, *The Environmentalism of the Poor: A Study of Ecological Conflicts and Valuation* (Cheltenham: Edward Elgar Publishing Ltd, 2003).

[12] I myself have used this category, however, in a deviant or heterodox way. Dissatisfied with the cultural turn of critical theory in the 1980s, and particularly with its excessive focus on civil society (a very problematic concept for me), Boaventura de Sousa Santos, *Toward a New Legal Common Sense. Law, globalization, and emancipation* (London: Butterworths, 2002), at p. 457 [hereafter, Santos 2002], and the corresponding abandonment of the problematic of the state, transformed into the privileged topic and target of conservative thinking, I wrote on the 'state as the newest social movement' in the hope of steering critical theory and left politics into the direction of 'rethinking' and 'refounding the state'. See also Boaventura de Sousa Santos and José Luis Exeni, ed., *Justicia Indígena, Plurinacionalidad e Interculturalidad en Bolivia* (Quito: Ediciones Abya Yala y Fundación Rosa Luxemburg, 2012) [hereafter, Santos and Exeni 2012] and Boaventura de Sousa Santos and Agustin Grijalva, ed., *Justicia Indígena, Plurinacionalidad e Interculturalidad en Ecuador* (Quito: Ediciones Abya Yala y Fundación Rosa Luxemburg, 2012) [hereafter, Santos and Grijalva 2012].

[13] Pereira Feixa and Juris 2009 (emphasis added).

[14] Richard Day, *Gramsci is Dead: Anarchist Currents in the Newest Social Movements* (London: Pluto Press, 2005), at pp. 1–15 [hereafter, Day 2005].

Generally speaking, these mobilizations are of the same type as those that inspired the use of the Spinozian concept of 'multitude' by Toni Negri and Michael Hardt in *Empire*.[15] But Day rejects the concept because, in his view, 'a global proletariat seems very difficult to reconcile with postmarxist critiques of a politics that gives centrality to the struggles of the working class, and with anti-racist feminist calls for the decolonization of theory and the practice of solidarity across all axes of oppression.'[16] According to Day, 'contemporary radical activism does not seek a return to the theory and practice of the Old Left of the nineteenth and early twentieth centuries, or even to the New Left of the 1960s to 1980s. There is something else going on here, something different, which I try to indicate by sometimes using the term *newest social movements* to describe those currents in which I am most interested.'[17]

Day argues further that the newest social movements are radical in that they seek fundamental change. They want to address not just the *content* of current modes of domination and exploitation but also the *forms* that give rise to them. Thus, for example, rather than seeking self-government within a settler state, a radical indigenous politics challenges the European notion of sovereignty upon which the system of states is built. Contemporary radical activism, then, pushes beyond the possibilities and limits of liberal reform, while not entirely discrediting attempts to alter the *status quo*. It rejects any politics of integration or inclusion in the existing political and social structures and, therefore, any attempt at reforming or transforming the state. It focuses on small-scale experiments in the construction of alternative modes of social, political and economic organization as they offer a way both to avoid waiting forever for the Revolution to come, *and* perpetuating existing structures through reformist demands. 'By avoiding making demands in the first place, it offers a way out of the cycle through which requests for "freedom" or "rights" are used to justify an intensification of the societies of discipline and control.'[18] Day echoes John Holloway's[19] manifesto on changing the world without taking power, inspired by the Neo-Zapatistas. Day emphasizes that rather than getting involved in power politics, the new radical activists strive to recover, establish or enhance their ability to determine the conditions of *their own* existence, while allowing and encouraging others to do the same.[20]

This analysis has been criticized on several grounds.[21] Although it captures well the autonomist, neo-anarchist nature of some of the collective actions of

15 Michael Hardt and Antonio Negri, *Empire* (Cambridge, MA: Harvard University Press, 2000).

16 Day 2005, at p. 5. 17 Day 2005, at p. 5. 18 Day 2005, at p. 15.

19 John Holloway, *Change the World without Taking Power: The Meaning of Revolution Today* (London and Sterling, VA: Pluto Books, 2002) [hereafter, Holloway 2002].

20 For other analyses along the same lines, see, besides Holloway 2002, A. K. Thompson, 'You Can't Do Gender in a Riot: Violence and Post-Representational Politics', *Berkeley Journal of Sociology* (2008) 52, pp. 24–49.

21 See, for instance, Patnaik's critique of the critique of the Gramscian concept of hegemony undertaken by Day: Patnaik, Arun Kumar, 'Gramsci is Dead But Ressurected', *Economic and Political Review* (2008) 13, pp. 25–7. See also Ruth Reitan, 'Review Essay. A Global Civil Society

recent decades, it fails to offer an adequate picture of contemporary activism as a whole, a criticism that may equally be made of Negri's and Hart's analysis in *Empire*. In my own work on contemporary social and political struggles and mobilizations, I have adopted a more open-ended, epistemologically self-conscious and empirically-grounded approach, emphasizing the diversity and heterogeneity of the different forms of collective action.[22] Indeed, if we focus on the social movements and struggles that have occurred in the global South, many of the analytical categories (materialist versus cultural; old versus new versus newest; state- or community-oriented; autonomous versus power-oriented) are either inadequate or totally irrelevant. In the end, it is the epistemology guiding the analysis that must be subjected to critical scrutiny. This much I have been doing while proposing the 'epistemologies of the South'.[23] Along these lines, I tried to show in my analysis of the World Social Forum, and of the movements and organizations gathered around it, how the celebration of diversity does not prevent the emergence of some forms of convergence and articulation, however limited.[24]

For my purpose here, it is important at this point to raise the following issues. First, in order to do justice to the different forms of collective action occurring both in the global North and global South, we must understand that they are contemporary only in the trivial sense that they occur simultaneously. At a deeper level, each one of these actions is only contemporaneous with its own historical, social and political context, even if this context may be related in complex ways to other contexts. Different histories cannot sit comfortably with one single way of being in the here and now. A thick conception of contemporaneity must recognize the co-existence of different ways of being contemporaneous. The categories used to describe collective action emerging from different contexts must be used with some caution. As Edward Said[25] cautioned us in relation to theories, the categories do travel, but, if we do not pay attention to the conditions of the travel, we may end up with reductionist analyses; the methodological or categorial overload may barely hide the poverty of empirical understanding. If the present of different collective actions responds to different pasts (and probably calls for different futures), the description of action in the present involves also the description of present differences in these actions. An unreflective analysis of a given type of identity-oriented collective action may ignore the fact that identity means different things in different contexts and for different groups of people, and that, accordingly, political economy may be called upon to ground identity as much as culture or religion.

in a World Polity, or Angels and Nomads Against Empire?', *Global Governance* (2007) 13 (3), pp. 445–60.

[22] Santos 2006. [23] Santos 2014. [24] Santos 2006.

[25] Edward Said, 'Traveling Theory', *The World, the Text, and the Critic* (Cambridge, MA: Harvard University Press, 1983), pp. 226–47.

The second issue is that we must distinguish between protests and mobilizations, on the one hand, and movements and associations, on the other. The protests and revolts I am dealing with here can hardly be conceived of as social *movements*, since in general they lack the minimal institutionalization that guarantees the sustainability of action over time. Of course, movements, associations and organizations may be behind the protests (be they the Muslim Brotherhood in the Egyptian Arab Spring or the different 'barrio collectives' in the *indignados* movement in Spain). Moreover, protests and mobilizations may *lead* to new movements, association or organizations. Some of the autonomist-anarchist initiatives that Day mentions evolved from or were strengthened by the protests and mobilizations of the early 2000s. These autonomist associations or movements represent one of the paths of resistance against capitalism, colonialism and patriarchy, but they are far from representing the totality of 'contemporary radical activism' (more on this below). In terms of social activism (or lack of social activism, depending on expectations and frustrations), our time is a palimpsest in which different social experiences have been inscribed, one on top of the other; the new or even newest experiences reveal or hide the remnants of old experiences, either by selective recurrence or erasure, or by unrealistic promises of rupture and innovation. Such an accumulation of superimposed experiences should prepare us to be confronted with either the surprising resurrection of the dead or the premature death of hitherto exhilarating possibilities.

I have given the general name of 'indignation revolts' to the protests and mobilizations that took place in different regions of the world in 2011–13. I have designated them as collective presences,[26] rather than as movements, to underline several features that characterize them: their extra-institutional character, minimal organization, surprising appearance, real or apparent spontaneity of aggregation, volatility (the immense capacity to move from limited or local demands to ample and national demands) and, in general, ephemeral presence. The words 'dignity', 'indignation' and 'indignity' were used extensively in the protests. As used here, 'indignation' does not refer exclusively to the indignant (*indignados*) movement of Southern Europe. It is, rather, a general designation covering all the protests between 2011 and 2013 mentioned earlier, and it may be used to express the revulsion against an extremely unjust state of affairs ('indignation') and to characterize a state of affairs that deprives a person or a group of her or his basic human dignity ('indignity'). In Spinoza,[27] indignation is connected to the revolt of the multitude against unjust laws. Indignation is the anger generated in us by a wrong done to us or to another; there is no indignation without the belief that one has been wronged.[28] The register is ethical and mobilizes reasons and passions,

[26] Santos 2014, at p. 192.

[27] Benedictus de Spinoza, *Political Treatise* (trans. Samuel Shirley) (Indianapolis: Hackett, 2000).

[28] Given the frequency with which the idea of indignation appears in the protests and in current political affairs, it may be useful to elaborate on the concept as it is understood by Spinoza, one

both abundantly present in the protests. It puts the emphasis of the collective action on the radical rejection of a given *status quo* rather than on the imagination of a future, better society. It calls for rebellion or revolt rather than for revolution or reform. This negativity is at the core of the conception of law that is implicit in many of the protests, even though the significant differences between them may invite greater specification.

In general, we can identify in the protests the following features with more or less primacy or intensity.[29] First, there was indignation at the extreme social inequality in contemporary capitalist societies. The intensity of the denunciation is expressed in the polarization between the 1% society and the 99% society. This is a very old denunciation indeed. Consider the following quotation: 'If a man knew nothing about the lives of people in our Christian world and he were told, "There is a certain people who have set up such a way of life, that the greater part of them, ninety-nine per cent, or thereabouts, live in

of the modern Western philosophers who gave it more weight in ethical and political matters. Though indignation (*indignatio*) only appears nine times in Spinoza's writings (in Ethics and Political Treatise – see Emilia Giancotti, (1970) *Lexicon Spinozanum* (La Haye: Nijhoff) – it is a crucial concept in Spinozian philosophy. See Ted Stolze, 'Indignation: Spinoza on the Desire to Revolt', *Marxism 2000* (University of Massachusetts: Amherst, 2000); Pierre Macherey, *Introduction à l'Ethique de Spinoza, La cinquième partie: les voies de la liberation* (Paris: Presses Universitaires de France, 1994); and Alexandre Matheron, 'L'indignation et le conatus de l'état spinoziste' in Myriam Revault and Hadi Rizk (eds), *Spinoza: Puissance et Ontology* (Paris: Kimé, 1994), pp. 153–65; Alexandre Matheron, *Individu et communauté chez Spinoza* (Paris: Minuit, 1988). According to Spinoza, indignation is a passion that consists in 'a hate toward someone who has done evil to another', Benedictus de Spinoza, *Ethics, and Treatise on the Correction of the Intellect* (London: J. M. Dent, 1993), it is a sadness with the accompanying idea of an external cause. Whenever tyrants or, in general, oppressive regimes, act in such a way that incites general indignation, the latter may lead to revolt and the consequent destabilization of the regime. If it were not for indignation, tyrants could go on committing excesses and feel secure, as subjects would remain more and more afraid and isolated. As justly emphasized by Stolze, indignation is responsible for both the fall and the rise of states. Indignation is thus intimately related to both fear and hope. Being a sad passion, affect or emotion, indignation can only be converted into an active one if submitted to what Spinoza calls 'cognitive therapy' in the *Ethics*. Given the fact that passions contain elements of insight and belief, it is possible to transform them, through reason, into positive, richer or better insights and beliefs. Stolze speculates on how this cognitive therapy might work in the case of indignation: 'We would not so much try to purge ourselves of the effect of indignation as try to use reason to engage in an imaginative reconstruction of indignation's underlying causes in as a complete a manner as possible. Such reconstruction would have the dual effect of (a) transforming indignation as a sad affect into a joyous affect and (b) increasing our power to understand, act on, and perhaps even uproot the source of indignation' (Stolze, at p. 14). This may sound too optimistic, given the limits of rational knowledge in Spinoza. We should remember that the highest knowledge in Spinoza, the 'third kind of knowledge', is the intuitive knowledge of our emotions. On the limits of rational knowledge in Spinoza, see Herman DeDijn, 'Ethics IV: the ladder, not the top. The provisional morals of the philosopher' in Yovel, Yirmiyahu and Segal, Gideon (eds), *Ethics IV: Spinoza on Reason and the 'Free Man'. Papers Presented at the Fourth Jerusalem Conference* (New York, Little Room Press, 2004), pp. 37–56. For a psychological analysis of indignation see, for example, Daniel Kahneman and Cass Sunstein, 'Indignation: Psychology, Politics, Law', *John M. Olin Program in Law and Economics Working Paper* (2007) 346.

29 The following is an interpretive summary of the documentation found in the references mentioned in notes 4, 5, 6 and 7.

ceaseless physical labor and oppressive need, and the rest one per cent lives in idleness and luxury now, if that one-hundredth has its own religion, science and art, what would that religion, science and art be like?" I think that there can only be one answer: "A perverted, a bad religion, science and art".' Was this written in the aftermath of the Occupy movement? No, it was written by Leo Tolstoy, in his diary on 17 March 1910.[30]

Second, there was indignation at the rise and endurance of dictatorship, be it in the form of personal dictatorship (in the Arab Spring) or at the impersonal dictatorship (disguised as democracy) of financial markets and global finance capital (Occupy and the *indignados* movements). It dominates a democratic imaginary (not a socialist one), based on the distinction between the ideal of democracy (or 'real democracy') and the low intensity democracies in the realpolitik of our time.

Third, there was distrust of state and non-state institutions, and hence a preference for extra-institutional means of struggle. The protestors in democratic societies start from the assumption that democratic institutions have been 'occupied' by non-democratic dominant groups and interests. The institutions are in place but they are not performing the roles for which they were created. In light of this, we are entering a post-institutional epoch, in which political rather than civil disobedience is justified. The protesters take to the streets and squares because they are the only public spaces that have not been occupied by financial capital. Moreover, the deliberations to be made in the process of protesting and resisting must ideally be taken by means of direct democracy, assembly democracy, distrustful of leaders and spokespersons.

Fourth, the protests are in most cases peaceful, even when they have to resist police brutality. The cyberspace social networks were a key instrument for the aggregation and articulation of such resistance.

These general characteristics must not be understood as understating the significant differences among the protests and mobilizations of 2011 and 2013. I distinguish three genealogies: the Arab Spring; Southern European and Brazilian indignation; and the Occupy movements in the United States. The Arab Spring (itself comprising quite distinct protests and mobilizations) emerged out of the ruins of the Arab nationalism, a kind of populist nationalism whose most prominent leader was Gamal Abdel Nasser, President of Egypt from 1958 to 1970. In a Western world dominated by Islamophobia, the demand for democracy on the part of protestors and the associations supporting them was a comforting surprise. The *indignados* movements in Southern European emerged out of the serious crisis (the coming ruins?) of European social democracy. Social and economic rights, which seemed to be part of the DNA of the post-WWII European polity, began to be questioned, particularly after the financial crisis of 2008. In a few years, these were converted from being viewed as a necessity into becoming an unsustainable luxury that left the

[30] Leo Tolstoy, *Last Diaries* (New York: G. P. Putnam's Sons, 1960), at p. 66.

old and new middle classes on the verge of poverty and their children, the majority of whom with many years of schooling, without the prospect of a dignified future. In Brazil, the protests were also related to the crisis of the 'rights package' of social democracy. But while in Europe social democracy was older and based on universal entitlements, in Brazil social democracy was ten years old and was based on massive compensatory policies (means-tested bonuses of different types). Through these, some 50 million Brazilians entered the consumer society. But many of them became protesting citizens, once they were confronted with the contradiction between access to consumer products and lack of access to public services (health, education, transportation). In the United States, the protests and mobilizations represented the social and ideological bankruptcy of neoliberalism. Among all the protests and mobilizations, the Occupy movement was the one in which the negative politics of indignation reached its most intense formulation. The radical denunciation of extreme inequality and of the degeneration of democracy into a plutocracy, if not a kleptocracy, was so intense that no demands were made on the state. One may however wonder if, in an insidious way, neoliberalism was present with a vengeance in the protests in the vehement protestors' denunciation of the predator state, as well as their defence, as a core value, of individual and collective autonomy.

2. New challenges to the critical theories advanced by Twining and Santos

Critical theory is any kind of intellectual practice that does not reduce reality to what exists. It is based on the claim that much of non-existent reality is actually rendered non-existent by dominant, and even hegemonic, power-knowledge technologies and practices. Such suppressed reality consists of present and past experiences of unjust suffering, and of resistance against them in the name of alternative modes of being, knowing and living which might lead to putting an end to or minimizing this unjust suffering. Critical theory, to use my own terms, involves always an exercise in a sociology of absences and a sociology of emergences.[31] It is about memory (and history) as well as anticipation. Concerning memory, critical theory conceives of contemporary societies as more and more divided between two groups: on the one hand, those that cannot forget past wrongs; on the other, those that do not want to remember. (This is at a time of intense contradiction between postcolonial or decolonial thinking and activism, on the one hand, and the relentless reproduction, in old and new guises, of colonial and neocolonial global politics, on the other.) These groups enact, and are enacted by, opposing politics of individual and collective subjectivization of the past as either a solved or as an unsolved part of the present. Concerning anticipation, critical theory conceives of contemporary

[31] Santos 2014, at pp. 164–87.

societies as divided between two groups: between those that see the current state of affairs as the only game in town (the cynics) or as an irremediably corrupt game (the resigned), and those that either imagine and struggle for other possible games (the revolutionaries) or believe in and struggle for the possibility of fair rules in the existing game (the reformists). (This is at a time of aggressive ideological, political and military technologies aimed at ratifying the past of the present by converting the future in an endless repetition of the present.) These groups enact and are enacted by opposing politics of individual and collective subjectivization of the future as either a given or as a task.

Both in the case of memory (and history), as in the case of anticipation, the contradictory politics of subjectivization are enmeshed in conflicting knowledges and emotions. Concerning these epochal conditions and the politics they give rise to, critical theory distinguishes between objectivity and neutrality.[32] It seeks to produce trustworthy knowledge, both as a sociology of absences and as a sociology of emergences, that will potentially promote or strengthen the stances and struggles of those that cannot forget past wrongs, and those who either imagine and struggle for other possible games or believe in and struggle for the possibility of fair rules in the existing game.

I consider that Twining and I are both critical theorists in the broad sense defined above. We are both concerned with suppressed, 'absent' realities, non-Western experiences and 'Southern voices'. By not being recognized, our Western canons of certified reality and knowledge end up being impoverished and we fail to grasp how false the supposed globality or universality of such canons is. Both of us are unreconciled to this 'cognitive injustice', as I would call it,[33] and take an activist stance in giving voice to suppressed, silenced or simply neglected voices.[34] Our common ground of inquiry is 'law in society' or 'law in context', even if, in my case, law shares my field of interests with politics and modern science. Our disciplinary loyalties are different: legal theory and jurisprudence, in the case of Twining, and sociology of law, in my case. Our

[32] Boaventura de Sousa Santos, 'A Critique of Lazy Reason: Against the Waste of Experience' in Wallerstein, Immanuel, ed., *The Modern World-System in the Longue Durée* (London: Paradigm Publishers, 2004), pp. 157–97 and Santos 2014.

[33] Santos 2014, at pp. 19–46.

[34] William Twining, *Globalisation and Legal Theory* (London: Butterworth, 2000) [hereafter, Twining 2000]; William Twining, ed., *Human Rights: Southern Voices* (Cambridge University Press, 2009) [hereafter, Twining 2009a]; William Twining, *General Jurisprudence: Understanding Law from a Global Perspective* (Cambridge University Press, 2009) [hereafter, Twining 2009b]; Boaventura de Sousa Santos, *Toward a New Common Sense: Law, Science and Politics in the Paradigmatic Transition* (New York: Routledge, 1995) [hereafter, Santos 1995]; Santos 2002; Boaventura de Sousa Santos and César Rodríguez-Garavito (eds), *Law and Globalization from Below. Towards a Cosmopolitan Legality* (Cambridge University Press, 2005) [hereafter, Santos and Rodríguez-Garavito 2005]; Boaventura de Sousa Santos, ed., *Democratizing Democracy. Beyond the Liberal Democratic Canon.* (London: Verso, 2005); Boaventura de Sousa Santos, ed., *Another Production is Possible. Beyond the Capitalist Canon* (London: Verso, 2006); Boaventura de Sousa Santos, ed., *Another Knowledge is Possible. Beyond Northern Epistemologies* (London: Verso, 2007); Boaventura de Sousa Santos, ed., *Voices of the World* (London: Verso, 2010), and Santos 2014.

differences are both substantive and the product of our intellectual and professional trajectories.

As regards our similarities, both of us had a strong extra-European experience (in Africa, in Twining's case; in Latin America, in mine), which helped us to contextualize (relativize) the Western canon of law. We both had a solid training in Western legal theory: Twining at Oxford and myself at the University of Coimbra and the Free University of Berlin; Twining in the common law tradition and myself in the continental law tradition. We both experienced the cultural and scientific shock of North America: Twining at Chicago Law School and myself at Yale Law School. In this respect, we arrived in the USA at crucially different times. I arrived at Yale eleven years after Twining, at the climax of the protests against the Vietnam War and civil rights movements. I had the opportunity of becoming a Marxist at Yale, while Twining had to forget at Chicago the Marxism he had reluctantly encountered at Oxford.

Before I engage in our differences, the question of postmodernism must be set straight. Twining strongly disagrees with what he takes to be my postmodernism.[35] In the interview with Manuel Atienza and Raymundo Gama, in this volume, after declaring his 'ambivalences about "post-modernism"', Twining adds: 'I value multiple perspectives, I recognize almost infinite complexity, I believe that imagination is required for understanding, but underneath I am an old-style cognitivist, who distinguishes between epistemology and ontology.'[36] The problem is that if I were the 'postmodernist' he portrays me to be, I would not be a critical theorist, since I don't consider postmodernism, in the sense he uses the term, as part of the Western critical tradition. In my work, I have insisted on the distinction between celebratory and oppositional postmodernism, and made clear that only the latter deserves to be included in the critical tradition. While celebratory postmodernism assumes that the modern problems of freedom, equality and fraternity are irresolvable and therefore should not concern us, the oppositional postmodernism affirms the validity and even the cogency of the modern problems, but claims that the modern solutions are not available any more (assuming that they were ever available) and other solutions have to be looked for. That is why, for instance, 'non-state law must be taken seriously'.[37] Although Twining acknowledges this difference,[38] he apparently gives no value to it. However, this difference is crucial and does not escape Gavin Anderson's attention (in this volume).

But I must concede a point to Twining in this regard. The term 'postmodernism' was so overloaded by the celebratory conception of it that I, frustrated with my incapacity to impose the oppositional conception, decided to abandon

[35] For instance, Twining 2009a, at pp. 194–244.

[36] See *An Intellectual Journey with William Twining (An Interview)*, Manuel Atienza and Raymundo Gama, in this volume.

[37] Twining 2009b, at p. 362. [38] Twining 2009b, at p. 320.

the concept in 2004. This was also the time at which my critique of capitalism was more and more intertwined with my critique of colonialism – my postcolonial turn; hence the title of my piece 'From postmodernism to postcolonialism and beyond both'.[39]

The substantive differences between our critical theories of law have been brilliantly laid out by Gavin Anderson (in this volume) and I do not have much to add. I would just like to stress the following points. Concerning globalization, Twining considers that my 'ideological conception of globalization' limits my agenda,[40] in particular, my insistence on the bottom-up approach, and the distinction between regulatory and emancipatory law. For me, the suppressed, invisible or silenced experiences, voices, practices and knowledge are not the product of scholarly inertia or innate myopia or deafness; they are, rather, the direct or indirect result of the systemic contradictions and inequalities caused by capitalism, colonialism and patriarchy throughout the modern era. In particular, colonialism (articulated with capitalism) caused forms of radical exclusion and invisibility grounded on the separation between metropolitan and colonial societies. I have metaphorically described this separation as drawn by an abyssal line according to which the social realities on the other side of the line (colonies) could in no way compromise the universality of the conceptions developed to characterize the social realities on this side of the line (metropolitan societies).[41] This explains why, in the late nineteenth century, labour law could be part of embryonic welfare law on this side of the line (in Europe) and part of penal law (*chibalo*) on the other side of the line (in the colonies), without this discrepancy implying any analytical flaw or contradiction.[42] In my view, a position is ideological which prefers not to remember this past and the wrongs it caused.

[39] The paper was presented at *the Luso-Afro Brazilian Congress of Social Sciences* held in Coimbra on 16 September 2004. The German version was published in 2005: Hauke Brunkhorst and Sérgio Costa, *Jenseits von Zentrum und Peripherie. Zur Verfassung der fragmentierten Weltgesellschaft* (Mering: Hampp Verlag, Buchreihe Zentrum und Peripherie, 2005); the Spanish version in 2008: Boaventura de Sousa Santos, *Conocer desde el Sur. Para una cultura política emancipatória* (La Paz: Plural Editores, 2008); CLACSO; CIDES-UMSA and the English version in 2010: Boaventura de Sousa Santos, 'From the Postmodern to the Postcolonial – and Beyond Both' in Encarnación Gutiérrez Rodríguez, Manuela Boatca and Sérgio Costa (eds), *Decolonizing European Sociology. Transdisciplinary Approaches* (Farnham: Ashgate, 2010), pp. 225–42), too late to be considered by Twining in his *General Jurisprudence*.

[40] Twining 2009b, at pp. 242, 447–8.

[41] Boaventura de Sousa Santos, 'Beyond Abyssal Thinking: From Global Lines to Ecologies of Knowledges', *Review* (2007), XXX (1), pp. 45–89 [hereafter, Santos, 2007] and Santos 2014, at pp. 118–36.

[42] Modern Western thinking is an abyssal thinking. It consists of a system of visible and invisible distinctions, the invisible ones being the foundation of the visible ones. The invisible distinctions are established through radical lines that divide social reality into two realms, the realm of 'this side of the line' and the realm of 'the other side of the line'. The division is such that 'the other side of the line' vanishes as reality becomes nonexistent, and is indeed produced as nonexistent. Nonexistent means not existing in any relevant or comprehensible way of being. Whatever is produced as nonexistent is radically excluded, because it lies beyond the realm of what the accepted conception of inclusion considers to be its other. What most fundamentally

Concerning the Western legal canon, both Twining and I are critical of conventional understandings. Twining defines his general jurisprudence as critical jurisprudence.[43] In this respect, our differences are both substantive and of emphasis. I agree with Twining that the West has a very 'rich heritage of texts and ideas'[44] and commend him for his brilliant effort to expand, revise and reinterpret the canon and the mainstream, on the basis of a critical assessment of its assumptions.[45] I think, however, that revising the canon may not suffice, since much of the modern world experience, in particular the one on the other side of the line, never entered the canon. This explains why the canon, no matter how expanded and revised, cannot to this day accept that the understanding of the world by far exceeds the Western understanding of the world, a key assumption of my critical theory since 1995.[46] My emphasis on the bottom-up approach and grass-roots movements with impact on law is based on my conviction that, in spite of all the much-needed revisions of the canon, so masterly crafted by Twining, in the end it will be necessary to re-found the canon if we want to expand the 'conversation of the world' that John Dewey called for.[47] One of my most recent empirical studies on bottom-up constitutionalism, a concept that Gavin Anderson so perceptively underlines,[48] deals with the recent constitutional processes and movements in Bolivia and Ecuador, unfortunately not yet available in English.[49]

This leads me to the final point of difference between Twining and Santos. It concerns epistemology; that is to say, the inquiry into the identification of and the conditions for the production of valid knowledge. Our difference does not lie in whether there is a difference between epistemology and ontology. We both distinguish between epistemology and ontology, but we subscribe to

characterizes abyssal thinking is thus the impossibility of the co-presence of the two sides of the line. To the extent that it prevails, this side of the line only prevails by exhausting the field of relevant reality. Beyond it, there is only nonexistence, invisibility, absence... In the field of modern law, this side of the line is determined by what counts as legal or illegal according to the official state or international law. The legal and the illegal are the only two relevant forms of existing before the law and, for that reason, the distinction between the two is a universal distinction. This central dichotomy leaves out a whole social territory where the dichotomy would be unthinkable as an organizing principle; that is, the territory of the lawless, the a-legal, the non-legal, and even the legal or illegal according to non-officially recognized law. Thus, the invisible abyssal line that separates the realm of law from the realm of non-law grounds the visible dichotomy between the legal and the illegal that organizes, on this side of the line, the realm of law (Santos 2007, at pp. 45–89 and Santos 2014, at pp. 118–35).

[43] Twining 2009b, at p. 449. [44] Twining 2009b, at p. 449.

[45] I myself have done this with Western philosophy: Boaventura de Sousa Santos, 'A Non-Occidentalist West?: Learned Ignorance and Ecology of Knowledge', *Theory, Culture & Society Special Issue: Occidentalism: Jack Goody and Comparative History* (2009), 26, pp. 103–25. See also Santos 1995.

[46] Santos 1995 and Santos 2014.

[47] John Dewey, 'Common Science and Science' in John Dewey and Arthur Bentley, *Knowing and Know* (Boston: Beacon Press, 1949), pp. 270–86.

[48] In this volume and also Gavin W. Anderson, 'Societal Constitutionalism, Social Movements, and Constitutionalism', *Indiana Journal of Global Legal Studies* (2013) 20 (2) pp. 881–906.

[49] Santos and Exeni 2012 and Santos and Grijalva 2012.

different epistemologies and ontologies. I cannot address this difference in any detail here. Suffice it for me to say that, for me, scientific, scholarly knowledge is a crucially important type of knowledge but not the only one; that most people around the world conduct their lives and conceive of their laws in non-scientific ways. These other knowledges have to be brought into the analysis through two procedures that I designate as ecology of knowledge[50] and intercultural translation.[51] Unless this is done, we, the critical theorists, will face the dilemma of reproducing cognitive injustice in the process of drawing attention to it. In my view, there is no global social justice without global cognitive justice. Of course, mainstream theorists do not even understand the dilemma, much less care about it. According to them, cognitive justice is an obnoxious concept; ignorant people are just ignorant, and it is our duty to teach them about our Western-centric scientific, scholarly knowledge, which is the only valid form of knowledge.

It would be fascinating if Twining and I could have a dialogue on the challenges posed by the 2011–13 indignation revolts to our critical theories. In its absence, in the following I briefly present my own response. In the final section, I venture some speculative notes on what Twining's response might look like. I hope that this will clarify even further our convergences and divergences.

3. Law and the indignation revolts

As one might expect, the protesters were not in the least interested in entertaining a reflection about the law and its role in society. If law, like no other attribute of the modern state, symbolizes the idea of institution and institutionalization (law and order), it is to be expected that the indignation movements would have very little to say about law, even when they had a lot to say about rights. After all, most of the protests were declared illegal and, from the very beginning, there were several attempts to ban them. The protesters' recourse to the direct action of occupation underlined the anti-institutional or extra-institutional impulse behind their protests. Moreover, the justification for recourse to direct action, particularly in democratic contexts, was that state institutions, supposedly at the service of citizens and charged with protecting their citizenship rights, were not performing the functions for which they were designed. They had been taken over by the power elite to serve their interests. What I propose here is, therefore, a hypothetical reconstruction. If the indignation revolts would have had time or interest in developing a critical theory of law underlying their struggles, what would it have looked like? How would they conceive of law? According to them, what would the role of law in society be? What was the concept of law underlying their collective action? In their understanding, how was law related to the state and the civil society?

[50] Santos 2014, at pp. 188–211. [51] Santos 2014, at pp. 212–35.

My interest in these questions was both political and analytical. I participated as an activist in some of the mobilizations in Portugal and held several meetings with the protestors in Coimbra, Lisbon and Madrid, and showed my solidarity with them to the best of my ability, including through writing newspaper articles and participating in TV and radio interviews and debates. I shared many of their concerns and struggles and experienced a similarly intense sense of indignation, and for the same reasons. As far as the critical theory of law and the questions formulated above are concerned, I had a specific analytical interest. The indignation revolts seemed to contradict the critical sociological theory of law that I have been developing over the years. One of the main features of such a theory is the idea that, under certain conditions, law can be used to promote progressive social transformation: what I have been designating as the counter-hegemonic use of law. Elaborating on such a possibility, the last chapter of my book *Towards a New Legal Common Sense*[52] is entitled: 'Can Law be Emancipatory?'[53] To this question, the indignation revolts seemed to answer with a resounding 'no'. Reading or listening to their declarations, I sensed that they were confronting me with the idea that I was entertaining a liberal reformist fantasy with no bearing in real life. If they were right, was I wrong?

In light of the differences between the three types of revolts and mobilizations I identified above, there is no monolithic conception of law implicit in them. There are, however, some 'elective affinities'[54] among various elements present in all of them, albeit with differing intensity. Central to the conception of law underlying the indignation revolts is the configuration of power relations prevailing in society. The law of the state is a crucial component of such configuration. Law is not autonomous in relation to prevailing power relations in society in any relevant sense. Law is politics by other means. But the embeddedness of law in power relations and politics (and *vice versa*) may be viewed from three different perspectives. In order to identify them,

[52] Santos 2002. I conceive of globalization as an internally fractured and indeed contradictory process, not only because it generates processes of localization (for example, the globalization of English Language localizes the German language, as much as the globalization of Hollywood filming 'ethnicizes' French filming) but also because globalization itself mirrors the contradictions of capitalist development. Concerning the latter, side by side with the by far dominant and hegemonic globalization of capital (neoliberal globalization), there is a globalization from below which I designate as counter-hegemonic. I define as 'counter-hegemonic globalization' the vast set of networks, initiatives, organizations and movements that fight against the economic, social and political outcomes of hegemonic capitalist globalization, challenge the conceptions of world development underlying the latter, and propose alternative conceptions. Boaventura de Sousa Santos, 'Beyond Neoliberal Governance: The World Social Forum as Subaltern Cosmopolitan Politics and Legality' in Boaventura de Sousa Santos and Rodríguez-Garavito, César (eds), *Law and Globalization from Below. Towards a Cosmopolitan Legality* (Cambridge University Press, 2005), p.29 . See also Santos 1995 and Santos 2006.

[53] Santos 2002, at pp. 439–66.

[54] The well-known title of Goethe's novel was later adopted by Max Weber in analyzing the elective affinities between the rise of capitalism and the protestant ethics: Max Weber, *The Protestant Ethic and the Spirit of Capitalism* (London & Boston: Unwin Hyman, 1930).

I distinguish among three types of law: configurative law, reconfigurative law and prefigurative law. 'Configurative law' is law as it reflects a given configuration of power relations. If these power relations are unequal and bound to produce injustice and oppression, law will be equally unjust and oppressive. 'Reconfigurative law' is law in the process of being resorted to in order to change power relations, and to reconfigure the correlation of forces in society. Reconfigurative law is law underlying what I have been calling the counter-hegemonic use of law. 'Prefigurative law' is expressive or performative law, law that expresses in its practice the anticipation of a different society based on a totally different set of power relations. In the following I will refer to them separately.

4. Configurative law: the abyssal duality of law[55]

According to the indignation revolts, in current capitalist societies there is an abyssal legal duality, a kind of legal pluralism that legal scholars have failed to recognize. Rather than being a duality between state and non-state law, it is an entrenched duality at the core of capitalist state law. To conceive it as the discrepancy between law in books and law in action, as conventional sociology of law does, implies that we face a contingent deviation and that the discrepancy could be overcome. For the indignant, both assumptions are wrong. The official state law has been pre-occupied by the power elites, the oppressors, whoever they are. This pre-occupation operates through a radical divide between two legal systems: the law of the 1% and the law of the 99%, the law of the oppressor and the law of the oppressed. This divide is both radical and invisible. They are incommensurable and intrinsically bounded together. They are bounded together not just because they coexist in the same geopolitical space. They are, indeed, produced by the same legislative power and adjudicated by the same judicial system. They both operate through systematic deviations from the general principles in which they are supposed to be grounded. And yet they remain incommensurate. The discrepancy between law in books and law in action, rather than a deviation or aberration, is constitutive of this type of pre-occupation. By negating the constitutive character of the discrepancy between law in books and law in action and, on the contrary, by proclaiming the unity, neutrality, autonomy and universality of the law, dominant political ideology and expert legal knowledge cannot possibly imagine the coexistence of the two legal systems. Any attempt at alternative ways of occupying the law by those excluded from power – the oppressed, by far the large majority of the population – is thus neutralized as unintelligible or simply outrageous.

However, the invisibility of such legal duality is not an exclusive product of the still-strong hegemony of legal liberalism. It has been favoured by the

[55] On the concept of the abyssal line, see note 42 above.

tendency of people to underestimate the signals of a major incoming destructive event or disaster only because they have never experienced it and have difficulty in figuring out its full consequences. We can call this 'a normalcy bias', and it is strongly reinforced by the corporate media.[56] Intoxicated by the promises of infinite progress, people tend to view as irreversible any improvement whatsoever that they experience in their life histories.[57] They tend to interpret in the most optimistic possible way any warnings that reversibility may be on the horizon, let alone that it is already taking place. Against evidence to the contrary, they go on believing that law represents a sovereign project and that it defends the common good through democratic government. As far as the duality between the law of the 1% and the law of the 99% is concerned, people have tended to view the changes occurring (above all, the concentration of wealth and the 'pre-occupation' of the state and its law by minoritarian powerful interests) as not compromising the fundamental unity of law. Indeed, the normalcy bias leads common citizens to believe that, in spite of all its shortcomings, democracy still works to the benefit of all the citizens, and that law is still behind David whenever Goliath tries to impose his rule. This belief is reinforced by a companion one, which I will call 'pre-emptive damage bias': this is the idea that more serious evils and disasters will be prevented from occurring tomorrow if people agree to endure today comparatively minor damage to their welfare.

The abyssal line that divides the two legal systems bears some similarities with the one that divided the metropolitan law from the colonial law in the period of historical colonialism, except that now the two laws are exercised in the same geopolitical territory. In the play of legal mirrors prevalent in society, there is no way that law could be reflected in its entirety. As a result, it remains invisible that 'law and order 1' is the other side of 'law and order 2' (which the 99% consider to be the disorder imposed on them by the 1%), and that in our societies 'the rule of law 1' goes side by side with 'the rule of law 2' (which the 99% consider to be the illegality imposed on them by the 1%).

[56] The concept of 'normalcy bias' has been developed in the theories of risk and disaster. The normalcy bias, or normality bias, refers to people entering a mental state when facing a disaster. It causes people to underestimate both the possibility of a disaster occurring and its possible effects. This often results in situations where people fail to prepare adequately for a disaster, and on a larger scale, the failure of governments to include the populace in its disaster preparations. The assumption that is made in the case of the normalcy bias is that, since a disaster never has occurred, then it never will occur. It also results in the inability of people to cope with a disaster once it does occur. People with a normalcy bias have difficulty reacting to something they have never experienced before. People also tend to interpret warnings in the most optimistic way possible, seizing on any ambiguities to infer a less serious situation. As a tragic example, see the normalcy bias at work in the case of the cyclone of 1991 that claimed the life of 140,000 people in Bangladesh. See Iware Matsuda, 'Loss of Human Lives Induced by the Cyclone of 29–30 April, 1991 in Bangladesh', *Geo Journal* (1993) 31 (4), pp. 319–25.

[57] As I hope it will be easily understood, I am here reconstructing the implicit discourse of the indignant on these issues.

In the last sixty years, the abyssal divide at the heart of law in capitalist societies has never been as radical and damaging for the vast majorities of our societies as it is today. It is the result of a thirty-year-long counter-revolution of the 1% against the social gains the 99% had obtained in previous decades through struggles carried out within the boundaries of the liberal democratic process. Through such struggles, some measure of social redistribution was achieved, partly through the expansion of enforceable social and economic rights. Prevailing power relations were thereby changed in the core countries of the world system; the best expression of such change was the creation of European-style social democracy and the Welfare State. In the last thirty years, the power elites, seconded by the global financial capital, have managed to reverse this historical process, hijacking democracy and putting it at the service of their exclusive interests. As a result, we live today in societies that are politically democratic but socially fascist.[58] This political split is the mirror image of the legal split.

The workings of dual legality

Let us now examine in greater detail the duality between the law of the 1% and the law of the 99%. In spite of its radical nature, this split has been achieved without any suspension of the Constitution, and without any declaration of the state of exception.

The law of the 1% is a status law, a personal law in the Weberian sense.[59] The law of the 99% is territorial law; it is the way of operation of the law when it addresses the needs and the aspirations of the 99%. The law of the 1% is conceived by the powerful as its own; as a consequence, the application of law is ruled by the idea of who does what against whom, rather than by the idea of what is done against no matter whom. According to the indignation conception of law, the balanced articulation among the three structural elements of modern state law – rhetoric, bureaucracy and violence[60] – is today completely absent, if it ever existed. On the contrary, there is now a structural imbalance between the three components. The law of the 1% operates almost exclusively through rhetoric. In recent years, the proliferation of soft law and forms of

[58] The present fascism is not a political regime. It is rather a social and civilizational regime. Rather than sacrificing democracy to the demands of capitalism, it trivializes democracy to such a degree that it is no longer necessary, or even convenient, to sacrifice democracy in order to promote capitalism. It is a type of pluralist fascism produced by the society rather than by the state. The state is here a complacent bystander, if not an active culprit. We are entering a period in which democratic states coexist with fascistic societies. This is, therefore, a form of fascism that never existed (Santos 2002, at p. 453).

[59] Referring to the patrimonial monarchical codification of Central Europe, Max Weber writes: 'essentially constituted merely the status law of the small privileged strata and left untouched the special institutions of the other estates, especially the peasantry, i.e., the great majority of the subjects'. Max Weber, *Economy and Society. An Outline of Interpretive Sociology* (Berkeley: University of California Press, 1978), at p. 858.

[60] On the three structural components of modern state law, see Santos 1995 at p. 430.

governance based on voluntary compliance has dramatically shown the prevalence of rhetoric in the law of the 1%.[61] On the contrary, the law of the 99% operates through bureaucracy and violence, and in recent times more through violence than bureaucracy, as illustrated by the criminalization of social protest.[62] Rhetoric is at most used to induce resignation by those faced with the excessive use of bureaucratic violence[63] by state bureaucracies or physical violence by the police.

Two illegalities

As there are two laws, there are two illegalities: the illegality of the powerful and the illegality of the powerless. The illegality of the powerful operates in two ways: first, through impunity or, in a few cases, through resort to the granting of immunity, and, second, through the adoption of illegitimate legal changes to suit their interests. In the first case, they use their overriding interpersonal, financial and organization resources to twist legal adjudication to their advantage; in the second case, they manipulate the legislative process either by engaging in illegal corruption (bribes, traffic of influences) or in legal corruption (lobbying). Only when an illegality committed by some powerful person or group affects the interests of some other powerful person or group, is it treated according to the principle of equality before the law. On the contrary, the illegality of the powerful committed against the powerless remains largely without punishment, be it, for example, wage theft, salary and pension cuts in violation of contracts and agreements, excessive credit commissions or overcharging, illegal foreclosures or excessively long prison sentences for minor offences.

[61] I have addressed this issue in Santos and Rodriguez-Garavito 2005 at pp. 29–64.

[62] In the last fifteen years many countries have promulgated anti-terrorism laws that have often been used to repress and punish peaceful social protests. For instance, throughout Latin America indigenous peoples have been punished under the severe anti-terrorism laws for blocking roads in protest against the transnational corporations, thus impeding the trucks of mining or timber companies from entering their ancestral territories. On the criminalization of social protest see, among many others, 'TADA: Hard Law for Soft State', *Economic and Political Weekly* (2000) 35 (13), pp. 1066–71; Paula Abal Medina and Mariana Ortega Breña, 'Thoughts on the Visual Aspect of the Neoliberal Order and the Piquetero Movement in Argentina', *Latin American Perspectives* (2011) 38 (1), pp. 88–101; Xavier Flores Aguirre, 'Criminalización de la Libertad de Expresión: Protesta Social y Administración Local en Guayaquil', *Iconos. Revista de Ciencias Sociales* (2007) 27 Quito, pp. 65–75; Paula Daibert, 'To Protect or Punish: New Anti-Terrorism Law Proposed in Brazil Could Curb Right To Protest', *Witness* (2014), blog.witness.org/2014/06/proposed-anti-terrorism-law-brazil accessed 14 June 2014; CONAIE, 'Ecuador Indigenous Leaders Charged with Terrorism and Sabotage Correa Administration Seeks to Criminalize Dissent and Peaceful Protest', *Amazon Watch* (2010), amazonwatch.org/news/2010/0701-ecuador-indigenous-leaders-charged-with-terrorism-and-sabotage accessed 1 July 2010; 'Pakistan protest leaders charged under anti-terror act', *World Watch*, www.worldbulletin.net/nawaz-sharif/143513/pakistan-protest-leaders-charged-under-anti-terror-act accessed 1 September 2014.

[63] As in the case of using the rhetoric of the war on terror to justify secret laws, disproportionate punishments, restriction on defendants rights, secret detention camps, Guantanamo etc.

By contrast, the law of the 99% treats the illegality of the powerless with excessive harshness. Minor violations of the criminal, civil or administrative law tend to be severely punished. The outstanding example in recent years is the criminalization of social protest.[64] The application of severe anti-terrorism laws against political dissent or social activism has become the norm, involving not only severe punishment for minor disturbances of public order, but also police brutality and the grotesque violation of privacy through the most intrusive forms of surveillance. Moreover, in many instances, the protesters act in self-defense, resisting illegal acts of the powerful, which the law of the 1% leaves unpunished. This is dramatically illustrated in the cases of peasants and indigenous people blocking roads to prevent the devastation of their forests by agri-business or timber industries, or resisting expulsion from their lands and territories by promoters of large-scale mining, industrial agriculture, dams or other megaprojects being carried out without their consent or consultation, as required by international law and, in most cases, with the complicity of corrupt governments.

The legal, the illegal and the alegal

Configurative law also has a propensity to engage in forms of social control that do not fit the conventional legal–illegal dichotomy. These are forms of social control in which the only effective behaviour is considered to be unbounded discretionary behaviour and, indeed, the more arbitrary the more effective. This is the field of alegality. Just two examples from different areas of social control will suffice. While managing the financial and budgetary crisis, the power elite may resort to emergency measures of dubious constitutional legality, imposing immense sacrifices on the 99%, while exempting the 1%, even when a minor sacrifice on the part of the latter would have diminished considerably the overall negative effects of the crisis.[65] The other example is taken from the so-called war on terror.[66] In this case, the controls on behaviour introduced in its name may become so arbitrary that to consider them illegal does not capture the full extent to which they are completely

[64] See note 62.

[65] This has been most notably the case of the 'austerity measures' imposed by conservative governments in Greece, Portugal and Spain since 2011. See, on this, Boaventura de Sousa Santos, *Portugal. Ensaio contra a Autoflagelação* (Coimbra: Almedina, 2012).

[66] There is an immense bibliography on the topic. See, for instance, Patrick P. Garlinger, 'Privacy, Free Speech, and the Patriot Act: First and Fourth Amendment Limits on National Security Letters', *New York University Law Review* (2009) 84 (4), pp. 1105–47; Susan Herman, 'The USA Patriot Act and the Submajoritarian Fourth Amendment', *Harvard Civil Rights-Civil Liberties Law Review* (2006) 41 (1), pp. 67–132; X. Besar, *Journal of International Commercial Law and Technology* (2012) 7.2, pp. 121–35; Alan Rubel, 'Privacy and the USA Patriot Act: Rights, the Value of Rights, and Autonomy', *Law and Philosophy* (2007) 26 (2), pp. 119–59; Mark Fenster, 'The Implausibility of Secrecy', *Hastings Law Journal* (2014) 65 (2), pp. 309–62; Michael Sall, 'Classified Opinions: Habeas at Guantanamo and the Creation of Secret Law', *Georgetown Law Journal* (2013) 101 (4), pp. 1147–70.

outside legal controls. Secret laws and secret interpretation of the laws result in the accused before a secret court not being allowed (and his or her lawyer likewise) to know the law on the basis of which he or she is being accused and eventually condemned. The secret services are able to access much of the electronic communications of most people, whether they are suspected of any wrong-doing or not, as recently exposed by Edward Snowden. The cyber-space, Guantánamo, and the transit lounges of international airports all seem to be privileged sites and spaces of alegality, twilight zones beyond the legal–illegal dichotomy that grounds modern legal principles. These alegal spaces and courses of action are bound to expand as democracy gets hollowed out, the state of exception gets normalized, and citizenship slides into servitude.

International law and international relations

In the field of international relations, the law of the 1% is the law of plundering and dispossession. International law is the most blatant and violent instance of the abyssal division between the law of the 1% and the law of the 99%. As far as international law is concerned, the law of the 1% is the law that protects at the transnational level the interests of the power elites of the core countries and their satellite elites in the periphery and semi-periphery of the world system. This law operates by underwriting the particular forms of capital accumulation that Marx called primitive accumulation.[67] According to Marx, these forms of capital accumulation were particularly violent and illegal, consisting of actions such as taking over communal lands followed by the expulsion of peasants in order to expand the nineteenth-century textile industry in England, thus creating the conditions for the more normal, peaceful, legal and sustainable reproduction of capitalist economic relations. Marx, therefore, conceived these as part of an initial phase of capitalism.

It is now evident, however, that such primitive accumulation, rather than merely a phase, is a constant feature of capitalism when analyzed on a global scale, and it continues today under different forms.[68] First, and foremost, neocolonialism and imperialist warfare guarantee access to natural resources. Second, land grabbing throughout Africa and Latin America, and the massive expulsion of peasants and indigenous peoples from the land they had cultivated for generations, pave the way for the unprecedented (in both scale and intensity) exploration of natural resources. These consist of mega infrastructure projects (huge dams and highways), large-scale open pit mining and new plantation industrial agriculture for agro-fuels and animal feed. Third, there is the unprecedented transfer of wealth from impoverished middle and popular

[67] Karl Marx, *Das Kapital I* (New York: International Publishers, 1970), at part VIII.

[68] This argument was presented initially by Rosa Luxemburg, *The Accumulation of Capital* (London: Routledge & Kegan Paul, 1951 [1913]). In recent times it has been elaborated upon most cogently by David Harvey, *The Limits to Capital* (London and New York: Verso, 2006) and *A Companion to Marx's Capital* (London and New York: Verso, 2010).

classes to the 1% by stealing salaries and pensions, cutting social benefits and forcing people out of their foreclosed homes, all in order to 'solve' the financial crisis; that is, by bailing out banks and remunerating speculators – the same ones that caused the crisis in the first place by their irresponsible, if not criminal, behaviour.

From the perspective of those taking part in the indignation revolts, law is basically configurative law; law is split in two with the purpose of oppressing majorities in the name of the common good, which in real terms is the exclusive good of the 1%. Configurative law is thus intrinsically a hostile ground for protesters who should have no illusions about the possibility of resorting to it to further their causes.

5. Prefigurative law

The indignation revolts have generated prefigurative law, the law of the occupation, which is self-given and thus not imposed. This is bottom-up law generated in the exercise of occupation itself.[69] The occupation of the public space involves the creation of an alternative conception of that place, during a certain period of time, by a sizeable number of people. Such an occupation requires the adoption of some regulation and ordering, rules facilitating legitimate behaviour and punishing the illegitimate one, as well as some kind of law enforcement mechanism in order to guarantee the implementation of such rules. To the extent that they involved occupation or sustained resistance, the indignation revolts tended to generate these rules in assembly-based forms of participation and deliberation brought about by consensus. However, in order to prevent small minorities from transforming their dissent into a veto power, some movements have adopted majority rule and even secret voting. Such rules and rulemaking are the foundational social contract of the occupation. Like the law of the 1%, this occupation law is self-given – it is a self-rule – and operates on the basis of rhetoric; it is almost devoid of bureaucracy and violence.

This law is prefigurative in the sense that, in both its design and its exercise, it bears witness to a real preview or anticipation of an alternative law in an alternative society where democracy, justice and equality are actually living experiences.[70] This is the only form of legal pluralism to which the indignation

[69] Inspired by Hermann Kantorowicz, *The Definition of Law* (Cambridge University Press, 1958), I have defended throughout my work a broad conception of law: first formulations in Boaventura de Sousa Santos, *Law against Law: Legal Reasoning in Pasargada* (Cuernavaca, México: Centro Intercultural de Documentación, 1974) and Santos, 'The Law of the Oppressed: The Construction and Reproduction of Legality in Pasargada Law', *Law and Society Review* (1977), 12, pp. 5–126. Referring to a more recent period, Twining 2009b, at p. 362 says, 'Recently some jurists interested in the implications of "globalisation" – including Glenn, Santos, Tamanaha, and Twining – have advanced arguments in favour of broader conceptions of law that include at least some examples of "non-state law".' As he rightly adds: 'this, not surprisingly, has met with some resistance.'

[70] This idea of real preview or anticipation is similar to the concept of real utopia put forward by Erik Ohlin Wright, *Envisioning Real Utopias* (London: Verso, 2010) to refer to really-existing

movement grants some positive value. In spite of its precarious, inchoate or embryonic appearance, this prefigurative law belongs to the same type of prefigurative law that existed in some liberated zones during the anti-colonial liberation movement[71] and has been in force for some years in the autonomous territories of the neo-Zapatistas.[72]

6. Reconfigurative law: can law be emancipatory?

In previous writings I have claimed[73] that the counter-hegemonic use of law presupposes, among other conditions, that legal mobilization must be part of a broader political mobilization. Legal mobilization involves going to courts to advance demands rather than to defend against criminal charges, putting pressure on the state bureaucracies in charge of implementing rights or mobilizing for legislative change. Political mobilization may involve different kinds of peaceful political activism, including direct action to advance causes in the political agenda. What the indignation revolts are saying is that the conditions for *legal* mobilization either do not exist or are deteriorating to such an extent that political mobilization must take unequivocal precedence over legal mobilization. According to the protestors, the impossibility of legal mobilization is the result of the rise of authoritarianism that has led to top-down extra-institutionalism or deinstitutionalization, disguised by the invisible split between the law of the 1% and the law of the 99%. As a result, social transformation through legal and judicial activism cannot be achieved under the current conditions of global capitalism.

According to the protestors, the conditions for a counter-hegemonic use of law, if they ever existed, have deteriorated to such an extent that nothing is left but a sad liberal fantasy, a hollow hope. Liberal democracy has proved impotent to neutralize the impulses of neoliberal capitalism to ever greater

practices that deviate in fundamental ways from conventional or hegemonic modes of conceiving of the economy or politics.

71 For the case of the liberated zones in Guiné-Bissau in the struggle against Portuguese colonialism conducted by Amílcar Cabral, see Boaventura de Sousa Santos, *A Justiça Popular em Cabo Verde* (Coimbra: Almedina, 2015).

72 For the case of the neo-Zapatistas see Subcomandante Marcos, *Nuestra Arma es Nuestra Palabra. Escritos Selectos* (New York: Seven Stories Press, 2001); Subcomandante Marcos, *Ya Basta!: Ten Years of the Zapatista Uprising: Writings of Subcomandante Insurgente Marcos* (Oakland, CA: AK Press, 2004).

73 The counter-hegemonic conception of the law involves a search into subaltern conceptions and practices, of which I distinguish three types: 1) conceptions and practices that, though being part of the Western tradition and evolving in Western countries, were suppressed or marginalized by the liberal conceptions that came to dominate; 2) conceptions that evolved outside the West, mainly in the colonies and later in the postcolonial states; 3) conceptions and practices that are today being proposed by organizations and movements that are active in advancing forms of counter-hegemonic globalization. In sum, in a period of paradigmatic transition away from dominant modernity, subaltern modernity provides some of the instruments that will allow us to travel along in a progressive direction; that is, in the direction of a good order and of a good society that is not yet here (Santos 2002, at p. 446). See also Santos, 1995.

concentration of wealth and undemocratic political power. Citizenship and human rights are being eroded, even in the core countries of the world system; surveillance destroys privacy beyond recognition; elected governments respond to rating agencies rather than to citizens; corruption seems endemic; transfers of wealth from the poor to the rich reach scandalous levels that were previously thought to be possible only under dictatorship; and imperialist wars are being reinvented incessantly. All this takes place without constitutional rules and guarantees being formally suspended. Under these conditions, no significant reconfigurative law is possible.

Law can only be recovered as an emancipatory tool if democracy is refounded and, in a sense, reinvented. This explains the centrality of the calls for 'real democracy' in the indignation movement.[74] Essentially, 'real democracy' means a political regime that effectively promotes political, social and economic equality and respect for equal difference, by transforming unequal power relations into relations of shared authority in society at large and not just in the political realm. In other words, without profoundly reconfiguring power relations in a more equitable and democratic way, no reconfigurative law is possible. The appeal is not, therefore, to constitutional lawyering as usual, but rather to a radical democracy and a profound state reform brought about by a bottom-up, participative, political process through which the 99% will exercise a robust constituent power. Some have called this process 'transformative constitutionalism', having in mind some recent constitutional processes in Latin America, such as in Ecuador and Bolivia.[75]

7. Conclusion: is it possible to occupy the law? Challenging Twining and Santos

In the preceding sections I outlined the main traits of the conception or conceptions of law and legal transformation that were implicit in the 2011–13 indignation revolts. I presented them as a challenge to the critical theory of law I have been proposing over the years. In order to refine the challenge, I offered a rough comparison between the critical legal theory formulated by Twining (as I understand it) and my own. Would these theories be equally disproved or challenged by the implicit understandings of the law present in the discourses and practices of the protestors?

[74] According to the *Carta por la Democracia* (Letter for Democracy), the framework proposed by the politics of austerity is, therefore, not to be accepted. Quite the opposite. There has never been so much wealth, but never has it been so badly divided and according to such antidemocratic and unfair criteria. This is why a complete reconsideration of the role of economic policies is needed in order to establish the principle of the populations' well-being above private, financial and corporate interests. At stake is the real, and not just formal, recognition that the laws of the market must be subordinated to the social role of the economy (movimientodemocracia.net). See also, Objetivos Politicos del 15M Barrio del Pilar (Madrid) barriodelpilar15m.wordpress.com/2014/06/28/objetivos-politicos-del-15m.

[75] See Boaventura de Sousa Santos, *Refundación del Estado en América Latina* (Bogotá:Siglo del Hombre Editores, 2010) [hereafter, Santos, 2010] and the bibliography cited there.

In his insightful comparative analysis of Twining and Santos in this volume, Gavin Anderson offers two possible readings: one that underlines the opposition between the two theories and one that shows the complementarity between them. Anderson opts for the second reading and convincingly shows the potential of such reading in guiding our analyses of the current transformations undergoing law and legal theory as a result of globalization and the emergent visions of cosmopolitanism. According to this reading, the top-down, sub-paradigmatic, statist (reformist) legal cosmopolitanism, defended by Twining, and the bottom-up, paradigmatic, grass-roots (revolutionary) legal cosmopolitanism, defended by me, complement each other in offering powerful – even if partial – accounts of current socio-legal transformations. As Anderson emphasizes: 'Crucially, on this approach, each possesses an implicit awareness of the limitations of their own perspective, and so we can see their respective accounts of cosmopolitanism as the result of a mutual exploration of those limits.' Moreover, Anderson suggests that the methodological consonance presupposed in the complementarity 'should not hide the political divergence between the two: whereas Twining is content to join Santos in beginning to examine the implications of a bottom-up approach, his political commitment to the utility of modern law as a solution to globalization means that they part company as Santos ventures further into the territory of "uncivil and strange society" which sees modern law as part of the problem to be overcome.'

I agree with Anderson's favoured reading and go further in the hypothesis of complementarity. I see it not only in the dialogue between Twining and me (external complementarity), but also among the different dimensions or layers of my own critical theory (internal complementarity). What I mean by the latter is the following. I have been defending in recent years the idea that we are in need not so much of alternatives to the *status quo* but rather of an alternative thinking of alternatives.[76] If this is true, we should envisage ways of overcoming the old distinctions between reform and revolution, or between sub-paradigmatic and paradigmatic and social transformation. As the 2011–13 protests show, social struggles are becoming more volatile and less structured in their organization, goals and means of struggle. They may combine limited reformist objectives and broad revolutionary ones, and may rapidly move from one type to another. Moreover, however extra-institutional in their initial impulses and forms of mobilization, some protests' mobilizations have evolved towards forms of institutional political action. This is most notably seen in the case of the political party *Podemos*, formed by some groups within the *indignados* movement in Spain, and considered today one of the most successful political parties in Spain, poised to win the next legislative elections.[77] In both

[76] Santos 2014, at p. 42.

[77] According to the public opinion poll published by the daily newspaper *El País* on 11 January 2015, if the elections were held now, the party *Podemos* would get 28.2% of the vote, beating the socialist party (PSOE) with 23.5% and the conservative party (PP) with 19.2%, available at www.publico.pt/mundo/noticia/partido-podemos-a-frente-das-sondagens-em-espanha-ciudadanos-ganha-expressao-nacional-1681857 accessed 14 January 2015.

my recent empirical studies[78] and in my theoretical work (developed in greater detail in my chapter 'Can law be emancipatory?'),[79] I try to account for both possibilities, however sceptical I may increasingly be in relation to small-scale, reformistic, subparadigmatic legal transformations. Someone that lived part of his life under dictatorship will never fail to recognize that, depending on the circumstances, the most limited reformist moves may take revolutionary energy and involve the risk of illegal behaviour, if they are to be brought about successfully.[80] Different historical contexts may also explain why, in the Arab Spring, the protestors were fighting *for* a Western-type democracy, while the *indignados* movement, and especially the Occupy movement, viewed the practice of this type of democracy as irremediably corrupted and unusable for progressive purposes.

What mostly distinguishes my work from Twining's is my emphasis on the grass-roots, bottom-up movements of excluded groups in society as the prime movers of social transformation, be it paradigmatic or sub-paradigmatic. As far as I am concerned, such movements are bound to comprise more and more extra-institutional and even illegal forms of mobilization. In the end, it was this characteristic of the 2011–13 protests that attracted my attention. It is difficult for me to imagine that Twining might have been attracted in a similar way. Our differences are probably not only theoretical and political, but also temperamental and affective.

Coming back to my conception of the counter-hegemonic use of law, I do not view the indignation revolts as evidence of a complete rebuttal of my theory, but rather as demanding a critical revision: without effectively changing the most political dimension of the law – constitutional law, founding both the state and the political system – no other progressive social transformation through law is to be expected. In the end, the indignation revolts, rather than supporting the counter-hegemonic use of law in general, focus their struggles on one specific counter-hegemonic use of a specific branch of law: constitutional law. The goal of transformative constitutionalism is premised upon such counter-hegemonic use. Only a reconfigurative constitutional law, combined with the continued bottom-up pressure that led to it, will reinstall in society the general possibility of a counter-hegemonic use of law.

78 Santos 2010 and Boaventura de Sousa Santos and Flávia Carlet, 'The movement of landless rural workers in Brazil and their struggles for access to law and justice' in Yash Ghai and Jill Cottrell (eds), *Marginalized Communities and Access to Justice* (Abingdon: Routledge, 2010), pp. 60–82.

79 Santos 2002, at pp. 439–66.

80 I spent part of my adult life in Portugal under the dictatorship of Salazar, which lasted for 48 years and only ended in 1974 in the aftermath of the Carnation Revolution.

7

Towards a cosmopolitan pluralist theory of constitutionalism

Gavin W. Anderson

1. Introduction

Globalization is remaking the constitutional paradox afresh, placing at the centre of debate the viability of constitutionalism itself. This new paradox revolves around the apparent contradiction between constitutionalism's ubiquity and its impossibility. From one perspective, constitutionalism has achieved global saturation as witnessed by a dizzying explosion of constitution-making over the past few decades,[1] accompanied by a broad-ranging international consensus in favour of the institutions and norms of liberal democracy.[2] At the same time, many pressing political and social issues are now ventilated through constitutional processes, whether campaigns for greater Scottish or Catalan autonomy,[3] expressions of religious faith in multicultural societies[4] or the allocation of social goods such as housing or medical care.[5] Perhaps the most striking development has been the leap which constitutionalism has taken beyond the nation-state, evidenced most volubly in debates over the constitution of the EU,[6] but which is also joined, for example, with regard to the constitutionalization of the rules of international trade[7] or the governance of the United Nations.[8] Within the academy, this ubiquity is reflected in the development of a distinct discourse of global constitutionalism, and a proliferation of prestigious scholarly outlets for considering these issues,[9] culminating in constitutional law perhaps now being regarded as the pre-eminent legal discipline.[10]

[1] Ran Hirschl, *Towards Juristocracy: The Origins and Consequences of the New Constitutionalism* (Cambridge, MA: Harvard University Press, 2004) [hereafter, Hirschl].

[2] Boaventura de Sousa Santos, *Toward a New Legal Common Sense* (London: Butterworth, 2002) [hereafter, Santos 2002], at p. 315.

[3] Stephen Tierney, *Constitutional Law and National Pluralism* (Oxford University Press, 2004).

[4] *R (Begum) v Denbigh High School* [2006] UKHL 15.

[5] Hirschl, at pp. 131–3.

[6] Grainne de Búrca and Joanne Scott (eds), *The EU and the WTO: Legal and Constitutional Issues* (Oxford and Portland, OR: Hart Publishing, 2001).

[7] Christian Joerges, Inger-Johanne Sand and Gunther Teubner (eds), *Transnational Governance and Constitutionalism* (Oxford and Portland, OR: Hart Publishing, 2004).

[8] Bardo Fassbender, *The United Nations Charter as the Constitutions for the International Community* (Leiden: Martinus Nijhoff, 2009).

[9] E.g. *International Journal of Constitutional Law (I-CON); Global Constitutionalism.*

[10] David Kennedy, 'The Mystery of Global Governance', 34 *Ohio Northern University Law Review* 827 (2008) [hereafter Kennedy 2008], at p. 845.

However, while being acknowledged for its worldwide salience, constitutionalism has also been undergoing something close to an existential crisis, calling into doubt whether the very enterprise can survive the disruptive forces of globalization. The language of the time is often revealing, and there has been intense speculation in the literature, with the disaggregation of law, people and place,[11] on what comes 'after public law'[12] and whether we have reached 'the twilight of constitutionalism'.[13] For some, this focuses on conceptual clarity, and they consider the idea of taking constitutionalism outside its traditional bounds to be a categorical error – constitutions regulate the institutional structure of the nation-state, pure and simple; whatever is happening at the transnational level, and however significant it may be, it is not constitutionalism, and it may fatally dilute the concept to misapply it in this way.[14] For others, of a critical disposition, the specific path which ubiquitous constitutionalism has taken renders it impossible in a more fundamental political sense: the entrenchment of the values of neoliberalism through binding multilateral investment rules makes potentially obsolete constitutionalism's capacity to remake the social order, thus compromising, in classical terms, the expression of democratic constituent power.[15]

It is perhaps not surprising, as its focus shifts to the global plane, that constitutional discourse should join the recent upsurge of interest in cosmopolitanism within the social sciences, both as a means of understanding contemporary globalization and for fashioning responses to its predicaments. At the core of constitutionalism's engagement with cosmopolitanism is the complex relationship between the local and the global. Some openly advocate a 'cosmopolitan turn' with regard to constitutionalism, seeing the latter's continued feasibility as inextricably linked to embracing a cosmopolitan paradigm that moves beyond the 'statist paradigm' of constitutionalism.[16] For others, the 'cosmopolitan dream' remains a chimera, unable to deliver its universalist vision when confronted with *realpolitik*.[17] Within these debates, there is a

[11] James Tully, 'The Unfreedom of the Moderns in Comparison to their Ideals of Constitutional Democracy', 65 *Modern Law Review* (2004) 204, at p. 209.

[12] Cormac Mac Amhlaigh, Claudio Michelon and Neil Walker, *After Public Law* (Oxford University Press, 2013).

[13] Petra Dobner and Martin Loughlin (eds), *The Twilight of Constitutionalism*? (Oxford University Press, 2010) [hereafter Dobner & Loughlin].

[14] Martin Loughlin, 'What is Constitutionalisation?' in Dobner and Loughlin (eds) 47 (2010).

[15] David Schneiderman, *Constitutionalizing Economic Globalization: Investment Rules and Democracy's Promise* (Cambridge University Press, 2008) [hereafter, Schneiderman], at pp. 13–17. See also Stephen Gill and A. Claire Cutler (eds), *New Constitutionalism and World Order* (Cambridge University Press, 2014), ch. 1.

[16] Mattias Kumm, 'The Cosmopolitan Turn in Constitutionalism: On the Relationship between Constitutionalism in and beyond the State' in J. L. Dunoff and J. P. Trachtman (eds), *Ruling the World? Constitutionalism, International Law and Global Governance* (Cambridge University Press, 2009), 258 [hereafter, Kumm 2009] at p. 263.

[17] David Kennedy, 'One, Two, Three, Many Legal Orders: Legal Pluralism and the Cosmopolitan Dream', *New York University Review of Law & Social Change* 641 (2007) [hereafter, Kennedy 2007], at p. 645.

general tendency for the cosmopolitan to be mapped onto the global or universal, and often unfavourably contrasted with the local or particular. On this approach, cosmopolitanism is an answer to a question about the default level of analysis: its proponents regard abandoning the traditional state-based framework as essential to bringing about the necessary 'revolution in legal thinking' which can guarantee constitutionalism's future prospects.[18]

There is, though, another understanding of cosmopolitanism. If we call the impetus to transcend methodological nationalism **cosmopolitanism I**, then **cosmopolitanism II** embodies an ethos of cosmopolitan pluralism, which highlights the creative potential that lies *in the space between* the local and the global. This brings us to the contribution of William Twining's thought to debates on constitutionalism and globalization. Twining regards 'a healthy cosmopolitan discipline of law' as an essential component of his theory of general jurisprudence in the global age.[19] The argument presented in this chapter is that Twining's understanding of cosmopolitanism is much closer to cosmopolitanism II, and, moreover, that exploring why this is the case shows the truly radical work which a cosmopolitan perspective brings to constitutional theory. This goes significantly further than the choice (or even relation) between different levels, going instead to the very nature of constitutionalism itself. As such, cosmopolitanism II reveals the extent to which what we take for granted in constitutional discourse is based on the systematic exclusion of much that properly belongs there. This suggests that those seeking to overcome the tension outlined above are looking in the wrong places: instead, we need to see constitutionalism's ubiquity and impossibility as both necessary and important, and furthermore, that their interaction supplies the critical energy to harness constitutionalism to more transformative ends. This leads to a more richly textured picture of constitutionalism which adds to the familiar account of 'constitutionalism from above' privileged by Western discourse, the generally occluded phenomena of '*constitutionalism from below*' found variously in innovative governance practices in the global South, non-institutional forms of politics, and the struggles of the marginalized and relatively powerless.

The structure of this chapter is as follows. We first set the scene by considering in more detail what is at stake in Twining's cosmopolitan discipline of law. Borrowing the term 'complementarity' from debates in science, we suggest, reading Twining alongside Boaventura de Sousa Santos, that this underscores the advantages for legal theory of a cosmopolitan pluralism which acknowledges that a theoretical perspective 'from above' should be read – and is only fully adumbrated in relation to – a counter-perspective 'from below'. We then focus more directly upon debates in constitutionalism and

[18] Kumm 2009, at p. 261.

[19] William Twining, *General Jurisprudence: Understanding Law from a Global Perspective* (Cambridge University Press, 2009) [hereafter, Twining 2009], at p. xi.

outline the contribution of cosmopolitanism I in responding to the challenges of globalization: whilst aware of the limitations of the Kantian framework, cosmopolitanism I retains a universalist aspiration which sits uneasily with the empirical complexity of globalization highlighted by both Twining and Santos. Following this, we offer an innovative approach, building upon the work of Seyla Benhabib, which applies cosmopolitanism II to constitutional theory. Reflecting more general developments in globalization theory which endorse the complementarity practised by Twining and Santos, we outline how 'top-down' and 'bottom-up' approaches to constitutional theory are necessary in navigating between cosmopolitanism's universal aspirations and the intransigence of the particular. We conclude by outlining the nature of the research agenda which this cosmopolitan pluralist approach generates.

2. Twining (and Santos) on cosmopolitanism

The resurgence of interest in cosmopolitanism in political and legal theory has appeared alongside, and largely in response to, the key geopolitical changes generally, albeit loosely, captured under the rubric of globalization. The fall of the Berlin Wall, and with it the bipolar world of the Cold War era, opened the conceptual space to imagine the pursuit of politics, and the crafting of solutions to problems of governance, on a global canvas.[20] In its initial articulation, contemporary cosmopolitanism sought to rework its original Kantian understanding for the present world of 'overlapping communities of fate'.[21] Central to the appeal of this enterprise was the potential for democratic governance to be carried from the national to supranational level, leading some proponents to speculate that cosmopolitanism might tame globalization.[22] More recently, though, something very interesting has happened to cosmopolitan discourse: those who are most wary of its past as a means of universalizing European values and power (including Santos) have sought to reclaim the language of cosmopolitanism to advance more insurgent projects. Indeed, one of the more remarkable developments has been the express adoption of the language of cosmopolitanism by those advocating radical resistance to the dominant, neoliberal, mode of globalization.

Here, we introduce the key issues in this debate by considering how ideas of cosmopolitanism have informed Twining's – and Boaventura de Sousa Santos' – efforts to reformulate legal theory to meet the exigencies of globalization. At first glance, the connection between the two may not be self-evident.

[20] Daniele Archibugi, 'Cosmopolitan Democracy' in Daniele Archibugi, ed., *Debating Cosmopolitics* (London: Verso, 2003), 1.

[21] David Held, 'From Executive to Multilateral Cosmopolitanism' in David Held and Mathias Koenig-Archibugi (eds), *Taming Globalization: Frontiers of Governance* (Oxford: Polity, 2003), p. 160 [hereafter Held 2003a], at p. 168.

[22] David Held, 'Cosmopolitanism: globalisation tamed?', *29 Review of International Studies* 465 (2003) [hereafter, Held 2003b].

Twining styles himself as an 'English jurist' concerned with law as it is institutionalized in the West,[23] while Santos is a scholar of the global South, and champion of the non- and a-legal, who seeks to replace the paradigm of modern law. Furthermore, the link with constitutionalism may also not be readily apparent, given that it does not feature prominently in either Twining's or Santos' work. However, reading them together crystallizes the fundamental tension underlying debates in cosmopolitanism between the normative appeal of the universal and the empirical stubbornness of the particular to resurface within any posited universal. Moreover, it provides the basis for understanding how this dilemma is replicated within constitutional theory. For Twining and Santos, it should be seen less as a choice between local and global levels of analysis and more as confronting the implications of cosmopolitanism's 'unresolved contrasts'.[24] In this section, we sketch the respective ways in which Twining and Santos embody cosmopolitanism before introducing the key idea of *complementarity*, borrowed from debates in science, to argue that although they emerge from scholarly traditions broadly characterized as, respectively, (Western) top-down and (Southern) bottom-up models of legal analysis, *taken together* they show that both models are necessary answers to a shared problem.

Twining's 'healthy cosmopolitan discipline of law'

In many ways, William Twining personifies the territory of cosmopolitanism that we are mapping here. As stated above, he self-identifies as a 'mainstream English jurist', writing 'within the tradition of [Western] modernity',[25] whose standpoint in debates on law and globalization is to advance the well-being of 'the institutionalised discipline of law, especially in common law countries'.[26] Anyone with even a passing knowledge of Twining's biography and scholarship – his extensive connections to Africa, his championing of 'Southern voices' – will soon realize that this self-portrait tells only a small part of the story. For one commentator, it is the relationship between the centre and periphery that has been the central preoccupation of his life's work.[27] While Twining's background and training may be seen as gravitational pulls towards the centre, much of his recent mission has been to rouse that centre from parochial complacency; thus, he advocates a 'radical rethink' in Anglo-American legal theory's response to globalization through a commitment to a 'healthy cosmopolitan discipline of law'.[28] Unpicking what this

[23] Twining 2009, at p. xiv.

[24] Seyla Benhabib, *Dignity in Adversity: Human Rights in Troubled Times* (Cambridge: Polity, 2011) [hereafter, Benhabib 2011], at p. 2.

[25] William Twining, *Globalisation and Legal Theory* (London: Butterworth, 2000) [hereafter, Twining 2000], at p. 198.

[26] Twining 2009, xiv.

[27] Harry Arthurs, 'Introduction', 18 *International Journal of the Legal Profession* 3 (2010), at p. 3.

[28] Twining 2009, at pp. xviii and xi.

cosmopolitanism entails brings us closer to the heart of the matter. In doing so, and without discounting the complexity at work here, I suggest that we should take Twining at his initial word and see his project as seeking to qualify important aspects of the Western model of law, whilst nonetheless retaining that model in setting its broad framework of inquiry.

Twining's scholarship employs cadences and tropes which will be instantly familiar to those schooled – and teaching – within the Western legal academy. For common law theorists in particular, Twining's conversation is one of which they can readily feel part, in a way that would be much more difficult to contemplate in the case of Santos. For example, Twining is perfectly at home calling, as he does in his Hamlyn lectures, for a reinvigoration of the legal treatise.[29] He is also content to situate himself within the Anglo-American analytical positivist tradition as exemplified by Herbert Hart, insisting on the importance of, 'draw[ing] a clear distinction between describing, explaining and interpreting legal phenomena', as they are and evaluating, criticising, recommending and prescribing conditions for legitimating such phenomena.[30]

For Twining, the truly interesting questions are not, turning to Santos' terms, whether law should be conceived as regulation or emancipation, or whether the paradigm of Western modernity has exhausted itself. One can imagine most Western scholars acceding to Twining's characterization of his own work as 'unashamedly subparadigmatic' (while shifting uneasily at the idea that it could be otherwise). As such, Twining measures the value of legal theory in terms of how it helps address 'urgent, real life, historically specific problems'[31] and has no problem endorsing Julius Stone's rendition of jurisprudence as that which 'seeks detailed empirical understanding and solution of *ad hoc* practical problems'.[32]

However, while acknowledging his intellectual roots, Twining is no apologist for Western jurisprudence, and views the latter's insularity as an impediment to the central task of the 'elucidation and construction of concepts'[33] which can enable legal theory to respond more effectively to globalization. In this connection, placing the adjective 'general' prior to 'jurisprudence' in the title of his most recent intervention in the globalization debate is highly informative, and underscores what distinguishes his approach from the mainstream. For Twining, 'general jurisprudence' signifies a focus on legal phenomena across jurisdictions, as opposed to the general aspects of a particular legal system.[34] Thus, a focus on state law alone, or even a global perspective that is confined to one type of legal ordering, is too restrictive for making sense

[29] William Twining, *Blackstone's Tower: The English Law School* (London: Sweet & Maxwell, 1994) [hereafter, Twining 1994].
[30] Twining 2009, at p. 27. [31] Twining 2009, at p. 5 [32] Twining 2009, at p. 5.
[33] Twining 2009, at p.xix.
[34] Thus, Twining suggests that 'modern jurists' such as Hart and Joseph Raz should be regarded as '*examples* of general jurisprudence' as 'their *conception* of "general jurisprudence" is quite narrow in being largely confined to state law viewed from what is essentially a Western perspective.' (Twining 2009, at p. 21, emphasis in original.)

of globalization. Instead, and in contrast with the centralizing tendency which has dominated Western law schools, Twining commends a pluralistic outlook for jurisprudence in a time of globalization, based in 'the theoretical study of two or more legal traditions, cultures, or orders . . . from the micro-comparative to the universal'.[35]

It is Twining's relationship to the idea of the universal that makes clear that his conception of cosmopolitanism is imbued with the pluralism associated with cosmopolitanism II, as outlined in the introduction. Indeed, his cosmopolitanism starts from the position that any claim to universality is to be treated with a healthy dose of scepticism, particularly if this claim is generated from within a single legal tradition.[36] This counsel of caution against an uncritical embrace of universalist modes of discourse extends to methodological, political and pragmatic concerns. Methodologically, Twining's unease is directed towards a tendency to regard the principal subject matter of law as the norms that have developed within official European and Anglo-American legal systems. His cosmopolitanism seeks to prevent this normative universalism from taking hold by encouraging legal theory to embrace the 'empirical study of social facts'[37] in order to reveal the rich variety of legal ordering in the contemporary world. In political terms, Twining highlights how a disdain for the empirical often flows from a belief that 'the fundamental values underlying modern law are universal',[38] which in practice lapses into an unreflective ethnocentrism.[39] He contrasts this with the 'fact' of belief pluralism in today's world.[40] Twining's more pluralist cosmopolitanism here questions whether the universalist aspirations of cosmopolitanism I can be reconciled with the recurrent danger of a totalizing particular masquerading as a false universal. This leads to the pragmatic consideration of how to harness law to social justice, and foster co-operation, in a world characterized by 'very different cosmologies and values.'[41] While Twining recognizes that this affords no simple answers, he sees openness to comparison and the influence of non-Western legal cultures as an indispensable element in developing a 'healthy cosmopolitan discipline of law'.[42]

Santos' subaltern cosmopolitanism

Boaventura de Sousa Santos' account of cosmopolitanism is located within his complex analysis of globalization and its relation to Western modernity. Globalization, he suggests, has both hegemonic and counter-hegemonic dimensions. Hegemonic globalization, on this view, reached its apotheosis in a global consensus based on neo-liberal economic models, weak state political models and liberal democratic constitutional models. This consensus, Santos

[35] Twining 2009, at p. 21. [36] Twining 2009, at p. xviii. [37] Twining 2009, at p. 6.
[38] Twining 2009, at p. 6 [39] Twining 2009, at p. xi. [40] Twining 2009, at p. 7.
[41] Twining 2009, at p. 7. [42] Twining 2009, at p. xx.

argues, marked the demise of Western modernity's promise of emancipation through enlightened management of the tension between order (or regulation) and good order (or emancipation), as the latter has been folded back into the former. Santos is emphatic that this is not the whole story, and alongside hegemonic globalization we should also include counter-hegemonic globalization, to capture the diverse range of acts of resistance to neo-liberalism, such as the new forms of political activism like the World Social Forum. A key component of this resistance is what he calls *subaltern cosmopolitanism*, which highlights the innovative and myriad ways in which 'subordinate nation-states, regions, classes or social groups and their allies' have been organizing to defend their common interests.[43]

Santos' cosmopolitanism can be seen as the obverse of Twining's. For Santos, the traditional Western understanding of law is an integral part of the problem of hegemonic globalization, and so he seeks to reorient the debate to how law and globalization might look from a Southern perspective. While his subaltern cosmopolitanism speaks to the same range of concerns as Twining, in each case he offers what he terms a more radical paradigmatic approach. In methodological terms, his diagnosis is that the reduction of law to *modern state* law is a crucial aspect of the collapse of emancipation into regulation. This leads him to argue for nothing less than the 'unthinking' of modern law. He finds in the interstitial places of subaltern cosmopolitanism forms of legal knowledge that were previously suppressed, and that expand the legal canon from the state to the non-state, and also to the non-legal, illegal and a-legal.[44] Santos' political analysis also seems to go further than Twining's, seeing the universalization of rational, Western law as part of a neoliberal strategy for depoliticizing social conflict by making formal legal processes the single criterion for global legality.[45] Accordingly, Santos contends, subaltern cosmopolitanism expands the potential fields of legal and political contestation through its epistemological openings, providing a vital form of counter-hegemonic agency. His view of the best strategy for advancing social justice is necessarily tied to his call for paradigmatic renewal, and is perhaps better described as programmatic rather than pragmatic. For Santos, anything other than a wholesale reconceptualization of law from the bottom up risks tinkering at the edges, and missing the opportunity for change provided by what he calls 'the most intellectually challenging and politically compelling aspect of globalization'.[46]

[43] Santos 2002, at p. 180. [44] Santos 2002, at p. 180. [45] Santos 2002, at p. 316.

[46] Boaventura de Sousa Santos and César A. Rodríguez-Garavito [hereafter, Santos 2005b], 'Law, Politics and the Subaltern in Counter-Hegemonic Globalization' in Boaventura de Sousa Santos and César A. Rodríguez-Garavito (eds) [hereafter, Santos and Rodríguez-Garavito 2005a], *Law and Globalization from Below: Towards a Cosmopolitan Legality* (Cambridge University Press, 2005), 1, at p. 2.

Twining and Santos: complementary cosmopolitanisms?

On one reading, Twining and Santos offer contrary accounts of the possibilities of legal cosmopolitanism in a time of globalization. While Twining acknowledges that the top-down model of Western legal theory has serious limitations, his approach is to modify and improve that model by opening it to an 'empirically grounded comparative'[47] understanding of other legal cultures. This is a cosmopolitanism marked by continuity: new perspectives are to be synthesized within a still-recognizable whole. In contrast, Santos' approach is more self-consciously critical, imbued with a deep wariness over the very idea of cosmopolitanism, seeing in its 'unconditional inclusiveness' more often than not an enterprise that 'pursue[s] the exclusionary interests of a particular social group'.[48] Thus, he presents instead a bottom-up cosmopolitanism of rupture that may appear to change the concept beyond all recognition. Moreover, there is a clear difference in sensibility between the two, underscored by the contrasts implied by Twining's description of his own approach as 'mundane, cautious and rather apolitical'.[49] Moreover, Twining is more receptive to the force of the argument against extending the scope of legal analysis entailed by Santos' subaltern cosmopolitanism, observing that these concerns 'deserve to be taken seriously'.[50]

However, it is important to move beyond surface impressions. To paraphrase Santos, another reading is possible: one that sees their respective positions as complementary rather than oppositional. This reading borrows the concept of *complementarity* from the scientific literature. In his Gifford lectures, neuroscientist Michael Gazzaniga explains the problem this idea seeks to address in the context of debates over the nature of causation in cognitive science.[51] Gazzaniga recounts how reductionist ideas which explain actions as always-already predetermined by physical conditions in the brain have been challenged by the notion of 'emergence', which sees consciousness as formed in the interaction between neural circuits and the social environment. For present purposes,[52] what is most interesting about Gazzaniga's work is his employment of Howard Pattee's concept of complementarity to denote:

> complementary models [which] are formally incompatible but both necessary. One model cannot be derived from, or reduced to the other. Chance cannot be

[47] Twining 2009, at p. xx. [48] Santos 2002, at pp. 459, 460. [49] Twining 2000, at p. 198.

[50] Twining 2009, at p. 375. It is interesting to compare the lengths to which Twining goes in seeking to persuade e.g. Simon Roberts that there may not be such a distance between the idea of legal pluralism and Roberts' anxiety that the latter would unnecessarily 'broaden representations of law to include negotiated orders' (at p. 371) with Santos' cursory 'why not?' response to those who ask why 'complementary forms of social ordering' should be designated as legal (Santos 2002, at p. 91).

[51] Michael S. Gazzaniga, *Who's in Charge? Free Will and the Science of the Brain* (New York: HarperCollins, 2011) [hereafter, Gazzaniga], at pp. 123–42.

[52] More broadly, whichever side one comes down on can make a huge difference to questions of free will and determinism, and the implications are becoming of increasing interest, for example, to questions of culpability in criminal law.

derived from necessity, nor necessity from chance, but both concepts are necessary.[53]

So, rather than, for example, extrapolating a top-down model of causation from findings that the brain acts before we have conscious awareness of a situation, a complementary approach questions the very nature of 'cause', seeing any course of action as driven not by a single physical system but potentially by 'hundreds, thousands, and perhaps millions' of such systems.[54] Thus, Gazzaniga sees a binary choice between upward and downward models of causation as misunderstanding the nature of the inquiry.[55] An important corollary of this stance is that each side, although *prima facie* incommensurate with the other, can be seen to be interdependent aspects of a shared problem. Gazzaniga's conclusion is that 'responsibility and freedom are found . . . in the space between brains, in the interactions between people'.[56] Returning to the discussion of cosmopolitanism, complementarity also provides us with a potentially more interesting and helpful reading of Twining's and Santos' contributions than the oppositional perspective outlined above. In particular, it enables us to view each as complemented by the other, developing the inquiry along paths that the intellectual conditioning of each, taken by itself, would not generally take. Crucially, on this approach, each possesses an implicit awareness of the limitations of their own perspective, and so we can see their respective accounts of cosmopolitanism as the result of a mutual exploration of those limits.[57]

While Twining acknowledges his roots in the Western legal tradition, he is highly critical of the narrowing of perspective that its 'top-down' statist world-view brings about. Interestingly, one of the ways in which he suggests that law is becoming more cosmopolitan in practice is through the persistence of 'post-colonial subaltern perspectives'.[58] In arguing that legal theory needs to adopt a more inclusive approach in its response to globalization, encompassing such perspectives, Twining comes close to Santos' position that their absence within the Western mindset is, and has been, actively produced.[59] Thus, and consistent with his rejection of any definitional long-stop in favour of viewing law more as a continuum, for Twining any top-down conception of law necessarily includes its bottom-up complement, and *vice versa*. But this methodological consonance should not hide the political divergence between the two: whereas Twining is content to join Santos in beginning to examine the implications of a

[53] Gazzaniga, at p. 123 (quoting Howard Pattee). [54] Gazzaniga, at p. 141.

[55] Gazzaniga, at p. 133. [56] Gazzaniga, at p. 137.

[57] This suggestion should not necessarily be taken as speculative, given Santos' acknowledgement in the preface to *Towards a New Legal Common Sense* that not only was it Twining's idea that Santos write a second edition, but that his criticism of Santos' work from a modern, Western perspective in his 'excellent book *Globalization and Legal Theory*' was 'persuasive enough to make [Santos] attempt a better book' (Santos 2002, at p. xxi).

[58] Twining 2009, at p. 7.

[59] Boaventura de Sousa Santos, 'Beyond Abyssal Thinking: From Global Lines to Ecologies of Knowledge', XXX *Review* (Fernand Braudel Center, 2007) 45 [hereafter, Santos 2007].

bottom-up approach, his political commitment to the utility of modern law as a solution to globalization means that they part company as Santos ventures further into the territory of 'uncivil and strange society'[60] which sees modern law as part of the problem to be overcome.

For Santos, any refolding of subaltern cosmopolitan legality back into the institutional clutches of modern law will undermine its counter-hegemonic possibilities. However, while 'reimagining legal institutions from below',[61] by mapping the new legal forms produced, for example by social movement struggles, rhetorically sharpens the political distinctions Santos wishes to draw, he does not see such a shift as wholly replacing top-down analyses. Rather, his concern is that if such approaches provide the *exclusive* focus of study, we will miss the 'moment of counter-hegemony',[62] thereby conceding too much to hegemonic readings of globalization. Moreover, for Santos, in a time of transition, the old paradigm of modernity does not simply disappear but is the shell from which the new insurgent paradigm emerges, and so the two must be understood in a (necessarily ambiguous) relation to each other.[63] Although Santos is deeply critical of law's excess of regulation under the paradigm of modernity, law is not theorized away in the new paradigm (unlike what he terms 'celebratory post-modernism'[64]); suitably reconfigured, it remains an important artefact in shaping social change.[65] Thus, Santos also appears to accept, at least during the present transitional moment, that aspects of the top-down conception of law remain in play, and indeed, that it is by transforming (while in large part retaining) the forms of that conception from the inside out, that the new paradigm comes into being.

Extending the idea of complementarity to debates on globalization and law, we can characterize legal cosmopolitanism as located *in the space between* the top-down Western model of legality and the bottom-up conception that Santos associates with developments in the South. This enables us to see both the extent of and the potential for interaction between these models in Twining's and Santos' work. For example, by outlining the shortcomings of the false universalism attributed to human rights from within the limits of conventional legal theory,[66] Twining can be seen to be preparing the way for an otherwise sceptical audience with respect to Santos' emancipatory 'new universalism of cosmopolitanism'.[67] Twining's pragmatic engagement of the possibilities within current institutional forms may also provide some practical resources for grounding Santos' theoretical inquiry into the nature of the paradigmatic transition. One advantage of this approach is that it enables

[60] Santos 2002, at p. 469. [61] Santos and Rodríguez-Garavito 2005 b, at pp. 14, 15.
[62] Santos and Rodríguez-Garavito 2005 b, at p. 6. [63] Santos 2002, at p. 11.
[64] Santos 2002, at p. 18. [65] Santos 2002, ch. 9. [66] Santos 2002, at p. xxi.
[67] Boaventura de Sousa Santos [hereafter, Santos 2008b], 'Human Rights as an Emancipatory Script? Cultural and Political Conditions' in Boaventura de Sousa Santos, ed. [hereafter, Santos 2008a], *Another Knowledge is Possible: Beyond Northern Epistemologies* (London: Verso, 2008), 3, at p. 24.

top-down or bottom-up approaches to gain insights from the other without resolving whether or not the framework of modern Western law needs to be replaced. In fact, it raises the prospect of Twining and Santos enlisting each other in their respective causes.

3. Cosmopolitanism and constitutionalism

In the remainder of this chapter, we consider the implications of cosmopolitanism for constitutional theory. We sketch the far-reaching implications of a complementarity-based approach with regard to constitutional theory, and argue that the exchange between constitutionalism from above and constitutionalism from below widens our conception of the subject: in particular, we consider the important contribution which reading Twining and Santos together makes to the ongoing debate.

The foregoing discussion sharpens what is at stake in the distinction drawn between the two conceptions of cosmopolitanism outlined in the introduction when applied to the constitutional realm. Under cosmopolitanism I, the key problem to be addressed is the enduring hold of methodological nationalism; in its place, a 'cosmopolitan turn' in constitutionalism has been advocated by some theorists, which, insofar as it transcends statist thinking, is said to hold out the promise of a revolution in constitutional thought on a par with the development of modern constitutionalism itself.[68] The complementarity approach outlined above, though, questions whether the key challenge that cosmopolitanism poses to constitutional theory is how '*national* constitutional lawyers imagine constitutional law'.[69] Instead, we explore the possibility that a broader challenge is presented by cosmopolitanism II, which sees the main difficulty to be overcome being how *modern Western* constitutional lawyers imagine constitutional law. In the remainder of this chapter, we outline first how some leading proponents of cosmopolitanism within constitutional theory can be seen to retain key aspects of the top-down approach identified by Twining and Santos. We then advance an alternative approach under which cosmopolitanism potentially reformulates our basic understandings of constitutionalism, by positing the latter as necessarily produced by the relationship between the (thus far) predominant conception of constitutionalism from above and the generally occluded, but increasingly visible, discourse of constitutionalism from below.

Cosmopolitanism I and the problem of methodological nationalism

In its classical form, cosmopolitanism is seen as the counterpoint to nationalism: what we have termed cosmopolitanism I. The choice between 'methodological nationalism' and 'methodological cosmopolitanism' is the subject of

[68] Kumm 2009, at p. 261. [69] Kumm 2009, at p. 261 (emphasis added).

Robert Fine's influential recent monograph.[70] The focus of Fine's analysis is the 'new cosmopolitanism' that accompanied the immediate aftermath of the fall of the Berlin Wall. This sought to revive the Kantian projects of universal history and perpetual peace through the abandonment of methodological nationalism, the recognition of greater mutual interdependence, and the normative pursuit of ideas of global justice.[71] He doubts whether this is sufficiently 'new' or 'cosmopolitan'. He sees the retention of a natural law teleology as leading to 'inflated claims' about the end of ideological conflict which it is difficult to justify when confronted with the empirical reality of global violence over the past few decades.[72] Even more pressing are the difficulties of transcending the framework of methodological nationalism, and here he suggests that new cosmopolitanism is insufficiently cosmopolitan, conceding too much to a 'conventional notion of belonging'.[73] For Fine, theorists such as Rawls and Habermas are open to the charge that their versions of cosmopolitanism are in practice grounded in American rights discourse and German constitutionalism respectively, but presented with a universalist supplement.

In Fine's view, though, the conclusion to draw from these challenges is not to abandon the cosmopolitan project but to reconstruct it on more robust theoretical foundations. In this connection he advocates a more thorough-going cosmopolitanism which, in contrast to the new cosmopolitanism, sets the conceptual frame as always operating at the global level and does not make any concessions to its supposed national origins. Accordingly, he unequivocally grounds this cosmopolitanism in the presupposition that 'the human species can only be understood if it is treated as a single subject.'[74] In this way, Fine suggests that cosmopolitanism can best live up to the ideal of 'the substantive unity of all human beings', which for him remains central in overcoming particularistic problems such as racism and xenophobia.[75]

Fine's caution against being unwittingly ensnared in the traps of methodological nationalism, while seeking to reconcile the universalist aspirations of cosmopolitanism with a more contingent view of political history, has considerable resonance for contemporary constitutional debates. While few theorists seek to conceptualize a unifying global constitutionalism, the statist frame has long been viewed by many as inadequate in both descriptive and normative terms for precisely the reasons advanced by Fine.[76] If methodological nationalism is, in the constitutional context, seen as unappealing, a growing number of constitutional scholars are finding in cosmopolitanism

[70] Robert Fine, *Cosmopolitanism* (London and New York: Routledge, 2007) [hereafter, Fine], at p. xi.

[71] Fine, at p. 4. [72] Fine, at p. xvi. [73] Fine, at p. x. [74] Fine, at p. x. [75] Fine, at p. xvii.

[76] Neil Walker, 'Taking Constitutionalism Beyond the State', 56 *Political Studies* (2008) 519 [hereafter, Walker].

the requisite tools for responding to the complexity of contemporary governance. Mattias Kumm has been at the forefront of this movement, and his work is a particularly important example given his claim that a cosmopolitan outlook brings about a qualitative shift in how we understand constitutional discourse.[77] As such, he enables us to evaluate whether grappling with the problem of methodological nationalism is the most far-reaching challenge that cosmopolitanism presents to constitutional theory.

According to Kumm, the basic mistake of conventional theory is to conflate the constitutional part as it has developed within the nation-state with the whole. This presents difficulties for contemporary times as what he calls 'big C' constitutionalism, fixated upon the establishment of ultimate legal authority, has dwindling relevance for those seeking to explain the 'deeply pluralized and fragmentary' forms of authority operating beyond the state.[78] However, recasting constitutionalism in 'small-c' terms, which seeks to describe the structures of international or global governance as part of a coherent legal order but which lacks the indicia of state sovereignty, is problematic for those who see such moves as giving up too many of the gains for the legitimate management of political power achieved by 'big C' constitutionalism in the state context.[79] Kumm argues that this tension can only be satisfactorily resolved by means of a cosmopolitan paradigm which, *contra* the sharp division just outlined, insists that there 'is only constitutionalism in different institutional contexts'.[80] In this way, Kumm sees cosmopolitan constitutionalism as establishing 'an integrative basic conceptual framework for a general theory of public law that integrates national and international law'.[81]

Kumm's project focuses welcome attention on what demarcates the scope of the constitutional once we move outside the statist frame, and there are some interesting parallels with Twining's approach in terms of conceiving of constitutionalism as a continuum. However, despite the Copernican claims made on behalf of his cosmopolitan approach, it can be regarded as occupying a relatively limited range of points on that continuum, leading us to question whether it fully articulates the potential for cosmopolitanism to open up our understandings of constitutionalism. Kumm sees his cosmopolitan paradigm as a 'unifying' framework for four key phenomena of the international legal order: doctrines for managing the relation between national and international law, the spread of novel global governance structures such as Global Administrative Law, 'the functional reconceptualization of sovereignty' and the international human rights regime.[82] But while this approach broadens the constitutional focus to include the relation between national and transnational

[77] Kumm 2009, at p. 261. [78] Kumm 2009, at p. 262.

[79] Mattias Kumm, 'The Cosmopolitan Turn in Constitutionalism: An Integrated Conception of Public Law', 20 *Indiana Journal of Global Legal Studies* (2013) 605 [hereafter, Kumm 2013)], at p. 608. Cf. Martin Loughlin, 'Constitutional Pluralism: An Oxymoron?' 3 *Global Constitutionalism* (2014) 9 [hereafter, Loughlin 2014].

[80] Kumm 2009, at p. 263. [81] Kumm 2009, at p. 264. [82] Kumm 2009, at p. 262.

norms, the list enumerated very much takes, in Twining's terms, the 'top-down' perspective of 'rulers, officials, legislators and elites'.[83] It is also Northocentric, with Kumm expressly citing the American and French constitutional innovations of the late eighteenth century as the antecedents from which he seeks to generalize.[84] Furthermore, the cosmopolitan constitutionalism posited is held out as a 'universally-applicable' framework for assessing the decisions and processes of those in authority.[85]

To non-Western eyes, the key features of constitutionalism before and after taking the cosmopolitan turn recommended by Kumm may seem remarkably similar, and moreover highly reminiscent of modern Western law's self-image.[86] Thus, if we adopt the empirically grounded comparative viewpoint commended by Twining, Kumm's cosmopolitanism may pluralize the sites of constitutionalism, but it does not necessarily pluralize our understanding of the constitutionalism which unfolds there. There are two important points to make in this connection. First, while Kumm may represent the most fully worked out version in the academic literature, his top-down, elite-focused, universalist focus is by no means unique to those seeking to flesh out the parameters of cosmopolitan constitutionalism. For example, transnational courts adjudicating international treaties occupy, for some, 'a central strategic position in the [cosmopolitan legal order]'[87] with the key 'discursive battles' occurring between their and national (legislative and judicial) institutions' interpretation of human right provisions.[88] For others, cosmopolitan constitutionalism is the key to ensuring that the highly technical rules of transnational trade ensure respect for 'common market freedoms' and basic property rights.[89] The point here is not to deny such positions their place within the cosmopolitan panoply, but rather to observe that the dualist focus on the relation between official legal orders appears of the same genus as Twining's black box of municipal and international law; consequently, the latter is not being prised apart by this version of cosmopolitan constitutionalism to the extent that is sometimes suggested.

To be clear: what we are tracking here goes beyond idiosyncratic takes on constitutional theory, but – and this is the second broad point – instead returns us to the potential limitations of orienting to cosmopolitanism through the prism of transcending methodological nationalism. Cosmopolitanism necessarily operates on the border between inclusion and exclusion. Thus, Fine grounds his cosmopolitan social theory in Hannah Arendt's concept of 'the right to have rights', informed by how this right's downfall in the twentieth

[83] Twining 2009, at p. 6. [84] Kumm 2009, at p. 322. [85] Kumm 2009, at p. 263.
[86] Twining 2009, at p. 6.
[87] Alec Stone Sweet, 'A cosmopolitan legal order: Constitutional pluralism and rights adjudication in Europe', 1 *Global Constitutionalism* (2012) 53 [hereafter, Stone Sweet], at p. 60.
[88] Stone Sweet, at p. 84.
[89] Ernst-Ulrich Petersmann, 'Human Rights require "Cosmopolitan Constitutionalism" and Cosmopolitan Law for Democratic Governance of Public Goods', EUI Working Paper 2013/14 (2013) [hereafter, Petersmann], at p. 8.

century was tied to totalitarian national movements' exploitation of 'pariah' peoples as stateless and so unable to possess such rights.[90] Without in any way trivializing the weight of the historical argument being made by Fine, in a contemporary setting it is important to ask whether the logics of exclusion should be exclusively or even primarily attributed to methodological nationalism. Twining and Santos direct us to the ways in which the modern Western conception of law is built upon the exclusion of others' experiences. If this conception of law, as suggested above, has transcended the nation-state, it would follow that its logics of exclusion are also at work at the supranational level. Accordingly, if we wish to address questions of power relations, then the critique of (or even the 'critique of the critique of'[91]) methodological nationalism may not be enough. In this regard, Santos argues that cosmopolitanism is only possible interstitially, at the margins.[92] On this view, conceiving of cosmopolitanism as normative universalism can be seen as an impediment to addressing unequal power relations insofar as it directs attention away from the contingent processes by which cosmopolitanism itself draws the line between inclusion and exclusion. In the following section, we consider how a cosmopolitanism that explores those interstices opens up constitutionalism to a more radical reformulation than has so far been contemplated.

Cosmopolitan II: constitutionalism as a 'field of unresolved contrasts'

An alternative account of cosmopolitanism which bears fruitful study for the constitutional debate is offered by Seyla Benhabib. Benhabib identifies an unanswered conundrum at the heart of present-day cosmopolitan theory which she attributes to its failure to address 'the paradox of bounded communities'.[93] This paradox speaks to the 'inevitable and necessary tension' between the duties and obligations which flow from being members of such bounded communities, and as members of the human race.[94] She traces this to Kant's ambiguous legacy which, while positing a right to hospitality as inherent in being human, retains elements of sovereign authority, not least to establish the intentions (hostile or otherwise) of the guest seeking such hospitality.[95] For Benhabib, it is important to go beyond the Kantian framework if cosmopolitanism's value for the present time is to be fully realized. In contrast with those who embrace cosmopolitanism as a positive ideal which can dissolve national borders, she commends a critical conception of cosmopolitanism as 'a negative ideal aimed at blocking false totalization'.[96] Cosmopolitanism II so understood

[90] Fine, at p. xvi. [91] Fine, at p. 9. [92] Santos 2002, at p. 180.

[93] Seyla Benhabib, *Another Cosmopolitanism* (Oxford University Press, 2006) [hereafter, Benhabib 2006], at p. 18.

[94] Benhabib 2006, at p. 19.

[95] This ambiguity, she argues, is reflected in Kant's own endorsement of the expansion of European mercantile capitalism overseas while at the same time opposing an imperial right to conquer with regard to colonial ventures in the Far East: Benhabib 2011, at p. 7.

[96] Benhabib 2011, at p. 5.

depicts 'a field of unresolved contrasts,' and views the positive conception as unable to transcend intractable antinomies between:

> particularistic attachments and universalist aspirations; between the multiplicity of human laws and the ideal of a rational order that would be common to all human cities; and between belief in the unity of humankind and the healthy agonisms and antagonisms generated by human diversity.[97]

Thus, unlike Fine, her response to the deficiencies in the actual record of cosmopolitanism is *not* to elevate a universalist conception that dissolves national borders as the most authentic form which alone can remedy its shortcomings: instead, she regards these shortcomings as unavoidable; the cosmopolitan ideal can best be salvaged, rather, by cultivating a different attitude towards these shortcomings.

Benhabib's account leads to a quite different understanding of the relevance of cosmopolitanism for constitutional scholarship than that outlined earlier. Instead of seeing constitutionalism in terms of a unifying framework, it considers what it would mean to extend this view of 'cosmopolitanism as struggle' to the constitutional realm. In doing so, it focuses attention on whether under cosmopolitanism I, by masking ongoing antagonisms, there may be a confluence of universalist tropes with the legitimation of existing concentrations of power.[98] A constitutional theory that does not encompass Benhabib's 'unresolved contrasts' is necessarily partial, both in its analytical scope and normative orientation.

How might a theory that does include this perspective be constructed, and what would it look like? An important starting point is to develop Twining's notion of law as continuum, but locate this in the space between the antinomies identified by Benhabib. On this approach, any posited account of constitutionalism is always to be seen in relation to how it distinguishes the non-constitutional. In prevailing conceptions of cosmopolitan constitutionalism, the top-down outcome of this process is assumed and provides the baseline for theorizing: for cosmopolitanism II, the interrogation of this process lies at the heart of the matter.

Cosmopolitanism II leads to a complementarity-based understanding of constitutionalism. Specifically, this argues that what is generally taken to be 'constitutionalism' is more accurately to be seen as constitutionalism from above, which is produced, and only becomes meaningful, through the active exclusion of constitutionalism from below. A fuller understanding of constitutional phenomena necessarily comprehends both constitutionalism from above *and* below. This is not to posit some essentialist notion to which all accounts of constitutionalism should conform rather, what we are highlighting are the contingent ways in which constitutional discourse is generated in practice. This builds on the germ of an approach outlined by Twining in a

[97] Benhabib 2011, at p. 2. [98] Santos 2002, at p. 460.

rare excursion into constitutional territory in 1993. Discussing the seemingly exponential spread of constitutionalism defined in terms of the rule of law, human rights, limited government and judicial review, he asks:

> Do these terms suggest that there is a widely shared agenda of problems with a limited range of solutions, as some constitution-mongers suggest? Or does an ambiguous discourse conceal a much greater range of issues that are more context-dependent and more sensitive to local knowledge than the common vocabulary reveals?[99]

Against a 'thin' conception of constitutionalism, which broadly equates to the precepts of liberal democracy, Twining favourably contrasts a 'more complex "realist" conception [which] combines the normative and the empirical'.[100] This 'thick' conception includes a '*de facto* map of political power' but also '*a good deal more*', which extends at least to 'an account of local legal culture and tradition, and of personnel and their ways of doing things'.[101] This view provides the basis for pluralizing our understandings of constitutionalism beyond the top-down conception associated with cosmopolitanism I, broadening what is encompassed within constitutional discourse beyond formal or even functional indicia. Nothing is ruled in or out as to the possible reach of the constitutional axes of inclusion and exclusion, and so there can be nothing immutable about the subject of constitutional discourse.

Twenty years later, much valuable assistance in fleshing out Twining's 'good deal more' in constitutional discourse can be found in Santos' analysis of contemporary globalization. It should be recalled that, for Santos, subaltern cosmopolitanism provides the necessary counterbalance to accounts that equate globalization with hegemonic globalization from above. For him, this reduction is not simply the incident of methodological myopia, but part of a strategy to legitimate neoliberalism by portraying it as 'the only game in town'.[102] In this connection, Santos makes two points that are highly relevant for our present purposes. By identifying its success in terms of 'silencing' alternative accounts, globalization from above sees itself as part of a broader conception of globalization. But, despite globalization from above's best efforts to bracket them out, questions of 'unequal exchanges and power relations',[103] which have been at the heart of legal and political theory, nonetheless persist through the rise of globalization from below. Underlying this process is a set of related challenges to the dominant top-down narrative, which argues that it is complemented from below in three important, and related, senses: geopolitical, focusing on the crucial context of North–South relations; institutional,

[99] William Twining, 'Constitutions, Constitutionalism and Constitution-Mongering' in Irwin P. Stotzky, ed., *Transition to Democracy in Latin America: The Role of the Judiciary* (Boulder CO: Westview Press, 1993) [hereafter, Twining 1993], at p. 383.

[100] Twining 1993, at p. 384. [101] Twining 1993, at p. 384 (emphasis added).

[102] Boaventura de Sousa Santos, 'Beyond Neoliberal Governance: The World Social Forum' in Santos and Rodríguez-Garavito (eds), 29 (2005a) [hereafter, Santos 2005], at p. 43.

[103] Santos 2005, at p. 29.

adverting to insurgent forms of law and politics outside formal settings, and; hierarchical, elucidating the perspective of those who live at the margins.

4. Conclusion: a constitutional research agenda 'from below'

We conclude by outlining some of the ways in which adopting this approach transforms the constitutional research agenda. Simply posing the question of what the West can learn from the South effects a fundamental shift of constitutional focus. The theory and practice of constitutionalism in the global age has tended to view the channel of transmission in top-down terms. Thus, whether celebrating the ultimate triumph of liberal democracy, or critiquing the attainment of a neoliberal hegemony, local traditions of governance are seen to be remade to accord with the constitutional imperatives of the West. Moreover, following Upendra Baxi, this is often presented in the language of endings,[104] indicating the closing down of constitutional innovations which depart from the emerging global norms.[105] However, notwithstanding the fatalistic tone of this analysis of globalization, others chart the vibrant and widespread patterns of resistance across the global South,[106] which some see as constituting a counter-hegemonic paradigm of globalization.[107] Thus, in representing the idea that there can be an alternative, the South provides an important counter to some of the more fatalistic readings of globalization. The invitation here is to consider how it would transform constitutional discourse by reversing the usual direction for the exchange of knowledge and including these developments within its scope.

One crucial way in which globalization from below opens up constitutional research is by bringing into the frame a wide range of bottom-up initiatives originating in the South, and which, according to Santos, provides a distinct 'matrix of governance'.[108] This includes the activism of social movements and civil society groups under the umbrella of the World Social Forum,[109] new forms of grass-roots politics such as participatory budget-making[110] and transnational solidarity campaigns in areas such as health and the environment.[111] These and other ongoing sites of struggle question the idea that global governance consists solely or primarily of the top-down imposition

104 Upendra Baxi, *The Future of Human Rights*, 3rd edn (New Delhi: Oxford University Press, 2008), at p. 244.

105 Schneiderman; Danny Nicol, *The Constitutional Protection of Capitalism* (Oxford and Portland, OR: Hart Publishing, 2010).

106 Ronaldo Munck, *Globalization and Contestation: the new great counter-movement* (London: Routledge, 2007); Geoffrey Pleyers, *Alter-Globalization: Becoming Actors in the Global Age* (Cambridge: Polity, 2010).

107 Santos and Rodríguez-Garavito. 108 Santos 2005, at p. 43. 109 Santos 2005a.

110 Boaventura de Sousa Santos, 'Two democracies, two legalities: participatory budgeting in Porto Alegre, Brazil' in Santos and Rodríguez-Garavito (eds) (2005a) 310.

111 Heinz Klug, 'Campaigning for Life: Building a New Transnational Solidarity in the Face of HIV/AIDS and TRIPs' in Santos and Rodríguez-Garavito (eds) (2005 b) 118; João Arriscado Nunes, Marisa Matias and Susana Costa, 'Bottom-up environmental law and democracy in the

of neoliberalism. Santos suggests that neoliberal governance follows a strategy of depoliticization, which defuses oppositional politics by converting them into technical questions to be presided over by the legal experts of international trade.[112] However, the alternative governance matrix of globalization from below resists this, and seeks to interrogate processes of marketization and liberalization which neoliberalism prefers to place beyond democratic reach. Thus if, as is increasingly the mainstream position, globalization from above is to be theorized in constitutional terms, ignoring its crucial relationship with globalization from below necessarily leads to a partial, and possibly misleading, picture. Instead, a fuller constitutional account takes note of how the future trajectory of globalization depends in large part on the interaction between top-down and bottom-up modes of governance. This approach directs research towards Benhabib's unresolved contrasts as themselves a source of constitutional generation, and, by keeping their dynamic tension in play, guards against any unnecessary foreclosure as to the outcome of that process. For Santos, globalization from below brings with it new forms of legality, such as inventive cross-fertilization between judicial and extra-judicial strategies of resistance.[113] Accordingly, an important area of future research explores the new forms of constitutional legality uncovered when we include the perspective from below. This includes redrawing the very borders of the constitutional itself.[114]

The agency through which these developments are generally prosecuted connects us to the second sense of 'below'. This speaks to the non-formal, unofficial levels of constitutional engagement not captured by a focus on formal institutions. This opens up a number of new scholarly frontiers, including the constitutional relevance of global social movements.[115] One of the most exciting innovations in the South, under the rubric of plurinational constitutionalism, has been the recognition within national constitution-making processes of the customary governance practices of indigenous peoples.[116] But, adopting a broad understanding of constitutionalism as the ongoing management of social differentiation through processes of abstraction and

risk society: Portugese experiences in the European Context' in Santos and Rodríguez-Garavito (eds) (2005) 363.

[112] Santos 2005, at p. 37.

[113] Santos 2002, at p. 467. See also César A. Rodríguez-Garavito and Luis Carlos Arenas, 'Indigenous rights, transnational activism, and legal mobilization: the struggle of the U'wa people in Colombia' in Santos and Rodríguez-Garavito (eds) (2005 b), 241.

[114] Gavin W. Anderson, 'The New Borders of the Constitutional', 50 *Osgoode Hall Law Journal* (2013) 737 [hereafter, Anderson 2013a]. For a highly stimulating account which explores the border between the legal and the a-legal in constitutional theory, see Hans Lindahl, *Fault Lines of Globalization: Legal Order and the Politics of A-Legality* (Oxford University Press, 2013).

[115] Gavin W. Anderson, 'Societal Constitutionalism, Social Movements and Constitutionalism from Below', 20 *Indiana Journal of Global Legal Studies* (2013) 881 [hereafter, Anderson 2013b].

[116] Pascal Lupien, 'The Incorporation of Indigenous Concepts of Plurinationality into the New Constitutions of Ecuador and Bolivia', 18 *Democratization* (2011) 774.

generalization,[117] we can see this non-institutional dimension of below as present in all constitutional arrangements, not just a selective few in Latin America. For example, the September 2014 referendum on Scottish independence can be seen, from one viewpoint, as a classic debate over the location of sovereignty, definitively settled by the 55%–45% vote in favour of the No side. However, in the immediate aftermath of the referendum, many commentators have suggested that the Union has been irrevocably changed in the process, not least because of the energizing of citizens who had become highly sceptical about effecting social change through traditional institutional routes.[118] The effect of this mass participation remains to be seen, but, writing in November 2014, opinion polls point both to a large-scale withdrawal of support from the traditional party of social reform in Scotland, the Labour party, with potentially enormous consequences for the outcome of the 2015 UK General Election. A top-down analysis cannot, on its own, explain the nature of this change, or its potential moment. Rather – and this is a point of wider application – to grasp fully how the constitutional horizons envisaged by these official processes shifted in ways unanticipated by their authors, it is necessary to include in the analysis the catalytic force of their interaction with grass-roots movements.[119]

Perhaps, though, the greatest impact of adverting to 'below' is to effect a profound change in the sensibility of constitutional scholarship. For Santos, the South is not only a geographical place, but a metaphor for 'all forms of subordination'.[120] The pervasiveness of suffering has emerged as an important theme in international law[121] and human rights[122] scholarship in recent years, addressing questions of the role of current international legal practices in sustaining poverty, and how it would transform international legal doctrine to start from the moral imperative of alleviating suffering.[123] There are few, if any, parallels in the constitutional literature, but it is instructive to reflect upon its absence and consider whether this denotes complicity in, or more problematically the constitutionalization of, suffering. What does it tell us about constitutional law as a discipline, that it is more at home exploring synergies with the rules of international trade than asking questions about the homeless and the hungry? Underlying most instinctual responses to this question is probably some notion that it is not constitutional law's business. However, the

[117] Christopher Thornhill, *A Sociology of Constitutions: Constitutions and State Legitimacy in Historical-Sociological Perspective* (Cambridge University Press, 2011), at p. 13.

[118] Iain MacWhirter, 'We can't leave Scotland's Future in the Hands of Politicians', *Sunday Herald* (2014): www.heraldscotland.com/comment/columnists/we-cant-leave-scotlands-future-in-the-hands-of-the-politicians.25445269 accessed 27 October 2014.

[119] Gerry Hassan, *Caledonian Dreaming: The Quest for a Different Scotland* (Edinburgh: Luath Press, 2014).

[120] Santos and Rodríguez-Garavito 2005b, at p. 14. [121] Baxi, at pp. 222–6.

[122] Andrew Williams, 'Human Rights and Law: Between Sufferance and Insufferability', 123 *Law Quarterly Review* (2007) 133.

[123] Thomas Pogge, *World Poverty and Human Rights*, 2nd edn (Cambridge: Polity, 2008).

broader framework of inquiry advanced here suggests that there is always more to be gained by exploring constitutionalism's connectedness than by assuming its separation. A constitutionalism that takes the perspective of the marginalized might, for example, elucidate the implicit hierarchies of social voice and representation underpinning ostensibly neutral constitutional baselines which have tolerated the global financial crisis and subsequent austerity. It might take a different approach to the priority of constitutional rights, expounding the constitutional case for an unconditional basic income.[124]

What better place to begin the process of bringing together constitutional perspectives from above and below than at the very bottom?

[124] Erik Olin Wright, *Envisioning Real Utopias* (London and New York: Verso, 2010), at pp. 217–20.

8

The state and constitutionalism in postcolonial societies in Africa

Yash Ghai and Jill Cottrell

1. Introduction

William Twining begins his monumental *General Jurisprudence: Understanding Law from a Global Perspective* with a short story about the dilemmas of a new constitution in a developing country. It concerns clean water.[1] The constitution – 'legitimated and validated by an admirably democratic constitutive process' – had a provision that 'No one shall be subjected to any form of torture, cruel, inhuman or degrading treatment or punishment.' A team of foreign and local consultants had been commissioned by an international agency to advise the government on the expenditure of foreign aid to promote 'democracy, human rights, and good governance'. Among the issues that the consultants focussed on was the right of prisoners to 'clean water'. One consultant argued that the failure to provide prisoners with the basic necessities was 'inhuman' and therefore unconstitutional. Others expressed scepticism with this approach. One objection was that there was no local judicial ruling to this effect (though there were such precedents from other jurisdictions). Another objection was that nearly half of the population had no access to clean water (and presumably their claims were stronger than those of prisoners, though seventy percent of them were on remand). Others argued that prisoners might have other priorities. One said, given the poverty in the country, it simply could not afford the constitution. Most consultants were not happy with this assertion and felt that the country had to define its own standards within its means, not necessarily copying the high standards in the West.

This fictitious story captures well the dilemmas poor countries face in redesigning their political, social and economic systems through the medium of the constitution, whether after a period of civil war, military regime, one-party rule, or secession. Although Twining says little about constitutions or constitutionalism, there are several aspects of his interests and his work that bear on the making, the scope and the implementing of constitutions. Many of them occur in regions of the world with which he is familiar. The processes of making the contents and the implementing of constitutions have become

[1] Cambridge University Press, 2009 pp. 3–5.

truly global (the team of consultants in Twining's story is all too familiar). What we call in our chapter the 'new constitutionalism' is global in a number of ways. There is foreign participation in negotiations to bring the country to a settlement and in the making of the constitution; in some extreme cases the country has been literally taken into receivership and the approval of its new constitution by the UN Security Council is the condition for the restoration of its sovereignty. There is the influence of international or regional norms, including human rights and protection of the environment; at the same time it must accommodate considerable diversity, internal to the country, of ethnicity, religion, language, customs and culture, and the constitution struggles to cope through forms of legal pluralism, balancing individual and communal rights – a national representation of universalism. There is considerable knowledge of the experiences of other countries with similar problems and borrowing of ideas from them and others; nor does this cease with the adoption of the constitution – a new trade in legal precedents then starts on broadly similar provisions. Central to the new constitutionalism, therefore, is the diffusion of laws, internal pluralism, multi-culturalism, and 'law and development', general topics on which Twining has written so well amongst others, and which have become more salient both globally and within national boundaries. The careful reader will find many resonances with his theoretical framework in this chapter.

In this chapter, we discuss the 'new constitutionalism' in Africa, after a brief review of the diversity of governance systems before colonialism. Constitutions cover a wider range of issues and institutions than before. They increasingly play a key role in linking the state to the international community and its norms and procedures. Domestically, they connect aspects of customary law and practices to the legal order. Increasingly, what were once regarded exclusively as differences between different regions, states and cultural traditions happen within one sovereign state, and not only in Africa. Dealing with these matters is no longer merely a matter of international relations and international law; it is crucial to governance within individual states.

2. Constitutions

The constitution is a set of rules and institutions that regulate the governing of the country. Constitutional*ism* is an ideology based on certain values, practices and procedures. At one level, the concept of a written constitution is very simple: it is text that is the supreme law of the land. A constitution was a way of consolidating power – as is well illustrated not only by colonial constitutions, but also those of European states. The concept of constitutionalism at first focussed on the supremacy of the constitution as a means of controlling the power of the state. A pioneering scholar of constitutionalism, Charles Howard McIlwain, said that, 'in all its successive phases, constitutionalism has one essential quality: it is a legal limitation on government; it is the anti-thesis of arbitrary rule; its opposite is despotic government, the government of will instead of law.'[2] Today, constitutionalism, though focused principally on the exercise of state power, encompasses a wide set of values and principles that must determine the governance of the country. These values and principles concern not only limits on state power, but may require that state power be exercised positively to promote ideas like equity, equality and other human rights, social justice and fair procedures.

In this chapter, we explore the precolonial and postcolonial constitutions, trying to understand the legacy in Africa of the colonial state. This issue is examined in the context of the new post-Cold War constitutions that seek to replace the model of the colonial state as well as its authoritarian successors. This approach enables us also to understand the changing nature of the state and its relationship to the constitution. We begin with a brief account of governance before colonialism and move to a short history of the objectives and orientation of constitutions during and since colonial occupation. The new constitutions are based on different values, procedures and institutions, with the emphasis on nation building, participatory democracy, sharing of state power and resources, a strong regime of rights – particularly social and economic rights – with a view to eliminating poverty, and preventing corruption. This is a new constitutionalism based on transformative constitutions.

3. Precolonial governmental systems

The most important generalization about precolonial systems in Africa is that it is almost impossible to generalize. When the European powers colonized Africa, Africans were living in largely self-contained and self-regulating communities, occupying relatively well-defined territory. It is tempting to divide the political systems in these communities into two broad categories – kingdoms and others – as T. O. Elias did:[3]

> These peoples may be classified into the two main African political patterns (a) the monarchical or chiefly societies with highly centralised administrative machinery, judicial institutions and military organisation. . .and (b) the republican or chiefless societies in which kinship supplies the bonds of social cohesion and where rules rather than rulers secured the essential mechanism of administrative and economic order.

In Nigeria there were the famous empires or kingdoms of the Fulani (Sokoto), the Hausa (swallowed by the Fulani), the Kanuri, the Nupe, the Yoruba and Benin, as well as the non-chiefly Igbo, Ibibio, people of the Delta and of the

[2] C. H. McIlwain, *Constitutionalism: Ancient and Modern* (Ithaca, NY: Great Seal Books, 1947) pp. 21–22.

[3] In *Nigeria: The Development of its Laws and Constitutions* (London: Stevens and Co., 1987) at p. 1.

'middle belt' (mostly non-chiefly). In Uganda there were the very dominant Buganda kingdom, some smaller kingdoms such as Toro, and various non-chiefly groups. Tanganyika was predominantly non-chiefly and Kenya almost entirely so (though the coastal strip was part of the realm of the Sultan of Zanzibar).

Inevitably, things were much more complex than that. One author observes:[4]

> In one region, Senegambia, [one] scholar discusses 'states', 'kingdoms', 'autocracies', 'vice-royalties', 'confederations', coastal and island 'peoples', and 'theocracies'.[5] Another scholar refers to 'city states', 'empires', 'sultanates', 'states', 'dynasties', and 'nomadic confederations' in North Africa and Central Sudan.[6] Others note 'pastoral societies', 'clans', 'tribes', 'war lords' and 'semi-autonomous vassal states', and still others, 'cities' and 'houses'.[7]

'States' varied enormously in terms of extent (which might wax and wane, as the Fulani empire did), the matters over which the ruler had power, the extent to which power was shared, the bureaucratic complexity of the system, the way in which rulers were identified and how they ruled, and how they left office. Non-kingly societies also varied tremendously. They might be nomadic and pastoral, hunter-gatherers or farmers. Their forms of organization might be clan based, age-set based or family based.

The fortunes of communities depended on natural resources, rains, disease, the ebb and flow of trade and also on internal conflicts. Most of them had some contacts with neighbouring communities, with exchanges as well as raiding or even war between them. Among communities engaged in cultivation, there were usually abundant resources and so there was little conflict over them, but this was not always true of pastoral communities. Community boundaries were porous[8] but organizations or rules did not usually extend beyond the community. Differences between communities were settled through negotiations, perhaps leading to reparations – and sometimes by force.

When anthropologists wrote of a category of 'states', what did they mean? H. F. Morris and James Read summarized some of that writing about the Baganda. The Baganda had a system of clans, each with its own geographical area, but successive Kabakas had superseded the powers of clan heads, creating

4 Carolyn M. Warner, 'The rise of the state system in Africa' (2001), 27 (05) Review of International Studies, pp. 65–89 at p. 70.

5 Citing B. Barry, 'Senegambia From the Sixteenth to the Eighteenth Century: Evolution of the Wolof, Sereer and Tukuloor' in Bethwell Ogot, ed., *General History of Africa* Oxford : Heinemann ,1992, pp. 262–99.

6 Citing J. O. Hunwick, 'Songhay, Borno and Hausaland in the Sixteenth Century' in J. F. Ade Ajayi and Michael Crowder (eds), *History of West Africa*, London : Longman ,1976 vol. I, 2nd edn, pp. 264–301.

7 Citing Murray Last, 'Reform in West Africa: the Jihād Movements of the Nineteenth Century' in J. F. A. Ajayi and Michael Crowder (eds), *History of West Africa*, vol. II (London: Longman Group, 1974), pp. 1–29, at pp. 10–13, S. F. Nadel, 'The Kede: A Riverain State in Northern Nigeria' in Fortes and Evans-Pritchard (eds), *African Political Systems*, pp. 165–96, at p. 166 and E. J. Alagoa, 'The Niger Delta States and Their Neighbours to 1800' in Ajayi and Crowder (eds), *History of West Africa*, vol. I, pp. 331–73, at p. 341.

8 See e.g. Bethwell A. Ogot, *History as Destiny and History as Knowledge: Being Reflections on the Problems of Historicity and Historiography* (Kisumu: Anyange Press Ltd, 2005) at p. 273.

a highly centralized kingdom with a monarch 'whose will was law'. Ten geographical/administrative areas (translated as 'counties') were each headed by a senior chief who, in this capacity, held land of the Kabaka, administered justice and collected taxes. In fact, these chiefs spent much of their time at court and participated in the Kabaka's council, which was both an advisory body and an appellate judicial body. The Kabaka also had an official directly accountable to him in each county.[9] The Baganda themselves were one people with a common origin myth; a nation, one might say.[10] But other 'states' were rather different. The Sokoto caliphate was the result of a combination of proselytization and *jihad*. Its extent was very great but its system of administration was very different from Buganda. It has been described as[11] 'a congeries of "emirates', or local governments, which were united 'by common membership of one Umma [community of believers] dedicated to the upholding of Islam and of Dar al-Islam',[12] who agreed that the Caliph was the supreme temporal and spiritual authority'.

The colonial powers did not think they were creating states. Indeed, this was precisely what they would *not* want to create, at least so long as they were thinking in terms of obedient colonial subjects. So state-building was definitely not on their agenda, much less nation-building. This absence has hindered the change of the colonial legacy to constitutionalism.[13] Almost every colony comprised a number of communities, with boundaries drawn in a somewhat random way. These boundaries depended, perhaps, on a river (less irrational), or on where conflicts were resolved, or on negotiations in Berlin, or even sometimes drawn with a ruler (Kenya's northern and Nigeria's eastern boundaries were clearly so drawn). Several 'states' had not really existed as a unit (or not for long) before they emerged at independence. Striking examples were the yoking together of Northern and Southern Rhodesia with Nyasaland into a federation, the referendum that finalized the boundary between Nigeria and Cameroun, the very existence of Cameroun itself, the referendum that sought to determine the boundary between Somalia and Kenya (but didn't), and the settlement that did confirm the coastal strip as part of the latter.

How relevant all this history may be is unclear. Various studies have shown how hard it is to know what precolonial societies were really like, and how the colonial regimes invented local custom in each colony, whether deliberately or not.[14] During the colonial period, if the authorities ignored traditional

[9] H. F. Morris and James S. Read, *Uganda: The Development of its Laws and Constitutions* (London: Stevens and Co., 1966) at p. 5.

[10] See Elliott Green, 'Ethnicity and Nationhood in Precolonial Africa: The Case of Buganda' (2010), 16 *Nationalism and Ethnic Politics* 1–21.

[11] Carolyn M. Warner, 'The rise of the state system in Africa' at p. 75.

[12] Citing R. A. Adeleye, 'The Sokoto Caliphate in the Nineteenth Century' in Ajayi and Crowder (eds), *History of West Africa*, vol. II, pp. 57–92, at 75.

[13] 'The Theory of the State in the Third World and the Problematic of Constitutionalism' in Douglas, Greenberg, and eds.,*Constitutionalism and Democracy : Transition in Contemporary Word* (New York: Oxford University Press ,1993) pp.186 –196.

[14] E.g. Francis Snyder, 'Colonialism and Legal Form; The Creation of "customary law" in Senegal' (1981), 19 *Journal of Legal Pluralism* 49–90.

institutions and ideas they would necessarily change, if not atrophy. If incorporated by methods of 'indirect rule' they would necessarily change because they were made to play different roles, with different resources, and a different legitimating foundation. And, either way, they would change because of changing modes of production and economic and political context generally. Formal education changed who had the knowledge and the skills, if not to rule, at least to interpret what was happening. So, what people might be inclined to perceive as 'tradition' was something very different from that past reality. Just as the colonial powers might use or invent local tradition in the colonies, and indeed invent metropolitan tradition to serve a local purpose, so those who would want, in constitution making or critique, to appeal to indigenous traditions of 'governance' might at best misunderstand and at worst manipulate or invent them. As Bruce Berman says,[15]

> Colonial officials, missionaries and anthropologists combined in an 'invention of tradition' through efforts to define clearly bounded tribal societies and identities that would preserve social stability and facilitate political control. Africans, for their part, responded through a process of cultural imagining based on real cultural experiences and resources, created and refashioned out of both old and new elements.

We shall see subsequently that it is no longer the case that postcolonial constitutions are closely modelled on those of the colonizing powers (at least in Anglophone African countries). There is still a recurrent complaint in the literature, and in elite meetings about new constitutions, that countries ought to have constitutions rooted in their own conditions, and that Western systems and democracy (the object of complaint varies) are unsuitable. But 'new constitutionalism' constitutions do not noticeably incorporate elements of *precolonial* governance either. If precolonial realities were really powerful influences on modern realities, one would expect countries with different precolonial pasts to have very different presents. But there is no discernible difference between countries' current systems of government in terms of their dominant precolonial governance. Carolyn Walker comments that 'it is clear that the myriad historical structures of precolonial Africa were eclipsed by the Westphalian state model.'[16] Most Anglophone sub-Saharan countries have various types of presidential system, though some have parliamentary characteristics, such as South Africa and Namibia. Only Mauritius has a classic parliamentary system. Where a model of constitutionalism is chosen to replace the colonial model, the models adopted are often still alien in origin. For example, Nigeria and Kenya are notable for having adopted clearly a US constitutional model. Nor is there any sense that they did this because they somehow thought of this as an anti-colonial model.

[15] Bruce J. Berman, 'Ethnicity and Democracy in Africa', JICA-RI Working Paper No. 22 Nov. 2010 at p. 9 jica-ri.jica.go.jp/publication/assets/JICA-RI_WP_No.22_2010.pdf.

[16] 'The Rise of State System' p. 79.

Carolyn Walker has commented, in relation to some similarity of policies adopted by non-colonized Ethiopia and former colonies, that 'the colonial state had less to do with these postcolonial states' activities than did elites' interests in making their entities into Western-style sovereign states and in "modernizing" the economy.'[17] It is suggested that, for constitution-making also – though in some countries there are attempts at local levels to use traditional leadership models – the focus is on the here-and-now with little harking back to the past, at least in the formation of structures of national government. One of the critical elements that plays a role is that almost all African countries are also ethnically heterogeneous, partly because of the curious boundary drawing mentioned earlier. That diversity may involve a majority ethnic group and various other smaller ones, but very commonly no group has an overall majority. This is not the place to go into the complexities, the myths, the fluidities and the politics of ethnicity, except to say that, whatever the 'ethnic reality' may be (if there is such a thing), ethnicity looms very large in the modern political realities of most countries and that political manipulation has all too often increased the salience of ethnic divisions. Although ethnic diversity may have a variety of empirical impacts, our concern is with the sorts of impact and perceptions that affect constitution making. Various constitutions have wrestled with the issue in a variety of ways, including trying to forbid political appeals to ethnic sentiment,[18] devolving power to units where ethnicity is less diverse and groups may feel a greater sense of control,[19] recognizing all local languages,[20] non-discrimination provisions[21] and guaranteeing to minorities representation, or at least voice,[22] sometimes all in the same constitution. Consociationalism – that is, the sharing of power among ethnic groups especially in the executive – though popular in some countries has proved less so in Africa, except in Burundi, and as an occasional transitional expedient elsewhere.[23]

[17] Ibid. p. 83.

[18] Kenya bans political parties formed on ethnic or religious bases (Art. 91(2)(a)); Tanzania's Constitutional Review Commission Draft said that elections must have 'no pronouncements which signal tribalism, provincialism, religious bias' (Art. 180(2)(d)(iii)).

[19] Nigeria's federal structure is ethnic to a considerable degree – it also depends on splitting up the big groups; Kenya's devolution is also ethnically related; Ethiopia's federalism is explicitly ethnic.

[20] The South African Constitution recognizes eleven languages as official and others as demanding promotion and respect.

[21] Kenya specifically mentions race, ethnic or social origin, religion, and language or birth, among others.

[22] See the Tanzanian draft 2013 45.-(1): The authority of the land shall specify legal procedure enabling the minority groups in society to: (a) participate in leadership in the authorities of the land. . .; the 2015 draft added, however, 'taking into account the resources and capacity of country'.

[23] South Africa and Sudan had elements of consociationalism in their transitional arrangements (1993–6 in the former and 2005–11 in the latter). Kenya, Zimbabwe and Ivory Coast have had short-lived power-sharing arrangements in crisis situations. None of these has been full-fledged consociationalism.

4. Stages of constitutions and constitution making in Africa

For our purpose, the significance of the arrival of the colonial powers was that it created the concept of a colony, with defined boundaries, within which were included the many communities that had lived there for a long time. The colonizers brought the concept and organization of the state and of the constitution. By virtue of the administrative and legislative acts of the colonizer, there emerged the beginnings of common rule over these communities as well as immigrants who made their way to the colony, for trade or other purposes. Traditional local ways of organizing and regulating the community were gradually displaced by colonial regulations, and thus began the end of one system of governance and the beginning of another, alien and powerful, which has become the starting point for modern African governance. The legal system showed a curious dichotomy: that part of the system that applied to Europeans and other external settlers had some resemblance to the law as administered in Europe but, as far as Africans were concerned, the system was arbitrary and depended more on the whims of the colonial administrators than the imperatives of the law – which demonstrated that the essential objective of colonialism was the exploitation of Africans and their resources.

Colonial rule was administered through institutions established by the British or other colonizers, but it also relied on alliances with members of friendly communities. Armed force played the most critical role at the beginning of the British occupation. A police force was established, not to protect the people but to coerce them into submission to British rule. The police as an aggressive force played a key role in the foundation of the structures of British administration – a role that has continued up to the present. In colonies settled by Europeans, vast areas of land were appropriated by the colonizers, pushing some communities from their traditional habitations in disregard of local rules and justified by alien concepts of ownership.[24] Indeed, the British colonial state was rooted in violence and the exploitation of African peoples. In the scramble for Africa, much depended on the might of the European powers, and little regard was paid either to the integrity of the peoples who were colonized or to the geographic rationality of the territory. The colony was based on organizational principles very different from those of the colonized. It was founded on violence and the violations of the rights of communities.

No state can long survive on force and violence, however, and gradually the colonizers set up a civilian administration, built on district officers and 'native administration', still the foundational system in many African countries. The idea of a written constitution was introduced. The constitution reinforced colonial claims to the colony and defined state boundaries (to ward off other

[24] On land, with reference to Kenya, see H. W. O. Okoth Ogendo, *Tenants of the Crown: Evolution of Agrarian Law and Institutions in Kenya* (Nairobi: African Centre for Technology Studies, 1991); Christopher Leo, *Land and Class in Kenya* (Toronto: University of Toronto Press, 1984), especially the first three chapters.

colonial powers). It regulated the relationship of the government of the colony with the metropolitan state and established the system of administration of the colony, including the judiciary. The constitution was essentially a device of delegated authority by the imperial power. There were two sources of constitutional powers: Parliament and the executive in London and, beneath them, the governor in the colony. These biased the constitution in favour of the executive. Despite the steady expansion in the scope of the colonial constitution, the overwhelming powers of the governor remained largely intact until the end of colonial rule. The governor's legislative powers were gradually transferred to a legislature, at first dominated by his officials and, with the move towards the representation of communities, by European settlers where these existed, or local elites in other colonies.

Colonial authorities enjoyed considerable immunity for their acts under the common law. The metropolitan government also reserved to itself the power to direct the colony's administration as to the exercise of its powers. The colony's constitution could easily be amended or abrogated by the colonial government, and thus the system of government could be adjusted periodically. The ultimate sovereignty of Whitehall and the considerable legislative and executive powers of the resident governor over the colony prevented the emergence of the rule of law. And missing from the constitution was any acknowledgement, much less regulation, of the police and the army, both of which constituted the underlying basis of colonial rule. Their deployment was purely an administrative matter. The courts, whether in the colony or in Britain, refused to exercise any real control over the powers of the British administration. Lord Denning said, as late as 1956: 'The courts rely on the representatives of the Crown to know the limits of its jurisdiction and to keep within it. Once jurisdiction is exercised by the Crown the courts will not permit it to be challenged.'[25] Courts thus abandoned, for the most part, attempts to ensure legality on the part of the government – another feature that was carried over into the post-independence period.

Few colonial constitutions came remotely close to constitutionalism, as defined earlier. There was no consultation with the local people on constitution making. There were few restrictions on the powers of the governor. Human rights and the participation of the local people in the system of government were missing from the colonial constitution (although over the years a measure of representation was given in the legislature to indigenous people). There was no notion of a nation or citizenship. It was hard, therefore, for a subject people to think of the constitution as protector of their interests; indeed, it completely disempowered them.

The state was the source of patronage, favours and wealth, which facilitated British co-optation of local collaborators. To begin with, different local communities lived in fairly compact and discrete areas, and were often

[25] *Nyali Bridge Ltd v Attorney-General* [1956] KB 1 at p. 15.

administered as such, so that for most Africans, local administration rather than central government mattered more. Towards the end of colonial rule, urbanization was beginning to grow in importance, but cities were places of temporary sojourn even for long-term inhabitants. Development in rural areas varied greatly, depending not only on resources, terrain and climate but also on colonial polices and the extent of settlement of white immigrants.

Administration by the British affected the social and economic structures of the African communities. The rhythm of their lives was seriously disrupted. Their self-sufficiency gave way to new forms of political economy. Although the colonial intention was to preserve a measure of traditional systems and to restrict movement of local people out of their traditional lands, many political, social and economic forces drove society in new directions. The colonial system led to uneven development of groups and regions – with great significance for postcolonial ethnic relations. It produced greater contact among communities as well as competition among them for access to the newly developing economy and state largesse. Driven by the market as well as administrative practices, it undermined the basis of egalitarianism, leading to differentiation among and within communities. These tendencies accelerated with the approach of independence, destroying trust within as well as between communities – not without the connivance of the colonial power.[26]

In settler-based colonies, because of their vested interests, the only way to challenge colonial power was by counter-force. The response of the colonial power to that counter-force exposed its moral bankruptcy, highlighting its lack of legitimacy, and ultimately led to independence, but not before a deal had been struck between the outgoing power and the incoming elite: an elite fashioned in no inconsiderable part by the outgoing power, rather than as an agreement among the people of the colony.

Far from independence and the accompanying constitution solving the problems generated by colonialism, it left many unsolved, and often generated several more (as with land in South Africa, Kenya and Zimbabwe).[27] Fears of some about the differential development of communities led to fragmentation among the political leaders and anxieties about power passing to a few privileged groups. Other colonies suffering from uneven development experienced similar disquiet, leading sometimes to resistance to independence itself among some groups. The bureaucracy and armed forces remained entrenched, and State House (formerly Government House) was able to exert its powers across

[26] Thus, colonial administration remains one of the important factors that contributed to current horizontal inequality; see Daniel Branch, *Kenya; Between Hope and Despair, 1963–2011* (New Haven: Yale University Press, 2011).

[27] Michael Cowen, 'The British State and Agrarian Accumulation in Kenya' in Martin Fransman, ed., *Industry and Accumulation in Africa* (Nairobi: Heinemann, 18982); Hastings Okoth-Ogendo, 'Land Ownership and Land Distribution in Kenya's Large-Farm Areas' in T. Killick, ed., *Papers on Kenya Economy: Performance, Problems and Policies* (Nairobi: Heinemann, 1981); and Karuti Kanyinga, *Redistribution from Above: The Politics of Land Rights and Squatting in Coastal Kenya* (Uppsala: Nordiska Africainstitutet, 2000).

the country through the networks of provincial commissioners, district officers and chiefs.

The fact that independence constitutions were negotiated distinguished them from previous colonial constitutions that were always external impositions. Independence constitutions made some attempts to redistribute state power, usually inserted a bill of rights, aimed to strengthen the independence of the judiciary, and in some instances made the police both more autonomous and more accountable. The question was whether these embellishments would do anything to change the logic and dynamics of the colonial state. When Britain annexed territory in Africa, it found, as we have said, numerous self-sufficient communities, leading their lives separately, with their own systems of governance and economy. What it bequeathed to the people on Britian's departure was a country with these communities tied together by political structures and the economy devised for their subordination, but with the additional problems of finding and creating a common identity and destiny: a state without a nation.

5. Independence constitutions

The kind of constitution that the colonial government preferred for independence could not have been more different from the one under which it ruled the colony. [28] To begin with, it was to be a negotiated agreement between the colonial power and local political groups, not the people directly. The constitution was to prescribe a democratic order with a Bill of Rights and an independent judiciary, similar to that in the metropolitan state. The draft constitution would have to be approved by the British parliament; this was probably a reason for the government's insistence on a democratic system. Often it was not possible for the colonial power to get its way on all issues, principally due to divisions within the local leadership.

The prospect of independence led to divisions among the people, or, more accurately, within their leadership. Most colonies were, as mentioned above, a conglomeration of ethnic groups, divided by language, religion, social traditions – and life styles. The larger groups looked forward to independence as a means to take over state power while the smaller ones were uneasy about independence as they feared that it would bring them under the domination of their larger neighbours. Internal divisions on the eve of independence broke out in most colonial possessions, going back as far as the Canadian confederation; in more recent times, they were manifested in India, where they led to the splitting of the country into two independent units: India and Pakistan. In other places, to avoid the splitting of the colony, intense discussions were

[28] For an excellent account of independent and subsequent constitutions and the states that fostered them, see Crawford Young, *The Postcolonial State in Africa: Fifty Years of Independence, 1960–2010* (Madison, Wisconsin: University of Wisconsin;, 2012).

held to find a settlement that satisfied minorities and was acceptable to the majority – with the colonial power sometimes acting as a mediator and sometimes as an interested party.

What we might call the ethnic factor (involving local communities, but sometimes also immigrant communities) was a major issue in most cases of decolonization. The demands of minority communities varied from secession to autonomy or federalism, equal citizenship, various forms of representation and power sharing at the national level, guarantees of religious freedom and other rights, joint control of security forces, and use of their language, according to the circumstances of the country. Several of these were adopted. Key features of many constitutions to accommodate diversity included guarantees of religious freedom among other civil and political rights, the continued use of a foreign language as official language (for the most part), the maintenance of personal laws, land provisions acknowledging traditional holdings and ownership and some form of power sharing (in terms of territorial divisions, or in terms of representation in legislature and/or government). So Nigeria remained a federation (and soon after independence created a fourth state) and became independent with a Bill of Rights originally introduced to reassure minorities. Kenya became independent with a blueprint to become a semi-federal country, with a standard colonial Bill of Rights and other measures to reassure the white population, as Zimbabwe was to do seventeen years later.

It is obvious that these demands are not all fully consistent with a regime of common citizenship and human rights and freedoms, which for the most part are oriented towards the individual. Nor are some of them consistent with the unitary system of government through which the colonial authorities ruled the people. These demands were frequently backed by the colonial power but resisted by the majority community; however, its leaders ultimately accepted them as the price of independence. Most of these provisions did not last long: once in power, the leaders of the majority community removed them, protests notwithstanding. However, ethnicity has been a key factor in politics and economy, and a major influence on the working of the constitution and the legal system. Many of these minority reassurance measures had short lives, therefore, as pressures towards centralization of power, especially in the hands of particular groups – even particular individuals – led to the adoption of radical changes.

6. Post-independence constitutions

The table in the Appendix to this chapter (mostly of Anglophone countries) shows how short-lived was the independence constitution in most countries. It was certainly not abrogated or replaced everywhere, but processes of amendment by politicians soon whittled down the original conception and the protections for certain groups, while a good number were abrogated by the military or radically changed to accommodate one-party states. Only a very few outliers retained their original designs more or less intact: Botswana and Mauritius stand alone in this respect.

The constitutional surgery was justified on various grounds, though three themes predominated. Firstly, to use the language of Julius Nyerere, first president of Tanzania, the constitution was a brake on development, while what was needed was an accelerator. Secondly, what was needed was 'our' constitution, based on their ideas, experiences and needs; the constitution was not based on African ideas of governance. Thirdly, a related point, the independence constitution was a colonial imposition.[29] In addition, the military often justified their takeovers in terms of corruption and abuse of power by the politicians, promising clean government and, almost always, a new constitution 'soon' (though 'soon' was often much delayed).

Military rule did not necessarily purport to do away with the constitution entirely. But what remained was there by courtesy of the military – a total negation of constitutionalism. Regimes that remained civilian in form (though some, including Swaziland, had the military in the background) showed two tendencies, with some commonalities: basically, they were aimed at the concentration of power. They changed parliamentary into presidential systems – not itself a necessarily autocratic tendency, of course, but it demonstrated some impatience with the idea of power being in any way divided. And they emasculated systems of autonomy, such as they were, in Ethiopia, Kenya and Uganda. One party states, *de facto* or *de jure*, were common, including in Tanzania, Zambia, Kenya, Ethiopia, Malawi, Ghana and Uganda. Even when the new constitution may have had democratic elements in it, the executive acquired or exercised vast powers without any accountability. The legislature was subservient to the executive, as was the judiciary.

Opponents of the regime were treated most brutally; many were killed or forced into exile. The personalized nature of these tendencies is shown by how few heads of government/state there were during the first thirty years or so of independence.[30] This was the period when African Heads of Government did not step down voluntarily – they either died in harness or were 'couped' out of office. Military regimes were no better, despite the aura of self-righteousness with which they, or at least the early ones, took over power. As Okoth-Ogendo wrote,[31]

[29] For a detailed account of the excuses and devices used to delegitimize the independence constitution, see H. W. O. Okoth-Ogendo, 'Constitutions without Constitutionalism Reflections as an African Political Paradox' in Douglas Greenberg et al. (eds), *Constitutionalism and Democracy: Transitions in the Contemporary World* (New York: Oxford University Press, 1993) pp. 65–82.

[30] Kenya (Kenyatta 1963–78(d), Moi 1978–2002); Tanzania (Nyerere 1962–85 (r)); Zambia (Kaunda 1961–91 (r)); Zimbabwe (Mugabe 1980–); Cameroun (Ahidjo 1960–82 (r), Biya 1982–); Malawi (Banda 1964–94). Key: d=died in office, r=retired (whether 'pushed' or not).

[31] *Constitutions without Constitutionalism* (above), p. 78.

> Military regimes have never been able to avoid the tendency towards an imperial presidential style... [they] reproduced the system by adopting the old civilian system, but assuming presidential power.

Bruce Berman says,[32]

> In spite of their extravagant claims to be the real agents of national unity and their suppression of all 'divisive' political parties and organizations, military regimes have represented little change in the state-focused patronage system. Instead, the military magnates incorporated themselves into a dominant position within the patrimonial networks of patronage and appropriation of state resources.

Samuel Nolustshungu has explained this 'failure of constitutional government to develop' in the following way.[33] It was:

> not the result of popular needs or demands but of governments seeking to escape the constraints imposed by the constitutions, laws, and the rights and expectations of citizens. . . .[T]here was little protest on constitutional grounds against the usurpation of power. In short, people have supported or opposed particular claimants to power and specific political programs with rather scant regard for the principles and procedures under which those claimants would rule.

He attributed this partly to largely peasant populations, or even urban groups, being difficult to organize politically, and many being variously dependent on the state for livelihood. We can add to these points the absence of an effective political opposition in most countries. So-called political parties are often merely reflections of ethnic alliances, happy to make accommodations with other groups if this will achieve office for leaders, and perceptions of benefit for their communities.

This massive accumulation of power was also possible partly because of the international politics of the Cold War. Both the West and the communist regimes were seeking allies to fight, or ward off, the other. They wanted friendly states to have enough weapons for this purpose, which they provided in considerable volume (mostly used, in practice, to fight local dissidents). In many instances it could be said that it was this Cold War support that sustained the regime, even as opposition to it among the people grew. The Russians massively armed Ethiopia and Mozambique, while the West armed Kenya, Uganda, Zaire and Egypt. The end of this period (which lasted for over thirty years) was heralded by the demolition of the Berlin Wall. That set the stage for the collapse of dictatorial and authoritarian regimes and paved the way for the return to democracy – now with the enthusiastic support of the West.

[32] Bruce J. Berman above at p. 15.

[33] 'Constitutionalism in Africa: Some Conclusions' in Greenberg et al. (above), pp. 366–78, at p. 366.

7. New constitutions: return to democracy and human rights

In some ways, the new constitutions bore a resemblance to the independence constitutions, particularly in the restoration of democracy. But the world had changed since the time of independence. There was the beginning of a new phase of globalization: political, economic and legal, which was to have a significant impact on the making and content of the new constitutions. Education had spread with more people achieving higher qualifications; there were more professionals, including lawyers; urbanization had increased exponentially; and civil society had emerged (despite, perhaps because of, past repression). The return to democratic orders of former communist states in Eastern Europe, as well as in former dictatorships in Asia, emboldened educated groups in Africa to demand full participation in the new instruments of 'governance' (a term popularized by the World Bank). New international norms on human and community rights had emerged or been consolidated, special conventions on the rights of the minorities and marginalized groups had been adopted, and there was growing concern with social justice and the eradication of poverty.[34]

In Asia and Africa (but not in Eastern Europe), the people won the right to participate in the making of the new constitutions. The initiatives of civil society for constitutional reform and their participation in the making of the new constitution marked major differences between these constitutions and their predecessors. A large number of organizations – religious, professional, political, gender, economic and social – developed an agenda of constitutional reform and were instrumental in forcing a review process on state authorities, in which most of them participated. Another change from the past was the scope of these constitutions, which deal not only with state institutions, but also with the values and principles that should underpin their policies and practices. The democracy that they seek to establish is participatory, opening space for legislative initiatives by the people, as well as recall of their representatives. They contain extensive Bills of Rights. These often balance individual with community rights and aim at ensuring social justice, as part of a fresh push for national integration, while respecting the diversity of cultures and traditions. High standards of integrity and competence are set out and compliance expected from public officials, from the president downwards. Independent commissions are established to ensure the accountability of government bodies. An independent judiciary is given wide powers to interpret and to act as the ultimate custodians of the constitution. The more ambitious of the constitutions also seek the reform of society, especially to

[34] Amartya Sen, *Development as Freedom* (Oxford University, 1999); Bård A. Andreassen and Stephen P. Marks (eds), *Development as a Human Right: Legal, Political and Economic Dimensions* (Antwerp: Intersentia, 2010) 2nd ed. which contains a chapter by Yash Ghai, 'Redesigning the State for "Right Development"' (one of the first articles relating radical human rights norms to constitutions – the original version was published in the 1980s); Thomas Pogge, *World Poverty and Human Rights* (Cambridge: Polity Press, 2008) 2nd ed.

ensure justice for women, the disabled, the young and the elderly – and marginalized communities. Both the state and society are bound by the constitution.

In these ways, the constitutions measure up to the highest standards of constitutionalism. It is easy to discern in these new constitutions responses to the problems of the past as well as aspirations for the future. There is often implicit in the text a theme of 'We've had enough of this and we don't want any more of it'. They represent a sharp and radical break from the administration of the state since the birth of colonialism and the era of independence. Precisely because of this they face formidable difficulties of implementation and enforcement.

8. Constitutionalism: then

Constitutionalism is a complex concept, being both source and limiter of power. It transcends the text and the supremacy of the constitution. The origins of what we call constitutionalism today lie outside the legal text. Constitutions were largely about the allocation of public power and the structure of the state, rather than values and principles. The ideas that we now associate with constitutionalism emerged in society, not the state, and reflected to a great extent the changing economic and class structures. These ideas served to mould the working of the constitution; they became the basis of 'conventions'. Conventions were the understandings in society on how state powers and constitutional procedures would be exercised or applied. Conventions reflected public morality and values, legitimacy of the political order, and relations of citizens to the state and with each other. The values underlying conventions became in a sense more important than the text; these values were internalized and became the rules of the political game.

In its origins, constitutionalism meant little more than that the law must be observed, even by the highest state officials – an idea sometimes encapsulated in the concept of the 'rule of law'. By the time Charles McIlwain wrote the classic study mentioned earlier (written, it must be noted, in 1940, at the time of victories of Nazi terrorism and aggression) the concept had expanded: 'it is a legal limitation on government; it is the anti-thesis of arbitrary rule; its opposite is despotic government, the government of will instead of law.'[35] By that time it encompassed a government limited by certain values, as well as one that respects the law. McIlwain does not mention democracy, the separation of powers, checks and balances, and judicial review of laws and acts of government – but being a US academic, his list, to be comprehensive, would have

[35] He begins by reminding his readers that 'perhaps never in its long history has the principle of constitutionalism been so questioned as it is today, never has the attack upon it been so determined or so threatening at it is just now. The world is trembling in the balance between the orderly procedure of law and the processes of force which seem so much more quick and effective', op. cit. at p. 1.

included them – and perhaps federalism as well, as a means of fragmenting state power.

Historically, constitutionalism preceded democracy.[36] Constitutionalism emerged in Europe as part of the bourgeois revolutions. The overthrow of temporal papal authority was engineered to bolster emerging national monarchies in Europe. The nationalization of power was necessary to advance the cause of national bourgeoisies, especially in competition with foreign ones. Constitutionalism also catered for other needs of capitalism: predictability, calculability and security of property rights and transactions. Capitalism also required the conversion of peasants into wage earners and the expansion and consolidation of national markets, thus compelling an alliance of the bourgeoisie with the monarchy against feudalism. Most of all, it needed the limitation of the arbitrary or discretionary powers of the state (usually the monarchy) against the intervention in property and other contractual rights. For this purpose, the concept of general rules was particularly well suited. Generality of rules prevented both discrimination and arbitrary action (important for competitive capitalism); it prevented the subordination of the judge to the legislature in specific disputes. General rules also prevent the possibility of state favouritism (and indeed corruption). Indeed, part of the movement for general rules was the reaction to special privileges and monopolies accorded in royal charters and instruments of incorporation. There is considerable tension between the needs of capitalism in general and the specific interests of individual enterprises or sections of industry.[37]

The old constitutionalism reached its apogee in the nineteenth century, not only because the capitalism that then existed was still competitive, but also because the propertied class had achieved political dominance. It exercised its dominance essentially through the autonomous and decentralized economy, the state merely providing the framework for it. This enabled a neat separation of public and private spheres. It may indeed be a condition for constitutionalism that there is a significant congruence of economic and political power. Since the nineteenth century, constitutionalism (as the 'rule of law') has certainly receded from its high water mark for a variety of reasons: the need to accommodate new economic and social interests (especially those of the working class), the broadening of the franchise, the internationalization of

[36] The following account of the history of the link between constitutionalism and the emergence of capitalism is based on Yash Ghai, 'The Theory of the State in the Third World and the Problematic of Constitutionalism' in Douglas Greenberg et al., op. cit. pp. 186–196.

[37] Mahmood Mamdani says that 'historical routes to the rule of law and a concept of constitutionalism are several and contradictory. The terrain of constitutionalism has never been and cannot now be an uncontested one.' Whereas in Western Europe the rule of law was seen as a check on an arbitrary and capricious royal power, in the US tradition it emerged as a limitation on popular sovereignty, in 'Social Movements and Constitutionalism: The African Context' in David Greenburg et al., op. cit. p. 174. In the same book Yash Ghai says, 'Constitutionalism represented the victory of particular groups and classes: but the victory itself was often the result of violence, exploitation, and repression.' (p. 191).

capital and the rise of multinationals and other corporate groups (diminishing the scope for national policy making), periodic economic crises leading to state intervention in the economy and undermining the regime of general rules through discretion, and a larger role for the state. These developments have not seriously affected the other ideological functions of the rule of law or constitutionalism. The ideology increasingly emphasizes the choices open to the people, the protection of economic rights and the impartial role of the state. By proclaiming its adherence to the rule of law, it seeks legitimacy for the state. And to some extent, perhaps, the ideology does have some impact on governments.

9. Constitutionalism: now

Constitutionalism was originally largely directed towards what the state could *not* do. In the course of time, the desirability of democracy and judicial review was acknowledged and they were added to the understanding of constitutionalism. Gradually, new features, including human rights, protection of minorities, justice for marginalized groups and gender equality, were incorporated. Others began to conflate constitutions with constitutionalism (provided the constitution embraced the principal positive features). It is often difficult to work out whether an author who uses the word 'constitutionalism' is referring to a set of values or merely to the 'constitution'.

What is obvious is that there is now increasing convergence towards certain values in national constitutions. In a number of countries, mostly in Europe and a few in Africa, this movement in favour of democracy and human rights followed the demise of communism (except that the new East European emphasis on markets is replicated to considerable extent in Africa). A certain striking similarity of new constitutions in a large number of countries is due to several factors. There was increasingly an international consensus on liberal constitutions, democracy and human rights. Western liberal states, directly or through intermediaries such as international agencies, influenced the constitution-making processes in many countries. There was an increasing commitment to a number of international and regional conventions on human rights, including those concerning social and economic rights. The people played a significant role in the making of these constitutions. Constitutional experts who advised on constitution making – some in more than one country – often studied the process and substantive provisions of the constitution of other states. A number of international public and private agencies set up special units or organizations to help in the making of constitutions. Consequently there was much copying of constitutions, leading, at least to a degree, to common approaches and orientation. Just as the movement for independence of British and French colonies in the 1960s, itself a sort of globalization, led to somewhat similar instruments, so did the new globalization of the 1990s lead to common approaches.[38]

New African constitutions were not merely liberal in espousing democracy and civil and political rights, but dealt also with broader problems facing the countries, past and future, including social justice and equity. As a result they gave prominence to social, economic and cultural rights, national integration, the sharing of state power, people-driven democracy, gender equality, integrity in public life, principles and values for the exercise of state power, protection of the environment and eradication of poverty. Not all constitutions dealt with such a large number of issues, but there is such a substantial common core of values and institutions that it would be justified to talk of a new concept of constitutionalism; political scientists and legal academics already do so.[39] There is a renewal of interest in comparative constitutional law. In most cases, the judiciary has been given special responsibility for the interpretation and custodianship of the new constitutions. There is already a brisk trade in legal precedents across oceans and legal traditions. There is a sense of triumphalism about the new constitutionalism, given its rapid spread globally and its orientation towards participatory democracy, social justice and the human dignity of individuals and communities. There is a degree of international and regional consensus surrounding these values, and there is talk of the constitutionalization of international laws and procedures.[40] There certainly has been internationalization of national constitutionalism, manifested in access of citizens to redress in regional and international tribunals (including trials for crimes against humanity in the International Criminal Court), the oversight responsibilities of UN agencies such as the Human Rights Council and the application of regional norms incorporated in the national constitution.

Another factor is the new globalization of the internet. Not only constitutional 'experts', but also ordinary citizens, can be aware of developments around the world, and effective use is made of that awareness by organized

[38] We have to admit that we (together with Michele Brand and Anthony Regan) wrote a handbook on constitution making which set out options for both negotiations for and participation in constitution making, and also how some critical issues had been or could be resolved. It has been translated into a few languages and used in a number of countries. Michele Brand, Jill Cottrell, Yash Ghai and Anthony Regan, *The Processes of Constitution Making: A Handbook of Options* (published on the web by Interpeace: see www.interpeace.org/constitutionmaking).

[39] Morris Kwindi Mbondeni and Tom Ojendwa (eds), *Constitutionalism and Democratic Governance in Africa: Perspectives from Sub-Saharan Africa* (Pretoria University Law Press, 2013); David Robertson, 'The Judge as Political Theorist' in *Contemporary Constitutional Review* (Princeton University Press, 2010); Denis Davis and Karl Klare, 'Transformative constitutionalism and the common and customary law', *South African Journal on Human Rights* (2010) Vol. 26:3, 403

[40] See, for example, Michel Rosenfeld, 'Is Global Constitutionalism Meaningful and Desirable?' (2014), 25 (1) *European Journal of International Law* 177–99; Zaid Al-Ali and Arun K. Thiruvengadam, 'The Competing Effect of national uniqueness and comparative influences on constitutional practice' in Mark Tushnet et al., *Routledge Handbook of Constitutional Law* (Abingdon, Oxon; New York: Routledge, 2013) pp. 427–42.

civil society, admittedly often assisted by foreign and international funding and assistance. Women's groups are very aware not just of the Convention on the Elimination of All Forms of Discrimination Against Women but of provisions in other countries' constitutions. The same is true of persons with disabilities and indigenous groups.

The new constitutionalism requires an activist state: the state doing things rather than restraining itself. A huge agenda is set for state authorities to fulfil, including eradicating poverty, dealing with past injustices, ensuring the basic necessities of dignified life to all, promoting public participation in state decisions and policies, protecting the environment and much more. Some constitutions build in mechanisms to ensure that the state does not abuse the additional powers given to it, as well as ensuring that the listed objectives are met. Here is a very clear and striking difference from the old constitutionalism. By the same token, there are some serious contradictions in the new, revolutionary, constitutionalism. Only a few new constitutions are the result of a revolution. In many instances, as a result of quirks of history, the ordinary people, many suffering from extreme deprivation, have been able to impose the constitution on the old ruling class. The latter will no doubt resist it. Is it possible to implement a constitution in this paradoxical situation? In the next section we examine this question by studying the nature of the African state and its ability to promote or sabotage new constitutionalism.

10. Africa and the new constitutionalism: will the promise hold?

By and large, the new constitutions in Africa have not fared as well as some people had expected. The most well-known and studied, that of South Africa, got off to a good start, with a very distinguished Constitutional Court providing useful guidance on implementation and observance of the constitution. Under the authority of President Nelson Mandela, the ANC government was fully committed to the constitution's reform agenda (which coincided largely with the ANC's own agenda, for which it had waged a struggle for decades). But after Mandela left the government, it did not pursue the reform agenda as vigorously as when he was its leader. Now under President Zuma, the government appears to have lost the will to pursue the reform agenda. However, the judiciary and some other independent commissions have declared some acts of the government unconstitutional; they have at least provided avenues for complaints, investigations and redress.

There are at least two factors that influence the pursuit of the constitutional agenda in South Africa: the leadership factor and the institutional factor (by which we mean the broad structure of society and economy). Regarding the first, South Africa had outstanding leaders of great ability and determination, totally committed to reform. As long as they were in charge, progress was made. Their successors did not have the same commitment, and reform was not pursued with the same vigour. In the long run, the second factor was more critical. In order to win the support of the white community, particularly conservatives among the Afrikaner community, the ANC did not push for fundamental economic and social reforms, which its partners and followers were keen to pursue. There was the danger that, without fundamental reform, the new political leaders would be co-opted into the old economic system and lose enthusiasm for change, and this is what appears to have happened.

If a country with such a long history of struggle and exceptional leadership, a strong civil society, and a people fully aware of the injustices of the system, has not fully succeeded in following through the agenda of its new constitution, what hope is there in other countries where the leadership is weak, without a long history of opposition to the old regime (indeed many were senior members of it), and with a somewhat docile and ill-informed public? The record of the institutions is uneven, but disappointing on the whole, especially after the first flush of enthusiasm at the adoption of the new constitution. All too often, leaders of the old regime are re-elected under the new constitution and so the lack of reform is understandable. The constitution may be revolutionary, but there has been no revolution. The old state remains intact, with its existing bureaucracy and an unreformed economy; there is often also the domination of ethnic politics and free use of the coercive force of the state inherited from the colonial days. The values and practices connected with the economic aspects of globalization undermine new constitutionalism (and now, particularly, with the entry of China into Africa's politics and economy).

11. The Kenyan example

There is no space here to examine in detail the impact of new constitutionalism in all the countries that have adopted it. In many cases, too, it is too early to make such an assessment. So we conclude the chapter with a brief analysis of Kenya, which adopted a new constitution in August 2010. This is widely acknowledged as the most radical constitution in Africa. It was inspired largely by the South African constitution, and the independence constitution of India (1950), with their deep commitments to social justice and the welfare of marginalized and disadvantaged communities. The Kenyan experience, we believe, has resonances elsewhere – and perhaps lessons. We have focussed on Kenya because we know it best. But the obstacles and the glimmers of hope are, so far as we are able to detect, similar in other countries.

The Kenya constitution was adopted overwhelmingly by Kenyans in the 2010 referendum. At the time, the President was Mwai Kibaki, an old-style politician who had long fought against its enactment, and succeeded in postponing it for some seven years, being forced into acquiescence as a result of ethnic conflict due to the old electoral system, and subsequent pressure from the international community. A large majority of politicians and the bureaucracy were also opposed to it. Yet they were given the responsibility to carry out its radical agenda. Despite the wide support among the people for it, and the specific steps provided for in the constitution that must be taken to implement it, the progress has been limited, as shall see. To explain why, we initially present a brief analysis of the political economy of the state in Kenya.

The independence and post-independence constitutions in Kenya, as in other African states, followed colonial precedent in creating and sanctioning an extraordinary aggregation of power, which only then did they try to regulate, modulate and control. Control over the powers of the state has proved exceedingly hard. The state is outside of, and stands over, civil society; those who accede to it seldom have a sufficiently strong base in society or economy. So they use the apparatus of the state to accumulate power and wealth (what Marx called 'primitive accumulation') – and in due course establish their dominance also over civil society. State violence, through the police and the army, has been key to the dominance of politicians who control it.

The politics of the state have had very negative impact on society and economy. The government and politicians have not only sanctioned violence; they have also ethnicized politics and violence.[41] No political or civic group has pursued promotion of national unity in a country of many ethnic, religious and cultural communities. Politicians have a keen interest in fomenting ethnic tensions and conflicts, pitting one community against another. In this way they expect to consolidate their support among members of their own community – regardless of what damage they do to the nation.

This lack of national unity and the ethnicization of politics are responsible for many ills. The economy has become closely intertwined with state patronage and ethnic politics, and leads business people to become architects of violence and to collude in other violations of the law. There is little accountability for the exercise of public power. Impunity for the friends of the regime and for compliant state officials is rampant – despite public outcry. All these demonstrate the absence of the rule of law. The way successive presidents have governed (or rather misgoverned) Kenya is proof that these violations are the norm, rather than the exception, in the functioning of the state. Consequently, the state suffers from a loss of legitimacy. Few perceive it as a social and political force for the common good. It is regarded, accurately, as partisan, throwing its weight behind specific communities and interests. The subordination of the notionally independent electoral commission, the police and the judiciary to the executive resulted in their inability to resolve national problems. The police were particularly singled out by the Waki Commission on the 2007-8 post-election violence for their failure to ensure Kenyans' security, and are held responsible for numerous murders, rapes and the displacement of the people.[42] They are no

[41] The extent of ethnicization of politics and government can be seen, among other sources, in contributions in a recent book: Yash Pal Ghai and Jill Cottrell Ghai (eds), *Ethnicity, Nationhood and Pluralism*. Ottawa and Nairobi: Global Centre for Pluralism and Kabba Institute, 2013, especially Karuti Kanyinga, 'Pluralism, Ethnicity and Governance in Kenya' pp. 47–73.

[42] *Report of the Commission of Inquiry into Post Election Violence* (Nairobi: Government of Kenya, 2008) (Chairman, Justice Philip Waki)

longer able or willing to protect the people against violence and plunder by private, politician-sponsored militias. The judiciary was so discredited that no-one believed that it was capable of impartial adjudication of election disputes. The Commission concluded that: 'Over time, this deliberate use of violence by politicians to obtain power since the early 1990s, plus the decision not to punish perpetrators has led to a culture of impunity and a constant escalation of violence'.[43]

A combination of the dominance of ethnicity and the state's role in accumulation led to intense competition for the capture of the state, resulting in the abuse or subversion of the democratic aspects of a constitution, such as publicly financed political parties, an independent electoral system, the operational independence of the police, freedoms of expression and association, and judicial impartiality. The rise of a commercial class is built on ethnic foundations, based on favours from a still-exclusionary state. Consequently, the new commercial elite does not want what capitalists are supposed to want: some respectable distance between themselves and the state. As the business class rises on the back of an 'ethnic' state, it finances, in return, its political sponsors' electoral campaigns. Both the state's ethnic favours and the state–capital alliance militate against any generalized rules defining relations between state and market economy, or at least the even-handed application of such rules. Ethnicized politics also weaken any commitment to human rights and encourage the evasion or distortion of any of the democratic procedures listed above.

Despite the postcolonial rise of an incipient bourgeoisie and other social forces, the overwhelming political factor has been the passivity of the majority of the people despite their exploitation and marginalization. Although peasants and workers constitute a majority, they cannot translate their grievances into political clout or pressure, since they have allowed themselves to be divided by the politicization of ethnicity. Thus to prevent the growth of their class consciousness is a critical goal of the strategy of the political class, the one class united by its many common interests. The most active popular political actions take ethnic forms and occur most blatantly at election times. There are few political parties in the classical sense of aggregating, articulating and protecting the interests of key sectors of the public – despite legislation that requires these objectives from political parties, on pain of dissolution.

Massive unemployment heightens worker vulnerability. Trade unions, once of some political significance, now wield little power, in part because of the globalization that tilts the balance in favour of capital, and partly because of their co-optation by the political class. Peasants once organized themselves into co-operatives but now have few means to express their concerns and demands. The youth also find themselves powerless, even if educated, and are easily recruited into militias by gangsters or politicians. And the fact that most

[43] At p. 22.

people work in the 'informal sector' heightens their vulnerability, and the irrelevance of organization.[44] The result of the economic system that arises is increasing the number of those who live in poverty and are unable to live a life in dignity. The constitutional commitment to fair working conditions is very hard to achieve.[45]

The new Kenyan constitution in operation

The new constitution tries to deal with all these and other problems facing Kenya. It gives great importance to promoting national unity through common identity, national values and an inclusive state. The slogan is 'unity in diversity', which is expressed in different ways: recognition of different languages, religion and culture, special representation of minorities and disadvantaged groups in state institutions, and – through the Bill of Rights – balancing the interests of the individual with those of the community. Many provisions seek to enhance the quality (and quantity) of democracy. Through devolution, state powers will be shared between the central and county governments, creating new centres of authority and democracy. There is to be greater accountability of state institutions, through classic checks and balances and right to information.[46] Participation of people in the making of laws and in policy decisions is required.[47] Political parties are encouraged to transcend ethnicity by becoming national, indeed forbidden to be narrowly regional or otherwise sectarian, and to practise internal democracy.[48] And the electorate was given the power to remove non-performing legislators.[49]

There are other reforms to improve the electoral system. The quality of democracy should be enhanced by a clearer separation of powers and a bicameral legislature so that counties will have, for the first time, direct representation at the national level. The roles of the police, armed forces and other security forces have been redefined in fundamental ways: through their mission as to protect the rights and freedom of Kenyans, and in compliance with the law, democracy, human rights and fundamental freedoms.[50] A major effort has been made to eradicate corruption in the public sector, through high

[44] It has been estimated that 34% of the economically active are in formal employment and 61% in informal. The economically active were 64% of the relevant age group, while 6% were unemployed but wanting to work. Taken from Debbie Budlender, 'Statistics on Informal Employment in Kenya' WIEGO Statistical Brief No. 5 (2011) at wiego.org/sites/wiego.org/files/publications/files/Budlender_WIEGO_SB5.pdf.

[45] Article 41.

[46] The latter is in Article 35. The authors wrote an account of the Constitution for the ordinary citizen: Yash Pal Ghai and Jill Cottrell Ghai, *The Constitution of Kenya; An Instrument for Change* (Nairobi: Katiba Institute, 2011). The first major academic book on the Constitution is PLO Lumumba and Luis Franceschi, *The Constitution of Kenya, 2010: An Introductory Commentary* (Nairobi: Strathmore University Press, 2014).

[47] Articles 10 (national values), 69 (environmental decision making), 118 (Parliament), 196 (county assemblies), 201 (public finance).

[48] Articles 91–2. [49] Article 104. [50] Chapter 14 on National Security.

standards of integrity and service as well as accountability,[51] through the creation of an open procurement system,[52] and through the establishment of an independent commission to investigate suspicions or allegations of corruption.[53] A number of other independent commissions are established to ensure that constitutional values and rules are observed.[54] For the protection of rights and freedoms under the constitution and to maintain the systems of integrity and accountability, a strong and independent judiciary is established, with wide jurisdiction, and as the ultimate interpreter and custodian of the constitution.[55]

This is indeed an ambitious agenda: there are many changes to be brought about, almost simultaneously, in a short period of time. As we write (January 2015), the constitution has been in force for four-and-a-half years, though the provisions concerning the setting up of an entirely new layer of government, the counties, came into effect only in April 2013. On an interim assessment of the realization of the objectives of the constitution, we conclude that the record is mixed, despite the fact that there is a remarkable amount of constitutional discourse in official documents and rhetoric.

The Kenyan experience shows how hard it is to shake off the experiences, attitudes and habits of the past, and indeed the actors of the past, at least when there is no true revolution. If anything, the abuse of ethnic diversity has become more intense, with politicians manipulating ethnic sentiments, especially at election time.[56] Certain sections of the community remain marginalized on ethnic grounds, and ethnic favouritism continues to characterize appointments. The constitution's agenda of increased national unity, integration and inclusion takes a distinctly back seat. Ethnicity is a major factor in the lack of progress on democracy. So are habits of rigging elections and bribing voters. Elections – and politics generally – are not about policies but about who is in power. The legislatures at the national and county levels have done themselves little credit. The public image is one of excessively greedy people, insisting on huge salaries and allowances. Personal status and benefit is the dominant concern.

Public participation, including in the legislative process, has been a largely new development, though lawmakers have facilitated participation grudgingly and minimally.[57] On integrity and corruption, the record has been little better – if at all – than in the past, and accountability mechanisms generally have been disappointing. A recent Public Service Commission report says that: 'On

[51] Especially in Chapter 6 on Leadership and Integrity. [52] Article 227. [53] Article 79.
[54] Chapter 15. [55] Chapter 10.
[56] See Jill Cottrell Ghai and Yash Pal Ghai, 'Ethnicity, Pluralism and the 2013 Elections' in Ghai and Ghai (eds), *Ethnicity, Nationhood and Pluralism* (above) pp. 75–135.
[57] A striking example was in December 2014, when a set of major reforms to legislation in the interests of 'security' were introduced, unheralded, into Parliament on 9 December, notice inviting public comment published in the print media on 10 December with a deadline of 15, passed on 18 and assented to on 19 December. A constitutional challenge failed before the High Court, and an appeal is pending.

average, 77.0 per cent of the persons prosecuted for corruption between 2009 and 2013 have been acquitted.'[58] A plethora of independent commissions and offices – an important feature of the constitution – have made little impact. The new model electoral commission started with high expectations but has been unable to convince many of its electoral impartiality, and has recently experienced the embarrassment of having a British company convicted in an English court of paying bribes apparently destined for the commission.[59] The anti-corruption commission has disappointed, as have those who should be on the front line of defence of the constitution, the Director of Public Prosecutions and especially the Attorney General.[60]

The parliamentary lawmaking processes were somewhat opaque, and there have been repeated allegations of members being bribed. There is very limited scrutiny of bills. And some legislation required by the constitution has been designed to thwart the constitutional intention: notably that on recall of legislators.[61]

There seems little progress in tackling inequality, whether between parts of the country[62] or within urban areas, despite official figures that insist that growth in the economy is healthy.[63] The state of the economy has been the major concern of people;[64] youth unemployment (up to age thirty-five) is several times greater than for other age groups. The high birth rate and the poor educational achievement of the great majority of those entering the job market defeat efforts to improve the situation.[65]

The judiciary, purged of some corrupt or incompetent colleagues, and under the leadership of a new Chief Justice, has discharged its obligations with much credit. It has stood up to the executive in a number of critical cases, giving clear and learned judgments. Civil society has made ample use of the procedure for public interest litigation, winning much of the time. There is better protection of human rights than before.

[58] *Public Service Compliance with Values and Principles in Articles 10 and 232 of the Constitution* (Nairobi: PSC, December 2014) p. 20.

[59] See the Serious Fraud Office account at www.sfo.gov.uk/press-room/latest-press-releases /press-releases-2014/uk-printing-company-and-two-men-found-guilty-in-corruption-trial .aspx

[60] See chapters on these by, respectively, Waikwa Wanyoike and Yash Ghai in Yash Pal Ghai and Jill Cottrell Ghai (eds), *The Legal Profession and the New Constitutional Order in Kenya* (Nairobi: Strathmore University Press/International Commission of Jurists Kenya, 2014).

[61] Ss. 45–48 of the Elections Act 2011 being designed to make it pretty well impossible.

[62] A good source on inequality is a recent report by the Society for International Development; see inequalities.sidint.net/kenya/overview-document.

[63] E.g. and IMF assessment see www.imf.org/external/np/sec/pr/2014/pr14455.htm.

[64] Ipsos surveys at www.ipsos.co.ke/home/index.php/downloads.

[65] 'Unemployment Rate in Kenya increased to 40 percent in 2011 from 12.70 percent in 2006': www.tradingeconomics.com/kenya/unemployment-rate. '12.7% of the working age population is unemployed. About 67% of Kenya's unemployed are youth between 15 and 34 years of age. The highest unemployment rates are for people around 20 years old at 35%.' – Kenya Country Report for the 2014 Ministerial Conference on Youth Employment: www.adeanet.org/min _conf_youth_skills_employment/sites/default/files/u24/Kenya%20Country%20Report_0.pdf.

An area of deficit is the use of the coercive power of the state, in the most brutal colonial style. Government reaction to security challenges has been largely to crack down, especially on certain communities, and to tighten executive control over the security forces.[66] The courts seem to be unable to do much about it.[67] People have little faith in the police or in the fairness of the criminal justice system.[68]

The lesson of this dismal record is that a radical constitution cannot change the foundations of state and society unless the powerful elements of the regime, politicians, bureaucrats, security forces, and the businesses and religious groups are sidelined. This did not happen in Kenya, despite the widespread support for the constitution from most sectors of the people. All these groups had a deep vested interest in the ways the old system worked. They found that, despite some fundamental changes in the constitutional system, they were able to continue old practices because the networks that sustained them all remained in place. Few of the influential groups, including the international community, challenge these practices and politics. The emergence of China as a key economic and political player in Africa, with no regard for human rights or democracy, merely buttressed the government. The government was able to fend off without much difficulty the few challenges it faced, alleging a violation of the constitution, principally by a weak, ill organized, civil society. One common tactic of the government was simply to disregard court orders or rulings by other bodies. The people who are victimized by the continuation of old practices are divided, ethnically and otherwise, handicapped by the lack of understanding of the ways of the government, and therefore unable to mount a real challenge to the regime.

However there are positive factors. People have a greater understanding of their rights and, among some, of how to mobilize them. Democracy is beginning to take root in some counties, and the county executives are under considerable pressure. Shifting responsibilities for much of government to the counties is having some impact, despite a good deal of corruption, wastage and inefficiency. These three factors, the institutional change to a more devolved system of government, and greater public consciousness, coupled with a more active and committed judiciary, may be what are necessary to make the difference between constitutionalism in the first forty or so years of an independent Kenya and the next.

66 '"Do not fear anyone," Nkaissery [Cabinet Secretary for Interior] tells police', *Standard* newspaper, 12 January 2015.

67 Though the High Court did hold some of the recent security laws amendment unconstitutional as limiting human rights more than was justified: *Coalition for Reform and Democracy and others v Republic of Kenya and the Director of Public Prosecutions* [2015] eKLR at kenyalaw.org/caselaw/cases/view/106083/.

68 Ipsos' SPEC (Social, Political, Economic and Cultural) Barometer December 2014.

12. Conclusion

Our chapter concerns a period covering close to a century. Inevitably, Africa has experienced many fundamental changes in that period. There are few traces of the traditional systems of government. We have seen major changes in most spheres of life and organization. Africa is now poised at the start of further major economic and social changes, with the greater involvement of outside, global, forces influencing – indeed shaping – its society and economy, and therefore politics. All this is bound to reshape the state. How will these changes affect the mass of the people, and will they be for better or worse?

Writing at the time of the two-hundredth anniversary of the US constitution, and applying Weberian analysis of the movement from a patrimonial to a legal rational state, Ghai saw the reverse: that change in Africa was moving from the legal rational (brief though it was) to the patrimonial. He cautioned himself, however, to be careful not to push these Weberian parallels too far. He pointed to the dynamics of change in Africa (writing before the Arab Spring), reminding the reader that

> there is no inevitability in my model that represents a certain conjuncture of social and economic change in the future. The collapse of colonialism promoted latent divisive tendencies, but its structures nourished an authoritarianism. Perhaps there is no straight route from [post] colonialism legality to constitutionalism, perhaps it must pass through a new process of state building [and nation building] . . . Circumstances may so change that the vested interests of the dominant class (and interests of foreign states and capital) are better served through a democratic rather than an authoritarian polity. The forms of development generated though frequently give rise to their own contradictions, for instance, the development of a propertied and professional middle class that values democracy and human rights for their own pragmatic and ideological reasons [having shifted to Marxist analysis!]. . . .(although it is as well to temper our optimism by reminding ourselves that dissatisfaction with one form of authoritarian regime does not necessarily lead to a democratic order).[69]

We are uncertain what the author of *General Jurisprudence* would make of this. Perhaps Twining studies change, but does not predict it. He certainly saw the contradictions that can befall the state when he wrote, 'Where power and authority diverge, as any realist knows, there tends to be a gap between what in fact happens and what is meant to happen. Giving a realistic account of a constitution as a kind of institution is accordingly problematic.'[70] How right he is, although we are not sure whether a state constitution is what he had in his mind. But we do know that Twining has always stood for justice and fairness.

[69] Yash Ghai, in Douglas Greenberg et al., op. cit, pp. 195–6.

[70] William Twining, *Globalisation and Legal Theory* (London: Butterworths, 2000) p. 77.

Appendix: The trajectory of constitutionalism in Africa

Country	Independence constitution	Change and decline of independence constitution	Revival of constitutionalism
Eritrea	1993 free from Ethiopia. 1994 process begins. 1995 Constitution	President does not bring into force. Autocracy	Awaited
Ethiopia	NA (not applicable)	Absolute rule of Haile Selassie ended with coup 1974. Dictatorship overthrown 1991	Process 1991–94 new constitution
Gambia	1965	1970 Presidential constitution. 1994 coup (against President Jawara after nearly 30 years). 1996 return to civilian rule – elections won by coup leader; weak human rights period etc. 2014 attempted coup	Awaited
Ghana	1957	1960 (amendment: one-party state) 1966, 1969, 1972, 1978, 1979 and 1981 (coups etc.)	1981 process towards democracy. 1993 new constitution 2010 – process towards revised constitution (not complete)
Kenya	1963	1964–1982 (amendments to focus power in President, reduce independence of judiciary etc. ultimately one party state)	1992 (multi-party) to new constitution 2010
Malawi	1964 (on dissolution of federation)	1966 constitution (Republican). No Bill of Rights. One party state. Later amendment – Banda President for life.	1993 referendum: return to multi-partyism; 1994 interim constitution; 1995 new constitution

Country	Independence constitution	Change and decline of independence constitution	Revival of constitutionalism
Nigeria	1960 (1963 republic but no radical change)	1966 (coup)	1979 and 1989 (followed by coups) and 1999
Sierra Leone	1961	1971 new constitution (presidential). 1978 Constitution (one-party)	1991 New constitution (multi-party). 1991–2002 civil war. 1991 constitution reinstated; review process ongoing
Somalia	1961	1969 coup (Siad Barre). 1991 Siad Barre overthrown; collapse of Somali state	2004 process under UN leads to constitution draft 2010. Adopted but undergoing review. Constitutionalism not fully restored
Swaziland	1968	1973 King abrogated constitution. Current constitution 2006: absolute monarchy remains, no parties.	Awaited
Tanganyika	1961	1962 (consolidated power in president)	
Tanzania		1964 and 1965 Interim constitution; one-party state. 1977 first union constitution	1984 Bill of Rights. 1992 multi-party. 2012 Ongoing troubled process
Zanzibar	1963	1963 (coup)	
Uganda	1962	1963 republican constitution rubber stamped by parliament. 1966 PM Obote abrogated constitution. New constitution (1967) did away with powers for kingdoms. State of emergency declared. One party state. 1971 Amin coup. 1979 Amin overthrown. 1985 Museveni coup	1988 process began. 1995 constitution adopted

Country	Independence constitution	Change and decline of independence constitution	Revival of constitutionalism
Zambia	1964 (on dissolution of federation)	1973 one-party state constitution	1991 transitional multi-party constitution 1996 and 2003 failed attempts to get new constitution. New process leads to 2013 draft (process incomplete)
Zimbabwe	1980	To 2005 17 amendments including abolition of seats for white minority. De facto one-party state. Referendum rejected draft constitution 2000	2007 process begins, abortive. New process 2009 leads to 2013 constitution. Full realization of constitutionalism still awaited (Mugabe still in office)

Sources: various including Mbondenyi and Ojienda, *(eds), Constitutionalism and Democratic Governance in Africa: Contemporary Perspectives from Sub-Saharan Africa* (Pretoria: Pretoria University Press, 2013 and www.constitutionnet.org).

9

Comparative law, rights and the environment

John McEldowney[1]

Introduction

William Twining's 2011 Montesquieu Lecture at Tilburg University[2] articulates the underlying ideas that have for many years[3] informed his approach to globalization and the role of comparative law in maturing a cross-jurisdictional understanding of law and legal systems.[4] While admitting that he is not a specialist in comparative law, he advances the case for a global perspective that is 'genuinely world-wide'[5] and is focused on 'broad geographical pictures' that take account of 'long historical time frames'.[6] He recognizes the degree of interdependence of the world under globalization, while acknowledging deep respect for the distinctive values and ethics of indigenous societies and peoples.[7] Setting boundaries on this endeavour is not easy. Refreshingly, Twining offers an open invitation to a broad diaspora of theoretical and doctrinal legal scholars, drawn to a common endeavour based on intellectual curiosity about the role of law and its imperfections.

The main focus of this chapter is on Twining's general discourse on law, justice and rights in environmental debates. We begin, in the first part, with Twining's ambition to develop analytic concepts that foster a broad critique of existing legal scholarship in the age of globalization. He sees how predominantly Western legal theories have failed adequately to address a global perspective when the world is becoming more interdependent, especially when faced with environmental problems. This is followed, in part 2, by a discussion of Twining's categorization of the sub-field of environmental law in

[1] I would like to thank Professors Christopher McCrudden and Abdul Paliwala for comments on earlier versions.

[2] William Twining, *Globalisation and Legal Scholarship* (Woolf Legal Publishers, 2011).

[3] See William Twining, *General Jurisprudence: Understanding Law from a Global Perspective* (Cambridge University Press, 2009) contains many of his thoughts and ideas written and published over the past fifty years.

[4] See William Twining, 'Comparative Law and Legal Theory, the Country and Western Tradition' in Ian Edge, ed., *Comparative Law in Global Perspective* (New York: Transnational Publishers, 2000). ch. 2.

[5] William Twining, *Globalisation and Legal Scholarship* op. cit., fn 2 p. 24. [6] Ibid, p.28.

[7] William Twining, *The Place of Customary Law in the National Legal Systems of East Africa* (University of Chicago Law School, 1964). William Twining, 'Some Aspects of Reception' (1957), *Sudan Jo. And Law Reports* 229. William Twining, *The Taylor Lectures* 1975, printed as *Academic Law and Legal Development* (Faculty of Law, University of Lagos, Nigeria 1976).

the context of philosophical debates about justice, rights and the environment. Twining casts doubt on reliance on the language of justice, but favours broad engagement with the jurisprudential context of the globalization debate. He observes that normative jurisprudence is often lacking a global perspective, particularly relevant to environmental law scholarship. His alternative is based on a 'cosmopolitan'[8] approach that is inclusive of both non-Western and Western traditions. Twining is sceptical about addressing environmental issues through an exclusively human rights approach. Part 3 draws together Twining's contributions to debates about multidisciplinary and interdisciplinary approaches that might inform the theory and practice of environmental law scholarship. The common feature of such approaches is its pervasive normativism. Twining sets high expectations for the future of environmental law scholarship: that it should be more self-critical; that it should engage with both Western traditions and schools of thought to be found in other legal traditions – underlining the relevance of both the global South and global North; and that the boundaries of disciplines including law should be expanded – encouraging contributions from many disciplines[9].

The effect of globalization on environmental law scholarship has been recognized in scholarship on climate change, ozone depletion and biodiversity[10] but with only limited success in changing orthodox legal analysis.[11] Twining's globalization analysis offers the potential for a reconfiguration of legal thinking that is both more responsive to change and more stimulating to study, with consequent benefits in understanding environmental problems.

1. Twining's ambition: the development of general analytical concepts in legal scholarship

Twining's ambition to develop analytic concepts that foster a broad critique of existing legal scholarship in the age of globalization invites scholars to question their own underlying assumptions and preconceptions. Acknowledging frustration with existing legal scholarship,[12] Twining draws inspiration from a broad conception of law, and the treatment of institutionalized normative systems or sets of rules more generally, as meaningful and relevant to

[8] William Twining, *Globalisation and Legal Scholarship* op. cit., fn 2 p. 24.

[9] Twining's use of globalization is broadly defined to go beyond economics to include any processes that tend to make human relations – economic, political, cultural, communicative etc. – more interdependent. See: William Twining, *Globalisation and Legal Scholarship*, Woolf Legal Publishers, 2011 p. 22.

[10] Daniel A. Farber, 'The Challenge of Climate Change Adaptation: Learning from National Planning Efforts in Britain, China and the USA' (2011), *Journal of Environmental Law* 23(2) pp. 359–82.

[11] William Twining, 'Law, justice and rights: some implications of a global perspective' in J. Ebbesson and P. Okowa (eds), *Environmental Law and Justice in Context* (Cambridge University Press, 2009), p. 78.

[12] William Twining, 'Rethinking law schools' (1996) 21 *Law and Social Inquiry* 1007.

theoretical inquiry. This is both open-ended and challenging but also unsettling for those who are mainly focused on the domestic law of sovereign states or on the public international law that deals almost exclusively with relations between such states. Twining articulates a legal theory that has, as part of its foundations, 'a quite pragmatic and flexible method for rethinking the potential implications of so-called "globalisation" (note the scare quotes).'[13] He is keen that we should see the endeavour as defining the broad area of inquiry, rather than presenting a specific view of jurisprudence or being judgemental about 'outputs' or results. It is a path to a better and more informed scholarship that has the potentially transformative effect of making law less ghettoized.

Central to Twining's challenge to legal scholars is to advance a legal pluralism that facilitates lawyers in addressing globalization and engaging with socio-legal as well as economic and political culture. This is similar to the underlying multidisciplinary and interdisciplinary approaches that informed much legal scholarship since the 1960s. Twining advances this discussion, however, by arguing that his particular globalization perspective engages not only with interdisciplinary approaches but also with legal pedagogy. As Twining concedes, this may give rise to labels such as Globalization, Jurisprudence, Legal Theory and Legal Scholarship being rejected by specialists in other legal sub-disciplines.[14] Twining's central thesis that the world is becoming more interdependent raises questions about the breadth of the scholarly endeavour beyond legal theory. It also resonates with Montesquieu's[15] pioneering of empirical investigation as providing evidence to justify conclusions and his location of scientific study in a global context.[16] Twining strongly suggests the necessity both to examine underlying assumptions that are found in the Western tradition of academic law and to take account of the global South as well as the global North.[17] Twining's ambition is to embrace the spatial dimensions of the earth irrespective of time spans[18]. The concepts of justice and nature might facilitate engagement with many of the main problems associated with any scholarship that seeks to address globalization and law.[19] Twining's

[13] William Twining, 'Globalisation and Legal Scholarship – response' (2013) 4(4) *TLT* pp. 714–25 at 715.

[14] Ibid. p. 725. [15] Montesquieu, Charles-Louis de Secondat (1689–1755).

[16] Montesquieu, *Consideration and the Causes of the Greatness of the Romans and Their Decline*, 1734.

[17] See William Twining, ed., *Human Rights: Southern Voices* (Cambridge University Press, 2009). Also see the writings of Boaventura de Sousa Santos. 'Law; A map of Misreading, Toward a Postmodern Conception of Law' (1987), 14 *Journal of Law and Society* 279. Twining's use of globalization is broadly defined to go beyond economics to include any processes that tend to make human relations – economic political, cultural, communicative etc. – more interdependent. See: William Twining, *Globalisation and Legal Scholarship* (Woolf Legal Publishers, 2011), p. 22.

[18] See William Twining, *Globalisation and Legal Scholarship* (Woolf Legal Publishers, 2011), p. 28

[19] See Peer Zumbansen, 'Why Global Law is Transnational; remarks on the Symposium around William Twining's Montesquieu Lecture' (2013), 4(4) *TLT* pp. 463–75 at 463.

contemporary vision of global comparative law, influenced by the American legal realist, Karl Llewellyn,[20] urges us to understand the background and context of a problem, and to develop a practical sense of what has worked or failed, and a pragmatic response as to how to take matters forward.

2. Twining's ideas on justice, rights and the environment

Environmental legal scholarship is an appropriate sub-field in which to consider Twining's globalization analysis where his advocacy for systematic re-thinking has the potential to inform general philosophical debates in environmental law on a number of levels: the methodology most suited to address globalization; the nature of the interdisciplinarity of the subject; and the incentives required for sustainability. Areas such as climate change, ozone depletion and biodiversity are examples of scholarship that addresses globalization. Yet these specialist areas have limited impact on environmental scholarship and approaches to environmental law too readily retain old traditions at national, international and EU law levels. Twining's project of analyzing a global perspective goes further by setting the scene for one of the most difficult issues, namely the interaction between the Western and non-Western legal traditions, especially in the context of the global environment. Economic disparity between regions and countries as well as in legal education and legal systems are all part of the mix. Threats to human existence from climate change, pandemics, war, drought and food shortages are issues that should be addressed within the framework of analytical jurisprudence.[21] Twining's analysis of the environment, rights and justice reiterates his main concerns, namely the excessive state-based focus of much legal thinking, the presence of too many unexamined assumptions that make it difficult to respond to concerns about globalization, and the potential contribution of legal theory.

How scholarship in these areas may be taken forward requires more self-critical analysis by scholars of the assumptions that have underlined the traditional state-focused disciplines. Twining's reflective essay on 'Law, justice and rights: some implications of a global perspective'[22] confronts the challenge of addressing major concerns about the environment from a global perspective. Twining acknowledges that there is new scholarship in sub-fields such as human rights law and environmental law[23] but this has not eased the difficulty

[20] William Twining, *Karl Llewellyn and the Realist Movement* (London: Weidenfeld and Nicolson; Norman: University of Oklahoma Press, 1985).

[21] See: Keith Culver and Michael Giudice, 'Complementing Comparison: Renewing Analytical Legal Theory to Meet the Explanatory Challenge of Globalisation' (2013), 4(40 *TLT* pp. 700–713 at 710.

[22] William Twining, 'Law, justice and rights: some implications of a global perspective' in J. Ebbesson and P. Okowa (eds), *Environmental Law and Justice in Context* (Cambridge University Press, 2009), p. 78.

[23] Also included are areas such as trade law and anti-terrorism law.

of adapting to globalization. Culver and Giudice recognize Twining's contribution to future scholarship:

> Where Hart illustrated the logical contingency of the content of apparently necessary rules, pointing to much different, yet stably different possible basic facts about the nature of humans, Twining opens the way to considering whether and how legality might exist under continually varying physical and social conditions following satisfaction of physical and social preconditions for legality.[24]

For Twining, environmental justice *prima facie* falls within the province of normative jurisprudence. His preliminary observations restate some of the common themes found in his writing.[25] Three points are particularly helpful in developing global perspectives on environmental law. First, lawyers need to be sensitive to boundaries, jurisdictions and levels of ordering. He warns against oversimplification of the relationship between the global and local. It is necessary to take account of diversity in culture, including 'other alliances, networks, religions, cartels and spheres of influence – all of these cut across simple vertical hierarchies and greatly complicate the picture of ordering and the diffusion of legal ideas'.[26] This is particularly important in developing policy responses to threats to humanity such as climate change, nuclear proliferation, war and peace, and extreme poverty. Second, comparative law should be broadened in order to avoid neglecting other aspects of interaction. Cross-level diffusion, different forms of inter-legality and, above all, legal and normative pluralism should be central concerns as the discipline of law becomes more cosmopolitan. Third, there are new avenues to be considered, such as the developing sub-field of law-and-geography. The idea of 'legal geography', corresponding to mapping law, applies to spheres of justice as well as the study of 'law in action'.

Twining's agenda for discussion pulls back from predominantly Western-dominated legal theories, which fail to explain the post-Westphalian world and are out of touch with practical realities. Data and fact finding are essential if the environmental justice debate is to develop. The absence of a truly global perspective has resulted in a failure to look beyond the confines of state borders in setting theories of justice and this results in the failure to provide an adequate theoretical basis for environmental law. There is evident disappointment of the work of John Rawls, which may fall short of what is needed or expected of the work of John Rawls, which fall short of what is needed or expected. This is the case particularly in Rawls' liberal theory of international justice,[27] which "rejects any principle of distribution, treats an outdated

[24] Ibid. p. 710.

[25] William Twining, *General Jurisprudence: Understanding Law from a Global Perspective* (Cambridge University Press, 2008), especially chapter 10, pps. 161–3.

[26] William Twining, 'Law, justice and rights: some implications of a global perspective' in J. Ebbesson and P. Okowa (eds), *Environmental Law and Justice in Context* (Cambridge University Press, 2009), p. 78.

[27] John Rawls, *The Law of Peoples* (Cambridge, MA: Harvard University Press, 1999).

conception of public international law as satisfactorily representing principles of justice in the global arena, and says almost nothing about extreme poverty, the environment, increasing inequalities, or American hegemony (and how it might be exercised), 'let alone about transnational justice or reparations or other issues that are now high on the global agenda'.[28] Twining senses Rawls' theory as parochial and conservative and is disappointed that Rawls fails to take account of the role of affluent societies and the global poor.[29] Thomas Pogge,[30] while accepting the main values underpinning Rawls' theories, adapts Rawls' ideas and expands them, shaping a more outward-looking analysis that is capable of addressing the interdependent world. Pogge concludes that the current global institutional scheme is unjust and world poverty is an important focus for global justice.[31] The recognition that global justice has to address extreme poverty is significant, although Pogge's discussion of the main environmental issues is limited; perhaps understandably, in view of his goal of devising a general theory. Twining is sceptical about how far a theory of environmental justice is sufficiently open-ended to accommodate values that lie outside the mainstream.[32] The language and nature of the subject may simply not afford a suitable way to express major concerns about the environment.

Academic writing on environmental justice[33] is a fast developing area. Concepts such as the 'precautionary' principle, the 'polluter pays' principle, and sustainable development have to be accommodated, when they are in conflict and when they converge. The challenges of globalization and international law have resulted, as Vel P. Nanda suggests, in an emerging mix of ideas and concepts:

> The forces of globalisation have indeed changed the world and the changing international landscape has fundamentally altered international law... What has also resulted is the emergence of concepts such as sustainable development, environmental justice, the rule of law and good governance which will no doubt shape the future of global existence.[34]

Human rights may yet provide an appropriate language for expressing arguments and claims, and its expansionist tendency globally makes it a powerful rhetorical tool that facilitates analysis and discussion. This leaves largely

28 Twining op. cit. fn. 2 p. 86 .

29 Twining op. cit. fn. 3 p. 163., William Twining, ed., *Human Rights: Southern Voices* (Cambridge University Press, 2009).

30 See T. Pogge, *World Poverty and Human Rights* (Cambridge: Polity Press, 2002) and also T. Pogge, 'Real World justice', 8(2005) *Journal of Ethics* 29.

31 Ibid.

32 Twining cites Peter Singer, an advocate of animal liberation, as an example of how values may not be commonly shared but are worth considering. P. Singer, *Animal Liberation* 2nd edition (New York: Random House, 1972).

33 Ole Pedersen, 'Environmental Principles and Environmental Justice' (2010), 12(1) *Environmental Law Review* pp. 26–49.

34 Vel P. Nanda, 'The challenges of globalisation and international law' in Shawkat Alam, Natalie Klein and Juliette Overland (eds), *Globalisation and the Quest for Social and Environmental Justice* (Routledge, 2011), pp. 254–74 at 274.

unresolved the question of the appropriateness of human rights discourse and contested values beyond Western societies.[35] Twining is not convinced 'that secular human rights can become a universal moral language', warning that 'human rights are perhaps overstated and need to be treated with great caution.'[36] Human rights discourse does not easily fit with the language of many major religions and other belief systems. There is a fear that human rights are a convenient tool for too many interested parties to use for their own purposes.[37] It may also prove difficult to resolve ownership issues in the context of protecting the environment.[38]

Twining concedes that the discourses of justice, human rights and utility have their place in the general environmental law discourse, in terms of arguments and negotiations, but this falls short of addressing the full range of issues raised by globalization.[39] Twining also addresses a mainstream debate in environmental literature of even wider impact, namely whether the focus of attention of environmental law and policy should be the benefit to human beings (anthropocentric) or the benefit to the environment (ecocentric). Most of the mainstream thinking adopts an anthropocentric approach. This may lead to doubts about whether ecocentric concerns are adequately considered in the main thinking on human rights and justice. Twining argues for pragmatism, the practical politics of coexistence and co-operation as well as the need for compromise.[40]

There are many lessons for environmental law scholarship that come from Twining's analysis, notably the necessity of embracing multiple standpoints and perspectives that need to be addressed in mainstream scholarship on environmental issues.[41] Scholars have to be willing to share the enterprise of their inquiry beyond their subject discipline. Twining's plea to go beyond traditional thinking in order to deal with general questions about values and law finds support from environmental lawyers interested in challenging the limits of environmental law.[42]

[35] Jan Hancock, 'The Human Right to Natural Resources' in *Environmental Human Rights, Power, Ethics and Law* ch. 6, pp. 137–56.

[36] Twining ibid. p. 89.

[37] U. Baxi, *The Future of Human Rights* 2nd edition (New Delhi: Oxford University Press, 2006), Y. Ghai, *Human Rights and Asian Values* (1998) 9 *Public Law Review* 168.

[38] J. Crawford, ed., *The Rights of Peoples* (Oxford: Clarendon Press, 2012). V. Baird, 'Land Rights and Wrongs' (1987) *The New Internationalist* no. 177 November, pp. 4–6.

[39] William Twining, 'Law, justice and rights: some implications of a global perspective' in J. Ebbesson and P. Okowa (eds), *Environmental Law and Justice in Context* (Cambridge University Press, 2009), pp. 87–88.

[40] This view is largely influenced by the work of the French Philosopher Jacques Maritain. See also C. McCrudden, 'Human Dignity and Judicial Interpretation of Human Rights', 20 (2008) *European Journal of International Law* 1.

[41] Legal education has an important role – see William Twining, 'A Cosmopolitan Discipline? Some Implications of "Globalisation" for legal Education', 8 (2001) *International Journal of the Legal Profession* 23.

[42] Hanne Petersen, 'Gender and environmental law and justice; thoughts on sustainable masculinities' in J. Ebbesson and P. Okowa (eds), *Environmental Law and Justice in Context* (Cambridge University Press, 2009), p. 98.

3. Multidisciplinarity and interdisciplinarity and the practice of environmental law scholarship

The sub-field of environmental law also raises the possibility of multidisciplinary and interdisciplinary approaches. It is important to distinguish between interdisciplinary and multidisciplinary. The former is an attempt to find a way to integrate discrete bodies of knowledge or disciplines to create a new knowledge synthesis. The latter is used to mean the joining together of one or more disciplines with little or no attempt to integrate them. It is clear that to date there has been a recognizable multidisciplinary approach adopted by lawyers interested in science.[43]

Twining's analysis argues for a 'healthy cosmopolitan discipline' that is widely drawn to include 'all social relations' and the 'legal orderings of the world'.[44] As well as engaging in a contextual discussion of the law, he promotes a widely-drawn methodology that encompasses theoretical and practical distinctions, encourages debates within and between disciplines, and explores different perspectives.[45] Twining favours broad cross-disciplinary approaches that challenge underlying assumptions. This may prove quite challenging to the discipline undertaking the inquiry. It may also be resisted by those who fear that the integrity of the specific discipline may be undermined or usurped.[46] Environmental legal scholarship is a good example of Bradley's point that 'law's relations with globalization are reflexive: laws promote globalization, and laws are a response to globalization.'[47]

The sub-field of environmental law offers a good example of the opportunity for multi-disciplinary research that is identified in Twining's methodology. This is commensurate with a technical approach that views environmental law as a means of administration endowed with discrete analytical tasks, which enables law to address scientifically knowable and manageable technological risks, if performed methodologically and rigorously. Such a methodologically technical approach is frequently employed in environmental legal analysis. It may occasionally be embedded in law directly but is more frequently found in environmental policymaking, which is eventually translated into law.

In an interdisciplinary approach, however, there is a common sharing or exploration of each other's methodology and approach. Environmental legal

[43] J. Vogler, *The Global Commons: Environmental and Technical Governance* (Chichester: John Wiley, 2000); O. Young, 'The Architecture of Global Environmental Governance: Bringing Science to Bear on Policy' (2008) 8 (no.1) *Global Environmental Politics* 14–33.

[44] William Twining, *Globalisation and Legal Scholarship* op. cit., fn 2 p. 46.

[45] See C. McCrudden, 'Legal research and the Social Sciences' (2006), 122 *Law Quarterly Review* 632.

[46] One example is R. Deech, 'Divorce Law and Empirical Studies' (1990), 106 *Law Quarterly Review* 229.

[47] Caroline Bradley, 'Book review: Globalization and Legal Theory' (2001), *University of Miami Inter-American Law Review* 31(3) (2001) 463–5.

scholarship has recently discussed the use of interdisciplinarity[48] and its place in the future direction of environmental law scholarship. This discussion provides a useful case study of some of the pitfalls and limitations of interdisciplinarity for both policy making and legislation.[49] It also provides an opportunity to find many common threads with Twining's analysis of working with different disciplines.

The historical intersection between the sub-field of environmental law and science provides support for collaboration between scientists and lawyers.[50] The two disciplines, especially the natural sciences, share some common characteristics that proved influential in their development. The early English common law drew from practitioners' interest in procedural formalities and adaptation to different forms of actions. Systemizing English law came from a number of influences. The 'science of law' attributed to William Blackstone[51] makes clear how law shares with science the application of logical reasoning and predictability, which in judicial terms sets the foundation for *stare decisis* and precedent. Scientific method came to use technical and formal rules applied to evidence gathering and analysis, and this was reflected in empiricist legal tradition rooted in the logic of judges. The collection and assessment of evidence and its use as a tool to mould ideas is a critical part of scientific thought and legal reasoning. Blackstone favoured adapting continental ideas and rights into common law practices.[52] He reasoned that English law was 'a science which distinguished the criteria of right and wrong'. Bentham offered codification and principle-based analysis from general acceptance of a utilitarian sociology. Prevailing *laissez faire* economics were gradually remodelled under the influence of political economists. J. S. Mill's influential *Principles of Political Economy*, first published in 1848, brought practical aspirations while analytic jurisprudence offered law reform as a means of addressing social and economic problems.

Developing a common methodology was not straightforward, and often contested, leading to disciplines developing in their own way rather than coming together. Originally, classical political economy favoured abstract, deductive and universal rules that conveyed respect for objectivity and conserving what was achieved. The sociological methodology of Augustus

48 Elizabeth Fisher, Bettina Lange, Eloise Scotford and Cinnamon Carlarne, 'Maturity & Methodology: Starting a Debate about Environmental Law Scholarship', *Journal of Environmental Law* 21(2) pp. 213–250(2009).

49 E. Fisher, *Risk: Regulation and Administrative Constitutionalism* (Oxford: Hart Publishing, 2009).

50 John McEldowney and Sharron McEldowney, 'Science and Environmental Law: Collaboration across the Double Helix' (2013), 13(3) *Environmental Law Review* pp. 169–198.

51 See William Twining, 'Globalisation and Legal Scholarship – response' (2013), 4(4) *TLT* pp. 714–25 at 719; W. Blackstone, *Commentaries* vol. X, 5–6.

52 William Blackstone (1723–1880), scholar and legal intellectual.

Comte[53] (1798–1857), whose influence was later absorbed in Mill's writing and became popularized by Frederic Harrison,[54] further advanced the cause of a realistic analysis as an alternative to abstract reasoning that took account of changing and often unpredictable outcomes. It also favoured a more subjective judgement.[55] German legal writers, such as Gustave von Hugo[56] (1764–1844), F. K. von Savigny[57] (1779–1861) and K. F. Eichorn[58] (1781–1854), varied in their adaptation of such ideas but were prominent figures favouring a broader social or national economics that would address the needs of the nation. Rather than seeing matters as 'static' they favoured greater pragmatism based on a rejection of the abstract method of reasoning in favour of a more realistic approach to the evolving nature of social problems. Maine's influence was also important[59] in terms of looking at how nature and law evolved and, in that evolution, how some relative standard for law might emerge.[60] It should come as no surprise that statistical study[61] and the innovations that accompanied mathematical and statistical analysis were applied to social problems, including public health, pollution and waste.[62] Theodore Porter observed[63] that the intellectual character of science-based statistical study had been transformed by the end of the nineteenth century and thereafter it had crystallized into a 'wealth of applications'. Porter, in his later work,[64] also observed how science is often made up by communities of researchers insistent on objectivity and resilient to external criticism. This gave science its cohesiveness, quest for objectivity and aloofness to outside investigators. It has contributed to the exclusiveness of the subject and is, perhaps, partly responsible for a failure of non-scientists to engage in debate with scientists.

[53] Auguste Comte (1798–1857), French philosopher Cours de Philosophie positive 6 volumes 1930–1842 and Systéme de Politique positive (1851–1854). His positivism and vision for humanity brought religious zeal and enthusiasm without formal religious beliefs.

[54] Frederic Harrison (1831–1923).

[55] Charles de Secondat Montesquieu, Baron de la Brede et de (1689–1755) French philosopher and author of *De l'espirit des lois* (1748).

[56] Gustave von Hugo (1764–1844).

[57] Fredrich Karl von Savigny (1779–1861), Law Professor at Marburg, engaged in the Commission for revising the Prussian Code (1810–42).

[58] K. F. Eichorn (1781–1854).

[59] Sir Henry Maine (1822–88), Jurist and historian, H. Maine, *Early Law and Custom* (1883).

[60] William Twining, 'Academic Law and legal philosophy: The significance of Herbert Hart' (1979), 95 *Law Quarterly Review* 557. William Twining, 'The Great Juristic Bazaar' (1976), 14 *Journal of the Public Teachers of Law* 185.

[61] A general historical analysis may be found in C. Bell and R. Bell, *City Fathers: The Early History of Town Planning in Britain* (Penguin, 1972); M. W. Flinn, ed., *The Medical and Legal Aspects of Sanitary Reform* (Leicester University Press, 1969).

[62] On science, see John Gribbin, *Science: A History* (Penguin, 2003); A. Wohl, *Endangered Lives: Public Health in Victorian Britain* (London: Methuen, 1984) and also C. Ponting, *A Green History of the World* (London: Sinclair-Stevenson, 1991).

[63] Theodore M. Porter, *The Rise of Statistical Thinking 1820–1900* (University of Princeton Press, 1986), p. 315.

[64] Theodore M. Porter, *Trust in Numbers* (University of Princeton Press, 1996), pp. 217–19.

Legal scholarship inevitably overlaps and merges with scientific research and scholarship in environmental law and, indeed, in environmental science. The intersection between law and science is not new, and has grown deeper in recent centuries with the growth of applied science and technology.[65] Porter has shown how the quantification of data is an important aid to understanding as well as transforming our knowledge, and informs many different approaches and disciplines.[66] There is a synergy between disciplinary objectivity familiar in law and to lawyers, with the objectivity claimed by science and for environmental data. Knowing 'things' as they really are appeals to philosophers, and counters claims based on the metaphysical. Lewis Wolpert has claimed that science is the best way to understand how the world works, a crucial building block towards protecting the environment and scientific advance.[67]

Recognition of this has given environmental law a particular trajectory in answering the challenge of new scientific discoveries. The industrial revolution produced a legacy of risk assessment, pollution controls and public health protection. It also fostered new processes and manufacturing of scientific instruments, which coincided with assessments based on numeracy and the quest for objective data. Science and objectivity spilled into other disciplines, including the social sciences, and had a major influence on policy makers. Twining's advocacy of data collection and mapping, combined with the underlying assumptions on which this is based, fits this approach to studying 'the law in action'.[68]

There are obvious examples where the tools of another discipline are both necessary and useful in the environmental area. The methods of Pareto efficiency are regularly used, and have proved useful, in assessing environmental regulation.[69] Few would deny that there is a gradual rise in interest in interdisciplinary scholarship. This is reflective of the importance of science and empirical legal scholarship. Normative analysis also favours an environmental law scholarship that recognizes the importance of science and its formative role in legitimating environmental law and policy.[70] New scientific advances constantly challenge the existing knowledge base in environmental science and the adequacy of environmental law and regulation. Responsive and flexible approaches are required to address environmental problems,

[65] See Roy Porter, *Flesh in the Age of Reason* (London: Allen Lane, Penguin, 2003), ch. 5.

[66] Theodore Porter, *Trust in Numbers* (Princeton: Princeton Press, 1996).

[67] Lewis Wolpert, 'What Lawyers need to know about science' in H. Reece, ed., *Law and Science* (1998), 1 *Current Legal Issues* 189; Lewis Wolpert, *The Unnatural Nature of Science* (London: 1992); also see J. McEldowney, 'The Environment, Science and Law' (1998), 1 *Current Legal Issues*, 109.

[68] William Twining, *Globalisation and Legal Scholarship* (Woolf Legal Publishers, 2011), p. 45.

[69] Jan Smits, *The Mind and Method of the Legal Academic* (Cheltenham: Edward Elgar, 2012).

[70] Stephen Yearley, 'Green Ambivalence About Science: Legal Rational Authority and the Scientific Legitimation of a Social Movement' (1992), 43 *British Journal of Sociology* 511; J. F. McEldowney and S. McEldowney, *Environmental Law and Regulation* (London and Oxford: Blackstone and Oxford University Press, 2001).

both new and old. Inevitably, responses will have to engage with the assessment of risk for environmental and human health.[71] An interdisciplinary relationship between law and science that is supported by reflexive learning between the disciplines[72] will require environmental lawyers to develop 'interactional expertise' with other disciplines,[73] as articulated in Elizabeth Fisher and others.[74] An interdisciplinary approach also sets priorities, assists in recognizing and admits difficulties when scientific solutions fail to mesh with legal outcomes or where the law appears irrelevant or is ignored in policy making.

For Twining, law has lagged behind other disciplines in thinking globally, but, in endeavouring to address global issues, 'we are not starting from scratch'.[75] Striving for shared understandings between relevant disciplines that address globalization sets a formidable challenge. It has to be admitted that such a goal may prove overambitious and unrealizable, but many scholars see this as a necessary step to take if environmental scholarship is to reach a new maturity.[76] Both disciplines have much to gain from the successful development of interdisciplinary working and the outcome may lead to better, proactive management of environmental problems. Law and science, however, offer contrasting styles of engagement with contested boundaries and fears about capture.[77] This inevitably raises barriers to dialogue. Reflexive learning is ambitious and demanding.[78] It can be facilitated through improvements in how environmental lawyers are trained[79] and

[71] Brian Wynne, 'Uncertainty and Environmental Learning: Preconceiving Science and Policy in the Preventative Paradigm' (1992), *Global Environmental Change* 111.

[72] See P. Lowe and J. Phillipson, 'Reflexive Interdisciplinary Research: The Making of a Research Programme on the Rural Economy and Land Use' (2006), 57(2) *Journal of Agricultural Economics* 165–84.

[73] J. Greaves and W. Grant, 'Crossing the Interdisciplinary Divide: Political Science and Biological Science' (2010), *Political Studies* Vol. 58 no. 2 pp. 320–339; R. Macrory, 'Regulating in a Risky Environment' [2001], *Current Legal Problems* 619; R. Macrory, *Modernising Justice: Regulation and the Role of an Environmental Tribunal* March 2003 Centre for Law and the Environment, Faculty of Laws, University College, London (available through Defra); R. Macrory, *The Environmental Justice Report* Environmental Law Foundation 2004 (available through Defra).

[74] Elizabeth Fisher, Bettina Lange, Eloise Scotford and Cinnamon Carlarne, 'Maturity & Methodology: Starting a Debate about Environmental Law Scholarship', *Journal of Environmental Law* 21(2) pp. 213–250 (2009).

[75] William Twining, *Globalisation and Legal Scholarship* (Woolf Legal Publishers, 2011), pp. 27–8.

[76] See Elizabeth Fisher, Bettina Lange, Eloise Scotford and Cinnamon Carlarne, 'Maturity & Methodology: Starting a Debate about Environmental Law Scholarship', *Journal of Environmental Law* 21(2) pp. 213–250 (2009); P. Lowe and J. Phillipson, 'Reflexive Interdisciplinary Research: The Making of a Research Programme on the Rural Economy and Land Use' (2006), 57(2) *Journal of Agricultural Economics* 165–84.

[77] See *R (on the application of Amvac Chemical UK(Ltd) v. Secretary of State for the Environment, Food and Rural Affairs* [2001] EWHC Admin 1011 is a good example.

[78] J. Phillipson and P. Lowe, 'Special Issue Guest Editorial: The Scoping of an Interdisciplinary Research Agenda' (2006), 57(2) *Journal of Agricultural Economics* 163–4.

[79] The range of science subjects today is very broad, encompassing geology, genetics, molecular biology and ethology, and incorporates ever more specialized areas such as ecotoxicology etc. Contemporary issues, such as climate change, flood defence and biodiversity loss, all have an

educated[80] in order to foster the necessary collaboration with science.[81] Mathematical and statistical studies are also important because of the quantification of data, while engineering makes a crucial contribution through the development and calibration of scientific instruments. But, as Nicholas de Sadeleer has observed:

> this marriage of law and reason is not entirely free of strife: legal rules are meant to provide predictability, yet nature is unpredictable; whilst the jurist seeks certainty, the scientist points to the uncertainty inherent in ecological risk.[82]

Today, scientific uncertainty as to the existence or recognition of a risk is not considered a good reason for delaying the adoption of laws or regulations aimed at preventing risk. Since the adoption of the precautionary principle in the 1990s, a preventative approach to environmental law is the underlying philosophy.[83] However, the adoption of preventative approaches is not necessarily evidence of embracing precaution in practice. As a consequence, in practice, various forms of prevention and deterrence have become the main drivers in the relationship between science and law.

The adoption of the precautionary principle constituted a refocusing that is to be found in international, European and domestic law.[84] Scientific uncertainty sits uneasily with traditional approaches to law that are premised on the need for legal certainty. Conventional science is most challenged when facing a new generation of risks that are linked to new technologies and leave considerable uncertainty as to how to anticipate and prevent harm.[85] Controversial areas include the science of climate change, CFCs, GMOs, hormone-disrupting chemicals and electromagnetic fields. The application of the precautionary principle has wider implications for the effectiveness of environmental law, much of which is predicated on the need for certainty and predictability. This much is already recognized, as environmental law is subject to many different approaches and even definitions.

important science input. Science informs us about the quality of air, drinking and bathing water and the impact of pollutants that threaten all forms of life.

[80] See Mark Huxham and David Sumner, *Science and Environmental Decision Making* (Essex: Pearson Press, 2000); R. Attfield, *Environmental Ethics: An overview for the Twenty-First Century* (Cambridge: Policy Press, 2003).

[81] P. Godfrey-Smith, *Theory and Reality: An introduction to the Philosophy of Science* (University of Chicago Press, 2003), p. 236.

[82] Nicolas de Sadeleer, 'The principles of prevention and precaution in international law' in M. Fitzmaurice, D. Ong, P. Merkouris (eds), *Research Handbook on International Environmental Law* (Edward Elgar, 2010), p. 185.

[83] Elizabeth Fisher, 'Precaution, Precaution Everywhere: Developing a "Common Understanding" of the Precautionary Principle in the European Community' (2002), 9 *Maastricht Journal of European and Comparative Law* 7.

[84] Nicolas de Sadeleer and Frank B. Cross, 'Paradoxical Perils of the Precautionary Principle' (1996), 53 *Washington and Lee Law Review* 859 p. 184.

[85] Stephen Breyer, *Breaking the Vicious Circle: Towards Effective Risk Regulation* (Harvard University Press, 1993).

Twining's 'mapping exercise' is evident where there are mutual benefits in accumulating scientific data and sharing risk assessment strategies, which are illustrated by examples of EU legislation such as REACH,[86] the Water Framework Directive (WFD) and the demands of regulating new developments such as GMOs. The existing epistemological and methodological framework should accommodate a different perspective on evaluation and justification that is sufficiently reflexive to promote effective learning specifically linked to solutions that correspond with identified environmental problems. There are governance and related regulatory issues that will also benefit from collaboration between environmental lawyers and scientists.

Access to environmental information and knowledge, not only for experts but also for the citizen, is a key component in environmental justice narratives. Environmental law scholarship has undoubtedly advanced considerably under the influence of cross-disciplinary study and is a practical example of Twining's advocacy of trend spotting as trend setting.[87] Maturity in environmental law scholarship, however, also offers an incalculable aid to help scientists understand their responsibilities as well as the legal constraints that apply to their work. The hurly-burly of collaboration is not unidirectional but a two-way exchange, and legal scholarship can bring valuable insights towards socially responsible science.[88]

Wyn Grant and Justin Greaves[89] have usefully defined the role of justification in interdisciplinary collaboration. Drawing on philosophical[90] and political scientific analysis,[91] they argue that:

> As academics and researchers what is important is not the pursuit of knowledge *per se*, but whether our conclusions are justified given the evidence (or arguments) we produce to support them. Or rather that they are backed up by sufficient evidence to justify the confidence to which they are asserted. For example, if we claim our conclusions are *likely* rather than certain or definitive,

[86] REACH (Registration, Evaluation, Authorization and restriction of CHemicals) refers to the European Regulation to provide human health and environmental protection. See S. McEldowney, 'EU Chemicals Policy – a Foundation for Environmental Protection or a Missed Opportunity?' (2004), *Yearbook of European Environmental Law Vol. 4* (Oxford University Press, 2004) pp. 85–116.

[87] William Twining, *Globalisation and Legal Scholarship* (Woolf Legal Publishers, 2011), p. 57.

[88] Kees Van Kersbergen and Frans Van Waarden, '"Governance" as a bridge between disciplines: Cross-disciplinary inspiration regarding shifts in governance and problems of governability, accountability and legitimacy' (2004), 43 *European Journal of Political Research* pp. 143–71.

[89] J. Greaves and W. Grant, 'Crossing the Interdisciplinary Divide: Political Science and Biological Science' (2010), *Political Studies* Vol. 58 no. 2 pp. 320–39.

[90] K. Popper, *Untended Quest: An Intellectual Autobiography* (London: Routledge, 2002); R. Scruton, *Modern Philosophy: an Introduction and Survey* (London: Pimlico, 2004).

[91] P. Lowe and J. Phillipson, 'Reflexive Interdisciplinary Research: The Making of a Research Programme on the Rural Economy and Land Use' (2006), 57(2) *Journal of Agricultural Economics* 165–84; L. M. Ashworth, 'Interdisciplinarity and international relations' (2009), 8(1) *European Political Science* 16–25; P. Burnham, K. Lutz Gilland, W. Grant and Z. Layton Henry, *Research methods in Politics* 2nd edition (Basingstoke: Palgrave–Macmillan, 2008).

> our arguments should be required to support the claim that they are probable.[92]

This gives rise to the desirability of a shared understanding of what constitutes a justified belief that is the true mark of successful interdisciplinary research.[93] Justification must crucially connect with evaluation, which provides the basis for an evidence-based focus that leads to accountability and appropriate audit.

Climate change, resilience, ozone depletion and biodiversity have created a risk literature in environmental law.[94] However, Ole Pedersen raises some important caveats about the contemporary drive towards interdisciplinarity in the practice of environmental law scholarship.[95] While accepting that interdisciplinarity produces some tangible benefits in terms of 'expanding the perimeters of a discipline', he claims that the effects of interdisciplinary work are often exaggerated. Pedersen argues that interdisciplinary work still adheres to disciplinary boundaries and that a 'perhaps unintended consequence of this ratification is that scholars, rather than becoming more interdisciplinary, become more entrenched in their discipline'. He observes that, at the end of a day of working on interdisciplinary engagement and scholarly debate, 'the lawyer returns to the law department and the community of fellow scholars'.[96] Pedersen argues for a 'flexible, open-minded and broadly defined approach to environmental law scholarship', which echoes Twining's enthusiasm for the examination of assumptions.[97]

More problematic for interdisciplinarity, however, is Pedersen's concern that environmental law scholarship is primarily focused on a specific community of scholars in which it is likely to thrive and develop.[98] This may be too confining for the global scholar and too restrictive of the discipline of comparative law that has to address global interconnections.[99] Perhaps interdisciplinarity is too demanding and time-consuming, requiring technical and specific expertise that is not easily absorbed or understood by the non-specialist.[100] The significant expansion in academic writing and its availability

[92] Ibid.

[93] A. Lijphart, 'Comparative Politics and the Comparative Methods' (1971), Vol. 65(3) *American Political Science Review* pp. 682–93; W. Grant and D. Chandler, 'Working Together Across Disciplines: Challenges for the Natural Sciences' (2007), British Association for the Advancement of Science, York.

[94] Elizabeth Fisher, Pasky Pascual and Wendy Wagner, 'Understanding Environmental Models in their Legal and Regulatory Context' (2010), *Journal of Environmental Law* 22(2) pp. 251–83.

[95] Ole W. Pedesen, 'The Limits of Interdisciplinarity and the Practice of Environmental Law Scholarship' (2014), 26 *Journal of Environmental Law* pp. 423–41.

[96] Ibid. p. 428.

[97] See William Twining, 'Social Science and Diffusion of Law' (2005), 32 *Journal Law and Society* 203.

[98] William Twining, 'Normative and Legal Pluralism: A Global Perspective' (2010), 20 *Duke Journal Of Comparative and International Law* 473.

[99] Generally see G. Teubner, ed., *Global Law without a State* (Aldershot: Dartmouth, 1997).

[100] Roger Cramton, 'Demystifying Legal Scholarship' (1986), 75 *Geo. LJ* 1 and also see Richard Posner, *Overcoming Law* (Harvard University Press, 1995).

worldwide that deters the faint-hearted may also be a factor to consider. Borrowing from other disciplines also requires rigorous academic standards as well as self-confidence. These concerns reflect the serious challenges and difficulties that confront a scholar seeking to go beyond the narrow technical boundaries of their own discipline to share knowledge derived from others. Pedersen's analysis serves to remind us how challenging Twining's plea for 'systematic rethinking' really is, and the demands it places on scholars and scholarship.[101] The tools of continuous mapping and the encouragement of cross-disciplinary debate are the means of addressing many of these concerns.[102] Environmental law may become caught up in debates about its own existence that are likely to be counterproductive, and this would be a missed opportunity to address transnational developments that embrace globalization.

Conclusions

Twining's emphasis on a global perspective inspires his desire to place environmental concerns in a broad framework, enabling them to be addressed at a theoretical and practical level outside the constraints of narrow, technical and territorial state-centred law. Legal scholars are encouraged to think about decision-making and the changing evolution of law outside and across national borders.[103] His overall analysis of environmental justice considers how concepts such as justice, utility and rights provide a platform for negotiation and discussion of a global perspective.[104] Addressing global environmental concerns in this way opens up a rich mixture of competing legal and regulatory systems that engage with social, cultural and economic aspects of the problem and may have to be reconsidered in the light of failures in the politics of decision-making. Globalization is readily recognized in climate change, ozone depletion and biodiversity, but has limited impact in the normative analysis of the subject.

Environmental legal scholarship is an appropriate sub-field in which to consider Twining's advocacy of systematic rethinking. This has the potential to inform general philosophical debates in environmental law on a number of levels: the methodology most suited to address globalization; the nature of the interdisciplinarity of the subject; and the incentives required for sustainability. Perhaps most important is his plea to reveal and critique assumptions, and adopt innovation in problem solving. This sets far-reaching challenges for legal

[101] See, for example, Sally Falk Moore, *Law as Process: An Anthropological Approach* (1978), *LIT Verlag* 2000, 54–81.

[102] See, for example, Paul Anderson, *Reforming Law and Economy for a Sustainable Earth* (Routledge, 2014).

[103] Bjorn Lomborg, *The Skeptical Environmentalists* (Cambridge University Press, 2001).

[104] J. Ebbesson and P. Okowa (eds), *Environmental Law and Justice in Context* (Cambridge University Press, 2009).

scholars and legal scholarship. These perceptions fit Twining's general understanding of the world's greater interdependence; a position that views the 'world and humankind as a whole'[105] in the context of 'broader geographical pictures and long historical time-frames'.[106] This is entirely consistent with an alternative vision and agenda of legal theorizing that crosses disciplinary boundaries and encompasses all levels of social relations.

Pedersen and others[107] have shown that achieving interdisciplinarity is challenging and may sacrifice the integrity of the subject discipline. Yet Culver and Giudice[108] have acknowledged that Twining has shown the way in taking forward the importance of global law and in advancing the case for a broader spectrum of comparative law. As Twining himself acknowledges, 'theories of law are not, and certainly should not be, the only outcomes of legal theorising.'[109] His belief that an understanding of the way social facts are preconditions or conditions of legality, his call for a renewed analytical approach to legality at normative and institutional levels, and his recognition that many changes in the environment may be fatal to the continuity of law and the legal system, bring Twining to the forefront of developing legal scholarship in this area. Building on Twining's globalization perspective, it is possible to see a new, more radical agenda for environmental scholarship: one embracing comparative analysis, reviving scholarship that often confronts the failures of law to address social and environmental concerns. Responses to the globalization phenomenon offer a critique of many assumptions held by legal scholars, especially in the sub-fields of environmental law, rights and environmental justice. This may even lead to questions about globalization itself, and it is this that may become a more lasting legacy than even Twining could have expected.

105 William Twining, *Globalisation and Legal Scholarship* (Woolf Legal Publishers, 2011), p. 24.

106 Ibid.

107 Ole W. Pedersen, 'The Limits of Interdisciplinarity and the Practice of Environmental Law Scholarship' (2014), 26 *Journal of Environmental Law* pp. 423–41.

108 Culver and Giudice, op. cit. p. 712.

109 William Twining, 'Globalisation and Legal Scholarship – response' (2013), 4(4) *TLT* pp. 714–25 at 716.

10

Homage and heresy from a licensed subversive: theorizing paradigm change in transnational economic regulation

Jane Kelsey

Reading jurisprudence through the lens provided by William Twining takes us on a journey of humble self-reflection, respectful in equal measure to those with whom he agrees and disagrees, never claiming to have the definitive answer.[1] In contrast with those who stoically defend an iconic canon throughout their careers, Twining urges us constantly to question the prevailing orthodoxy and re-evaluate the value of legal theorization in its context. Twining is not a revolutionary. His conversation with Boaventura de Sousa Santos in *Global Legal Theory* reveals a restrained, almost conservative, champion of a jurisprudence whose mission is to ensure that the conceptual foundations of law are sufficiently sophisticated and robust to stand the test of time.[2] Yet, by unshackling law from its orthodoxies, he has helped to liberate scholars and students in traditional law schools from the fetters of what we have come to call 'liberal legalism'. Twining's special contribution to those who are immersed in the interstices of 'globalization' as scholars, activists or practitioners is to push us beyond the immediate and the particular to theorize that complex, multidimensional legal domain.

This tribute to Twining proposes an active role for legal theory in analyzing the ferment in the global regime of economic regulation (a ferment that has intensified since the global financial crisis (GFC) began in 2007), and in articulating the conceptual foundations for a more ethical and socially just alternative. My standpoint is that of an engaged and partisan critic of transnational economic regulation, one informed by the political economy of law. My point of departure for the substantive discussion of that regime is Twining's first treatise on *Globalisation and Legal Theory*, in particular his use of Santos' work to tease out the challenges posed by transnational capitalism.

Borrowing from Twining's toolkit, transnational economic regulation is mapped on four interrelated planes: geopolitics, legal architecture, corporate power and sites of dissent. The resulting picture of complexity and fracture creates a sense of the dynamic challenges legal theory needs to address. One

[1] William Twining, *Globalisation and Legal Theory* (Butterworths, 2000) 247. [2] Ibid., ch. 8.

major source of ferment is the empowerment of capital through international investment rules and 'behind the border' disciplines on governments, and the burgeoning recourse by foreign investors to private international arbitration against states. There is a rapidly escalating crisis: some states are exiting their existing agreements and either eschewing new ones or developing their own new templates, while the patron states of capital are promoting more far-reaching rules. Other sites, such as conflicts over financial re-regulation and capital controls, presage similar crises. The discussion culminates in reflections on how legal theory in the hands of the 'licensed legal subversive' might aid the process of progressive transformation and suggests a programme of steps, drawn from Twining's work, to that end.

1. The licensed legal subversive

I have always relished William Twining's idea of the jurist as 'licensed subversive', although his version is somewhat more restrained than mine. In *Global Legal Theory* Twining enumerates various functions of legal theory:

> By standing back one can survey the field, or some sector of it, as a whole and see how different parts are related to each other: one might call this the *mapping or synthesizing function.*
>
> Theorizing can help us to construct and clarify conceptual frameworks, models, ideal types and other thinking tools – this might be called the *conceptual or analytical function.*
>
> Constructing general concepts, principles, taxonomies and hypotheses can also save repetition and be economical – one might call this the *simplifying function.*
>
> [T]ranscending of boundaries between institutionalized fields of learning might be called the *cross-disciplinary function.*
>
> However, the most important theoretical function of all is the sustained teasing out, articulation and critical examination of the general assumptions and presuppositions underlying the discourse of the discipline or praxis *at a given moment in history.* In this view, one of the main jobs of jurisprudence is the critical exploration and evaluation of prevailing assumptions underlying legal discourse.[3]

The prior question for me is: what is the object of such theorization? Twining sees no necessary correlation between generality and practical utility. If the purpose is simply to articulate a general theory that has intellectual rigour and integrity, it does not matter whether it has any prospect of influencing the dynamics that are driving the contemporary direction of the law. Twining's subversive is 'as much concerned with questioning assumptions and opening up lines of enquiry – more or less gently stirring – as with defining and

[3] Ibid., 11–12 [emphasis added].

defending entrenched positions or striking artificially rigid postures'.[4] 'Stirring', by Twining's subversive, amounts to questioning assumptions and generating debate. In my view, the legal subversive can also advocate and strategize for change. The role of analytical theorist and informed partisan need not be mutually exclusive, provided both are pursued with integrity and intellectual rigour. Critical enquiry is an essential precursor to effective and responsible advocacy. Equally, an in-depth understanding of the problematic is a prerequisite to then standing back and theorizing it.

A jurist's standpoint frames what kind of legal subversive they choose to be: the objects of their inquiry, the questions they ask, the tools selected for analysis, and the use to which the argument and its conclusions might be put. Twining describes his own standpoint as 'that of an English jurist, who is concerned about the health of the institutionalized discipline of law, especially in common law countries, during the next fifteen to twenty years in the face of "globalisation"'. He then acknowledges that a 'jurist from a different tradition, or with a different personal background, would almost inevitably present a significantly different picture. Few of us can break away very far from our intellectual roots.'[5]

My own standpoint is central to the argument I want to make. Like Twining, my work on globalization grew out of critiques of law and colonization, as indigenous Maori reasserted their sovereign authority in Aotearoa New Zealand in the late 1970s and early 1980s. The advent in 1984 of a virulent form of neoliberalism progressively closed the political, economic, legal and ethical spaces for Maori to achieve redress and empowerment outside the neoliberal model. My initial study of New Zealand's 'neoliberal experiment' focused mainly on the domestic domain, broadening beyond Maori to critique its general socio-legal impacts, and was refracted through the political economy of law.[6]

In 1990, I was invited with other critical thinkers and activists to a forum that ran parallel to the Brussels ministerial meeting at the mid-point of the Uruguay round of negotiations. The ministerial talks were nominally about the General Agreement on Tariffs and Trade (GATT). But it became clear that their proposed new 'trade' agreement on services, including foreign investment, was an extraterritorial version of what we were seeing at the domestic level, and sought to lock future governments into maintaining and extending that neoliberal paradigm. The interests of capital would be advanced and the broader populace in Aotearoa New Zealand, especially Maori, would remain distressed and disempowered.

[4] Ibid., 247.

[5] William Twining, *General Jurisprudence. Understanding Law from a Global Perspective* (Cambridge University Press, 2009) xiv.

[6] Jane Kelsey, *Economic Fundamentalism. The New Zealand Experiment. A World Model for Structural Adjustment?* (Pluto, 1995).

What we observed in 1990 was embryonic and inchoate.[7] Clearly, something momentous was happening. The corporate lobbyists and beneficiaries were a visible and powerful presence in the halls, disappearing to work alongside their patron states in the opaque process of constructing the new international 'trade' rules. When the World Trade Organization (WTO) came into being in 1995, the General Agreement on Trade in Services (GATS) was a major pillar. Governments of the global South had secured some concessions,[8] which would later be attacked during the Doha round and the secretive plurilateral negotiations for a Trade in Services Agreement (TISA) outside the WTO.[9]

The WTO Director General Roberto Ruggiero famously proclaimed they were now 'writing the constitution of a single global economy'.[10] But few of us who were grappling with the power politics of WTO and the novelty of its agreements[11] had any idea how expansive and intrusive the transnational regime of economic regulation would become. Twenty years later, the WTO seems a *comparatively* transparent and orderly institution with a finite set of rules. We now face a much more complex and multilayered transnational regime that imposes enforceable rules on diverse areas of domestic law and policy through a range of formal and informal arrangements.

Activists from both the global North and South have continued to track these secretive negotiating processes, educate politicians, academics, NGOs, trade unions, journalists and students, and try to block the adoption and expansion of this particular legal domain. That work is cross-disciplinary, multilayered and largely unco-ordinated, undertaken by individuals and organizations with diverse skills and politics. We variously: deconstruct the arcane technical treaty texts and their implications for the constitutions and legal rules of nation states; research and expose the relationships between agents of capital and their patron states; analyze the geopolitics that drives the strategic positions of states, and explain their alliances and conflicts; reveal the

[7] This was before the internet and worldwide web became a source for almost instant dissemination of information. Our main source of information on the secretive negotiations was Gestetnered copies of South–North Development Monitor (SUNS) newsletter produced by veteran Indian journalist Chakravarthi Raghavan and mailed out internationally.

[8] Jane Kelsey, *Serving Whose Interests? The Political Economy of Trade in Services Agreements* (Routledge Cavendish, 2008) pp. 58–60.

[9] Public Services International, 'Brief on the Trade in Services Agreement (TISA) July 2013' (2013) www.world-psi.org/sites/default/files/documents/research/en_psi_tisa_policy_brief_july_2013_final_web.pdf accessed 30 December 2014; Global Services Coalition, 'Global Services Coalition Paper on the Trade in Services Agreement' (2014) servicescoalition.org/images/GSC_Statement_on_TiSA_Sept_2014_FINAL.pdf accessed 30 December 2014.

[10] Quoted in Charan Devereaux, Robert Lawrence and Michael Watkins, *Case Studies in US Trade Negotiations. Volume 1: Making the Rules* (Institute for International Economics, 2006), pp. 163–4.

[11] These analysis of the WTO quickly merged with critiques of the proposed Multilateral Agreement on Investment negotiated at the OECD from 1995–8 and the Asia Pacific Economic Cooperation forum (APEC); see, for example, Jane Kelsey, *Reclaiming the Future. New Zealand and the Global Economy* (Bridget Williams Books, 1999), chs. 7, 8 and 9.

mysteries of evolving technologies and the reorganization of supply chains; expose the social realities of how these agreements affect local communities and support their resistances to them; and much more. There were, and still are, tensions among those who do this work. Some seek to mitigate the harm being caused, especially to vulnerable countries and communities, by influencing negotiations. Others believe that national and international social movements can force governments to exit these arrangements and shut down the institutions.

My own approach sees transnational economic regulation as an integral part of the neoliberal continuum that nurtures and supports a financialized global economy and the unjust distribution of power and resources that this entails. In a forthcoming book, I argue that the world is on the cusp of a period of transformation equivalent to the epochal shifts in the capitalist economy and the role of the state that began in the 1930s[12] and again in the late 1970s.[13] We are now entering an interregnum – the old is dying, the new is yet to be born.[14] We do not know what shape it will take. As Santos observes,[15] the energy that drives a paradigm change will be rooted in social conditions and political mobilization. The private beneficiaries and political patrons of the current paradigm will vigorously defend their gains from the past four decades and will resist any transformation.

History tells us that a post-neoliberal world will not necessarily be more ethical or socially progressive. Legal theorists have a role to play in helping to ensure that it is. Understanding the antagonisms can help identify potential sites of tension and catalysts for change. Imagining the principled foundations of something new can fuel the hunger and momentum for change. Hence, the task of the jurist as a legal subversive in the domain of transnational economic regulation is to delegitimize the agreements, defeat new ones and propagate a general theoretical basis for progressive alternatives within a broader theorization of the interrelated crises of financialized capitalism and neoliberalism.

The notion of legal pluralism that informs this approach differs from Twining's. In *Globalisation and Legal Theory* Twining describes legal pluralism in a normatively neutral way, as either 'the co-existence of multiple legal orders in the same context of time and space or the recognition of different legal traditions and sources of law within a single legal system'.[16] However, he acknowledges that the plurality of perspectives and standpoints generates multiple descriptions of a single legal order.[17] A standpoint based on political economy privileges the relationship between capitalism and law in understanding single legal orders and inter-legality, and suggests a more partisan

[12] Karl Polanyi, *The Great Transformation: The Political and Economic Origins of Our Time* (2nd edn, Beacon Press, 2001).
[13] David Harvey, *A Brief History of Neoliberalism* (Oxford University Press, 2005).
[14] Jane Kelsey, *The FIRE Economy* (Bridget Williams Books, forthcoming 2015).
[15] There are many aspects of Twining's critique of Santos with which I concur.
[16] Twining (n 1), 216. [17] Ibid.

role for the intellectual. Different approaches to theorization do not mean that similar tools cannot be used to develop them.

2. A point of departure

Law is intrinsically complex. It occupies a multilayered legal landscape that is shaped by non-linear processes and contradictory forces that shift over time. When it is liberated from the narrow confines of Western jurisprudence it can be seen to be infused by diverse influences. These include: colonialism and imperialism; the enduring and the reinvented traditions and resistances of indigenous law; and the inter-sectionality of feminism, class, sexuality, culture and belief systems. Twining captures that broad canvas in his suggestion in *General Jurisprudence* that

> a reasonably inclusive cosmopolitan discipline of law needs to encompass all levels of legal ordering, relations between those levels, and all-important forms of law including supra-state (e.g. international, regional) and non-state law and various forms of 'soft law' and legal orders.[18]

A transformative approach to legal theory is clearly not what Twining envisaged. General theories are not constructed for particular conditions or as strategic contributions to paradigm change. Nor are they driven by the urgency of contributing to an imminent debate. My concern is that a general theory of law along the lines that Twining suggests in *General Jurisprudence,* one that seeks to encapsulate all these dimensions, becomes so general that it serves little expository value and loses its critical edge. Indeed, the tone of *General Jurisprudence,* written in 2009, conveyed a sense that globalization had become regularized.

At the same time, the dynamic nature of legal theory is precisely Twining's point. His work on globalization recognizes that general theories are framed by their context and of their time. His earlier work, *Globalisation and Legal Theory,* published in 2000, was spurred in part by the increased prominence of 'globalization' in popular and scholarly lexicons. I prefer Twining's efforts to grapple with the challenges posed by globalization in the earlier book. There, he directly engaged with questions of power, including economic power and transnational capital, in particular when deliberating on Santos' magnum opus *Toward a New Common Sense.*

Santos had identified seven types of legal transnationalization as particularly warranting attention. Three related to global capitalism: transnationalization of nation state law; development of legal regimes of regional integration; and transnational commercial regulation, ranging from *lex mercatoria* to commercial arbitration to the WTO. Twining concurred that these areas needed theorizing within a broad contextual framework and more

[18] Twining (n 5), 275.

locally.[19] Those three elements of legal transnationalization remain pivotal to global capitalism, but have become inseparably intertwined. They are also still under-theorized. Clearly, that theorization needs to reflect their new contextual framework, as law and globalization is rethought in light of the global financial crisis and other contemporary challenges.[20]

Since 2007, the tenor of debates about the institutions, ideologies, regulatory models and practices associated with neoliberalism has shifted. Predictions of continuing crises in the material economy are accompanied by trenchant critiques of transnational economic regulation. Ideas that were once unthinkable heresies are now being uttered from within the bastions of neoliberal 'orthodoxy'.[21] As discussed below, a growing number of states that find themselves bound to international rules that harm their economy and society and deny their sovereignty are voicing their dissent. Some are developing exit strategies and advocating alternatives, but are confronted by a thick and deeply embedded global regime. The patron states of financialized capitalism have responded to this ferment by promoting even more radical rules through a multiplicity of plurilateral, regional and bilateral arrangements. Some, largely affluent, states are willing fellow travellers; others that are more vulnerable seem defenceless to resist. The private beneficiaries who participate formally and informally in these arenas are exacerbating tensions as they push the legal boundaries to extract maximum gains.

3. Mapping the domain

Mapping the transnational legal domain allows the analyst to stand back and see how different parts of the whole relate to each other. I argue that it also has a strategic function for transformative theorizing. But legal cartography is a complex task. The transnational legal order is dynamic and changing at a pace and on a scale that is impossible to track in precise detail. Yet it is not the particulars that are important for theorizing; it is mapping the trends, dynamics and contradictions with enough breadth and robustness to provide a sound foundation to work from. This analysis necessarily spans many different geographies. Four interrelated dimensions of transnational economic regulation are focused on here: geopolitics, the legal architecture, corporate power, and sites of dissent within the 'orthodoxy'.

[19] The other four forms of legal transnationalization related to mobility of people, linkages and coalitions among indigenous peoples, human rights, and 'the common heritage of mankind'. Twining, *Globalisation and Legal Theory*, 239–41.

[20] Other developments outside the sphere of transnational economic regulation, including the Czech and Arab Springs, the resurgence of Cold War tensions between Russia and 'the West', and the emergence of the non-territorialized Islamic State, are equally pertinent.

[21] Christine Lagarde, 'Economic Inclusion and Financial Integrity' (Conference on Inclusive Capitalism, London, 27 May 2014) www.imf.org/external/np/speeches/2014/052714.htm accessed 30 December 2014.

Geopolitics

The United States of America and Europe dominated the story of the GATT and its expansion into the WTO, the proliferation of bilateral investment treaties, the expansion of bilateral and regional free trade and investment agreements, and the current negotiation of mega-arrangements whose economic and strategic significance are intended to reshape the global legal landscape. The US and EU compete and collaborate in what Raj Bhala describes as 'competitive imperialism'.[22] Their objectives are strategic as well as commercial. Each has its own preoccupations. The US strategic 'pivot' to the Asia Pacific since 2009 is an explicit strategy to neutralize the rise of China,[23] while the EU focuses its attention on its internal disarray and conflicts on its Eastern borders.

The US and the EU are the driving force behind the three complementary mega-arrangements currently under negotiation. The twelve-country Trans-Pacific Partnership Agreement (TPPA) began in 2008 and is the most advanced.[24] Negotiations for the Trade in Services Agreement (TISA) among twenty-three parties began in early 2013.[25] The first talks for a proposed Transatlantic Trade and Investment Partnership (TTIP) between the US and EU were held in July 2013.[26] All three purport to create gold standard, twenty-first century rules through new behind-the-border disciplines on governments, enhancing regulatory coherence, facilitating global supply chains, and ensuring unimpeded cross-border flows of goods, services, capital and data.

The US is the common party to all three. The EU is a key player in two, alongside Japan, Canada, Chile, Australia and New Zealand. Whether any of these deals is concluded will depend on the commercial interests and domestic politics of the major players. The existing participants control the terms of entry for others under similarly one-sided rules to accession as the WTO. The US demanded a heavy price for Japan's entry into the TPPA negotiations[27] and

[22] Raj Bhala, 'Competitive Liberalization, Competitive Imperialism, and Intellectual Property' (2007), 28 *Liverpool LR* 77.

[23] Hillary Clinton, 'America's Pacific Century' (2011) Foreign Policy foreignpolicy.com/2011/10/11/americas-pacific-century accessed 30 December 2014.

[24] Negotiating parties are: Australia, Brunei Darussalam, Canada, Chile, Japan, Malaysia, Mexico, New Zealand, Peru, Singapore, US, Vietnam. See Jane Kelsey, *Hidden Agendas. What we Need to Know about the TPPA* (Bridget Williams, 2013); C. L. Lim, Deborah Elms and Patrick Low, 'Introduction' in C. L. Lim, Deborah Elms and Patrick Low (eds), *The Trans-Pacific Partnership. A Quest for a Twenty-first-Century Trade Agreement* (Cambridge University Press, 2012).

[25] Negotiating parties are: Australia, Canada, Chile, Chinese Taipei, Colombia, Costa Rica, EU (counts as one), Hong Kong, Iceland, Israel, Japan, Liechtenstein, Mexico, New Zealand, Norway, Republic of Korea, Pakistan, Panama, Paraguay, Peru, Switzerland, Turkey, United States. See Public Services International (n 9); Global Services Coalition (n 9).

[26] European Commission, 'The Transatlantic Trade Investment Partnership' ec.europa.eu/trade/policy/in-focus/ttip accessed 30 December 2014; US Trade Representative, 'Transatlantic Trade and Investment Partnership' www.ustr.gov/ttip accessed 30 December 2014.

[27] Jane Kelsey, 'Terms of Japan's entry to TPPA talks bad news for NZ, "surrender of sovereignty" for Japan' (Press release, 15 March 2013) www.itsourfuture.org.nz/terms-of-japans-entry-to-tppa-talks-bad-news-for-nz accessed 30 December 2014.

blocked China from coming to the TISA table.[28] These arrangements, and the rapid expansion of other regional and bilateral deals since 2000, are often attributed to the paralysis in the WTO and the determination of the major players to circumvent opposition to their demands.

An equally potent related motivation is the emergence of the BRICS – Brazil, Russia, India, China and South Africa – as potential competitors for economic and strategic influence, and as a galvanizing force for the global South within and outside the WTO. Some of these ascending powers are themselves seeking to firm up their geopolitical alliances and lock in access to resources. Notably, China has been negotiating a range of bilateral trade and investment agreements with individual states and regions, and is co-sponsoring with the Association of South East Asian Nations (ASEAN) their own sixteen-country mega-arrangement, the Comprehensive Regional Economic Partnership Agreement (RCEP).[29] Many participants in RCEP overlap with the TPPA, creating the potential for conflicting obligations under inconsistent models and rules. Old alliances are also being fractured, with only some ASEAN members participating in the TPPA. Support from traditional US allies such as Australia, Britain and South Korea for the China-led Asia Infrastructure Investment Bank is further evidence of the shifting geopolitics of global capitalism.[30]

Large parts of the world are invisible from this map. Defensive regional and sub-regional arrangements in Africa, Asia and the South Pacific are peripheral to the geopolitics that frames transnational economic regulation.

Legal architecture

The second mapping exercise is more technical and more difficult. It seeks to synthesize the multiplicity of co-existing agreements, including their scope, the content of the rules, and the implications for domestic legal systems and affected communities. Superficially, these arrangements involve a broadly coherent set of rules that are underpinned by the legal requirements of WTO compatibility in goods and services. But the 'spaghetti bowl' of arrangements that have proliferated, especially this century, both supplement and fragment the multilateral regime.[31] In particular, there are problems of overlap and incoherence where the same states are parties to more than one agreement with different rules. The

[28] 'Congressional Trade Leaders Criticize China's ITA Stance, Nix TISA Participation for Now', *Inside US Trade Daily News,* 9 July 2014.

[29] Negotiating parties are: the member states of ASEAN (Brunei, Burma, Cambodia, Indonesia, Laos, Malaysia, the Philippines, Singapore, Thailand, Vietnam), Australia, China, India, Japan, New Zealand and South Korea. Neither the EU nor the US is a participant.

[30] 'Support for China-led development bank grows despite US opposition', *The Guardian* (13 March 2015), www.theguardian.com/world/2015/mar/13/support-china-led-development-bank-grows-despite-us-opposition-australia-uk-new-zealand-asia accessed 25 May 2015.

[31] Richard Baldwin, Simon Evenett and Patrick Low, 'Beyond Tariffs. Multilateralising Deeper RTA Commitments', (2007) Working paper to WTO-HEI Conference on 'Multilateralising

cross-fertilization of existing and subsequent treaties is compounded by the application of most-favoured nation clauses. The difficulty in mapping this architecture highlights the practical problems for domestic legislators and officials to catalogue the country's obligations and exposure.

The pace with which new arrangements are concluded makes any detailed map quickly out of date.[32] Official repositories, such as the WTO's register of notified Regional Trade Agreements[33] and the United Nations Conference for Trade and Development (UNCTAD) record of known investment treaties,[34] are never up to date. Hard copies of old treaties may simply be lost. It becomes impossible for governments to predict their exposure. For example, Egypt maintains it is party to sixty-nine bilateral investment treaties, ICSID refers to ninety-three treaties and the US puts the number at one hundred and eleven.[35] The secrecy that surrounds the negotiation of many agreements makes it impossible to identify fully those that are pending or their potential coverage. Once completed, their *travaux preparatoire* and working documents may remain publicly unavailable.[36]

All this uncertainty gives private players, especially well-connected international law firms and their corporate clients, added leverage over states by being able to threaten to initiate a dispute under one or more of the multiplicity of treaties. Mapping disputes, identifying the parties and interests involved (corporate and state), and the outcomes of these disputes is equally problematic. Secrecy is built into most state–state and investor–state disputes outside the WTO, although many recent free trade and investment agreements provide some more disclosure. Some documents and even awards are impossible to access.[37] Settlements usually remain private and confidential.[38] In some cases the parties may never disclose the existence of a dispute.[39]

Most economic treaty arrangements have a broadly similar architecture, scope and content, which reflect the influence of the major players. The US has

Regionalism', 10–12 September 2007, WTO, Geneva, www.wto.org/english/tratop_e/region_e/con_sep07_e/baldwin_evenett_low_e.pdf accessed 30 December 2014.

32 For example, Christopher Dent, *New Free Trade Agreements in the Asia-Pacific* (Palgrave Macmillan, 2006).

33 WTO, 'Regional Trade Agreements Information System', rtais.wto.org/UI/PublicMaintainRTAHome.aspx accessed 30 December 2014.

34 UNCTAD, 'International Investment Agreements Navigator', investmentpolicyhub.unctad.org/IIA accessed 30 December 2014.

35 Hatem Zayed and Heba Khalil, 'Egypt and International Arbitration. Protection of Investors. No Consolation for Public Money' (Egyptian Centre for Economic and Social Rights, 2013), 8.

36 The negotiating parties to TPPA and TISA have agreed that all documents aside from the final text will remain confidential after the agreement comes into force, or the negotiations are terminated, for four and five years, respectively. In some countries, such as New Zealand, official information laws would allow those documents to remain confidential.

37 Nathalie Bernasconi-Osterwalder and Martin Dietrich Brauch, 'The State of Play in Vattenfall II: Leaving the German Public in the Dark', Briefing Note (International Institute for Sustainable Development, 2014).

38 Ibid.

39 UNCTAD, *Investor–State Disputes Arising from Investment Treaties: A Review* (UN 2005) 5–6.

a template for free trade agreements and model bilateral investment treaty (BIT) that can only be negotiated at the edges, with the final text subject to US congressional approval and to presidential certification of compliance by the other party or parties.[40] The EU has shown some greater flexibility, first with its template reflecting the 'technocratic' Global Europe strategy to externalize its internal regime, and then the Europe 2020 strategy to 'defend European interests worldwide'.[41] The expansion of the EU's mandate under the Lisbon Treaty to investor protections and enforcement both introduced new offensive opportunities and generated more internal dissent. The new mega-treaties include novel chapters that are intended to create precedents for other negotiations, as with the state-owned enterprises and regulatory coherence chapters in the TPPA,[42] or to become exported back into the WTO, as the EU has proposed in relation to the TISA.[43]

Corporate power

A third layer of the map plots the roles and activities of private capital. Neoliberalism has systematically created new opportunities for private interests to influence the decisions of national and sub-national governments. Behind the neutral terminology of non-state actors, civil society, third sector partnerships and co-regulation is a regime of concepts, norms, processes, techniques and opportunities that confer asymmetrical power on private élites, especially capital.[44] That regime has become incorporated into global arrangements, ensuring a genuinely transnational sphere of corporate

[40] Jane Kelsey and Sanya Reid Smith, 'Memorandum on the US Legal Requirement for "Certification" of Trade Partners Compliance before an Agreement Like TPPA Comes into Effect' (2014) tppnocertification.org/wp-content/uploads/2014/08/Certification-memorandum.pdf accessed 30 December 2014.

[41] European Commission, 'Communication from the Commission to the Council, The European Parliament, The Economic and Social Committee and the Committee of the Regions, *Global Europe. Competing in the World*', (Communication) COM (2006) 567 europa.eu/legislation_summaries/external_trade/r11022_en.htm accessed 30 December 2014; Roberto Bendini, 'The European Union's trade policy, give years after the Lisbon Treaty', (In-depth Analysis), Directorate-General for External Policies, European Commission, DG EXPO/B/PolDep/Note/2014_76, 5–9.

[42] Jane Kelsey, 'The Risks of Disciplines on State-Owned Enterprises in the Proposed Trans-Pacific Partnership Agreement' (Stakeholder programme at the eleventh round of TransPacific Partnership Agreement negotiations, Melbourne, 4 March 2012) www.itsourfuture.org.nz/wp-content/uploads/2013/09/Kelsey-TPP-SOE-paper.pdf accessed 30 December 2014; Jane Kelsey, 'Preliminary Analysis of the Draft TPP Chapter on Regulatory Coherence' (2011) www.itsourfuture.org.nz/wp-content/uploads/2013/09/JK-Memo-on-Reg-Coh.pdf accessed 30 December 2014.

[43] European Union, 'A Modular Approach to the Architecture of a Plurilateral Agreement on Services', September 2012, 5–7 trade.ec.europa.eu/doclib/html/152686.htm accessed 30 December 2014.

[44] Despite purported influence of labour and environment groups over a Democratic Party President and members of Congress in the US or in the European Parliament, from my observation they wield comparatively little influence over the final outcome of negotiations.

influence. The lobbying power and influence of commercial interests over the drafting of WTO treaties is well documented, especially on intellectual property[45] and services.[46] The leaked draft chapter of TISA on financial services[47] and the leaked US proposal for e-commerce[48] both directly align with the wish list of the relevant corporate lobbies. Some countries have institutionalized the influence of their major corporations. The US Trade Representative consults over texts and negotiating positions with more than 500 citizens who sit as cleared advisers on twenty-seven advisory boards.[49] Almost all are corporate representatives.

The introduction of novel chapters into the TPPA is the direct result of industry influence, often drawing legitimacy from precedents they have established in other international forums. The state-owned enterprises[50] and regulatory coherence chapters are based on corporate-led initiatives developed in the Asia Pacific Economic Co-operation forum and the OECD.[51] This tactic is not new. In the late 1970s the US finance industry seeded the idea of a trade in services agreement in the OECD, gradually securing support from the European Economic Community and other affluent countries for its inclusion in the Uruguay round.[52]

Aside from influencing negotiations, foreign investors benefit from special protections and the power to enforce them against host governments through international arbitration. These rights and protections were initially set out in BITs and are now routinely incorporated as investment and related chapters in free trade and economic integration agreements. The sheer number of these agreements is magnified by the ability of investors to mix and match across treaties through their most favoured national provisions. The definition of investment has also become more expansive, commonly including intellectual property rights, procurement contracts, equities, securitized financial

[45] Peter Drahos and John Braithwaite, *Information Feudalism. Who Owns the Knowledge Economy?* (The New Press, 2003), 12.

[46] Kelsey, 'Case study 3: The Services Mafia' in (n. 8) pp. 76–82.

[47] Jane Kelsey, 'Memorandum on Leaked TISA Financial Services Text' (2014) wikileaks.org/tisa-financial/Analysis-of-secret-tisa-financial-annex.pdf accessed 30 December 2014.

[48] Jane Kelsey and Burcu Kilic, 'Briefing on US TISA Proposal on E-Commerce, Technology Transfer, Cross-Border Data Flows and Net Neutrality' (2014) data.awp.is/data/filtrala/15/analisis.cleaned.pdf accessed 30 December 2014.

[49] USTR, 'Advisory Committees', www.ustr.gov/about-us/intergovernmental-affairs/advisory-committees accessed 30 December 2014.

[50] OECD, *Guidelines on Corporate Governance of State-owned Enterprises* (OECD 2005); 'US Business Groups Push for New SOE Disciplines in TPP Negotiations', *Inside US Trade*, 24 March 2011; 'USTR using OECD Work As Guide For TPP Proposals On SOE Disciplines', *Inside US Trade*, 21 July 2011.

[51] APEC and OECD, *APEC-OECD Integrated Checklist on Regulatory Reform* (OECD 2005) www.oecd.org/regreform/34989455.pdf accessed 30 December 2014; APEC, *APEC Information Notes on Good Practice for Technical Regulation* (APEC 2000) www.jisc.go.jp/eng/apec-asem/pdf/grp_info.pdf accessed 30 December 2014; APEC, *APEC Principles to Enhance Competition and Regulatory Reform* (APEC 1999) www.oecd.org/gov/regulatorypolicy/2371601.doc accessed 30 December 2014.

[52] Kelsey (n 8), 61–70.

instruments, bonds and even sovereign debt instruments. Other chapters facilitate the making of these investments and constrain their regulation, especially for financial services, e-commerce, internet and data services, telecommunications and intellectual property. 'Umbrella clauses' allow investors to enforce contracts with a state party through the investor–state enforcement provisions where there is no breach of treaty rules, even where the contract specifies the use of domestic courts or some other means of enforcement. They are common in bilateral investment treaties and the US demands them in its free trade treaties.

The behaviour of capital has also changed. The dispersal of production and supply chains has increased the number and location of investors who can bring disputes, without them needing to reincorporate or engage in treaty and forum shopping.[53] US consumer group Public Citizen identified the presence of 54,000 US multinational corporations across the twelve TPPA countries.[54] As discussed below, some private equity and hedge funds, known as 'vulture' funds, specialize in buying distressed assets during financial or political crises and demanding payment at full face value. Boutique international law firms are equally aggressive and unscrupulous in expanding their lucrative business.

Mapping these various forms of corporate power is an uneven affair. International and national corporate lobbies can be remarkably frank about some of their activities, although when corporations are cleared advisers they are sworn to secrecy. The more subtle influence through public–private governance bodies, co-regulation, private consultants, revolving doors and other forms of state–corporate intimacy is much more difficult to identify. By definition, covert lobbying and influence is intended to remain invisible. It is almost impossible to document the chilling effect on governments of a threat to litigate. Information about investment arbitrations may be kept totally or partially secret, even where governments are happy to release the full documentation, as are the terms of settlements.

Sites of dissent within the 'orthodoxy'

Mapping shifts in ideology and policy preferences among the institutions and voices of the 'orthodoxy', and their post-crisis critiques of financialization and the neoliberal regime, provides an invaluable picture of how the paradigm is changing. Intellectual stalwarts of the global financial regime are rethinking their positions. In a 2009 review of the UK's Financial Services Authority, its former chair, Lord Adair Turner, proposed a 'more intrusive and more systemic' approach to financial regulation.[55] *Financial Times* columnist

[53] Foreign firms may strategically incorporate or transfer their legal identity to those countries to take advantage of investment treaties.

[54] Public Citizen, 'TPP Investment Map: New Privileges for 54,000 Companies?' citizen.org/Page.aspx?pid=4083 accessed 29 December 2014.

[55] Adair Turner, *The Turner Review: A Regulatory Response to the Global Banking Crisis* (Financial Services Authority, 2009) 86.

Martin Wolf argues that the world economy is set on an unsustainable course and calls for radical reforms in his 2014 book *The Shifts and the Shocks*.[56]

For three decades international institutions like the IMF, OECD and WTO have designed, propagated and legitimized an ideologically coherent and complementary neoliberal regime, including the main pillars of economic regulation. That consensus is now fragile. There are significant differences in strategy within the international organizations themselves. On the one hand, the IMF is grappling with the challenges in a very public way. In a speech on 'inclusive capitalism' Managing Director Christine Lagarde described 'recent excesses of risk-taking, leverage, opacity, complexity, and compensation'.[57] A steady stream of papers from its research economists has recanted core tenets of the neoliberal orthodoxy.[58] In a major about-face, the IMF has also supported the limited use of capital controls.[59] By contrast, the WTO is in total denial. The major powers have suppressed calls from a number of member states to debate the relationship between the financial services rules and the GFC.[60] The OECD launched a consultation on investor-state arbitration in 2012 in recognition of the emerging crisis of legitimacy, but otherwise remains largely reconstructed.[61]

These shifts create tensions with the transnational regime and between the major institutions. The rehabilitation of capital controls as a means of reducing or deterring the destabilizing cross-border flows of 'hot' money directly conflicts with US free trade agreements that prohibit governments from using them, on pain of costly disputes and economic or financial penalties.[62] The UNCTAD *Trade and Development Report 2011* also expressed concern that international agreements 'may severely limit not only the application of capital controls, but also other measures aimed at re-regulating or restructuring financial systems'.[63] The 2014 report was equally outspoken on

[56] Martin Wolf, *The Shifts and the Shocks: What We've Learned – and Have Still to Learn – from the Financial Crisis* (Penguin Press, 2014).

[57] Lagarde (n 21).

[58] Discussed in Cornel Ban, *Austerity versus Stimulus? Understanding Fiscal Policy Change at the International Monetary Fund Since the Great Recession* (2014) Global Economic Governance Initiative, Boston University, www.bu.edu/pardee/research/global-economic-governance-2/austeritystimulusworkingpaper accessed 30 December 2014.

[59] Kevin Gallagher and Yuan Tian, 'Practicing What They Preach: The IMF and Capital Controls' (*TripleCrisis*, 13 June 2014), triplecrisis.com/?p=9934 accessed 30 December 2014

[60] Jane Kelsey, 'The Conundrum of Shifting Orthodoxies: FTAs and Korea's Currency Controls', (2011) *JIEL*, 1, 6–7

[61] OECD, *Investor State Dispute Settlement. Public Consultation 16 May–23 July 2012* (OECD 2012); OECD, *Government Perspectives on Investor State Dispute Settlement. A Progress Report*, 14 December 2012 (OECD 2012); D. Gaukrodger and K. Gordon, *Investor-State Dispute Settlement: A Scoping Paper for the Investment Policy Community*, OECD Working Papers on International Investment, 2012/03 (OECD 2012).

[62] Sarah Anderson, 'Trans-Pacific Partnership and Capital Account Regulations: An Analysis of the Region's Existing Arrangements' in Kevin Gallagher and Leonardo Stanley (eds), *Capital Account Regulations and the Trading System; A Compatibility Review* (Pardee Center Task Force Report, 2013), 81–90.

[63] UNCTAD, *Trade and Development Report 2011* (UNCTAD 2011) 100.

the issue.[64] These collisions will become increasingly important sites of contest between the discredited old paradigm and embryonic alternatives.

4. The international investment regime

The most volatile site of contest at present is the special rights and powers conferred on foreign investors under BITS, investment chapters of free trade treaties, and specialist agreements like the Energy Charter Treaty. These rights and protections are designed to constrain governments' autonomy. Requirements to reduce or eliminate restrictions on foreign investment, remove preferences for nationals or investors of other countries, or guarantee unfettered capital transfers have to be internalized into domestic law. Governments also surrender important development tools, such as local preferences, economic needs tests, requirements for technology transfer or establishment through joint ventures. Investor protections, such as requirements of fair and equitable treatment and protections against direct and indirect expropriation apply to new measures, from legislation to administrative decisions and court judgements. Some tribunals have interpreted those rules to apply an effective standstill on domestic regulation.[65]

Investor–state dispute settlement (ISDS) provisions in these agreements mean that foreign investors can enforce these special protections directly against the host government, rather than relying on their parent states to do so. Foreign investors do not face the same political, legal and diplomatic constraints as states when they consider such action. The UNCTAD's annual data on *known* investment arbitration disputes shows an exponential increase over the past decade.[66] As of 2014, there were 568 known treaty-based cases involving ninety-eight governments. The majority were lodged since 2007. Investors from EU states have brought more than half the disputes, a legacy of Europe's colonial powers securing treaties with their former colonies to protect investors' interests after decolonization. The US accounts for one-fifth of cases.[67] As China's growing offshore investments faced anti-Chinese sentiment, insurance company Ping An launched China's first known investment dispute in 2013.[68] The insurer had invested in Belgium company Fortis Bank,

64 UNCTAD, *Trade and Investment Report 2014* (UNCTAD 2014).

65 Matthew Porterfield, 'A Distinction without a Difference? The Interpretation of Fair and Equitable Treatment Under Customary International Law by Investment Tribunals', *Investment Treaty News*, 22 March 2013, www.iisd.org/itn/2013/03/22/a-distinction-without-a-difference-the-interpretation-of-fair-and-equitable-treatment-under-customary-international-law-by-investment-tribunals accessed 30 December 2014.

66 UNCTAD, 'Recent Developments in Investor–State Dispute Settlement' (2014) 1 *IIA Issues Note* 7, Figure 6.

67 Ibid., 8.

68 Cruyplants Eloy Wagemans and Partners, 'First Chinese Investment Arbitration Case against Belgium' (Legal Knowledge Portal, 23 April 2013) legalknowledgeportal.com/2013/04/23/first-chinese-investment-arbitration-case-against-belgium-2 accessed 30 December 2014.

which the Belgian government partially nationalized in a bailout during the financial crisis, and then on-sold the shares. Ping An claimed $2.3 billion in compensation.

Available data suggests about forty-three per cent of the 274 concluded cases were decided in favour of the State and thirty-one per cent in favour of the investor. However, another twenty-six per cent were settled, which implies some payments to investors (the details of settlements are rarely published).[69] These percentages overstate the wins for states because, in the words of one prominent arbitration lawyer, many of those claims 'should never have seen the light of day'.[70] Applying what has been described as a 'cavalier approach to legal principles' arbitrators have embarked on 'tribunal adventurism', issuing awards that appear to lack any rational foundation.[71]. Remedies can include compensation for loss of future profits even if the actual investment was minimal, with compound interest dating back to the date of the government's action.[72]

Moreover, bringing an actual case is not the investor's first choice. Foreign investors play the treaty card, using the *threat* of a dispute to have a chilling effect on the government to abandon a proposed measure. There are strong incentives for governments to capitulate. Costs of disputes average $8 million,[73] but can be much higher, and disputes can drag on for years before tribunals with a perceived pro-investor bias.[74] Recent controversial disputes have sought hundreds of millions of dollars of compensation for a whole range of regulatory initiatives: for the Canadian federal court's rejection of a medicine patent for failing the domestic 'promise of utility' test;[75] for the Quebec government's moratorium on fracking;[76] for the Indian Supreme Court's cancellation of telecommunications licenses it said were corruptly

[69] Ibid., 10.

[70] George Kahale, 'Keynote Speech' (Eighth Annual Juris Investment Treaty Arbitration Conference, Washington DC, 28 March 2014), 17 www.curtis.com/siteFiles/Publications/8TH%20Annual%20Juris%20Investment%20Treaty%20Arbitration%20Conf.%20-%20March%2028%202014.pdf accessed 30 December 2014.

[71] Ibid., 10–11.

[72] As of December 2014 the second-highest known award was $930 million against Libya in favour of a Kuwaiti investor for termination of a land lease for a tourism project that the investor had not started four years after gaining the lease. The original claim was for $55 million, but was amended during the process. The final award was $5 million for actual loss and expenses, $30 million 'moral damages' for harm to the investor's reputation, and $900 million for lost future opportunities. Mohamed Abdulmohsen Al-Kharafi & Sons Co. v. Libya and others, Final Arbitral Award, 22 March 2013. www.italaw.com/cases/documents/2199 accessed 4 January 2014.

[73] OECD (n 60), 19. [74] A view shared in Kahale (n 69), 17.

[75] The dispute is essentially a challenge to the 'utility doctrine' in Canadian law. Public Citizen, 'U. S. Pharmaceutical Corporation Uses NAFTA Foreign Investor Privileges Regime to Attack Canada's Medicine Patent Policy, Demand $100 Million for Denial of a Patent', www.citizen.org/eli-lilly-investor-state-factsheet accessed 30 December 2014.

[76] Pia Eberhardt, Timothé Feodoroff, Emma Lui, Cecilia Olivet and Stuart Trew, 'The Right to Say No: EU Canada Trade Agreement Threatens Fracking Bans' (Transnational Institute, Corporate Europe Observatory and Council of Canadians, 2013).

granted;[77] for tobacco control laws in Australia and Uruguay;[78] and for Germany's phasing out of nuclear power generation after the Japanese Fukushima disaster.[79]

The arbitration process

Investor–state disputes are almost always heard by *ad hoc* panels of arbitrators. The most common mechanism is that provided by the International Centre for the Settlement of Investment Disputes (ICSID) attached to the World Bank. Other options include arbitration according to the rules of the United Nations Commission on International Trade Law (UNCITRAL), the International Chamber of Commerce (ICC) or through *ad hoc* processes. There is no equivalent in these arbitration panels of due process or the rule of law as it operates in domestic courts. Decisions of these private tribunals are not based on any system of binding precedent and there are no formal appeals. The proceedings are often held in secret. As noted, evidential documents, legal arguments and even full decisions and amounts of the awards may never be made public. In some cases it is impossible to discover that a dispute has even been brought. There are no effective conflict of interest rules for arbitrators. According to a study on the investment arbitration industry in 2012 it 'has become normal for investment arbitrators to constantly switch hats: one minute acting as counsel, the next framing the issue as an academic, or influencing policy as a government representative or expert witness'.[80]

Boutique law firms who bring disputes (and supply arbitrators)[81] have become legal adventurers, drumming up business from potential claimants, including in conflict zones.[82] Three top law firms were involved in 130 investment arbitrations in 2011 alone.[83] Private investment funds are even underwriting the legal costs for investors – effectively leasing the dispute – in exchange for a share of any final award, or buying the award from the successful claimant to enforce it.[84]

Speaking to conference of arbitrators in March 2014, senior investment lawyer George Kahale described investor–state arbitration as 'fundamentally

[77] K. M. Gopakumar, 'India: Investment Treaties Stifle Public Policy Objectives' (2012) 7357 *South North Development Monitor*, www.ftamalaysia.org/article.php?aid=285 accessed 30 December 2014.

[78] Government of Australia Attorney-General's Department, 'Tobacco Plain packaging – Investor–state Arbitration', www.ag.gov.au/internationalrelations/internationallaw/pages/tobaccoplainpackaging.aspx accessed 30 December 2014.

[79] Bernasconi-Osterwalder and Brauch (n 36).

[80] Pia Eberhardt and Cecilia Olivet, *Profiting from Injustice: How Law Firms, Arbitrators and Financiers are Fuelling an Investment Arbitration Boom* (CEI/TNI, 2012), 43.

[81] Ibid., 20–21.

[82] Cecilia Olivet and Pia Eberhardt, *Profiting from Crisis: How Corporations and Lawyers are Scavenging Profits from Europe's Crisis Countries* (CEI/TNI, 2014).

[83] Eberhardt and Olivet (n 79), 8. [84] Ibid., 9.

flawed' and needing 'a complete overhaul'.[85] Kahale identified a long list of failings:

- Governments often do not understand the consequences when they sign these treaties. One bad treaty through 'the magic wands' of the most-favoured nation rule and treaty shopping can provide 'protections never imagined for virtually an entire world of investors'.
- Investors and their lawyers have pushed the boundaries to the point that virtually any governmental act, gesture or statement can ground a claim.
- Third party funders are turning arbitration into an industry. By making a small initial investment they can decide whether the likely returns are worth proceeding with the claim.
- Arbitrators are giving core rules of minimum standard of treatment and expropriation meanings that were never intended, but it is hard to eliminate those rules when existing treaties have long durations, and they give rights to investors that hang over for a further lengthy period. The lack of proper appeals makes it impossible even to correct decisions that are based on manifest errors.
- Claimants grossly exaggerate their claims and mega-claims are seeking sums that exceed many nations' GDP. The amounts actually awarded are arbitrary. A claimant may even receive damages when they have lost substantive argument. Kahale cites another renowned independent arbitrator, Professor Abi-Saab, who dissented in an award of $67 million to mining company ConocoPhillips against Venezuela. Abi-Saab described the case as 'a legal comedy of errors on the theater of the absurd, not to say travesty of justice, that makes mockery not only of ICSID arbitration, but of the very idea of adjudication'.[86]
- The bar for disqualifying an arbitrator is set very high. As a result, conduct wholly unacceptable of a national judicial officer is commonplace and conflicts of interest are rife. Such flaws matter when 'arbitrators feel free to follow their preferred school of thought or even to invent law without fear of appellate review'.[87]
- Private arbitrators now develop public international law, with huge implications for governments, by applying questionable legal reasoning in processes designed for private commercial arbitration. 'Legally bankrupt decisions are cited in subsequent cases involving the same issues in the hope that a new legal principle will emerge . . . and be imbued with a certain legitimacy'.[88]
- Such behaviour is predictable in a system where arbitrators depend on the interested parties or the appointing authorities for their future appointments. The outcome of a dispute can be predicted once the arbitrators are known.

[85] Kahale (n 69), 2. [86] Ibid., 11. [87] Ibid., 14. [88] Ibid., 5–6.

Financial crisis cases

Recent financial crises have exacerbated concerns about international investment arbitration. Argentina has faced fifty-three (almost a tenth) of the known disputes,[89] with billions of dollars in unresolved claims. Nearly all relate to Argentina's measures to contain the economic crisis in the early 2000s.[90] Tribunals have made broad and inconsistent interpretations, from which there is no appeal.[91] The government has argued 'necessity', based on treaty provisions that allow it to take action to maintain public order and protect its essential security interests, and customary international law.[92] Tribunals have been notoriously inconsistent in their rulings, which have gone predominantly against Argentina.[93]

The most controversial claims relate to Argentina's sovereign debt restructuring. One claim was lodged by 60,000 bondholders under an investment treaty with Italy.[94] However, Argentina has also been sued in the US courts, because much of its debt was US-dollar denominated and subject to US law. As of 2012, 158 such suits were pending.[95] The most infamous is led by vulture fund NML Capital, a subsidiary of Paul Singer's hedge fund Elliott Management Ltd, which specializes in buying distressed debt with the intention of claiming payment in full.[96] NML Capital bought Argentine bonds with a face value of $220 million for an estimated $48.7 million.[97] It successfully petitioned the US domestic courts for payment in full plus interest, commission and penalties.[98] In October 2012, Ghana, which was not a party to this dispute, impounded an Argentine frigate after NML Capital secured a court

[89] UNCTAD (n 65), 8.

[90] 'Argentina Settles Five Investment Treaty Awards' (Allen & Overy, 7 November 2013) www.allenovery.com/publications/en-gb/Pages/Argentina-settles-five-investment-treaty-awards.aspx accessed 30 December 2014.

[91] Nathalie Bernasconi-Osterwalder, 'ICSID's Annulment Decision in Impreglio v. Argentina: Finality of Awards v. Legal Correctness' (*Investment Treaty News*, 14 May 2014) www.iisd.org/itn/2014/05/14/icsids-annulment-decision-in-impregilo-v-argentina-finality-of-awards-v-legal-correctness accessed 30 December 2014.

[92] E.g. Italy–Argentina Bilateral Investment Treaty 1990 (opened for signature 22 May 1990, entered into force 15 October 1993), art. XI.

[93] José Alvarez and Tegan Brink, 'Revisiting the Necessity Test: *Continental Casualty v Argentina*', (2010–11) *Yearbook of International Law and Policy*, 319; Kelley Chubb, 'The "State of Necessity" Defense: A burden, not a blessing, to the international investment arbitration system', (2013) 14 *Cardozo J of Conflict Resolution* 531.

[94] Jessica Beess und Chrostin, 'Sovereign Debt Restructuring and Mass Claims Arbitration Before the ICSID: The *Abaclat* Case', (2012) 53(2) *Harvard ILJ* 505.

[95] Ibid., 507.

[96] 'Gauchos and Gadflies', *Economist* (22 October 2011) www.economist.com/node/21533453 accessed 30 December 2014.

[97] UNCTAD, 'Argentina's Vulture Fund Crisis – Global Implications' (*International Debt Observatory*, 4 July 2014) www.oid-ido.org/imprimer.php3?id_article=1459 accessed 30 December 2014.

[98] Felix Salmon, 'Elliot vs Argentina: The Second Circuit's Dangerous Game' (*Reuters*, 4 March 2013) blogs.reuters.com/felix-salmon/2013/03/04/elliott-vs-argentina-the-second-circuits-dangerous-game accessed 30 December 2014.

order to enforce an unpaid award of $1.6 billion. A law of the sea tribunal ordered Ghana to release the ship.[99] The NML saga continued in 2014 when a US court ordered Argentina to pay the holdouts the full estimated $1.33 billion plus interest[100] before any more regular payments could be made to the nearly ninety-two percent of bondholders who had agreed to the restructuring of their debt.[101] As a result, Argentina was pushed into default again in September 2014. Argentina's situation is not unique. As of 2014, Greece faces an investment dispute over a retrospective restructuring of sovereign debt bought by a Slovak bank in 2010.[102] Spain faces at least eight claims from renewable energy investors whose subsidies were withdrawn as part of Spain's austerity package.[103]

These cases have exposed how arguments about the need to protect foreign investment have skewed even basic economic assumptions about risk. Default on debt is part of the risk associated with financial investments. The massive sums being awarded mean desperately needed public money, including bailout funds, is being siphoned off to foreign investors. In September 2014 the UN General Assembly passed a resolution moved by the Group of 77 and China that recognized that recurring sovereign debt crises involve 'very serious political, economic and social consequences' and should not be impeded by measures emanating from another state. It sought a new multilateral framework for 'the orderly and predictable restructuring of sovereign debt'. Eleven members, including the US, UK, Canada and Japan, voted against.[104]

The backlash

Legal scholars have long recognized the legitimacy crisis facing international investment agreements.[105] The incursions on regulatory sovereignty have also

[99] Liz Ford, 'Maritime Tribunal Orders Ghana to Set Argentina's Libertad Frigate Free' *Guardian* (17 December 2012) www.guardian.co.uk/global-development/2012/dec/17/maritime-tribunal-ghana-argentina-libertad accessed 30 December 2014; Agustino Fontevecchia, 'The Real Story of How a Hedge Fund Detained a Vessel in Ghana And Even Went For Argentina's "Air Force One"', *Forbes* (5 October 2014) www.forbes.com/sites/afontevecchia/2012/10/05/the-real-story-behind-the-argentine-vessel-in-ghana-and-how-hedge-funds-tried-to-seize-the-presidential-plane/print accessed 30 December 2014.

[100] UNCTAD (n 96).

[101] Hugh Bronstein, 'Argentina Wants Bond Payment Unfrozen if Debt Talks to Go On', *Reuters* (2 July 2014) usa.news.net/article/1574248/argentina-wants-bond-payment-unfrozen-if-debt-talks-to-go-on&referid=138 accessed 30 December 2014.

[102] Luke Eric Peterson, 'In New Procedural Decision, Arbitrators in Greek Sovereign Debt Case Clarify Possible Merits Process', (2014) 7(3) *International Arbitration Reporter* 9–10.

[103] Luke Eric Peterson, 'As With Earlier Argentine Cases, Avalanche of Claims Against Spain Look Set to be Resolved by Diversely-Composed Arbitral Tribunals', (2014) 7(17) *International Arbitration Reporter*, 19–20.

[104] Oscar Ugarteche and Ariel Noyola Rodriguez, 'Argentina's Default: Vulture – Funds and Sovereign Debt Restructuring' (*Madhyam*, 23 September 2014) www.madhyam.org.in/argentina-default-vulture-funds-sovereign-debt-restructuring (accessed 25 November 2014).

[105] Susan Franck, 'The Legitimacy Crisis in Investment Treaty Arbitration: Privatizing Public International Law Through Inconsistent Decisions' (2005) 73(4) *Fordham LR* 1521.

made such agreements a domestic political issue in many countries, although governments have not always made good their promises. After the French and German governments objected to inclusion of investor–state dispute settlement in the proposed US–EU Transatlantic Trade and Investment Partnership, the new President of the European Commission, Jean-Claude Juncker, announced that the 'commission will not accept that the jurisdiction of courts in the EU member states be limited by special regimes for investor-to-state disputes. The rule of law and the principle of equality before the law must also apply in this context.'[106]

The Australian Senate debated, but rejected, a law to prevent a future government from including ISDS in any future agreement.[107] In 2005 the Australian government had refused to accept investor–state dispute settlement in the Australia–US FTA. A challenge by Philip Morris Asia to Australia's plain packaging tobacco law strengthened the Labor Government's resolve. However, the Liberal-led government elected in 2013 had opted for a 'case-by-case' approach.[108] The chief justices of Australia and New Zealand have both expressed concern that investment arbitration may trump the national legal system.[109]

Public interest advocates, such as jurists,[110] have written open letters opposing such provisions, while health professionals[111] have echoed concerns expressed by the head of the World Health Organization.[112] Environmental

[106] 'New European Commissioners suggest that ISDS may be shut out of the TTIP' (*Investment Treaty News*, 19 November 2014), www.iisd.org/itn/2014/11/19/news-in-brief-17 accessed 30 December 2014.

[107] Australian Senate Foreign Affairs, Defence and Trade Legislation Committee, 'Inquiry into the Trade and Foreign Investment (Protecting the Public Interest) Bill 2014', August 2014, www.aph.gov.au/Parliamentary_Business/Committees/Senate/Foreign_Affairs_Defence_and_Trade/Trade_and_Foreign_Investment_Protecting_the_Public_Interest_Bill_2014/~/media/Committees/fadt_ctte/trade_foreign_investment/report.pdf accessed 30 December 2014.

[108] The Bill to exclude ISDS from future international treaties was considered by a Senate select committee in 2014 but defeated by the government majority. Ibid.

[109] R. S. French, 'Investor–State Dispute Settlement – A Cut Above the Courts?' (Supreme and Federal Courts Judges' Conference, Darwin, 9 July 2014) www.hcourt.gov.au/assets/publications/speeches/current-justices/frenchcj/frenchcj09jul14.pdf accessed 30 December 2014; Sian Elias, 'Barbarians at the Gate: Challenges of Globalization to the Rule of Law' (World Bar Association Conference, Queenstown, 4 September 2014) www.courtsofnz.govt.nz/speechpapers/BarbariansattheGate_2014_09_04.pdf accessed 30 December 2014.

[110] 'An Open Letter from Lawyers to Negotiators of the TransPacific Partnership Urging the Rejection of Investor–State Dispute Settlement', 8 May 2012, tpplegal.wordpress.com/open-letter 30 December 2014.

[111] For example, Joshua Freeman, Gay Keating, Rhys Jones, George Laking, Marilyn Head, Alexandra Macmillan, 'The impact of the Trans-Pacific Partnership on health: Why an independent, comprehensive health impact assessment is crucial prior to signing', *NZDoctor*, 28 November 2014, www.nzdoctor.co.nz/un-doctored/2014/october-2014/28/the-impact-of-the-trans-pacific-partnership-on-health-why-an-independent,-comprehensive-health-impact-assessment-is-crucial-prior-to-signing.aspx accessed 30 December 2014.

[112] Margaret Chan, 'Health Has an Obligatory Place on any Post-2015 Agenda' (67th Health Assembly, Geneva, 19 May 2014) www.who.int/dg/speeches/2014/wha-19052014/en accessed 30 December 2014.

NGOs, unions, indigenous peoples and social movements have continuously mobilized against specific cases and investment laws in general.[113]

Governments began asking, out loud, what would be lost, and who would lose, if these treaties were renounced unilaterally or by consent. As of 2014 Brazil's legislature had never ratified an investment agreement, but it hardly starved for investment. In January 2013 Argentina announced it would follow the examples of Bolivia, Ecuador and Venezuela and withdraw from ICSID. The chief legal advisor to Argentina's Treasury described ICSID as 'a tribunal of butchers' that rules only in favour of multinational companies and said quitting the centre would be a key move to recover Argentina's legislative and jurisdictional sovereignty.[114] Indonesia began withdrawing from BITS that provide a window for it to do so.[115] South Africa decided to terminate most of its BITS and develop domestic legislation as an alternative.[116] India designed a new model BIT.[117]

The contest

UNCTAD's World Investment Forum in October 2014 hosted a session on reform to investment arbitration.[118] The UNCTAD has a long-held concern about these treaties. The discussion was framed by its proposal in June 2013 of five main reform paths: promoting alternative dispute resolution; limits on investor access to investor–state dispute settlement; negotiation of individualized rather than template agreements; an appeals facility; and a standing investment arbitration court.[119] Several governments cautiously supported moves along UNCTAD's lines.[120] Others observed that these steps would not

[113] See generally www.citizen.org/trade, www.bilaterals.org, www.itsourfuture.org.nz, aftinet.org.au/cms/trans-pacific-partnership-agreement accessed 30 December 2014.

[114] 'Argentina in the Process of Quitting from World Bank Investment Disputes Centre' (*Merco Press*, 13 January 2013) en.mercopress.com/2013/01/31/argentina-in-the-process-of-quitting-from-world-bank-investment-disputes-centre accessed 30 December 2014.

[115] Ben Bland and Shaun Donnan, 'Indonesia to terminate more than 60 bilateral investment treaties', *Financial Times* (26 March 2014) www.ft.com/intl/cms/s/0/3755c1b2-b4e2-11e3-af92-00144feabdc0.html#axzz3NLtGkLP2 accessed 30 December 2014.

[116] Jackwell Feris, *International Arbitration Newsletter*, 10 December 2014, www.dlapiper.com/en/asiapacific/insights/publications/2014/12/international-arbitration-newsletter-q4-2014/challenging-the-status-quo accessed 30 December 2014.

[117] Deepshikha Sikarwar, 'New bilateral investment treaties will help India avoid arbitration' *The Economic Times* (New Delhi, 16 December 2014) articles.economictimes.indiatimes.com/2014-12-16/news/57112387_1_investment-treaty-coal-india-tci-cyprus-holdings accessed 30 December 2014.

[118] The author was present and took notes of the statements delivered at the Session. Most statements referred to below can be accessed at UNCTAD World Investment Forum, 'Reforming the International Investment Agreements Regime', unctad-worldinvestmentforum.org/programme/sessions/reforming-the-international-investment-agreements-regime accessed 30 December 2014.

[119] UNCTAD, 'Reform of Investor–State Dispute Settlement. In Search of a Roadmap', (2013) 2 *IIA Issues Note*.

[120] For example, Egypt, Germany and Turkey; see (n 117).

address the existing stock of agreements, unless the parties agreed to renegotiate or vary them, and called for more fundamental reforms to protect the state's regulatory sovereignty.[121] Representatives of ICSID, UNCITRAL and the Stockholm Chamber of Commerce acknowledged there were concerns,[122] noting they had been making incremental modifications (although they fell short of UNCTAD's proposals).

The problem is that any substantial changes led by UNCTAD or the arbitral forums would require support from the capital exporting states that protect the interests of investors, as well as from the corporate lobby groups and the arbitration industry itself. That seems unlikely. Capital exporting states, including the US, EU, Switzerland and Canada consider that they are already including new best practices in their agreements to address legitimate concerns.[123] The private beneficiaries of ISDS that spoke at the forum were also in a state of denial. The chair of the Business and Industry Council Investment Committee at the OECD complained that 'the well co-ordinated, emotional, internationally-widespread debate' was 'totally out of proportion' to the issues.[124] The United States Council for International Business went further, making a series of assertions: strong investment agreements are more important than ever; gold standard BITS require core investor protections; these protections must apply before the investment is made; investors must have direct access to investor–state dispute settlement. Above all, the system works: 'We reject the premise that the international investment regime is in crisis, is fundamentally flawed, or in need of radical revisions.'[125]

Growing investors leverage

Even if investment arbitration were effectively reformed, the substantive rules would still be partisan in favour of foreign investors. The new mega-agreements are adding further layers to benefit foreign corporations. The twelve-country TPPA appears to be the most far-reaching. Behind-the-border disciplines on domestic policy and regulatory decisions aim to create coherent pro-market and pro-business processes, criteria and choices, and the right of affected interests to have their say.[126] A draft Regulatory Coherence chapter leaked in

[121] Especially Argentina, Bangladesh, Barbados, Bosnia Herzegovina, Brazil, Croatia, Ecuador, Namibia, South Africa, Sri Lanka; see (n 117).

[122] unctad-worldinvestmentforum.org/programme/sessions/reforming-the-international-investment-agreements-regime accessed 30 December 2014.

[123] Attempts to constrain the legal adventurism of arbitral tribunals through new wording in the Central American Free Trade Agreement failed in the first two cases: Public Citizen, 'ISDS Cannot be Fixed', December 2014, www.bilaterals.org/spip.php?page=print&id_article=26494 accessed 30 December 2014.

[124] Winand Quaedvlieg, chair of the BIAC Investment Committee; see (n 117).

[125] Peter Robinson, United States Council for International Business; see (n 117).

[126] Jane Kelsey, 'The Trans-Pacific Partnership Agreement: A Gold-Plated Gift to the Global Tobacco Industry?' (2013), 39 *AJLM* 237, 246–252.

2011 would provide a range of opportunities for other TPPA states and their corporations to influence policy and legislative decisions in their favour, and for cross-Party oversight of compliance with the chapter.[127] These obligations were cross-referenced to parties' obligations in the transparency chapter. Although not leaked, that chapter is expected to further enhance the participation of commercial interests in decisions affecting them.

These two chapters must be read in conjunction with the rules, processes and arrangements mandated through other TPPA chapters. They include a separate annex on transparency for healthcare technologies, technical barriers to trade, sanitary and phytosanitary measures, telecommunications, cross-border services, financial services, investment, state enterprises, government procurement and dispute settlement. The cumulative effect would constrain sovereign governments from deciding their own criteria, priorities and processes for policy and regulation. They would also ensure that foreign players, both states and corporations, can enter into the domestic policy and legislative domain to influence decisions in their favour. These expanded investor rights turn full circle back to ISDS, with the threat of an investor–state dispute if a government fails to listen. The Philip Morris tobacco dispute against Australia shows how a private corporation and supportive researchers can use the opportunities for intervention and requirements for disclosure to generate an evidence portfolio they can use in an investor–state dispute if the chilling effect fails.[128]

5. The challenge

I have suggested there is a legitimate role for the licensed subversive in developing a general theory that not only seeks to examine critically the praxis at this moment in history, but also contributes to its transformation.

When Twining concluded his engagement with Santos in *Global Legal Theory* he articulated a series of steps as a starting point for a general theory. My aim in this chapter has been to take Twining's methodology seriously, and to seek to identify the steps that a general theory of global economic law requires, if it is both to identify the flawed present and provide the opportunity for radical readjustment. Each step would be an important contribution to influencing the intellectual climate in a way that would pre-empt pragmatic and cosmetic adjustments and inform a principled reworking of the international economic regime.

Adapted to the current context, and applied to the global financial, investment and trade systems, those steps are:[129]

[127] Kelsey (n 41). The author understands that this version of the text was subsequently diluted.
[128] Kelsey (n 125), 252–62. [129] Ibid., 242.

1. Construct a coherent 'total picture' of transnational economic regulation, synthesizing the multilateral, regional, bilateral and national economic institutions, regulations, norms and practices as dynamic and contested.
2. Clarify values, develop general normative principles, and construct alternative conceptual frameworks that reflect those values and principles.
3. Locate these dynamics in an intellectual history that helps identify continuities and disjunctures, and enduring concepts of general importance.
4. Generate middle-order empirical hypotheses and general working theories for participants, with a methodology that might work on a transnational basis.
5. Critically examine the assumptions that underlie the general and specific legal discourse on transnational economic regulation.

These would need to be refracted through mapping of the following dynamics that were sketched out above:

6. Trends in the financialized mode of capitalism.
7. The geopolitical positions of major players in transnational economic regulation, with special attention to alliances and dissonances within and between the global North and global South, broadly defined.
8. Initiatives by transnational corporations, corporate lobbies and professional firms that seek to shape the future direction of transnational economic regulation.
9. Significant national and international trends in international organizations, regional and national legislatures, academia, professions, public interest groups, indigenous nations and social movements at all levels, which affect the legitimacy of transnational economic regulation and advance the potential for transformation to a new paradigm.

This is an exceptional moment for legal theorists who are inspired by Twining. In 'normal times' there would be almost no prospect for critical insights from legal theory to influence, let alone reshape, a legal regime that is dominated by the power of capital and its patron states. However, these are not normal times. Recent developments indicate that new spaces and unique opportunities are opening up. Much of the diagnostic and analytical work is already being done. The big theoretical question is what concepts and assumptions might underpin viable alternatives, recognizing that the regulatory regime and prevailing mode of capitalism are intertwined. For me, that is the exciting, urgent and daunting challenge for global legal theory today.

Part III
Legal theory

11

Digital thoughtways: technology, jurisprudence and global justice

Abdul Paliwala[1]

Prologue

On arrival in Belfast for my first academic post in 1968, I was asked by the head of department, William Twining, what I was interested in. Blithely I replied 'computers, jurimetrics and law'. I was quite surprised to find a positive response from William. 'That's excellent! We can start a Law Faculty Computer Committee and you can co-ordinate it!' Somewhat non-plussed by this response, I put in my next bid. 'But we will need a programmer!' William responded, 'How much of a programmer?' I said, off the top of my head, 'one-third.' William said OK.

We developed the first IT and Law project, which was a computerized law citator for Northern Ireland Law Reports. William's encouragement did not stop there. I took a part-secondment to the First Parliamentary Draftsman's Office, to learn legislative drafting and also promote computerization. In Northern Ireland, we introduced the first word processor. In the UK, we promoted computerization of the statute book through the Stow-Hill Committee.[2] I taught an innovative jurisprudence module on computers and law. Our research paper for the Law Commission seminar on Classification of Law suggested that computerization would lead to transcendence of traditional conceptual categories of law as people would be able to search contextual or functional categories.[3]

William inspires people by engaging with people's own visions. He is clearly aware of the role of technology in the law and jurisprudence of globalization, including challenges posed by Internet law and the potential role of artificial intelligence on rule-making.[4] Of particular significance is his suggestion that mathematical modelling and programmed learning may promote a shift away

[1] I would like to thank [TO ADD AT PROOF] for comments on an earlier version.

[2] Stow-Hill Committee, *Statute Law: the Key to Clarity* (Sweet & Maxwell, 1972)

[3] William Twining, Katherine O'Donovan and Abdul Paliwala, 'Ernie and the Centipede' in J. A. Jolowicz, ed., *Division and Classification of Law* (Butterworths, 1970), 10.

[4] William Twining, *General Jurisprudence: Understanding Law from a Global Perspective* (Cambridge University Press, 2009), 13; William Twining, *Globalization and Legal Theory* (Butterworths, 2000), 2; William Twining and David Miers, *How to Do Things with Rules*, 5th edition (Cambridge University Press, 2010).

from sociological to more positivist jurisprudence.[5] Beyond that, however, the importance of the role of technology finds little recognition.

This chapter uses Twining's key analytical, realist, contextual, spatial, pluralist and social justice concerns of globalized general jurisprudence to address the impact of digitization on society and law or the digitization of 'thoughtways' on 'lawways'.[6] A brief account of Twining's ideas on jurisprudence and globalization is followed by an account suggesting that digitization promotes new forms of networking on a global scale with implications for globalization and social justice. The following two sections consider the impact of digitization on law. The first section considers the digital globalization of law-jobs with an emphasis on legal information and processes at national and global levels. It argues that where digitization has involved information and communication, it has met with relative but globally uneven success, with implications for social justice. However, where it has tried to engage with specific legal decision making processes, it has so far made very little progress. This is attributed to the inappropriate conceptualization of law. The second section argues that while digitization brings about paradigmatic changes in law and the nature of law, cyberspace's complex plural spaces give rise to contested pluralities in the mode of regulation. There are contestations between promoters of cyberspace as free space and corporate interests which demand new property rights including rights in intimate information; between citizens and national and transnational surveillance by states; and between dominant and less powerful states.

1. Twining's general jurisprudence in a global perspective

Twining's work derives its impetus from two main mentors, H. L. A. Hart and Karl Llewellyn, and a third spiritual mentor in Jeremy Bentham.[7] From Hart he derives his abiding but circumscribed adherence to a liberal positivism on the basis of Hart's distinction between the positive 'is' and the liberal 'ought'.[8] From Llewellyn he derives his greater attachment to realism suggesting 'that there is more to the study of law than the study of a system of rules; that for most purposes legal doctrine should be seen in the context of legal processes and legal processes should be seen in the context of social processes'.[9] From Bentham he derives a utilitarianism that he translates into contemporary approaches to law and global social justice.[10]

[5] Twining, *General jurisprudence* (n 4), 204; Twining, 'Argumentation, Stories and Generalisation: A Comment' (2009), 6 *Law Probability and Risk* 169.

[6] The terms 'thoughtways' and 'lawways' are used in the wider realist sense used by Karl Llewellyn.

[7] Twining, *Globalization & Legal Theory* (n 4) 3. [8] Ibid.

[9] *William Twining, Karl Llewellyn and the Realist Movement* (Cambridge University Press, 2012), 407.

[10] Twining, *General Jurisprudence* (n 4) 149–73; Twining, Globalization and Legal Theory (n 4), 102.

For Twining there is no real contradiction between Hart and Llewellyn in spite of their mutual lack of appreciation. The former belongs in the world of concepts and the latter in the world of context. 'Hart tells us what (state) law is; Llewellyn provides a lens on what law (more broadly conceived) does, and a way of conceiving of non-state law, legal pluralism, and the how of the actual operation of laws, lawyers and legal orders.'[11]

Twining envelopes the conceptual within his realist derived contextual frame, but then gives a dynamic twist to the consolidated frame by challenging jurisprudential scholars (or 'jurisprudes') to reconfigure jurisprudence at both conceptual and contextual levels by becoming more genuinely cosmopolitan in the era of globalization:

> Collectively we have generally been ignorant of other legal traditions and belief systems and generally indifferent to legal phenomena and problems in other parts of the world. My argument is not that our discipline should abandon its local roots and its concern with immediate detailed practical problems, but rather that building on the strengths of our heritage it should broaden its vision to include other levels of ordering, other forms of law, understandings of other legal traditions and belief systems, and to engage more with pressing global and transnational issues. Insofar as our discipline has already been responsive to such challenges, the role of general jurisprudence is to take stock of these responses and make sense of them, as well as to guide, suggest, stimulate, and criticize.[12]

Thus he suggests that a global jurisprudential perspective needs to account for transnational legal fields such as Internet law; the global dimensions of phenomena such as climate change; the transnational dimensions of subjects such as Intellectual Property (IP) law; the significance of religious movements and the position of diasporic communities, especially through migration; the development of comparative law to meet the challenges of pluralism; and the radical rethinking of law based on feminism, human rights, critical theory and postmodernism.[13] More particularly, he suggests taking account of 'Southern Voices'.[14]

There is a distinct difference between Twining's essentially modified Kantian perspective, which suggests an enrichment and some questioning of the Western liberal canon through consideration of Southern voices, and the more radical position taken by others: Boaventura de Sousa Santos, who develops a 'counter-hegemonic' dimension to Southern epistemologies;[15] Upendra Baxi, who promotes 'voices of suffering'[16] and Peter Fitzpatrick,

[11] *Twining, Karl Llewellyn and the Realist Movement* (n 10), 409.

[12] Twining, *General Jurisprudence* (n 4), 444–5. [13] Ibid,. 446–7.

[14] William Twining, *Human Rights: Southern Voices* (Cambridge University Press) and Twining, *General Jurisprudence* (n 4), Ch. 13.

[15] Boaventura de Sousa Santos, *Epistemologies of the South: Justice Against Epistemicide* (Paradigm, 2014).

[16] Upendra Baxi, *The Future of Human Rights* (Oxford University Press, 2012)

who provides a transgressive voice as a deconstructor of the culture of the West.[17] That is, Twining is an empathetic advocate from an essentially Western enlightenment location, whereas the others challenge that Western location.

2. On digital thoughtways

Digitization may be seen as the paradigmatic indicator of the late twentieth and twenty-first centuries and has spawned imageries such as Marshall McLuhan's Global Village, Daniel Bell's Information Society and Jean-François Lyotard's Network Society.[18] Manuel Castells took the transformationist idea further by highlighting the communication capabilities of digital networking in developing a social economic notion of a Network Information Society, a society in which previous hierarchical organizational forms were increasingly subordinated to pluralist networking facilitated by digital media:

> Networks constitute the new social morphology of our societies, and the diffusion of networking logic substantially modifies the operation and outcomes in processes of production, experience, power, and culture.[19]

For some, such as Michael and Ronda Hauben, the network logics promoted a new cosmopolitanism of cyberspace that transcended national boundaries:

> Welcome to the 21st Century. You are a Netizen (a Net Citizen), and you exist as a citizen of the world thanks to the global connectivity that the Net makes possible. You consider everyone as your compatriot. You physically live in one country but you are in contact with the world via the global computer network. Virtually you live next door to every other single Netizen in the world. Geographical separation is replaced by existence in the same virtual space.[20]

The ideologies of net neutrality and netizen and network governance emerge from the technical structure of the internet, in which governance rules were created by open organizations including the Internet Society, the Internet Engineering Task Force and the Internet Architecture Board.[21] Governance groups are not appointed; only chairs are appointed. Membership is open to all

[17] Peter Fitzpatrick, *The Mythology of Modern Law* (Routledge, 1992); Peter Fitzpatrick, *Modernism and the Ground of* Law (Cambridge University Press, 2001).

[18] Marshall McLuhan, *The Gutenberg Galaxy: The Making of Typographic Man* (University of Toronto Press, 1962); Daniel Bell, *The Coming of Post-Industrial Society* (Basic Books, 1976), 127, 348; Jean-François Lyotard, *The Postmodern Condition* (Manchester University Press, 1984), 5.

[19] Manuel Castells, *The Information Age: Economy Society, Culture. Vol 1: The Rise of the Network Society* (Blackwell, 2000), 500.

[20] Michael Hauben and Ronda Hauben, *Netizens: An Anthology* 1996 www.columbia.edu/~rh120 accessed 9 September 2014

[21] Abdul Paliwala, 'Netizenship, Security and Freedom' (2013), 27:1 *International Review of Law, Computers and Technology* 104; Mathieu O'Neil (2009), *Cyberchiefs: Autonomy and Authority in Online Tribes* (Pluto, 2009).

interested parties. Anyone can propose a new technical rule through a memo that is subject to comments and amendments. This radical non-bureaucratic system of self-governance is what has given the internet community its peculiar strength during a period of profound cultural change. The culture of self-governance has seeped into and led to strong ideological and economic positions in fields such as the development of Free and Open Software (FOSS) and Content and phenomena such as crowdsourcing and communal authoring. These ideologies support opposition to the extension of Intellectual Property rights and electronic surveillance by states and corporations. For some, such as Yochai Benkler, there is a new mode of production, or Network Information Economy, resulting in a radical new culture with emphasis on the new global commons, which nevertheless co-exists with the market economy.[22]

The early redemptive vision of the digital age as a solution to many of the problems of the social and physical environment has been replaced by more sober notions in which there is recognition that the transformations wrought by the digital may bring about new dilemmas as well as promises. Thus Castells uses the term 'informational capitalism' to indicate that capitalism also takes on new cyber-capitalist forms such as Google and Facebook, which utilize the power of network information society and in particular enhance its global potential.[23] These transformations involve not only new modes of network production, such as global commodity chains, but also new capitalist business models which enable the Googles of the world to become dominant economic forces by providing free access to information for users. Kaushik Rajan suggests that in these transformations pre-existing political economic power structures 'overdetermine' the Network Information Society.[24] Thus, new forms of capital and ways of working often emerge in contestation with traditional forms of 'industrial capital', but they tend to be dominated by the power of global capital or, in the case of surveillance, by agencies of global capital and the state.

The dominant role of global corporations in digitization further exacerbates forms of digital exclusion. For Castells, access to the digital was a vital part of access to key cultural, political and economic networks.[25] Earlier notions of digital divides, as being seen purely in terms of access to technology, have been

[22] Yochai Benkler, *The Wealth of Networks: How Social Production Transforms Markets and Freedom* (Yale University Press, 2006), www.benkler.org/Benkler_Wealth_Of_Networks.pdf accessed 9 September 2014.

[23] Castells (n 19); Christian Fuchs (2012), 10:1 'Google Capitalism', *Triple Communication, Capitalism & Critique* www.triple-c.at/index.php/tripleC/article/view/304 accessed 10 September 2014.

[24] Kaushik Rajan, *Biocapital: The Constitution of Postgenomic Life* (Duke University Press, 2006); see also Baxi, *The Future of Human Rights* (n 16), 156.

[25] Manuel Castells, 'Information technology, globalization and social development', *Conference on Information Technology and Development* Geneva, United Nations Research Institute for Social Devlopment. www.unrisd.org/infotech/conferen/castelp1.htm accessed 25 July 2014.

replaced by notions of the quality of access to, use and control of the digital environment.[26] While many previously developing countries have shown great advances in technology use and the Eastern Tiger economies can no longer be considered 'developing', great masses of people, especially in the global South, are excluded from quality access to the digital environment.[27] What is equally significant is that power and control, whether in property rights, organization or governance and surveillance of the digital environment, are exercised largely by global corporations, state or international agencies and non-state organizations.

There are therefore strong resonances between Twining's reformulation of general jurisprudence to take into account pluralism, globalization and issues such as social justice and the role of the digital in social transformations.

3. The digital globalization of law-jobs

In a consideration of digitization and globalization, the specific contribution of Llewellyn's law-jobs theory as elaborated by Twining is to broaden the horizons of law to include contextual, plural and global dimensions.[28] Law-jobs exist in any human social context: they are not uniform; for example, they do not require states, formalized systems of rules, courts or specific forms of decision making. Nor is there a monopoly of law-jobs; there can be pluralism. Finally, they exist co-terminously in global, national, regional and local planes providing a complexity of regulatory forms.[29]

This broad perspective provides a liberating framework for considering the impact of digitization on law-jobs. Is there merely a change in efficiency of service provision, or is there a change in the nature of law-jobs and of law? What is digitization's impact on globalization and in differential social justice between the North and the South?

In the book, *A History of Legal Informatics*, several pioneers in the field suggest that the results are very mixed.[30] Richard Susskind is the most enthusiastic exponent of the proposition that computers have the potential for fundamental transformation of legal work, but suggests that lawyers have 'insufficiently adapted' to legal informatics. He writes:

[26] Anteneh Ayanso, Danny Cho and Kaveepan Lertwachara, 'Information and Communications Technology Development and the Digital Divide: A Global and Regional Assessment' (2014), 20 *Information Technology for Development*, 60–77; Mark Warschauer, *Technology and Social Inclusion: Rethinking the Digital Divide* (MIT Press, 2004); Abdul Paliwala, 'Digital Divide: Globalization and Legal Regulation' (2004), *UTS Law Review* 26–38.

[27] Ayanso Ibid.

[28] Twining, *Karl Llewellyn and the Realist Movement* (n 10), 175–184; Twining, *General Jurisprudence* (n 4), 103–16; Karl Llewellyn, 'The Normative, the Legal and Law-Jobs: The problem of Juristic Method' (1940), 49 *Yale L J* 1355.

[29] Twining, *General Jurisprudence* (n 4), Ibid.

[30] Abdul Paliwala, ed., *A History of Legal Informatics* (Prensa Universitarias de Zaragoza, 2010).

> The market is increasingly unlikely to tolerate expensive lawyers for tasks (guiding, advising, drafting, researching, problem-solving, and more) that can equally or better be discharged by less expert people, supported by sophisticated systems and processes. Therefore the jobs of many traditional lawyers will be substantially eroded and often eliminated. At the same time, new law-jobs are likely to emerge which may be highly rewarding, even if very different from those of today. The market will determine that the legal world is inefficiently resourced and is likely to drive out excesses and unnecessary friction and, in turn, we will witness the end of outdated legal practice and the end of outdated lawyers.[31]

While Susskind espouses the transformative potential of technology but blames lawyers for their head-in-the-sand attitude, Philip Leith and Kate Hoey advance the opposite perspective. They appreciate the transformative potential of technology but are concerned with the 'disastrous' reality of many projects led by computer technicians and enthusiasts and suggest that 'luckily most lawyers have been sceptical about the advantages of the computer and have not been overly keen to take the lead in the implementation of technology'.[32] Even though Susskind's provocative work is titled *The End of Lawyers*, his gaze, as of Leith and Hoey, is largely directed towards lawyers.[33] They represent two dimensions for exploration of the changes taking place in current lawyers' and judges' roles and the manner in which other professionals, businesses and citizens are involved in law-jobs previously done by lawyers.

Major changes are taking place in the world of law and in law-jobs, of which only some may be attributed to technology. Perhaps the most significant changes have been the rise of neo-liberal approaches that have liberalized the provision of legal services. Thus, the United Kingdom *Legal Services Act 2007* has loosened the monopoly in provision of legal services and promoted restructuring of the legal professions. Alternative Business Structures (ABS) permit businesses which are not necessarily led by lawyers to provide legal services. Furthermore, recent severe funding cuts and restructuring of legal aid have deeply affected the poorer sectors. Susskind's argument that lawyers have to face the challenges of such liberalization by becoming more techno-competent is based on the ideologies of a neo-liberal market and emancipatory information technologies, both of which need questioning.

4. The uneven globalization of legal information retrieval

Perhaps the greatest legal transformation has been in electronic legal information retrieval, which has produced a Gutenbergian transformation in access to legal information. Thus the development of LEXIS in the US and similar

[31] Richard Susskind, 'Legal Informatics: A Personal Appraisal of Context and Progress' in Paliwala, ed. (n 30), 119.

[32] Philip Leith and Kate Hoey, *The computerised Lawyer: A Guide to the Use of Computers in the Legal Profession*, 2nd edn (Springer, 1998), ix.

[33] Richard Susskind, *The End of Lawyers?* (Oxford University Press, 2008).

systems in Europe gave lawyers expensive access to legal information previously available only through costly hard copy in law libraries.[34] Prior to digitization, research relied on the indexing, cataloguing and memory capacity of publishers, librarians and lawyers, thus reinforcing specialism. The development of electronic retrieval systems led to an explosion of information extending to unreported decisions and other jurisdictions. Equally substantial was the transformation of navigation techniques. Previously conceptual approaches were replaced by Key Word in Context (KWIC) searches whether by a name such as News International, or beings such as dogs or a place such as Zanzibar, thus transcending conceptual boundaries and leading to a profound shift in the approaches to division and classification of law and enabling the development of contextual subjects such as refugee law, investment law and information technology law.[35] Other refinements include hypertext, which has enabled the user to move between documents through clicks on links; medium-neutral or court- or legislature-assigned citation systems enabling hypertexting between datasets, and natural language searches which have simplified the search process.[36] However, expensive proprietary datasets were a resource exclusively for rich lawyers and state claims for copyright obstructed access to legal information. The rise of the internet, and with it the culture of freedom of the net, including ideologies of open source and free access to information, resulted in a transformation. The Free Access to Law Movement promoted free provision of web-based legal information.[37] State agencies and courts finally succumbed to political pressure and the desire to improve their legitimacy in an era of e-governance by publishing material free on the internet. But the main providers of electronic free legal information were academics. Pioneered by Cornell's Legal Information Institute's (LII) publication of US Supreme Court decisions, there quickly developed a global phenomenon of LIIs epitomized by the worldwide Legal Information Institutes (LIIs) which are loosely co-ordinated in WorldLII and by the Free Access to Law Movement.[38]

There are obvious implications in this for law-jobs. There has been a significant shift in legal work culture with the arrival of efficient information retrieval. But non-lawyers have also benefited, thus loosening the hold of traditional lawyers. In particular, ordinary citizens also now have free access to legal material.[39] While much use of online systems has been by law professionals and

[34] Jon Bing, 'Let there be LITE: A brief history of legal information retrieval' in Paliwala (n 30), 21.

[35] Twining, 'Ernie and Centipede' n 10–30.

[36] Peter Martin, 'How Structural Features of the U.S. Judicial System have affected the take-up of Technology by the Courts' in Paliwala (n 30), 83–96; Graham Greenleaf 'The Global Development of Free Access to Legal Information' in Paliwala (n 30) 53, 74

[37] FALM Website: www.falm.org accessed 10 Sept 2014; Greenleaf ibid.

[38] AUSTLII www.austlii.edu.au; WorldLII www.worldlii.org accessed 10 September 2014; FALM Website Ibid.

[39] Bing (n 34), 49; Cedric Spencer, *How the Plain English and Free Access to Law movements may have opened up an area of opportunity previously unavailable to most small businesses* (DBA thesis, Southern Cross University, Lismore, NSW 2011); Daniel Poulin, 'Free Access to Law in

students and other professionals, and while citizens prefer secondary information about law rather than primary, there is significant evidence of use by ordinary citizens.[40]

Online legal information has promoted globalization of law and legal practice. Initially, online legal information systems were very solo-jurisdictional proprietary systems that could not talk to each other. The major commercial systems such as LEXIS and WESTLAW realized the problems with this in an era of globalization and themselves became global information providers, but with an emphasis on the developed world.[41] Yet, major credit for innovative research and development in globalization of access to legal information belongs to the global family of LIIs signified by WorldLII and the Free Access to Law Movement. The development of medium-neutral citation systems promotes not only searching and hyperlink navigation across proprietary systems but across jurisdictional boundaries. Innovations include attempted transcendence of global linguistic issues such as different meanings of concepts in jurisdictions and searching across languages. Remarkably, the availability of English translations of legal texts is being used for cross-linguistic searches even across Chinese, Japanese and Korean common Eastern character sets.[42]

However, these remarkable developments in the globalization of law camouflage the reality of digital exclusion. Many countries, such as Malaysia, Singapore, Brazil, Uruguay and Chile, have developed or even taken the lead in digitization. Nevertheless, the less-developed countries suffer from inequality in the extent and quality of online access, including incomplete and precarious websites.[43] For global corporate law firms, the globalization of law provides a real globalization of access to developing country material. This is not the case for ordinary developing country practitioners and citizens who are often

Canada' (2011) 12 *Legal Information Management*' 165–72 lexum.com/en/publications/free-access-law-canada accessed 8 September 2014.

40 Greenleaf (n 36).

41 See e.g. LEXIS/NEXIS Global Legal Searches support.lexisnexis.com/ilexis/record.asp?ArticleID=10823&ALid=eldc_global; Daniel Poulin, 'Open Access to Law in Developing Countries' [2004] 9 *First Monday* firstmonday.org/htbin/cgiwrap/bin/ojs/index.php/fm/article/view/1193/1113 accessed 10 September 2014.

42 Amy Shee, 'TaiwanLII – Past, Present, Prospects' www.taiwanlii.ccu.edu.tw/taiwanlii/en accessed 10 September 2014; Yoshiharu Matsuura and Amy Shee, 'Sharing of Legal Information: Korea, China, Taiwan and Japan' www.slideserve.com/jory/20-may-2011-seoul-yoshiharu-matsuura-jalii-amy-h-l-shee-taiwanlii accessed 10 September 2014.

43 The instability of sites is illustrated by the ending of the Droit Afrique Francophone portal, portail.droit.francophonie.org. For issues involved see Yates, K. et al., 'Establishing a Sustainable Legal Information System in a Developing Country: A Practical Guide' www.ejisdc.org/ojs2../index.php/ejisdc/article/view/702 accessed 20 September 2014; Abdul Paliwala 'Free Access to Law in Africa: Issues for Network Society' in Ginerva Peruginelli and Mario Ragona (eds), *Law via the Internet: Free Access, Quality of Information, Effectiveness of Rights* (Florence: European Press Academic Publishing), 253–60.

denied these services by issues of cost, technical access and lack of knowledge.[44]

5. Law office systems

Information Technology has brought about remarkable changes in lawyers' work practices, though many of these changes are a reflection of changes in businesses generally. Starting with word processing, legal information retrieval and email, lawyers have increasingly adopted office automation and knowledge management systems.[45] The use of intranets for intra-firm work, the internet and social media have become so common that there are claims that no respectable law firm can be without a web presence.[46] A multiplicity of hardware devices, including the PC, laptops, tablets and smart phones have become common tools of trade. Paper documents are being replaced by e-documents and scanning has enabled easy integration of paper documents into document management systems. But the opposite perspectives of Susskind and Leith/Hoey suggest a paradox.[47] Lawyers are either not aware of the fundamental transformative potential of technology and the threat to their work or are pragmatically avoiding overhyped technology promoters.

Nevertheless, Information Technologies have enabled innovative law firms to transcend physical geographical limitations of intra-firm or external communication, whether with clients, other law firms or courts, enabling the rise of large national and global corporate firms that increasingly outsource ancillary services. Most law firms merely use the web as an advertising device, but others provide online legal advice with the carrot of free advice being used to lure customers into paid relationships. A greater innovation is the online virtual practice.[48] *Law on the Web, LegalZoom* and *Rocket Lawyer* typify online service providers that provide information about law and documents, and may provide some online advice, but refer you to a private practitioner in case of need.[49] These services may employ lawyers and para-legals on a different basis to traditional law firms. An equally significant phenomenon is the growth of non-traditional legal practices. The UK *Legal Education and Training Review* highlights the rise of the 'unregulated sector' in the provision of legal services

[44] See e.g. Robert Hinson, Raymond Atuguba, Dan Ofori, Julius Fobih, 'The Internet and Lawyers in Ghana: Some Initial Qualitative Perspectives' (2007), 56:4 *Library Review* 311–22; see also Poulin (n 41) and Paliwala (n 41).

[45] Martin Apistola and Petter Gottschalk, *Essential Knowledge and Management Issues in Law Firms* (Universal Publishers, 2012).

[46] This is of course a common claim of those marketing websites; see e.g. WebJuris www.webjuris.com/cle_script.pdf accessed 18 December 2014.

[47] Susskind (n 31); Leith and Hoey (n 32).

[48] Stephanie Kimbro, *Virtual Law Practice: How to Deliver Legal Services Online* (ABA/LPM Publishing, 2010).

[49] Law on the Web www.lawontheweb.co.uk; LegalZoom www.legalzoom.com; Rocket Lawyer www.rocketlawyer.com accessed 10 December 2014.

by a variety of unregulated organizations and people, including businesses and non-governmental organizations.[50] Traditional law firms (including paralegals) provide only forty-four per cent of advice services in justiciable issues. Over fifty per cent of advice seekers in justiciable issues relied on unregulated providers. Furthermore, the change in the State's position on electronic provision of information as a service, and emphasis on simplification of instructions and forms, has resulted in the development of e-governance state information systems which allow reasonably able internet users to obtain information and submit documents online that previously required lawyers' services.[51]

But do these changes mean more than the fact that law-jobs are being done by different persons? This may be the case with the automation of some law-jobs. Firstly, the more information a user can obtain for herself, the greater the level of user control in a transaction, whether face to face or online. A consumer filling in an automated will or other document on a website is in a different position from a relationship with a face to face lawyer, in the sense that it is the user who is taking responsibility. Secondly, the nature and level of regulation is affected in the new types of legal service. Thirdly, Alternative Business Structures (ABS), which enable the development of enterprises which combine legal and non-legal services, promote greater commodification of legal work by parcelling out different aspects of the same job to a variety of specialists who may or may not have legal expertise. There are resulting problems for legal ethics and regulation as well as for the survival of professional monopolies.[52]

The combination of communications, document management and intranet systems has enabled teamwork across the globe in both synchronous and asynchronous manner, thus ameliorating time differentials.[53] Commodification has also enabled the development of global legal commodity chains in which different aspects of a law-job can be spread across the globe.[54]

Information Technology has also promoted global legal pluralism. Online Dispute Resolution (ODR) systems mushroomed to deal with increasing

[50] UKCLE Independent Research Team, *Final Report of the UK Education and Training Review* 2013, (LETR) Report Table 3.4, S3.122 letr.org.uk/wp-content/uploads/LETR-Report.pdf accessed 11 September 2014.

[51] Kimberley Stolzfus, 'Motivations for implementing e-government: an investigation of the global phenomenon' *Proceedings of the 2005 National Conference on Digital government research dg.o '05* (2005, 333–338) dl.acm.org/citation.cfm?id=1065343 accessed 11 Sept 2014; Anuj Subharwal and Payal Lamba, 'Building Blocks of E-Governance: Strengthening the Democratic System' (2014), 07:02 *OIDA International Journal of Sustainable Development* 25–32.

[52] LETR (n 51), Report S2.71, 2.72.

[53] David Brock, Tal Yaffe, Mark Dembrowski 'International diversification and performance: A study of global law firms' (2006), 12:4 *Journal of International Management* 473–489.

[54] Ibid.; Laurel Terry, 'The Legal World Is Flat: Globalization and Its Effect on Lawyers Practicing in Non-Global Law Firms' (2007–8), 28 *Nw. J. Int'l L. & Bus.* 527; James Faulconbridge, Jonathan Beaverstock, Daniel Muzio and Peter Taylor, 'Global Law Firms: Globalization and Organizational Spaces of Cross-Border Legal Work' (2007–8) 28 *Nw. J. Int'l L. & Bus.* 455.

transnationalization of e-commerce.[55] Thus, most online retailers use ODR methodologies, which suit user needs as users have transacted online, most of the data is held online and decisions can therefore be made conveniently.[56] This may be the case especially where the service provider, such as eBay or Amazon, is acting as a neutral third party. Most websites utilize electronic form-filling and e-communication; some may use Intelligent Agents.[57]

If the globalization of legal information was uneven, the globalization of legal work is considerably more so. Global corporate law firms, which work mainly for global corporations, dominate litigation through their combination of electronic global and local expertise.[58] Public interest law firms with global expertise and network links provide a counter-trend in operating successfully on behalf of subaltern groups and sufferers from oppressive conduct by states and global corporations.[59] Thus a global network of NGOs, lawyers, academics, students and activists was responsible for the request to extradite General Pinochet from the United Kingdom.[60] Information technology is as essential to such networking as it is to the crowdsourcing of evidence of atrocities: for example, in Argentina's disappearances, where large numbers of victims may be involved.[61] Similarly, electronic-networking has been key to the work of global public interest law firms such as Leigh Day.[62] The remarkable electronic contribution to human rights work was observed as early as 1991 in events in the former Yugoslavia:

> Every turn of political fortunes was reported immediately by journalists able to file stories and photographs through electronic media beamed across the world by CNN and other satellite news networks. News reports accompanied by digital photographs were available instantaneously to Internet users on the World Wide Web (WWW), and discussed ad infinitum on Internet user-groups and discussion groups. Concerned Internet users established links with the inhabitants of Sarajevo through 'Sarajevo on-line,' a World Wide Web site allowing Internet users to pose questions directly to identified students (whose photographs and biographies were featured on the net) who posted answers regularly.

[55] Mohamed Wahab, Ethan Katsh and Daniel Rainey (eds), *Online Dispute Resolution: Theory and Practice* (Eleven International Publishing 2012) www.mediate.com/articles/ODRTheoryandPractice.cfm accessed 10 December 2014; Davide Carneiro, Paulo Novais and Jose Neves (eds), *Conflict Resolution and its Context: From the Analysis of Behavioral Patterns to Efficient Decision Making* Dordrecht (Springer, 2014)

[56] Wahab (n 56). [57] Carneiro (n 15) 237. [58] Terry (n 55).

[59] John Bonine, 'Public interest environmental lawyers – global examples and personal reflections' (2004) 10 *Widener L. Rev.* 451; Scott Cummings and Louise Trubek, 'Globalizing Public Interest Law' (2008), 13 *UCLA J. Int'L L. & Foreign Aff.* 1; See generally Boaventura de Sousa Santos and Cesar Rodriguez-Garavito (eds), *Law and Globalization from Below: Towards a Cosmopolitan Legality* (Cambridge University Press, 2005).

[60] David Sugarman, 'From unimaginable to possible: Spain, Pinochet and the Judicialisation of power' [2002] 3 *Journal of Spanish Cultural Studies* 1.

[61] Iain Guest, 'Behind the Disappearances: Argentina's Dirty War Against Human Rights and the United Nations' *University of Pennsylvania Studies in Human Rights* 1990.

[62] The Leigh Day Trainee Statement: 'To maximise the use of IT systems introduced to assist in the management of cases' www.leighday.co.uk accessed 20 September 2014.

> Action alerts were sent across the Internet directly to concerned observers by groups like Amnesty International, which led to letter writing campaigns and popular pressure on Western government officials to act. . . . In the same time that it had taken to produce the single 1914 Carnegie report, a seemingly infinite stream of words had emerged which brought the Balkan conflict of the information age to life.[63]

Social media have had a tremendous impact on developments such as the Arab Spring and Gaza.[64] The impact goes beyond mere speed and efficiency of processing. A key to the digitization of human rights work is the manner in which non-legal professionals such as clients, witnesses, students and NGOs become integrated in law-jobs in previously inconceivable forms of teamwork.

Internet Fatwas (Islamic Legal Pronouncements) provide a remarkable example of changing relationships between those seeking legal pronouncements and those providing it.[65] Previously, a woman seeking a legal pronouncement would only have recourse to one authority through a male intermediary. Online Fatwas go beyond ease of access, as women can seek a Fatwa from any authority, wherever located, and they forum shop for Fatwas by obtaining second and third opinions. The resulting power shift has implications for Islamic gender justice.[66]

6. An inadequate jurisprudence?

The significant changes in law-jobs have resulted mainly from ordinary information technology processes such as data processing, data storage, retrieval and management in combination with the information rich, rapid and global communication and networking capabilities of the internet. However, when information technology has been applied to deeper legal processes, which involve the very nature of law, the result has not been very successful. This is especially so in relation to the application of artificial intelligence (AI) systems to law. Leith blames the meagre and unsatisfactory results of costly AI and law research on faulty jurisprudence and especially on almost exclusive reliance on analytical positivism and ignorance of user needs and requirements.[67]

> However, what became clear to me . . . was why lawyers of the time were so keen on expert systems in law: they had been brought up in the context of a simplistic rule oriented view of law of the sort promoted by Hart, and such a perspective

[63] Jamie Metzl, 'Information Technology and Human Rights' (1996), 18:4 *Human Rights Quarterly* pp. 705–46 at 705.

[64] Paliwala, *Netizenship, Security and Freedom* (n 21).

[65] Shaheen Ali, 'Behind the Cyberspace Veil: Online Fatawas on Women's Family Rights' in Shaheen Ali, Anne Hellum and Ann Griffiths (eds), *From Transnational Relations to Transnational Laws: Northern European Laws at the Crossroads* (Ashgate, 2011) 117.

[66] Ibid.

[67] Philip Leith,'The Rise and Fall of the Legal Expert System' in Paliwala ed. (n 30) 179–203.

neatly dovetailed with the approach used in rule based expert systems. In effect, there was a culture in law of denying the complexity of law.[68]

Many involved with AI and law still refuse to acknowledge that there are underlying problems with the nature of legal reasoning. Thus Eric Engle suggests that AI can solve the problems of legal complexity:

> Because procedural rules are mechanical, they lend themselves to computer modelling. The complex yet mechanical nature of procedural laws, particularly in the context of international law, explain why computer modelling of complex mechanical rule structures such as civil procedure, conflicts of laws/private international law may be a useful tool for practitioners. The computer is less likely than a human to overlook any of the Byzantine exceptions or exceptions to exceptions that may result in the application or non-application of a foreign or domestic procedural or substantive law.[69]

Unfortunately, the author's attempt at yet another rule-based expert system involves very little analysis of the theoretical problems underlying the relationship between law and technology.

In spite of the general decline in research, there are ways in which AI and law decision making systems are being employed; for example, in automated motor-speed fining systems which automate the process from the road speed camera to the issue of fine notices to the speeder.[70] The crucial factor with such systems is that the law is remodelled to suit the needs of AI, whereas other approaches attempt to develop systems that reflect the law. The result is a fundamental cybernetic transformation of legal relationships with important social implications.[71]

Does AI in law have a future, then? Engle suggests that the reason for lack of interest in AI may be economic; that none of the systems is of value in the marketplace as yet, with greater emphasis being given to applications such as the web, communication systems and online information retrieval.[72] While he may have a point, the real reasons for relative failure may be ignoring user needs and inadequate jurisprudence.

More nuanced approaches attempt to deal with these issues.[73] Instead of considering AI as the basis decision making systems, the emphasis has been on decision support systems, with the development of intelligent assistants or

[68] Ibid., 182.

[69] Eric Engle, 'An introduction to artificial intelligence and legal reasoning: using xtalk to model the alien tort claims act and torture victim protection act' (2014), 11 *Rich. J.L. & Te* ch. 2, 2.

[70] Arno Lodder and Anja Oskamp (eds), *Information Technology and Lawyers: Advanced Technology in the Legal Domain, from Challenges to Daily Routine* (Springer, 2006).

[71] Abdul Paliwala, 'An Intellectual Celebration: A Review of the Jurix Legal Knowledge Based Systems Scholarship' (2001), 8 *Artificial Intelligence and Law* 317–335; Oskamp and Lodder (n 71).

[72] Engle (n 70).

[73] Lodder and Oskamp (n 71); Giovanni Sartor, Pompeu Casanovas, Mariangela Biasiotti, Meritxell Fernández-Barrera (eds), *Approaches to Legal Ontologies* (Springer, 2011); Davide Carneiro, Paulo Novais, Francisco Andrade, Johan Zeleznikow and Jose Neves Carneiro,

agents.[74] More sophisticated techniques include attempts to emulate the legal process with the use of argument systems.[75] Case-based reasoning systems emulate common law case methods.[76]. Kevin Ashley claims that HYPO can countenance a variety of factors and standpoints, including judges, plaintiffs and defendants, and instead of making decisions, provide the most significant precedents or precedent-based arguments. However, Ashley's experiment does not utilize the potential for a sophisticated theoretical analysis of contextual, temporal and sociological factors relevant to decisions. Cass Sunstein uses Dworkinian positivism to suggest that, while thin artificial intelligence ideas might be useful in improving legal search facilities to provide a more intelligent version of LEXIS/Westlaw, contemporary AI techniques are currently incapable of making the sort of value judgments implied by case-based reasoning.[77] Twining, in a sympathetic exploration of a criminal investigation AI project, warns of the tendency of even contextual AI 'to treat programs designed as aids to thinking as if they were substitutes for thinking' but above all to oversimplify when his own 'Modified Wigmorian Approach' to fact analysis stresses complexity of argumentation and legal reasoning.[78]

In a rethinking of jurisprudential approaches to AI and law, Twining's ideas on general jurisprudence, and its relationship to the particular as well as on rules, provide a way forward, especially that AI and law rules should not be taken out of their context as 'rule-handling is only one aspect of the crafts of law'.[79] AI and law have thus to be related to a realist social economic and political context.

It is necessary to particularize projects into simple doable objectives, which fit the real practice of law-jobs rather than formal concepts, and user needs and ways. For example, information retrieval systems have been improved through AI-based techniques of natural language searching as users prefer such systems to the complexities of Boolean logic.[80] The best research integrates AI into general technological and human approaches to problem solving, as is the case with the successful development of neutral citation systems based on the court

'Online dispute resolution: an artificial intelligence perspective' (2014), 41 Artif Intell Rev 211–240; Carneiro (n 15).

[74] Anja Oskamp and Arno Lodder, 'Introduction: Law, Information Technology, and Artificial Intelligence' in Lodder and Oskamp (n 71) 1 and Bench-Capon T. and Prakken H. (2006) 'Argumentation' in Lodder A. and Oskamp (n 71) 61.

[75] Ibid.

[76] Kevin Ashley, *Modeling Legal Argument: Reasoning with Cases and Hypotheticals* (MIT Press, 1990); Kevin Ashley, 'Case Based Reasoning' in Lodder and Oskamp (n 71), 23.

[77] Cass Sunstein, 'On Artificial Intelligence and Legal Reasoning' (2001), *Chicago Public Law and Legal Theory Working Paper* No 18.

[78] Twining (n 5), 170. The paper critiqued Floris Bex, Susan van den Braak et al., 'Sense-Making Software for Crime Investigation: How to Combine Stories and Arguments?' (2007), 6 *Law Probability and Risk* 145–68.

[79] Twining and Miers were not averse to expert systems: *How to Do Things with Rules* (n 4) viii, 254 viii.

[80] See e.g. Natural Language Searching Wiki in Lexis/Nexis wiki.lexisnexis.com/academic/index.php?title=Natural_Language_Searching accessed 25 Aug 2014.

or other institution producing the document, rather than secondary publishers. The system enabled users to search across datasets. The main tasks involved were political in convincing institutions such as judiciaries and legislatures to adopt the system. However, the underlying technical basis involves AI-based techniques of hypertext and intelligent pattern-matching.[81]

The most important task is to take into account the social political and economic context in which law operates. As AI becomes ubiquitous in society generally, there is need to question its effect on relationships between humans and machines, employment and work practices, human rights and social justice:

> For instance, when decision support systems are used to decide whether an applicant will get social benefit, the system will set the standard. Deviations from this standard will be rare, since they will imply more work for the decision maker and it might mean he will have to justify the deviation.[82]

Unfortunately, most AI and law research has tended to commence with AI technology and attempted to apply it without any research into social and political implications, context, real practice or user ways or needs. Even Oskamp and Lodder, cited above, commence with an AI system rather than attempting to solve socio-legal problems in which AI may be a component.[83] Some recent attempts go beyond the previously dominant simple analytical approach to a broader notion of legal ontology and its application in the new 'semantic web' era. However, legal onotologies are affected by the same issues of diversity of understanding the nature of reality as is jurisprudence.[84] While most current ontological work on AI and law deals with analytical concepts, Pompeu Casanovas et al. provide an alternative framing for the development of 'empirically grounded' legal ontologies with an ambitious attempt to develop a decision support system for judges. Thus the basis for the *Juriservis* system includes notions of legal culture, including 'attitudes, ideas, expectations and values' that are to be discovered through qualitative socio-legal research.[85] There is a similar approach to awareness of context in Davide Carneiro et al's work on the role of AI in Online Dispute Resolution systems with an emphasis

[81] Needle J. (2000), 'The Automatic Linking of Legal Citations', Commentary 2000 (3) *The Journal of Information, Law and Technology (JILT)* www2.warwick.ac.uk/fac/soc/law/elj/jilt/needle accessed 25 August 2014.

[82] See e.g. Oskamp and Lodder (n 75), 17. This tendency for AI to transform power relations between technology and humans can be seen in the devastating use of AI-based systems in drone warfare. Noel Sharkey, 'Automating Warfare: Lessons Learnt from the Drones' (2011) 21 *J. L. Inf. & Sci.* 140.

[83] Oskamp and Lodder ibid.

[84] Amselek P. and MacCormick N. (1989), *Controversies about Law's Ontology* (Edinburgh University Press); Oskamp and Lodder (n 70); Sartor (n 73); Richard Benjamins, Pompeu Casanovas, Joost Breuker and Aldo Gangemi (eds), *Law and the Semantic Web: Legal Ontologies, Methodologies, Legal Information Retrieval, and Applications* (Springer, 2005)

[85] Pompeu Casanovas, Nuria Casellas and Joan-Josep Vallbé, 'Empirically grounded developments of Legal Ontologies: A Socio-Legal Perspective' in Sartor (n 74) 52.

on understanding the context of the user.[86] Though fraught with difficulties, the wider pluralist realist rights-conscious approach and an emphasis on decision support rather than decision making may point us in the right direction.

7. Cyberspace and the globalization of substantive law

The unevenness noted in the technological transformation of legal information and law-jobs is even more pronounced in technology's impact on substantive law, specifically intellectual property (IP) rights and surveillance. Technology has resulted in the creation of new domains of substantive law, such as internet law and e-commerce law, and transformed established areas such as IP law.

Technology has also promoted globalization and legal pluralism and is affecting the nature and culture of law.[87] This can be seen especially in the development of the new *Lex Mercatoria* and cyberspace law. Both locate themselves in complex legal spaces in which national and international legal institutions interact with plural legal and quasi-legal networks involving not mere contestations of norms but of ideologies which raise issues of uneven global social justice. Thus, cyberspace is asserted as transcendent space, a new cosmopolitan universe democratically ruled by netizens; at the same time, global corporations and states assert new forms of digital domination, the former through property rights and surveillance and the latter through surveillance. The objective of this section is to consider these modes of digital dominance and the complex relationship between ideologies of control through property and surveillance, and oppositional ideologies of resistance through the principle of netizenship.

8. The uneven globalization of IP rights

A sceptical perspective suggests that, in a similar fashion to the historic enclosure of the English commons, the contest over digital property rights would favour the US, developed countries and global corporations, to the extent that their interests would lead to global advancement of their IP rights.[88] This globalization has coincided with the commodification and digitization of information to the extent that not only did IP rights in relation to software and hardware become a major aspect of all IP, but digital elements became key aspects of IP in information, medicines, bio- and nano-technologies and

[86] Carneiro D. et al. (2014) (n 56) ch. 5 and ch. 9.

[87] Ramesh Subramanian and Eddan Katz (eds), *The Global Flow of Information: Legal, Social and Cultural Perspectives* (NYU Press, 2011).

[88] Abdul Paliwala, 'Regulating Cyberspace: Modes of Production, Modes of Regulation and Modes of Resistance' in Ali et al. (n 66) 227.

manufactured goods and processes.[89] The WTO Trade Related Intellectual Property Rights (TRIPS) Agreement globalized IP rights by obliging each state to follow global IP standards. In a form of globalized localism,[90] US economic interests shaped the negotiations and text with the assistance of the United States Trade Representative.[91]

Resistant cultures

This extension has not gone uncontested. New cybercapitalism is based on the notion of free access, whether to communication such as email, information such as Google or social media such as Facebook and Twitter.[92] Cybercapital's new dynamic business models initially rely on advertising, but increasingly rely on new forms of surveillance policing. 'Free' users are being bio-powered into selling their souls for intimate information. With the advent of tethered appliances and data mining, this has become the most significant new market commodity.[93] Cybercapitalists such as Google and Amazon and 'old' capitalists such as media and book publishers have conflicted; for example, in Google's attempt to provide a free searchable library of book contents and the clash between Hachet and Amazon over e-book prices.[94] While either side may win a particular skirmish, the economic power belongs to the new cybercapitalist corporations.

The netizen culture of openness and commonwealth provides a more dynamic alternative to both industrial and cybercapital with the underlying notion of information as a global public good being used to contest the demands of capital within and without the law. We noted the remarkable successes of the free software and content movements in relation to legal information. 'Free' culture promotes a collaborative commons in which creativity is produced through co-operative activity, whether in the production of collaborative works of art or literature or crowdsourcing of research. The culture of individual property rights, on the other hand, constrains this collaboration.[95] The result has been an attempt to restrain a flourishing digital culture by copyright extension

[89] See e.g. the US Digital Millennium Copyright Act in relation to copyright and extension of patenting over life processes by the US Supreme Court. Lawrence Lessig, *Free Culture: The Nature and Future of Creativity* (Penguin, 2005), esp. 187.

[90] Boaventura de Sousa Santos, *Toward a New Legal Common Sense* (2nd ed Butterworths, 2002), 179.

[91] Peter Drahos, 'Negotiating Intellectual Property Rights: Between Coercion and Dialogue' in Peter Drahos and Ruth Mayne (eds), *Global Intellectual Property Rights: Knowledge, Access and Development* (Oxford University Press, 2002), 161.

[92] Eric Wilson, 'Criminogenic Cyber-Capitalism: Paul Virilio, Simulation, and the Global Financial Crisis' (2012), 20:3 *Critical Criminology* September 249–74; Pamela Samuelsen, 'Mass Digitization as Fair Use' (2014), 57:3 *Communications of the ACM* 20–22.

[93] Jonathan Zittrain, *The Future of the Internet: And How to Stop It* (Yale University Press, 2008), ch. 5.

[94] Samuelsen (n 93); Andrew Albanese, *The Battle of $9.99: How Apple, Amazon, and the Big Six Publishers Changed the E-Book Business Overnight* (Google eBook, 2013).

[95] Rosemary Coombe, *The Cultural Life of Intellectual Properties: Authorship, Appropriation and the Law* (Duke University Press, 1998); Benkler (n 22).

reinforced by propaganda that 'copyright violation is piracy' and highly publicized prosecutions of 'pirates'.[96] These conflicting ideas came to a head in a series of cases in the US and abroad in relation to sharing of music across the internet. The resulting decisions in the US courts and abroad have tended to favour the media content corporations and the closing down of sharing sites.[97] Nevertheless, both at national and global levels a resisting society has refused to comply with the demands of capital and law, iconized by the worldwide Pirate Party Movement.[98]

The globalization of IP rights has been perceived as most socially unjust, with the greatest controversy in the case of pharmaceuticals in relation to the global HIV/AIDS pandemic. Yet, another global social injustice is the exacerbation of the digital divide in the context of the global growth in the economic, cultural and social importance of digital forms. While some former developing countries have digitally leapfrogged Western countries, their rise was often based on avoidance and evasion of Western IP claims.[99] There have been global advances in digitization, with digital technology being increasingly available to the elites in developing countries. While cell phones are becoming globally ubiquitous, the poor cannot afford other technology. The qualitative digital divide has been increasing both in terms of access and control over digital technologies, information and processes.[100] Therefore the Right to Development is asserted in counterpoint to WTO/TRIPS and other Western global property interests and became the focus of the World Summit on the Information Society.[101] However, the Summit's proposals were in the main anodyne. Lobbying by global corporate interests led to lukewarm support for Free and Open Software and content movements, but there was no challenge to IP rights other than a muted call for a better balance between developing country interests and IP rights.[102] This led to the

[96] Lawrence Liang, 'Piracy, Creativity and Infrastructure: Rethinking Access to Culture' in Subramaniam and Katz (n 88), 54–89; Lessig (n 90), 53.

[97] Kathy Bowery, *Law and Internet Cultures* (Cambridge University Press, 2005), ch. 5; Paliwala (n 89).

[98] Pirate Parties International: www.pp-international.net accessed 20 September 2014.

[99] Stephen Chen, 'Pirate Production, Intellectual Property and Informal Sectors in Developing Countries' in Tony Fu-Lai Yu, Yuen Wai-Kee, Diana Kwan, *International Economic Development: Leading Issues and Challenges* (Routledge, 2014), 93.

[100] Ayanso (n 26).

[101] World Summit on the Information Society (WSIS) (2003) Declaration of Principles, Building the Information Society: a Global Challenge in the New Millennium, WSIS-03/GENEVA/DOC/4-E 12.12.2003; (2004) Report of the Geneva Phase of the World Summit on the Information Society WSIS-03/GENEVA/9(Rev.1)-E 18.2.2004; (2005a.) Tunis Agenda for the Information Society WSIS-05/TUNIS/DOC/6 (Rev. 1)-E 18.11.2005; (2005b) Tunis Commitment WSIS-05/TUNIS/DOC/7-E 18.11.2005.

[102] Assafa Endeshaw, 'Intellectual property and the digital divide' (2008), (1) *The Journal of Information, Law and Technology* (JILT) www2.warwick.ac.uk/fac/soc/law/elj/jilt/2008_1/endeshaw accessed on 25 July 2014; World Intellectual Property Organization *Proposal by Argentina and Brazil for the Establishment of a Development Agenda for WIPO*(WIPO 2004) www.wipo.int/edocs/mdocs/govbody/en/wo_ga_31/wo_ga_31_11.pdf accessed 20 September 2014.

formation of a 'Friends of Development' Group of fifteen countries (now the WIPO Development Agenda Group) at the World Intellectual Property Organization (WIPO). This Group initiated the proposition that 'IP protection is a policy instrument the operation of which may, in actual practice, produce benefits as well as costs, which may vary in accordance with a country's level of development'.[103] The Group has worked in close collaboration with the netizen community in asserting the development of a fairer global IP policy, leading to the adoption of a Development Agenda by WIPO in 2007. Nevertheless, as with similar developments in the WTO, developed country resistance has meant that there has been no substantial realignment of IP rights.[104]

The most effective form of resistance has been what global corporations term 'piracy'. Liang points to the encroachment of the Global Commons in the digital age as similar to resistance in the eighteenth century to the Black Acts closing common land in Britain.[105] From the perspective of the excluded, especially of the developing countries, who have benefitted from both commercially- and non-commercially-motivated 'piracy', the notion of 'piracy' needs to be challenged. Where commercial 'pirates' are promoting effective transcendence of digital divides, the contestation of rights claims within a context of disobedience to unjust laws raises issues of porous legality or concurrence of illegalities.[106]

9. State surveillance

The state has an even more comprehensive armoury of surveillance than cybercapital, provided that digital corporations comply legally or informally with state demands. Hilary Clinton's call for internet freedom challenged the extensive surveillance practices of undemocratic regimes, whether in China – with its extraordinary Great Firewall of China and a complex system of surveillance maintained by hard legal and soft measures – or in 'Arab Spring' countries:

> So let us recommit ourselves to this cause. Let us make these technologies a force for real progress the world over. And let us go forward together to champion these freedoms for our time, for our young people who deserve every opportunity we can give them.[107]

[103] WIPO ibid.

[104] Catherine Saez (2013), 'Concerns Arise Over Implementation Of WIPO Development Agenda' [2013] *IP Watch* www.ip-watch.org/2013/05/14/concerns-arise-over-implementation-of-wipo-development-agenda accessed 10 September 2014.

[105] Liang (n 97); Chen (n 100); E. P. Thompson, *Whigs and Hunters: Origin of the Black Act* (Harmondsworth, 1985).

[106] Liang (n 97); Paliwala (n 89); cf Lessig (n 90).

[107] Hilary Clinton, 'Remarks on Internet Freedom', *The Newseum*, Washington, DC, 21 January 2010 www.state.gov/secretary/rm/2010/01/135519.htm accessed 5 August 2014.

Unfortunately, this freedom call has been largely undermined by revelations of the practices of Western governments, especially of the US itself, in instituting unconstitutional surveillance and persecution of whistleblowers and other challengers of these activities. Some of these developments were chronicled as early as 2010 by Strossen, but the Wikileaks and Snowden revelations have emphasized the extent to which the state also acts with a range of legal, semi-legal, illegal and formal/informal measures to produce a surveillance state.[108] The basic surveillance framework involves a combination of the National Security Act, the Patriot Act, the Homeland Security Act and the Foreign Intelligence Surveillance Act (FISA) but reinforced by directions and practices of questionable legality. For example, the Patriot Act (S212) provided a defence in civil suits for Internet Service Providers if they voluntarily gave information upon request by state agencies. The National Counter-Terrorism Centre Guidelines issued under the National Security Act provided for wide information on citizens and non-citizens even when there is no information that they are connected to terrorism.[109] The legislative structure suggests a principle that for US citizens there will be protection of constitutional rights to free speech and privacy. However, such rights are not available to foreigners who are governed by FISA. Significantly, Snowden has revealed various devices for the blurring of differences between citizens and foreigners, including sharing by intelligence agencies of Western countries' surveilled information.[110]

The new surveillance transcends traditional forms. Bulk data collection is different from traditional spying, in which specific subjects are pinpointed; all data and data subjects become the object of espionage with the information being provided voluntarily or involuntarily by a network of airlines and digital corporations involved in search engines, emails, cloud computing and social networks. There is blurring of differences between state and private agencies in their roles as information policers – surveillance becomes pluralized. Finally, data collection transcends national boundaries and becomes a global activity involving a network of state and private agencies.

[108] Nadine Strossen, 'Free Speech in an Era of Terrorism, The Regulation of Extremist Speech in the era of Mass Digital Communication: Is Brandenburg Tolerance Obsolete in the Terrorist Era?' (2009) 36 *Pepperdine Law Review* 361; Yochai Benkler, 'A Free Irresponsible Press: Wikileaks and the Battle over the Soul of the Networked Fourth Estate' (2011), 46 *Harv. C.R.-C.L. L.* Rev. 311; Susan Landau, 'Making Sense from Snowden: What's Significant in the NSA Surveillance Revelations' [2013], July Spotlight July 2013, p66; Susan Landau, *Surveillance or Security? The Risks Posed by New Wiretapping Technologies* (MIT Press, 2011).

[109] David Medine, Rachel Brand, Elisabeth Cook, James Dempsey and Patricia Wald, *Report on the Telephone Records Program Conducted Under Section 215 of the USAPATRIOT Act and on the Operations of the Foreign Intelligence Surveillance Court* (Privacy and Civil Liberties Oversight Board, 2014) www.fas.org/irp/offdocs/pclob-215.pdf accessed 12 March 2014.

[110] Susan Landau, Zigmunt Bauman, Didier Bigo, Paulo Esteves, Elspeth Guild, Vivienne Jabri, David Lyon and RBJ Walker, 'After Snowden: Rethinking the Impact of Surveillance' (2014), 8 *International Political Sociology* 121, 130–31.

Sites of resistance

The very porosity between the legal and illegal in these surveillance activities has led to forms of resistance which have also been complex and multidimensional. The legal basis for the resistance has involved constitutional rights, especially in the US, but resistance has transcended national frontiers, sovereignty and human rights.[111] The sites of resistance have been complexly located in individualized evasion of state surveillance, whistle-blowing organizations and individuals, such as Wikileaks and Snowden, netizen organizations which use constitutional and civic resistance devices, national politics of left and right orientation and global political coalitions.

Thus, if we take individual forms of resistance, citizens in countries such as China have used a variety of technical devices to avoid surveillance.[112] Unsurprisingly, Tor[113], one of the main software network anonymity devices, was originally developed by the US navy as part of the quest to promote freedom of the internet in undemocratic countries, but is now used to evade surveillance:

> We've been thinking of state surveillance for years because of our work in places where journalists are threatened. Tor's anonymity is based on distributed trust, so observing traffic at one place in the Tor network, even a directory authority, isn't enough to break it. Tor has gone mainstream in the past few years, and its wide diversity of users – from civic-minded individuals and ordinary consumers to activists, law enforcement, and companies – is part of its security.[114]

Political Netizen resistance has included the electorally successful Swedish and worldwide Pirate Party Movement and the less successful Kim DotCom's New Zealand Internet Party.[115] Transnational political resistance has involved a plural alliance of netizen organizations such as Electronic Frontier Foundation, Western developed countries such as Germany and developing countries such as Brazil. The Alliance has worked successfully to promote a UN General Assembly resolution calling for respect for privacy and free

[111] Landau, 'Making Sense from Snowden' (n 110); Bauman et al. Ibid.; for current legal and other actions see Electronic Frontier Foundation, 'NSA Spying on Americans' Blogsite www.eff.org/nsa-spying accessed 14 September 2014; The TOR Blog 'On Being Targeted by the NSA' blog.torproject.org/category/tags/nsa accessed 20 August 2014.

[112] Giovanni Ziccardi, *Resistance, Liberation Technology and Human Rights in the Digital Age* (Springer, 2012).

[113] The Tor website suggests: 'Tor helps to reduce the risks of both simple and sophisticated traffic analysis by distributing your transactions over several places on the Internet, so no single point can link you to your destination' www.torproject.org accessed 15 December 2014.

[114] Tor blog (n 113).

[115] Pirate Parties International www.pp-international.net; New Zealand Internet Mana Party internet.org.nz; for conflict between the Internet Mana Party and New Zealand Government over surveillance see David Meyer (2014), 'Snowden weighs into New Zealand election with surveillance claims' gigaom.com/2014/09/15/snowden-weighs-into-new-zealand-election-with-surveillance-claims all sites accessed 18 December 2014.

expression rights, a review of surveillance laws and practices and a report from the UN High Commissioner for Human Rights.[116]

However, underneath the complex alliance between netizens seeking cyberspace freedom and countries with questionable surveillance practices lies a paradox:

> The digitized geopolitics assumes that cyberspace is a battlefield and that states must build up their own cyber capabilities in order to defend themselves and/or must engage in international coalitions in order to face the challenges posed by mass surveillance and digital espionage. The paradoxical effect of this particular game seems to be that states' resistance against mass surveillance ultimately reinforces the digitized reason of state regime. Reproducing the opposition between security and freedom, while playing the digitized geopolitics game, states might end up subsuming citizenship and rights to the positional logic of a data subject. While fighting against mass surveillance, states may create the appropriate conditions to conduct mass surveillance themselves.[117]

Thus the principles of netizenship and human rights are threatened by both US dominated globalization of surveillance and its re-territorialization by developed and developing countries in the interests of sovereignty and state security. A more positive transnational coalition of state and netizen groups was formed out of disaffection with corporate and state IP and surveillance practices. This is the 'media haven' of the International Multi-Media Institute in Iceland; a 2010 resolution of the Iceland Parliament intends to protect it through the world's freest media laws.[118]

10. Conclusion

This chapter has used William Twining's broad perspective on general jurisprudence to interrogate the manner in which digitization is affecting legal information, processes and substantive law. Twining has enveloped Hart's analytical positivism with Llewellyn's realism and developed an approach that is contextual and positivist and encompasses globalization. He uses pluralism to illuminate the complex relationships between various levels of formal and informal laws and processes. Global social justice issues, as illustrated by Southern voices, become key concerns of Twining's general jurisprudence.

This has provided an excellent basis for framing an inquiry into the nature and role of digitization on legal information, processes and substantive law, especially because the digitization era requires a reimagining of the formal and

[116] UN General Assembly Resolution on The Right to Privacy in the Digital Age 2013 www.hrw.org/sites/default/files/related_material/UNGA_upload_0.pdf accessed 12 December 2014; UN News Centre 'General Assembly Backs the Right to Privacy in the Digital Age'www.un.org/apps/news/story.asp?NewsID=46780#.VBoB18stC00 accessed 12 December 2014.

[117] Bauman et al. (n 112) 130–31.

[118] International Modern Media Institute, Iceland en.immi.is accessed 20 October 2014.

conceptual legal categories due to the rise of what Castells has termed the Network Information Society. Thus, the weaknesses of analytical positivism become apparent when attempts are made to translate complex legal tasks to the digital mode. Digitization is recasting not only the who and how of doing law-jobs, but the relationships involved among the law users, including law professionals, non-professionals and advice seekers. It also contributes to globalization and pluralization of law-jobs with increasing roles for global plural networks of actors. Finally, this has social justice implications of uneven and often unjust globalization.

There is an equal need for a wider jurisprudential consideration of digitally induced changes in substantive law. This is necessary not merely because of the globalization of, for example, IP law, but also in order to understand the contestations between the North and South, old and new forms of capital, and between ideologies of property rights and commons. Similarly, the extension of surveillance by cybercapital and states, and the struggle against such extension, requires a broader jurisprudential perspective. This has to account for complex networks of global and national state and non-state agencies, digital and transportation corporations, the use of hard and soft power, and formal, informal, technological and legally questionable mechanisms. On the other side stand similarly complex transnational/local netizen interests involved with a variety of forms of legal, porous quasi-legal, illegal and technological forms of resistance.

Twining's contribution is to provide a framework for exploration of these questions. His adherence to realism and positivism enables those who follow his approach to ask a wide variety of questions from very different perspectives. In particular, he is open to, if not deeply engaged with, feminism, post-modernism and critical studies. If there is an apparent contradiction between his positivism and his great intellectual concern with social justice, human rights and 'Southern Voices', there is a possible resolution.[119] By placing great emphasis on these matters within a general jurisprudential context, Twining requires all those constructing a jurisprudential inquiry to address these issues. The challenge of jurisprudence is to enable the broadest inquiry and not to stifle it.

[119] Cf. Alan Norrie, 'Book Review: William Twining, "General Jurisprudence: Understanding Law from a Global Perspective"', *Warwick School of Law Research Paper* (2010) ssrn.com /abstract=1676121 or dx.doi.org/10.2139/ssrn.1676121 accessed 12 September 2014. Norrie acknowledges Twining's main contribution to broadening jurisprudence, but is critical of his positivist distancing of it, and considers his adherence to Hart contradictory and limiting of critical inquiry.

12

Twining on Llewellyn and Legal Realism

*Frederick Schauer**

I

Legal Realism is contested terrain.[1] And it is contested not because of disagreements around the edges of an accepted core idea. Rather, the very nature of Legal Realism is contested, and there exist widely divergent views about just what lies at the core, and about what the central claims and commitments of Legal Realism really are.

A sample of the various positions claiming to ride under the Legal Realist banner will make the extent of this disagreement clearer. Thus, some theorists believe that Legal Realism is centrally about the relative importance of facts in adjudication, in contrast to a traditional view allegedly holding that abstract rules are more important determinants of legal outcomes than are the facts of particular cases.[2] Those who subscribe to this understanding of Legal Realism's core commitments do not, of course, saddle the traditional view with the implausible position that abstract legal rules can be applied to particular cases without regard to the facts presented in those cases. Nevertheless, there remains an important difference in emphasis between a more traditional view that the determination of which facts are relevant comes from pre-existing legal rules, and a more Legal Realist view holding that judicial and other legal decisions are made primarily on the basis of all the facts of a particular

* This chapter is a substantially modified version of the author's *Foreword* to the second edition of William Twining's *Karl Llewellyn and the Realist Movement* (Cambridge 2012)

[1] In this essay, 'Legal Realism' will be capitalized, in large part to emphasize the differences between Legal Realism as a view about some or many aspects of law on the one hand, and the various forms of philosophical realism on the other. In metaphysics and meta-ethics, for example, realist perspectives are associated with a belief in an external or objective reality, as opposed to the view that what we perceive as moral or physical reality is principally the creation of human cultures or the minds of individual human beings. By stressing the mind-independence of an external reality, therefore, most embodiments of philosophical realism stand in contrast to Legal Realism, at least insofar as Legal Realism is ordinarily and properly understood to stress discretion, indeterminacy, non-objectivity and the human element in legal decision-making.

[2] See Brian Leiter, *Naturalizing Jurisprudence: Essays on American Legal Realism and Naturalism in Legal Philosophy* (Oxford 2007); Brian Leiter, 'American Legal Realism,' in Martin P. Golding and William A. Edmundson (eds), *Blackwell Guide to the Philosophy of Law and Legal Theory* (Blackwell, 2005), 50–66; Brian Leiter, 'Legal Realism' in Dennis Patterson, ed., *A Companion to Philosophy of Law and Legal Theory* (Blackwell, 1996), 261–79.

controversy that a particular judge deems relevant, without regard to whether some array of pre-existing legal rules makes those facts relevant or not.

If the facts that some legal decision-maker deems relevant are largely independent of legal rules, then we can perceive the related but different (at least in emphasis) understanding of Realism that focuses substantially on the sequencing of decision-making and justification. Going back at least as far as Judge Joseph Hutcheson's famous 1929 article about the role of the 'hunch' in judicial decision-making,[3] and continuing as the primary focus of Jerome Frank's *Law and the Modern Mind*,[4] theorists and commentators often understood to be Legal Realists have insisted that judges do not first consult the law and thereafter reach a decision on the basis of that law, as the traditional picture would have it. Rather, so Hutcheson and Frank and many others have claimed, judges, like lawyers with a client, initially reach a decision about which party ought to prevail, often on the basis of a full range of both legal and non-legal facts and factors, and then, and only then, do they consult the law in order to justify – or 'rationalize', as Frank was fond of putting it – a decision made substantially on non-legal grounds.

Still another view of Realism contrasts realism with formalism, or at least something claimed to be formalism.[5] Here Realism's target is said to be the view that law is often, usually or almost always determinate, such that the law dictates a particular result, or at least renders ineligible most of the outcomes that would be otherwise eligible on moral, political, economic or pragmatic grounds.[6] The Realist challenge to this view, a challenge sometimes described in terms of indeterminacy[7] and sometimes in terms of functionalism or instrumentalism,[8] is the view that in all, most or many cases, and especially in the controversies that wind up in court or wind up in appellate courts, the law does not uniquely determine a result, with the consequence that the law leaves open to the judge or other decision-maker a broad field of possible results, with the decision-maker then selecting her preferred result on non-legal grounds.[9]

[3] Joseph J. Hutcheson, Jr, 'The Judgment Intuitive: The Function of the "Hunch" in Judicial Decision' (1929), 14 *Cornell Law Journal* 274.

[4] Jerome Frank, *Law and the Modern Mind* (Brentano's, 1930).

[5] See Laura Kalman, *Legal Realism at Yale 1927–1960* (North Carolina, 1986). See also Theodore M. Benditt, *Law as Rule and Principle: Problems of Legal Philosophy* (Stanford, 1978), 2–5; Brian Bix, *Jurisprudence: Theory and Context* (3rd edn, Sweet & Maxwell, 2003), 179–80; Robert S. Summers, *Form and Function in a Legal System* (Cambridge, 2006), 28–9; Anthony J. Sebok, *Legal Positivism in American Jurisprudence* (Cambridge, 1998), 75–83; Brian Z. Tamanaha, *Beyond the Formalist–Realist Divide: The Role of Politics in Judging* (Princeton, 2010).

[6] Perhaps like 'positivism', the term 'formalism' has attracted so many different (and usually pejorative) meanings that it might be better to discard the term entirely. But for an analysis and qualified defense of at least one form of formalism, see Frederick Schauer, 'Formalism' (1988) 97 *Yale Law Journal* 509.

[7] See Kent Greenawalt, *Law and Objectivity* (Oxford 1992), 11; Roger Shiner, *Norm and Nature: The Movements of Legal Thought* (Oxford 1992), 217; Mark Tushnet, *Red, White, and Blue: A Critical Analysis of Constitutional Law* (Harvard, 1988), 191–6.

[8] Kalman, note 5, 29–31.

[9] See Brian Leiter, 'Law and Objectivity' in Jules Coleman and Scott Shapiro (eds), *Oxford Handbook of Jurisprudence and Philosophy of Law* (Oxford, 2002), 969.

The Realist perspectives just described are about judicial decision-making, but other Realist perspectives are about academic method, and in particular on the importance of empirical inquiry in understanding the nature of law and legal decision-making. Thus, Legal Realism is often thought of as the empirical (and largely external[10]) examination of law and its processes, with the aim of allowing lawyers and others to predict legal outcomes,[11] or of offering social science insights or conclusions about the nature of law itself, or, more commonly, of identifying the determinants of legal outcomes. And thus one of the pre-eminent contributions of Legal Realism is commonly claimed to be that social science inquiry about law and legal decision-making is often preferable and more accurate as prediction than the close textual and doctrinal analysis that still pervades legal education and legal scholarship.[12]

One modern characterization of Realism goes in a quite different direction, focusing less on judicial decision-making or academic method and more on the substance of law. More particularly, this view, which sees Robert Hale[13] as a central figure in the Realist tradition,[14] understands Legal Realism as denying

[10] External *not* in the sense of denying the existence of an internal point of view, *pace* H. L. A. Hart, *The Concept of Law* (3rd edn, Penelope A. Bulloch, Joseph Raz and Leslie Green (eds), 2012), but in the far more plausible sense of not taking the testimony of a judge or other legal decision-maker as conclusive evidence of just which rules or norms or values she has in fact internalized. There are many ways of finding out just which rules a judge has internalized, and which thus guide a judge's decision, but the judge's own announcements are hardly the only or even the best of these ways. See Frederick Schauer, 'Legal Realism Untamed' (2013) 91 *Texas Law Review* 749.

[11] The importance of seeing law substantially in terms of predicting legal outcomes is a major theme of Oliver Wendell Holmes, 'The Path of the Law' (1897), 10 *Harvard Law Review* 457. The Realists embraced this idea, as is apparent in Karl N. Llewellyn, *The Theory of Rules*, Frederick Schauer, ed. (Chicago, 2011), 55–60, but took it one step further. Holmes believed that knowledge of legal rules and legal categories would facilitate accurate prediction, but the Realists, *contra* Holmes, stressed that identifying various non-legal factors would often make for better predictions. And thus those modern political scientists who emphasize the role of non-legal factors in determining and predicting Supreme Court decisions are properly understood as heirs to this strand of Realism. See Saul Brenner and Harold J. Spaeth, *Stare Indecisis: The Alteration of Precedent on the Supreme Court, 1946–1992* (Cambridge, 1996); Jeffrey J. Segal and Harold J. Spaeth, *The Supreme Court and the Attitudinal Model Revisited* (Cambridge, 2004). A valuable analysis of the relationship among prediction, Holmes and Realism is William Twining, 'The Bad Man Revisited' (1972), 58 *Cornell Law Review* 275.

[12] See John Henry Schlegel, American Legal Realism and Empirical Social *Science* (North Carolina 1995); Brian Z. Tamanaha, *Realistic Socio-Legal Theory* (Oxford, 1997).

[13] See Robert L. Hale, 'Coercion and Distribution in a Supposedly Non-Coercive State' (1923), 38 *Political Science Quarterly* 470. On Hale and his connection with Realism, see especially Barbara H. Fried, *The Progressive Assault on Laissez Faire: Robert Hale and the First Law and Economics Movement* (Harvard 2002). See also Morton J. Horwitz, *The Transformation of American Law 1870–1960: The Crisis of Legal Orthodoxy* (Harvard, 1992).

[14] Hale, an economist and lawyer, was a Columbia colleague of Llewellyn's, but Llewellyn does not list him among the Realists in Karl Llewellyn 'Some Realism About Realism' (1931), 44 *Harvard Law Review* 1222. This exclusion may or may not be telling about the core commitments of Realism, or Llewellyn's view of those core commitments, and thus the exclusion of Hale may be no more dispositive than the inclusion of Edwin Patterson, whose work bears few earmarks of any Realist perspective. See William Twining, *Karl Llewellyn and the Realist Movement* (2nd edn, Cambridge, 2012), 73–83.

law's alleged neutrality. Legal rules and doctrines, according to this critique, are traditionally thought to be either natural or neutral, or both.[15] To the extent that this view exists, rather than being a caricature or straw man, then the contrasting view – that legal rules, or legal baselines, are actually the product of political and economic choices – is claimed to be the true version of Legal Realism.[16]

II

Although there is thus disagreement about the core commitments of Legal Realism, there is far less about the place of Karl Llewellyn within the Realist canon. Indeed, it would not be much of an exaggeration to claim that any understanding of Legal Realism that did not prominently feature the life and writings of Llewellyn would be defective for just that reason. And that is why any examination of Realism must start with William Twining's enduring project of recovering, explaining and interpreting Llewellyn.

Twining's work on Llewellyn, although commonly associated with Twining's magisterial *Karl Llewellyn and the Realist Movement*,[17] in fact has earlier origins. As a graduate law student and then visiting scholar at the University of Chicago Law School, Twining devoted several years and countless hours to sorting and arranging all of Llewellyn's published and unpublished writings, culminating in the 1968 publication of *The Karl Llewellyn Papers*.[18] This volume remains an essential work for anyone interested in Llewellyn and Realism, not only because Twining's extensive textual commentary provides important context and interpretive commentary, but also because it contains important descriptions of and excerpts from unpublished works.

Indeed, although *Karl Llewellyn and the Realist Movement* is primarily a work of history, biography and interpretation, it also presents summaries of two of Llewellyn's most important works, neither of which had been published when Twining published his book. One, *The Theory of Rules*, has since been published,[19] but the other, one even more important in Twining's view

[15] Blackstone is a particularly common target. See Duncan Kennedy, 'The Structure of Blackstone's Commentaries' (1979) 28 *Buffalo Law Review* 209. It is not at all clear, however, just who actually believed (or believes) that the substantive baselines of legal doctrine are either natural or neutral. Most of the standard suspects, including Joseph Beale (see Twining, note 14, 38–9) and Herbert Wechsler, 'Toward Neutral Principles in Constitutional Law' (1959), 73 Harvard Law Review 1, turn out on close inspection to either have had more complex views or to have believed nothing of the kind.

[16] See Neil Duxbury, *Patterns of American Jurisprudence* (Oxford, 1995); Fried, note 13; Horwitz, note 13, 169–246; Gary Minda, *Postmodern Legal Movements: Law and Jurisprudence at Century's End* (New York University Press, 1995). This substantive conception of Realism is also apparent in the Introduction, chapter introductions, and organization (which does not get to issues of legal reasoning and decision-making until Chapter 6) of William W. Fisher III, Morton J. Horwitz and Thomas A. Reed (eds), *American Legal Realism* (Oxford, 1993).

[17] Note 14. [18] William Twining, *The Karl Llewellyn Papers* (Chicago, 1968).

[19] Llewellyn, note 11.

to understanding Llewellyn, is the still-unpublished *Law in Our Society* manuscript, intended (and used by Llewellyn) as a set of teaching materials, but also an important scholarly contribution to the Realist perspective itself.[20]

Finally, a full grasp of Twining's views on Legal Realism, and on Llewellyn, would have to include Twining's *How to Do Things with Rules*, co-written with David Miers,[21] and like Llewellyn's *Law in Our Society*, designed initially for teaching purposes but containing valuable and original academic insights. Even the briefest glance at the index of *How to Do Things with Rules* makes it clear that Llewellyn is a prominent figure in Twining's view of the nature of legal reasoning, and thus of the actual practice of rule-making, rule-following, precedent and common law adjudication and method.

III

In using Llewellyn in so much of his own work, Twining goes far beyond the role of cataloger, archivist and historian, however invaluable those roles are. For in Twining's understanding of Llewellyn we find a particular point of view, both about Llewellyn and about Legal Realism. With respect to Llewellyn, Twining sees substantial continuity where others see significant change. That is, some number of commentators, including this author,[22] see the later Llewellyn, especially the Llewellyn of *The Common Law Tradition*[23] and perhaps also of *Law in Our Society*, as more moderate, less iconoclastic, more focused on the tempering and stabilizing influences of common law method, and indeed less Realist, than the Llewellyn who in 1930 described rules in *The Bramble Bush* as 'pretty playthings'.[24] It is true, of course, as Llewellyn insisted throughout his career, that even *The Bramble Bush* contained important qualifications often ignored by the critics of Realism.[25] And much the same can be said about many of Llewellyn's other writings of the 1930s and even earlier. But there remains an important question of emphasis and tone, and this is where the disagreement lies. For some, the later Llewellyn so dampened his earlier Realism that the sharpest edges of the Realist perspective seem to have been rounded off, and perhaps unfortunately so. But for Twining, Llewellyn throughout his career recognized the stabilizing forces of law as well as the leeway, even if those stabilizing forces often came from legal culture rather than from formal rules. And thus, although Llewellyn early on aligned himself with virtually all of Jerome Frank's perspectives except for

20 See Twining, note 14, 170–202.

21 William Twining and David Miers, *How to Do Things with Rules* (4th edn, Butterworth's, 1999).

22 See Llewellyn, note 14, Editor's Introduction.

23 Karl N. Llewellyn, *The Common Law Tradition – Deciding Appeals* (Little, Brown, 1960).

24 Karl N. Llewellyn, *The Bramble Bush: On Our Law and Its Study* (Columbia, 1930), 5.

25 As is apparent from a 1942 correspondence with Lon Fuller (provided to me by Kenneth Winston) and also from Karl N. Llewellyn, 'Some Realism about Realism' (1931), 44 *Harvard Law Review* 1222.

Frank's infatuation with psychoanalysis[26] Twining presents us with a moderate and complex Llewellyn whose differences with Frank, Thurman Arnold, Fred Rodell, and the other iconoclastic Realists are more important than the similarities.

Twining's views about the essential consistency over time of Llewellyn's thinking can be seen as well in Twining's views about Realism itself. Although Twining has his share of criticisms of *The Common Law Tradition*,[27] he does not see it as an anti-Realist work as much as Realism in its more sophisticated, nuanced and well-developed form. And again here it is impossible to say that Twining is either right or that he is wrong, in large part because we are talking about matters of emphasis. It is of course true, as both Llewellyn and Twining stress, that the various factors that make law 'reckonable' (Llewellyn's word) stand in some contrast to the caricatured 'what the judge had for breakfast' view of Realism often attributed (although almost certainly erroneously) to Jerome Frank and the other extreme Realists. But given the tendency of lawyers, judges and legal academics to overstate law's reckonability, predictability and doctrinal moorings, it may well be that emphasizing judicial discretion, the psychological and political influences on judicial decision-making and the variability of judicial behaviour is a useful corrective, and a corrective perhaps slighted by those who, like Twining, see in Realism and in much of Llewellyn's work a focus on stability and predictability that is often more absent than both of them appear to believe.

This short essay is hardly the place to engage in a full analysis of these questions about Llewellyn and about Realism. Suffice it to say here that Twining, both in his own work and in his understanding and interpretation of Llewellyn, gives us a sophisticated, subtle and balanced view of legal and judicial decision-making that is properly considered to be part of the Realist canon itself. As with the parable of the blind men and the elephant, determining which aspect of Realism we choose to emphasize is itself a question of standpoint. Indeed, recognizing the importance of standpoint is one of Twining's own enduring contributions.[28] To understand Realism is thus to understand the various standpoints from which Realism can be perceived and evaluated. One of those standpoints gives us the emphasis on predictability, reckonability and the non-formal factors that produce them, as Twining and Llewellyn have stressed, just as another standpoint provides the emphasis on variability and unpredictability so associated with Frank, Rodell and the caricatured Llewellyn. And thus these contrasting emphases can themselves be seen as part of the essentially contested terrain of Legal Realism itself.

[26] Karl N. Llewellyn, 'Frank's Law and the Modern Mind' (1931) 31 *Columbia Law Review* 82.

[27] Twining, note 14, 203–7.

[28] See Twining, note 11. See also William Twining, 'Other People's Powers: The Bad Man and English Positivism, 1897-1997' (1997), 63 *Brooklyn Law Review* 189.

IV

Each of the many understandings of Legal Realism has its adherents. Members of and sympathizers with the Critical Legal Studies Movement, for example, tend to promote the last-mentioned of the various interpretations described in Section I above,[29] insisting that Legal Realism was centrally about recognizing the non-neutrality and consequent political choices implicit in substantive legal doctrine.[30] Moreover, both the qualitative and the quantitative social scientists who study the operation of law with empirical methods claim to be fostering the 'new legal realism', even as their methods (and home disciplines) vary widely.[31]

It would be tempting to dismiss as irrelevant or distracting these contrasting perspectives on the allegedly 'true' nature of Legal Realism. The disputes, some might be tempted to say, are merely contests about a label, and labels are just that – labels with no intrinsic reality. But the temptation should be resisted. Labels often make a difference in terms of how we perceive, categorize and organize the world, and the battle over how we should understand Legal Realism and the tradition that created it is in reality a battle over ownership of the legacy of perhaps the most important strand of American legal theory, or, at the very least, the most characteristically American strand of American legal theory. Any attempt to frame or to reframe Legal Realism, therefore, is best understood not as one side of a debate about labels, but rather as an offer or attempt to reach an understanding of a large component of the American legal tradition.[32]

[29] See Horwitz, note 13; Guyora Binder, 'Critical Legal Studies' in Patterson, *A Companion to Philosophy of Law*, note 2, 280. See also Andrew Altman, *Critical Legal Studies: A Liberal Critique* (Princeton, 1990), 106–17.

[30] It is worth noting, however, that one goal of the Critical Legal Studies movement is/was also to continue the more conventionally understood dimensions of the Realist project, in particular the focus on law's indeterminacy and the consequent choices open to a judge in any particular case. See Duncan Kennedy, 'Freedom and Constraint in Adjudication: A Critical Phenomenology' (1986) 36 *Journal of Legal Education* 518; Mark Tushnet, 'Critical Legal Studies: An Introduction to Its Origins and Underpinnings' (1986), 36 *Journal of Legal Education* 505.

[31] Compare Howard Erlanger et al., 'Is It Time for a New Legal Realism?' (2005) 2005 *Wisconsin Law Review* 335, with Daniel A. Farber, 'Toward a New Legal Realism' (2001), 68 *University of Chicago Law Review* 279, with Thomas J. Miles and Cass R. Sunstein, 'The New Legal Realism' (2008) 75 *University of Chicago Law Review* 831. See also Victoria E. Nourse and Gregory C. Shaffer, 'Varieties of New Legal Realism: Can a New World Order Prompt a New Legal Theory?' (2009), 95 *Cornell Law Review* 61.

[32] It is worth noting that the connections between American Legal Realism and the Scandinavian Legal Realism of Axel Hägerström, A. Vilhelm Lundstedt, Karl Olivecrona and Alf Ross (see Gregory S. Alexander, 'Comparing the Two Legal Realisms – American and Scandinavian' (2002) 50 *American Journal of Comparative Law* 131) are, at best, attenuated. Although the Scandinavian Realists shared some political goals with many of the American Realists, the fundamental core of Scandinavian Realism is a scepticism about the objectivity (or even the point) of morality, a view that was drawn from the logical positivism that flourished during the period when many of the Scandinavian Realists were writing. See Patricia Mindus, *A Real Mind: The Life and Work of Axel Hägerström* (Springer 2009). Some of the American Realists may

Of course, the various perspectives on or strands of Legal Realism need not be thought of as necessarily mutually exclusive. The importance of an external empirical study of the determinants of legal decisions, for example, is fully compatible with the view that non-legal factors are pre-eminent among those determinants; and the view that non-legal factors are of principal importance is similarly compatible with the view that the equities of the particular facts of particular cases are among the most important of the non-legal factors. On the other hand, the view that legal rules are indeed causally important in judicial decision-making, but that the rules that are causally important diverge from the 'paper rules' found in law books, a view most attributable to Llewellyn,[33] is in some tension with the fact-focused particularism of Hutcheson, Frank and others. Even putting such tensions aside, however, matters of emphasis are important. Consequently, the question of the true or central nature of Legal Realism persists. It was a question that much concerned Llewellyn in 'Some Realism about Realism',[34] and it is a question whose importance should not be so easily dismissed as simply being about 'mere' labels.

Asking about the 'real' nature of something, however, is fraught with perils. Famously, J. L. Austin treated 'real' as his primary example of what he (unfortunately) called a 'trouser-word', in the sense of there being some other word, the negation, that 'wore the trousers' by virtue of playing the leading role.[35] Thus, we do not really know what it is for something to be 'real' unless we have an understanding of the particular form of unreality that the designation of something as 'real' is intended to reject. A coat that is said to be made of real fur, for example, is an assertion that the coat is not made out of imitation fur, but it is not an assertion that the fur is not toy fur, yet in other contexts 'real' means 'not a toy', as when in some contexts we talk about a real car when we mean precisely to say that it is not a toy car.

In the context of law, therefore, it is interesting to wonder just what form of unreality the various claims of Legal Realism to be real are attempting to deny. There are numerous candidates for such claimed unrealities, and each of the characterizations of Realism described above is premised on a belief that there is a certain kind of unreality that would be usefully disabused by accepting the Realist challenge. Thus, and as noted in Section I above, for some the relevant unreality is the belief that legal decision-making is rule- rather than fact-intensive; for others it is the belief that judges do not decide on an outcome until after consulting the relevant legal rules; for still others it is the belief that

have been similarly sceptical about the objectivity of morality, but the American Realist enterprise was far removed from addressing such issues.

[33] See Karl Llewellyn, 'A Realistic Jurisprudence: The Next Step' (1930), 30 *Columbia Law Review* 431; Schauer, note 10.

[34] Note 9. It is important to note, however, that Llewellyn, both in this article and elsewhere, had a decidedly non-essentialist view about the nature of Legal Realism, believing that it was more a state of mind than a program or a movement, and believing that multiple and partially divergent perspectives could all properly be characterized as Realist.

[35] J. L. Austin, *Sense and Sensibilia* (G. J. Warnock, ed., Oxford, 1962), 15–19, 63–77.

judicial opinions are an accurate description of the thinking and reasoning processes of judges,[36] and there is also the form of unreality represented by the belief that the best way to understand law is by engaging in the largely non-empirical analysis of reported appellate opinions.[37] And so on. And thus when Holmes observed, famously, that 'the life of law has not been logic, it has been experience,'[38] he not only established himself as a Realist precursor in seeking to debunk a long-held belief about the nature of common law reasoning, but emphasized that we understand legal perspectives substantially by what they seek to reject. Had there not been a tradition of treating common law development as a process of logical discovery, Holmes's quip would have made no sense. It gets its bite precisely from the existence of what it seeks to rebut. And so too with much of Legal Realism, whose enduring importance stems largely from the cluster of traditional views about legal thought and judicial decision-making that it has sought, from the beginning, to challenge.

V

But given that there are competing conceptions of Legal Realism, and thus competing conceptions of just which accepted beliefs about the nature of law and legal decision-making are in need of debunking, how are we to resolve the controversy? One possibility is that there is no need to resolve it at all. If Legal Realism is more a state of mind than a concrete position, as Llewellyn long insisted,[39] then it could well be that the various positions associated with

[36] Even outside of the Realist canon and explicit discussions about Realism, there is a normative debate about whether judges are, or should be, candid in their opinions. Compare David Shapiro, 'In Defense of Judicial Candor' (1987) 100 *Harvard Law Review* 731, with Scott C. Idleman, 'A Prudential Theory of Judicial Candor' (1995), 73 *Texas Law Review* 1307. And Richard A. Wasserstrom, *The Judicial Decision: Toward a Theory of Legal Justification* (Stanford 1961), distinguishes the role of law in causing legal decisions – the logic of decision – from its role in justifying them – the logic of justification.

[37] It is often said that 'we are all Realists now', Gary Peller, 'The Metaphysics of American Law' (1985), 73 *California Law Review* 1151; Joseph William Singer, 'Legal Realism Now' (1988), 76 *California Law Review* 465, 467, but it is far from clear that that is actually so. Obviously the truth of the claim that we are now all Realists depends on the conception of Realism that the claimant holds, but there are some indications that the main lines of the Realist critique remain resisted. For one example, consider the torts casebook developed by Leon Green, a central Realist figure. Green believed that the determinants of outcomes in torts cases were not formal doctrines, such as foreseeability and proximate cause and reasonable care, but rather the factual situations in which claims arose. As a result, he organized his casebook not around the traditional legal categories of tort law but instead around the factual categories of the world, such as railways and animals. Leon Green, *The Judicial Process in Torts Cases* (West, 1931). Yet it is noteworthy that no modern torts book takes a similar approach. Is this rejection of Green's approach based on the view that Green was empirically mistaken, and that the formal categories of tort law have more to do with outcomes in tort cases than the factual situations in which tort claims arise, or is it perhaps because there is more resistance to the core claims of Legal Realism than the common incantation of 'we are all Realists now' appears to imagine? On the latter possibility, albeit with a somewhat different conception of Realism in mind, see Hanoch Dagan, 'The Realist Conception of Law' (2007) 57 *University of Toronto Law Journal* 607.

[38] Oliver Wendell Holmes, Jr, *The Common Law* (Little, Brown, 1881), 1.

[39] See note 34.

Realism are connected by nothing more than a family resemblance, a cluster of related positions sharing no common features among all. And it is also possible that the claims of Legal Realism become appropriately transformed over time, adapting to the needs and issues and concerns of the present, rather than being limited to the topics and questions that happened to have occupied a certain group of people at a particular time. Just as history, even the history of the same events, is (or must be) rewritten for each generation, maybe so too is the history, the meaning, the legacy and the importance of Legal Realism different now than it was in the 1980s, and different in the 1980s from what it was in the 1950s, and different in the 1950s from what it was in the 1930s.

Yet however we seek to define the task of understanding Realism, we cannot, or at least should not, avoid an inquiry that is at least in part historical. After all, there existed real Realists. Llewellyn and Frank and Oliphant and many others were real people who had real thoughts and who wrote real books and real articles. And while there might be genuine debates about whether certain figures were or were not Legal Realists – Oliver Wendell Holmes, John Chipman Gray, Benjamin Cardozo, Robert Hale and others are often the subject of such debates – these debates about inclusion or exclusion are debates at the periphery, debates about figures whose entitlement to the Realist label is open to legitimate disagreement. But no-one seriously doubts that Jerome Frank, Karl Llewellyn, Felix Cohen, Herman Oliphant, Hessel Yntema, William Douglas, Wesley Sturges, Thurman Arnold, Max Radin, Leon Green and Underhill Moore, among others, existed at the historical core of American Legal Realism from the 1920s to the 1940s, and an understanding of Legal Realism that does not recognize the centrality of at least most of these major figures is more usefully understood as an attempt to hijack the Legal Realist legacy rather than as an effort to understand or continue it.

Once we acknowledge the importance of history in understanding Legal Realism, and once we acknowledge as well the central position of a small group of principal players in defining what Realism was and remains, we are led to still another aspect of the importance of Twining's *Karl Llewellyn and the Realist Movement.* It would be tempting to describe the book as a 'classic', but that description understates its importance. Although others have written about Karl Llewellyn,[40] and although the work of numerous scholars has illuminated Llewellyn's special role in the development of commercial law as we know it,[41]

[40] See N. E. H. Hull, *Roscoe Pound and Karl Llewellyn: Searching for an American Jurisprudence* (Chicago, 1997); Wilfrid E. Rumble, *American Legal Realism: Skepticism, Reform, and the Judicial Process* (Cornell, 1968); Brian Leiter, 'Karl Nickerson Llewellyn (1893–1962)' in *International Encyclopedia of the Social and Behavioral Sciences*, Karl Ulrich Meyer, ed. (Elsevier, 2001), 8999.

[41] See Douglas G. Baird, 'Llewellyn's Heirs' (2002), 62 *Louisiana Law Review* 1287; Ingrid Michelsen Hillinger, 'The Article 2 Merchant Rules: Karl Llewellyn's Attempt to Achieve The Good, The True, The Beautiful in Commercial Law' (1985), 73 *Georgetown Law Review* 1141; Allen R. Kamp, 'Karl Llewellyn, Legal Realism, and the UCC in Context' (1995), 59 *Albany Law Review* 325; Gregory E. Maggs, 'Karl Llewellyn's Fading Imprint on the Jurisprudence of the

nothing even approaches Twining's book in its comprehensiveness. If nothing else, it is the definitive intellectual biography of an enduring figure in American legal theory, and the most penetrating analysis of the ideas of one of the small number of people who, from the 1920s until the 1960s, were at the pinnacle of American legal thought.[42]

But the volume's title is accurate. This is a book not only about Llewellyn, but also, and perhaps more importantly, about American Legal Realism. Implicit in the title, of course, is Twining's view that one cannot understand Realism without understanding Llewellyn's thought,[43] and Twining's implicit assumption that Llewellyn was arguably the most important of the Realists. Some – Herman Oliphant,[44] Underhill Moore[45] and Joseph Hutcheson,[46] as well as the aforementioned and more complex Holmes and Gray[47] – may have been earlier. And others – Jerome Frank,[48] Thurman Arnold[49] and Fred Rodell[50] – may have

Uniform Commercial Code' (2000), 71 *University of Colorado Law Review*, vol. 71 (2000); James Whitman, 'Commercial Law and the American Volk: A Note on Llewellyn's German Sources for the UCC' (1987), 97 *Yale Law Journal* 156; Zipporah Barshaw Wiseman, 'The Limits of Vision: Karl Llewellyn and the Merchant Rules' (1987), 100 *Harvard Law Review* 465.

42 I will not list those who I believe are the others, for fear of treating and ranking legal theorists and thinkers as if they were movie actors or footballers.

43 For a similar view about the importance of biography to understanding Realism, see Roy Kreitner, 'Biographing Realist Jurisprudence' (2010), 35 *Law & Social Inquiry* 765.

44 Oliphant's 'A Return to Stare Decisis' (1928), 14 *American Bar Association Journal* 71, is based on a speech given in 1927, and Oliphant had been active in Realist-sounding curricular reform at the Columbia Law School from the early 1920s. See Kalman, note 5, 68–75.

45 Moore's empirical Realism was evident as early as his 1923 'The Rational Basis of Legal Institutions' (1923), 23 *Columbia Law Review* 609, and he too was involved in the curricular upheavals at the Columbia Law School that started even earlier. See Schlegel, note 8.

46 Hutcheson's most memorable writing was in 1929, Hutcheson, note 3, and the roots of his thinking and writing go back somewhat earlier. See Charles L. Zelden, 'The Judge Intuitive: The Life and Judicial Philosophy of Judge Joseph C. Hutcheson, Jr.' (1998), 39 *South Texas Law Review* 905.

47 More complex in the sense that they are better thought of as precursors to Realism than Realists themselves. See Frederick Schauer, *Thinking Like a Lawyer: A New Introduction to Legal Reasoning* (Harvard, 2009), 124–8.

48 Especially in *Law and the Modern Mind*, note 4, but also in Jerome Frank, *If Men Were Angels* (Harper & Brothers, 1942), and Jerome Frank, 'Are Judges Human? Part One: The Effect on Legal Thinking of the Assumption That Judges Behave like Human Beings' (1931), 80 *University of Pennsylvania Law Review* 17. It is common to dismiss Frank as a comparatively unimportant figure in Realist thought, partly because of the infatuation with the naïve and crude version of psychoanalytic theory represented in *Law and the Modern Mind* and other early works, and partly because of his combative and flamboyant language. But Frank's views about the importance of particular facts in particular cases and about the order of decision and justification are important aspects of Realist thought as to which Frank was one of the initial contributors. See Charles Barzun, 'Jerome Frank and the Modern Mind' (2010), 58 *Buffalo Law Review* 1127.

49 See Thurman W. Arnold, 'The Jurisprudence of Edward S. Robinson' (1932), 41 Yale Law Journal 1282. See also Spencer Weber Waller, *Thurman Arnold: A Biography* (New York University Press 2005); Neil Duxbury, 'Some Radicalism about Realism? Thurman Arnold and the Politics of Modern Jurisprudence' (1990), 10 *Oxford Journal of Legal Studies* 11.

50 See Fred Rodell, *Woe Unto You, Lawyers!* (Reynal & Hitchcock, 1935). And see the description of Rodell in Charles Alan Wright, 'Goodbye to Fred Rodell' (1980), 89 *Yale Law Journal* 1456.

produced more shock value by the boldness of their arguments, the extravagance of their prose, and the nature of their personalities. But Llewellyn (who had no need to yield to anyone with respect to colourful prose or noteworthy personal characteristics) was a presence at something close to the beginning, and – by virtue of his positions at Yale, Columbia and Chicago, of his anthropological work,[51] and of his role in the creation of modern commercial law[52] – was the pervasive presence of Legal Realism for at least thirty years. To understand Llewellyn is simply to understand Realism, and to understand Realism is to begin to understand Llewellyn, Twining insists, and in that he is plainly correct.

Karl Llewellyn and the Realist Movement was, when first written, the right book on the right topic to understand Legal Realism, and it remains so forty years on. The book is comprehensive, meticulously researched from original archival sources, engagingly presented, and, perhaps most importantly, jurisprudentially sophisticated. Twining started his academic career with and immersed in Llewellyn and Realism, but he has continued as a substantial figure in legal theory in his own right. His work on the theory and history of evidence and proof remains definitive;[53] he has made major contributions to thinking about legal reasoning.[54] In much of his recent work he has attempted, with much success, to try to understand legality in a world of highly diverse cultures and legal systems.[55] As the Afterword to *Karl Llewellyn and the Realist Tradition* makes stunningly clear, Twining thinks and writes about the nature of law in a way that situates him at an angle from the mainstream of contemporary analytic jurisprudence, and in this respect he is not only Llewellyn's biographer, curator, and interpreter, but also his heir. But like Llewellyn, who knew his Austin and Kelsen thoroughly, it would be a mistake to confuse Twining's iconoclasm with a lack of sophistication or a lack of knowledge. When *Karl Llewellyn and the Realist Movement* was first written 1971, Twining was very much a part of the world of jurisprudence, and it is a world with which he remains connected and one he understands well. And thus one of the things that sets *Karl Llewellyn and the Realist Movement* apart from most of the other books and articles about Llewellyn and about Legal Realism is that the meticulous and exhaustively documented historical account that Twining provides is combined with an understanding of legal theory that is evident

[51] Karl Llewellyn and E. Adamson Hoebel, *The Cheyenne Way* (University of Oklahoma Press, 1941). Various other works with an anthropological orientation, most published in the 1940s and 1950s, are listed in Twining's definitive bibliography of Llewellyn's published and unpublished works. *The Karl Llewellyn Papers*, note 18. See also Ajay K. Mehrotra, 'Law and the "Other": Karl N. Llewellyn, Cultural Anthropology, and the Legacy of *The Cheyenne Way*' (2001), 26 *Law & Social Inquiry* 741.

[52] See note 41.

[53] See especially William Twining, *Rethinking Evidence: Exploratory Essays* (2nd edn, Cambridge, 2006); William Twining, *Theories of Evidence: Bentham and Wigmore* (Weidenfeld & Nicolson, 1985).

[54] Twining & Miers, note 21.

[55] William Twining, *General Jurisprudence: Understanding Law from a Global Perspective* (2009).

from Twining's other work, but which in this book frames and informs his analysis of Legal Realism in unique and important ways.

VI

As set out in Section II above, Twining's Llewellyn and Twining's Realism are both very much informed by a particular point of view. Thus, although there are those – this author among them – who are inclined to see a substantial shift in Llewellyn's thought over the years, and who are inclined to take seriously what some think of as the more extreme claims of Legal Realism, Twining sees mostly consistency in Llewellyn's thought throughout the years, and he is at pains to emphasize that many of the seemingly more guarded conclusions of Llewellyn's later work were present even from the beginning.[56] For Twining, Llewellyn was never as extreme as the opening pages of *The Bramble Bush* suggest, and never as narrowly focused on appellate adjudication as some have thought. And thus Twining argues that the full compass of Llewellyn's thought and contributions were there to be found by the careful reader more or less from the very beginning. Similarly, therefore, a full appreciation of Realism is, for Twining, an appreciation of Realism's focus on legal culture as well as appellate adjudication, and an empirical and sensitive understanding of law's determinacies as well as its indeterminacies.

Twining's account thus takes a strong position, and that is part of its value, both for those who agree and those who disagree. For those who disagree, and I am among them, at least in part, Twining's accurate excavation of the origins of Llewellyn's later thought in Llewellyn's earlier writing may slight important differences of emphasis. Yes, there are connections between the Llewellyn of *The Bramble Bush* and 'Some Realism About Realism' on the one hand, and the Llewellyn of the Uniform Commercial Code and *The Common Law Tradition* on the other, but there may also be discontinuities. And this should not be surprising. Over the course of a long and complex career, Llewellyn not only grew older (and maybe wiser), but become more immersed in the world of practice and the world of law reform, and became more aware of the role of law in other cultures. It would be surprising if such a wealth of experiences over thirty years did not change the thought of someone with as curious and fertile a mind as Llewellyn, and consequently it may tell only part of the story to emphasize the undoubted continuities over time without also noting the numerous changes over the span of a long and productive career in different institutions in different places.

[56] Thus, there are themes in Llewellyn's later work that are foreshadowed, and in a more understated way than in *The Bramble Bush*, in *The Case Law System in America*, Michael Ansaldi (trans.), Paul Gewirtz (ed.) (University of Chicago Press, 1989), originally written in German as *Präjudizienrecht und Rechtssprechung in Amerika*, published in Germany in 1933, and based on lectures that Llewellyn delivered in Leipzig in 1928.

Perhaps more significantly, it may be important to recognize that Llewellyn at his most extreme may have been more correct than either Twining or many others have recognized. Rules may not be 'pretty playthings', as Llewellyn, to his regret, noted in the opening pages of *The Bramble Bush*, but the extent of their causal contribution to legal outcomes may still be exaggerated by those who make their living thinking and teaching about legal rules and legal doctrine. Indeed, although Llewellyn was insistent throughout his life that 'real' legal rules diverged in important ways from the literal meaning of the 'paper rules' that one could find in statute books and summarized in black letters in hornbooks and casebooks,[57] he did subscribe to the view that the real rules were causally important in determining legal outcomes, and that various non-rule factors of professional craft and culture exercised a stabilizing and moderating influence on the operation and development of law.[58] But perhaps Llewellyn, whose admiration for the culture of real lawyers and real judges was considerable, and who respected the collective wisdom of the legal establishment (he called them 'the lawmen'), overestimated, whether always or eventually, the determinacy of even law broadly conceived, and underestimated the role that ephemeral personal, psychological, political and economic factors played in causing legal results. Perhaps, therefore, the less qualified utterances of the earlier Llewellyn, along with the even less qualified utterances of Jerome Frank, for example, and others, still have more to teach us then Twining's Llewellyn, or even anyone else's Llewellyn, or possibly even the later Llewellyn, may have imagined.

VI

That Twining's picture offers falsifiable hypotheses and strong but debatable conclusions is, of course, an unqualified virtue and not a vice. *Karl Llewellyn and the Realist Movement,* as well as Twining's other writings on Llewellyn and on Legal Realism, provide not only a wealth of historical detail and interstitial insight, but also stake out a position about the meaning of Legal Realism and about the nature of Llewellyn's thought that no legal theorist or historian of American legal thought can afford to ignore. But now, with the addition to the Twining corpus of his genuinely new and lengthy Afterword to the second edition of *Karl Llewellyn and the Realist Movement*, Twining's most recent writing on Realism, the importance of that book is even greater. But the Afterword also situates Llewellyn and Realism within the modern jurisprudential terrain, a terrain that was just beginning to develop in the late 1960s and early 1970s. This is a terrain that tends, by and large, to ignore Llewellyn and to ignore Legal Realism, with most of its inhabitants remaining largely in the thrall of H. L. A. Hart's misreading of Llewellyn and misunderstanding of

[57] See Schauer, note 10. [58] See especially, Llewellyn, *The Theory of Rules*, note 11.

Legal Realism in *The Concept of Law*.[59] Moreover, it is a terrain, as Twining emphatically believes, that has achieved a degree of philosophical sophistication at the expense of the empirical Realism that was central to Llewellyn's thought, and, more importantly, at the expense of understanding the phenomenon of law as it exists in the world we know.

As with his interpretations of Llewellyn and Realism, Twining's concerns about the directions of modern legal theory will undoubtedly attract objections as well as agreement. But this is to be applauded and not dismissed. In offering, in the Afterword, new and important historical data along with crisp and challengeable claims about the nature of legal theory as it is practiced today, Twining has combined the historical with the jurisprudential in a way that makes him not only our foremost interpreter of Legal Realism, but a central figure himself in Realism's enduring legacy.

[59] In Chapter Seven of *The Concept of Law*, note 10 above, Hart not only ignores Llewellyn's qualifications of the early passages of *The Bramble Bush*, qualifications that Hart himself had acknowledged several years earlier in H. L. A. Hart, 'Positivism and the Separation of Law and Morals' (1958), 71 Harvard Law Review 593, 615 note 40, and thus not only too easily brands Llewellyn as a 'rule sceptic', but also makes several more substantive blunders. He characterizes Realism as being concerned only with the external prediction of judicial decisions, although Llewellyn and others had long recognized the internal as well as external points of view. And he accuses the Realists of conflating the disputed edges of legal rules with all of law, although once again Llewellyn and others had explicitly insisted that their claims about legal indeterminacy were limited to litigated or appellate cases, and that litigated cases bear the same relationship to the underlying pool of disputes 'as does homicidal mania or sleeping sickness, to our normal life'. *The Bramble Bush,* 58. A valuable modern edition of *The Bramble Bush* is Karl N. Llewellyn, *The Bramble Bush: On Our Law and Its Study* (Oxford, 2009).

13

Theorizing as activity: transnational legal theory in context♠

*Peer Zumbansen**

1. Conceptual adequacy: never just about the 'words'

> [T]here is a need for sustained critical analysis of the adequacy of our existing stock of concepts for transnational legal discourse, both law talk (the discourse *of* rules and its presuppositions) and talk about law (discourses *about* any legal phenomena).[1]

A set of questions that is plaguing legal scholars today concerns the degree to which well established, legal doctrinal categories and concepts may or may not continue to retain meaning in a transnational, in itself highly contested context of regulatory institutions, processes and ideas. Depending on one's affiliation with either a 'private' or a 'public' law mindset, the answers seem to differ quite markedly. Whereas the scholars close to the private law camp appear to be quite relaxed about the prospect,[2] public lawyers, by contrast, evince considerable skepticism.[3] Can it be that transnational private lawyers are more at ease with the idea of making the global world their oyster than public lawyers? And, if so, why? Is it because public lawyers – more systematically than private lawyers – investigate the prospect of law beyond the

♠ The title of this essay is inspired by William Twining's self-depiction as 'a late convert to the idea of treating theorizing as an activity rather than as a subject'. See his article: 'Reading Law', 24 *Valparaiso University Law Review*, 1–35 (1989), 19. See also William Twining, *General Jurisprudence. Understanding Law from a Global Perspective* (2009), 9–10, 'Jurisprudence as activity', and 242ff, for a succinct engagement with the related, 'transnationalisation of empirical legal studies'.

* I am grateful for valuable comments from Upendra Baxi, Priya Gupta and Christopher McCrudden.

1 William Twining, *Have concepts, will travel: analytical jurisprudence in a global context*, 1 *International Journal of Law in Context* 5 (2005), 6.

2 J. H. Dalhuisen, 'Legal Orders and their Manifestation: The Operation of the International Commercial and Financial Legal Order and its Lex Mercatoria', 24 *Berkeley Journal of International Law* 129 (2006); Klaus-Peter Berger, 'Transnational Commercial Law in the Age of Globalization', 42 *Centro di studi e ricerche di diritto comparato e straniero* 1 (2001).

3 Armin Bogdandy, Philipp Dann and Matthias Goldmann, 'Developing the Publicness of Public International Law', 9 *German Law Journal* 1375 (2008); Anne Peters, 'The Merits of Global Constitutionalism', 16 *Indiana Journal of Global Legal Studies* 397 (2009); Martin Loughlin, 'The Constitutional Imagination', 78 *Modern Law Review* 1 (2015).

nation-state using both 'administrative'[4] and 'constitutional'[5] law principles and ponder on the essential and collateral damages that globalization processes inflict on state institutions? This apparently less worried state of mind displayed by private lawyers would, indeed, be cause for concern, but less for surprise. It too much echoes the divide between the cavalier attitude by the 'law and economics' generation of domestic private lawyers towards preserving the twentieth century interventionist and welfare state, and those who want to extend and productively transform it.[6] Today's contested transnational legal efforts to regulate global business now appear as little more than a replay of the struggle for domination between state and market that has marked Western states since the late nineteenth century.[7] The stark polemics governing this debate can hardly hide the deep-seated political positions of the participants, and the stakes are, indeed, high now that the regulatory aspirations once associated with the state need a new institutional framework. A design of such scope is daunting and cuts across the skills and competences, and surely also the imaginations, of lawyers, social theorists and political philosophers. Each discipline is trying to make sense of what has emerged and might emerge in the future under the label of 'globalization'.

Law becomes entangled with its legal instruments and its concepts in very concrete historical, socio-economic, regional and local settings. This prompts the question – well known, of course, to all those who set out to both *relativize* law's connection to the state[8] and *provincialize* the Western experience – of whether a Weberian narrative of state and law modernization is still appropriate.[9] Both relativization and provincialization have tremendous consequences for just about any engagement with 'law', from the way we look at which 'facts' are considered as *relevant*[10] to any attempt at delineating the scope and boundaries of a

[4] Benedict Kingsbury, Nico Krisch, Richard B. Stewart and Jarrod Wiener, 'Global Governance as Administration – National And Transnational Approaches to Global Administrative Law', 68 *Law & Contemporary Problems* 1 (2005).

[5] Michel Rosenfeld, 'Rethinking constitutional ordering in an era of legal and ideological pluralism', 6 *International Journal of Constitutional Law* 415 (2008); Neil Walker, 'Taking Constitutionalism Beyond the State', 56 *Political Studies* 519 (2008).

[6] David Campbell, 'The End of Posnerian Law and Economics', 73 *Modern Law Review* 305 (2010); Peer Zumbansen, 'Law After the Welfare State: Formalism, Functionalism and the Ironic Turn of Reflexive Law', 56 *American Journal of Comparative Law* 769 (2008); David Charny, 'Illusions of a Spontaneous Order: "Norms" in Contractual Relationships', 144 *University of Pennsylvania Law Review* 1841 (1996).

[7] Daniela Caruso, 'Private Law and State-Making in the Age of Globalization', 39 *New York University Journal of International Law & Politics* 1 (2006).

[8] See e.g. William Twining, *Globalisation and Legal Theory* (2000), 10–13, and Boaventura de Sousa Santos, *Toward a New Legal Common Sense: Law, Globalization, and Emancipation* (2002).

[9] Dipesh Chakrabarty, *Provincializing Europe. Postcolonial Thought and Historical Difference*, 2nd ed. [orig. 2000] (2007).

[10] William Twining, 'Taking Facts Seriously', 34 *Journal of Legal Education* 22 (1984), 41: 'There is more to the study of law than the study of rules.' William Twining, 'Taking Facts Seriously – Again', 55 *Journal of Legal Education* 360 (2005), 367: 'As the discipline of law becomes more

'legal' order.[11] One of the central contentions I would like to put forward in this regard is that such a declared 'socio-legal' approach never just arises out of pure interest in how things look, taste or operate. Studying the tensions – indeed the rifts and wilful demarcations – between a private and a public 'lawyer's' universe in the muddy realm of contracting social norms and self-regulation, we are inescapably confronted with the 'why'. We must ask 'in whose name', 'in whose interest' is this zone of 'market self-regulation' being promulgated and effectively shielded from state 'intervention'? In other words, our investigations in legal and normative pluralism prompt us to explore the lines between legal and political thought and the fragile state of balance between them, as we constantly negotiate the demands of each. Just how this should be done is something that engages us as scholars, teachers, mentors, activists and humans.

It is against this background that the interventions and contributions, teaching methods and engagements of a towering figure such as William Twining should be understood and appreciated. His work is carried out simultaneously on numerous fronts and is marked above all, perhaps, by a commitment to seriousness: seriousness in trying to understand, before advancing a proposal; seriousness in listening to others, as well as making their voices heard.[12] There are, for example, numerous examples in today's engagements with so-called 'soft law', 'self-regulation' and 'private ordering', where drawing the line between what Twining calls 'normative' and the 'legal pluralism' becomes *impossible* as a definitional exercise.[13] It becomes *necessary*, however, to point out the stakes and the interests in such demarcations and the associated fights over territory, as they play out in the real world. The following remarks, albeit in too cursory a manner, aim to point to a number of contexts in which these stakes become tangible and where we are challenged more than usual to formulate a position, as scholars and as teachers. By engaging with Twining's immensely perceptive discussion of a number of categories and application fields that are key here – 'facts', 'cases', 'narratives' and 'skills' – I hope to draw several preliminary conclusions regarding the still-evolving contours of socio-legal scholarship and teaching in *a transnational* context.

cosmopolitan, more attention will inevitably have to be paid to the European, international, transnational and comparative aspects of evidence.'

[11] William Twining, 'Normative and Legal Pluralism: A Global Perspective', 20 *Duke Journal of Comparative & International Law* 473 (2010), 510ff, highlighting the importance of carrying out 'transnational' studies of sub-state or sub-national phenomena and pointing to Walter Weyrauch's research of 'Gypsy Law'.

[12] See e.g. William Twining, *Human Rights, Southern Voices*. Francis Deng, Abdullahi An-Na'im, Yash Ghai and Upendra Baxi (2009).

[13] Twining, *Normative and Legal Pluralism*, above.

2. Globalization! As within, so outside of the state: law's ambiguous functions

Much of William Twining's research, writing and teaching engages with law. It is situated both 'before' and 'after' globalization, as well as within and outside the Western nation state's boundaries. Reading, and re-reading, Twining's awe-inspiringly sophisticated, precise and thought-provoking scholarship on 'evidence', 'concepts', 'Legal Realism' (K. Llewellyn, in particular), 'globalization' and 'jurisprudence' works as a pertinent reminder of a particular quality of academic interventions that prompt us to emulate it. It is a rare kind of scholarly engagement: rare because its scope and simultaneous commitment to depth, clarity and provocation is admirable and rather singular, and rare because the combination of – or, rather, the intertwinement of – 'theory' and 'practice' is rendered as an art form. Such theoretical, conceptual as well as pedagogical and institution-building work[14] does not just happen. Twining's interest and investment in 'evidence', both in scholarship[15] and teaching[16], is just an illustration of a long-standing commitment to carry out *theory as activity*; to expose oneself and one's students and readers to ever more perplexing facts, data and iterations, that – strikingly enough – might have come from today's newspaper.[17] His famous 'newspaper exercise' ('Read the paper, take a minimum of four, a maximum of six hours to identify the role of law in the stories you read') is, of course, a wonderful example which combines practical facility with a terrific level of complexity.

His drilling for the impact of globalization on law (doctrine, concepts and curricula) results in pertinent contributions to some of today's most pressing debates in law, legal theory and legal education.[18] All this is set against the background of a deep-rooted, comparative and cosmopolitan understanding of law, the Western representations of which he urges us to see only as a smaller part of the bigger picture, Whether it is his inaugural lecture in Belfast[19], the Dewey lecture at NYU[20] or the Montesquieu lecture in Tilburg[21], Twining is securely located in the here and now, with both eyes

[14] Peter Tillers, 'Introduction to William Twining', 38 *Seton Hall Law Review* 871 (2008), 873. 'He, more than anyone else, has taken steps to institutionalize the evidence revolution – he has worked to establish programs and communities in order to ensure that scholarship about evidence will continue to deepen, broaden, and evolve'.

[15] William Twining, *Theories of Evidence* (Bentham & Wigmore, 1985).

[16] William Twining, 'Taking Facts Seriously', 34 *Journal of Legal Education* 22 (1984), 30ff.

[17] William Twining, 'Reading Law', 24 *Valparaiso University Law Review* 1 (1989), 15ff.; William Twining, *Globalisation and Legal Theory* (2000), 1–3, and see William Haltom and Michael McCann, *Distorting the Law. Politics, Media and the Litigation Crisis* (2004). I am grateful to Upendra Baxi for directing me to this work.

[18] See hereto also the observations by Harry W. Arthurs, in: 18 *International Journal of the Legal Profession*, 3–5 (2011).

[19] William Twining, 'Pericles and the Plumber', 83 *Law Quarterly Review* 396 (1967).

[20] William Twining, 'Talk About Realism', 60 *New York University Law Review* 329 (1985).

[21] William Twining, *Globalisation and legal scholarship*, with an introduction by Willem J. Witteveen (2011).

set on the 'What and Where and When, and How and Why and Who'.[22] And it is these paradigmatic framings, programmatic architectures or axiomatic restatements that Twining puts on the agenda, either to continue or initiate an inquiry of crucial importance. In this endeavour, he sometimes acts as interpreter and conveyer of fresh perspectives on old debates. For example, in 1973 he concluded his landmark study of American Legal Realism not only with an insightful discussion of, but with a forward-looking engagement with, the questions the Realists had struggled with.[23] At other times, as in Tilburg or in the context of his 'Southern Voices' project,[24] he acts as *agent provocateur*, trying to push his audience to look beyond the confines of their own doctrine- and concept-heavy legal 'science', and beyond their Western-cultural framings.[25]

Twining[26] has long been a traveller between worlds. With a keen mind and an admirable sensibility he depicts the communication gaps that mark the space separating different legal (political and economic) cultures.[27] In sketching the dimensions of legal doctrine's engagement with globalization in a variety of contexts,[28] he constantly underscores the need to shift perspectives and viewpoints[29] and to revisit, reconsider and reassess the insights that were gained along this unpredictable path.[30] Meanwhile, he has been a fervent advocate of the need to keep legal education, curricular reform and law school innovation in close touch with these theoretical developments.[31] In his 2009 Montesquieu lectures in Tilburg, for example, he built on his most recent major work, *General Jurisprudence*.[32] He masterfully drew these different strands together and formulated a succinct and yet highly complex list of

[22] Kipling, 'The Elephant's Child' (from *Just So Stories*, 1902), cited in Twining, 'Reading Law', above note 17, at 14.

[23] William Twining, *Karl Llewellyn and the Realist Movement* [1973] (2nd ed 2012), 'The Significance of Realism', 375–6: '(1) What should law schools be teaching, by what methods? (2) What should be the scope and methods of legal research? Is an empirical science of law possible and, if so, how can it be developed? (3) How far are legal institutions, concepts, principles, and rules adequately performing their proper role in a rapidly changing American society? In particular, what is the actual and potential role of courts, especially appellate courts, as agencies of legal change? (4) What is the relationship between law as a discipline and other social sciences such as economics, sociology, psychology and anthropology? How can communication and cooperation between law and the social sciences be extended?'

[24] William Twining, *Human Rights, Southern Voices*. Francis Deng, Abdullahi An-Na'im, Yash Ghai and Upendra Baxi (2009); William Twining, *General Jurisprudence. Understanding Law from a Global Perspective* (2009), 376ff.

[25] William Twining, *Globalisation and legal scholarship*, with an introduction by Willem J. Witteveen (2011), 37.

[26] The following section draws on ideas developed in Peer Zumbansen, 'Lochner Disembedded: The Anxieties of Law in a Global Context', 20 *Indiana Journal of Global Legal Studies* 29 (2013).

[27] See William Twining, 'Other People's Power: The Bad Man and English Positivism, 1897–1997', 63 *Brook L. Rev.* 189 (1997).

[28] See Twining, above. [29] See *Human Rights, Southern Voices* (William Twining, ed., 2009).

[30] See William Twining, *General Jurisprudence: Understanding Law from a Global Perspective* (2009).

[31] See Twining, above, at 257–263. [32] Twining, above, 32.

challenges that had been ‘identified inductively in over ten years of thinking about globalisation and law and general jurisprudence’.[33] These challenges identify some of the central concerns of legal theory in the context of globalization with remarkable precision. Twining notes that:

- the whole Western tradition of academic law is based on several kinds of assumptions that need to be critically examined in a changing context;
- we lack concepts, and data to generalise about legal phenomena in the worlds as a whole: analytic concepts that can transcend, at least to some extent, different legal traditions and cultures;
- comparison is the first step to generalisation and more sophisticated and expansive approaches to comparative law are critical for the development of a healthy discipline of law;
- we need more sophisticated normative theories that are well-informed and sensitive to pluralism of beliefs and differences between value systems; and,
- especially, we need improved empirical understandings of how legal doctrines, institutions and practices operate in the "real world".’[34]

While it is not possible in the narrow confines of the present paper to do justice to the programme of research, inquiry and imagination that Twining sets out for us, we may still want to underline the complexity of the constellation he identifies. His assessment reflects a sure grasp of multilayered and difficult-to-unravel problems: unchecked yet influential assumptions that lack analytic concepts; the need to elaborate an adequately sophisticated theory of comparative legal studies; and more sophisticated normative theories. This ambitious, theoretical–intellectual agenda is accompanied by as well as grounded and embedded in a passionate call for improved empirical understandings of the real world workings of legal doctrines, institutions and practices. What is striking in Twining's identification of the work to be done is, above all, the humility and caution with which the programme is formulated. This is why his depiction of law's challenges is so useful in setting the stage for a contemporary assessment of how law, in dialogue with other disciplines, sets sail on this journey. There is, indeed, much to be humble and cautious about. The emerging, and quickly overwhelming, world of transnational governance needs to be treated as more than a new playground for well-worn and established rules, principles and order concepts. Instead, law is faced with a multiplication of cases, locally and comparatively, as well as with a proliferation of sites of norm production and legal conflict.[35] But, as Twining notes, there is not much security to be had in a world where lawyers (and others) witness the erosion of dearly held distinctions such as public/private,

[33] William Twining, *Globalisation and Legal Scholarship* (2011), at 36.

[34] Id. at 37 (bullet points added).

[35] See *Handbook of Transnational Governance: Institutions and Innovations* Thomas Hale and David Held (eds), 2011 (bringing together individual studies on fifty-one distinct regulatory regimes in the area of transnational governance).

state/non-state, and even law/non-law, prompting them to contemplate 'law's fading coordinates'.[36] *Que faire*, in such a situation?

While four of the challenges identified above direct our attention to the undone theoretical and conceptual work, the fifth one – improved empirical understandings of how legal doctrines, institutions and practices operate in the real world – is key. In the search for an analytical framework for law in this new, transnational landscape of new actors, norms and processes, it is the need for an improved empirical understanding that harkens back to a dimension of law intimately linking the old and the new, the national, transnational and global. Twining's pointer to law's operations in the real world is sensitive to longstanding concerns among perceptive observers as well as real world inhabitants about law's and lawyers' blindness regarding the impact and consequences of legal decisions (or of the absence of such effects).

The disregard by law and its personnel for the temporality and effect of law's operation[37] is a crucial component of any attempt to ground and to contextualize law, and its role and relation to society.[38] Such issues are taken up, predominantly, by legal sociologists, criminologists[39] or legal anthropologists[40] whose insights carry particular significance for today's efforts to demarcate law's role in a context of disembeddedness. What emerges clearly is that conceptual elaborations of law must remain closely connected to an evolving methodology that tests theoretical assumptions and presuppositions.[41] This goes some way in explaining the degree to which today's legal sociological and legal anthropological scholarship on law and globalization is adamant that possible patterns of neglect, exclusion and omission in some models of global law be identified and monitored, as they

36 See Marc Amstutz, 'The Letter of the Law: Legal Reasoning in a Societal Perspective', 10 *German L. J.* 361 (2009); Walker, above.

37 See generally Austin Sarat, 'Vitality Amidst Fragmentation: On the Emergence of Postrealist Law and Society Scholarship', in *The Blackwell Companion to Law and Society* 1 (Austin Sarat, ed., 2004) (tracing the development of the study of law and society).

38 See generally, Mariana Valverde, *Everyday Law on the Street: City Governance in an Age of Diversity* (2012) (evaluating the role of law in city governance on both a local and global scale); John Paterson and Gunther Teubner, 'Changing Maps: Empirical Legal Autopoiesis', 7 *Soc. & Legal Stud.* 451 (1998) (outlining an approach to developing an empirical understanding of legal autopoiesis); Peer Zumbansen, 'Law's Knowledge and Law's Effectiveness: Reflections from Legal Sociology and Legal Theory', 10 *German L. J.* 417 (2009) (discussing the present and future state of legal sociology and theory).

39 See e.g. Mariana Valverde, *Law's Dream of a Common Knowledge* (2003).

40 See e.g. Sally Falk Moore, *Law as Process: An Anthropological Approach* (1978).

41 See e.g. Stewart Macaulay, 'Elegant Models, Empirical Pictures, and the Complexities of Contract', 11 *Law & Soc'y Rev.* 507 (1977) (analyzing the fact that contract law has developed theoretical foundations based on litigation despite the fact that few contract disputes are resolved via litigation); Stewart Macaulay, 'Non-Contractual Relations in Business: A Preliminary Study', 28 *Am. Soc. Rev.* 55 (1963) (analyzing the role that occupation plays in determining the amount of planning and legal action that takes place in the context of business). See also Marc Galanter, 'In the Winter of Our Discontent: Law, Anti-Law, and Social Science', 2 *Ann. Rev. L. & Soc. Sci.* 1 (2006) (critiquing what the author perceives to be a prevailing, and unjustified, negativity towards the law).

rapidly become fashionable. The critical response by scholars working within the realm of Third World Approaches to International Law (TWAIL)[42] to Global Administrative Law[43] is noteworthy in this regard,[44] as is the scrutiny of the recent turn by global governance institutions such as the World Bank[45] to the use of indicators[46]. What connects such inquiries to the socio-legal project of 'law in context', which has always been central to Twining's endeavours, is the effort to formulate adequate descriptive and evaluative standards to capture the present state of disembedded transnational governance.[47]

3. Facts, stakes, interests: law in context

> Reading a newspaper in this way illustrates the point that legal lenses are essential to understanding society as much as non-legal lenses are necessary to understanding law.[48]

How best can this analytical enterprise be connected to the pedagogical one? Taking Twining's newspaper exercise seriously prompts a number of questions with regard to the kind of information, data and facts that we draw on to make sense of law in a global context. What are the building blocks of transnational regulatory governance? Is such a question descriptive or normative, or both? The (Western) nation-state has been transformed through processes of Europeanization, globalization and

[42] For background, see, for example, James Thuo Gathii, 'Third World Approaches to International Economic Governance', in *International Law and the Third World: Reshaping Justice* 255 (Richard Falk et al. (eds), 2008); Obiora Chinedu Okafor, 'Critical Third World Approaches to International Law (TWAIL): Theory, Methodology, or Both?', 10 *Int'l Community L. Rev.* 371 (2008).

[43] See generally Benedict Kingsbury et al., 'The Emergence of Global Administrative Law', 68 *Law & Contemp. Probs.* 15 (2005) (identifying the new field of Global Administrative Law and proposing next steps for its development).

[44] See generally B. S. Chimni, 'Co-Option and Resistance: Two Faces of Global Administrative Law', 37 *N.Y.U. J. Int'l L. & Pol.* 799 (2005) (evaluating the effect of Global Administrative Law from a third world perspective).

[45] See generally Galit A. Sarfaty, *Values in Translation: Human Rights and the Culture of the World Bank* (2012) (evaluating the marginalization of human rights concerns within the World Bank); Sally Engle Merry, 'Measuring the World: Indicators, Human Rights, and Global Governance', in *Law in Transition: Rights, Development and Transitional Justice* Zumbansen and Buchanan (eds), 2014 (exploring the use of indicators as representations of complex phenomena for the purposes of global governance).

[46] This is, of course, a variation of David Kennedy's magisterial treatment of international institutional development. David Kennedy, 'The Move to Institutions', 8 *Cardozo L. Rev.* 841 (1987).

[47] William Twining, 'Diffusion and Globalization Discourse', 47 *Harvard International Law Journal* 507 (2006); William Twining, 'Responding to Globalisation [Review Essay on Rafael Domingo, The New Global Law, Cambridge UP 2010]', 49 *Osgoode Hall Law Journal* 353 (2011); Peer Zumbansen, 'Transnational Law, Evolving', in *Elgar Encyclopedia of Comparative Law* (2nd ed.) 898 (Smits, ed., 2012); Peer Zumbansen, 'Administrative law's global dream: navigating regulatory spaces between "national" and "international"', 11 *ICon International Journal of Constitutional Law* 506 (2013).

[48] Twining, *Reading Law*, above note 17, at 18.

privatization;[49] but do we set out to describe this process of institutional change, or do we engage with this transformation with a view to shifting the foundations of political legitimacy, agency and control? Do we contemplate the contours of the emerging transnational regulatory landscape when we draw up the syllabus for a basic course in constitutional or in public law,[50] or would this be better taught in an advanced course in transnational legal theory? Again and again, we are confronted with the porous lines between description and evaluation.

There is a similar permeability, it seems, between 'technical' and 'theoretical' in our curricular design of courses in law school. The former are seen as teaching the basic skills needed to apply doctrine to facts, while the latter are seen as offered to the happy few who are interested in going beyond what is necessary. Twining, of course, has revealed such distinctions as artificial through his conceptual and pedagogical writing. The pressing questions for any law teacher today, regardless of whether we are planning a first year or upper year course, are: '*what* is the law we ought to be teaching our students in the present context?'; and 'how are we to illustrate the challenges arising from this very context for law?'

One of the key insights that can, in my view, be gained from the 'law in context' work supported and executed by Twining is the importance of the local. Despite our interest in the interrelations between the domestic–municipal and the global–transnational, our usage of and our adherence to particular concepts and understandings is never just borne out of nostalgia for the local. Instead, as Twining so aptly describes in the first, largely autobiographical section of his new *Afterword* to the 2012 republication of the Llewellyn study,[51] the concrete circumstances of one's exposure to and one's engagement with a living legal culture are crucial for the way in which we develop a 'general' understanding of law.[52] I too have come to think about the challenges of globalization for law, against a particular background in latter twentieth-century German law, legal education and welfare state political economy.[53] A defining feature of 'becoming a lawyer' in that context, especially when given the opportunity to study and to work at the

49 Ralf Michaels and Nils Jansen, 'Private Law Beyond the State? Europeanization, Globalization, Privatization', 55 *American Journal of Comparative Law* 843 (2007).

50 For two noteworthy examples, see Sabino Cassese, 'New paths for administrative law: A manifesto', 10 *International Journal of Constitutional Law* [I.Con] 603 (2012), and, before that, Alfred C. Aman Jr, 'Administrative Law for a New Century', in *The Province of Administrative Law* 90 (Taggart, ed., 1997).

51 William Twining, *Karl Llewellyn and the Realist Movement* [1973] (2nd edn 2012), 388ff.

52 William Twining, *General Jurisprudence. Understanding Law from a Global Perspective* (2009), Preface, xiii–xiv.

53 See the individual, comparative observations by Christian Joerges, David Trubek and myself on the occasion of the 2011 republication of the landmark volume, 'Critical Legal Thought: A German–American Debate' (Nomos, 1986), in 12 *German Law Journal*, 1–33 (2011), available at www.germanlawjournal.com/pdfs/Vol12-No1/PDF_Vol_12_No_01_01-33_Articles_Joerges_Trubek_Zumbansen.pdf.

Faculty of Law in Frankfurt, across the street from the Institute for Social Research and the Department of Philosophy, where Adorno and Horkheimer had worked and where Habermas spent the majority of his career, was a sense of urgency in learning the law with an eye to Germany's history before and after 1945. So, among other things, we needed to be attentive to the institutional transformation underway in the 1970s and 1980s, its historical roots and contemporary political as well as socio-economic conditions, and how the 'Roaring Nineties' (as Joseph Stieglitz termed them) turned out to accentuate and amplify these domestic developments in a very particular way.[54] For lawyers who, like me, grew up in this context, the 'challenges of globalization for law' have, quite naturally, always been both descriptive *and* evaluative, 'legal' *and* 'normative'. As a result, any depiction of the state of globalization in legal terms is always already coloured by particular interest in the 'stakes' behind a particular case, in the institutional embeddedness of a legal process in the larger political context, and motivated by a deeper scepticism towards the neat separation of public and private law. The formula that leading, yet 'peripheral' lawyers – to use Twining's phrase – employed was that of 'economic law' ('*Wirtschaftsrecht*').[55] When one begins to identify the contours as well some of the structural features of today's transnational context in contrast to a particular version of the Weberian state, and what Tony Judt described as 'Postwar', this background matters. It then seems appropriate to look for the origins of the fast-evolving transnational regulatory order in domestic legal (and socio-economic, historically evolved) cultures, in their interaction and in the processes that cut across jurisdictional boundaries. The increasing proliferation of non-state actors involved in the preparation and production of regulatory norms had already been a central feature of the modern Western welfare state throughout the course of the late twentieth century.[56] The transnationalization of regulatory governance has dramatically amplified and exacerbated these dynamics. In Germany, as in France or the United States, against the fading contours of different variations of the welfare state,

[54] For very insightful observations and commentary, see Christian Joerges, 'The Science of Private Law and the Nation-State', in *The Europeanization of Law. The Legal Effects of European Integration* 47 (Snyder, ed., 2000), and Wolfgang Streeck, 'German Capitalism: Does it exist? Can it survive?', in *Political Economy of Modern Capitalism* 33 (Crouch and Streeck (eds), 1997). And see Wolfgang Streeck's analysis of the correlations between German economic policy and European market governance in Wolfgang Streeck, *Buying Time. The Delayed Crisis of Democratic Capitalism* (orig. German, *Die gekaufte Zeit*, 2012) (2014).

[55] Rudolf Wiethölter, 'Die Position des Wirtschaftsrechts im sozialen Rechtsstaat', in *Wirtschaftsordnung und Rechtsordnung, Festschrift für Franz Böhm zum 70. Geburtstag* 41 (Coing, Kronstein and Mestmäcker (eds), 1965); Rudolf Wiethölter, 'Proceduralization of the Category of Law', in *Critical Legal Thought. An American–German Debate* 505 (Joerges and Trubek (eds), 1989).

[56] Colin Scott, 'Private Regulation of the Public Sector: A Neglected Facet of Contemporary Governance', 29 *Journal of Law and Society* 56 (2002); Bronwen Morgan and Karen Yeung, *An Introduction to Law and Regulation. Texts and Materials* (2007).

concepts such as responsive[57] and reflexive,[58] even learning,[59] law were mobilized in the hope of capturing and preserving the essence of law as an instrument of people's egalitarian self-government. Pertinent to such efforts was a diagnosis of 'crisis', which touched not only the instrumental nature of legal regulation but reached much deeper, in fact, into the normative and institutional foundations and processes of a political society.[60] Even before a more engaged analysis of 'globalization' processes took off, socio-economic scholars had grown deeply concerned about the ways in which the welfare state's capacity to develop and deliver social safeguards had become precarious, both financially and conceptually. This 'exhaustion' of the Welfare State, as Jürgen Habermas called it,[61] resulted in a normative and institutional ambiguity that indeed encapsulates much of the structure we are confronted with in our present-day transnational constellation.[62] The diffusion of norm creation processes has ranged from 'hard' forms, such as treaties and laws, through more 'soft' forms, including conventions, codes and guidelines, to even more elusive, possibly out-of-legal-bounds norms, such as recommendations, suggestions and public relations statements. This illustrates the richness of a regulatory wonderland, but the politics of it all remain, well, all over the place. The questions about legitimacy and agency of transnational governance become exponentially more pressing the more we recognize the historical continuities of state transformation, now depicted

[57] Gunther Teubner, 'Substantive and Reflexive Elements in Modern Law', 17 *Law & Society Review* 239 (1983).

[58] Philippe Nonet and Philip Selznick, *Law and Society in Transition. Toward Responsive Law* (1978).

[59] Charles F. Sabel and Jonathan Zeitlin, 'Learning from Difference: The New Architecture of Experimentalist Governance in the EU', 14 *European Law Journal* 271 (2008); Peer Zumbansen, 'Law's Effectiveness and Law's Knowledge: Reflections from Legal Sociology and Legal Theory', 10 *German Law Journal* 417 (2009).

[60] This is excellently captured by Jürgen Habermas, *Legitimation Crisis* [orig. German 1973: *Legitimationskrise im Spätkapitalismus*] (1975). An amazing commentary on this line of thinking – and its inability to keep the economy, market-governance and the ubiquitous turn to 'financialization' at the centre of an analysis of 'crisis' – is now provided by Wolfgang Streeck, *Buying Time. The Delayed Crisis of Democratic Capitalism* [orig. German 2013: *Gekaufte Zeit. Die vertagte Krise des demokratischen Kapitalismus*] (2014). Chapter 1, and see p. 2: 'Underestimating capital as a political actor and a strategic social force, while at the same time overestimating the capacity of government policy to plan and to act, they thus replaced economic theory with theories of the state and democracy; the penalty they paid was to forgo a key part of Marx's legacy.' With regard to the efforts in legal theory to address the exhaustion of the welfare state, I have myself attempted to trace the Left's loose grip on "'law and economics' hijacking of socio-legal studies' interest in bottom-up governance and social ordering in: Peer Zumbansen, 'Law After the Welfare State: Formalism, Functionalism, and the Ironic Turn of Reflexive Law', 56 *American Journal of Comparative Law* 769 (2008).

[61] Jürgen Habermas, 'The New Obscurity: The Crisis of the Welfare State and the Exhaustion of Utopian Energies [1985]', in *The New Conservatism. Cultural Criticism and the Historians' Debate* [ed. and transl. by Shierry Weber Nicholsen] 48 (Habermas, ed.), 1989).

[62] See e.g. Kenneth W. Abbott and Duncan Snidal, 'Strengthening International Regulation Through Transnational New Governance: Overcoming the Orchestration Deficit', 42 *Vanderbilt Journal of Transnational Law* 501 (2009).

through the lens of globalization. In consequence, our efforts to identify the relevant *actors, norms* and *processes* that make up the DNA of transnational regulatory governance[63] become entangled with parallel projects in democratic and political theory and political philosophy. Well-known analytical categories are making their reappearance. Who counts as *competent* and as *legitimate* actors in this hybrid, pluralistic norm-creation universe? Is it the individual or the organization with the *expertise*, competence and most adequate understanding of the problem at hand? Or is it the he or she who is *authorized* to deliver (and, enforce) binding norms of law?

4. Transnational law pedagogy

> February, 1962. [. . .] This was the period in which a Scottish philosopher could justify his transfer to the Sudan on the ground that Khartoum was more central than Aberdeen. Almost every week we entertained at least one visiting fireman from the United States who was clocking up mileage, buying local carvings, selling American legal education, and passing gossip along the circuit.[64]

Considering this, we open our curriculum catalogues and course programmes and begin to ask questions. What is it that we are doing? What should lawyers study today? What should law professors teach them?[65] Why are we constantly both disturbed and intrigued by calls to introduce more Business School-like 'case studies' in legal education?[66] Maybe our scepticism has its roots in a stubborn insistence on law's embeddedness in a long history that is, above all, a treasure trove of discursive and political struggles over the very meaning of the words which are traded on today's market of attention. The awareness of this history and background leads to Hercules being caught between a feeling of humility and a stubborn aspiration still to 'get it right'.[67]

Verba docent, exempla trahunt. Rather than teaching law from Abraham, Raskalnikov or H. L. A. Hart, why not – as Twining famously suggested – '*read the news*'? Why not confront students with the reality and complexity of 'cases' as they are unfolding right before our eyes? Why not try to facilitate students to discern the 'legal aspects' of stories reported by the media; stories that centrally implicate competing visions of justice, human rights and social order? Why not, for example, 'teach' Jack Goldsmith's op-ed[68] rather than Bruno Simma's

63 For an elaboration of this triad, see Peer Zumbansen, 'Law and Legal Pluralism: Hybridity in Transnational Governance', in *Regulatory Hybridization in the Transnational Sphere* 49 (Jurcys, Kjaer and Yatsunami (eds), 2013).

64 William Twining, *Karl Llewellyn and the Realist Movement* [1973] (2nd ed 2012), Afterword, 'Framing Llewellyn', id. 388–443, 394.

65 The following section draws in part on Peer Zumbansen, 'What lies Before, Behind and Beneath a Case? Five Minutes of Transnational Lawyering and the Consequences for Legal Education', in *Stateless Law: Evolving Boundaries of a Discipline* (ssrn.com/abstract=2370428 Van Praagh and Dedek (eds), 2015).

66 www.law.harvard.edu/academics/degrees/jd/pos/law-and-bus accessed 21 November 2013.

67 Ronald Dworkin, *Law's Empire* (1986). 68 Above, note 19.

and Antonio Cassese's 1999 stand-off in *European Journal of International Law*?[69] Like a client walking into a law office with a simple story about a complex situation, the former, a short newspaper article that appeared on the morning that US President Obama was contemplating an invasion of Syria, held the key to the larger questions raised by the latter, penned by two world-renowned international law experts debating the adequacy of the UN Charter's provisions on the use of force in the face of a humanitarian crisis. How to combine the accessibility, sharpness and in-the-midst-of-it-all nature of the op-ed with the formidably rich yet succinct restatements of legality as the ultimate boundary (Simma) versus legitimacy as the necessary herald of a new legality (Cassese)?

To learn about a case, its 'parties', interests and stakes from the newspaper, would potentially enhance one's imagination about the case beyond the confines of studying a case in, say, contract, tort or family law. The newspaper story would already dissolve the boundaries between the 'legal' case and the messy social context out of which it is soon to be plucked. The newspaper story has the potential to help us situate the case in a broader context of social interaction and, in so doing, open our eyes to dimensions of the case we so often no longer see when reading a decision on its own. Importantly, reading an emerging 'case' through the lens of journalism illustrates agency and voice. It serves to highlight the role of the one telling the story, framing the case, identifying and qualifying the facts. The significance, both conceptually and practically, of such a reversal of perspective from judge to lawyer is the one thing that law teachers so frequently fall short of conveying to their students. Students, in turn, can hardly be blamed for sitting in class after class on a particular 'topic' or 'field', consuming thousands of judgments (or, comparatively, law reports) through their time at law school.

Unsurprisingly, then, identifying the stakes and the possible solutions to a case that is tethered only to a particular legal 'field' problematically limits the scope of engaging with all that the 'case' could actually be. Indeed, some of these *cases*, arguably, are not even '*cases*' yet, and there is perhaps no easy way to include them in the curriculum. The examples come to mind of the egregious human rights abuses at the Chinese Apple supplier, Foxconn[70] or, even more recently, the long-brooding struggle over labour and human

[69] Bruno Simma, 'NATO, the UN and the Use of Force: Legal Aspects', 10 *European Journal of International Law* 1 (1999); Antonio Cassese, 'Ex inuiria ius oritur: Are We Moving towards International Legitimation of Forcible Humanitarian Countermeasures in the World Community?', 10 *European Journal of International Law* 23 (1999).

[70] Malcolm Moore, 'Inside Foxconn's suicide factory', *The Telegraph* (27 May 2010) online: The Telegraph www.telegraph.co.uk/finance/china-business/7773011/A-look-inside-the-Foxconn-suicide-factory.html; Jenny Chan, 'A suicide survivor: the life of a Chinese worker' (2013) 28:2 *New Technology, Work and Employment*, 84–99; Jeffrey G. Huvelle and Cecily E. Baskir, 'A Fair Labor Future for Foxconn? The 2012 FLA Audit of Apple's Largest Supplier', 1(2) *Peking University Transnational Law Review*, pp. 212–59.

rights for the Bangladeshi ready-made-garment industry,[71] 'Skill training', clinical legal education,[72] 'experiential learning'[73] – all these are but tips of an iceberg, representing deeper disputes over the aims of legal education, the roles of lawyers in a changing, transnationalizing[74] society and precarious employment and long-term security.[75] The task of reforming legal education, thus regarded, becomes an exercise in reflection upon the nature of legal knowledge[76] and the scope of the ethical and political responsibility of lawyers.[77]

Take one more example as illustration of this challenge: that of the *Canadian Residential Schools Settlement* (IRSSA). Following years of public and legal advocacy and litigation to address Canada's deeply problematic role in the installation and maintenance of Residential Schools for First Nations' children, an agreement was reached to create a compensation scheme and a foundation whose mandate includes several different educational projects.[78] Numerous questions arise from this example; questions regarding both the nature and function of law in this context, as well as questions concerning legal pedagogy. What is the legal 'field' in which the different dimensions of this 'case' could best be addressed? To make this line of inquiry even more poignant: which course at a law school would be likely to include a session on the Settlement for its students at all? Is the IRSSA a (Canadian) example of an increasingly transnational concern with so-called Transitional

[71] See e.g. Edward Bearnot, 'Bangladesh: A Labor Paradox', *The World Policy Institute*, 2 May 2013 'Join the Conversation', www.worldpolicy.org/journal/fall2013/Bangladesh-Labor-Paradox. See also 'Steven Greenhouse, Bangladesh Labor Leader arrested during Rana Plaza Protest in New Jersey', *The Guardian*, 15 March 2015, www.theguardian.com/us-news/2015/mar/15/bangladesh-kalpona-akter-arrested-rana-plaza-new-jersey (accessed 25 May 2015).

[72] Nadia Chiesa, 'The Five Lessons I learned Through Clinical Legal Education', (2009) 10:7 *German Law Journal*, 1113–24, online at germanlawjournal.com/pdfs/Vol10No07/PDF_Vol_10_No_07_SI_1113-1126_Chiesa.pdf; Richard Wilson, 'Western Europe: Last Holdout in the Worldwide Acceptance of Clinical Legal Education', (2009) 10:7 *German Law Journal*, 823–46, online at germanlawjournal.com/pdfs/Vol10No07/PDF_Vol_10_No_07_SI_823-846_Wilson.pdf.

[73] Lorne Sossin, *Experience the Future of Legal Education*, CLPE OHLS Research Paper No. 47/2013 ssrn.com/abstract=2337521 (2013).

[74] Helge Dedek and Armand de Mestral, '"Born to be Wild": The "Trans-systemic" Programme at McGill and the De-Nationalization of Legal Education', 10 *German Law Journal* 889 (2009); Rosalie Jukier, 'Challenging the Existing Paradigm: How to Transnationalize the Legal Curriculum', 24 *Penn State International Law Review* 775 (2006); Phillip B. Bevans and John S. McKay, 'The Association of Transnational Law Schools' Agora: An Experiment in Graduate Legal Pedagogy', 10 *German Law Journal* 929 (2009).

[75] Guy Standing, *The Precariat. The New Dangerous Class* (2011); see, in this vein, Richard Sennett, *The Culture of the New Capitalism* (2006).

[76] Peer Zumbansen, 'Law's Effectiveness and Law's Knowledge: Reflections from Legal Sociology and Legal Theory', 10 *German Law Journal* 417 (2009); Margaret Thornton, 'The Law School, the Market, and the New Knowledge Economy', 10 *German Law Journal* 641 (2009).

[77] Harry W. Arthurs, 'Law and Learning in an Era of Globalization', 10 *German Law Journal* 629 (2009).

[78] www.aadnc-aandc.gc.ca/eng/1332949137290/1332949312397.

Justice?[79] If so, what are the lessons of the IRSSA for law students? How, and in which course, should they learn about the procedural intricacies, the access to justice challenges and the law and reconciliation dimensions that are at the heart of the Settlement?[80] What will happen, perhaps, is that this 'problem' (not case) will be addressed, if at all, in a new, small seminar on 'Transitional Justice'. Alternatively, we could imagine it playing a role in courses on 'Legal Professionalism' or 'Legal Foundations', 'Legal Sociology' or perhaps 'Legal History'. In the context of such courses, presumably taught at the start of the increasingly condensed[81] and simultaneously overburdened legal programme, the Settlement may at least function to provide some historical context for those students aware of these events, as well as stimulating an interest in 'Aboriginal law' or 'Transitional Justice'. At its best, however, the Settlement could serve as an illustration of the many complex layers of a problem as they become visible when lawyers attempt to find a legal solution to a deeply ingrained and only very incompletely 'worked through' historical experience.[82]

We can already recognize that the established ways of *not* associating these non-cases with a particular, neatly circumscribed, legal 'field' are intimately tied to a denial of Utopia. This is not because the utopian lawyer pushes against the citadel of a self-assured, parochial doctrinal framework in the name of the yet impossible, unthinkable, out-of-the-world legal imagination. Rather, it is because the line drawing, which is done through the identification of what belongs to a legal 'field' and what falls through the cracks of all legal (doctrinal) fields, denies any such Utopia to begin with by establishing an entire universe of self-sufficient legal reproduction.[83]

Such definitional challenges existed long before lawyers were asked to confront globalization processes and their impact on the law. Take the example of domestic tort and environmental law, both prime examples of how law deals with extreme cases of societal, technical complexity and risk. We can well remember how environmental law had to break through the shells of tort law

[79] See e.g. the contributions to R. Buchanan and P. Zumbansen (eds), *Law in Transition: Rights, Development and Transitional Justice* [with an epilogue by Bryant Garth] (Oxford/Portland: Hart, 2014).

[80] Rosemary L. Nagy, 'The Scope and Bounds of Transitional Justice and the Canadian Truth and Reconciliation Commission', 6 *International Journal of Transitional Justice* 1 (2012).

[81] www.insidehighered.com/news/2013/08/26/president-obama-calls-cutting-year-law-school accessed 21 November 2013.

[82] Robert W. Gordon, 'Undoing Historical Injustice', in *Justice and Injustice in Law and Legal Theory* 35 (Sarat and Kearns (eds), 1999); Richard M. Buxbaum, *From Paris to London: The Legal History of European Reparation Claims 1946-1953*, UC Berkeley Public Law Research Paper No. 1914802 works.bepress.com/richard_buxbaum/1 (2012).

[83] This is exactly the direction into which Twining points when he refers to 'memory' as a 'fact' in transitional justice contexts, that we need to learn to grasp through an evolving evidence framework: William Twining, 'Taking Facts Seriously – Again', 55 *Journal of Legal Education* 360 (2005), 377.

in order to develop legal concepts and instruments that would be adequate to the emerging 'risk-society'. Yet the specialization in both fields places particular demands on the respective classroom instructor to work against the perception that 'tort law' and 'environmental law' are separate legal *fields* which capture the ways in which law deals with a particular segment of societal activity and conflict. By continuing to highlight the interrelations between tort and environmental law, we confront students with the stakes of law's engagement with a reality that is never just 'found' but always constructed. Because tort law has a relatively long history in both legal practice and legal education, it has to be presented to students as the subject of conceptual, as well as political, reform.

How well do we infuse into our teaching a sense that not only is law in a constant state of change, but that lawyers are crucial agents of such change? Do we do enough to train our students to feel comfortable in their roles as stakeholders in a continuing debate over the aims and outcomes of legal battles? How can we train them even better to understand (tort, but also contract, corporate, constitutional etc.) 'law in context', which means today including a more than superficial introduction to the changing dimensions of post-industrial, globally integrated markets, the proliferation of expert standard-setting, and the resulting pressures on public oversight. In short, how well do we introduce students to the current realities of globalized market organization? It would be against such a background as this that students would come to appreciate the stakes involved in imagining, creating and developing a new field – for example, environmental law. While similar contentions can be made regarding the development of, say, internet law or, more recently, of transitional justice,[84] the question remains of how best to give students even a hint of such challenges during their legal classroom education. When it comes to breaking down barriers between neatly contained 'fields' that we use to control reality,[85] as well as between legal fields and different disciplinary demarcations of meaning, how, indeed, can we train students to understand and to assume their roles as 'game changers', as agents of change and critical reflection?

5. Politicizing transnational legal theory

But if one's view of law extends beyond appellate courts to trial courts, and beyond trial courts to pre-trial and post-trial events, and beyond litigation to dispute prevention and resolution, and beyond these to the kind of pervasive transnational phenomenon that is illustrated by the newspaper exercise, then a conspectus of legal theories that uses a case study set in the peculiar institutional context of a common law appellate court will not do. It is too narrowly focussed,

[84] See R. Nagy, above note 80.

[85] See the inspiring comments by Rama Mani, 'Dilemmas of Expanding Transitional Justice, or Forging the Nexus between Transitional Justice and Development', 2 *International Journal of Transitional Justice* 253 (2008).

> too unrepresentative, and too culture-bound to provide a basis for capturing a balanced overview of the range of general questions that need to be asked and tackled as part of a general understanding of the subject-matter of the discipline of law.[86]

Behind these questions on field boundaries and pedagogy lies, of course, the bigger concern that is still outstanding concerning the role of socio-legal studies in the transformation of mainstream legal scholarship and legal education. This is even more pressing now, as – at least in the United States and, arguably in the transnational field of corporate, contract and commercial law – 'law and economics', in terms of institutional and political impact, may come to be seen as the most successful 'law and society' sub-discipline, *tout court*. But, perhaps, not all is lost. An encouraging number of scholars have persistently been pushing for possible ways to reinvigorate 'law and society' approaches in ways that would further strengthen its interdisciplinary footing.[87] At the same time, we see developing what Twining has called a 'sustainable critique' that might grow into a conceptual–semantic apparatus through which a cross-cultural, transnational regulatory dialogue could become possible.[88] Echoing and encouraged by such efforts, some of us have been interested in seeking out and elaborating possible building blocks of what is, by its nature, perhaps best qualified as a 'transnational legal theory in context',[89] which I hope eventually to integrate and conceptualize as *Transnational Sociological Jurisprudence*. Central to such an undertaking are processes of '*translation*', of dialogue and reciprocal engagement, that become necessary in order to more adequately grasp the dynamics as well as the consequences of (allegedly clearly defined) legal-regulatory areas with their corresponding epistemologies. In *Reading Law*, for example, Twining includes a perfect observation of how a tort law case does not walk into one's legal practice labelled as such. The identification of the law – and, as it turns out to be, the case 'before, behind and beneath the

[86] Twining, *Reading Law*, above note 17, at 27.

[87] Recent, promising illustrations are offered by Eve Darian-Smith, 'Ethnographies of Law' in *The Blackwell Companion to Law and Society* 545 (Sarat, ed. 2006), Eve Darian-Smith, *Laws and Societies in Global Contexts. Contemporary Approaches* (2013), David Nelken, 'Transnational Legal Processes and the (Re)construction of the "Social": The Case of Human Trafficking' in *Exploring the 'Social' of Socio-Legal Studies* 137 (Feenan, ed., 2013), Prabha Kotiswaran, 'Do Feminists Need an Economic Sociology of Law?', 40 *Journal of Law and Society* 115 (2013), Elizabeth Mertz and Jothie Rajah, 'Language-and-Law Scholarship: An Interdisciplinary Conversation and a Post-9/11 Example', 10 *Annual Review of Law and Social Sciences* 9.1 (2014), and Rebecca Johnson, 'Justice and the Colonial Collision: Reflections on Stories of Intercultural Encounter in Law, Literature, Scupture and Film', 9 *NoFoundations* 68 (2012).

[88] For an early iteration of this task, see, of course, Boaventura de Sousa Santos, 'Law: A Map of Misreading. Toward a Postmodern Conception of Law', 14 *Journal of Law & Society* 279 (1987).

[89] Here, I am much inspired by Rudolf Wiethölter's longstanding analysis of the correlation between political, sociological and economic analysis of law. See e.g. Rudolf Wiethölter, 'Social Science Models in Economic Law', in *Contract and Organisation. Legal Analysis in the Light of Economic and Social Theory* 52 Daintith and Teubner (eds), 1986b, as well as Rudolf Wiethölter, 'Materialization and Proceduralization in Modern Law', in *Dilemmas of Law in the Welfare State* 221 Teubner, ed., 1986a.

case'[90] – falls into the hands of the lawyer (as well as her colleague on the other side, and the judge).

The crucial questions have been just *how* the lawyer(s) and judges end up *doing* this (a classical Legal Realist concern), but how we may *teach* students to understand this issue. Regarding the client who does not have the words 'tort case' written on his or her forehead, one of the crucial aspects is the almost inconceivable gap between the way in which we press students into classrooms, teaching them one 'area' of law in usually drastic isolation from all the others, and an ordinary litigator's experience of having to come up with coherent and effective answers to a 'case' with a million layers, edges and corners. Echoing William Twining's parallel field work in the domestic sphere of law's episteme and in the transnational and comparative world of diffusion and transplantation,[91] scholars who work in transnational law and transnational regulatory governance have repeatedly found themselves returning to explore the grey zones of interaction, tension and replay between the allegedly separate universes of the nation-state and 'global law'.[92] What seems to continue to inform this work are relatively widely-shared concerns over the divide between often overly descriptive socio-legal studies of transnational regulatory dynamics offered by lawyers, on the one hand, and rather dark and perhaps too pessimistic Cassandra-like depictions of an irreversible neo-liberalization of global market governance, on the other.[93] What, we may ask then, would 'law in transnational context' look like? Is it a field, a movement, a topic for research or a curricular innovation?

Writing today, well into the second decade of the new millennium, hardly anyone would aptly describe his or her research as being on 'globalization' without straight away identifying the particular strand of globalization research one was actually pursuing. That train of a general engagement with 'globalization' as such, it seems, has moved on. And we are all on it, here or there. That means that things have only become more complex and more complicated. Most of us now are globalization scholars by default, just as we are – at least in most areas – post-9/11 scholars. There are, at the same time, not

[90] Peer Zumbansen, 'What lies Before, Behind and Beneath a Case? Five Minutes of Transnational Lawyering and the Consequences for Legal Education' in *Stateless Law: Evolving Boundaries of a Discipline* 215 ssrn.com/abstract=2370428 Van Praagh and Dedek (eds), 2015.

[91] William Twining, 'Diffusion and Globalization Discourse', 47 *Harvard International Law Journal* 507 (2006); William Twining, 'Have concepts, will travel: analytical jurisprudence in a global context', 1 *International Journal of Law in Context* 5 (2005), and William Twining, *Globalisation and Legal Theory* (2000), ch. 6.

[92] Peer Zumbansen, 'Sustaining Paradox Boundaries: Perspectives on the Internal Affairs in Domestic and International Law', 15 *European Journal of International Law* 197 (2004); Gunther Teubner, 'The King's Many Bodies: The Self-Deconstruction of Law's Hierarchy', 31 *Law & Society Review* 763 (1997); Harry W. Arthurs, 'Labor Law Without the State', 46 *University of Toronto Law Journal* 1 (1996).

[93] David Schneiderman, 'Realising Rights in an Era of Economic Globalisation: Discourse Theory, Investor Rights, and Broad-Based Black Economic Empowerment' in *Redefining Sovereignty in International Economic Law* 429 (Shan, Simons and Singh (eds), 2008).

so many who manage to keep their eyes on so many different developments simultaneously. Twining is one of these exceptional scholars who, through a rare combination of intellectual curiosity and generosity,[94] has been able to be a highly effective thinker, innovator, interpreter, connector, facilitator and mentor. Much of such work happens outside the purview of keynote lectures or significant publications. As is evident, in Twining's case, it happens through his interaction with authors, colleagues, students and lawyers, near and far.

Some of my colleagues and I have been pursuing the hope of reinvigorating what in earlier times would have been called 'political' legal theory, and which we might today most fittingly pursue through a combination of socio-legal studies and research in political economy, economic sociology of law and critical theory. Such work has more in common with the socio-legal work of William Twining than might be readily obvious. While he never makes very explicit the exact level of his enthusiasm for the larger political and transformative dimensions of Legal Realism, Twining's astoundingly detailed and careful reconstruction of the Realist project does indeed suggest a deeper level of substantive sympathies. The concluding chapter *The Significance of Realism* fails, in that regard, to do this commitment adequate justice; a commitment which is more strikingly apparent over the course of the study itself and, certainly, in the erudite and spirited *Afterword* of 2012. What is evident, however, throughout the 1973 book its 2012 republication and, surely, from numerous other writings, is Twining's unswerving commitment to a jurisprudence of *law in context*. This commitment, again, is serious and thorough. Its rigour is illustrated in just about all of the cases, scenarios, examples and sites of engagements he has chosen to address. In my view, such law in context, *in action*, as it were, can hardly be detached from a genuine interest in the *political* texture in which these instantiations are occurring. How else are we to understand Twining's ever-recurring warnings against engaging in ultimately never-ending and fruitless definitional battles over the nature of law, or over where to draw the lines between law and non-law? What appears to motivate him (and us) is the '*why*' and the '*how*' of the human, and institutional, interactions that give rise, among other things, to such jurisprudential inquiries as how law/legal pluralism and non-law/normative pluralism can be separated from each other. It is against this background that we should look, very briefly, at the emerging contours of a transnational *political* jurisprudence, on the one hand, and a brief didactical illustration of classroom strategy, on the other.

[94] Compare his description of Llewellyn in William Twining, *Karl Llewellyn and the Realist Movement* [1973] (2nd ed 2012), Preface, p. xxv. Compare, also, his responses to the 2013 Symposium, organized by graduate students at Osgoode Hall Law School, and published in Transnational Legal Theory, tltjournal.blog.com/2014/03/31/twining-symposium.

Actors, norms, processes: translation categories in transnational political legal theory

The transnational regulatory landscape that forms the backdrop of current investigations into the nature and functions of legal ordering is above all characterized by an intriguing, if often bewildering, array of different *actors, norms* and *processes (ANP),* sometimes operating side by side and sometimes interacting with each other.[95] But what are we to make of these terms, ANP? Do they constitute 'new' versions of 'old', Western Welfare State institutional–conceptual frameworks, such as the Rule of Law, Separation of Powers, the normative hierarchy and unity of law? Or are they bloodless word-phrases, loosely attached to the madness of global un-law with a piece of gum? In previous work, I have been interested in qualifying and using the triad of ANP as 'translation categories', in order to capture the theoretical and conceptual challenges arising in a context where they are called upon to offer legal analysis and doctrinal assessments in a framework very different from that of a (Western) nation state – particularly in a context marked by evolving conceptions of the state, the rule of law and notions of the separation of powers, as well as a system of normative hierarchy with some form of constitutional text or order at the pinnacle of the pyramid.[96] In the present context, this *translation* or engagement is seen to occur in two ways: first in the form of the Legal Realist confrontation of legal norms with their invisible social realities; and secondly through a close study of the ways in which the content and boundaries of legal fields are being drawn and justified. The key here is a contextualization of lawyers' demarcation discourses regarding the function and boundaries of particular legal areas ('fields') in a never fully disclosed or disclosable realm of epistemological conceptualization. For example, what – in the domestic context – would justify a strict separation between labour law on the one hand and corporate law on the other? What, in a different domestic context, are the connections between the 'modernization' of law (and the state) and the marginalization and exclusion of those who are considered not to be part of it?[97] We should know, and have already known for some time,[98] that the justification of distinguishing between these two legal fields, despite its 'functional' persuasiveness,[99] is at its core *political.*

But this attention to politics does not go far enough. What is most frequently associated today with the need to expand law's interdisciplinary

[95] Peer Zumbansen, 'Transnational Private Regulatory Governance: Ambiguities of Public Authority and Private Power', 76 *Law & Contemporary Problems* ssrn.com/abstract=2252208 (2013).

[96] Peer Zumbansen, 'Lochner Disembedded: The Anxieties of Law in a Global Context', 20 *Indiana Journal of Global Legal Studies* 29 (2013), 54–60.

[97] Priya S. Gupta, Judicial Constructions: Modernity Economic Liberalization and the Urban Poor in India, 42 *Fordham Urban Law Journal* 25 (2014).

[98] Adolf A. Berle, *The 20th Century Capitalist Revolution* (1954).

[99] John Dewey, 'The Historic Background of Corporate Legal Personality', 35 *Yale Law Journal* 655 (1926); William W. Bratton, 'The "Nexus of Contracts" Corporation: A Critical Appraisal', 74 *Cornell Law Review* 407 (1989).

capacity[100] is only the surface of a more comprehensive crisis of law's epistemological foundations. On the one hand, from a legal–sociological perspective, we find an increasingly fuzzy relationship between allegedly 'public' and 'private' actors involved in the formulation and implementation as well as the enforcement of norms. But while this proliferation of private regulatory actors is not such a novelty, given its historical precursors,[101] its particular appearance in the context of the continuing crisis and transformation of the regulatory aspirations of the New Deal and the post-war Welfare State, requires a comprehensive analysis that would effectively revisit and reinvigorate the pondering by the Legal Realists on the hidden politics of de-politicizing markets,[102] contracts[103] and families.[104] What seems to me to be a crucial dimension of *transnational legal theory as activity* is to consciously draw out different local narratives of historically evolving legal and normative pluralisms, regulatory cultures and socio-economic conditions, in order to appreciate more fully the way in which they shape different understandings of 'the global'. This is a matter of considerable urgency, precisely because too much theorizing of 'global law' occurs in a manner that takes the particular background of (Western) nation-state history as universal.[105]

From cases to 'before the case'

In a seminal article from 1977, Oscar Schachter wrote about the then-current state of legal training. He argued that '[t]he traditional training and preoccupations of most lawyers may not provide an adequate basis for the kind of broadly based inquiry into needs and possible solutions in areas which are economic, political or technical.' He suggested, however, that it 'is also pertinent to recall that in many national legislative inquiries, the lawyer is recognized as the appropriate "generalist" for carrying out the necessary investigation into needs and legal solutions. In these situations, lawyers perform an organizing and critical role by gathering and scrutinizing relevant data and opinion from a wide variety of sources.' He went on to say: 'I do not

[100] See e.g. NYU's 2012–2013 Hauser Colloquium program, focusing on an interdisciplinary analysis to place legal theory in the interdisciplinary context of global governance: www.law.nyu.edu/academics/colloquia/hauserglobal.

[101] Louis Jaffe, 'Law Making by Private Groups', 51 *Harvard Law Review* 201 (1937).

[102] Robert L. Hale, 'Coercion and Distribution in a Supposedly Non-Coercive State', 38 *Political Science Quarterly* 470 (1923).

[103] Clare Dalton, 'An Essay in the Deconstruction of Contract Doctrine', 94 *Yale Law Journal* 997 (1985); Danielle Kie Hart, 'Contract Formation and the Entrenchment of Power', 41 *Loyola Chicago Law Journal* 175 (2009).

[104] Frances E. Olsen, 'The Family and the Market: A Study of Ideology and Legal Reform', 96 *Harvard Law Review* 1497 (1983).

[105] This is strikingly still the case in much of the work on 'global administrative law'. For critical comments, see – *inter alia* – B. S. Chimni, 'Co-option and Resistance: Two Faces of Global Administrative Law', 37 *New York University Journal of International Law & Politics* 799 (2005), Carol Harlow, 'Global Administrative Law: The Quest for Principles and Values', 17 *European Journal of International Law* 187 (2006), and Susan Marks, 'Naming Global Administrative Law', 37 *New York University Journal of International Law and Politics* 995 (2005).

suggest that this role can be performed only by lawyers, or, that they can necessarily carry it out better than others. [. . .] It is, of course, obvious that this kind must extend far beyond the usual lawyer's analysis of legal rules and precedent with its implicit assumptions about causal relations and the ends to be served. In order to carry out the international legislative task in an adequate manner, it is essential that nonlegal materials be examined and evaluated, and that expertise in nonlegal fields be drawn upon and utilized in a comprehensive manner.' He concluded: 'Experience has shown that this can be done by international lawyers through informal means, but much room remains for systematic collaboration with other scientific and professional groups.'[106]

Practicing lawyers are often confronted with the limitations of having to rely on precedent or legislation when advising clients in areas of 'new' law, or where court decisions and statutory regulations are not yet sufficiently available. While this might be due to the fact that the law – in a domestic setting – regularly adapts to a newly-emerging regulatory problem, this governance lag is amplified in the context of transnational activities, where issues of sovereignty, jurisdiction and forum pose additional obstacles to the creation of effective legal regulation. Practically speaking, lawyers in such cases frequently resort to teamwork, to experts, stakeholders and other relevant parties 'on the ground', eventually shifting their strategy from litigation to a combination of legal consultancy, advocacy, coalition building and even public awareness building. This type of lawyering requires considerable flexibility, competences and resources, which are not readily available to every lawyer. From a theoretical perspective, the lawyer might find herself overwhelmed by what can be the technical, cognitive as well as moral complexity of the case setting she is working on.

Bringing about a shift in perspective – from judge to lawyer, from lawyer to advocate, from expert to citizen – emerges as a task for legal pedagogy in the times ahead. On a general scale, not just selectively, students must be invited, from the moment they enter law school, to become aware of and to take on the perspective of the lawyer, advocate and activist involved in 'building' a case from a set of diverse, inchoate and constantly evolving facts and data. This can be achieved by introducing 'practice' modules, experiential and group work segments or clinic requirements into everyone's legal training. It is through such engagement that students are given the opportunity to work on examples of concrete, real-world developments in law and governance from the perspective of a practising lawyer, a rights advocate or rights activist. In the spirit of Professor Schachter's quotation, above, such lawyers need to be 'generalists', competent to see the bigger picture, and at the same time specialists, willing to engage with material outside their doctrinal areas of expertise. Accordingly, at the centre of such undertakings is the decisive shift away from training lawyers

[106] Oscar Schachter, 'The Invisible College of International Lawyers', 72:2 *Northwestern University Law Review*, 217–226 (1977), 224–225.

in learning and interpreting the law primarily through the study of jurisprudence (case law, as in the common law tradition) or through the interpretation of statutory law (legislation – civil law tradition) towards the development of different, significantly more practice- and context-related perspective. This shift is a crucial element in confronting students as future practitioners with the real-world challenges of an effective 'access to justice'. Assuming the position of legal practice and rights advocacy, students immerse themselves into a case from the 'bottom up' by identifying and *negotiating* the affected and involved interests, finding and *navigating* the applicable law, including – possibly – soft law, codes of conduct, social norms etc. and developing a Legal Interest Representation Strategy ('LIRS'). In contrast to giving legal advice to a client in a more or less confined and concrete legal question regarding, say, liability, entitlement, conviction or acquittal, the development of a LIRS might include a variety of avenues, including but not limited to designing a litigation or defense strategy, to the enhancing of legal and political rights, to engaging in coalition and public awareness building or to contributing to a sustainable stakeholder interest representation process. Students who are involved in such practice-related training modules are asked to look beyond the otherwise narrowly confined boundaries of the case through the lens of the legal decision. Instead, they are constantly confronted with cases that are 'not yet' cases and those which might never get to court. Such cases raise intriguing questions regarding litigation design, but perhaps – more importantly – advocacy, mobilization, community and coalition building.

Training lawyers for the transnational context through a significantly enlarged spectrum of engagements with law and competing approaches to conflict resolution emerges as a pressing concern for today's legal education reform efforts. Meeting the challenges of law in *transnational* contexts remains very much on the agenda; examples are ubiquitous and, arguably, promising. Legal clinics, experiential learning and transnational law programmes are gaining a stronger foothold in law schools, and 'socio-legal studies' might just offer the right critical substance to keep everyone involved on their toes.

14

Does global legal pluralism need a concept of law?

Roger Cotterrell

1. Introduction

Among William Twining's scholarly contributions, one of the most important has been his effort to enlarge the scope of analytical jurisprudence in the light of challenges posed by 'globalization'[1] for legal theory. He has argued for a new focus for conceptual inquiries, to help to shape a legal theory appropriate to contemporary socio-legal conditions. Part of his project seems to be to restate, from a certain standpoint, the full potential of jurisprudence and legal theory against some agenda-limiting tendencies of recent legal philosophy.

These tendencies are not present in his own work. He sees law as a discipline but he adopts a consciously eclectic approach to legal study, seeking insights from diverse knowledge-fields. So, juristic legal theory can draw on resources from many disciplines. He notes: 'By no means all questions in legal theory are in first instance philosophical questions and not all jurists are philosophers'[2] – philosophy has no monopoly of legal theory. Theorists are concerned not only with the largest questions about law, its contexts and methods, but also with synthesizing legal ideas and providing frames of reference for studies in and beyond particular legal systems.[3] Different levels of generality are needed for different kinds of interpretive, comparative or explanatory legal studies.

This approach suggests that jurisprudence should be a restless, outward-looking enterprise, focused on law but inseparable from historical, philosophical and social scientific studies and driven by practical questions.[4] Indeed, what is advocated is the antithesis of the imaginary 'legal philosophers' circle' that Twining once entertainingly satirized, in which issues set from within the circle (in his satire, a select group of people in a balloon floating high above the ground) are addressed in a kind of self-sufficient, self-justifying discourse.[5] His

[1] On the difficulties of using this and related concepts see W. Twining, *General Jurisprudence: Understanding Law from a Global Perspective* (2009) 13–18.

[2] W. Twining, *Law in Context: Enlarging a Discipline* (1997) 137.

[3] Twining, *General Jurisprudence* (op. cit.) 9–10.

[4] On the identity of jurisprudence as a knowledge field and a practice see R. Cotterrell, 'Why Jurisprudence is not Legal Philosophy' (2014) 5 Jurisprudence 41–55; and 'Professing Jurisprudence' in A. Diduck, N. Peleg and H. Reece (eds), *Law in Society: Reflections on Children, Family, Culture and Philosophy. Essays in Honour of Michael Freeman* (2015).

[5] W. Twining, *The Great Juristic Bazaar* (2002) 375–6.

proposal for an expanded analytical jurisprudence gets its sharpest focus when linked to a very practical need to understand law's loosening of some of its ties to the nation state – and, especially, the proliferation of forms of transnational law and regulation. He refers now to his project on global legal theory as reviving aspirations for a 'general jurisprudence'[6] capable of studying legal ideas across the jurisdictional boundaries of particular systems. Such a jurisprudence will recognize the immense plurality of legal orders that now exist – not only as state legal systems but also as legal regimes unbounded by or traversing state borders.

This chapter[7] seeks to celebrate William Twining's work by addressing basic questions that his advocacy of general jurisprudence opens up. Is a general concept of law needed to embrace the range of regulatory regimes developing in a world in which transnational and intra-national regulation are increasingly significant – a world that many writers have characterized as one of global legal pluralism?[8] What purposes might such a concept serve? If (as will be argued here) such a concept can have value, what approach should be taken in trying to formulate it? Taking the social rule approach of H. L. A. Hart's concept of law as a starting point, the chapter examines limitations of this approach – in particular, ones brought to light by reinterpreting politically and sociologically Hart's analogy between legal rules and the rules of sports and games. Finally, in the light of the above, it suggests key elements (political, communal, institutional) that must be present in any concept of law that can recognize appropriately the full range of contemporary national and transnational regulation.

2. Controversies about conceptualizing law

Hart famously insisted that trying to define law in general terms is fruitless.[9] Yet, even if much legal philosophy, following Hart's lead, now discards the quest for definition in favour of an effort to understand how law is talked about in specific

[6] Twining, *General Jurisprudence* (op. cit.).

[7] A different and shorter version of this text has been published in S. P. Donlan and L. H. Urscheler (eds), *Concepts of Law: Comparative, Jurisprudential and Social Science Perspectives* (2014).

[8] See e.g. F. G. Snyder, 'Governing Economic Globalization: Global Legal Pluralism and European Law' (1999), 5 *European Law Journal* 334; Snyder, Economic Globalisation and the Law in the Twenty-first Century, in A. Sarat ed., *Blackwell Companion to Law and Society* (2004); O. Perez, 'Normative Creativity and Global Legal Pluralism: Reflections on the Democratic Critique of Transnational Law' (2003), 10 *Indiana Journal of Global Legal Studies* (no 2) 25; P. S. Berman, *Global Legal Pluralism: A Jurisprudence of Law Beyond Borders* (2012); M. Giudice, 'Global Legal Pluralism: What's Law Got To Do With It?' (2014), 34 *Oxford Journal of Legal Studies* 589. The term is used in various ways. I adopt it here because it suggests the diversity and polycentricity of transnational regulation. It does not imply any single globalizing process in relation to law, any emerging unified global legal regime, any homogeneity of transnational regulation, or any theoretical presuppositions about the form or scope of this regulation.

[9] H. L. A. Hart, *Essays in Jurisprudence and Philosophy* (1983) ch. 1.

contexts, it still seeks to describe or explain the characteristics that typically, even universally, identify practices, forms or ideas as legal. Scholars engaged in this task suggest many reasons why such marks of law's distinctiveness need clarification: for example, to explain (i) the possible or necessary bases of authority of law,[10] (ii) the criteria that give legal systems their identity[11] or distinguish law from other forms of normative regulation,[12] (iii) the forms of understanding essential to law as an intellectual and social practice,[13] (iv) the nature of law's distinctive kind of normativity,[14] or (v) the basic moral or political implications of law's existence.[15] These kinds of issues, which, it is often assumed, can be raised wherever and whenever law is thought to exist, inspire attempts to explain its typical or essential features.

The effort to explore such questions clearly need not require a search for a universal or global juristic concept applicable to what jurists might recognize as 'law' in any time or place. Austin restricted his project of general jurisprudence to 'the ampler and maturer [legal] systems of refined societies'[16] – a practical, culturally-conditioned limitation of scope, hardly different from that assumed since his time in much comparative law scholarship[17] and legal philosophy.[18] The appropriateness of a concept of law will surely depend on its intended scope of application, and this matter cannot be settled in the abstract but only by reference to the aims and cultural contexts of particular inquiries.

If, for example, the aim is to generalize or compare 'across two or more legal traditions or cultures (or even jurisdictions)',[19] rather than to develop an idea of law applicable in all times and places, a concept of law to inform the inquiry will surely still be needed. But many elements in it may be self-evident and shared between the traditions, cultures or jurisdictions compared; they will not require explicit statement. To articulate such a concept may, however, seem

10 See e.g. B. Leiter, *Naturalizing Jurisprudence: Essays on American Legal Realism and Naturalism in Legal Philosophy* (2007) 129–31.

11 See e.g. J. Raz, *The Authority of Law*, 2nd edn. (2009) ch. 5.

12 See e.g. A. Marmor, 'Legal Conventionalism' in J. Coleman ed., *Hart's Postscript: Essays on the Postscript to the* Concept of Law (2001); D. Howarth, 'On the Question, "What is Law?"' (2000) 6 *Res Publica* 259.

13 H. L. A. Hart, *The Concept of Law*, 2nd edn. (1994) 81.

14 H. Kelsen, *Pure Theory of Law*, transl. M. Knight (1967).

15 See e.g. L. Murphy, 'The Political Question of the Concept of Law' in Coleman, *Hart's Postscript* (op. cit.).

16 John Austin, *Lectures on Jurisprudence or the Philosophy of Positive Law*, 5th edn. (1885) lect. XI.

17 For example, among leading early modern comparatists, Raymond Saleilles saw useful legal comparison as restricted 'to the civilised world'; Edouard Lambert saw its scope as practically restricted to modern European civil law systems: see C. Jamin, 'Saleilles' and Lambert's Old Dream Revisited' (2002), 50 *American Journal of Comparative Law* 701, at 715–6.

18 Discussion of the issue seems relatively rare in Anglo-American legal philosophy, but Joseph Raz explicitly acknowledges the primacy of 'contemporary municipal legal systems' in informing his concept of law. See Raz, *Authority of law*, op. cit. 50.

19 W. Twining, 'A Post-Westphalian Conception of Law' (2003), 17 *Law and Society Review* 199 at 202, 246.

important when apparently fundamental characteristics of law in one environment are absent in another (which nevertheless seems worthy of juristic or socio-legal comparison) or else take such radically different forms as to make their nature or significance as legal phenomena controversial. In fact, in any theoretical generalization or comparison of phenomena selected for their legal relevance, a concept of law will be implicit or explicit in the inquiry.

Studies of, for example, the nature of dispute processing, norm enforcement or various kinds of regulation which, William Twining has suggested, could be undertaken in a renewed general jurisprudence[20] must rely, insofar as they are studies in *legal* theory, on their reference to a concept of law appropriate to the inquiry in hand. The problem will be to specify the nature of 'the legal' flexibly enough to allow for revision in the light of research experience. A concept of law will have to be adequate to organize a project as an inquiry related to law, but not so fully elaborated as to close off inquiry in advance about diverse phenomena that it might be illuminating to treat as legal in some sense.

For some scholars, such as Ronald Dworkin, the search for a concept of law to help describe or explain the nature of law has seemed fundamentally misguided, at least as a legal philosophical project in the tradition of analytical jurisprudence. Dworkin saw the juristic task as to understand and engage reflexively in interpretive practices by which law's validity or truth in specific contexts is determined. A jurisprudential project aimed at theorizing generally about or systematically comparing legal phenomena may seem remote from this task. When such a project seeks descriptive knowledge of law through comparison, generalization and conceptual clarification, it will consider what gives practices or rules their identity as legal phenomena. It will ask 'what makes a particular structure of governance a legal system rather than some other form of social control?'[21] But Dworkin characterized this question as 'sociological', marginalizing it from legal philosophy; he saw it as having 'neither much practical nor much philosophical interest'.[22]

Whatever the merits of this last claim, it at least raises the issue of why general conceptual inquiries about the nature of law are significant. From a Dworkinian standpoint, they do not help to resolve practical questions about whether rules are valid as part of a specific legal order or whether statements of the law in such a context are true; they do not aid juristic practice in this sense. Another way of putting the matter is that they do not resolve, or even help to resolve, questions about the ultimate location of the authority that validates law for the purposes of juristic or official practice.[23] Dworkin argued that the impossibility of using a Hartian concept of law to explain the sources of legal validity reveals the difficulty for any such explanatory concept of

[20] Ibid. 242.

[21] R. Dworkin, 'Hart and the Concepts of Law' (2006), 119 *Harvard Law Review Forum* 95 at 97.

[22] Ibid. 97–8, and see Dworkin, *Justice in Robes* (2006) ch. 8.

[23] See also D. Dyzenhaus, 'The Demise of Legal Positivism?' (2006), 119 *Harvard Law Review Forum* 112 at 114.

law.[24] The open-textured, potentially incomplete and plural character[25] of the rule of recognition – as the ultimate criterion of law's validity – in Hart's concept of law may support claims that efforts to identify the basis of legal authority by means of a general, descriptive, explanatory concept of law have been unproductive. And disagreements between 'inclusive' and 'exclusive' legal positivists about the rule of recognition's theoretically-possible content may point in the same direction.

Those stressing such difficulties often claim that practical problems of legal authority or validity are resolved not by applying pedigree tests of 'the legal' (derived from a concept of law) but, rather, in a collectively-understood process of argument about provisionally-identified legal materials. Nevertheless, it should be emphasized that any such process of argument presupposes certain conditions. It presupposes especially a *discursive arena* in which it can take place. For Dworkin, for example, it presupposes a particular community, which in some way sees itself as the author of its law.

For distinct territorially-bounded legal systems, such as those of nation states, it may seem easy to assume the scope and character of a discursive arena in which legal argument and interpretation takes place. But the matter is much more complex when many kinds of intersecting transnational regulatory regimes are under consideration. Then it may be important, and perhaps difficult, to define the discursive arenas in which interpretation of regulation, and debates about the validity and authority of law, occur. Who is included in the various communities of interpreters? What collective understandings about methods of attributing validity and authority to regulation link them? Assumptions of normal legal practice may be hard to make. Questions about the scope, identity and differentiation of regulatory regimes become practically important. If they are not answered, the claim that law is a matter of interpretation becomes an unenlightening truism. Everything depends on the assumptions on the basis of which that interpretation takes place.

3. Some purposes of a concept of law

Conceptual inquiries about law's *identity* (in Dworkin's terms, how far it is 'a particular structure of governance' distinguishable from any 'other form of social control')[26] surely have juristic significance, whether or not they are philosophically interesting. And certainly, as Dworkin notes, they are sociologically interesting. Indeed, the fact that he characterizes them as sociological, while many Hartian positivists see them as central to legal philosophy, suggests that clear demarcation lines between juristic, legal philosophical and sociological inquiries cannot now be drawn without controversy. This is hardly a new claim. Eugen Ehrlich, setting out his programme for sociology of law early

[24] Dworkin, *Justice in Robes* (op. cit.) ch. 7. [25] Raz, *Authority of Law*, op. cit. 93–7.
[26] Dworkin, 'Hart and the Concepts of Law' (loc. cit.) 97.

in the twentieth century, saw the comparative conceptual inquiries of Austin's general jurisprudence as indicating 'a part, at least, of the material which the practical science of law will be able to pass on to the sociological science of law',[27] though he sought a distinctively sociological way of understanding law's identity.

Juristically, the development of a concept of law as a marker of law's identity can serve at least two distinct purposes. First, it can be used to make explicit the underlying *framework of legal understandings* in relation to which comparisons of law-related ideas and practices across or between different regulatory regimes or jurisdictions can be undertaken. Secondly, it can be used to conceptualize *boundaries of 'the legal'* (legal doctrine, institutions, arguments, methods, problems, etc.) in relation to non-legal or extra-legal considerations. Such a conceptualization does not necessarily suggest either (i) that the boundaries of the legal are fixed (so that they cannot change, or are similarly located whatever legal order is considered), or (ii) that they should be fixed in a particular way (as a timeless, context-free ideal).

Reasoning out the boundaries of law in a certain way with certain criteria in mind can be, instead, a challenge to consider how to relate those boundaries to particular contexts.[28] This challenge can be accepted not only by theorists seeking to understand the nature of law, but also by lawyers asking how far, for example, moral or economic efficiency arguments might be legitimately made in particular contexts of legal reasoning, or how far various kinds of public or private regulation, 'soft law' or 'persuasive' authority[29] might be relevant as legal material. A concept of law might, in other words, offer a framework for arguing out boundary problems of law systematically and comparatively.

For both juristic and sociological purposes (whatever their exact relation), a practically useful general concept of law is likely to have similar qualities. It will not be a definition of the subject-matter that marks an endpoint of inquiry. It will be, rather, a starting point: a framework for study, a provisional setting of parameters, a means of identifying and clarifying key questions about law that can be raised in a variety of contexts.

Viewed in this way, a concept of law is relevant to inquiries about law's authority or validity. Such a concept drawn up on the basis of observation and experience of law in a range of settings may not answer questions about the validity of specific rules or other precepts as law, or about the truth of statements of the law in a particular jurisdiction. But it may provisionally suggest the *parameters* in which legal authority and validity can be debated or their sources located. Indeed, it may suggest conditions required for legal authority and validity to be meaningful ideas at all. Its main contribution may be to

[27] E. Ehrlich, *Fundamental Principles of the Sociology of Law*, transl. W. L. Moll (1936) 485.

[28] See Howarth, 'On the Question, "What is Law?"' (loc. cit.).

[29] H. P. Glenn, 'Persuasive Authority' (1987), 32 *McGill Law Journal* 261; cf. G. Lamond, 'Persuasive Authority in the Law' (2010), 17 *Harvard Review of Philosophy* 16.

inspire challenges to assumptions made in particular legal contexts about any of these matters.

While these are practical juristic considerations, they are relevant also to sociological studies of the authority structures of law. Indeed, juristic and sociological inquiries are often interrelated. Practising lawyers need, as part of their professional skill, to be able to make sociological sense of their observations of the environments in which law is practised, and incorporate those observations as part of their juristic understanding of law. Correspondingly, many sociological inquiries about law as an aspect or field of social experience will need to synthesize the practical understandings of professional and other participants in legal processes.

Dworkin attacks positivist efforts to specify a concept of law for descriptive or explanatory purposes in a general jurisprudence on the grounds that there is no 'neutral', 'uncommitted' or value-free standpoint from which such a concept can be proposed.[30] This is an appropriate reminder that any concept of law will reflect specific values or experiences. But such a concept can still aid communication with people who have different regulatory experiences and value commitments insofar as expressing the concept helps to reveal the standpoint it embodies. And, in fact, the viewpoint reflected in a concept of law is not necessarily confined by the legal environment in which it has emerged. Limits may certainly be set by the project for which it has been created (how much generalization of legal experience is envisaged? how extensive are the legal comparisons to be made?), but it is not pointless to seek a concept of law to suggest an indefinite, broadening range of regulatory contexts. The insurmountable limits of any such concept are not those of experience but of imagination. A concept of law might be a means to broaden perspectives beyond those gained through any particular practical legal experience. It might also express an aspiration towards such a broadening.

4. 'Law' in global legal pluralism

Contemporary transnational regulation presents a striking image of normative diversity. Referring mainly to economic transnational regulation, Francis Snyder notes 'a startling variety of new legal forms and regimes', 'a variety of institutions, norms and dispute resolution processes located and produced, at different structured sites, around the world'.[31] There is now a (surely far from level) 'global legal playing field', including 'a novel regime for governing global economic networks'.[32] But the many sites of global legal pluralism 'do not

[30] Dworkin, *Justice in Robes* (op. cit.) ch. 6.

[31] Snyder, 'Economic Globalisation and the Law' (loc. cit.) 624; Snyder, 'Governing Economic Globalization' (loc. cit.) 342. See further G.-P. Calliess and P. Zumbansen, *Rough Consensus and Running Code: A Theory of Transnational Private Law* (2010); R. Cotterrell, 'What is Transnational Law?' (2012), 37 *Law & Social Inquiry* 500.

[32] Snyder, 'Governing Economic Globalization' (loc. cit.) 343, 372.

make up a legal system'.[33] There is no uniform jurisdictional reference point, no single discursive arena in which legal reasoning takes place. Instead, regimes of different kinds intersect, conflict, compete and overlap. Legal authority is relative and contingent.

It is not necessarily clear what, following a positivist approach, should be looked for as appropriate 'pedigree tests' of normative validity in these diverse areas of regulation. Wolf Heydebrand writes of a need to redefine notions of 'law' and 'legal' in considering 'quasi-legal regulatory mechanisms at the global level'.[34] Much significant transnational regulation is 'soft law'[35] and the legal quality of the contemporary *lex mercatoria* is subject to 'seemingly eternal dispute'.[36] Similarly, the 'legal substructure of international finance and banking is remarkably underdeveloped, characterized for the most part by a set of recommended "best practices" exhibiting little formality or clarity', while regulation emphasizes 'open-ended, flexible guidelines'.[37] In fact, '[m]any of the substantive norms of international business law are directly determined by the huge "industry leaders" who dominate the market... More and more, [multi-national] corporations exercise "sovereign" powers of law-making.'[38] Codes of practice, operating in some respects like multilaterally negotiated treaties, are 'applied as standard-form contracts laid down by the leading firms in a particular market.'[39]

In general, in transnational arenas, regulatory regimes of great diversity – public and private, state and international, 'soft' and 'hard', legislated and negotiated, centralized and diffuse – co-exist, often in very unclear relations with each other. While some are rooted in territorial jurisdiction, the scope of others is functionally defined. Some operate through 'horizontal' co-ordination (especially by standardization of contractual terms in the process of transnational business dealings) while others operate more 'vertically' through hierarchies of authority located in specific rule-making or adjudicatory institutions.

[33] Ibid. 374.

[34] W. Heydebrand, 'From Globalisation of Law to Law under Globalisation' in D. Nelken, ed., *Adapting Legal Cultures* (2001) 120.

[35] Snyder, 'Economic Globalisation and the Law' (loc. cit.) 630; L. Senden, 'Soft Law, Self-Regulation and Co-Regulation in European Law: Where Do They Meet?' (2005), 9 *Electronic Journal of Comparative Law* (no 1); D. M. Trubek and L. G. Trubek, 'Hard and Soft Law in the Construction of Social Europe: The Role of the Open Method of Coordination' (2005), 11 *European Law Journal* 343; A. Schäfer, 'Resolving Deadlock: Why International Organisations Introduce Soft Law' (2006), 12 *European Law Journal* 194.

[36] P. Zumbansen, 'Piercing the Legal Veil: Commercial Arbitration and Transnational Law' EUI Working Paper LAW 2002/1 (2002) 2.

[37] W. E. Scheuerman, 'Globalization and the Fate of Law' in D. Dyzenhaus, ed., *Recrafting the Rule of Law* (1999) 255. For reasons see e.g. T. Rixen, 'Why Reregulation after the Crisis is Feeble: Shadow Banking, Offshore Financial Centers, and Jurisdictional Competition' (2013), 7 *Regulation and Governance* 435; M. Titolo, 'Privatization and the Market Frame' (2012), 60 *Buffalo Law Review* 493.

[38] Scheuerman, 'Globalization and the Fate of Law' (loc. cit.). 257.

[39] Snyder, 'Governing Economic Globalization' (loc. cit.) 363.

The inclination to deny that some, or perhaps much, of this regulation is law derives from deep-rooted assumptions about law's nature: for example, that it can only be created or controlled by state institutions and agencies; that it is essentially public and not private regulation; that it aims (even if sometimes unsuccessfully) to achieve clarity and relative constancy in the form of fixed rules, not flexible standards; that it is a supreme form of regulation, dominating other regulatory regimes; that it is comprehensive in its social field; and that it consists of imperative demands or specified permissions, not negotiated understandings. Each of these assumptions about law is challenged by developments in transnational regulation, insofar as this regulation is now often labelled 'law', seen as legally important, or increasingly integrated with national or international law.[40]

Is it possible and useful to impose, as a template on this diversity, a general transnational concept of law? Would this help to broaden perspectives on the significance of new or newly prominent regulatory regimes that do not fit traditional ideas of nation-state law? As William Twining has argued, it is not fruitful just to accept theoretically as law whatever regulatory practices are given the label 'law' by those who participate in them.[41] That would be to abandon the analytical purposes for which a concept of law should be designed. It would be to provide no guiding framework on which comparative or theoretical inquiries could be built. At the same time, there is no reason (from either juristic or sociological points of view) to give up the effort to conceptualize law in the face of growing transnational regulatory complexity, and as part of an effort to understand that complexity.

Juristically, the most obvious problem that transnational regulation poses is that of structuring meaningful argument about the validity of regulation and its sources of authority – a problem of knowing how to reason normatively and systematically in transnational arenas. How is it possible to create a discourse to integrate transnational normative structures and impose juridical order on them? By contrast, from a *sociological* point of view, the need is to conceptualize law in ways that are helpful (i) in tracking the continuing (but reducing) power of nation-state regulation and (ii) in surveying the field of transnational regulation in relation to the social, economic and political forces shaping it.

5. Hart and the rules of games and sports

In contemporary Anglophone legal theory, an approach informed by Hart's legal philosophy might seem initially promising as a basis for addressing analytical problems of transnational regulation. Hart's concept of law has been found useful not only by jurists but also by some legal sociologists and anthropologists. Neil MacCormick explored its usefulness in characterizing

[40] Cotterrell, 'What is Transnational Law?' (loc. cit.).

[41] Twining, 'A Post-Westphalian Conception of Law' (loc. cit.).

the transnational law of the European Union, and escaping limits imposed by traditional ideas of sovereignty.[42] Yet, for MacCormick, '[d]espite the pluralistic or polycentric potentialities [Hart. . .] points to in developing his theory, pluralism remains more a potential than an actual virtue of his own work.'[43] Like most other legal philosophers, Hart largely assumes that nation-state boundaries correlate with legal system boundaries and limit the discursive arena of legal reasoning on questions of legal validity. The pluralist potential of his theory lies only in the fact that he does not *explicitly* tie his concept of law to the state's territorial jurisdiction. Unlike, for example, Hans Kelsen, Hart offers no analysis of the relation of law and state,[44] the closest he comes to this being the important role his theory gives to 'officials'. But these are theoretically identified not as state officials but only as officials in relation to the legal system they serve.

In considering the kind of concept of law that could be useful in global legal pluralism it is worth noting the limits as well as the advances of Hart's concept of law. It replaces Austin's theory of sovereign and subject, linked by legal commands, with the idea of an impersonal structure of rules making up a legal system. The main advance here for legal theory is to make it possible to separate the concept of law from particular structures of state-centred political power. It becomes possible to imagine, for example, international law and customary law as, in some sense, law, even if less developed than the law of nation states. But the price paid for this – the remarkable vacuum at the centre of Hart's concept of law – is the *difficulty of clearly distinguishing legal rules from many other obligation-imposing social rules.* It is necessary briefly to illustrate this problem before showing how it arises and how it must be avoided in studying global legal pluralism. My illustration is in terms of the relationship of legal rules and rules of games or sports.

Having identified law as the union of primary and secondary rules, Hart specifies minimum conditions for a legal system to exist as being: (i) that citizens in general regularly obey the primary rules, and (ii) that 'officials' adopt an internal (critical, reflective) view of secondary rules, applying them as meaningful guides for their own conduct and that of others.[45] Rejecting the idea of defining law, he claims only that this conceptualization identifies central cases of typical invocations of the idea of law. Yet he has been widely assumed to be concerned with identifying law in contrast to other social phenomena. Frederick Schauer claims, for example, that 'Hart helped us see why law is different not only from the state-sanctioned application of force, but also from norms, values, habits, practices, and a host of other determinants of

[42] N. MacCormick, 'Beyond the Sovereign State' (1993), 56 *Modern Law Review* 1; and see MacCormick, *Questioning Sovereignty* (1999) ch. 8. A conceptualization of legalization in international relations that finds some inspiration in Hart's concept of law is suggested in K. W. Abbott et al., 'The Concept of Legalization' (2000), 54 *International Organization* 401.

[43] MacCormick, 'Beyond the Sovereign State' (loc. cit.) 9.

[44] Raz, *Authority of Law* (op. cit.) 98.

[45] Hart, *Concept of Law* (op. cit.) 116.

behaviour that . . . remain crucially different from law.'[46] The sophistication of Hart's approach has often been seen to lie partly in his refusal to identify law in political terms as Austin did. Instead of tying law to sovereign power he emphasizes its normativity (as rules) and its reality as social (especially linguistic) practices.

As is well known, this emphasis leads him (and other legal philosophers) to make frequent analogies between legal rules and the rules of games. But, remarkably, at no point does he clearly identify what distinguishes law as a species of social rules from the rules of games.[47] He discusses games only to explain common features of rules, including legal rules. This seems odd. Legal sociologists (unlike most jurists) are sometimes prepared to recognize 'private legal systems'[48] and many varieties of social rules as law but they would usually not hesitate to distinguish law from rules of games or sports. It is surely strange if Hart's concept of law gives no theoretical resources to make this distinction. Yet this matter has received little comment.

Legal rules for Hart are obligation-imposing, but rules of games can also have this character for the players. In any case, not all legal rules have all the attributes that Hart sees as creating obligations.[49] Further, organized games or sports certainly do not necessarily lack secondary rules, the emergence of which marks, for Hart, transition 'from the pre-legal to the legal world'.[50] Often there are elaborate, rule-governed processes supervised by 'officials' for creating, recognizing, debating, changing and adjudicating on the primary obligation-imposing rules of games and sports (e.g. in cricket, bridge or chess). Rules of games, no less than of law, are viewed from internal and external viewpoints. Indeed, the rules of some sports and games (e.g. cricket, bridge, croquet) are typically called laws.

Could it be said that games and sports are essentially, in some sense, trivial while law is concerned with matters of fundamental social importance? Joseph Raz emphasizes law's dominant social importance, its regulatory comprehensiveness, its claim to supremacy over other norm systems and its role in supporting them.[51] But he admits these are traits of 'the legal' that can vary in degree,[52] and, in fact, each of these suggested marks of law's distinctiveness can be challenged with regard to law's actual social conditions of existence in

[46] F. Schauer, '(Re)taking Hart' (2006), 119 *Harvard Law Review* 852 at 871. For an argument that Hart's concept of law can embrace social rules without an institutional structure of secondary rules see D. Von Daniels, *The Concept of Law in Transnational Perspective* (2010) and, for criticism of this argument, see Cotterrell, 'What is Transnational Law?' (loc. cit.) 504–8.

[47] Dworkin notes that Hart's concept of law as the union of primary and secondary rules does not distinguish legal systems from such institutions as organized sports: see Dworkin, 'Hart and the Concepts of Law' (loc. cit) 100. For an elaborate discussion of the nature and organization of rules of games see J. Raz, *Practical Reason and Norms* (1975) 113–23.

[48] W. M. Evan, *Social Structure and Law: Theoretical and Empirical Perspectives* (1990) 123–37. See also Calliess and Zumbansen, *Rough Consensus and Running Code* (op. cit.) 120–1.

[49] Hart, *Concept of Law* (op. cit.) 174, 175, 229. [50] Ibid. 94.

[51] Raz, *Authority of Law* (op. cit.) 116–20. [52] Ibid. 116.

particular contexts.[53] Many acknowledged laws address only highly specialized, technical matters of minor regulation.[54] On the other hand, often much turns on the outcome of games or sporting contests, in terms of reputations, prizes, opportunities, sponsorship and careers. Much attention is often paid to management of the rules of sports and the adjudication of disputes. Much money may be at stake in organized sports. Indeed, the outcome of some sporting contests may be a matter of national economic, cultural or political importance, and of popular interest, in a way that decisions on issues of law rarely are.[55]

The point to be made here is not that the rules of games and of law cannot be theoretically distinguished in a satisfactory way. It is that an approach to conceptualizing law that seeks to remove from this conceptualizing process a consideration of *empirical questions* about law's specific social contexts and to address it more abstractly – for example, by exploring the structuring of rules or norms – may not provide resources for understanding legal experience in general, or the variety of forms of law that currently exist. A concept of law that, for example, cannot clearly show that, for all their similarities, legal systems and the normative organization of sports events are fundamentally different social phenomena lacks the power to guide appropriate studies of law, both by those who practise it juristically and those who study its character sociologically (two not necessarily distinct categories of people).

6. A concept of law in its contexts

The 'games problem' in the concept of law points to what is missing from some contemporary approaches to legal philosophy – an adequate recognition of the inseparability of any practically useful idea of law from its political and social contexts of application.[56]

Dworkin implied interestingly, in his early work, that law can be distinguished from the rules of games because rules *dominate* games as enterprises in a way that is not true of law;[57] by contrast, rules do not dominate law because other standards (e.g. legal principles) are fundamental. Again, for Dworkin, games (or at least some of them) are *autonomous* institutions,[58] existing for

[53] B. Z. Tamanaha, *A General Jurisprudence of Law and Society* (2001) 139–40.

[54] Hart notes (*Concept of Law*, op. cit. 170) that game-rules concern 'activities for which there are only intermittent opportunities, deliberately created.' But this applies, no less, to many activities regulated by law. Elsewhere (see the references in note 46, above) he admits the insignificance of many laws.

[55] For a critique of the idea that sports regulation does not involve matters of general governmental significance see J. Anderson, 'An Accident of History: Why the Decisions of Sports Governing Bodies are not Amenable to Judicial Review' (2006), 35 *Common Law World Review* 173.

[56] Cotterrell, 'Why Jurisprudence is not Legal Philosophy' (loc. cit.).

[57] R. Dworkin, *Taking Rights Seriously* (1977) 24–5. [58] Ibid. 101.

their own sake, whereas law is not; it is thoroughly implicated in its wider social and moral context.

I think this is not quite correct, though it hints at something of great importance. It is surely not true that games are regulated only by rules; they are often also considered to be governed by other standards. The 'spirit of the game' may be very important,[59] and related to a sense of purpose, fairness and of playing properly rather than undermining the game or 'bringing it into disrepute'.[60] Again, games are not necessarily autonomous institutions: they may be pursued for many wider purposes, including the development of skills, fitness, or social contacts, and may be viewed, like law, from many perspectives.[61] But it is right to stress that law cannot be fully understood in terms of rules entirely divorced from the specific moral contexts of their development and use.

The problem in following Dworkin's approach to emphasizing this law–morality connection is that, for him, it is to be pursued entirely within the confines of experience of a particular legal community. But contemporary regulatory complexity requires the recognition of an intense *interaction* between many different regulatory communities often with fluctuating, partly shared memberships. It is this interaction (not necessarily governed by any shared authority or common understandings) that now produces the complex global legal pluralism discussed earlier. Global legal pluralism can only be understood, and conceptualized, by recognizing that the participant experience of interpreters in any particular regulatory regime must co-exist with (and will shape and be shaped by) their observation of other regulatory regimes that overlap, relate to and possibly conflict with it. Participants in global legal pluralism will experience a variety of regimes, jurisdictions and systems, and will do so simultaneously as both observers and interpreters.

While Hart's expulsion of political power, in the form of Austinian sovereignty, from his concept of law explains its strange inability to relate law and state, or even to see law as more than a game of rules, Dworkin's distinguishing of law from game-rules in terms of law's wider moral significance points to law's essential ties to structures of community; that is, its deep immersion in the social. The lesson to be learned is that a convincing concept of law must emphasize directly and explicitly law's *political* dimensions or its *communal* dimensions, or both. And it must do so sociologically, recognizing (especially

[59] See D. Fraser, *Cricket and the Law: The Man in White is Always Right* (2005), especially chs. 6 and 7.

[60] A classic case is the notorious 1933 'body-line' controversy in cricket. For a brief account see R. Blythe, *The Age of Illusion* (1983) ch. 7. It has been suggested that 'law, unlike a game, purports to bind us morally': see J. Gardner, 'Legal Positivism: 5½ Myths' (2001), 46 *American Journal of Jurisprudence* 199 at 227. But this purported distinction begs the question of what morality can be. The idea of 'the spirit of the game' indicates a morality of its practice which it is not difficult to see as analogous to the morality that holds other kinds of networks of social relations together.

[61] M. Weber, *Critique of Stammler*, trans. G. Oakes (1977) 116–24.

in the contexts of global legal pluralism) the variety of law's practices and the empirical variability of its political and communal conditions of existence. It is to these matters that it is necessary, finally, to turn.

A concept of law should be judged by its fitness for the specific purpose for which it has been created. Whether treated as a model, framework, ideal type[62] or embodiment of a 'focal meaning',[63] it should be seen less as making 'a claim to truth'[64] about the nature of law than as organizing efforts towards solving specific problems, whether of legal discourse or in social research on legal phenomena. The tendency to present concepts of law as embodying truth about law may explain the radical inconclusiveness of some debates in legal philosophy. Behind this tendency is an assumption that all scholars are engaged in the same inquiry, about the same legal experience, with the same ends in view. When the participants in debates are theorists whose shared experience is of modern Western state legal systems, this assumption may be understandable. But in confronting the challenges posed by the interaction of many kinds of national, transnational and international regulation, as well as by intimations of legal pluralism in unitary nation states[65] and a new 'jurisprudence of difference' in legal thought,[66] it seems increasingly untenable.

Various concepts of law could be helpful in understanding global legal pluralism depending on the tasks in hand. Perhaps the most urgent task at present is to be able to map this pluralism, to use legal theory to show the interrelating legal structures that exist and to explore the kinds of legal reasoning possible (and hence the possibilities for a transnational rule of law) given this regulatory diversity. A concept of law serving such purposes would need to be able to represent not only legal thinking familiar to lawyers in modern nation-state legal systems, but also relationships between regulatory regimes not identified in terms of nation-state jurisdictions. The experience to be represented in a transnational concept of law will be simultaneously that of 'internal' participation in the use and interpretation of regulation and 'external' observation of how potentially conflicting or competing regulatory structures and practices interact. But legal interpretation – increasingly, interpretation *across* as well as within normative regimes – will not be possible except in the context of this observation. And observation of global legal pluralism will require *interpretive understanding* of its diverse normative practices. Thus, the distinctions between 'internal' and 'external' views of law, so familiar in legal philosophy, will be hard to maintain.

[62] M. Weber, *Economy and Society*, transl. E. Fischoff et al. (1968) 20–22.

[63] J. Finnis, *Natural Law and Natural Rights* (1980) 276–81.

[64] Cf. A. Marmor, 'Legal Positivism: Still Descriptive and Morally Neutral' (2006), 26 *Oxford Journal of Legal Studies* 683 at 692.

[65] See e.g. R. Grillo et al. (eds), *Legal Practice and Cultural Diversity* (2009).

[66] R. Cotterrell, *The Politics of Jurisprudence* 2nd edn (2003) ch. 8.

7. Politics, community, doctrine, practices

Beyond the need for this kind of responsiveness to a plurality of regimes of legally-relevant regulation, two other general suggestions about a transnational concept of law can be made, both of them developing points made earlier about problems of Hart's concept of law.

First, a Hartian concept of law that draws close analogies between legal rules and the rules of games, rather than emphasizing radical differences between them, is useful for many purposes; but in the complex, rapidly evolving, political and social contexts of global legal pluralism, concepts of law emphasizing law's links to political structures or its roots in various kinds of community structures seem especially important.

The *political* link suggests a need to consider new arguments about structures of national and international sovereignty, and more generally to examine the extent to which a useful concept of transnational law must incorporate a sharp awareness of the power structures of globalization and international relations. Correspondingly, linking law with structures of *community* would address a need to explore the many new and diverse networks of social relations that support various forms of transnational regulation. For example, it might reflect the ways in which transnational business and financial networks, as well as segments of legal and other professions operating transnationally, both shape and give authority to transnational regulation; an authority that might, in some cases, be as significant as the traditional forms of state-based legal authority. More generally, this approach would portray transnational law as representing networks of different types of social relations of community with different (often competing or conflicting) legal implications and problems.[67]

A second suggestion also relates to the emphasis on impersonal rules in Hart's concept of law. If this focus has a disadvantage in directing attention away from a search for what is distinctive about law in favour of emphasizing what may be common to many systems of social rules, a good strategy in developing a transnational concept of law might be to reintroduce the personal element by emphasizing not only rules, but also the institutionalized *practices of managing them*. Indeed, the emphasis should be on these practices in relation to legal doctrine in general, including not only rules, but also principles, concepts or values of law. The emphasis should be on relatively stable, recognized, established processes or agencies existing for the purpose of creating (including changing), interpreting or enforcing doctrine.[68]

[67] R. Cotterrell, 'Transnational Communities and the Concept of Law' (2008), 21 *Ratio Juris* 1. On law as the regulation of networks of community see Cotterrell, *Law, Culture and Society* (2006), and Cotterrell, *Living Law* (2008) ch. 2 and Part 4.

[68] R. Cotterrell, *Law's Community* (1995) ch. 2. The approach here can be compared with 'The Concept of Legalization' (loc. cit.) of Abbott et al. My concept of doctrine implies the idea of obligation which they also stress, and similarly embraces diverse normative phenomena (not just rules). But Abbott et al. address this diversity in terms of 'precision' as a variable, while I

To see law as *institutionalized* doctrine in this sense is to emphasize the specific, identifiable mechanisms by which legal doctrine is socially managed in organized, patterned ways. It is to emphasize that law is never normative ideas alone, but always ideas that are the focus of *specific practices* designed to serve them. Such an emphasis necessarily brings political or communal elements back into a concept of law, the nature of these depending on where the agencies or processes of doctrine-management are seen to be socially located, and by whom and in what ways they are controlled. Whatever their other roles and effects, these agencies or processes should be seen as controlling the *assertion of authority* by law. They are the primary institutional (that is, patterned, established and recognized) links between law as doctrine and its specific social contexts.[69]

In the context of global legal pluralism, it would be wise not to insist on the presence of *all* of these three kinds of institutionalized practices – for creation, interpretation *and* enforcement of doctrine – as necessary to the existence of law. Some degree of formal institutionalization is required to mark 'the legal'. But the purposes of a concept of law in this context might be best served by recognizing that, while the institutionalization of one or more of these functions of creation, interpretation or enforcement is necessary to law, not all of them may be found in every legal regime or legal type. For example, much well-developed and effective 'soft law' lacks formal enforcement mechanisms. And standards of various kinds that it might be very important to take into account in interpreting transnational regulation are not necessarily created by anything like orthodox courts or legislatures. Again, transnational doctrine sometimes lacks distinct adjudicatory or interpreting institutions or agencies; and where these exist they sometimes compete or conflict (a matter familiar in relation to international law as well as new transnational regulatory regimes).[70] The authority of transnational regulation as law might well vary depending on the extent of its institutionalization.

Concepts of law useful in analyzing transnational regulation are likely to be much more flexible and exploratory than many earlier characterizations of law

think types of doctrine may be differentiated in other ways. Their idea of 'delegation' refers to aspects of what I call institutionalization but begs questions about the diverse kinds of authority underpinning legal processes.

69 To talk of 'agencies', 'processes', 'practices' and 'institutions' is not necessarily to restate a Hartian emphasis on (secondary) rules since one should not assume, or emphasize, the rule-governed nature of these phenomena in all cases. Their customary, purposive, charismatic or prudential basis might not necessarily be best formulated in terms of governing rules (though in relation to many regulatory structures this will surely be possible). As Max Weber taught (*Economy and Society*, op. cit., 215–6, 226–54), not all legitimate authority is based on rules. A general concept of law taking account of the great variety of global regulatory structures will thus emphasize institutionalized practices from which rules may (or may not) emerge, or around which they may (or may not) cluster.

70 R. Higgins, 'A Babel of Judicial Voices? Ruminations from the Bench' (2006), 55 *International and Comparative Law Quarterly* 791; P. S. Berman, 'A Pluralist Approach to International Law' (2007), 32 *Yale Law Journal* 301.

in the literature of legal theory. Any such concept will be a work in progress, a provisional frame, a practical tool in organizing new fields, an idea tailored to specific contexts and projects. But it could serve new purposes of a reinvigorated general jurisprudence. It could help to re-direct analytical jurisprudence towards sustained engagement with the now pressing problems of understanding law's changing transnational arenas. Not least, it might dispel any lingering visions of the 'legal philosophers' circle', high up in its balloon, hardly connected to a turbulent, shifting legal reality on the ground.

15

How to do things with legislation, or, 'Everything depends on the context'[1]

David Miers

Introduction

When William Twining and I wrote *How to Do Things with Rules* (*Rules*),[2] our principal purpose was to develop an approach to the interpretation of rules of law that was premised on the unstartling but apparently overlooked idea that in spotting what might be one's doubt about a rule's interpretation and setting about a strategy to resolve it, any interpreter (but students of law in particular) would find it helpful first to focus on a range of factors beyond the text, however that might be formulated. Those factors included the various actors' standpoints, their perceptions of the problem or their understanding of the doubt raised by the facts and the potentially applicable rule(s), and the precision or otherwise of the normative context in which those rules had themselves been formulated and interpreted. During walks around Cardiff, Leamington Spa and Iffley, and with occasional time out to catch up with the Ashes or to support the local pub, it became clear that our approach could equally well apply to the interpretation of other written and unwritten rules of large and small societies, of clubs and communities, of national and international organizations, and of schools and universities. We also mulled over a more explicit extension of our approach to the interpretation of federal constitutions, but concluded that we would instead deploy these various texts more liberally at the outset of the book in order to engage the reader and to exemplify both the diversity of rules and rule-statements and the constant and common themes that attach to their interpretation and application.

Our primary focus throughout remained the domestic law of the United Kingdom, greatly changed by what in the last edition we called 'the European

1 Lord Steyn, *Effort Shipping v. Linden Management* [1998] 1 All ER 495, 508.
2 William Twining and David Miers, *How to Do Things with Rules: A Primer of Interpretation* (Cambridge University Press, 5th edition, 2010).

Dimension'. Published in 1976, the first edition was completed but three years after the United Kingdom's accession to what was then the European Economic Community, and more than twenty years before the Human Rights Act 1998 incorporated the European Convention for the Protection of Human Rights and Fundamental Freedoms (ECHR) into its law. But our central message remained consistent throughout: that to be a competent and effective interpreter of rules it is necessary first to develop an intelligent and enquiring understanding of the context in which those rules were made, and thus of the positions and arguments that interpreters may take about their application in any case. This understanding is initially based on an appreciation of the forms and functions of rules, of the nature of interpretation and its relationship with the rule's supposed or articulated purpose, and the impossibility of 'perfect' rules of law. We always regarded the central chapter on conditions of doubt as the fulcrum both of the book and of its message. Whether an interpreter's reading of a rule is routine or problematic depends in part on her understanding of its context, and it is for this reason that the chapters on legislation and its interpretation, and on reading cases, aimed to contextualize their origins and the interpretive communities that compete for attention.

I pursue this message here in the particular case of reading and interpreting legislation as my contribution to this celebration of the breadth and acuity of William's writings on law and jurisprudence, and in the more general sense of the intellectual and pedagogical themes that underpinned his groundbreaking work in the development of the *Law in Context* series, of which *Rules* was an early product. Nor is an understanding of a rule's context a desirable attribute only for those who inhabit Blackstone's Tower,[3] but as Lord Toulson made clear, it also has forensic value: 'in the area of statutory construction, context is critical.'[4] It is opportune, too, in the context of the government's 'good law' initiative launched in 2013. Promoted by the Office of the Parliamentary Counsel (OPC) and the Cabinet Office, 'good law' is 'necessary, effective, clear, coherent and accessible', qualities that ought to be achieved in legislation but are frustrated by a range of obstacles, of which perhaps the most debilitating is disproportionate complexity.[5] To understand its causes and possible remedies the good law initiative reflects many of the themes that William and I explored, in particular in chapters 7 and 8 of *Rules,* and that are reprised and updated here.[6]

[3] William Twining, *Blackstone's Tower: the English Law School* (1994).

[4] *R v. Massey* [2007] EWCA 2664 [15] (as Toulson LJ).

[5] See Office of the Parliamentary Counsel and the Cabinet Office, *When Laws Become Too Complex – A review into the causes of complex legislation* (March 2013).

[6] A fuller, referenced text is available on the Cambridge University Press Resources website www.cambridge.org/gb/academic/subjects/law/legal-skills-and-practice/how-do-things-rules-5th-edition?format=HB.

1. The political context: legislation is a political activity[7]

'Legislation affects us all.'[8] The ways in which the content, organization and the impact of any public general Act is determined have, with two significant exceptions – the formation of a Coalition Government following the General Election in May 2010, and the enactment of the Fixed-term Parliaments Act 2011 – hardly changed in the four years since the last edition of *Rules* was published in 2010. Since then, and at the time of writing (December 2014), 150 public general Acts had been passed, all marked by the same diversity in origin, subject-matter and intended effects. They variously give effect to the United Kingdom's obligations, within the European Union (EU) and under other international treaties, to recommendations of the Law Commission, and rectify earlier omissions, errors or unforeseen judicial interpretation revealed by litigation, public enquiries and rulings of the European Court of Human Rights. Some Acts are very short, others formidably long, and a few were highly controversial.

But the vast majority are products of government policy; some made by the previous government and others by the Coalition Government, a political arrangement unlike any previous British peacetime parliamentary experience. Much of its legislation comprised elements of its 'Programme for Government', but in form and content its legislation was very much in the mould, concerning single or connected policies on such matters as education, pensions, reform of the energy market and of welfare benefits; and, while legislation cannot of itself generate economic activity, responding to the 2008 financial crisis. A single Act will often group together a wide range of matters connected only by virtue of being to do with a broad conception of departmental policy. 'Christmas tree bills' have long been regarded as presenting obstacles to clarity in the organization of the statute book,[9] a feature particularly seen in the case of the Home Office, which has, with the Ministry of Justice, remained a dominant legislative force, many of their Acts touching on aspects of the rule of law and the separation of powers.

The Coalition Government introduced other changes to the United Kingdom's unwritten constitution, but without question the most significant was the Fixed-term Parliaments Act 2011. This ended the government's power to call a general election at a time of its own choosing and, unless repealed, has fixed the dates of all future general elections. In common

[7] 'At some level, all legislation is political; that fact is both an explanation for its controversial character and a source of its legitimacy'; D. Feldman, 'Beginning at the Beginning: The Relationships between Politics and Law', in D. Feldman, ed., *Law in Politics and Politics in Law* (2013; hereafter, *Feldman*), p. 7.

[8] *When Laws Become Too Complex*, p. 1. This succinct observation echoes the pervasiveness of the theme captured in the extract from the Renton Report (*The Preparation of Legislation*, 1975, Cmnd 6053; quoted at *Rules*, p. 196, and the analysis on pp. 197–8).

[9] House of Commons, Political and Constitutional Reform Committee (PCR Committee), *Ensuring Standards in the Quality of Legislation* (2013–14, HC 85), paras. 11–15.

with their predecessors, these further elements in a decade of constitutional change attracted no formally distinct parliamentary procedure, a deficit of which the House of Lords Constitution Committee (Constitution Committee) was highly critical. But the Coalition Government firmly rejected its recommendation that 'a clear and consistent process should apply to all significant constitutional change'. It acknowledged that clarity in the presentation of a Bill's effects is of central concern, but 'in this respect, constitutional change is no different from any other public policy. All policy development, whether or not leading to legislation, should go through a process of rigorous analysis.'[10] No special treatment was called for; nor, as the Committee itself recognized, is there a watertight definition of what is constitutional. There is here a theme that will repeat: there is little, if any, incentive for the executive to agree to reforms in the preparation or the scrutiny of legislation that may delay or otherwise constitute an obstacle to the application of the iron law of government, that it should always 'get its business'.

2. The preparatory context: precision and clarity in legislation

Along with the 'better legislation' agenda,[11] the good law initiative stands in the tradition of calls by parliamentary committees, academic writers and pressure groups to improve the clarity of legislation that commenced with the Renton Report,[12] but it is unique in being publicly led by the OPC. Its analysis of the causes of complex legislation centred, as did much of our consideration of the preparation of legislation, on three key dimensions: 'the volume of the statute book, the quality of legislation, and the perception of disproportionate complexity'.[13] For reasons of space, but noting the 2010 protocol between the Government and the Law Commission concerning its proposals for 'reform, consolidation or statute law revision',[14] I deal only with the second and third of these dimensions, as we did in *Rules*, in reverse order.

[10] Constitution Committee, *The Process of Constitutional Change* (2010–12, HL 177), paras. 115 and 126, and *The Government response to the House of Lords Constitution Committee report 'The process of constitutional change'* (2011, Cm. 8181).

[11] *Rules*, pp. 206–8. This agenda was a particular objective of the Commons Modernization Committee, established in 1997 but discontinued after the 2010 General Election. Its activities now fall within the wide terms of reference of the Political and Constitutional Reform Committee, discussed below.

[12] Supra, n. 8. [13] *When Laws Become Too Complex*, p. 6.

[14] The Law Commission, *Protocol between the Lord Chancellor (on Behalf of the Government) and the Law Commission* (2010; HC 499, Law Com No 321), para. 8, made under s. 2 of the Law Commission Act 2009. See Law Commission, *The Work of the Law Commission 2011–2015, Incorporating the Eleventh Programme* (July 2011), Part 3, and *Annual Report 2012–13* (Law Com 338), Part 2, Statute Law; *Rules*, pp. 224–9.

The perception of disproportionate complexity in legislation: who, what and why

One of the major developments in our understanding of the factors that bear on achieving precision and clarity in legislation has been the increasing transparency surrounding the conditions under which it is prepared. This is in part due to public accounts by current and former First Parliamentary Counsel, but substantially to the government's publication of the procedures to be followed from a department's wish to translate policy into law, through the drafting process, to the management of the Bill through Parliament.[15]

While the OPC's clients are the instructing government departments, the drafter's audience, as we discussed in the last edition, is much wider than that client relationship implies.[16] As between these various audiences – the department, MPs and peers, judges, users – the drafter's first responsibility is to the client department. Its responsibility, once the Cabinet's Parliamentary Business and Legislation (PBL) Committee has allocated its proposed Bill a slot in the government's legislative programme, is to produce a clear and detailed statement of what it is to do in policy terms. The main purpose of its drafting instructions is to say what is wanted. OPC's guide, *Working with Parliamentary Counsel*, suggests that their best structure emulates 'the elements of the so-called mischief rule of statutory interpretation', at whose core is the following analysis: 'This is something we want to happen; This is why it cannot happen without legislation; This is how we think the law needs to be changed in order for it to happen.'[17] These instructions' extent, complexity and impact on existing legislative or common law rules will vary from Bill to Bill. But the preparation of any Bill requires attention to its compatibility with the ECHR and with any EU legislation, to its impact on the devolved administrations, and to the conferral of any delegated powers likely to attract parliamentary scrutiny. For these purposes the Bill team must prepare memoranda for the PBL Committee, as well as Explanatory Notes and an Impact Assessment, both of which will become public documents, and all of which can be very useful aids to interpretation for both judicial and non-judicial interpreters.

The process of reducing policy to legislation – the narrowing down of high-level policy goals to precise, clear and enforceable rules of law – is a challenging task on which a former First Parliamentary Counsel singled out 'the problem of hitting a moving target from a moving platform' as deserving emphasis. This describes the process by which the drafter, in giving effect to policy, has to take account of how those whose behaviour is to be changed will respond, and possibly adjust what the legislation requires in order to correct their response to the desired course. But this adjustment must itself be calibrated to the

[15] Cabinet Office, *Guide to Making Legislation* (2013).

[16] *Rules*, pp. 203–6; see evidence of First Parliamentary Counsel, *Ensuring Standards in the Quality of Legislation*, EV 13, Q.36 (14 June 2012), and *When Laws Become Too Complex*, pp. 2, 21.

[17] The Office of the Parliamentary Counsel, *Working with Parliamentary Counsel* (2011), paras. 138, 165–6.

underlying policy with the result that the legislative solution may well now differ from the drafter's starting point, or becomes more complex. And because primary legislation 'is usually prepared on the basis that it will continue in place until it has been repealed, rather than expire when its purpose has been fulfilled', the drafter has to anticipate 'not only the immediate consequences of a change but also its longer term effect.'[18] Ensuring that those whose behaviour is to be affected by the Act will, by means of sanction or remedy, behave as the policy desires, means that 'from a legal point of view, law is written with those who might break it in mind. Politically, law is written for those who are expected to abide by it.'[19]

All of this can add to a Bill's complexity, on the causes of which the good law initiative provides a detailed analysis. In an echo of a point we made in the last edition, this commences with the observation that 'often, when complaining about poor legislation, commentators are really criticising the political and ideological considerations that lie behind the Bill.'[20] How does complexity, or, as OPC characterizes the question, the perception of complexity, arise? In part it is because 'the legislation that we produce covers an enormous area, and the area occupied by the statute book gets bigger and bigger year after year. That is for all sorts of reasons – partly European law, human rights law, the desire for society to address mischiefs and to get things regulated and to remove sources of injustice';[21] but there is no single cause. Complexity depends in part upon the user's standpoint, in particular their experience with those areas of statute law with which, for reasons of their profession, appointment or employment, they have familiarity: 'the likely audience for a specific law depends on the context.'[22]

The quality of legislation

Given the broadly accepted diagnosis that legislation can be disproportionately complex, the good law initiative, pursued at the preparatory and, later, the parliamentary stages of a Bill, prescribes remedies that contemplate, first, standards designed to satisfy fundamental constitutional norms that apply to any law making in a liberal democracy, and, secondly, more specific drafting standards designed to promote clarity alongside precision in the legislative text. As to the first, considerable attention has of late been given to the development of a code of constitutional standards to be applied to the preparation of legislation. These would prescribe how clauses dealing, for

[18] Sir S. Laws, 'Giving Effect to Policy in Legislation: How to Avoid Missing the Point', *Statute Law Review*, 32(1) (2011), 1–16, pp. 7–8.
[19] Sir S. Laws, 'Legislation and Politics' in *Feldman*, pp. 87–103, pp. 92–94. This echoes Stephen J.'s encomium, *Rules*, p. 142.
[20] *When Laws Become Too Complex*, p. 6; *Rules*, pp. 213–4.
[21] First Parliamentary Counsel, *Ensuring Standards in the Quality of Legislation*, Evidence, EV 13, Q. 34 (14 June 2012).
[22] *When Laws Become Too Complex*, pp. 19, 24–8.

example, with retrospective legislation, delegated powers, access to justice and the timing of pre-legislative scrutiny, should be formulated.[23]

More recently, the House of Commons Political and Constitutional Reform Committee (PCR Committee) proposed a somewhat different approach,[24] but one which resonates at some points with these constitutional standards. It proposed that a Code of Legislative Standards for good quality legislation be agreed between Parliament and the Government, and that a Joint Legislative Standards Committee of Parliament be established to ensure that Bills comply with agreed technical and procedural criteria.[25] The specific drafting techniques that the Committee identified, such as purpose or overview clauses, new definitions of existing legal concepts, index clauses for definitions and formulae, invite two comments. First, a number of them have been in use for some years, and are seen in recent enactments;[26] for example, the Bribery Act 2010 and the Immigration Act 2014 continue the use of symbols to identify the persons to whom a section refers.[27] Other examples include ss. 1–6 of the Flood and Water Management Act 2010 (a response to the floods of the summer of 2007), which are titled 'key concepts and definitions'; s. 1 of the Sunbeds (Regulation) Act 2010 (a government backed private Member's Bill), headed 'main interpretative provisions'); s. 1 of the Taxation of Pensions Act 2014, headed 'Provision for pension flexibility etc.' which lists the seven Parts of Schedule 1 containing the detail of that provision; the interpretation section of the Local Audit and Accountability Act 2014, which italicizes the words to be construed; s. 4 of the National Insurance Contributions Act 2014, which, in a clear echo of an explanatory leaflet, is titled, 'How does a person who qualifies for an employment allowance receive it?'; and s. 1 of the Corporation Tax Act 2010, headed 'Overview of Act', itself a further instalment of the *Tax Law Rewrite Project*.[28]

Secondly, the use of these and such other devices as preambles and purpose clauses (s. 1(2) of the Anti-Slavery Day Act 2010) is not uncontroversial. It is useful, initially, to distinguish two kinds of purpose clause. There are, first, those that set out a framework for the exercise of regulatory or executive discretion by Ministers, local government, or a statutory agency responsible for a given area of public policy. This kind of purpose clause, which is quite commonly used to set the parameters by which regulatory or executive decisions are to be made, should be distinguished from those

[23] These standards are helpfully summarized in J. Caird, R. Hazell and D. Oliver, *The Constitutional Standards of the House of Lords Select Committee on the Constitution* (2014).

[24] This was also an objective of the House of Commons Modernization Committee, established in 1997 (*Rules*, pp. 207–208), but it was discontinued after the 2010 General Election. Its activities now fall within the wide terms of reference of the PCR Committee.

[25] *Ensuring Standards in the Quality of Legislation* (2013–14, HC 85), Annex A.

[26] Flood and Water Management Act 2010, ss. 1–6 'key concepts and definitions'; Sunbeds (Regulation) Act 2010, s. 1 'main interpretative provisions'.

[27] The use of such symbols assists gender neutrality in drafting as much as it assists clarity.

[28] *Rules*, pp. 223–4, and see *Guide to Making Legislation*, paras. 28.20 and 40.11.

purpose clauses whose function is to resolve ambiguities in interpretation that the drafter ought to have resolved. In this instance, the public policy task is, in effect, being left to the judiciary to determine. In the last edition we discussed the theoretical and operational hazards that attend the use of purpose clauses (and also of statements of principle); debate about their value continues. For their supporters, purpose clauses can improve the Bill's drafting, assist parliamentary scrutiny, guide other users through the Bill's content and aid interpretation. For their critics, their typical generality means that they are of little value in assisting detailed understanding of the Act and may be a potential source of doubt about its interpretation.[29] But, as one critic has commented, the literature 'has two large gaps in it. The first is that there is little empirical evidence of the operation of objects provisions. The second is that there is very little treatment of the administration – where numerically far more application of the law occurs than in the courts.'[30]

More promising is the considered use of plain language drafting, where OPC 'has worked to make legislation more accessible';[31] but here too there are constraints. 'It is axiomatic that legislation can have only one function and that is to change the law';[32] the use of plain language may be the direction of travel, but provided only that it does not perversely obscure precision in what is to be achieved.[33] A second is political. These various drafting techniques are helpful but (like drafters) governments of all persuasions have always been reluctant to elevate the prudential to the prescriptive; in this the Coalition Government is no different. Accepting that improvements in the quality of legislation are both desirable and possible, it rejected both proposals as neither necessary nor effective.[34]

3. The parliamentary context

The widespread public disengagement with parliamentary government occasioned by the MPs expenses scandal triggered a period of intense self-scrutiny within the House of Commons, which we reviewed in Appendix 8 of *Rules* and do not rehearse here.[35] A major consequence was the *Wright* report, many of

[29] *Rules*, pp. 222–3; *Ensuring Standards in the Quality of Legislation*, para. 68; there are no references to 'purpose clauses' in the *Guide to Making Legislation*.

[30] J. Barnes, 'Statutory Objects Provisions: How Cogent is the Research and Commentary?' *Statute Law Review*, 34(1) (2013), 12–31, 29.

[31] *Ensuring Standards in the Quality of Legislation*, para. 39.

[32] 'Giving Effect to Policy in Legislation: How to Avoid Missing the Point', p. 3.

[33] *Rules*, p. 221; *Ensuring Standards in the Quality of Legislation*, Evidence, EV 13, Q. 35 (14 June 2012); see also J. Barnes, 'When "Plain Language" Legislation is Ambiguous – Sources of Doubt and Lessons for the Plain Language Movement', *Melbourne University Law Review*, 34 (2010), 671–707.

[34] PCR Committee, *Ensuring standards in the quality of legislation: Government Response to the Committee's First Report of Session 2013–14* (2013, HC 611), paras. 12, 18, and 21.

[35] Available on the Cambridge University Press Resources website.

whose recommendations have been successfully implemented,[36] but arguably only because there was here a 'constitutional moment',[37] or, as the Speaker of the House of Commons described it, 'the catalyst of the expenses scandal'.[38]

To understand the impact of the parliamentary context in which Bills are enacted, it is necessary to recognize that the principal driver is the executive's desire to control the process of enactment. The central importance of 'the usual channels' and of party management, especially in the case of the 650 MPs in the Commons to ensure that enough Members are present (or paired) to vote on government business, remain fundamentally unchanged, as do a Bill's formal stages.[39] In the case of the Lords, Ministers are advised to prepare a 'parliamentary handling strategy', to include a list of those peers 'likely to take a particular interest and what engagement with them is planned'.[40] Pre-legislative scrutiny conducted by joint committees of the Lords and Commons and the now better-informed Public Bill committees in the Commons both carry the potential for and have improved the scrutiny process. But their effectiveness depends upon the willingness of Members and inevitably, of government, to make them work. While successive governments have accepted the value of pre-legislative scrutiny in principle, and a Bill's progress is now better facilitated by 'programme orders',[41] the Coalition Government's desire to get its business meant that it rejected the PCR Committee's recommendation that pre-legislative scrutiny should be mandatory, as that would reduce flexibility in the management of its programme.[42]

There are very few Bills that do not confer power on a Minister to legislate, typically by means of a statutory instrument; some 3,500 or so are produced every year. As described in the last edition, Parliament's institutional arrangements for the scrutiny of those that are subject to parliamentary procedure (primarily affirmative procedure) have focussed separately on their technical qualities (Joint Committee on Statutory Instruments (JCSI))[43] and on their merits (House of Lords Merits of Statutory Instruments Committee). We also

36 PCR Committee, *Revisiting Rebuilding the House: the impact of the Wright reforms* (2012–13, HC 82).

37 D. Oliver, 'Politics, Law and Constitutional Moments in the UK', in *Feldman*, pp. 239–56, 241. No such moment has arisen for House of Lords reform; nor does one look likely.

38 The Rt Hon John Bercow MP, The Michael Ryle Memorial Lecture (30 June 2014); www.parliament.uk/business/commons/the-speaker/speeches/speeches/michael-ryle-memorial-lecture-/.

39 *Rules*, pp. 200–4. A Bill's stages are helpfully visualized and documented on the parliamentary website www.parliament.uk/about/how/laws/passage-bill.

40 *Guide to Making Legislation*, section 19.

41 House of Commons, Procedure Committee, *Programming* (2013–14, HC 767).

42 *Revisiting Rebuilding the House*, paras. 15–18. See also the previous government's response to the Constitution Committee's recommendations concerning 'fast-track' legislation: Constitution Committee, *Government Response to Fast-track Legislation: Constitutional Implications and Safeguards* (2009–10, HL 11), Appendix p. 7.

43 *Rules*, pp. 216–8. The JCSI now operates a process of pre-scrutiny of draft instruments subject to the affirmative procedure in order to 'help to avoid difficulties about powers, drafting, etc.' at a later stage.

noted the significant escalation in the intensity of parliamentary scrutiny of delegated legislation as successive governments sought to provide for executive law making without the paraphernalia of promoting a Bill. The threat posed to parliamentary sovereignty by legislation conferring on Ministers the power to dispense with primary legislation ('Henry VIII powers') is illustrated by the Coalition Government's Public Bodies Act 2011.

As drafted, the Bill contained powers authorizing Ministers by order to abolish or merge public bodies and offices, or to modify their constitutional or financial arrangements; the only parliamentary control was the affirmative resolution procedure. In a critical review, the Delegated Powers and Regulatory Reform Committee (DPRR Committee) commented that these powers 'would grant to Ministers unacceptable discretion to rewrite the statute book, with inadequate parliamentary scrutiny of, and control over, the process'.[44] On this occasion the government relented, amending the Bill to include an obligation on the Minister to consult, a sunset clause,[45] and a number of statutory conditions that must be met before a draft order can be laid.[46] The Act also introduced an 'enhanced affirmative procedure', which extends the scrutiny period if either House so resolves.

Viewed overall, parliamentary scrutiny of delegated legislation now comprises, in ascending order, and according to whether the legislation is an ordinary statutory instrument, a public bodies order or a legislative reform order, negative, affirmative, enhanced affirmative, and super-affirmative procedure. While they do provide for a strengthened scrutiny role for Parliament, the Coalition Government has acknowledged that this 'patchwork of procedures' may be unhelpfully complex; but, and as always, it has expressly reserved the right to develop a different approach where 'an existing model is not viewed as appropriate'.[47] Its desire to keep control extends also to the executive's cautious response to proposals to establish post-legislative scrutiny

[44] DPRR Committee, *Public Bodies Bill [HL]* (2010, HL 57) para. 1. See also criticism of the Draft Deregulation Bill, which underwent pre-legislative scrutiny during the 2013–14 session of Parliament, followed by the government's withdrawal of the offending clauses; Joint Committee on the Draft Deregulation Bill, *Draft Deregulation Bill Report* (2013–14, HL 101, HC 925), paras. 18 and 67; *Government Response to the Report of the Joint Committee on the Draft Deregulation Bill* (2014, Cm 8808), para. 14.

[45] 'Sunset' clauses, which provide for automatic expiry after a specified period of the Act (or a Part or sections of it), have rarely figured in United Kingdom legislation. They are now more widely used as an alternative to or in conjunction with 'review clauses', a novel requirement to review new or amended regulation; see HM Government, *Sunsetting Regulations: Guidance* (2011). Section 124 of the Police Reform and Social Responsibility Act 2011 provides an extensive example; see also the Enterprise and Regulatory Reform Act 2013, s. 59(2), inserting s. 14A in the Interpretation Act 1978.

[46] Ministerial compliance with the statutory conditions is monitored in the Lords by the Merits Committee, renamed the Secondary Legislation Scrutiny Committee in recognition of this new role, and in the Commons by the relevant departmental select committee.

[47] DPRR Committee, *Statutory Procedures for the Scrutiny of Delegated Powers* (2012-13, HL 19), para. 1; *Statutory Procedures for the Scrutiny of Delegated Powers: Government Response* (2012–13, HL 64), Appendix A.

as a routine aspect of the oversight of new legislation. Central to the issue is the question of who would conduct such scrutiny: the government of the day, or Parliament? The Constitution Committee recommended that, as with pre-legislative scrutiny, post-legislative scrutiny should be conducted by a Joint Committee on Post-Legislative Scrutiny, a view shared by the Law Commission.[48] Not persuaded by this particular proposal, but accepting that a new process for post-legislative scrutiny was desirable, the government introduced in 2008 new arrangements based on the combination of a published departmental memorandum on the Act's implementation and its scrutiny by the corresponding House of Commons select committee, should it choose to do so.[49] The problem is that the number and length of these memoranda would far exceed the departmental select committees' capacity to scrutinize each Act. A 2013 review noted that 'out of the 58 government post-legislative scrutiny memoranda published so far, only three have been the subject of dedicated reports by committees.'[50]

4. Interpretive contexts: *judicial interpretation: language, context and purpose*

Questions that concern what is meant by and how an interpreter, including judicial interpreters, might uncover 'the intention of Parliament' in any case continues to generate both puzzlement and discussion of its value for any interpretive exercise.[51] In respect of judicial interpretation, our approach was to analyze, within the court's overarching 'basic task' as conceived by Lord Bingham in the *Quintavalle* case,[52] decisions reported in one year of the *All England Law Reports* that illustrated how judges articulated their understanding of that task. Our results are confirmed by a similar exercise in which, of 162 decisions recorded in *Westlaw* in 2013, 117 (72%) related to questions concerning the application of one or more statutory provisions to the facts, and around a third of the total contained specific or more general normative propositions concerning the 'interpretation of statutes' or 'statutory interpretation'. One of these decisions, *Bloomsbury International Limited and others v Sea Fish Industry Authority and Department for Environment, Food and Rural Affairs* is a clear example of Supreme Court's application of what Lord Steyn earlier described as the modern approach to statutory construction, 'to have

48 Constitution Committee, *Parliament and the Legislative Process* (2003–04, HL 173-I), para 165; Law Commission, *Post-Legislative Scrutiny* (2008, Law Commission 302, Cm. 6945).

49 Office of the Leader of the House of Commons, *Post-Legislative Scrutiny: The Government's Approach* (2008, Cm. 7320); and see *Guide to Making Legislation*, para. 13.17 and Part 40.

50 House of Commons, Liaison Committee, *Select Committee Effectiveness, Resources and Powers: Responses to the Committee's Second Report* (2012–13, HC 911), p. 12.

51 R. Ekins, *The Nature of Legislative Intent* (2012); N. Duxbury, *Elements of Legislation* (2013).

52 *R (on the application of Quintavalle) v. Secretary of State for Health* [2003] UKHL 13; *Rules*, pp. 243–8.

regard to the purpose of a particular provision and interpret its language, so far as possible, in a way which best gives effect to that purpose'.[53]

The case concerned a statutory levy payable by their importers on sea fish and fish products that were, according to s. 4(3)(a) of the Fisheries Act 1981, 'landed in the United Kingdom'. The condition of doubt turned on an ambiguity in that phrase. Did it mean fish brought ashore for the first time, in this instance in the United Kingdom (the narrow meaning), or did it include fish brought into the territory of the United Kingdom, whether directly from the sea or indirectly after having been brought ashore in another country (the broad meaning)?[54] The importers' case was that the levy could only be imposed upon fish whose first 'landing', after being caught, was in the United Kingdom. Rejecting this in favour of the broad meaning, Lord Mance, speaking for the majority, observed that 'in matters of statutory construction, the statutory purpose and the general scheme by which it is to be put into effect are of central importance. They represent the context in which individual words are to be understood.' Here, the legislation's purpose and scheme was clearly set out in the Act: to promote the efficiency of the sea fish industry, specifically including importers of sea fish or sea fish products, and to impose a levy on importers in order to fund that purpose.[55] The narrow meaning would defeat the purpose since very few of such importers would be caught and thus contribute to the levy. Accordingly, the broader meaning, covering any form of bringing the fish into the United Kingdom, wherever the sea fish or fish product may have been first landed after catch, was to be preferred.

It is not possible to examine here the many dicta in the 2013 cases concerning the performance of the judge's basic task, but Lord Neuberger MR's observation, that 'the starting point for any exercise of statutory interpretation is that the language of the statute should be given its ordinary meaning',[56] is both typical and authoritative. This is so even where the definition of the word (or words) to be interpreted is very wide and thus the consequence for a person caught by them severe. 'Despite the undesirable consequences of the combination of the very wide definition of "terrorism" and the provisions of s. 117 [of the Terrorism Act 2000] it is difficult to see how the natural, very wide, meaning of the definition can properly be cut down by this Court.' Unless the natural meaning of the legislation conflicts with the ECHR, or with any other international obligation of the United Kingdom, 'our function', said

[53] [1997] 3 All ER 818, 825. Reaffirmed in *Barclays Mercantile Business Finance Ltd v Mawson (Inspector of Taxes)* [2004] UKHL 51 [28]; and IRC v. *Scottish Provident Institution* [2004] UKHL 52.

[54] Adapted from Lord Phillips [2011] UKSC 25 [56]. The case also involved the question of whether the levy constituted a customs duty under European Union law, in which case it would be void.

[55] [2011] UKSC 25 [10]–[11].

[56] *Crown Prosecution Service and Secretary of State for the Home Department v Gohil and Gohil* [2012] EWCA Civ 1550 [26].

Lord Neuberger P in *Gul*, 'is to interpret the meaning of the definition in its statutory, legal and practical context.' For this purpose, the court may, though the use of *Hansard* within the terms of Pepper *v Hart* is inapplicable,[57] 'find comfort' in parliamentary exchanges with the government Minister,[58] as well as, more generally, in the disputed section's legislative history.[59]

An important element in the Supreme Court's reasoning in *Hughes*, a case concerning the interpretation of s.3ZB of the Road Traffic Act 1988, was that the principle of legality requires that where Parliament does, as its sovereignty permits it to do, legislate contrary to fundamental principles of human rights, then it must do so in clear words: 'fundamental rights cannot be overridden by general or ambiguous words.'[60] But whereas in *Hughes* there was no unambiguous text indicating Parliament's intention to displace the principle against penalization under a doubtful law,[61] the statutory words under consideration in *Fowler v Commissioner of Police for the Metropolis* were 'sufficiently clear to indicate that Parliament intended them to bear their natural and ordinary meaning, despite the fact that such an interpretation involved overriding essential privacy rights.' The Court of Appeal added, 'the principle of legality is an important tool of statutory interpretation. But it is no more than that. When an issue of statutory interpretation arises, ultimately the question for the court is always to decide what Parliament intended.'[62]

If the principle of legality is defeasible when determining from the statute's purpose and the clarity of its language what the interpretation of a contested word or phrase ought to be, so too are the many canons of construction and other normative propositions that congregate around the matter of statutory interpretation; for example, when used in statutory texts, ordinary words of the English language should be interpreted according to their natural and ordinary meaning in context, unless that yields a result inconsistent with the statute's purpose. Not only may a particular canon of construction (or presumption) be displaced by the statutory language, but 'there will be many cases, where different canons will point to different answers'. The notion of normative ambiguity is familiar enough, but, as Lord Neuberger MR continued in *Cusack v London Borough of Harrow*, that does not call their value into question. They have a valuable part to play in interpretation, 'provided that they are treated as guidelines rather than railway lines, as servants rather than masters'.[63]

[57] [1993] AC 593; *Rules*, pp. 260–6.

[58] *R v Gul* [2013] UKSC 64 [38]–[39], *per* Lord Neuberger P.

[59] *The Queen (Oao) Omar & Ors v The Secretary of State for Foreign and Commonwealth Affairs* [2013] EWCA Civ 118.

[60] *R v Secretary of State for the Home Department Ex p Simms and O'Brien* [2000] 2 AC 115, 131E, per Lord Hoffmann, cited in *Hughes* [2013] UKSC 56 [27], *per* Lords Hughes and Toulson. They added, 'The duty of a court faced with legislation is faithfully to construe its meaning. It is not to impose upon it a judicial view of what it ought to have said' [13].

[61] F. Bennion, *Bennion on Statutory Interpretation* (2008) Part XVII.

[62] [2013] EWCA Civ 1342 [28], [31], *per* Lord Dyson MR.

[63] [2013] UKSC 40 [57]; *Rules*, p. 244.

The Court of Appeal's overarching comment in this case on the nature of interpretation warrants repetition. 'Interpretation of any document ultimately involves identifying the intention of Parliament, the drafter, or the parties. That intention must be determined by reference to the precise words used, their particular documentary and factual context, and, where identifiable, their aim or purpose. To that extent, almost every issue of interpretation is unique in terms of the nature of the various factors involved. However, that does not mean that the court has a completely free hand when it comes to interpreting documents: that would be inconsistent with the rule of law, and with the need for as much certainty and predictability as can be attained, bearing in mind that each case must be resolved by reference to its particular factors.'[64] The judiciary's self-imposed limitations on what would otherwise constitute a 'free hand' in interpretation may be analyzed in terms of the judicial interpretation of statutes being a 'disciplined activity'.[65] Our approach has been to characterize them as the product of the shared understandings of both the constraints and the freedoms implicit in the judges' position within the constitution that are made explicit in the interpretive community of which they are members.[66]

5. Broadening the study of law from within: the case of legal education

William Twining's contribution to our understanding of the use, scope, definition and interpretation of rules, and of rules of law, powerfully challenges much of the received wisdom concerning how legal education should go about its business of enabling students to become competent users and interpreters, in particular, of legislative and case law rules. Broadening the study of law within legal education means being alert to the contexts in which rules, whether in fixed or non-fixed verbal form, come to be identified and formulated as responses to perceived problems; and in these particular contexts, recognizing that judicial pronouncements about the doctrine of precedent and the role of interpretive norms, while constituting uniquely authoritative models of interpretation, are not the full story.[67]

Noting that a user study found that 'the comprehension level of legislative texts by both legally qualified and non-legally qualified users was generally quite low and that all users found it challenging to read legislation and demonstrate their understanding of it', the good law initiative remarked on a review conducted by the *Statute Law Society*, which indicated 'that until recently, legislation, legislative techniques and interpretation were often

[64] Ibid., [58]. [65] Duxbury, *supra*, n. 51, pp. xiv–xv.

[66] See for example *Benkharbouche v Embassy of The Republic of Sudan* UKEAT/0401/12/GE [38]-[40], per Langstaff J and *R (on the application of Prudential plc and another) v Special Commissioner of Income Tax and another* [2013] UKSC 1 [52]–[72] per Lord Neuberger P.

[67] William Twining, 'The Bad Man Revisited', *Cornell Law Review*, 58 (1973), 275–93; *Rules*, pp. 15–23 and passim.

neglected in undergraduate teaching'.[68] It may be that undergraduates find 'the interpretation of legislation', whether part of a first year introduction to the legal system or a legal skills course, or an element in a traditional jurisprudence course, to be dull. Law students may well miss in the legislative text the dialectic that sharpens the issues and makes reading cases in the core or their chosen optional areas of study live. But a legislative text is also the product of a dialectic process even if many more elements contributed to the formulation and eventual enactment of the policy, however modest. It was in part for this reason that we included in *Rules* a wide range of exercises that we considered might address this problem, and possibly engage their interest. At the very least, we considered that a fuller understanding of the legislation's origins, and of the various actors' standpoint, was a good place to begin the interpretive task. It may seem that there is nothing that is very novel in this; but the *Statute Law Society*'s conclusion, if of general application, suggests that if progress is to be made in legal education's grasp of what drives interpretation in any case, this central message in William Twining's jurisprudence continues to command attention.

[68] *When Laws Become Too Complex*, pp. 19–20. The Teaching of Legislation, www.statutelawsociety.org/teaching_legislation_materials/academic_papers_on_teaching_legislation.

16

How to do things with standards

Jeremy Waldron[1]

1

The distinction between rules and standards is nowadays a commonplace of American jurisprudence. A speed limit is a rule; a norm that requires drivers to take reasonable care is a standard. The distinction is between a norm that uses relatively precise, descriptive and perhaps even operationalized predicates in its protasis and apodosis, and a norm that, in its protasis and apodosis, uses evaluative or other vague terms whose application requires thought, evaluation or judgment on the part of the norm applier.

The distinction between rules and standards is less well known in the United Kingdom, in British jurisprudence. It doesn't really feature in William Twining and David Miers' book, *How to Do Things with Rules*: there is no entry for 'standards' in the index to that book.[2] In fact, Twining and Miers explicitly disavow any real interest in different types of norms. They seem to want to use 'rule' as a very general term, meaning 'a general norm mandating or guiding conduct or action in a given type of situation', and they agree that this definition is 'somewhat broader than the term is sometimes used in ordinary discussion'.[3]

They do cite (and criticize) Ronald Dworkin's distinction between rules and principles; but they concentrate mainly on his distinction between norms that apply in an all-or-nothing fashion ('rules', according to Dworkin) and norms that guide but do not necessarily determine a result ('principles').[4] (They do not pay attention to his account of the different modes of presentation of rules and principles in the law: rules present themselves, are recognized, and operate at the surface of enacted law whereas principles reside deep within the spirit of a legal system and are not easily discerned by a 'rule of recognition'.)[5] Dworkin probably erred in thinking

[1] An earlier version of this paper was presented at a conference on vagueness organized by the NYU Philosophy Department in 2013.

[2] William Twining and David Miers, *How to Do Things with Rules: A Primer of Interpretation*, 5th edition (Cambridge University Press, 2010).

[3] Ibid., pp. 80, 83.

[4] Ibid., pp. 82–5, responding to Ronald Dworkin, *Taking Rights Seriously* (Harvard University Press, 1977), at pp. 22–8.

[5] Dworkin, 'The Model of Rules', pp. 39–45.

that H. L. A. Hart was using the term 'rule' in the rather narrow sense that American jurists have in mind when they contrast rules and standards.[6] And Dworkin confused matters further by using the term 'standard' as a very general term, meaning roughly 'norm' and comprising both rules and principles. So terminology in this area is a bit of nightmare.

Even so, the distinction between rules and standards, as different kinds of surface-level or enacted norm, is pretty well known in America.[7] The constitutional norm in Article II of the US Constitution stipulating the age that a person must have attained before he or she can become President of the United States is a rule: 'neither shall any person be eligible to that Office who shall not have attained to the Age of thirty five Years'.[8] The use of a numerical predicate, 'thirty five', is typical of a rule, as is the existence of a clear and public method of establishing whether the norm condition applies – namely, the practice of issuing birth certificates and public and uncontroversial ways of counting the number of years that have elapsed since the day of a person's birth. And the constitutional norm that limits the punishments and exactions that may be inflicted by US authorities is a classic example of a standard: 'Excessive bail shall not be required, nor excessive fines imposed, nor cruel and unusual punishments inflicted.'[9] The word 'excessive' in both its occurrences is a term of evaluation, requiring normative judgment in its application; the same is true of 'cruel', though it is a slightly 'thicker' or more specific term of evaluation than 'excessive'. Both are enacted norms, and so they both differ from the norms that Dworkin called 'principles'. Dworkinian principles, however, usually have the characteristic that distinguishes standards from rules: they are best formulated, when they are formulated, with the use of evaluative terms. (The paradigm that Dworkin is famous for using, 'No one shall profit from his own wrongdoing', is an example. It requires evaluative judgment, not only to discern the principle but to apply it.)

The distinction between rules and standards is not hard and fast, partly because the term we are using to make the distinction – 'predicates that require evaluative judgment in their application' – is not itself precise: for example, is 'unusual' in the Eighth Amendment such a term? But the purposes for which we draw the distinction do not themselves require precision. We are interested in the distinction between rules and standards partly because of the different political responsibilities that they indicate. Doing things with norms involves acting or requiring action pursuant to certain value-judgments. In the case of rules, all the relevant value-judgments are

[6] Ibid., pp. 38–9; cf. H. L. A. Hart, *The Concept of Rules* (Oxford University Press, 1961), pp. 77–88 and 'Postscript' in H. L. A. Hart, *The Concept of Rules*, 3rd edition (Oxford University Press, 2012), pp. 254ff. See also Twining and Miers, *How to Do Things with Rules*, p. 84.

[7] See, for example, Duncan Kennedy, 'Form and Substance in Private Law Adjudication', *Harvard Law Review* 88 (1976), 1685, at pp. 1687–1701; Kathleen Sullivan, 'The Supreme Court, 1991 Term – Foreword: The Justices of Rules and Standards', *Harvard Law Review*, 106 (1992), 22.

[8] US Constitution, Article II, clause 5. [9] Ibid., Amendment Eight.

made by those who frame and enact the norm. In the case of standards, however, some of the relevant value-judgments are left to be made by those whose task it is to apply the norm. With rules, value-judgments are made upstream at the legislative level; with standards, some of the relevant value-judgments are made downstream on the streets or in the courtroom.[10]

We are also interested in the distinction between rules and standards, because of the particular problems that they pose. Standards pose problems of disparate and unpredictable application in a pluralistic society; what counts as 'cruel' or 'excessive' to some people in a given society may counts as 'entirely appropriate' to other members of the same society, and it may be impossible for the subject of a norm to figure out which group his actions will be at the mercy of. Rules pose problems of arbitrarily concocted precision in circumstances where precise application is sought for its own sake rather than for the sake of tracking boundaries that are in themselves morally relevant. There is nothing particularly significant about a thirty-five year age qualification for the presidency, as opposed to thirty-six or thirty-four-and-a-half; relative to those possibilities, the constitutional standard is arbitrary. We insist arbitrarily on precision here just because we want a bright-line distinction, not because the thirty-five-year cut-off has any moral significance in itself.

Thirdly, we are interested in whether adjudicators and other interpreters should see standards as 'inchoate' rules. Presented with a standard, as I have defined it, should a judge or a bench of judges see it as their task to convert the standard into a rule by pinning down its application in various determinate ways? Or are there ways of interpreting and elaborating a standard which keep faith with the fact that it was not promulgated as a rule – with the fact that it was, as Henry Hart and Albert Sacks put it, 'an *avowedly* indeterminate directive'?[11]

These interests do not presuppose a bright line between rules and standards. But their pursuit is interesting for jurisprudence nonetheless. The case of standards helps complicate and deepen our sense of how people can do things with norms.

I said that Twining and Miers do not make use of the distinction between rules and standards. They do talk briefly about the idea of a standard, even though they don't use that terminology. One interesting point they make is that norms whose expression embodies value predicates can sometimes operate categorically as rules (in the narrow sense). There is no necessary correlation between precision and prescriptive status.[12] So, for example, Article 3 of

[10] See Frederick Schauer, *Playing by the Rules: A Philosophical Examination of Rule-Based Decision-Making in Law and in Life* (Oxford University Press, 1991), pp. 158 ff.

[11] See Henry M. Hart and Albert M. Sacks, *The Legal Process: Basic Problems in the Making and Application of Law* (William N. Eskridge and Philip P. Frickey (eds), 1994), p. 150 (my emphasis).

[12] Twining and Miers, *How to Do Things with Rules*, p. 83.

the European Convention on Human Rights operates categorically to forbid torture and inhuman and degrading treatment; the fact that these terms are general and evaluative in character does not diminish the categorical character of the norm that embodies them. I think it is a pity that Twining and Miers did not explore the idea of standards beyond this. In the rest of the paper, I want to give a taste of what such exploration might reveal – of the different ways in which a lawmaker and the community for which he legislates can 'do things' with standards.

2

Let me begin with an American example, from the State of Montana in the north-western United States. Section 61–8–303(1) of the Montana Code – the part of Montana's law dealing with speed limits – used to provide as follows:

> [α] A person operating or driving a vehicle of any character on a public highway of this state shall drive the vehicle in a careful and prudent manner and at a rate of speed no greater than is reasonable and proper under the conditions existing at the point of operation, taking into account the amount and character of traffic, condition of brakes, weight of vehicle, grade and width of highway, condition of surface, and freedom of obstruction to the view ahead. The person operating or driving the vehicle shall drive the vehicle so as not to unduly or unreasonably endanger the life, limb, property, or other rights of a person entitled to the use of the street or highway.

But it now specifies numerical speed limits:

> [β] The speed limit for vehicles traveling: (a) on a federal-aid interstate highway outside an urbanized area of 50,000 population or more is 75 miles an hour at all times and the speed limit for vehicles traveling on federal-aid interstate highways within an urbanized area of 50,000 population or more is 65 miles an hour at all times; (b) on any other public highway of this state is 70 miles an hour during the daytime and 65 miles an hour during the nighttime; (c) in an urban district is 25 miles an hour.

The reason that Section 61–8–303(1) now specifies numerical speed limits is that in 1998, in a case called *State v. Stanko*, the Montana Supreme Court, by a vote of four to three, struck down the earlier version as 'void for vagueness on its face and in violation of the Due Process Clause of the Montana Constitution'.[13] The Montana court explained why it struck the statute down in terms provided by the federal void-for-vagueness doctrine. It cited the following prose from a decision of the US Supreme Court on void-for-vagueness:

> As generally stated, the void-for-vagueness doctrine requires that a penal statute define the criminal offense with sufficient definiteness that ordinary people can

[13] *State v. Stanko*, 292 Mont. 192, 974 P.2d 1132 (Mont., 1998).

> understand what conduct is prohibited and in a manner that does not encourage arbitrary and discriminatory enforcement.[14]

In the view of the Montana court, the problem appears to have been that Mr Stanko would have no idea which of a variety of possible conceptions of *reasonable speed* he would be at the mercy of, so far as his interactions with the law were concerned. And on the Montana Supreme Court, the position of the majority was that he was entitled to know this, so he could adjust his behaviour accordingly.

I have labelled these versions of the Montana speed limit as [α] and [β], respectively. Version [β] casts the speed limit in the form of a rule, using mostly numerical predicates along with references to various types of roadway. This was the version adopted after *Stanko* was decided, in order to avoid the problems that the pre-*Stanko* standard ran into. True, version [β] refers to 'daytime' and 'nighttime', but the apparent vagueness of these terms is offset by language elsewhere in the section: '"Daytime" means from one-half hour before sunrise to one-half hour after sunset. "Nighttime" means at any other hour.'

Version [α] by contrast – i.e. the provision under which Mr Stanko was charged – was cast as a standard using all sorts of terms that seem to require evaluative judgment on the part of anyone applying them: 'in a careful and prudent manner', 'at a rate of speed no greater than is reasonable and proper under the conditions', and 'to unduly or unreasonably endanger the life, limb, property, or other rights of a person entitled to the use of the street or highway'.

Was the problem here one of vagueness? Some of the terms used in traffic laws are no doubt vague in the familiar sense:[15] they suffer from Sorites vagueness, which occurs when the law confronts a continuous spectrum with its binary logic;[16] and some of them may suffer from Wittgensteinian vagueness – indeterminacy of criteria – like 'vehicle'.[17] But the vagueness of the terms used in version [α] is not of that sort – at least, not in the first instance; I shall say something in a moment about the entanglement of various different forms of vagueness. The Montana Supreme Court was particularly exercised by the phrase 'at a rate of speed no greater than is reasonable and proper under the conditions existing at the point of operation'. Consider 'reasonable' in this predicate. The primary difficulty here is not that velocities form a continuum that does not disclose any bright line between the reasonable and the unreasonable: that would be Sorites vagueness. The primary difficulty is that the ordinary citizen has no idea of what conception of reasonableness is being invoked here.

[14] *Kolender v. Lawson*, 461 US 352, 357–58 (1983), cited in *State v. Stanko* at 1136.

[15] See the discussion of vagueness in Twining and Miers, *How to Do Things with Rules*, pp. 167–72.

[16] See Jeremy Waldron, 'Vagueness in law and Language: Some Philosophical Issues', *California Law Review*, 82 (1994), 509, at pp. 516–7.

[17] See Ludwig Wittgenstein, *Philosophical Investigations*, trans. G. E. M. Anscombe (Basil Blackwell, 1974), pp. 31e–32e (para. 66). For the indeterminacy of 'vehicle', see the opinion of Justice Oliver Wendell Holmes in *McBoyle v. United States*, 283 US 25 (1931).

This is not really a matter of vagueness, at least not in anything like the philosopher's sense of vagueness. It is a matter of competing conceptions.

3

To make this problem vivid, I am going to exaggerate a little, endowing Mr Stanko with a set of rather Nietzschean views about driving. Mr Stanko, I will say, may have considered the issue of *reasonable speed* in terms that took account of the particular joys of driving fast on relatively deserted highways – the wind in your hair, the sense of freedom, perhaps even the exhilaration of a certain amount of risk.

But the Stanko conception of reasonable speed is not universally shared. The officer who pulled Mr Stanko over, Officer Breidenbach, may have developed a conception of reasonable speed oriented mostly to safety and the avoidance of the death and mayhem that are all too often features of the experiences that confront law-enforcement officers on highways with speeding drivers.

These disparate conceptions of *reasonable speed* may overlap in large areas of conduct. And, whatever conception one is using, one is directed by the Montana statute to refer to factors like the amount and character of traffic, condition of brakes, weight of vehicle, grade and width of highway, condition of surface and freedom of obstruction to the view ahead. Even so, Mr Stanko's driving at eighty-five mph in a new and mechanically perfect car on a sunny day on a road that was, for all practical purposes, clear of any other traffic, is exactly the kind of case to pose an issue between these two conceptions of reasonable speed. Apparently the road afforded an unobstructed view for some 300 feet; that was how far Breidenbach was behind Stanko and he never lost sight of him. But it was a mountain road and there were some broad and challenging curves: exactly the sort of road to generate what we may call Stanko-exhilaration of the most delightful sort. It was the sort of road that separates the good drivers from the bad, and Stanko may have been proud of his excellent driving. Officer Breidenbach might say there were risks associated with Stanko's driving. And so there certainly were: a person stepping onto the road from a concealed position might be mowed down by a vehicle approaching at eighty-five mph. But the event was unlikely; it was a wilderness area. And anyway, the statute did not direct the elimination of risk: it instructed the driver 'not to *unduly* or *unreasonably* endanger the life, limb, property, or other rights of a person entitled to the use of the street or highway', and the two conceptions of *reasonable speed* are likely to differ in their assessment of which abstract possibilities of endangerment are undue or unreasonable.

4

I talked earlier about the entanglement of different kinds of vagueness. The fact that there is a choice to be made between the Breidenbach and the Stanko conceptions of *reasonable speed* is not a matter of vagueness. But the application of *either one* of these conceptions might involve vagueness of the Sorites kind. For Stanko's conception still generates some sense of unreasonable speed – where the exhilaration gives way to terror, the wind rips rather than ruffles one's hair, and the risk to other road-users is massive. But where exactly Stanko-reasonableness fades into Stanko-unreasonableness will be quite vague. There will be gray areas; it will be impossible to draw a bright line. And there will be similar issues for Officer Breidenbach's more cautious conception. His conception too will array velocities on a continuum and it will not determine a bright line separating Breidenbach-reasonableness from a snail-like pace that even the officer would have to call Breidenbach-unreasonableness. However, we are not called to confront these issues of vagueness until we have chosen between the two conceptions.

The same may be said about any element of Wittgensteinian vagueness in my story. For example, the application of Officer Breidenbach's conception of reasonable speed may not involve checking off any tidy set of necessary and sufficient conditions. Judging two different vehicles to be each travelling at a reasonable speed may, in Breidenbach's view, involve the application of different sets of criteria that bear at best a family resemblance to one another.

All in all, this business of reasonable speed will often be a complex and delicate matter of judgment that is difficult to articulate. Backing up Officer Breidenbach at the hearing in *Stanko*, the Montana Attorney-General said this, when he was asked what speed would be reasonable in the circumstances in which Mr Stanko was pulled over:

> Again, that would be depending upon the – it will always be a question of judgment at the time based on the conditions at the time, if there were heavier traffic. I cannot give you a number that would have been reasonable and prudent at that – it ultimately may come down to a question to be determined by the jury. The officer will exercise his best judgment in applying the statute.[18]

But what I am arguing here is that it is possible to separate the background question of general evaluation that the use of a term like 'reasonable speed' involves from the difficult matters of judgment and line-drawing that are involved in the application of a given conception of reasonableness.

5

The idea of there being different conceptions of a given concept is familiar from the work of Ronald Dworkin.[19] It is a fairly straightforward idea. The application of certain value-laden predicates often involves the use of something like a normative theory or a principle, which one takes to be indicated by the use of the term. Considered in itself – in advance of any attempt to specify such a theory or principle – we may think of the predicate as designating a

[18] *State v. Stanko*, at 1137. [19] Dworkin, *Taking Rights Seriously*, pp. 134–6.

concept. The association of such a predicate with a particular theory or principle counts as a *conception*, and there may be multiple such conceptions competing with one another.

For example, anyone who is trying to figure out what is reasonable in some domain has to have a sense of the sort of reasons that are important to take into account and the weight to be given to them when they pull in different directions. The concept of *the reasonable* – or, in our example, the concept of *a reasonable speed* – doesn't tell them much beyond this, except that the concept of what it is reasonable for me to do does not neglect the interests of others and requires some fair balance among the interests of all affected.[20] A conception of the reasonable in some sphere fills out this schema, by indicating the interests that are to be particularly taken into account, the weight to be accorded to them, and the idea of a fair balance among them. Officer Breidenbach's conception of a reasonable speed differs from Mr Stanko's conception, in my story, by not according much weight to the exhilaration factor.

Some value-concepts that are used in law afford greater initial guidance than *reasonableness* does, for 'reasonable' is a very general value-term. Consider, for example, the use of the term 'cruel' (as applied to possible punishments) in the Eighth Amendment to the US Constitution. When we try to apply it to possible punishments – such as solitary confinement or capital punishment – we are aware that 'cruel' is concerned with the extent of suffering and the attitude towards suffering evinced by persons involved in its infliction.[21] Beyond that, different users have to develop different theories of how, through the use of this term, an upper limit on the harshness or painfulness of punishment is to be established. One theory might rivet its attention on the unhealthy and sadistic attitudes that can all too easily be associated with the international infliction of discomfort and distress that punishment inevitably involves. Another theory might focus on the occurrence of suffering that seems to be in excess of what is required as punishment, whether this occurrence is the result of anyone's intention or not. These generate disparate conceptions of cruelty. My point is that the concept of cruelty already sets us off along certain lines, but within those lines we may move in somewhat different directions. The Eighth Amendment does not require us to make a general evaluation (or just any old evaluation) of punishment; it is not concerned, for example, with the expensiveness or inefficiency of a form of punishment as a criterion of limitation.[22] So the predicate

[20] Cf. the discussion in Rawls, *Political Liberalism* (Columbia University Press, 1996), pp. 48–54.

[21] See Jeremy Waldron, 'Cruel, Inhuman and Degrading Treatment or Punishment: The Words Themselves' in my collection *Torture, Terror and Trade-Offs: Philosophy for the White House* (Oxford University Press, 2010), 276, at pp. 299–302.

[22] Even when a court reaches the conclusion that (say) disproportionate punishments fall foul of such a norm, they do so not because the norm invites us (under the auspices of 'cruel') to consider everything that might be relevant to the assessment of the punishment in question (including proportionality), but because we have a theory that a punishment becomes cruel when there is, so to speak, a surplus of suffering gratuitously inflicted that bears no proportional relation to reasonable penal goals.

already frames and begins to channel the work that we do under the auspices of this provision. This, of course, is how 'thick' moral predicates operate: their use requires an evaluation, but they channel and direct the evaluation that is required to a certain extent. The thicker the term, the greater the degree of channeling and direction. But it is seldom enough to eliminate the possibility of rival conceptions.

One additional complicating point is this. The use of a thick moral term already intimates a certain sort of evaluation, even if it does not settle its exact character. But the sort of evaluation it intimates may not command the support of those to whom the provision that uses the term is addressed. If a law is enacted that says, 'Women should not wear outfits that are unchaste', many of those to whom it is addressed (many women, for example) may not accept any norms of the sort that are embodied in the term 'chaste'. Even among those who do accept norms of this kind, there will be disparate conceptions of what chastity requires. But the disparity, the indeterminacy, will be heightened by some people offering and using conceptions whose aim it is to dilute the impact of the sort of norms traditionally embodied in the term. They may even essay what C. L. Stevenson called 'persuasive definitions' of the term, like 'Daring is the new chaste', etc.[23]

One reason for using rules rather than standards is to avoid this sort of thing. One commands a certain speed limit, or a certain determinate limit on punishment, or a certain length for women's skirts – and requires people to observe the rule, whether they agree with what they may think of as the underlying policy or not. But with a standard – whether it uses 'reasonable' or 'cruel' or 'chaste' – one cannot avoid the fact that users have to develop and apply a conception, and that conception may be informed not only by their particular take on how best to elaborate the standard but also by their particular view about the desirability of the norms that the standard appears to embody.

6

The decision of the Montana Supreme Court in the *Stanko* case was not unanimous. Three of the justices voted to convict Mr Stanko. Two of them said that his speed was so excessive that he lacked standing to impugn version [α] of the speed limit for vagueness: I guess the idea was that a whole array of conceptions of *reasonable speed* would overlap in condemning his velocity, so that *as applied* to his case the standard was not vague.[24] The other dissenting

[23] C. L. Stevenson, 'Persuasive Definitions', *Mind*, 47 (1938), 331.

[24] Justice Regnier, dissenting: 'In my view, Stanko's speed on the roadway where he was arrested clearly falls within the behavior proscribed by the statute. Operating a vehicle at eighty-five miles per hour on a two-lane highway with frost heaves, steep hills, and curves, where farm vehicles may unexpectedly appear, is not reasonable and proper under the conditions. Therefore, I conclude that Stanko has no standing to attack the facial validity of this statute.' (*State v Stanko*, at 1139).

judge, Chief Justice Turnage, was quite impatient with Mr Stanko's complaint about version [α] along different lines.

> This important statutory provision of our motor vehicle traffic regulations has been the law of Montana since it was enacted by the legislature in 1955... This important traffic regulation has remained unchanged as the law of Montana ... since that time. Appellant Rudy Stanko challenged this statute as being unconstitutional in 1998 because of vagueness. Apparently for the past forty-three years, other citizens driving upon our highways had no problem in understanding this statutory provision. Section 61–8–303(1) is not vague and most particularly is not unconstitutional as a denial of due process. Therefore, I dissent.[25]

That was all he wrote. Now, not only did Chief Justice Turnage suggest that the alleged indeterminacy of version [α] had never proved a problem for generations of Montanan drivers, he also suggested that the version was – as phrased – an '*important* statutory provision of our motor vehicle traffic regulations'. Why might he have thought that?

The Chief Justice did not elaborate. But in a much earlier case (*State v. Schaffer*, from 1917), another state Supreme Court, this time in Ohio,[26] said the following about a *reasonable speed* provision:

> The Legislature ... in this instance, saw fit to fix no definite rate of speed for the car. ... [A] rate of speed dangerous in one situation would be quite safe in another situation, and if the rate of speed were definitely fixed, naturally it would have to be the minimum speed at which cars might be safely driven, because that speed would have to be a safeguard against every possible situation... There is no place in all the public [roads] where a situation is not constantly changing from comparatively no traffic to a most congested traffic; from no foot travelers to a throng of them; from open and clear intersections, private drives, and street crossings, to those that are crowded; from free and unobstructed streets to streets filled with crowds of foot travelers and others getting off and on street cars and other vehicles. In order to meet these varying situations, and impose upon the automobilist [*sic*] the duty of anticipating them and guarding against the dangers that arise out of them, this statute was evidently passed in the interests of the public safety in a public highway.[27]

And the court went on to say that it was precisely the statute's 'adaptability to meet every dangerous situation' that commends it as a valid enactment.[28]

Notice, in this regard, the Ohio court's emphasis on the role of the driver ('the automobilist') in anticipating the varying situations that arise and adjusting his speed accordingly. When we discuss these situations of vagueness, it is

[25] *State v Stanko*, at 1139.

[26] *State v. Schaffer* 96 Ohio St. 215; 117 N.E. 220 (1917). I have discussed this case extensively in Jeremy Waldron, 'Vagueness and the Guidance of Action', in A. Marmor and S. Soames (eds), *Philosophical Foundations of Language in the Law* (Oxford University Press, 2013) 58–82.

[27] *State v. Schaffer*, at 230 and 234–5. [28] Ibid., at 236.

tempting to say that the allegedly vague law is 'applied' by law enforcement officials and courts and it is tempting to neglect the initial role of 'self-application' by the primary subject of the law.[29] But the driver is the first addressee of any traffic law and, for most of the cases to which the law applies, it is the driver's judgement, and only the driver's judgement, that is relied upon. The legislature determines that the objects of traffic policy will be better safeguarded in a varying environment by trusting to the judgement of the driver – with his or her eyes and ears there on the spot – to determine a reasonable speed, than to try to determine this itself from its lofty vantage point in the State Capitol. As I said in Section 1, that is how standards work: they represent a determination that some of the judgements that the law requires are better made downstream from the legislature, at street level (as it were) than upstream in the legislative chamber itself; that is why they use value language like 'reasonable' to indicate to the citizen that it is for him to make a judgement about the matter. The use of this language guides the driver's action, not directly by telling him exactly what the upper speed limit should be, but by instructing him that an exercise of judgement on his part is called for; this is guidance too.[30]

Now, in the *Stanko* case – the case we began with – the Montana Supreme Court did notice that a standard, such as version [α] of the Montana speed limit, transfers judgement downstream, out of the legislative chamber. But it saw this only as an unconstitutional delegation to law enforcement authorities. It said,

> A vague law impermissibly delegates basic policy matters to policemen, judges, and juries for resolution on an ad hoc and subjective basis, with the attendant dangers of arbitrary and discriminatory application.[31]

The trouble with this is that it entirely neglects the first moment of application: self-application of the norm by the driver. What it says about Montana drivers' self-application of version [α] is that 'the average motorist in Montana would have *no idea* of the speed at which he or she could operate his or her motor vehicle on this State's highways without violating Montana's "basic rule"' (my emphasis). Really? No idea at all? One is reminded of an observation by John Stuart Mill in his essay on *Utilitarianism*: 'There is no difficulty in proving any ethical standard whatever to work ill, if we suppose universal idiocy to be

[29] For the idea of self-application as a most important moment in the legal process, see Hart and Sacks, *The Legal Process*, at p. 120. Do Twining and Miers talk enough about self-application? They don't actually ignore it; they say that 'in legal processes there are a great many types of participant, but the main ones *apart from the parties themselves* are usually taken to be the legislator, . . . the advocate, the judge (or other decider), and the law enforcer' (Twining and Miers, *How to Do Things with Words*, p. 135; my emphasis). But they do not make much of interpretation and applications as processes that have to be undertaken in the first instance by those to whom the norms is addressed. Nor do they say nearly enough about the extent of law's reliance on self-application.

[30] See Waldron, 'Vagueness and the Guidance of Action', pp. 66–73.

[31] State v. Stanko, 1136.

conjoined with it.'[32] But, on any hypothesis short of that, most actual drivers will have some working hunches about reasonable speeds in various circumstances. And this presumably is what Chief Justice Turnage meant in his dissent, when he said that 'apparently for the past forty-three years, other citizens driving upon our highways had no problem in understanding this statutory provision'.

7

Of course, a difficulty arises when the driver's hypothesis about reasonable speed turns out to be incompatible with the views of law-enforcement and the courts. Law typically involves layers of application: the driver self-applies the standard; the police officer applies it in swearing out a complaint; and the judge applies it in convicting or acquitting the defendant.

In some cases, we might expect considerable variation. Three possibilities spring to mind. (1) In a pluralistic society, there may be areas of life where there are radically disparate ways of doing things, leading to radically disparate convictions about what is reasonable and unreasonable conduct in that area.[33] (2) In other cases, the views of a court, say, on what is reasonable and unreasonable may be influenced by information which in the nature of things the individual cannot have; so there would be an element of unfairness in judging the individual's assessment of reasonableness by the court's rather differently-informed conception.[34] (3) In still other cases, applications by individual law-enforcement officers may be contaminated by prejudice, leading them to apply differential standards to members of different groups in the community. The court in *Stanko* hinted at this when it worried about 'dangers of arbitrary and discriminatory application'.[35]

These possibilities help us understand the case against using value-predicates: in some areas of life and law, it may be difficult to align or co-ordinate the self-application of these norms with their secondary application by law enforcement officials and judges. They work better where there is substantial reason to expect such alignment, worse where there is good reason not to.

I think the Court in *Stanko* exaggerated the difficulties of using a *reasonable speed* statute. And I played along with that exaggeration, by

[32] John Stuart Mill, *Utilitarianism*, ed. George Sher (Hackett Publishing, 2001), p. 24.

[33] I am using 'pluralism' here in a sense different from the way it is used in Twining and Miers, *How to do Things with Rules*, p. 89. For them, 'pluralism' means the eclectic use of a variety of values and standards by a single person; for me it means the existence of different communities of evaluation in a given society.

[34] See the discussion of *Cline v. Frink Dairy Co.*, 274 US 445 (1927) in Robert Post, 'Reconceptualizing Vagueness: Legal Rules and Social Orders', *California Law Review*, 82 (1994), 491. In *Cline*, individual dairymen had to work out what a 'reasonable profit' was on their products; but the state's assessment of a reasonable profit involved macro-economic data that the individual dairymen could not have access to.

[35] State v. Stanko, 1136.

imagining an ethical disparity between Mr Stanko's Nietzschean conception of *reasonable speed* – wind in the hair, living on the edge, etc. – and Officer Breidenbach's more safety-oriented conception. I did this so that I could illustrate the difference between indeterminacy arising out of multiple conceptions of *reasonable speed* and indeterminacy arising out of the vagueness (the Sorites vagueness or the Wittgensteinian vagueness) of any one of these conceptions.

But there are ways of minimizing the disparities between the various conceptions in play here. Drivers have to remember that when they are implicitly invited by the law to apply a conception of reasonable speed, they are not asked to do this as a parlour game. They are invited to do this *as a matter of law*: it is law they are self-applying, something that is supposed to represent not just their own idiosyncratic views, but a view that can stand, even in their own self-application of it, in the name of the whole community. So if Mr Stanko is aware of the idiosyncrasy of his personal conception of *reasonable speed*, he may want to think twice before he self-applies *this* as a community norm (albeit a community norm that is, for the time being, in his hands). This is not just a matter of prudence – though a prudent driver will give some thought to the views that police officers are likely to have on the matter. (We all do this when we drive over the limit but within what we take to be the margin of tolerance – in my experience, twelve to fifteen mph over the limit on the New York State Thruway.) As I say, it is a matter of maintaining awareness that this is law, *for the community*, that we are talking about. Apart from anything else, it is important that drivers orient their sense of reasonable speed to one another's driving on the same roadways. Drivers have to share the road and it is desirable for them to share a sense of how this norm that they have is to be self-administered among them.

Officer Breidenbach must reflect on this too; perhaps his conception of *reasonable speed* has been too greatly informed by the traumas of the accident scenes he has attended, giving him a distorted view of the dangers of driving (say) above sixty-five mph. He has to enforce version [α] of the speed limit for the community, not just for himself; and he must ponder what conceptions of *reasonable speed* good and thoughtful drivers in his jurisdiction are likely to have come up with, and what outer limits of this shared sense of reasonableness he ought to regard himself as responsible for patrolling. I think this issue of reasonableness being treated as a legal standard, and thus as a shared standard, not just a matter of individual ethical conviction, is very important.

8

I have tried to show that the use of terms like 'reasonable' in some of the laws that apply to us should not be seen simply as instances of objectionable vagueness or indeterminacy. On the contrary, these standards often help to sponsor thoughtfulness and reflection in the law, on the part of those who are called on to apply it (including its primary addressees). People who are instructed to drive at a reasonable speed are credited with the ability to develop a conception of reasonableness in this regard and to apply it themselves to the diverse circumstances that led the legislature to refrain from issuing a numerical rule.

Elsewhere, I have argued that the sponsorship of this thoughtfulness is entirely compatible with the political ideal of the Rule of Law.[36] But It might be thought that the use of terms like 'reasonable' yields norms that suffer from a deficit of clarity – '[t]he desideratum of clarity', said Lon Fuller, 'represents one of the most essential ingredients of legality' – and that therefore it detracts from or undermine the Rule of Law. Because such norms do not let people know in advance exactly where they stand, they don't offer determinate guidance, and they empower those entrusted with the application of the law to impose their own judgments in a way that is not legally controlled, or at least not tightly controlled by law. People then seem to be at the mercy of the value judgments (the discretion) of officials and courts, second-guessing their own futile attempts to figure out how these norms will be authoritatively applied.

For example, it is F. A. Hayek's opinion, expressed in *The Road to Serfdom*, that '[o]ne could write a history of the decline of the Rule of Law . . . in terms of the progressive introduction of these vague formulas [like "reasonableness"] into legislation and of the increasing arbitrariness and uncertainty that results'.[37] I hope I have made clear why I disagree with this. It is true that the Rule of Law looks for some degree of certainty and predictability in the actions of the state, so that expectations can be nurtured and respected and so that people can know with some degree of assurance what rights they can count on and what their obligations are. In some areas this matters more than others.[38] But we should avoid any conception of the Rule of Law that requires law to be mechanically applicable in all circumstances; we should not diminish the role of law in focusing intelligence and facilitating the use of reasons, including moral reason, among its participants.[39] The use of standards as well as rules is one of the ways in which law does this.

So: I think we should resist the view that when standards are in play – norms like version [α] of the Montana traffic law – we might as well not have law at all,

[36] Jeremy Waldron, 'Thoughtfulness and the Rule of Law', Proceedings of the British Academy, 18 (2010), 1.

[37] F. A. Hayek, *The Road to Serfdom*, (University of Chicago Press, 1944), p. 78.

[38] The most important thing, we are told, that people need from the law that governs them is predictability in the conduct of their lives and businesses. Tom Bingham, in his book *The Rule of Law* (Allen Lane, 2010), p. 38, quoted Lord Mansfield:

> 'In all mercantile transactions the great object should be certainty: and therefore it is of more consequence that a rule should be certain, than whether the rule is established one way rather than the other.'

Lord Bingham went on to observe in his own voice that '[n]o one would choose to do business, perhaps involving large sums of money, in a country where parties' rights and obligations were undecided' (ibid.).

[39] Waldron, 'Thoughtfulness and the Rule of Law', at pp. 4–6.

or that the thoughtfulness which is sponsored in the use of standards represents the opposite of the Rule of Law. It is a mistake to regard these norms as simply blank checks for discretion, as though the most they told the person that they were addressed to was to prepare yourself for the arbitrary imposition of a value judgment by those in power. In fact the use of standards clearly represents an exercise in legal guidance. Think back to version [α]. Is it really the case that it gives the drivers of Montana no guidance? Only on the crudest behavioural conception of what it is to guide someone's action. Having one's action guided by a norm is not just a matter of finding out about the norm and conforming one's behaviour to its specifications. It can involve a more complex engagement of practical reason than that. The use of a standard credits a human agent not just with the ability to comply with instructions but with the capacity to engage in practical deliberation. The sign that says: 'Drive at a reasonable speed in the circumstances' tells the driver: 'Now is the time to check the weather and the road conditions and relate that information intelligently to your speed and moderate your behaviour accordingly. Now is the time to focus on this and do the thinking that the application of the standard requires.' It mobilizes the resources of practical intelligence possessed by the norm subject – a mobilization that might not take place if the law-maker had not promulgated the standard. It guides his agency in that way, even if it leaves it up to him to determine the appropriate behaviour. It is law that requires and triggers thoughtfulness, rather than law that supersedes thoughtfulness.

9

I have focused most of this discussion on standards that use broad evaluative terms like 'reasonable'. But in sections 1 and 5, I touched briefly upon the use of thicker terms like 'cruel' in the Eighth Amendment. I want to conclude by summarizing a couple of the points I have made by reference to this class of value-terms.

First, I think we can see clearly in the case of the prohibition on cruel punishment the distinction between possible indeterminacy, resulting from disparate conceptions of *cruelty,* and possible indeterminacy, resulting from the vagueness of any given conception of it. Indeed it is probably easier to see this in the case of *cruel punishment* than in the case of *reasonable speed*: there was something artificial about the rival Stanko- and Breidenbach-conceptions that I manufactured for the latter. As I said in section 5, we all know that cruelty is about inappropriate attitudes towards others' suffering. But some may have conceptions of this that are informed by a savage retributivism and regard nothing as cruel unless it goes beyond the demands of, say, *lex talionis,* while others may equate cruel punishment with the infliction or toleration of suffering that is unnecessary in light of a more humane penology. Clearly, once we have chosen one of these – and there are many other available conceptions – we will face further questions, which may be questions of vagueness, about their application. But the first step – the development of a working conception of cruel punishment – is not in itself the resolution of a vagueness problem.

A second point I made about reasonable speed is that the application of this norm is entrusted in the first instance to its primary addressees – drivers. Police and courts come later. Exploration of analogous points for the Eighth Amendment prohibition is interesting. In an exact analogy with version [α] of the Montana speed limit, it is a mistake to say that the Eighth Amendment is directed primarily to courts and that the problem with it is that it doesn't give enough guidance to judges. The Eighth Amendment is directed in the first instance to legislators. It is a constitutional provision and they are its primary addressees (along with prison officials who may be capable on occasion of acting cruelly without legislative authorization). Legislators are the ones who are to take care that the punishments they authorize are not cruel. In an interesting asymmetry, the analogue of the Officer Breidenbach figure will be some private petitioner who claims he is being cruelly treated. He and his lawyers make a complaint to the court about what the legislator has authorized, and the federal courts respond to that complaint (just as the Montana courts responded to Officer Breidenbach's complaint about Rudy Stanko).

Once again the possible disparity between the conception of *cruelty* held by the legislative majority, the conception of *cruelty* held by the petitioner, and the conception of *cruelty* held by the court may pose a problem. But it is a problem that can be mitigated in a number of ways, not least by the feedback given by the courts to legislators and potential petitioners through constitutional *stare decisis*.

I also believe that the point I made in section 8 about appealing not just to one's own personal and perhaps idiosyncratic conception of the concept being used in the law is important here. Elsewhere, I tried to distinguish the approach I am recommending here from the 'moral reading' of provisions like the Eighth Amendment recommended by Ronald Dworkin.[40] Dworkin's approach seems to suggest that each norm-applier should ask himself, as honestly as he can and in as objective a spirit as he can muster, certain quite specific evaluative questions: 'What attitudes towards suffering really are seriously inappropriate? What really is cruel?' On Dworkin's approach, the norm-applier is to ask these questions as complicated moral questions, and to try to get to the objective right answer – that is, to the moral truth about cruelty, inhumanity and degradation and about the other moral issues that they embed. Any sensible person will recognize, of course, that – as with all objective inquiries – what you get is the speaker's best opinion, and opinions will differ. But the formation of the opinion is supposed to be governed by the discipline of presenting the question and the answer in an objective spirit.

[40] Waldron, 'Cruel, Inhuman and Degrading Treatment or Punishment', pp. 313–19, criticizing Ronald Dworkin, *Freedom's Law: The Moral Reading of the Constitution* (Harvard University Press, 1996).

On Dworkin's account, the norm-applier engages his or her own critical views on what counts as inhuman and degrading. On the account I have suggested, one should be trying to articulate a conception of cruelty that can work for us all, as a standard for common conscience. Some may go further and say that these provisions purport to elicit some shared sense of positive morality, some 'common conscience' we already share, some code that already exists or resonates among us.[41] (Maybe the conjunction of 'unusual' with 'cruel' in the Eighth Amendment points us in that direction.) I have toyed with that position in the past,[42] but I think it goes too far. Still, I do want to insist that there is a difference between one's own personal view of what makes a punishment cruel, and a view that one articulates (as a legislator, as a petitioner, or as a judge) as something that can stand and be applied as constitutional law in the name of us all. Of course, even within this framework, there are plenty of options. All of the conceptions of cruel punishment I have mentioned – here and in section 5 – could work as attempts to articulate a conception of cruelty that can work as law. So we still have to face the question of indeterminacy at this level.

This brings me to my third and final point, which is, again, about the Rule of Law and thoughtfulness. I acknowledged in section 8 that the Rule of Law sometimes has to insist on clarity and predictability, which might call into question the use of evaluative terms like those I have been considering in this paper. But, in some cases, the craving for certainty matters less than the need for reflection, flexibility, reason and thought, sponsored by the law through its use of standards rather than rules. I can imagine an argument that traffic law is an area where clarity is important, though I tried to state the opposite case in section 7. I cannot imagine anyone saying that it is more important to be able to say with certainty what punishment an offence attracts than to suffer the indeterminacy occasioned by the use of predicates like 'cruel' in constitutional provisions.

For one thing, the primary addressee of these provisions is not an individual, as in the traffic case, but a legislature; and it is hard to get a sense of what the interest or expectation of predictability amounts to in this matter. It is not the predictability that a businessman craves, or the predictability needed for the autonomy of a Hayekian individual.

For another thing, it is the job of a legislature to deliberate thoughtfully and at length on the constitutional character of the laws that it passes. (It's a mistake to think this is only the function of the courts, not the legislature. Some countries require the Attorney-General to certify that a proposed bill is

41 We sometimes think of these standards as prohibiting conduct that 'shocks the conscience'. Again, I prefer to think of that not as an appeal to the moral sensibility of the solitary individual, but to the possibility of establishing some sort of shared conscience, ('con-science' in the etymological sense of 'knowing together').

42 Jeremy Waldron, 'Inhuman and Degrading Treatment: The Words Themselves', *Canadian Journal of Law and Jurisprudence*, 23 (2010), 269, at p. 284.

compatible with the constitution or the Bill of Rights and if necessary to open a debate devoted to this very issue.[43]) True, legislatures are perfectly capable of generating thought and debate when left to their own devices. But the legislative advantage of the Eighth Amendment is that it requires the legislature to address the question of the cruelty of the punishments it ordains, whatever else it talks about. You may say that, in light of the indeterminacy as between rival possible conceptions of cruel punishment, that will be an inconclusive debate, with members often talking at cross purposes, precisely because the crucial term is unclear; and if it is conclusive, it will yield different and incompatible results depending on whose conception of cruel punishment is in the majority.

Maybe so. But it is a mistake to think that the only value of such a debate lies in the clarity of its terms and the determinate and consistent conclusiveness of its outcomes. Sometimes, what matters is just that there should be a debate on cruelty, within at least the terms of reference that the concept affords, whether or not it is conclusive. The passage of a penal statute is better when it is accompanied by a debate about cruelty in these indeterminate terms, for the indeterminacy of the terms does not mean that the debate might as well not take place at all. Law can sponsor thoughtfulness of certain sorts – here, thoughtfulness about cruelty in the legislature – even when law does not tell us determinately what exactly to think about it.

10

What I have tried to do in this chapter is to indicate a numbers of ways in which we might think about the particular issue of standards in the law – standards in the sense that American jurists contrast with rules. The terminology of the distinction may be American, but the distinction itself and its significance apply to English law as well; indeed, to all legal systems. *How to Do Things with Rules* is a wonderful book, but I think it is a pity that it did not delve deeply into this problem.

I understand that Twining and Miers' book is intended primarily as an introduction to problems of interpretation for students to use early in their law school careers. It is, as the subtitle tells us, a 'primer' of interpretation. But the issues raised by the distinction between rules and standards are not just of scholarly interest. Anyone who confronts the norms that law uses ought to be aware of the different ways in which law tries to do things by using norms of different kinds, and the difference this makes to the way in which norms of different kinds are interpreted. I take my lead here from the remarkable discussion of interpretation and 'reasoned elaboration' in the Hart and Sacks legal process materials.[44] It seems to me that their discussion of the difference between rules and standards, and of the different challenges involved in

[43] See e.g. New Zealand Bill of Rights Act 1990, section 7.
[44] Hart and Sacks, The Legal Process, pp. 102–58.

'the process of reasoned elaboration of purportedly determinate directions' and 'the reasoned elaboration of avowedly indeterminate directions', is much more nuanced and infinitely preferable to an approach to interpretation that treats doing things with standards as simply trying to do things with vague and general language.

17

Glimmers of an awakening within analytical jurisprudence

Brian Z. Tamanaha

Analytical jurisprudents have neglected William Twining to their detriment. The Quain Professor of Jurisprudence Emeritus, University College London, Twining is a Fellow of the British Academy and member of the American Academy of Arts and Sciences, a recognized authority on evidence, and author of a leading text on American Legal Realism. He has written numerous jurisprudence books and articles, analyzing law across multiple spectra. Despite these achievements, rarely does a discussion of his work show up in the writings of analytical jurisprudents. Their failure to engage with Twining has contributed to the insularity of contemporary analytical jurisprudence.

Signs have appeared recently, however, that they might finally be waking up to issues Twining has raised for decades. In 'Why the State?', Joseph Raz, eminence grise of analytical jurisprudence, comes out 'critical of jurisprudential theories that focus more or less exclusively on the state'.[1] This is a stunning turnaround for Raz, who has himself been criticized for focusing exclusively on the state.[2] He continues:

> Furthermore, once we understand the relations between state law and other kinds of law-related systems we may well conclude that even if state law is in some ways theoretically and practically the most challenging or the most important kind of legal system, it is better understood alongside other such systems rather than through theories that focus on it to the exclusion of the others.[3]

Raz speculates that theorists have focused exclusively on state law because 'once this trend is established people keep the focus simply because that is how theory is done, and those who are interested in the theory of state-law flock to do legal philosophy for that reason'.[4] But owing to changes in the wake of globalization, Raz urges legal philosophers to break out of this narrow view to examine 'other kinds of law', including 'international law, or the law of organizations like the

[1] Joseph Raz, 'Why the State?' (2014) 1 (unpublished essay on file with author), available at papers.ssrn.com/sol3/papers.cfm?abstract_id=2339522

[2] See Brian Z. Tamanaha, *A General Jurisprudence of Law and Society* (Oxford University Press, 2001) 138–48, 151.

[3] Raz, 'Why the State?', 2. [4] Id. 3.

European Union, but also Canon Law, Sharia Law, Scottish Law, the law of native nations, the rules and regulations governing the activities of voluntary associations, or those of legally recognized corporations, and more, including many transient phenomena, like neighborhood gangs'.[5]

Raz is undoubtedly correct that legal philosophers must expand their horizons – finally arriving at a position Twining articulated a dozen years ago, in 'A Post-Westphalian Conception of Law':

> During most of the twentieth century, mainstream Anglo-American jurisprudence focused almost entirely on two forms of law: municipal law (of sovereign nation-states and subordinate legal orders) and public international law (largely but not exclusively treated as the law governing relations between states). From a global or a broad transnational perspective this 'Westphalian' focus is inadequate. It leaves out too much: if one were to try to sketch a broad overview of forms of legal orders in the contemporary world, one might quibble about including *lex mercatoria* or *ius humanitatis* or Pasagarda law or Gypsy law or Hindu law or Internet law, but it would be difficult to justify leaving out European Community law or Islamic law or major examples of 'traditional' or 'chthonic' law. Yet it would be strange to try to subsume all of these under municipal law or public international law. If one were to adopt an historical perspective, other candidates would press for attention, for example, classical Roman law, the medieval law merchant, canon law, to say nothing of major traditions of religious, indigenous, and chthonic law. This is not merely or mainly a semantic issue; rather it involves a judgment about what forms of legal ordering deserve sustained attention by our discipline.[6]

Twining has extensively developed the implications of this position in a number of books and articles over the past two decades.[7]

Raz does not mention Twining in this essay, nor any other theorists who have taken up these issues. He writes as if on a clean slate, figuring out matters analytically. That is Raz's prerogative, of course, and what he says is illuminating. By ignoring existing social-legal theory that covers the same ground, however, he risks falling into errors other theorists have already made and have since learned to avoid. In this essay, I recount Twining's lengthy struggle to expand the focus of analytical jurisprudence, lending support to his advocacy by addressing a few key issues on which legal philosophers have gone wrong owing to their narrowness.

[5] Id. 4.

[6] William Twining, 'A Post-Westphalian Conception of Law' (2003), 37 *Law & Society Review* 199, 199. This essay is an extended review article of *A General Jurisprudence of Law and Society*, which presses the same themes.

[7] See William Twining, *Globalization and Legal Theory* (Northwestern, 2000); William Twining, 'The Province of Jurisprudence Re-Examined' in Catherine Dauvergne, ed., *Jurisprudence for an Interconnected Globe* (Ashgate, 2003); William Twining, 'General Jurisprudence' (2006), 15 *U. Miami Int'l and Comp. L. Rev.* 1; William Twining, *General Jurisprudence: Understanding Law from a Global Perspective* (Cambridge University Press, 2009); William Twining, 'Normative and Legal Pluralism' (2010), 20 *Duke J. of Comp. and Int'l Law* 473.

1. Twining's long battle within analytical jurisprudence

A mischievous paper was delivered by Twining at the 1977 World Congress on Philosophy of Law and Social Philosophy. An allegory presented as a day-dream, it recounts the many sights a group of visitors encounter as they wander through 'The Great Juristic Bazaar: A General Theory of Law for the Modern Age'. Touring across jurisprudence, Twining vividly portrays it as an unruly blooming jumble: 'all attempts to impose some kind of order on this lavish, sprawling, anarchic scene had proved quite fruitless.'[8] The insights he offers up in this irreverent romp through the field defy recapitulation, but one passage bears quoting:

> [T]he Legal Philosophers' Circle, a spherical balloon, [was] floating high above the enclosure, kept up by a combination of warm air and long supple stilts. In sharp contrast with the previous exhibits, ordinary tourists were discouraged from entering, for serious philosophers prefer to speak only to or past each other. The ascent was arduous and, in order to gain admission, an applicant had to undertake to observe certain conventions: to think before speaking, to speak before listening, to write before reading, to confine himself to philosophical questions and, much to the disappointment of the serious student, never to expect any answers. Furthermore, no heavy books or footnotes were admitted, in case the balloon might become weighted down and descend to earth... From below it was not possible to tell whether what was being said was sense or nonsense, for the stilts were so tall as to put the speakers out of earshot, even if they had not all been speaking simultaneously.[9]

Tongue-in-cheek throughout, Twining poked good-natured fun not just at legal philosophers but across the jurisprudential bazaar, including at himself. The dream ends quizzically, wondering whether anything solid lies in these pursuits, while theorists carry on.

A couple of years later, in a review of the *festschrift* celebrating H. L. A. Hart's seventieth birthday, Twining praised Hart for infusing jurisprudence with the priorities and techniques of contemporary analytical philosophy, subjecting legal concepts and modes of reasoning to systematic analysis, bringing clarity and renewed vigour to jurisprudence. But Twining also expressed reservations about the tendency of Hart's followers 'to adopt a rather narrow and recondite view of jurisprudence and by implication either to treat jurisprudence as co-extensive with legal philosophy or to imply that philosophizing in the Oxford style is the only intellectually worthwhile kind of jurisprudential activity'.[10] 'Notions of what is philosophically interesting may also have a limiting influence; at worst this may take the form of a kind of intellectual snobbery about what concepts or issues are worthy of

[8] William Twining, 'The Great Juristic Bazaar' (1978), 14 *J. Society of Pub. L. Teachers* 185, 188.
[9] Id. 195.
[10] William Twining, 'Academic Law and Legal Philosophy: The Significance of Herbert Hart' (1979), 95 *Law Quarterly Review* 557, 656.

attention.'[11] Twining was especially critical of their single-minded devotion to conceptual analysis with little attention to how law operates in society. 'Yet if law is to be viewed as a social phenomenon,' he wrote, 'it would seem to be worthwhile at least to explore the relationship between legal theory and social theory, in particular possible connections between theories of law and theories of society.'[12] More pointedly, he remarked, 'Hart has not in a systematic way attempted to proceed beyond the confines of Bentham's expository and censorial jurisprudence into the kind of broader perspective that is encompassed by phrases such as "sociology of law".'[13] In closing, Twining worried that Hart's successors might 'contribute to a narrowing' of jurisprudence.[14]

Hart was 'was clearly displeased' by this essay, Twining recounts, their relationship civil but cool thereafter.[15] Subsequently confirming Twining's worry, Hart's successors have indeed paid little attention to broader social perspectives on law. Raz himself describes legal philosophy as *necessarily* insular and narrow:

> Since a legal theory must be true of all legal systems the identifying features by which it characterizes them must of necessity be very general and abstract. It must disregard those functions which some legal systems fulfill in some societies because of the special social, economic, or cultural conditions of those societies. It must fasten only on those features of legal systems which they must possess regardless of the special circumstances of the societies in which they are in force. This is the difference between legal philosophy and sociology of law. The latter is concerned with the contingent and with the particular, the former with the necessary and the universal. Sociology of law provides a wealth of detailed information and analysis of the functions of law in some particular societies. Legal philosophy has to be content with those few features which all legal systems necessarily possess.[16]

Other analytical jurisprudents have echoed this stance. 'Social sciences cannot tell us what the law is because it studies human society,' Scott Shapiro declares. 'Its deliverances have no relevance for the legal philosopher because it is a truism that nonhumans could have law. Science fiction, for example, is replete with stories involving alien civilizations with some form of legal system... Social scientific theories are limited in this respect, being able to study only human groups, and hence cannot provide an account about all possible instances of law.'[17] Rising high above the ground, their gazes firmly fixed on eternal stars, legal philosophers are after abstract universal truths, detached from the messy-complex-multifarious reality of law.

It is important to point out that Twining's criticisms – now nearly four decades on – have all along been made *within* analytical jurisprudence. 'I want

[11] Id. 570. [12] Id. 566–67. [13] Id. 578. [14] Id. 580.

[15] William Twining, 'Schauer on Hart' (2005), 119 *Harv. L. Rev. Forum* 122, 122n3.

[16] Joseph Raz, *The Authority of Law* (2nd ed. Oxford University Press, 2009) 104–05.

[17] Scott Shapiro, *Legality* (Harvard University Press, 2011) 406–07.

to make a plea for a revival of general analytical jurisprudence,' he explains, 'but much more broadly conceived than its nineteenth and twentieth century predecessors.'[18] Twining was drawn to legal theory as Hart's student and much of his work is analytical. His motivation was not to debunk Hart's work but to render it richer by instilling it with insights from social theory and social–legal studies. That Twining is treated as an outsider bespeaks the narrowness of analytical jurisprudence as currently practiced, as if defined wholly by the methods and goals of legal philosophy. He is in good company. Frederick Schauer, a philosophically sophisticated jurisprudent who likewise urges greater incorporation of sociological insights,[19] is also on the outside. What marks them as 'outsiders', though they have written extensively on the nature of law, is analytical jurisprudents in the prevailing Oxford–Yale orbit pay them little heed. Analytical jurisprudence has the appearance of an exclusive (in the bad sense of the word) ever-shrinking club, dominated by legal philosophers who prefer to speak only to each other.

But the ground has irrevocably shifted with Raz's announcement that legal philosophy must expand its focus beyond state law. By no means is he advocating an embrace of social legal work – that would be too much. Nonetheless, it is a substantial step in Twining's direction because it requires analytical jurisprudents to go beyond armchair intuitions about state law to read the abundant literature on other forms of law. Once they embark on this new inquiry, their oft-repeated claims about universal truths of the essential nature of law applicable to all places and times will be hard to maintain (as I will show shortly).

This belated shift was inevitable for two reasons emphasized by Twining. Since all theorists accept that law is a social institution, it makes no sense, like donning blinders while driving, to abstain from plumbing information provided by social–legal approaches.[20] The second factor behind this inevitability is the geo-political-legal changes wrought by globalization. Hart's concept of law was constructed mid-twentieth century at the pinnacle of the state legal system, brilliantly reducing state law to core elements, but it was inadequate from the outset because the state was never as dominant as legal philosophers assumed – globalization exposed this reality.[21] Writing about the implications of globalization for jurisprudence, Twining observed a decade ago,

> As the discipline of law becomes more cosmopolitan, there needs to be a geographical, cultural, and political broadening of its agendas. Contemporary legal theory needs to tackle issues relating to legal traditions, non-state law, legal pluralism, multiculturalism, human rights, transnational justice, diffusion of law, problems of comparison and generalization, and our collective ignorance

[18] Twining, 'Province of Jurisprudence Re-examined', supra 31.

[19] See Frederick Schauer, '(Re)thinking Hart' (2006), 119 *Harvard. L Rev.* 852.

[20] See Brian Z. Tamanaha, 'What is "General" Jurisprudence? A Critique of Universalistic Claims by Philosophical Concepts of Law' (2011), 2 *Transnational Legal Theory* 287.

[21] This argument is elaborated in Tamanaha, *A General Jurisprudence of Law and Society*, supra.

> of other legal traditions and cultures. Until recently, hardly any of these topics were dreamt of in Hart's legal philosophy or those of most of his followers. Yet nearly all of these topics deserve the scrutiny of philosophers and analytical jurists.[22]

Apparently Raz now agrees, opening up a brave new world for legal philosophers. This welcome, long-overdue, expanded focus will challenge some of their cherished verities.

2. The collapse of essential, necessary, universal truths about law

'A theory consists of necessary truths,' Joseph Raz asserts, 'for only necessary truths about the law reveal the nature of law. We talk of the "the nature of law", or the nature of anything else, to refer to those of the law's characteristics which are of the essence of law, which make law what it is.'[23] A true theory of law holds for all places and all times. 'Naturally, the essential properties of the law are universal characteristics of law... When surveying the different forms of social organization in different societies throughout the ages we will find many which resemble law in various ways. Yet if they lack the essential features of the law, they are not legal systems.'[24] Other analytical jurisprudents have made similar assertions. A theory of law must 'consist of propositions about the law which are necessarily true, as opposed to merely contingently true,' writes Julie Dickson, because 'only necessarily true propositions about law will be capable of explaining the nature of law.'[25]

Talk about essential and necessary features is puzzling in relation to social constructions like law – based on ideas, beliefs and actions – which come in a multitude of variations and change over time. 'Legal systems are not natural kinds . . . that have essences,' Ronald Dworkin objected. 'They are social kinds: to suppose that law has an essence is as much a mistake as supposing that marriage or community has an essence.'[26] When setting out their position on essential properties, Raz and Shapiro both cite H_2O as an example without addressing the manifest ontological differences between water and law.[27] Philosophers generally agree the essential properties of water are mind-independent internal properties: 'we are accustomed to thinking of essentialness as fixed by the laws of nature.'[28] Law is neither mind-independent nor fixed by

22 Twining, 'Schauer on Hart', supra 129.

23 Joseph Raz, *Between Authority and Interpretation* (Oxford University Press, 2009) 24, 17.

24 Id. 25.

25 Julie Dickson, *Evaluation and Legal Theory* (Hart Publishing Company, 2001) 18.

26 Ronald Dworkin, 'Hart and the Concepts of Law' (2006), 119 *Harvard Law Review* 95, 95 (2006).

27 Shapiro, *Legality*, supra 8–9, 406; Raz, *Between Authority and Interpretation*, supra 27, 23 n. 7. Noting this difference, see Brian Bix, 'Conceptual Questions and Jurisprudence' (1995), 1 *Legal Theory* 465, 468.

28 Crawford L. Elder, 'On the Place of Artifacts in Ontology', in Eric Margolis and Stephen Laurence (eds), *Creations of the Mind* (Oxford University Press, 2007) 37.

the laws of nature. Frederick Schauer has repeatedly challenged claims that law has essential and necessary properties.[29] Law is more aptly captured by Wittgenstein's notion of family resemblances, he argues, and is better thought of as a cluster concept.[30] Until analytical jurisprudents answer these large questions their claims about essential and necessary features of law will remain mysterious; statements of faith rather than analytically established.

The claim of universal truth is likewise dubious. Again, Raz:

> It is easy to explain in what sense legal philosophy is universal. Its theses, if true, apply universally, that is, they speak of all law, of all legal systems; of those that exist, or that will exist, and even of those that can exist though they never will. Moreover, its theses are advanced as necessarily universal... The general theory of law is universal for it consists of claims about the nature of all law, and of all legal systems, and about the nature of adjudication, legislation, and legal reasoning, wherever they may be, and whatever they may be. Moreover, its claims, if true, are necessarily true. Suffice it to say that *the truth of the theses of the general theory of law is not contingent on existing political, social, economic, or cultural conditions, institutions, or practices.*
>
> *The universality of the theses of the general theory of law is a result of the fact that they claim to be necessary truths*, and there is nothing less that they can claim... A claim to necessity is the nature of the enterprise.[31]

Multiple objections can be raised to these assertions,[32] but I will limit myself to showing that they are unconvincing on their own terms – and utterly collapse when Raz's newfound agenda is added to the mix.

Law is a folk concept, and there are different concepts of law, which can change over time. Raz recognizes this: 'While the general theory of law is universal, it is also parochial.'[33] What makes it parochial 'is that the concept of law is itself a product of a specific culture'.[34] 'Talk of *the* concept of law really means *our* concept of law. As has already been mentioned, the concept of law changes over time. Different cultures have different concepts of law. There is no one concept of law, and when we refer to the concept of law we just mean our concept of law.'[35] 'It follows that in working out a theory of law we are explicating our own self-understanding of the nature of society and politics [.]'[36] He acknowledges, furthermore, that 'our concept [of law] is liable to be forever in flux.'[37]

[29] See Frederick Schauer, 'On the Nature of the Nature of Law' (2011) at papers.ssrn.com/sol3/papers.cfm?abstract_id=1836494; Frederick Schauer, 'The Best Laid Plans' (2013), 120 *Yale Law Journal* 586, 613–19; Frederick Schauer, 'The Social Construction of the Concept of Law: A Reply to Julie Dickson' (2005), 25 *Oxford Journal of Legal Studies* 493.

[30] Schauer, 'On the Nature of the Nature of Law', supra 15.

[31] Raz, *Between Authority and Interpretation*, supra 91–92 (emphasis added), see also 97 (universal truth claim).

[32] A more detailed critique is articulated in Tamanaha, 'What is "General" Jurisprudence?', supra.

[33] Raz, *Between Authority and Interpretation*, supra 92. [34] Id. 95. [35] Id. 32. [36] Id. 97.

[37] Id. 98.

Let us set aside questions about who Raz speaks for with his royal 'our', to instead raise an obvious objection: a parochial concept of law that changes over time cannot produce timeless, universal truths about law. How does Raz square this circle? In effect, he holds time and space constant, identifying the essential features of the social institution picked out by 'our' concept of law in the here and now. 'What counts is the nature of the institution which the concept of law (i.e. the one we currently have and use) designates.'[38] If other societies, past, present and future, lack institutions with the essential features of law, he asserts, they do not have law according to our current concept of law.

If Raz's claim is only that the theory of law is universally *applicable*, then his analysis would be sound: one may take a concept abstracted from one context and apply it to examine other places and times (with proper caveats). His argument fails when he claims universal *truth*, however, because it is contradicted by his starting point. Raz asserts: 'Suffice it to say that *the truth of the theses of the general theory of law is not contingent on existing political, social, economic, or cultural conditions, institutions, or practices.*' To the contrary, the contingency of Raz's theory of law lies in its admittedly parochial origin in the here and now (global North). This contingent origin is not erased in the abstracting process of theory formation, but rather thereby becomes entrenched in the theory of law produced, with its origin concealed in elaborate philosophical clothing and talk of universality.

Already unpersuasive on its own terms, Raz's universal truth claim falls apart in light of his recent assertion that legal philosophers must take account of other forms of law, including Canon law, Sharia, etc., as well as the rule systems of corporations and sports leagues. For decades, his theory of law has been based exclusively on state law, which underlies his assertions about a singular, universally true theory of law. Recognition of multiple forms of law eliminates the singularity that undergirded his position.

As Twining and I have extensively shown,[39] moreover, various socially recognized manifestations of law do not share all the same basic features. This conclusion led Twining to a very thin formulation of law (one that can be varied depending on purpose and context[40]) – while I propose a conventionalist approach to identify different forms of law – because any concept of law with more robust elements cannot encompass the full range of legal phenomena. Multiple forms of law, when viewed through the logic of Raz's argument, potentially give rise to multiple universally true concepts of law which do not share the same essential features. This would make no sense.

[38] Id. 25.

[39] See Twining, 'A Post-Westphalian Conception of Law', supra; Twining, *General Jurisprudence*, supra; Twining, 'Normative and Legal Pluralism', supra; Tamanaha, *A General Jurisprudence of Law and Society*, supra.

[40] Twining, *General Jurisprudence*, supra 116.

3. Conflating rule systems within legal systems

Raz might hang on to his universal truth claim with the following riposte: it may be the case that beneath surface differences the multiple forms of law all share core essential features, which constitutes the universally true theory of law; so we must wait and see what legal philosophers produce after analysis.

Time will tell. The necessary inquiry cannot be based on analysis from intuitions, and it will be a monumental task that requires extensive study. Legal philosophers must examine not only each form of law, but also their myriad variations. Customary law, to offer just one prevalent example, takes different forms in communities prior to the presence of the state, when incorporated within the state, and when independent of the state.[41] Religious law also comes in multiple variations within and separate from the state. Legal philosophers must do what Twining has urged for decades: resort to social legal studies to learn about the social reality of law. This endeavour, should they embark on it, will enrich legal philosophy.

Meanwhile, it will assist their inquiry to keep in mind that Raz's list of kinds of law combines two distinct categories: 1) international law, Canon Law, Sharia, EU law, etc.; and 2) the rules and regulations of voluntary associations and corporations, among others. The first group consists of legal forms that are socially recognized as 'law', whereas members of the second group are generally not considered law. Raz included the latter, presumably, because they consist of rule systems that appear to share certain features with law. Legal philosophers will learn a great deal from examining both categories, as he urges. However, while he is correct to think of the former as forms of law, it is a mistake to consider the second category 'law'.

In treating the second group as law, Raz is headed down the same trail that legal pluralists followed for decades, though some have recently retreated. 'The [legal] institutions I have in mind are themselves rule governed,' he elaborates, 'ultimately governed by practice-based rules that determine if not all at least the most important aspects of their constitution, powers, and mode of operation. Perhaps the most elementary powers legal institutions have are enforcement and adjudicative powers, namely the powers to take measures to enforce other rules and to adjudicate disputes about their applicability.'[42] Based on this understanding, Raz asserts, 'the rules of the U.S. and of Columbia University *are legal systems*.'[43] 'There can be *law-based* systems governing members of a profession, co-religionists, inhabitants of a certain territory, and so on… *law-like* systems apply to groups, united by the rules, such as members of a university, a sports club, a profession, or a locality.'[44]

Before accepting these characterizations, we must determine what the most sensible general category is. Social institutions can be categorized along

[41] For a discussion of a range of manifestations of customary law, see Brian Z. Tamanaha, *Understanding Law in Micronesia: An Interpretive Approach to Transplanted Law* (Brill, 1993).

[42] Raz, 'Why the State?' supra 6. [43] Id. 7 (emphasis added). [44] Id. 8.

different dimensions so the category one selects should be based upon what best facilitates analysis and understanding. Are these better understood as *law*-based systems or *rule*-based systems? Are all rule-based systems types of law or is law just one type of rule-based system? Universities and sports leagues have various rule-making and judicial-type bodies, as do many social organizations. If those characteristics define legal systems, then society is overflowing with a profusion of 'law'.

Anthropologists and sociologists who identify themselves as legal pluralists arrived at this very position several decades ago. Marc Galanter (invoking Hart's concept of law) asserted law can 'be found in a variety of institutional settings – universities, sports leagues, housing developments, hospitals, etc.'[45] John Griffiths, who penned the most influential theoretical elaboration of legal pluralism, declared, 'all social control is *more* or *less* legal.'[46] Another leading theorist, Boaventura de Sousa Santos, offered this defense: 'It may be asked: why should these competing or complementary forms of social ordering be designated as *law* and not rather as "rule systems", "private governments", and so on? Posed in these terms, this question can only be answered by another question: Why not?'[47]

To call these social institutions 'legal systems', one might say in answer to Santos, is counter-intuitive and lacks theoretical justification. It amounts to a massive relabelling of social phenomena with no real conceptual gain. After a quarter-century of insisting that all rule systems are forms of law, Griffiths, late in his career, repudiated this position. Owing to irresolvable conceptual problems with isolating distinctively legal phenomena, he became convinced 'that the expression "legal pluralism" can and should be reconceptualised as "normative pluralism" or "pluralism in social control".'[48]

This branch of legal pluralism went wrong by fastening on features common among social institutions, which cannot serve to distinguish law. To see this, consider John Searle's account of the ontology of social institutions, which at the most basic level consists of sets of constitutive rules and regulative rules. 'Human institutions vary enormously, all the way from religions to nation-states to sports teams to corporations,' Searle observed, but beneath the surface lie 'purely formal features they have in common that enable them to function in human life.'[49]

[45] Marc Galanter, 'Justice in Many Rooms: Courts, Private Ordering, and Indigenous Law' (1981), 19 *Journal of Legal Pluralism* 1, 17–18.

[46] John Griffiths, 'What is Legal Pluralism?' (1981), 24 *Journal of Legal Pluralism and Unofficial Law* 1, 38. For a critique, see Brian Z. Tamanaha, 'Understanding Legal Pluralism: Past to Present, Local to Global' (2008), 30 *Sydney Law Review* 375.

[47] Boaventura de Sousa Santos, *Toward a New Common Sense: Law, Science in Paradigmatic Transition* (Routledge, 1995) 115 (emphasis added).

[48] John Griffiths, 'The Idea of Sociology of Law and its Relation to Law and to Sociology' (2005), *Current Legal Issues* 49.

[49] John R. Searle, *Making the Social World: The Structure of Human Civilization* (Oxford University Press, 2010) 123.

Notice that Searle identifies the *very same examples* as Raz and legal pluralists: religions, nation states, sports teams and corporations. Significantly, however, when invoking these examples Searle is not talking about *law* per se, but about social institutions generally that share formal features. When Raz (and legal pluralists) assert that universities, sports clubs and professions have 'legal systems' (or are 'law-based' or 'law-like'), he is picking up on the fact that they are constituted by rules and regulate the conduct of their members by rules which must be promulgated and applied. But these cannot be defining features of 'law' because a multitude of institutions have the same elements. Searle recognized this: 'The ontology I have given [for government or state] so far might also fit nonpolitical structures such as religions, corporations, universities, and organized sports.'[50] (Searle subsumes law within government.) What makes a particular institution 'law' or 'legal', as opposed to some other type of institution, operates at levels above the formal features they share. On his part, Searle eschews 'any kind of essentialism:' 'There is no set of necessary and sufficient conditions that define the essence of the political.'[51] Though he makes extensive use of legal institutions as examples in his analysis, Searle was not concerned with questions about the nature of law and does not address the issue; like Max Weber, he invokes the monopoly of physical force to help identify government.

These are complex issues and I do not purport to resolve the matter in this brief coverage. Nor do I suggest that Twining has all the answers, though he is well aware of, and avoids the pitfalls of, attaching the label 'law' to rule systems of corporations and sports clubs. Rather, my point is to show once again that legal philosophers can benefit from Twining's work, and from social legal theory more generally, which extensively engages these issues. Legal philosophers tend not to read social–legal literature on the unexamined assumption that they have nothing to learn therefrom. Jules Coleman states categorically, 'there is absolutely no reason to believe that the facts that interest us as philosophers and social theorists are the facts that social and natural scientific theories are interested in addressing or are designed to addressed.'[52] In this essay I hope to have shown that this stance is unwise and contrary to open-minded theoretical inquiry. Law is a social institution, after all, and it is odd that legal philosophers take apparent pride in denying that they might have something to learn from their more empirically-oriented theoretical colleagues who centre on law as a social institution. For decades, Twining has been urging them to think more broadly, though to little avail.

[50] Id. 170. Searle treats 'government' and 'states' equivalently for the purposes of his analysis. Id. 161 n. 12.

[51] Id. 171.

[52] Jules L. Coleman, 'Methodology' in Jules L. Coleman, Kenneth Einar Himma and Scott J. Shapiro (eds), *The Oxford Handbook of Jurisprudence and Philosophy of Law* (Oxford University Press, 2002) 350.

Conclusion

I will take the liberty of closing my contribution to this *festschrift* in honour of William with a few personal comments. In his theoretical discussions, William occasionally inserts biographical notes about theorists, implicitly suggesting that personal background has an influence on their theoretical views. William and I have quite similar theoretical views of law, which, in addition to the fact that I have learned a great deal from his work, might partially be explained by experiences we both underwent in the course of our early intellectual development. We both spent our childhood years at the margins of the West – William in Uganda and Mauritius and me on an outer island of Hawaii (before it became a tourist mecca) – which gave us an appreciation for other cultures and ways of life. After obtaining a law degree, William taught law for a number of years in Sudan and in Tanzania, and I worked as a lawyer in the Federated States of Micronesia.

While I cannot speak for William, my experiences in Micronesia thoroughly shook up my view of law. The transplanted state legal system in their society was not consistent with my previous assumptions about law, and highly effective customary law bodies governed everyday life independent of the state. A great deal of what I read in Hart, Raz and legal philosophers generally, while illuminating on its own terms – assuming the primacy of state law – simply did not fit the reality of law on Yap. Their pronouncements about the nature of law, frustratingly, were presented as universalistic, ruling out of existence alternative legal forms by philosophical fiat. Ever since, I have been trying to develop a theoretical framework that acknowledges the extraordinary complexity and variety of social–legal forms.

William has been pursuing much the same goal for decades, as his essays from the 1970s reflect, compelled by his own dissatisfactions with legal philosophy,[53] and I was delighted to find him as an intellectual guide. We are bonded by an additional similarity. We read a great deal of legal theory, legal sociology, legal anthropology, legal history and comparative law, as well as social theory and political theory – though he reads more moral theory than I do and he is vastly more learned in general. Notwithstanding these catholic interests, we have always seen ourselves as jurisprudence scholars and our intellectual home is squarely in legal theory. Yet we are misfits, outside the artificially constricted boundaries of analytical jurisprudence, not philosophical enough to be legal philosophers, not sociological enough to be legal sociologists; perhaps we are sociological jurisprudents, though that branch seemingly expired with Roscoe Pound.

This might seem like a trivial matter, but theoretical debates typically take place within and between theoretical schools or branches, and to be outside recognized categories leaves one homeless and excluded. Most contemporary

[53] For greater detail, see Twining, 'The Province of Jurisprudence Re-examined', supra.

jurisprudence texts do not include sections on social–legal theory; an omission that speaks volumes.[54] Jurisprudents who have made informative contributions to theories of law and society – from Julius Stone in the past, to Roger Cotterrell in the present – are consequently forgotten or largely ignored within mainstream legal theory. That is why William's effort to expand the horizons of analytical jurisprudence has enduring significance. Toward this end, despite the critical tenor of my comments, I should say I very much appreciate that Raz is now urging legal philosophers to consider multiple forms of law. This is a terrific development for jurisprudence, and I hope others follow his lead.

I am grateful to have William as a fellow traveller and mentor, and to be his friend. He is the most open-minded and generous scholar I know, and a truly lovely person. My aim in this essay is to help his pioneering ideas gain their due recognition. Legal philosophers are only now awakening to legal phenomena that he has wrestled with for decades. Alas, if the past is any guide, they likely will not read this piece; but others will know.

[54] I try to rectify this in Brian Z. Tamanaha, 'The Third Pillar of Jurisprudence' (forthcoming), *William & Mary Law Review*, papers.ssrn.com/sol3/papers.cfm?abstract_id=2256622

Appendix: A bibliography of William Twining

Penelope Twining

Books and other publications

Legal Fictions in Theory and Practice (ed. with Maksymilian Del Mar). Springer 2015.

Karl Llewellyn and the Realist Movement, Weidenfeld & Nicolson 1973, Oklahoma University Press, 1985, revised edition Cambridge University Press 2012.

Evidence, Inference and Enquiry (with Philip Dawid and Mimi Vasilaki, eds). British Academy/Oxford University Press 2011.

Globalisation and Legal Scholarship (Montesquieu Seminars Tilburg, Nijmegen) Wolf Legal Publishers 2011 Translation of earlier version (Brazil) Portuguese sub nom: *Globalização e estudos juridicos Meritum* v. 7 n.1 15-53 (2012)

Legal Theory and the Legal Academy (ed. with M. Del Mar and M. Giudice). Farnham: Ashgate 2010.

How to Do Things with Rules (with David Miers), 5th edition. Cambridge University Press 2010.

Human Rights: Southern Voices. Cambridge University Press 2009.

Uma Concepção Pós-Westfaliana de Direito (with Oscar Guardiola-Rivera, trans. C. Baldi). Rio de Janeiro: Lumen Juris 2009.

General Jurisprudence: Understanding Law from a Global Perspective. Cambridge University Press 2009.

Rethinking Evidence: Exploratory Essays, Blackwell 1990, Northwestern University Press 1994, 2nd edition. Cambridge University Press 2006.

Analysis of Evidence (with Terence Anderson). Little, Brown, and Weidenfeld and Nicolson, 1991; Northwestern U.P., 1998 (and Teachers' Supplement). (2nd Edition) (with Terence Anderson and David Schum) Cambridge University Press 2005.

Derecho y Globalización Estudio preliminar Oscar Guardiola-Rivera y Clara Sandoval Villalba. Biblioteca Universitaria 2003.

Evidence and inference in history and law: interdisciplinary dialogues (ed. with I. Hampsher-Monk). Northwestern University Press 2003.

The Great Juristic Bazaar: Jurists' Texts and Lawyers' Stories. Ashgate 2002.

Globalisation and Legal Theory. Butterworths 2000, Northwestern University Press/Cambridge University Press 2001.

Law in Context: Enlarging a Discipline. Oxford University Press 1997.

Blackstone's Tower: The English Law School (Hamlyn lectures). London: Sweet & Maxwell 1994.

Legal Records in the Commonwealth (ed. with Emma Quick). Aldershot: Dartmouth 1994.

Evidence and Proof (ed. with Alex Stein). Aldershot: Dartmouth 1992.

Issues of Self-determination (ed.). Aberdeen University Press 1991.

Learning Lawyers' Skills (ed. with Neil Gold and Karl Mackie). Butterworths 1989.

Access to Legal Education and the Legal Profession (ed. with Rajeev Dhavan and Neil Kibble). Butterworths 1989.

Sociological Jurisprudence and Realist Theories of Law (ed. with E. Kamenka and R. Summers). Berlin: Munich: Duncker & Humblot 1986.

Essays on Kelsen (ed. with Richard Tur). Oxford University Press 1986.

Legal Theory and Common Law (ed.). Blackwell 1986.

Theories of Evidence: Bentham & Wigmore. Weidenfeld & Nicolson and Stanford University Press 1985.

Facts in Law (ed.), Wiesbaden: Franz Steiner Verlag 1983.

Law Publishing and Legal Information (ed. with Jennifer Uglow). Sweet & Maxwell 1981.

Legal Literature in Small Jurisdictions (ed. with Jennifer Uglow). London: Canadian Law Information Council and Commonwealth Secretariat 1981.

Academic law and legal development (Taylor lectures). University of Lagos 1976.

How to Do Things with Rules (with David Miers). Weidenfeld & Nicolson 1976, 2nd edition 1982, 3rd edition 1991, 4th edition 1999, 5th edition Cambridge University Press 2010. Italian translation by Carlo Garbarino *sub. nom.* Come far Cose con Regole, Milan 1990.

The Karl Llewellyn Papers. University of Chicago Law School 1968.

Pericles and the Plumber (Inaugural Lecture). Belfast 1967 – a shortened version was published in 83 L.Q.R. 396.

The Place of Customary Law in the National Legal Systems of East Africa. University of Chicago Law School 1964.

Articles, book chapters and papers

Forthcoming

Introduction to reprint of K. N. Lewellyn, *The Bramble Bush: On our law and its Study*, (privately printed, New York 1930, Oceana Publications 1951) in series *The books that made Law in the Western World (13th century – 1940)*. Springer, forthcoming 2016.

"Evidential Reasoning in the International Criminal Tribunal Rwanda, A Case Study: Tharcisse Muvunyi" (with Terence Anderson), forthcoming in *International Journal of Criminal Justice.*

"McAuslan in Context: Early Days in Dar and Warwick" [Later Days in 43 countries] in Thanos Zartaloudis and Valerie Kelley (eds.), *Essays in Honour of Patrick McAuslan,* Birkbeck/Routledge, forthcoming 2015.

"Legal Realism and Jurisprudence: Ten Theses" in Elizabeth Mertz and Stuart MacAulay (eds), The New Legal Realism (Vol 1), Cambridge University Press, forthcoming 2015.

##

Preface to *Legal Fictions in Theory and Practice*, Maksymilian Del Mar and William Twining (eds). Springer, 2015.

"'Looking Back will still keep us Looking Forward'", A a letter from Arthur Corbin to Soia Mentschikoff upon the death of Karl Llewellyn, 47 *Yale Journal of Law and Humanities* (2015) 101–111.

Russian Translation of "General Jurisprudence" (2005), with comments by M. V. Antonov, in *Russian Yearbook of Legal Theory* No. 3 2010 IISSN 2077–5644 at pp. 229–79 (published 2015).

"Globalisation and Legal Scholarship: A Response", 4 *Transnational Legal Theory* (2014) 714–725 (in Symposium on William Twining's Montesquieu Lecture, Globalisation and Legal Scholarship).

"LETR: The Role of Legal Academics in Legal Education and Training: Ten Theses", 48 *The Law Teacher* (2014) 94–103.

"Francis Deng on Dinka Culture and Human Rights", 46 *Verfassung und Recht in Übersee* (2013) 197–214.

Review of Neil Walker (ed.), MacCormick's Scotland (2013) *C.L.J.* 437–442.

"Human Rights: Southern Voices: Yash Ghai and Upendra Baxi", in José Barreto (ed.) *Human Rights and the Third World Perspective* Newcastle-upon-Tyne: Cambridge Scholars Publishing, (2013) pp. 256–310.

"Donald Neil MacCormick 1941–2009", in *Biographical Memoirs of the Fellows of the British Academy XI* (2012) pp. 448–71.

"Globalization and Law Studies"/ "Globalização e studios juridicos", *Meritum Revista de Direito da Universidade Fumec V.7 no.*1 pp.15–53 2012.

"Globalisation and Law: Ten Theses" in *The Law of the Future and the Future of Law Vol, II* (Sam Muller, Stavros Zouridis, Morly Frishman and Laura Kistemaker (eds)) Den Haag: Torkel Opsahl Academic E Publisher 2012.

"What is the Point of Legal Archeology?" in *Transnational Legal Theory* 3(2) pp. 166–72 (2012).

"Legal Pluralism 101", in Brian Z. Tamanaha, Caroline Sage and Michael Woolcock, *Legal Pluralism and Development: Scholars and Practitioners in Dialogue* New York: Cambridge University Press, 2012, pp. 112–128.

"Professionalism in Legal Education", 18 *Int. Jo. Legal Profession* No. 1 and 2 (2011) pp. 165–72.

"Globalization and legal literature". *Osgoode Law Journal* 353–373 (2011) (review article of R. Domingo *The New Global Law* (2011)).

"Implicaciones de la Globalización Para el Derecho Como disciplina", in Pedro Mercado Pacheco (ed.) *Un Panorama de Filosofía Juridíca y Politíca* (50 años de acfs) *Anales de la Catedra Francisco Suárez* No. 44 pp. 341–68 (2010).

"Entrevista con William Twining" (Manuel Atienza y Raymondo Gama), *Doxa* 32, 713–727 (2010)j.

"Moving Beyond Law: Interdisciplinarity and the Study of Evidence", in Philip Dawid, William Twining and Mimi Vasalaki (eds.) *Evidence, Inference and Enquiry* British Academy/ Oxford University Press, 2010, pp. 73–118.

"Normative and Legal Pluralism", (Bernstein Lecture, 2009) 20 *Duke Journal of Comparative and International Law* (2011–12) pp. 473–517.

"Punching our Weight? Legal scholarship and public understanding" (The SLS Centenary Lecture), 29 *Legal Studies* (2009) pp. 519–33.

Introduction to Symposium on Robert B. Stevens, *International Journal of the Legal Profession*, 16, No.1, (2009), 1–3.

"De nuevo, los hechos en serio" [Taking Facts Seriously – Again], *Cuadernos de Filosofía del Derecho, DOXA* 32 (2009).

"*Institutions of Law*: Globalization, non-state law and legal pluralism", in Maksymilian Del Mar and Zenon Bankowski (eds) *Law as Institutional Normative Order* Ashgate 2009.

"Implications of Globalisation for Legal scholarship", in Andrew Halpin and Volker Roeben (eds) *Theorising the Global Legal Order* (Oxford: Hart, 2009), pp. 39–59.

"Alan Swan: The Chicago Connection", 64 *University of Miami Law Review* 9–14 (2009).

"Karl N. Llewellyn", in Roger K. Newman (ed.) *The Yale Biographical Dictionary of American Law* (New Haven: Yale University Press, 2009), pp. 346–8.

"The Law in Context Movement", in Cane and Conaghan (eds) *The New Oxford Companion to Law* (Oxford University Press, 2008), pp. 680–2.

"Law, Justice and Rights: Some Implications of a Global perspective" in Ebbeson & Okowa (eds) *Environmental Law and Justice* (Cambridge: Cambridge University Press, 2008) pp. 76–97.

"Surface Law", in Hanne Petersen, Anne Lise Kjær, Helle Krunke and Mikael Rask Madsen (eds) *Paradoxes of European Legal Integration* (Aldershot: Ashgate 2008) pp. 157–184.

"Address to Evidencers", 38 *Seton Hall Law Review* 879–83 (2008).

"Globalisation and Comparative Law", in E. Őrűcű and D. Nelken (eds), *Comparative Law: A Handbook* ch. 3 (Oxford: Hart, 2007).

"The Challenge of Authority – a Post-Modern Foundationalist?" *Public Law* 210 (2007) (Comment on Gearty's Hamlyn Lectures).

"General Jurisprudence", 15 *University of Miami International and Comparative Law Rev.* 1–59 (2007).

"Argumentation, stories and generalizations: A comment", 6 *Law, Probability and Risk* 169–185 (2007).

"Human Rights: Southern Voices (MacDonald Lecture, University of Alberta)", 11 *Review of Constitutional Studies* 203–279 (2007) reprinted in Abdul Paliwala (ed.) *Law, Justice and Social Development* (LGD), 1. www2.warwick.ac.uk/fac/soc/law/elj/lgd/2007_1/

"Upendra Baxi: A Tribute", in *Law, Justice and Social Development* (LGD) (2007), 1. www2.warwick.ac.uk/fac/soc/law/elj/lgd/2007_1/

"Two Kinds of Post-Modernism: Santos, Calvino, and Haack", in Cornelis de Waal (ed.) *Susan Haack: A Lady of Distinctions. A Philosopher Replies to Her Critics* 229–250 (Amherst, NY: Prometheus Books (2007).

"La Dufusión del Derecho: Una perspectiva Global", in Alfonso de Julios-Campuzano (ed.) *Ciudadania y Derecho en el Era de la Globalización* 131–64 Madrid: Dykinson (2007).

"Taking Facts Seriously – Again", in Paul Roberts and Mike Redmayne (eds) *Innovations in evidence and proof : integrating theory, research and teaching* at pp. 65–86. Hart Publishing, 2007.

"Taking Facts Seriously – Again", 55 *Journal of Legal Education* 360–80 (2006).

"Glenn on Tradition: An Overview", 1 *Journal of Comparative Law* 107–15 (2006).

Review of Cownie, *Legal Academics*, and Bradley, *Conversations Choices and Chances* 32 *Journal of Law and Society*, 667–72 (2006).

"Diffusion and Globalization Discourse", 47 *Harvard International Law Journal* 507–15 (2006).

"Schauer on Hart", 119 *Harvard Law Review Forum* 105–112 (2006).

"Have Concepts, Will Travel: Analytical Jurisprudence in a Global Context", 1 *Int. Jo. Law in Context* 5–40 (2005).

"Social Science and Diffusion of Law", 32 *Journal of Law and Society* 203–40 (2005).

"General Jurisprudence", in M. Escamilla and M. Saavedra (eds.), *Law and Justice in Global Society (XXII World Congress on Philosophy of Law and Social Philosophy).* (Universidad de Granada Press, 2005) pp. 645–688.

"Diffusion of Law: A Global Perspective", 49 *Journal of Legal Pluralism* 1–45 (2005).

"The Hutton Inquiry: Wider Legal Aspects", in W.G. Runciman (ed.) *Hutton and Butler: Lifting the Lid on the Workings of Power,* 30–50 British Academy/OUP, (2004).

"Por una teoria geral do direito revitalizada", 5 *Dereito e Democracia* 2 (2004), 509–537.

"The Province of Jurisprudence Re-Examined" (Julius Stone Memorial Lecture, Sydney, 2000), in (C. Dauvergne (ed.) *Jurisprudence in an Interdependent Globe*, pp. 13–42. Ashgate, 2003.

"A Post-Westphalian Conception of Law", 37 *Law and Society Review* 199–257 (2003).

"The Role of Academics in the Legal System (UK)", in P. Cane and M. Tushnet (eds) *Oxford Handbook of Legal Studies*, Oxford University Press, 2003, pp. 920–29

"Law Teaching as a Vocation", 1 *Speculum Iuris* 161–80 (2003).

"Evidence as a Multidisciplinary Subject" (Cardozo Conference, New York, April 2003), *Law, Probability and Risk* 2, pp. 91–107 (June 2003).

"Reviving General Jurisprudence", in M. Likovsky (ed.) *Transnational Legal Processes*, pp. 3–22. Butterworths, 2002.

"Bentham, Jeremy" in *International Encyclopedia of the Social and Behavioral Sciences* vol. 2, pp. 1145–51. Pergamon, 2001.

"Legal Reasoning and Argumentation", in *International Encyclopedia of the Social and Behavioral Sciences*, vol.13, pp. 8670–75. Pergamon, 2001.

"A Cosmopolitan Discipline? Some Implications of 'Globalisation' for Legal Education", 8 *International Journal of the Legal Profession* 23–36 (2001) (also in *1 Journal of Commonwealth Law and Legal Education* 13–29 (2001)) (translated into Italian in XXVII *Sociologica Del Diritto* 17–36 (2001/3).

"The Ratio Decidendi of the Parable of the Prodigal Son", in K. O'Donovan and G. Rubin (eds) *Human Rights and Legal History: Essays for Brian Simpson*, pp. 149–71. Oxford University Press, 2000.

"Good Stories and True Stories", in P. van Koppen and N. Roos (eds) *Rationality, Information and Progress in Psychology and Law: Liber Amicorum Hans F.M. Crombag*, pp. 43–51. Metajuridica, Maastricht, 2000.

"Comparative Law and Legal Theory: The Country and Western Tradition", (SOAS Law Dept. 50th anniversary lectures) in Ian Edge (ed) *Comparative Law In Global Perspective*, pp. 21–76. Transnational Publishers, 2000.

"Mapping Law" (MacDermott Lecture), 50 *Northern Ireland LQ* 12–49 (1999).

"Necessary, but Dangerous?", in Marijke Malsch and Hans Nijboer (eds) *Complex Cases: Perspectives on the Netherlands Criminal Justice System*, pp. 69–98. Thela Thesis, Amsterdam, 1999.

"Pericles Regained?", 1 *Legal Ethics*, 129–52 (1999) (revised version of ch. 16 of *Law in Context: Enlarging a Discipline*).

"Jeremy Bentham and General Jurisprudence", 112 *Tidsskrift for Rettsvitenskap*, 381–407 (1999) (First Eckhoff Memorial Lecture, 1998).

"Globalization and Comparative Law", 6 *Maastricht Journal of European and Comparative Law*, 217–43 (1999).

Review of Natalie Hull, *Roscoe Pound and Karl Llewellyn*, 115 *LQR*, 152–60 (1999).

"Narrative and Generalizations in Argumentation About Questions of Fact", 40 *S. Texas L. Rev.* 351–65 (1999).

"R. G. Collingwood's Autobiography: One Reader's Response", 25 *Journal of Law and Society* 603–20 (1999).

"Imagining Bentham: A Celebration", in Michael Freeman (ed.) *Current Legal Problems*. Oxford: Oxford Uuniversity Press, 1998, pp. 1–36.

"250th Anniversary of Jeremy Bentham", *Wig and Gavel* 10(1998), 26–8.

"Civilians Don't Try: A Comment on Mirjan Damaska's 'Rational and Irrational Proof Revisited'", 5 *Cardozo Journal of International And Comparative Law* 69–78 (1997).

"Other People's Power: The Bad Man and English Positivism 1897-97", 63 *Brooklyn Legal Review* 189–223 (1997).

"Narrative and Generalisations in Argumentation about Questions of Fact", in Ake Frandberg (ed) *Festkrift Till Stig Stromholm*, 821–833. Uppsala University, 1997.

"Freedom of Proof and the Reform of Criminal Evidence" 31 *Israel L. Rev.* 439–63 (1996).

"Recent Trends in Evidence Scholarship", in J. H. Nijboer and J. M. Reijntjes (eds), *Proceedings of the First World Conference on New Trends in Criminal Investigation and Evidence*. Lelystad: Konninklijke Vermande, 1996, pp. 13–22.

"Globalization and Legal Theory – Some Local Implications", 49 *Current Legal Problems* (1996), pp. 1–42.

"Rethinking Law Schools: A Response to Schlegel," 21 *Law and Social Inquiry* 1007–1016 (1996).

"General and Particular Jurisprudence – Three Chapters in a Story", in S. Guest (ed.) *Legal Positivism Today*, 119–46 (Dartmouth, 1996) (reprinted in *Law in Context: Enlarging a Discipline* at 149–79).

"A Nobel Prize for Law?" in Geoffrey Wilson (ed.) *Frontiers of Legal Scholarship* (John Wiley, 1996) (reprinted in *Law in Context: Enlarging a Discipline* at 339–53).

"What are law schools for?" 46 *N.I.L.Q.* 291 (2005) (revised version reprinted in *Law in Context: Enlarging a Discipline* at 292–311).

"Anchored Narratives – A Comment", *European Journal of Crime, Criminal Law and Criminal Justice* 106–114 (1995).

"Remembering 1972: The Oxford Centre in the Context of Developments in Higher Education and the Discipline of Law", in D. Galligan (ed.) *Socio-Legal Studies in Context* – Special Issue of *Journal of Law and Society*, vol. 22, No. 1 pp. 35–49 (1995) (reissued as a book by Blackwells).

"Postgraduate Studies in Law", in Peter Birks (ed), *Reviewing Legal Education*. Oxford University Press, 1994.

"Karl Llewellyn's Unfinished Agenda: *Law in our Society* and the Job of Juristic Method" (Chicago papers in Legal History, 1993; shorter versions published in 48 *University of Miami Law Rev.* 119 (1993)) and U. Drobnig and M. Rehbinder (ed.) *Rechtsrealismus, multikulturelle Gesellschaft und Handelsrecht*. Duncker & Humblot, Berlin 1994.

"Alternative to what? Theories of Litigation and Dispute-Settlement in Anglo-American Jurisprudence: Some Neglected Classics", 56 *M.L.R.* 381 (1993).

"The Initial Stage: Notes on the Context and a Search for Consensus", *Proceedings* of First Consultative Conference, Lord Chancellor's Advisory Committee On Legal Education and Training, 1993.

"Constitutions, Constitutionalism and Constitution-mongering", in I. Stotzky (ed.) *Transition to Democracy in Latin America: The Role of the Judiciary.* Westview, 1993.

"Intellectual Skills at the Academic Stage: Twelve Theses", in P. Birks (ed.) *Examining the Law Syllabus: Beyond the Core.* 93–5. Oxford University Press, 1993.

"The Rationalist Tradition of Evidence Scholarship: An Anglo-American overview and some speculations about Continental Europe", in J. Nijboer (ed.) *Forensic Expertise and the Law of Evidence.* Amsterdam Koninklijke Nederlandse Akademie, 1993.

"The Analysis of Evidence", in H. Lewis-Ruttley (ed.) *Skills Teaching and Assessment in Practice*, 5–20. Institute of Advanced Legal Studies, London 1991.

"Maine and Legal Education: a comment", in Alan Diamond (ed.) *The Victorian Achievement of Sir Henry Maine*, 209–16. Cambridge University Press, 1991.

"Reflections on Law in Context", in P. Cane and J. Stapleton (eds) *Essays for Patrick Atiyah*, 1–30, Oxford: 1991.

"Five Cheers for Tillers and Schum", 13 *Cardozo Law Review* 713–23 (1991).

"The New Evidence Scholarship", 13 *Cardozo Law Review*, 295–302 (1991).

"Lawyers' Stories", in *Action and Agency*, (Roberta Kevelson (ed.)) 317–89. New York: P. Lang, 1991.

"The Case Law System in America", 100 *Yale Law Jo.* 1093–1102 (1991).

"Evidence and Proof in Anglo-American Litigation" in M. Jakubowski (ed.) *Anglo-Polish Legal Essays*, 71–114. vol. 3. Warsaw: University of Warsaw. 1990.

"Reading Bentham" (Maccabean lecture), LXXV *Proceedings* of the British Academy, 97–141 (1989).

"Preparing Lawyers for the Twenty-first Century", *Proceedings* of the Eighth Commonwealth Law Conference, Auckland, New Zealand (April 1990) (reprinted in 3 *Legal Education Review* 35).

"Recent Trends in Legal Education in the Commonwealth: Beyond The Primary School Model", in R. Wacks (ed.), *The Future of legal Education and the Legal Profession in Hong Kong.* University of Hong Kong, 1989. (reprinted 2 *Legal Education Review* 35 (1990).

"Analysis of Evidence" (with T. Anderson), in Gold, MacKie and Twining (eds) *Learning Lawyers' Skills.* Butterworths, 1989.

"Reading Law" (Seegers Lectures), 24 *Valparaiso Law Review* 1 (1989).

"Rationality and Scepticism in Judicial Proof: Some Signposts", 2 *Int. Jo. Semiotics of Law* 69 (1989).

Soliloquoy (Twining on Jurisprudence), *Law Talk*, Summer 1988, 4–6.

"Il precedente nel diritto Inglese: una demistificazione", in Giovanna Visentini (ed.) *La Giurisprudenza per Massime e il valore del Precedente*, Padova: CEDAM, 1988, pp. 33–50, 455–504.

"Adjudication between freedom and proof: Freedom of proof at common law", *Conference Paper*, University of Trento (1988).

"Legal skills and legal education", 22 *The Law Teacher* 4 (1988).

"Hot Air in the Redwoods", 86 *Mich. L. Rev.* 1523–1547 (1988).

"Access to Legal Education and the Legal Profession, A Commonwealth Perspective", 7 *Windsor Yearbook of Access to Justice*, 157–208 (1987) (reprinted in Dhavan, Kibble and Twining eds, *Access to legal education and the legal profession*.Butterworths, 1989

"Legal Education and Training: Some Lessons of History", *Commonwealth Legal Education Newsletter, No* 52, (1988).

"The Camel in the Zoo" in Issa Shivji ed. *The Limits of Legal Radicalism* UDSM, Dar-es-Salaam, 1987.

"1836 And All That: Laws in the University of London 1836-1986", *Current Legal Problems* 261 (1987) (shorter version reprinted in *The University of London and the World of Learning*. F.M.L. Thompson ed., Hambledon Press, 1990.

"The Boston Symposium: A Comment", 66 *Boston University Law Review*, 391–99 (1986).

"Bentham's Writings on Evidence", *Bentham Newsletter*, No 10, 34–40 (1986).

"Taking Skills Seriously", *Commonwealth Legal Education Newsletter, No* 43, Appendix (reprinted in *Journal of Professional Legal Education*, (1986) *and Learning Lawyers Skills*, op. cit.).

"Cannibalism and Legal Literature", *Oxford Journal of Legal Studies, vol* 6, 423–30 (1986).

"Theory in the law curriculum" (with D. N. MacCormick), in *Legal Theory and Common Law* op. cit., 238–54.

"Talk About Realism", 60 *New York University L. Rev.*, 329–84 (1985).

"The Paperchase in England and Wales: An overview of Legal Education and Training", American Bar Association Conference, London, (July 1985).

"Some scepticism about some scepticisms", 11 *British Journal of Law and Society*. I. 137; II 285 (1984).

"Why Bentham?" *Bentham Newsletter, No.* 8, 34–49.

"Evidence and Legal Theory", 47 *MLR* 261–83 (1984) (Inaugural Lecture, UCL); reprinted in *Legal Theory and Common Law* op cit 62–80.

Entries in *Biographical Dictionary of the Common Law*, ed. A. W. B. Simpson, on C. K. Allen (6–7); W. W. Cook (125); John Dickinson (149–150); Jerome Frank (190–3); Karl Llewellyn (319–22); J. H. Wigmore (531–5); Samuel Williston (543–4) and Hessel Yntema (554–5). London, Butterworth 1983.

"Keeping up to date in Xanadu", *Seventh Commonwealth Law Conference Papers*, Hong Kong 235–40 (1983).

"Law for Non-Lawyers: Some Preliminary Reflections", *Commonwealth Secretariat* (1983).

"Identification and Misidentification: Redefining the Problem", in Sally Lloyd-Bostock and Brian R. Clifford (eds) *Evaluating Witness Evidence* 253–84 (Wiley & Sons 1983); revised version in Stein Evju (ed.) Samfunn Rett Rettferdighet. Tano, Norway 1986.

"The Rationalist Tradition of Evidence Scholarship", in Enid Campbell and Louis Waller (eds.) *Well and Truly Tried* 77. Law Book Company 1982.

"Rule-Scepticism and Fact-Scepticism in Bentham's Theory of Evidence", in *Facts in Law* op cit (1983), pp. 65–81.

"The Benson Report and Legal Education: A Personal View", in Philip Thomas (ed.) *Law in the Balance,* Martin Robertson. Oxford University Press, 1982, p. 186.

"Taking Facts Seriously", in Neil Gold (ed.) *Essays on Legal Education.* Butterworths (Toronto) 1982, 51–76 (reprinted 34 *Journal of Legal Education* 22–42 (1984)).

"Goodbye to Lewis Eliot: the Academic Lawyer as Scholar", Presidential Address, Society of Public Teachers of Law, 15 *JSPTL* (N.S.) 2–19 (1980).

"Debating Probabilities", *Liverpool Law Review* Vol II 51–64 (1980).

"Benson and the Academics", 48 *MLR* 558–66 (1980).

"Legal Education for All", in D. Mitchell (ed.) *Legal Studies and Legal Education for Non-Lawyers,* 1–13. Sydney: Butterworths, 1979.

"Academic Law and Legal Philosophy; the Significance of Herbert Hart", 95 *LQR* 557–80 (1979).

"Torture and Philosophy", *Aristotelian Society: Supplementary Volume LII,* 143–168 (1978).

"The Great Juristic Bazaar", 14 *JSPTL* (N.S.) 185 (1978).

"Information about Law", in Papua New Guinea (P.N.G.) Law Reform Commission 1977; re-issued *sub nom Law Information Centre,* (1977).

"The Contemporary Significance of Bentham's *Anarchical Fallacies*", 61 *ARSP* 325 (1975).

"Law and Social Science: The Method of Detail", *New Society,* 27th June 1974, reprinted in P. Barker (ed.) *The Social Sciences Today*. Edward Arnold, 1975.

"Some Jobs for Jurisprudence", 1 *British Journal of Law & Society* 149 (1974) (Inaugural Lecture, University of Warwick).

"Bentham on Torture" (with P. E. Twining), 24 *NILQ* 305 (1973), reprinted in M. James (ed.) *Bentham and Legal Theory*. Queen's University of Belfast, 1973.

"Treatises and Textbooks: a reply to T. B. Smith", 12 *JSPTL* (NS) 267 (1972).

Review of A Ehrenzweig's Psychoanalytical Jurisprudence 21 *Am Jo Comp Law* 348 (1973).

"Law and Anthropology: A case-study in Interdisciplinary collaboration", 7 *Law & Society Rev*, 561 (1973) reprinted in R. Luckham (ed.) *Law and Social Enquiry: Case studies of Research*. Scandinavian Institute of African Studies ICLD, 1981.

"The Way of the Baffled Medic", 12 *JSPTL* (NS) 348 (1973).

"Emergency Powers and Criminal Process: The Diplock Report", *Criminal Law Review* 406 (1973).

"The Bad Man Revisited", 52 *Cornell L. Rev.* 275 (1973).

"Is your Textbook Really Necessary?" 11 *JSPTL* (NS) 267 (1973).

"Ernie and the Centipede" (with K. O'Donovan and A. Paliwala), in Jolowicz (ed.) *The Division and Classification of the Law* (London: Butterworths, 1970), p. 10.

"Legal Eagles or Battery Hens?" (with D. Mitchell and K. O'Donovan) 10 *JSPTL* (NS) 6 (1968).

"Social Justice and the Law", in A. Sawyerr (ed.) *East African Law and Social Change* (1967).

"Two works of Karl Llewellyn", in 30 *MLR* 165 (1967–8).

"Legal Education within East Africa", in *East African Law Today* (1966).

"The Restatement of African Customary Law – A comment", 1 *Journal of Modern African Studies* 221 (1963).

"The English law Teacher in Africa", 7 *JSPTL* (NS) 80 (1962).

"Bibliography of Sudan Law I", (with A. R. Nasri and P. E. Twining), *SLJR* 313 (1960).

"Law Reporting in the Sudan" *JAL* 176 (1959).

"Khartoum Municipal Council v. Cotran – a study in judicial techniques", *Sudan Law Journal and Reports* 112 (1959).

"Some Aspects of Reception", *Sudan Law Journal and Reports* 229 (1957).

Miscellaneous shorter articles, case notes, reviews etc. are not listed.

Reports involving a substantial contribution

Review of Uganda Criminal Justice System (co-author, Crown Agents/ODA, 1996–7).

Report of Review Team of National Law School of India University (with Marc Galanter and Savitri Goonesekere, 1996).

Legal Education Tanzania (FILMUP Project) (Chief Consultant, 1994).

LL.M. Review, University of London – Interim and Final *Reports*, 1992–3.

Report on Judicial Records in Accra (London: Association of Commonwealth Archivists, 1991).

Law as an Academic Discipline (Heads of University Law Schools, 1983).

Law Publishing and Legal Scholarship (Final Report of SPTL Working Party, 1977).

Emergency Powers: A Fresh Start (The Queen's University, Belfast, Working Party on Emergency Powers, Fabian Trust No 416, 1972).

Legal Education in a Changing World (International Legal Center, New York 1975).

Legal Education in Botswana, Lesotho and Swaziland with J. C. N. Paul (Inter-University Council, 1970).

Documentation and Editorial Work

Records of International Commercial Arbitration (Preliminary project) [2013–14]

Records of Legal Education Project (Advisory Panel, Institute of Advanced Legal Studies, 1995–98).

Commonwealth Legal Records Project 1990–1994.

Editor, *Jurists series* 1979– (formerly Edward Arnold, Weidenfeld & Nicolson; now Stanford University Press).

Editorial work for the Bentham Project 1971–75.

Co-Editor, *Law in Context* series (Weidenfeld & Nicolson Ltd, Butterworths, now Cambridge University Press) 1966.

Director, Karl Llewellyn Papers Project, 1963–65.

Bibliography of Sudan Law I (with P. E. Twining and A. S. Nasri, 1960, (*SLJR* 313).

Secretary, East African Law Documentation Project, 1963–5.

Secretary, Sudan Law Project (legal archives), 1960–61.

General Editor, Sudan Law Journal and Reports, 1959–61.

Index

Abi-Saab, Professor, 230
abortion
  human rights and views on, 57
  margin of appreciation, 48
Abraham, A. Hayward, 291
abyssal line, 133
academic law
  limitations of, 99
access to justice
  real-world challenges of, 302
Accidents, Compensation and the Law (Atiyah), 5
accountability and transitional justice, 88
accountability mechanisms, 88
acknowledgement of harms, 82
activists
  for human rights, 53
actors
  legitimate, in pluralisitic world, 291
  non-state and regulatory norms, 289
  proliferation of private regulatory, 300
actors, norms, and processes (ANP), transnational political legal theory, 299–300
Adamson-Hoebel, E., 91, 96
adverse possession, 103
Advisory Committee of the Human Rights Council, 58
affirmative action, human rights, and views on, 58
affluent societies
  versus global poor, 201
Africa. *See also* former colonies
  constitution making in former colonies, 172–175
  constitutionalism, trajectory of, 193–195
  major economic and social changes, 192
  new constitutionalism, 166, 184–185
African National Congress (ANC), 184
Afrikaner community
  ANC compromises with, 185
agro-fuels, 137
All England Law Reports, 330
Allende, Salvador, 99, 100, 103, 105, 109
alterity. *See* otherness
alternative business structures (ABS), 247, 251
Amazon and cybercapitalism, 258
Amazon and Hachette conflict over e-book prices, 258
American Legal Realism, 4, 7, 274, 284, 354, *See also* Legal Realism
American Realists, 21
Amerindians
  cannibalism, and Eurocentric projections, 94
  Christian and Eurocentric views of, 92
  encounters with Europeans, 91
  gift economies, 93
amnesty
  human rights abuses, 75
  military and political actors, 86
Amnesty International, 253
Anaconda, 103, 105
Analysis of Evidence (Anderson, Schum and Twining), 9
analysis, conceptual
  legal philosophers and, 357
ANC. *See* African National Congress
ancestral rights, 119
Ancient Law (Maine), 4
Anderson, Gavin, 127, 129, 141
Anderson, Terry, 8, 10
Anglo-American legal theory
  response to globalization, 147
An-Na'im, Abdullahi, 21, 39, 59–62
ANP. *See* actors, norms, and processes

anthropocentric approach
environmental law, 202
anthropologists, legal
role of law in globalization, 286
anthropology
Eurocentric views on Amerindian cultures, 94
insights into globalisation, 96
anti-corruption commission
of Kenya, 190
Arab Spring, 115–125, 192
Egypt, 122
electronic surveillance of revolts, 260
indignation revolts of 2011–2013, 142
protests and mobilizations, 124
arbitration
arbitrators and switching hats, 229
disputes, data from UNCTAD, 227
foreign investors versus sovereign states, 214
investor-state, flaws of, 229
process, 229–230
protections for foreign investors, 224
arbitrators
investor-state disputes, 229–230
Arendt, Hannah, 157
Argentina
disappearances, and effect of IT, 252
economic crisis, early 2000s, 231
NML Capital and settlement for bonds, 232
withdrawal from ICSID, 234
argument systems, electronic, 255
arguments, moral or economic efficiency
legal reasoning, 308
Arnold, Thurman, 270, 274, 275
artificial intelligence (AI) and law research, 253–257
artificial intelligence
effect on rule-making, 241
role in online dispute resolution, 256
artificial intelligence (AI) systems
law and, 253
ASEAN. *See* Association of South East Asian Nations
Ashley, Kevin, 255
Asia and constitutions of former dictatorships, 179
Asia Pacific Economic Cooperation, 216
Assembly of Heads of State and Government of the Organization of African Unity, 42
Association of South East Asian Nations (ASEAN), 221
Atienza, Manuel, 127
Atiyah, Patrick, 5
Attorney General of Kenya, 190
attribution of authority to law, 318
austerity package, Spain, and energy investors, 232
Austin, J.L., 272, 276, 305, 308, 312, 313
Australia
Philip Morris Asia tobacco dispute, 233, 236
tobacco control laws, 229
authoritarianism
top-down institutions of law, 139
transitional justice, 74
automated motor-speed fining systems, 254
autonomy and liberty
interference with, in torture, 35

Badiou, Alain, 37
Baganda system of clans, 168
Banjul Charter on Human and People's Rights, 42
barrio collectives, 122
Bauman, Richard, 63
Baxi, Upendra, xiii, 21, 39, 68, 69, 70, 74, 101, 102, 105, 110, 161, 243, 371
behind the border disciplines on governments, 214
Being Against the World Guardola-Rivera, 98
Belgium
partial nationalisation on Fortis Bank, 228
belief
privatisation of, or fundamentalism, 93
religions without, 93
Bell, Daniel, 244
beneficiaries
unjustly acquired gains, 102
Benhabib, Seyla, 146, 158
Benkler, Yochai, 245
Bentham, Jeremy, 3, 8, 9, 12, 15, 242
fragments on torture, 22–24
Berlin Wall, fall of, 146, 155, 178
Berman, Bruce, 170, 178
Bhala, Raj, 220
bilateral investment treaties (BITs), 223
defence of, 235
foreign investors and special rights, 227
nations withdrawing from, 234
Bill of Rights
of Kenya, 188

bills of rights
post-colonial African nations, 179
biodiversity, 199
globalisation and environmental law, 197
risk literature in environmental law, 210
birth rate, high, in Kenya, 190
BITs. *See* bilateral investment treaties
Black Acts and closing of common land, 260
Blackstone, William, 204
Blackstone's Tower (Twining), 9
Blakeley, Ruth, 32
Bloomsbury International Limited and others v Sea Fish Industry Authority and Department for Environment, Food and Rural Affairs, 330
Blum, Walter, 5
Bolivia
constitutional process, 129
reconfigurative law and constitutional process, 140
withdrawal from ICSID, 234
Boolean logic
versus natural language searching, 255
Bosch, Juan, 100
Botswana and independence constitution, 177
bottom-up approach
effects on law, 129
bottom-up constitutionalism, 129
bottom-up law, 138
bottom-up, participative, political process, 140
Boudon, Raymond, 64
boundaries of 'the legal', 307–309
Bramble Bush, The (Llewellyn), 269, 277, 278
Brasenose College, Oxford, 2
Brazil
indignados movements, 125
indignation movement, 124
protests around public transport, 117
resistance to electronic surveillance, 262
response to digital exclusion, 249
Brazil, Russia, India, China and South Africa (BRICS)
global South and trade agreements, 221
breaking silence, 82
Breidenbach, Officer, 340
BRICS. *See* Brazil, Russia, India, China and South Africa
bright-line distinction
language used in rules for sake of precision, 337
British parliament
approval of constitutions in former colonies, 175
Brown, Kris, 77
bulk data collection, 261
Burke, Edmund, 50
Business and Industry Council Investment Committee, OECD, 235
Business School-like 'case studies'
transnational law, 291

Calvino, Italo, 8
Cameroun and boundary with Nigeria, 169
Campbell, Colm, 85
Canada, medicine patent and foreign investors, 228
Canadian Residential Schools Settlement (IRSSA), 293
Canon Law
examining different kinds of law, 355
capital
accumulation, 137
controls, 214, 226
empowerment of, 214
internationalisation of and multinationals, 182
old and new forms, 264
capital exporting states
interests of investors, 235
capital punishment
human rights, and views on, 58
capital transfers
trade agreements, 227
capitalism
abyssal divide between 1% and 9%, 134
and law, privileged relationship of, 217
cyber-capitalist forms, 245
financialized, 217, 219
inequalities caused by, 128
neoliberal, 71
primitive accumulation (amassing of wealth), 137
social movements and revolts, "new", 119
tension with individual enterprises, 181
wage earners, 181
capitalist realism, 101
capitalist state law
duality, entrenched in, 132
Cardozo, Benjamin, 274
Carneiro, Davide, 256
Casanovas, Pompeu, 256
case-based reasoning systems, electronic, 255

Cassese, Antonio, 292
Cassin, René, 108
Castells, Manuel, 244, 245
Castro, Eduardo Viveiros de, 96
causation, nature of, and complementarity, 151
cell phones, global use of, 259
Central African Republic
 reparations and attitudes toward, 82
CFCS. *See* chlorofluorocarbons
Chase-Dunn, Christopher, 115
Cheyenne Way (Lewellyn and Adamson-Hoebel), 91
Chicago Law School, 127
child marriages, 43
Chile
 actions of United States, 106
 political roles of writers, 100
 response to digital exclusion, 249
 transitional justice, 85
Chilean coup d'état, 99, 100–103
Chilean Decree, 103
Chilean Way, 100–103, 107
China
 avoidance of surveillance, 262
 economic and political player in Africa, 191
 offshore investments and indisputes, 227
chlorofluorocarbons (CFCs), 208
Christian theologians
 Eurocentric views of Amerindians, 92
Christianity
 human rights and, 54
citizen, ordinary
 concept of "reasonableness", 339
citizenship versus servitude, 137
civil liberties
 relations among humans and ecosystems, 105
civil rights movement (US), 119
civil society
 constitutional reform in Asia and Africa, 179
 litigation, in Kenya, 190
 non-state actor, 81
class structures
 changing, and constitutions, 180
clean break phenomenon, 81
climate change, 199, 208
 global dimensions of, 243
 globalisation and environmental law, 197
 policy responses to, 200
 risk literature in environmental law, 210
Clinton, Hillary, 260
Code of Legislative Standards (UK legislature), 326
codes of conduct, 302
coercive interrogation, 37
Cohen, Felix, 274
Cold War, 106
 effects on former African colonies, 178
Cold War era, 146
Coleman, Jules, 364
collaborative commons, 258
collective habits, 66
Collingwood, R. G., 8, 11
colonial authorities and immunity for acts, 173
colonial rule
 Africa and British occupation, 172
colonialism
 guilt of Western states, 43
 inequalities caused by, 128
common law countries
 institutionalized discipline of law, 147
common law development
 logical discovery, 273
Common Law Tradition, The (Llewellyn), 269, 270, 277
common rule
 colonies in Africa, 172
communism, collapse of, 45
communitarianism
 individualism versus, 41
community-led initiatives
 transitional justice, 77
comparative law
 challenges of pluralism, 243
 role of, and globalisation, 196–197
complementarity, 145, 147, 151–154
 views of cosmopolitanism, 151
Comprehensive Regional Economic Partnership Agreement (RCEP), 221
computerisation
 law offices and, 241
Comte, Augustus, 205
concept of law
 games problem, 314–316
 general and transnational, 311
 political or communal elements, 317–319
 transnational regulation, analyzing, 318
concept of law, Hart's
 problems with, 317–319
Concept of Law, The (Hart), 2, 3, 12
conceptual or analytical function
 theorizing, 214

configurative law
legal duality, 132–138
configurative law, reconfigurative law, and preconfigurative law, 132
ConocoPhillips
investor-state dispute with Venezuela, 230
consensus, 138
consensus and divergence
traditional values, 50
conservatism, defined, 50
consociationalism, 171
constituitions
defined, 166–167
constitution
independence and colonial imposition in African, 177
constitutional discourse
cosmopolitanism, 143–146
constitutional experts, 182
constitutional law, comparative, 183
constitutional processes
social issues and, 143
constitutional reform
post-colonial African nations, 179
constitutional rights to free speech and privacy
US citizens, 261
constitutional theory
complementarity-based approach, 154
constitutionalism
colonial constitutions versus, 173
complementarity-based understanding, 159
congruence of economic and political power, 181
cosmopolitanism II, 159
former colonies and, 169
global age and 'top-down' terms, 161
in nineteenth century, 181
in the past, 180–182
pluralism of discourse, 160
preceding democracy, 181
present day, 182–184
research agenda "from below", 161–164
transcending statist thinking, 154
constitutionalism from below
global South and innovative practices, 145
constitutions
copying of, by "experts", 182
new, and post-colonial and post-dictatoriship nations, 179
post-independent African countries, 176–178
constitutions, new
independence in former Afican colonies, 175
contemporary radical activism, 120
continuous mapping, 211
Convention on the Elimination of All Forms of Discrimination Against Women, 184
conventions
rules of political game, 180
co-operatives
Kenya's peasant population, 187
copper
Chile and nationalisation of resources, 103
Copper Department, 104
copyright extension
collaborative commons, 258
copyright violation, 259
Cornell, Drucilla, 71
corporate lobbyists and beneficiaries, 216
corporate media
reinforcement of 'normalcy bias', 133
corporate power
international, and mapping of, 225
corruption, illegal and legal, by 1%, 135
Cortázar, Julio, 100, 101, 102, 105, 109
cosmopolitanism
and constitutionalism, 154–161
bottom-up view of, 151
constitutionalism paradoxes of, 158–161
creative potential between local and global, 145
human race as unified subject, 155
in era of globalisation, 243
pluralism and, 149
resisting globalization, 146
subaltern, 150
subaltern and counterbalance to globalization, 160
two complementary views, 151–154
universalism, new, 153
versus localizers, 70
Cotterrell, Roger, 366
Council of Europe, 45
counter-hegemonic use of law, 132
court decisions
not sufficiently available, 301
Cowen, Denis, 6
Crime and Custom in Savage Society (Malinowski), 91

Criminal Investigation AI project, 255
criminal justice mechanisms, 88
criminal justice system
  and perceptions of unfairness, in Kenya, 191
criminalization of social protest, 135, 136
criminologists
  role of law in globalization, 286
critical enquiry, 215
Critical Legal Studies Movement, 271
critical theories of Twining and Santos, 125–130
Cross, Sir Rupert, 15
cross-disciplinary function, 214
cruel, as term used in Constitution, 342
cruelty, as aspect of torture, 34
cultural relativism, 51–52
  moderate, 52
  strong, 52
culture norms
  universal norms versus, 52
culture of freedom of the Net, 248
culture, common, as justification for repressing human rights, 46
cultures and parochial concepts of "law", 360
Culver, Keith, 200, 212
Cusack v London Borough of Harrow, 332
customary law
  variations of, 362
cybercapital
  versus netizen culture, 258
cybercapitalism and resistant cultures, 258–260
cyberspace
  and alegality, 137
  and globalization of law, 257
  free space, versus corporate interests, 242
  netizens and questionable surveillance, 263

data collection and mapping, 206
Davies, Kenneth Culp, 5
Davis, Jeremy, 27
Day, Richard, 119, 122
debt restructuring
  Argentina, 232
  Greece, 232
decision support systems
  use of IT in law offices, 254
"*Definition and Theory in Jurisprudence*" (Hart), 2
deforestation
  self-defense of indigenous people, 136
  social movements, "new", 119
Delegated Powers and Regulatory Reform Committee (DPRR Committee), 329
Dembour, Marie, 79
demilitarization, demobilization, and reintegration (DDR), 75
democracy
  compromised by multilateral investment rules, 144
  erosion of, in face of neoliberal capitalism, 139
  international law and emerging norms, 86
  participatory and post-colonial Africa, 179
  participatory, and new constitutions, 167
  post-colonial Africa, 191
  post-colonial and post-dictatorship nations, 179
  preceded by constitutionalism, 181
  real versus low intensity, 124
  reconfigurative law, 140
  separation of powers, in Kenya, 188
  transitional justice, 74
  versus plutocracy, 125
democratic governance
  national to supranational level, 146
Deng, Francis, 21, 39, 59–62
Denning, Lord Thompson, 173
deontological argument against torture, 36
Dependency school of economics, 102
derogable and non-derogable rights, 86
Dershowitz, Alan, 24
  torture and War on Terror, 29–33
development
  Free and Open Software (FOSS), 245
  legal regimes of regional integration, 218
  rural areas in Africa, 174
  sustainable, 201
development in rural areas
  former colonies in Africa, 174
Dewey, John, 7, 129
dheng (or *dheeng*)
  Dinka concept of traditional values, 49
diasporic communities, 243
Dickson, Julie, 359
dictatorship
  definitions of, in newest social movements, 124
  reformist moves and illegal behaviour, 142
dictatorships in Southern Europe

social movements, "old" and "new", 118
digital age
promises counterbalanced by dilemmas, 245
digital divides
access to technology versus quality of access, 245
commercial "pirates", 260
digital domination
global corporations and states, 257
digital environment
control over by global corporations and other agencies, 246
digital exclusion, 245
inequalities in digital access, 249
digital property rights
globalization and social inequalities, 257
digitization
law-jobs theory, 246–247
digitization, global, 244–246
dignified life
new constitutionalism, 184
dignity
defined, and human rights, 57
Dinka tribe, South Sudan, 49, 59
Director of Public Prosecutions of Kenya, 190
Director, Aaron, 6
discursive arena, 307
dispute processing, nature of
general jurisprudence, 306
diversity and pluralism
traditional values and human rights, 58
Divine Will, 28
doctrine of excess profits, 102, 105, 106, 109
domestic law
versus globalization and legal concepts, 197
Douglas, William, 274
Doxa, Cuadernos de Filosofía del Derecho (journal), 1
dual legality, 134–135
Due Process Clause of the Montana Constitution, 338
Durkheim, Emile, 93
Dworkin, Ronald, 3, 12, 306, 314, 335, 341, 351, 359
Dworkinian positivism, 255

Eastern character sets
cross-linguistic legal searches, 249
Eastern Europe
constitutions of post-communist states, 179
Eastern law
fanaticism and, 93
Eastern Tiger economies, 246
ecologism of the poor, 119
e-commerce law, 257
economic crises
and state intervention, 182
economic disparity
environmental law, 199
economic exploitation
global interventionism, 102
economic needs tests, 227
economic regulation, transnational, 213, 216, 217
economic rights
protection of, in constitutions, 182
economic transnational regulation
variety of new legal forms, 309–311
economy
of Kenya, and illegal activities, 186
Ecuador
constitutional process, 129
reconfigurative law and constitutional process, 140
withdrawal from ICSID, 234
education
and training
human rights, 58
formal, and colonial systems, 170
legal, aims of, 293
legal, and challenges of globalization, 288
legal, and economic disparities, 199
legal, and emphasis on "business" case studies, 291
legal, and role of socio-legal studies, 296
legal, and theoretical developments, 284
legal, broadening from within, 333–334
legal, reforming, 293
low achievement in Kenya, 190
post-colonial African nations, 179
e-governance state information systems, 251
Egypt
Arab Spring movement, 124
Cold War and Western powers, 178
investment treaties, 222
Ehrlich, Eugene, 307
Eichorn, K.F., 205
elections
post-colonial Kenya, 186
reform of system, in Kenya, 188
electromagnetic fields, 208
electronic provision of information, 251

electronic retrieval systems
study of law, 248
electronic surveillance, 260–263
digital era, 245
Elliott Management Ltd
distressed debt buyouts, 231
emergence, notion of, 151
Empire (Negri and Hardt), 120, 121
empirical investigation, 198
empirical questions
regarding law and social contexts, 314
enclosure of the English commons, 257
End of Lawyers, The (Susskind), 247
Energy Charter Treaty, 227
enforcement of norms
public versus private actors, 300
Engle, Eric, 254
Engle, Richard, 254
English translations of legal texts, 249
Enlightenment, the, 64
entitlements
social democracy and, 125
environmental issues
law scholarship and, 202
environmental justice
citizen knowledge, 209
realm of normative jurisprudence, 200
theory of, 201
environmental law
benefit of humans or nature, 202
legal scholarship and scientific research and, 206
limits of justice, human rights, and utility discourses, 202
methodological technical approach, 203
versus tort law, 294
environmental law scholarship
effect of globalisation, 197
future of, 196–197
multi-disciplinary and interdisciplinarity, 203–211
environmental legal scholarship, 199–202
environmental NGOs
objections to investment arbitration, 234
environmental policymaking, 203
epistemic gerrymandering, 111
equity
new African constitutions, 183
Esquirol, Jorge, 99
ethics of care, 37
Ethiopia
Cold War alliance with Russia, 178
military rule, 177
Ethiopia, as one-party state, 177
ethnic factor
issue in African decolonisation, 176
ethnicity
factor in former colonies, 176
lack of progress in democratic reform, 189
political parties in Kenya, 188
politics of, in Kenya, 187
ethnocentrism
assumption of universal values, 149
questions regarding, in international law, 90–96
ethnocentrism and Western jurisprudence, 90
Eurocentrism
questions of, in Western law, 90
European Convention for the Protection of Human Rights and Fundamental Freedoms (ECHR), 41, 45, 86, 321, 338
European Court of Human Rights, 45, 46, 47
European Dimension
and changes to UK domestic law, 321
European Economic Community, 321
European Journal of International Law, 292
European Union
international investments and arbitration disputes, 227
traditional values and UN resolutions, 53
European Union (EU)
and UK's obligations, 322
compatibility of UK legislation, 324–325
evidence
two rules of, 15
evidence, study of, 14–16
excess profits doctrine, 107
exchange economies versus gift economies, 93
exclusion and invisibility, 128
Executive Board of the American Anthropological Association, 40
exit strategies
for states caught in global regime, 219
expertise versus authorization in globalized law, 291

Facebook as cyber-capitalist form, 245
facts, stakes, interests, and law in context, 287–291
Fanon, Frantz, 109

Federal Republic of Germany (FRG), 85
female genital cutting, 42, 43
feminism
religious values, 54
social movements of 1960s, 119
Southern voices, 84
views on Bentham's fragments, 36
women's rights and localizers, 70
financial crises and effects on investment arbitration, 231–232
financial re-regulation, 214
Financial Services Authority, United Kingdom, 225
Fine, Robert, 155
FISA. *See* Foreign Intelligence Surveillance Act
Fisher, Elizabeth, 207
Fisheries Act (1981) and ambiguities in language of, 331
Fitzpatrick, Peter, 243
focal meaning as concept of law
organizing efforts toward solving problems, 316
forced marriages, 43
foreclosures
financial crisis and sacrifice of 99%, 138
Foreign Intelligence Surveillance Act (FISA) and electronic surveillance, 261
foreign investment
reducing restrictions on, in trade agreements, 227
foreign investors
favoured, in mega-agreements, 235–236
questions regarding special rights and powers, 227–236
former colonies
Africa and development in rural areas, 174
Africa and independence, 182
Africa and legal systems, 172
Africa, and approval of constitutions by British parliament, 175
Africa, and constitution making, 172
Africa, and police forces, 173
Africa, and Westphalian state model, 170
constitutionalism, 169
guilt of Western states, 43
in Africa, and independence, 169
local versus central government, 174
former Yugoslavia
human rights work nad electronic contributions, 252
Fortis Bank, 227
FOSS. *See* Free and Open Software
Foucault, Michel, 29, 35
Fowler v Commissioner of Police for the Metropolis, 332
Foxconn, Chinese Apple supplier
human rights abuses, 292
fracking, Quebec government and foreign investors, 228
Fragments (Bentham)
four caveats to Twining's analysis, 36–37
Frank, Jerome, 7, 8, 266, 270, 274, 275
Frankfurt School, 100
Free Access to Law Movement, 248, 249
Free and Open Software (FOSS), 245, 259
free trade agreements
tensions created by, 226
free trade and investment agreements, 220
free trade treaties, investment chapters of, 227
Free University of Berlin, 127
freedom of contact, 68
freedom of property, 68
Friedmanite economics, 6
Friedmann, Wolfgang, 4
Fukushima disaster, 229
Fuller, Lon, 4, 348
fundamentalism
Western projections on 'others', 95

Galanter, Marc, 363
Gama, Raymundo, 127
García Márquez, Gabriel, 100, 105
GATT. *See* General Agreement on Tariffs and Trade
Gazzaniga, Michael, 151
gender equality
incorporated in constitutionalism, 182
gendered harms, 80, 85
General Agreement on Tariffs and Trade (GATT), 215, 220
General Agreement on Trade in Services (GATS), 216
general jurisprudence
Austin's concept of, 308
cosmopolitan discipline of law, 145
focus on legal phenomenon across jurisdictions, 148
law's changing transnational arenas, 319
Twining's advocacy of, 304
Twining's definition of, 129
General Jurisprudence (Twining), 8, 13–14, 99, 192, 218, 242, 284

general jurisprudence glab
global perspective, 242–244
General Jurisprudence: Understanding Law from a Global Perspective (Twining), 165
genetically modified organisms (GMOs), 208
regulation of, 209
Genocide Convention, 25
geography
impact on traditional law making, 13
geopolitics, 220–221
Germany
resistance to electronic surveillance, 262
termination of nuclear power generation, 229
Ghai, Yash, 21, 39, 46, 105, 192
Ghana, 231
Ghana, as one-party state, 177
gift economies versus exchange economies, 93
Gilbert, Chief Baron, 15
Giudice, Michael, 200, 212
Glendon, Mary Ann, 41
Glenn, Patrick, 63
Global Administrative Law, 156, 287
global and local
oversimplification of relationship, 200
global business
legal efforts to regulate, 281
global capital
new forms of capital in digital era, 245
global capitalism, 110, 218
suppression of social transformation, 139
Global Commons, 260
global comparative law, 199
global corporate law firms
globalisation of law, 249
global corporations
digital exclusion, 245
global digital commons, 245
global economic networks
legal playing field, 309
global economy, 214–218
global economy, financialized, 217
global financial crisis of 2007–2008, 124
austerity as result, 164
law and globalisation, 219
sacrifices of the 99%, 136
global financialization
calls for reform, 225–227
global governance
legal order, and cosmopolitanism, 156
global hegemony
European claims to, 91
global interventionism
economic exploitation, 102
global law. *See* globalization
global law, theorizing of, 300
global legal pluralism, 251, 304, 312
distinguishing legal from social rules, 312
intersecting and conflicting law regimes, 309
law in, 309–311
limiting expectations of practices, 318
observation of and interpretive understanding, 316
understanding, through various concepts of law, 316
variety of regimes, jurisdictions, and systems, 315
global legal theory
Twining's project on, 304
global market governance
neo-liberalization of, 297
global North
collective actions, and differences from global South, 121
historical sequence of social movements, 118
interests in transitional settings, 74
liberalism, 87
global property interests, 259
global social injustice
digital divides, 259
global social justice, 100
global social movements
constitutionalism, 162
global South
bottom-up constitutionalism, 161
collective actions, and differences from global North, 121
digital exclusion, 246
ecological movements, 119
metaphor for subordination, 163
religious rights, 48
social movements ("new") in post-colonial era, 118
support for traditional values, 53
traditional values and human rights, 59–62
transitional justice, 85–88
global supply chains
trade agreements, 220
Global Village, 244
Globalisation and Legal Theory (Twining), 213, 217, 218

globalization
effect on new constitutions, 179
anthropologists' insights, 96–100
commerce and finances, 101
economic, and multinationals, 107
effects on law, 283
environmental concerns and law, 211–212
environmental law scholarship, 196–197
hegemonic and counterhegemonic, 149
hegemonic and Western understanding of law, 150
impact of digitization, 246
implications of, for jurisprudence, 358
law, different kinds of, 354
law's ambiguous functions in, 283–287
laws and responses to, 203
legal terms, 289
legal theory and inclusive approach, 152
legal theory and reformation of, 146
liberation versus suffering, 69
limitations of one type of legal ordering, 149
modern law as a solution to versus "uncivil" views, 153
pluralistic outlook for jurisprudence, 149
potential damages to public laws and regulations, 281
power structures of, 317
public versus private law responses to, 280–282
scholars, activists, or practitioners and Twining's contributions, 215
top-down and bottom-up governance, 162
top-down approach, 160
traditional law making and current trends, 13–14
undermining of new constitutionalism, 185
US intervention in Vietnam, 101
viability of constitutionalism, 143–146
Western modernity, 149
globalized market organization
realities of, and students of law, 295
GMOs. *See* genetically modified organisms
Goldsmith, Jack, 291
good law concept (UK), 321
good law initiative, 321, 323, 333
Google
as cyber-capitalist form, 245
cybercapitalism, 258
government
post-colonial Africa, and responsibility for, 191
Grant, Wyn, 209
grassroots movements
effects on law, 129
Gray, John Chipman, 274
Great Firewall of China, 260
Great Juristic Bazaar, The (Twining), 8
Greaves, Justin, 209
Greece
debt restructuring and investment disputes, 232
Green, Leon, 7, 274
Griffiths, John, 363
Gross, Oren, 33
Group of 77, 232
Guantánamo and alegality, 137
Guzmán, Jaime, 104

H. L. A. Hart
The Nightmare and the Noble Dream (Lacey), 3
Haack, Susan, 8
Habermas, Jürgen, 289, 290
Hachette and Amazon conflict over e-book prices, 258
Haitian Constitution and slave revolution of 1801, 108
Hale, Robert, 267, 274
"hard" forms of norm creation, 290
Hardt, Michael, 69, 120
Harrison, Frederic, 205
Hart, H.L.A., 2, 3, 12, 93, 148, 242, 278, 291, 304, 312, 315, 336, 337, 356, 365
concept of law and rules of games and sports, 311–314
Hart, Ronald, 357, 358
Hauben, Michael and Ronda, 244
Hayek, F.A., 348
health and the environment
transnational solidarity campaigns, 161
health professionals
objections to investment arbitration, 233
Heydebrand, Wolf, 310
hierarchy, normative
Western framework of law, 299
History of Legal Informatics, A (Susskind), 246
HIV/AIDS pandemic
global controversy over pharmaceuticals for, 259
Hobbes, Thomas, 104
Hoey, Kate, 247
Holloway, John, 120

Holmes, Oliver Wendell, Jr., 273, 274, 275
Homeland Security Act and electronic surveillance, 261
hormone-disrupting chemicals, 208
House of Commons (UK)
 self-scrutiny, 327–330
House of Commons Political and Constitutional Reform Committee (PCR Committee)
 legislation, quality of, in UK, 326
How To Do Things With Rules (Twining and Miers), 9, 269, 320, 335, 352
Hughes (Road Traffic Act 1988), 332
Hugo, Gustave von, 205
human
 defined, in sixteenth century, 91
human race, unity of, and cosmopolitanism, 155
human relations
 reciprocal, and anthropologists' insights, 96
human rights
 addressing violations, 74
 AI and its effects on, 256
 Arendt's 'right to have rights', 157
 based on traditional values, 52
 by virtue of being human, 44
 calling violators to account, 88
 challenging aspects of modernity, 70
 concepts of, examined, 40
 connected to humanitarianism, 72
 conventions, examples of, 25
 cultural approach to, 60
 different views of lawpersons and philosophers, 34
 discourse of suffering, 101
 dissatisfactions with, 68
 education and training, 58
 Enlightenment philosophers, 54
 erosion in core countries of world system, 140
 ethics of, and feminism, 37
 false universalism, 153
 female genital cutting, unaddressed by debates, 42
 freedom and liberty, 68
 future of, in post-human world, 109–111
 globalization and, 68
 human dignity, 54
 in Kenya, and balancing individual with community rights, 188
 in local context, 59
 incorporated in constitutionalism, 182
 individualism, 68
 international and "public" versus "private" spheres, 42
 international law and traditional values, 41
 international norms, and community rights, 179
 international standards, 43
 interpretations of, to legitimize traditions, 57
 laws and doctrinal developments, 41–43
 legitimacy in cultural contexts, 60
 missing in colonial constitutions, 173
 movement, and effectiveness of, 60
 multinationals and national resources, 106–109
 new constitutionalism, 183
 new synthesis with traditional values, 67
 new views on traditional values, 67–72
 non-democratic regimes, 86
 Nuremberg tribunals as model in 1970s Latin America, 100
 orthodox or naturalistic theories of, 44
 overlooked in transnational law pedagogy, 291–295
 political theories of, 44
 post-colonial and post-dictatorship nations, 179–180
 protected by state or state-sponsored bodies, 42
 religious rights, in Russia, 45
 resolutions of the UN Human Rights Council, 40–43
 rhetoric, used to justify repression, 46
 Southern Voices and Twining's work on, 98
 standards of, 52
 stateless people, or 'pariah' peoples, 158
 suffering as important 163
 threatened by globalization of surveillance, 263
 three approaches, 44–45
 traditional values and, 38–40, 51–52
 understanding of, in Kenya, 191
 universal acceptance, 56
 violations and transitional justice theory, 79
 violations and victims' needs, 82
 violations, and the fight against, 72
 Western conceptions of, and UN resolutions, 52
 women and sexual minorities, 53
human rights abuses
 Foxconn and Bangladeshi ready-to-wear factory, 292

Human Rights Act of 1998, 321
Human Rights Committee, 71
Human Rights Council, 72
human rights discourse
  free-market liberalism, 68
human rights NGOs
  objections to UN resolutions, 53
human rights project, 39, 41, 53, 67–72
Human Rights Watch, 71
human rights work
  effects of IT, 252
Human Rights, Southern Voices (Twining), 98, 101
humanitarian crisis
  UN Charter and "Use of Force", 292
Hutcheson, Judge Joseph, 266, 275
Hypertext, 248
HYPO, 255
hypothesis of complementarity, 141

ICC. *See* International Chamber of Commerce
ICSID. *See* International Centre for Settlement of Investment Disputes
ideological conflict versus reality of global violence, 155
immigration
  Western projections on "others", 95
imperialism, competitive, 220
"inchoate" rules
  definition of standards, 337
income, basic and unconditional, 164
independence
  ensuing problems in Africa, 174
  former colonies in Africa, 169, 182
  former colonies in Africa and new constitutions, 175–176
  former colonies in Africa and path to, 174
India
  independence and splitting of nation, 175
  new model BIT, 234
  telecommunications licence and foreign investors, 228
indigenous peoples
  human rights and, 42
  objections to investment arbitration, 234
  politics, radical, and challenges to Eurocentric notions, 120
  rights, 57
indignados movements, 122, 130
  Arab Spring revolts and, 116
  Southern Europe, 124
indignation revolts. *See also indignados* movements
  calls for 'real' democracy and reconfigurative law, 140
  configurative law, 132–138
  law and, 115–125
  occupation of public spaces, 138
  prefigurative law, 138–139
  reconfigurative law, 139–140
  theory of law, possible, 130
individualism
  communitarianism versus, 41
  human rights in support of, 68
  primary unit of society, 87
  social sciences and, 98
Indonesia and withdrawal from BITs, 234
industrial agriculture, 136
industrial revolution and environmental law, 206
industrial society and labour or ("old") movements, 118
inequalities in legal information retrieval, 247–250
inequality of wealth and Occupy movement, 125
information police
  state and private agencies, 261
information retrieval
  impact on law-jobs, 248
  natural language searching, 255
Information Society, 244
Information technology and legal systems, 250–253
information, personal
  and cybercaptialism, 258–260
  market commodity, 258
informational capitalism, 245
inseparability thesis, 101
Institute for Social Research, in Frankfurt, 289
intellectual property (IP) law
  transnational dimensions of, 243
intellectual property (IP) rights, 245, 257
  globalization of, 259
Intelligent Agents
  in online retail, 252
intercultural discourse, 52
interdependence, increasing, of the world, 212
interdisciplinary relationship
  law and science, 207
inter-legality, different forms of, 200

international airports and alegality, 137
International Centre for Settlement of Investment Disputes (ICSID), 222
  nations withdrawing from, 234
  reform of arbitration, 235
International Centre for the Settlement of Investment Disputes (ICSID), 229
International Chamber of Commerce (ICC), 229
international community and non-state actors, 81
International Covenant on Civil and Political Rights, 42
International Covenant on Economic, Social and Cultural Rights, 42
international economic regime
  steps to reforming, 236
international finance and banking
  legal substructure, undeveloped, 310
international investment agreements
  legitimacy, questions regarding, 232–234
international investment regime, 227–236
international investors
  special rights and powers, 227
  threat of disputes and "chilling effect", 228
international law
  benefits to private versus public lawyers, 280
  ethnocentricism, questions of, 90–96
  legal tribunals, 88
  private arbitrators and effects on, 230
  right to democratic governance, 86
  transitional justice, 74, 87
  versus globalisation and concepts of law, 198
international law firms
  role in financial or political crises, 225
international laws
  consensus building around human rights values, 183
International Monetary Fund (IMF), 69
  neoliberal regime, 226
International Multi-Media Institute in Iceland, 263
international relations
  law of the 1%, 137
international trade
  constitutionalisation of rules of, 143
  priority over questions of poverty and hunger, 163
internationalisation of capital
  rise of multinationals, 182
Internet
  community and self-governance, 245
  development of law of, 295
  freedom of, 260
  law and challenges posed, 241
  law of and global jurisprudential perspective, 243
  music sharing, 259
Internet Architecture Board, 244
Internet Engineering Task Force, 244
Internet Fatwas (Islamic Legal Pronouncements), 253
Internet law, 257
Internet Society, 244
interpretations of law
  actor's standpoints, 320–321
interpretive contexts
  language, context and purpose, 330–332
investment arbitration
  contending with national legal systems, 233
  reforms to, 234–235
investment rules, international, 214
investment treaties, 220
investment-state arbitration, reform of, 234
investor-state disputes, 236
  international arbitration, 229–230
  reform of investor-state arbitration, 234
  settlement of (ISDS), 227
  settlement, and access to, 235
IP protection, 260
IP rights
  inequalities in globalization of, 247–250
  software and hardware, 257
Iraq
  de-Ba'athification process, 85
  transitional justice, 87
  weapons of mass destruction justification for war, 86
Irish Rebellion of 1798, 27
Islam, militant, 41
Islamic dress and margin of appreciation, 48
Islamic gender justice, 253
Islamic states
  religious rights, 48
issue of reasonable speed, 340
IT and Law project, 241

Japan
  TPPA negotiations, 220
  transitional justice, 85
Joint Legislative Standards Committee of Parliament (UK), 326

judges
  current changes in role, 247
  decision support system, 256
  empiricist legal tradition, 204
  legal rules, consulting, 272
  versus case-based electronic reasoning systems, 255
judicial interpreters, 330–332
judicial opinions
  thinking processes of judges, 273
judiciary, independent, in Kenya, 189
Judt, Tony, 289
Juncker, Jean-Claude, 233
jurisprudence, 10–11
  and globalization, Twining's views on, 242
  definition by Julius Stone, 148
  global legal pluralism, 316
  global perspective, lack of, 196–197
  pluralistic outlook, 149
  reconfiguring at conceptual and contextual levels, 243
just compensation, 104
justice
  marginalised groups, and constitutionalism, 182
justice, cognitive, 130
justice, rights, and the environment, 199–202

Kahale, George, 229
Kalven, Harry, 5
Kant, Immanuel, 155
  hospitality versus sovereign authority, 158
Karl Llewellyn and the Realist Movement (Twining), 8, 268, 274, 276, 278
Karl Llewellyn Papers, The (Twining), 268
Kartashkin, Vladimir, 56–58
Kelly, Tobias, 79
Kelsen, Hans, 312
Kennecott, 103, 105
Kenya
  Cold War and Western powers, 178
  disputed boundary with Somalia, 169
  independence and colonial Bill of Rights, 176
  military rule, 177
  post-colonial constitutionalism, 185–191
  pre-colonial territories, 168
  unity in diversity in action, 188–191
Kenya, as one-party state, 177
Key Word in Context (KWIC), 248
Kibaki, Mwai, 185
Kircheimer, Otto, 107
Kirill, Metropolitan, 46, 54–55, 59, 61, 62, 67
knowledge building, 78
knowledge, scientific, and Westerncentric, 130
Koskenniemi, Martii, 68,
Kruse, Vinding, 4
Kumm, Mattias, 156, 157

labour law versus penal law (*chibalo*), 128
labour movement, as, 118
Lacey, Nicola, 3
Lagarde, Christine, 226
land grabbing
  expulsion of peasants and indigenous people, 137
Langlois, S., 63, 64
language, religion, and culture
  unity in diversity, in Kenya, 188
Latin America. *See also* Southern Voices
  authoritarian states, 80
  counterrevolutionary repression, 100
  locality of Southern voices, 99
  transformative constitutional processes, 140
  transitional justice, 76
Lautsi case, 46, 47
law
  and colonisation, critiques of, 215
  and living legal culture, 288
  and science, a multidisciplinary approach, 203–211
  authority of, 305
  broad conceptions of versus ephemeral factors, 278
  concept of and purposes supporting, 307–309
  concept of, to explain nature of, 306
  conceptualizing and controversies about, 304–307
  connection to the state, 281
  different kinds of, 354
  dominant social importance, 313
  economic, 289
  framework for, in globalization, 286
  identity of, 307–309
  in transnational contexts, challenges of, 302
  indignation revolts, 130
  mindset, private versus public, 280
  nature of, battles over definitions of, 298
  of native nations, examining different kinds, 355

law (cont.)
of the 1% and the 99%, 132, 133, 134–136, 137–138
of the 1%, and rhetoric as exclusive form, 134
of the 99%, based on bureaucracy and violence, 135
political context, 322–323
reconceptualisation from the bottom up, 150
social contexts, 314
study of, field boundaries and pedagogy stands, 296–298
two distinct categories of, 362
utopian, versus specialization of legal fields, 294
validity or authority, concepts of, 308
Law and Economics school, 98
law and *legal*
redefining for regulatory mechanism at global level, 310
Law and Social Change in Contemporary Britain (Friedmann), 4
Law and the Modern Mind (Frank), 266
law in action, new sub-field of, 200
law in context
facts, stakes, interests, 287–291
importance of the local, 288
project, socio-legal, 287
Law in Context movement, 5
Law in Context series, 9, 321
Law in Context: Enlarging a Discipline (Twining), 9
Law in Our Society (Llewellyn), 269
"Law, Justice and Rights: Some Implications of a Global Perspective" (Twining), 199
law libraries, and globalization of legal information, 248
Law of Evidence, The (Gilbert), 15
Law of Peoples, The (Rawls), 14
law office systems, 250–253
Law on the Web, 250
law research
AI technology and, 256
law school
cases beyond established "fields" of study, 293
technical versus theoretical in design of courses, 288
law students
challenges, beyond ordinary "fields" of study, 295
law-jobs
impact of digitization, 246
IT processes and changes to, 253–257
laws
unjust, and revolt, 122
Lawson, F. H. Z., 2
lawyer
as generalist and investigator, 300
lawyers
advising clients in "new" law, 301
challenges of liberalisation, 247
Lee Kuan Yew, 46
legal analysis, top-down and bottom-up models, 147
legal and political mobilization, 139
legal architecture and mapping trade agreements, 221–223
legal areas ('fields'), functions and boundaries, 299
legal canon, expanded from state to non-state, 150
legal cartography, 219–227
legal decision-making, rule- versus fact-intensive, 272
legal doctrine
institutions and practices in, 285
seen in context of legal processes, 242
legal education. *See* education: legal
Legal Education and Training Review, 250
legal exceptionalism, 107
legal fields and limitations of, 292
legal geography, new sub-field of, 200
legal information and law-jobs, technological transformation of, 257
Legal Information Institutes (LII), 248
legal information, free software and content movements, 258
legal information, retrieval of, and globalization, 247–250
legal interest representation strategy (LIRS), 302
legal interpretation and global legal pluralism, 316
legal liberalism, 132
legal phenomena and globalization, 285
legal philosophers
law as social institution, 364
Legal Philosophers' Circle, The (Twining's satire), 303, 356
legal philosophy

expanding beyond state law, 358
insular and narrow, 357
limitations of, 356–359
"Post-Westphalaian Conception of Law" (Twining), 355
Twining as guide to exploring, 365
legal pluralism, 217, 282, 363
legal pluralism and indignation revolts, 138
Legal Realism
competing conceptions of, 273–277
different understandings of, 271
dimensions, political and transformative, 298
disagreements of nature of, 265–268
empirical inquiry, 267
existing law used to "rationalize" decisions, 266
facts of case independent of legal rules, 266
legal rules as basis of, 268
Llewellyn's changing viewpoint on, 277–278
relative importance of facts in adjudication, 265
social science inquiry about law, 267
substance of law, 267
view of "what the judge had for breakfast", 270
Legal Realist
confrontation of legal norms, 299
Legal Realists
de-politicizing of markets, contracts, and families, 300
legal reasoning and evidence, study of, 14
legal rules and the rules of games
Hart's concept of law, 317
legal rules versus social rules, in transnational law, 312
legal rules, "real" versus "paper", 278
legal scholarship
analytical concepts in, 197–199
environmental law and, 206
multidisciplinary and interdisciplinary approaches, 198
socio-legal studies, 296
Legal Services Act 2007 (UK), 247
legal services and "unregulated sector", 250
legal services, neo-liberal approaches and digitalization, 247
legal subversive, role of the jurist, 217
legal system and former colonies in Africa, 172
legal system and minimum conditions specified by Hart, 312
legal systems compared to organization of sports, 314
legal theories, Western, and global perspective, 196
legal theory, global, 214–218
legal thinking, state-based, 199
legal traditions, 63
legal training, generalist and investigative skills, 300–302
legal transformation and indignation revolts, 140–142
legal transnationalization, 218
legal treatise, reinvigoration of, 148
legal understandings, framework of, 307–309
LegalZoom, 250
legislation (UK)
complexity, perceptions of, 324–325
purpose clause, 326
quality of and new techniques of drafting, 325–327
quality of, and recent enactments, 326
reform, consolidation, and improvements, 323–327
use of symbols in drafting, 326
legislation as political activity, 322–323
legislation, reading and interpreting, 321
legislative change
reconfigurative law, 139
legislatures
of Kenya, and perceptions of excessive greed, 189
Leigh Day, 252
Leith, Philip, 247, 253
Lenzerini, Federico, 57
lesbian, gay, bisexual, and transgender (LGBT) rights, 53
religious values, 54
Levi, Dean Edward, 5
Lévi-Strauss, Claude, 92, 96
Lex Mercatoria, 257
lex mercatoria, legal quality of, 310
LEXIS, 247, 249, 255
Leyla Sahin case, 48
liberal peace, 87
liberal values versus superstitious beliefs, 95
liberalism
individual as primary unit of soicety, 87
licensed subversive (Twining's idea of the jurist), 214, 236–237

Life of the Law, The (Nader), 91
life world issues
  social movements ("new" global movements), 118
Lindahl, Hans, 97
linguistic issues in legal searches, 249
Lisbon Treaty, 223
litigator's experience and effective answers, 297
Llewellyn, Karl, 3, 4, 6, 7, 9, 12, 21, 91, 96, 199, 242, 268–269, 274
  changing views on Legal Realism, 277
lobbying as legal corruption, 135
local and the global
  relationship between, 100
localizers, 70
  versus cosmopolitans, 70
  women's rights, 70
Lodder, Arno, 256
Luban, David, 34
Lyotard, Jean-Francois, 244

MacCormick, Neil, 8, 16–17, 311
Maine, Sir Henry, 205
Malawi, as one-party state, 177
Malaysia
  response to digital exclusion, 249
Malinowski, Bronislaw, 91, 96
Mance, Lord Jonathan Hugh, 331
Mandela, Nelson, 184
Maori and sovereign authority in New Zealand, 215
mapping exercise, 209
mapping or synthesising function, 214
Marcuse, Herbert, 107
margin of appreciation, 47
market freedoms, 157
market libertarianism, 107
market self-regulation
  versus state intervention, 282
marriage
  religious beliefs and, 48
Marsh, Robert, 47, 69
Martinez Alier, Joan, 119
Massoud, Mark Fathi, 73, 74
material economy, predictions of crisis, 219
materialistic versus non-materialistic issues
  global North versus global South, 118
Maudsley, Ronald, 2
Mauritius, 170
  independence constitution, 177
McAuslan, Patrick, 14
McIlwain, Charles Howard, 166, 180
McLuhan, Marshall, 244
mega-agreements and rules favouring foreign investors, 235–236
megaprojects
  self-defence of indigenous people, 136
  social movements, "new", 119
Meister, Robert, 105
memory and history and critical theory, 125
Mendieta, Eduardo, 94, 111
Mentschikoff, Soia, 6, 7, 10
metropolitan law versus colonial law, 133
metropolitan versus colonial societies, 128
Middle East
  Arab Spring revolts, 115–125
Miers, David, 8, 269
militancy, new, 119
Military rule
  post-colonial Africa, 177
militias, private
  in Kenya, 187
Mill, J.S., 204
mining
  copper, in Chile, 104
  megaprojects and indigenous peoples, 136
  megaprojects in global South, 137
  nationalisation in Chile, 103
  rents, Marxist views on, 102
minorities
  protection of, in constitutionalism, 182
modern commercial law
  Llewellyn and, 276
modern legal theory
  Twining's concerns about, 279
modern state law
  three structural elements, 134
modern world versus Western world views, 129
modernity, 111
Monreal, Novoa, 109
Monshipouri, Mahmood, 70
Montesquieu, 198
Montesquieu Lecture at Tilburg University (Twining), 196, 284
Moore, Underhill, 7, 274, 275
moral term, "thick", and indeterminacy, 343
Morris, H. F., 168
most-favoured nation clauses
  legal architecture of trade agreements, 222
Mozambique
  Cold War alliance with Russia, 178

multinational companies
international investment disputes, 234
multi-national corporations
exercising "sovereign" powers of law-making, 310
multinational vampires, 102
multinationals
economic globalization, 107
internationalisation of capital, 182
nationalisation of resources, in Chile, 102
rights of, versus indigenous peoples, 102
Russell II discussions, 106
Russell Tribunal, 106
multitude, concept of, 120
music sharing on Internet and "piracy", 259
Muslim Brotherhood, 122
Muvangua, Nyoko, 71

Nader, Laura, 91
Namibia, 170
Nanda, Vel P, 201
Nasser, Gamal Abdel, 124
nation building and new constitutions, 167
nation states
territorially-bounded legal systems, 307
national and international sovereignty
new arguments about structures of, 317
National Counter-Terrorism Centre Guidelines, 261
National Security Act, 261
National Security Act and electronic surveillance, 261
national unity
lack of, in Kenya, 186
nationalisation, 109, 181
Chile and copper resources, 103
nationalism
methodological, and cosmopolitanism I, 154–158
transcended by cosmopolitanism I and II, 145
versus cosmopolitanism, 154
nationalization
Chile and copper resources, 102
nation-state boundaries
correspondence with legal system boundaries, 312
nation-state jurisdictions
concept of law to serve in regulatory regimes outside of, 316
natural law, traditional values and, 58
natural resources. *See* resources
natural rights, 50
Negri, Toni, 69, 120
neocolonialism
access to natural resources, 137
extractive, 101
neoliberalism, 217
acts of resistance to, 150
calls for reform, 225–227
debates and predictions, 219
defeat of Maori claims of sovereignty, 215
global governance and top-down imposition of, 162
globalization, hegemonic, 160
in Latin America, 101
threats to constitutionalism, 144
Neo-Zapatistas, 120
net neutrality
ideologies of, 244
netizen culture
globalization of surveillance, 263
openness and common wealth, 258
netizen organisations, 262
Netizen status, 244
network governance, 244
Network Information Economy, 245
Network Information Society, 244, 245, 264
cyber-capitalism, 245
Network Society, 244
Neuberger, David, Baron Neuberger of Abbotsbury, 331
New Deal
regulations and, 300
New Evidence Scholarship, 16
new international economic order, 109
new legal realism
varied methods of practicing, 271
new movements
social movements and revolts, 119
News International, 248
newspaper exercise
Twining's practical exercise, 283, 287
Nicholas, J.B.K.M. (Barry), 2
Nigeria
boundary with Cameroun, 169
independence and colonial Bill of Rights, 176
pre-colonial kingdoms, 167
NML Capital, 231
distressed debt buyouts, 231

Nolustshungu, Samuel, 178
non-governmental organizations (NGOs)
  Human Rights Watch, 71
  Peoples' Welfare and Development Society, 72
non-positivist theories, 12 *See also* positivism
non-state actors, 81
  transitional justice, 80
non-state armed group, 81
norm creation
  religious beliefs, 48
  soft and hard forms of, 290
norm enforcement
  general jurisprudence, 306
normalcy bias, 133
normative, 282
normativity of tradition, 65–67
North Africa
  Arab Spring revolts, 115–125
Northern Ireland, 78
Northern Ireland and state and non-state terror, 22
Northern Ireland Law Reports, 241
Novoa Monreal, Eduardo, 107
nuclear proliferation, 200
Nuremberg principles, 104
  Satre and Russell I, 102
Nuremberg Trials, 100, 107, 110
Nyerere, Julius, 177

Obama, Barack, 292
occupation of public spaces
  indignation revolts, 138
Occupy movements, 124
  democracy as irremediably corrupted, 142
Occupy Wall Street
  Arab Spring revolts and, 115
OECD. *See* Organisation for Economic Co-operation and Development
Office of the Parliamentary Counsel (OPC), 321, 323, 324, 325, 327
Okoth-Ogendo, Hastings, 177
Oliphant, Herman, 274, 275
Onazi, Oche, 71
One percent society versus 99 percent society, 123
one-party states in Africa, 177
Online Dispute Resolution
  role of AI in, 256
Online Dispute Resolution (ODR) systems, 251
online legal services, 250–253
ontological positions on torture, 33
Organisation for Economic Co-operation and Development (OECD)
  neoliberal regime, 226
Orthodox Churches and views on human rights, 58
orthodoxy of law, questioning, 213–214
Oskamp, Anja, 256
otherness
  Eurocentric views and, 95
  human relations, 96
ownership issues
  human rights versus environmental law, 202
Oxford, style of philosophizing, 356
ozone depletion, 199
  globalisation and environmental law, 197
  risk literature in environmental law, 210

Pareto efficiency, 206
Parliamentary Business and Legislation (PBL) Committee, 324
parliamentary context (UK)
  legislation and procedures, 328
parliamentary government procedures (UK), 327–330
parlimentary scrutiny of legislation (UK)
  patchwork of procedures, 329
participatory budget-making, 161
patriarchy, inequalities caused by, 128
Patriot Act and electronic surveillance, 261
Pattee, Howard, 151
peasant populations
  organization of, 178
Pedersen, Ole W., 210, 211, 212
penal law (*chibalo*)
  labour law as part of, 128
people's rights, 106
Peoples' Welfare and Development Society, The, 72
Pepper v Hart, 332
permanent decolonisation, 106, 107
Permanent Sovereignty over Natural Resources, 103
persuasive authority and relevance as legal material, 308
Philip Morris Asia tobacco dispute, 233
  Australia and, 236
Ping An insurance company, 227
Pinochet, Augusto, 104
piracy, commercial and electronic, 260

Pirate Party Movement, 262
plain language drafting
in UK legislation, 327
plantation industrial agriculture, 137
plutocracy versus democracy, 125
Podemos political party, 141
Pogge, Thomas, 14, 201
police force
and brutality, 136
British colonies in Africa, 172
former colonies in Africa, 173
use of violence, in Kenya, 186
political activism, 150
politics of coexistence and cooperation
environmental law, 202
politics of law
anthropologists' insights into, 96
universality, and anthropologists' insights, 96
polluter pays principle, 201
pollution controls, industrial revolution and, 206
Porter, Theodore M., 205, 206
positivism, 11–12
positivist approach
validity tests of regulations, 310
Posner, Eric, 76
post–Cold War
constitutions, 167
post–Cold War era
transitional justice as fixer, 73
post-colonial constituionalism
Kenya, 185–191
post-colonial constitutionalism, 166–167
Kenya, 187
post-industrial society
social movements ("new" movements), 118
postmodernism
definitions of, 127
post-neoliberal world, 217
"Post-Westphalian Conception of Law" (Twining), 355
post-Westphalian world, 200
Pound, Roscoe, 365
poverty, extreme, 200
power relations
and unequal exchanges, 160
elites and control of configurative law, 132
indignation revolts, 131
nationalism, methodological, 158
privileged groups in former colonies in Africa, 174
pragmatism
politics of coexistence and cooperation, 202
Prebisch, Raúl, 109
precautionary principle, 201
pre-colonial systems in Africa, 167–171
preconfigurative law, 132
predetermination of action by cognitive conditions, notion of, 151
preemptive damage bias, 133
prefigurative law
indignation revolts, 138–139
primitive accumulation, 137
Principle of Utility, 27
Principles of Political Economy (Mill), 204
Principles of Proof, 15
private arbitrators
public law and, 230
private beneficiaries and pushing legal boundaries, 219
private ordering, 282
private versus public lawyers in transnational context, 280
project of modernity, 94
propertied class
political dominance in nineteenth century, 181
Property Law
reparations in post-colonial nations, 103
property rights, 157
cyberspace and corporate interests, 242
Public Citizen, 225
public general Acts (UK), 322–323
public health protection, industrial revolution and, 206
public interest law firms and subaltern groups, 252
public participation, democratic, in Kenya, 189
public power, allocated in constitutions, 180
Public Service Commission
in Kenya, 189
public spaces and social movement protests, 124
punishment
minor disturbances caused by 99%, 136
Putin, Vladimir, 45, 46

Qur'an, the, and conflicts in texts, 61

racism as aspect of extractive globalisation, 101
Radin, Max, 274
Rajan, Kaushik, 245
Rational Choice Theory, 98
Rationalist Tradition of Evidence Scholarship, The, 15
Raventos, Jorge, 100
Rawls, John, 200
Raz, Joseph, 313, 354, 355, 358, 359, 364, 365
  claim of universal truth in law, 360, 361, 362
  on true theory of law, 359–361
  universal truth versus Western theories of law, 361
RCEP. *See* Regional Economic Partnership Agreement
REACH (EU legislation), 209
Read, James, 168
"Reading Law" (Twining), 296
ready-made-garment industry
  labor and human rights issues, 293
realism and positivism
  Twining's adherence to, 264
realistic analysis as alternative to abstract reasoning, 205
realpolitik, 144
"reasonable speed," issues of, 340–341
receptor approach to human rights, 55
reconfigurative law, 132
  indignation revolts, 139–140
reductionism, 151
regime change
  and transitional justice, 86
  former colonies in Africa, 177
  new constitutionalism, 185
Regional Economic Partnership Agreement (RCEP), 221
Regional Trade Agreements, 222
regulations
  domestic, challenged by trade agreements, 227
  public or private and relevance as legal material, 308
  trade agreements, 220
  transnational and Hart's concept of law, 311
  transnational and open-ended, flexible guidelines, 310
  transnational and questions of validity and sources of authority, 311
  transnational and varying extents of institutionalisation, 318
  transnational, labelled as "law", 311
  various kinds of
    general jurisprudence, 306
regulatory practices
  labeled as "law", 311
religions
  norms based on subjectivity, 94
  pre-Columbian Ameridians, 93
  projections of, 94
  Western, and imperialism, 94
religious freedom, 48
religious laws, variations of, 362
religious movements, significance of, 243
religious practices
  traditional values, 48–49
religious rights
  global South, 48
  in Russia, 45
  Islamic states, 48
  practice of religion and traditional values, 48
religious values, human rights and, 54
religons, fundamentalist
  projections by Western nations, 94
remedial equality, 105
Renton Report, 323
reparations
  addressing historical injustice, 103
  Central African Republic, 82
  in transitional justice, 80, 82
  international institutions, 83
  post-colonial countries, 109
  post-colonial nations, 103
  women's voices in, 82
reparative justice, 103 *See also* transitional justice
Residential Schools for First Nations' children, 293
resilience
  risk literature in environmental law, 210
resistance
  across global South, 161
  judicial and extra-judicial strategies, 162
  piracy against global corporations, 260
  principle of netizenship, 257
  sites of, to surveillance, 262–263
  to neo-liberalism, 150
Resolution 12/21, 55
Resolution 16/3, 55
Resolution 21/3, 59
resources
  access to, in BRICS countries, 221
  cultivation versus pastoral communities, 168

depletion of, in global South, 119
exploitation of, in Africa, 172
financialized global economy and unjust distribution, 217
international community, 81
land grabbing, 137
nationalisation of, 102
neocolonialism and access to, 137
permanent sovereignty over, 103
sharing of, and new constitutions, 167
used to maintain elite interests, 74
warfare and access to, 137
responsibility doctrines, 93
Rethinking Evidence (Twining), 9, 16
revolution
resulting in new constitutions, 184
Rheinstein, Max, 5
Rhodesia, Northern and Southern and Nyasaland, 169
Right of Property, The (Kruse), 4
right to conquest versus restitutions, 103
Right to Development and counterpoint to WTO/TRIPS, 259
rights. *See also* feminism; women's rights; human rights
"natural", 50
cultural, 49, 69
cultural and indigenous, 42
education and training, 58
government abuse of, 68
indigenous peoples and "traditional" practices, 49
lesbian, gay, bisexual, and transgender, 53
marginalized peoples, 43
of women and sexual minorities, 42
religious, 45, 48
social and economic and new constitutions, 167
socio-economic, 42, 69, 71
rights advocate or rights activist
in legal training, 301
risk assessment, industrial revolution and, 206
risks, new generation of, 208
risk-society, emerging, 295
Road to Serfdom, The (Hayek), 348
Roaring Nineties and challenges to globalization, 289
Roberts, Simon, 96
Rocket Lawyer, 250
Rodell, Fred, 270, 275
Roman Catholic Church and views on human rights, 58
Rome Treaty, 31
royal charters and special privileges, 181
Ruggiero, Roberto, 216
Rule of Law
concept of, 180
ideal of reasonableness, 348
Western framework of law, 299
rule systems conflated with legal systems, 362–364
rules
and principles, distinctions between terms, 335
and standards, distinctions between, 337
example of, in U.S. Constitution, 336
games and sports and Hart's concept of law, 311–314
of games and of law, similarities and dissimilarities, 314
reasons for choosing over standards, 343
social, written and unwritten, 320
transnational concept of law, 317
versus standards, distinctions between, 335–338
rules of evidence, 16
Russell Tribunal (Russell I), 102
Russell Tribunal (Russell II), 99, 102, 105, 106, 107, 109–111
and Southern Voices, 110
Russell Tribunals (Russell I and II), 100–103
Russell, Bertrand, 100
Russia
acceptance of universal human rights, 45
religious rights after Communism, 45
UN Human Rights Council and resolutions, 39
Russia and Russian Orthodox Church, and new geo-politics, 45–46
Russian Orthodox Church, 45

Sacks, Albert, 337
Sadeleer, Nicholas de, 208
Said, Edward, 121
salaries and pensions transferred to the 1%, 138
Salmond on Torts, 5
same-sex marriage
human right to, 48
human rights, and views on, 58
traditional values and, 50

Santos, Boaventura de Sousa, 14, 68, 69, 96, 111, 125–130, 140–142, 149–150, 213, 217, 363
cosmopolitanism I and II and constitutionalism, 154–161
Southern epistemologies, 243
views on cosmopolitanism, 146
Sarajevo on-line, 252
Sartre, Jean-Paul, 100, 105, 111
Savigny, F.K. von, 205
Schachter, Oscar, 300, 301
Schauer, Frederick, 312, 358, 360
Scheffler, Samuel, 65–67
Schmitt, Carl, 104
scholars, socioeconomic, concern with welfare state, 290
scholarship, socio-legal, and transnational context, 280–282
Schum, David, 8
scientific fact research, 7
scientific method and empiricist legal tradition, 204
scientific research and environmental law, 206
scientific thought
evidence, collection and assessment, 204
Scottish Enlightenment, 17
Scottish independence
referendum in September 2014, 163
Scottish Law
examining different kinds of law, 355
Searle, John, 363, 364
secrecy
disputes outside the WTO, 222
investment arbitration, 225
security laws, 93
self-governance and digital territories, 245
self-regulation, 282
Separation of Powers
Western framework of law, 299,
separations, political, of fields of law, 299
September 11, 2001, terrorist attacks, 41
Shapiro, Scott, 357
Shari'ah Law
examining different kinds of law, 355
international human rights standards and, 41
Sharp, Malcolm, 6
Shaw, Rosaline, 79
Shifts and the Shocks, The (Wolf), 226
Shils, Edward, 62
Shklar, Judith, 34
"The Significance of Realism" (Twining), 298
Simma, Bruno, 291, 292
simplifying function, 214
Singapore and response to digital exclusion, 249
Singer, Paul, 231
Singer, Peter, 14
small-scale experiments
social movements, newest, 120
Snowden, Edward, 137, 262
Snyder, Francis, 309
social and economic rights and backlash by 1%, 134
Social Area
Chile's nationalisation of industries, 107
social benefits, reduced, for profit of 1%, 138
social change, positive, and civil society groups, 81
Social Choice theorists, 98
social control, beyond legal-illegal dichotomy, 136–137
social democracy
crisis of, and *indignados* movements, 124
rights package, in Brazil, 125
social inequality and contemporary capitalist societies, 123
social justice
global, 103–106
global North and global South and digitization, 246
Kenya's constitution, 185
new African constitutions, 183
programmatic rather than pragmatic, 150
uneven, and globalization, 257
social legal studies and reality of law, 362
social media
cybercapitalism, 258
effects on Arab Spring and Gaza, 253
law firms and web presence, 250
social movements
"*new* new", 119
objections to investment arbitration, 234
post-industrial society, 118
Western-centric theories, 117
social norms, 302
social problems
current, and crisis point in addressing, 69
social protests, worldwide, between 2011 and 2013, 115
social rule approach

law as a starting point, 304
social struggles, indignation revolts of 2011–2013, 141
social transformation, suppressed by global capitalism, 139
social-legal approaches and law as social institution, 358
societies, multicultural
expressions of faith, 143
socio-economic rights
human rights and, 42
socio-legal studies, transformation of mainstream legal scholarship, 296–298
socio-legal theory of law, 115
sociological methodology, 204
sociologists, legal
role of law for society in globalization, 286
sociology of emergences, 115
sociology of law, 307
'soft' forms of norm creation, 290
soft law, 282, 302
relevance as legal material, 308
transnational regulation, 310
Sokoto caliphate and system of administration, 169
solidarity among social movements, 120
Somalia and disputed boundary with Kenya, 169
"Some Realism About Realism," (Llewellyn), 272, 277
Sorites vagueness and spectrum of "reasonableness", 339
South Africa, 49, 170
leadership in new constitutionalism, 184
new constitutionalism, 184–185
reform agenda, 184
withdrawal from BITs, 234
South African Constitution, 70, 71
South African Constitutional Court, 70
southern Africa and views on human rights, 68
Southern European
indigination movements, 124
Southern European and Brazilian indignation movements, 124
Southern Voices, 68, 72, 243
considering, versus Western liberal canon, 243
globalization project, 110
human rights discussions in Latin America, 99, 100
implications for human rights, 98
in Africa, 147
in transitional justice, 73, 85–88
Latin America, 90–96
Twining's globalization project, 110
Twining's globalization project, 73, 284
Southern Voices (Twining), 21
sovereign debt crises
investment arbitration and, 231–232
response of UN General Assembly, 232
restructuring, new framework for, 232
sovereignty
of nations, reconceptualization of, 156
permanent, over natural resources, 103, 106
Spain
austerity package and energy investors, 232
indignados movement, 122, 141
speaking truth to power, 82
Special Review of Counterterrorism, Detention and Interrogation Activities (IG Report), 32
Spinoza, Baruch, 122
Sriram, Chandra Lekha, 87
standard, example of, 336
standards used in law, example of, 338–340
standpoint
importance of, 270
in legal education, 12
inseparability thesis, 101
Western discourses on human rights, 73
Stanko, Rudy, 339, 340
state and market, struggle for dominance, 281
state and non-state institutions, distrust of, 124
state of siege and use in Latin American countries, 101
state power
constitutionalism, 167
sharing of and new constitutions, 167
State v. Stanko, 338, 339, 341, 343, 345, 346
state, activist, and new constitutionalism, 184
state, role of
to support "tradition", 58
statistical studies and social problems, 205
Statue of International Court of Justice, 31
Statute Law Society, 333, 334
statute struck down for "void for vagueness", 338–340
statutory law
practice- and context-related perspective, 302
statutory regulations
not sufficiently available, 301

Stielitz, Joseph, 289
Stockholm Chamber of Commerce, 235
Stone, Julius, 148, 366
Story of a Death Foretold: The Coup Against Salvador Allende, 11 September, 1973 (Guardiola-Rivera), 98
student movement
  labeled as "new" movements, 118
student movements, 101
students of law
  as game changers, 295
  questions regarding current and future fields of study, 295
Sturges, Wesley, 274
sub-Saharan countries systems of governance, 170
suffering, unjust, and alternative modes of ending, 125
Sultan of Zanzibar, 168
Sunstein, Cass, 255
surveillance
  Arab Spring countries, 260
  bulk data collection, 261
  electronic, in digital era, 245
  erosion of citizenship and human rights, 140
  global corporations and agencies, 246
  legal and illegal acts of, 262
  national and transnational, 242
  policing and new business models, 258,
  resistance to, 262
  state, 260
  technology's impact on, 257
  Tor software, to evade, 262
  U.S. Acts and agencies, 261
  unconstitutional, in United States, 261
  violation of privacy, 136
surveillance, electronic, 245
Susskind, Richard, 246, 250
sustainable development, 201
Syria and vision of good society, 71
systematic rethinking, 211

Tamanaha, Brian Z., 14
Tanganyika and pre-colonial territories, 168
Tanzania
  as one-party state, 177
  constitution as delaying development, 177
Tax Law Rewrite Project (UK), 326
technology and the law, new views on, 241–242
technology transfer, requirements for, 227
Teitel, Ruti, 80
terminology, legal, and criticisms of, 335–338
territorial jurisdiction versus transnational arenas, various, 310
terror. *See also* War on Terror
terror, domestic versus international, 37
terrorism. *See also* War on Terror
  definition of, 331
  prevented by torture, 30
Terrorism Act 2000 (UK), 331
terrorism in Northern Ireland, 22
Theories of Evidence: Bentham and Wigmore (Twining), 15
theories of law and theories of society
  connections between, 357
theory and practice, Twining's intertwinement of, 283
theory as activity, 283
theory of harm, 80
Theory of Rules, The (Llewellyn), 268
theory of utility and torture as a case of, 36
Third World Approaches to International Law (TWAIL), 287
thoughtways, digital, 244–246
threats to human existence, 199
Tilley, Terrence, 64
TISA. *See* Trade in Services Agreement
Tolstoy, Leo, 124
Tor software, used to evade surveillance, 262
tort and environmental law
  interrelations of, versus separate legal fields, 295
torture
  civil society and, 25
  cruelty as aspect of, 34
  defined by Bentham, 22–24
  deontological argument against, 36
  fragments on, by Bentham, 22
  institutionalized, 36
  lethal versus non-lethal, 30
  ontological positions on, 33–35
  theory of utility, 36
  utilitarian "justification", 27
  view on justifications, 35–36
  War on Terror and justifications for, 29–33
"torture" fragments by Bentham, 22
Toward a New Common Sense (Santos), 69, 131, 218
TPPA's Regulatory Coherence chapter, 235
trade agreements, 220–221
  mapping of, 221–223

questions about transparency of, 222
Trade and Development Report 2011 (UNCTAD), 226
Trade in Services Agreement (TISA), 216, 220
trade unions in Kenya, 187
tradita, 65, 67
traditio, 65, 67
tradition versus custom, in definitions, 62
traditional practices and collective enterprises, 66
traditional thinking
going beyond, to answer questions about values and law, 202
traditional values
alternative understanding of, 63
appeal in less developed nations, 70
authority, assumed, 66
conflicts with human rights, 52
conservative interpretation, 54–58
defined, 56
dignity, freedom and responsibility, 56
doctrines versus social practices, 64
form of protest, 70
implications of UN resolutions, 72
international universalism, 58–59
new synthesis with human rights, 67
new views on, 67–72
normativity of tradition, 65–67
oppositions to UN resolutions, 53–54
orthodox understandings, 62
orthodox view, and limits of, 67
progressive agenda, potential for, 69
stereotypes and discriminatory practices versus, 59
traditio versus *tradita*, 64
two conceptions of, 62–67
Transatlantic Trade and Investment Partnership (TTIP), 220, 233
transformative constitutionalism, 140
transitional justice, 73, 74, 294
clean break phenomenon, 81
concessions and tensions, 88
from below, 76
global South, missing in debates, 78–84
Latin America, 76
liberal peace and criticisms of, 87
limitations of, versus restitution, 104
marginalization of social, economic, and cultural rights, 79
non-state actors, 80, 81
reparations in post-colonial nations, 80
short history of, 74–78
sites of transformation, 80
Southern Voices, 85–88
victimhood, 82
transitional societies
attention from powerful states, 88
transnational commercial regulation, 218
transnational concept of law, 317–319
transnational courts and international treaties, 157
transnational economic regulation, 217
transnational governance and effects on law, 285
transnational law
rules and practices of managing them, 317
social relations with differing legal implications, 317
transnational law pedagogy, 291–295
transnational legal domain
mapping of, 219–227
transnational legal theory, development of, 296
transnational political jurisprudence, 298
transnational regulatory governance, 297
transnational regulatory governance and globalization, 291
transnational regulatory governance and questions of building blocks, 287
Transnational Sociological Jurisprudence, 296
transnationalization of nation state law, 218
Trans-Pacific Partnership Agreement (TPPA), 220
rules favouring foreign investors, 235
transparency
TPPA chapters regarding, 236
UK legislation, 324–325
treaties and agreements, 219–227
treaty texts and questions of transparency, 216
trickle-down theory of economic justice, 104
Tristes Tropiques (Lévi-Strauss), 92
Trust Fund for Victims in the Central African Republic, 83
TTIP. *See* Transatlantic Trade and Investment Partnership
Turner, Lord Adair, 225
Twining, Penelope, 21, 22, 37
Twining, William, 21–22, 59, 68, 72, 73, 78, 89, 90, 91, 96, 115, 125–130, 140–142, 145, 192, 241, 282, 298
biographical information, 1
calls for renewed analytical approach, 212

Twining, William (cont.)
- cosmopolitanism I and II and constitutionalism, 154–161
- credentials of, 354
- fragments on torture by Bentham, 22–24
- healthy cosmopolitanism discipline of law, 147–149
- interpretations of Llewellyn's' works, 268–269
- interview with, 1–17
- law research and implications for era of globalization, 283–287
- view on justifications for torture, 35
- views on cosmopolitanism, 146–147

ubuntu
- human rights protections, 70–71
- traditional values and, 49

Uganda
- Cold War and Western powers, 178
- military rule, 177
- pre-colonial kingdoms, 168

Uganda, as one-party state, 177

UN Advisory Committee, 56, 58–59

UN Convention against Torture (CAT), 23, 24, 31, 32, 37

UN Declaration on the Granting of Independence to Colonial Countries and Peoples, 108

UN General Assembly
- Allende's speech on nationalization, 109
- debates on human rights, 109
- doctrine of excess profits, 106
- Resolution 1803/1962, 103
- response to electronic surveillance, 262
- response to sovereign debt crises, 232

UN High Commissioner for Human Rights, 263

UN Human Rights Committee, 43, 67

UN Human Rights Council, 51, 54, 55, 58, 183
- resolutions on human rights issues, 40–43
- resolutions on traditional values, 39, 53

UN Resolutions
- 12/21 of 2 October 2009, 55
- 16/3 of 24 March 2011, 55
- 1803/1962 on "Permanent Sovereignty over Natural Resources", 103
- 21/3 of 27 September 2012, 59
- objections to, 53

UN Special Rapporteur, 56–58, 59, 61

UNCITRAL. *See* United Nations Commission on International Trade Law

UNCTAD. *See* United Nations Conference for Trade and Development

unemployment
- Kenya and worker vulnerability, 187

Uniform Commercial Code, 277

unions
- objections to investment arbitration, 234

United Kingdom
- transitional justice, 86

United Nations
- approaches to human rights, 52
- debates traditional values, 62
- governance of, 143
- traditional values and synthesis with human rights, 67

United Nations Commission on International Trade Law (UNCITRAL), 229
- reform of investment arbitration, 235

United Nations Conference on Trade and Development (UNCTAD), 222, 227, 234

United States
- international investments and arbitration disputes, 227
- intervention in Vietnam, 101, 103, 127
- neoliberalism, collapse of, and Occupy movement, 125
- objections to UN resolutions, 53
- Occupy movements, 124
- template for free trade agreements, 223
- transitional justice justifications, 86
- use of force and transitional justice, 86

United States Council for International Business, 235

unity
- Eurocentric definition of, 93
- of law and Western framework, 299

Universal Declaration of Human Rights, 40, 58, 108

universal human rights, 60 *See also* human rights

universal truths about law
- criticisms of, 359–361

universalism, 52, 73
- international, versus traditional values, 58–59

University of Alicante, 1

University of Chicago Law School, 5

University of Coimbra, 127

University of Warwick Law School, 14
urbanisation and former colonies in Africa, 174
Uruguay
response to digital exclusion, 249
tobacco control laws, 229
utilitarianism
public interest versus vulnerability of the innocent, 29
torture, "justification" of, 27
Utrecht School of Law, 55

vagueness. *See also* Sorites-vagueness; Wittgensteinian-vagueness
vagueness and terms used in laws, 339
vagueness in laws and entanglements of, 340–341
value-concepts used in law, 342
value-judgments, and standards and norms, 336
values
conservative, 49–50
national, 47–48
religious, 51
traditional and human rights, 38
traditional, and divergent approaches at UN, 51–52
traditional, and religious practices, 48–49
traditional, appeal and understanding of, 47–51
values, national, 51
Venezuela
independent arbitrators and ConocoPhillips dispute, 230
withdrawal from ICSID, 234
Vermeule, Adrian, 76
victimhood and transitional justice, 82
Vietnam and US intervention, 101, 103, 127
violence, institutional, 36
voices of suffering, 243
"void for vagueness" statute, 338–340
vulture funds, 225

"Why the State?" (Raz), 354
Waki Commission and report on Kenya, 186
Walker, Carolyn, 170, 171
war and peace, 200
War on Terror, 30, 135, 136
water boarding, 37
Water Framework Directive (WFD), 209
wealth and resources, redefining of, 105
wealth inequality, 133
wealth inequality and neoliberal capitalism, 139
weapons of mass destruction, 86
Weber, Max, 14, 93, 364
Welfare State
elitist backlash against, 134
exhaustion of, 290
post-war, in U.S., 300
Western experience of law and globalization, 281
Western jurisprudence
diverse influences on, 218
Western jurisprudence and tendencies toward ethnocentrism, 90
Western law, liberal, 93
Western legal theory, top-down model and limitations of, 151
Western legal tradition, top-down worldview, 152
Western nation-state history, perceived as universal experience, 300
Western tradition of academic law
challenged by changing context, 285
Western traditions and ethnocentrism in international law, 90–96
Western welfare state. *See also* Welfare State
institutional-conceptual frameworks, 299
regulatory norms and non-state actors, 289
WESTLAW, 249, 255, 330
Westphalian state model
former colonies in Africa, 170
What If Latin America Ruled the World? (Guardiola-Rivera), 98
whistleblowers
encouragement of, 110
persecution of, 261
Why Terrorism Works (Dershowitz), 30
Wigmore, John Henry, 8, 15
Wigmorian approach, modified, to fact analysis, 255
Wikileaks, 261, 262
WIPO. *See* World Intellectual Property Organisation
Wirtschaftsrecht (economic law), 289
Wittgenstein, Ludwig, and family resemblances, 360
Wittgensteinian vagueness, 341
indeterminacy of criteria, 339
Wolf, Martin, 226
Wolpert, Lewis, 206

women and sexual minorities, human rights issues, 53
women's rights
  Convention on the Elimination of All Forms of Discrimination Against Women, 184
  localism of human rights, 70
  reparations and women's voices in, 82
  transitional justice and marginalization, 80
Woods, Michael, 2
Working with Parliamentary Counsel (OPC), 324
World Bank, 69, 229, 287
World Congress on Philosophy of Law and Social Philosophy, 356
world economy and calls for reforms, 226
World Health Organisation (WHO), 233
World Intellectual Property Organisation (WIPO), 260
World Investment Forum, October 2014, 234
World Revolution 2011, 115
World Social Forum, 121, 150, 161
World Summit on the Information Society, 259
World Trade Organization (WTO), 220, 260
  founding of, 216
  neoliberal regime, 226
  Seattle protests in 1999, 119
World Trade Organization Trade Related Intellectual Property Rights (TRIPS) Agreement, 258
World Wide Web (WWW)
  effect on reporting Balkan War, 252
WorldLII, 248, 249
worldviews
  post-colonial, subaltern perspectives, 152
  Western law and 'top-down' perspective, 152
Wright report on legislation in UK, 327
writers and political roles in Chile, 100–103
WTO. *See* World Trade Organization

Yale Law School, 127
Yntema, Hessel, 274, 375
youth of Kenya, and powerlessness, 187

Zaire, Cold War and Western powers, 178
Zambia, as one-party state, 177
Zimbabwe
  constitution, process of, 195
  independence and colonial Bill of Rights, 176
Zizek, Slavoj, 23
Zuma, Jacob, 184
Zwart, Tom, 39, 55, 59, 61, 62

CPSIA information can be obtained
at www.ICGtesting.com
Printed in the USA
LVOW03*1108171115
462964LV00006B/19/P

9 781107 116405